AMSCO® ADVANCED PLACEMENT®

UNITED STATES
GOVERNMENT
AND POLITICS

SECOND EDITION

David Wolfford teaches Advanced Placement® U.S. Government and Politics at Mariemont High School in Cincinnati, Ohio, and has served as an AP® Reader. He has a B.A. in Secondary Education and an M.A. in Constitutional and Legal History, both from the University of Kentucky. He has conducted historical research projects on school desegregation and American political history. David has published in historical journals, such as *Ohio Valley History* and *Kentucky Humanities*. He has written on government, politics, and campaigns for national magazines and Cincinnati newspapers. He is a James Madison Fellow, a National Board certified teacher, and a regular contributor to *Social Education*. David is editor of *By George: Articles from the Ashland Daily Independent* (Jesse Stuart Foundation) and associate editor of *Ohio Social Studies Review.*

Reviewers

Jenifer A. Hitchcock, NBCT, M.Ed
AP® Government and Politics Reader
James Madison Fellow '16 (VA)
Fairfax High School
Fairfax, Virginia

Jennifer A. Jolley, NBCT, M.A.
James Madison Fellow '10 (FL)
Palm Bay Magnet High School
Melbourne, Florida

David LaShomb, M.S.
College Board Consultant
AP® U.S. Government and Politics
Georgetown, Texas

Louis Magnon, M.A.T., M.Ed.
Department of History and Political
    Science
San Antonio College
San Antonio, Texas

Eileen Sheehy
Billings West High School
AP® U.S. Government and Politics
Billings, Montana

David M. Seiter, M.Ed.
Northridge High School
AP® U.S. Government and Politics
Layton, Utah

Brian Stevens, B.A., M.A.
College Board Consultant
Coldwater High School
AP® U.S. Government and Politics
Coldwater, Michigan

Barry L. Tadlock, Ph.D.
AP® Government and Politics Reader
Associate Professor of Political Science
Ohio University
Athens, Ohio

AMSCO® ADVANCED PLACEMENT®

UNITED STATES GOVERNMENT AND POLITICS

SECOND EDITION

AMSCO® SCHOOL PUBLICATIONS, INC. ,

a division of Perfection Learning®

Acknowledgment: "Letter from Birmingham Jail" is reprinted by arrangement with The Heirs to the Estate of Martin Luther King Jr., c/o Writers House as agent for the proprietor New York, NY. Copyright: (c) 1963 Dr. Martin Luther King, Jr. (c) renewed 1991 Coretta Scott King.

AMSCO® Advanced Placement® Government and Politics is one of a series of Advanced Placement® social studies texts first launched with the book now titled *AMSCO® Advanced Placement® United States History.*

© 2019 Perfection Learning®

Please visit our website at:
www.perfectionlearning.com

When ordering this book, please specify:

Softcover: ISBN 978-1-5311-1283-7 or **1314301**
Hardcover: ISBN 978-1-5311-1284-4 or **1314306**
eBook: ISBN 978-1-5311-1285-1 or **13143D**

6 7 8 9 10 11 12 DR 23 22 21 20 19 18

Printed in the United States of America

Contents

UNIT 2 Interactions Among Branches of Government

UNIT 3 Civil Liberties and Civil Rights

UNIT 4 American Political Ideologies and Beliefs

Essential Question: *What are the functions and impacts of
political parties, and how have they adapted to change?*

Preface

AMSCO® Advanced Placement® United States Government and Politics explains the American political system and will enhance student performance on the Advanced Placement® U.S. Government and Politics exam. The College Board has redesigned the course and national exam, and this new edition reflects those changes. The text includes a good mix of colorful history, modern political examples, and relevant statistics. Accounts of political personalities and memorable events aid understanding and provide examples for students to answer the exam's questions. The free-response and multiple-choice practice questions parallel those that appear on the national exam.

This redesigned and updated book reflects contemporary trends in Congress, the presidency, and the courts, and it includes data from the 2016 federal elections and more recent special elections. I draw from my research projects, political reporting, and years of teaching the AP Government course. I have provided a bibliography for those who want more information and insights.

This book fills the gap between a test prep handbook and a costly political science textbook. It is thorough enough to be a student's go-to book, especially if used in conjunction with other print and online resources. It can be read gradually over an entire term or reviewed in just a few weeks with the built-in review tools.

I would like to thank for their inspiration and good counsel my dad George Wolfford; history professor David Hamilton; and colleagues Luke Wiseman, Dan Ruff, and Matt Litton. Special thanks go to Brian Stevens, a reviewer of this volume and my first source for how to teach AP Government and Politics. Thanks to reviewers David LaShomb, Tony Magnon, and Eileen Sheehy for improving the first edition. Thanks to Brian, David LaShomb, Dave Seiter, Jenifer Hitchcock, Jennifer Jolley, and my first college-level Poli Sci instructor Dr. Barry Tadlock.

A special thanks to our editor-at-the-helm, Carol Francis, who kept this crew, and especially this author, on pace. And, of course, thanks to AMSCO/ Perfection Learning and Steve Keay for believing in me and for publishing my work. To more than any, thanks to Mika, Maya, and Miki for their sacrifices to allow this book to become a reality.

David Wolfford, May 2018

Introduction

Congratulations on accepting the challenge to learn and master United States government and politics at an accelerated level. *AMSCO® Advanced Placement® United States Government and Politics*, revised to align with the latest course and exam description from the College Board, will help you build mastery of the fundamental concepts of government as well as the disciplinary practices of political scientists. This introduction explains the redesigned course and new test format. Sixteen content and skills-building chapters follow, with extensive coverage of fundamental concepts, information and examples to bring them to life, required foundational documents and Supreme Court cases, and practice questions.

The College Board's Advanced Placement Program started in 1955. The U.S. Government and Politics course began in 1987. In 2017, nearly 9,500 high schools offered this course, and nearly 319,000 students took the national exam. The vast majority took this class in their senior year. Nearly 3,000 colleges accepted these scores and awarded credit in place of course work.

Taking an Advanced Placement course and exam in government and politics has many benefits. The depth and rigor will help you gain deep understanding of this relevant subject. The course will also help prepare you for college, sharpening your skills in analyzing and interpreting information from a variety of sources. Taking these types of courses may save time and money by bypassing college courses later, depending on how your prospective college regards these exams. Colleges also consider your enrollment and performance in these courses as they determine admissions and award scholarships. One College Board study found that 85 percent of colleges view students' AP experience favorably as they consider admissions decisions, and 31 percent report considering it when determining scholarship awards.

The exam is given in early May, but you must register earlier in the year. Check your school's guidance department or the College Board's website for details, fees, and deadlines.

Please note: This book focuses on the U.S. Government and Politics course, not the separate Comparative Government and Politics course, which compares various national governments.

The Design of the Government and Politics Course

The College Board redesigned the United States Government and Politics program and will base the exam on the redesigned program starting in 2019. The changes focus on depth rather than breadth, concepts rather than rote learning, and five "Big Ideas" that animate American government: (1) Constitutionalism, (2) Liberty and Order, (3) Civic Participation in a Representative Democracy, (4) Competing Policymaking Interests, and (5) Methods of Political Analysis. Interactions—among the three branches of government, between the federal and state governments, and between citizens and their government—are highlighted.

The new course has less emphasis on content and more on skills. Noticeable is the College Board's expectation that students be well versed in 15 landmark Supreme Court cases—the only ones on which students will be tested. There will be no more predicting which obscure case might appear somewhere on the exam.

The Board has selected nine foundational documents, eight of which are from the time of the nation's founding and the ninth, Dr. Martin Luther King Jr.'s "Letter from a Birmingham Jail," is from 1963. Like the Supreme Court cases, these nine sources are "must-know" documents. A feature within the chapters introduces each one, focusing on the key concepts, and the full document can be found in the Foundational Document Sourcebook at the end of this book, with questions to get you thinking about the documents and providing opportunities to develop and apply political science disciplinary skills and practices.

Since policy and policymaking are ever-present in understanding government, the policymaking process, once a separate unit, has now been interwoven throughout the course. In this way, policymaking can be tied directly to the concepts in the course.

The course also develops **political science disciplinary practices**, such as analyzing arguments and relating concepts to political institutions, behavior, or policies. In addition, the course provides many opportunities to develop and strengthen **reasoning processes**—defining, understanding stages in processes, comparing, and understanding causation.

Finally, the program requires the completion of a project through which students will make a civic connection. The course emphasizes citizen participation as the bedrock of American representative democracy.

Government and Politics Content

This course is like a college-level introductory course in government and politics. The key themes include the creation and design of government, the three branches, civil rights and liberties, political ideology, and how the citizens interact with government. Overarching questions include the following: How do elections work and how are they won? How do the three branches interact to create law and policy? How are people in this democracy linked to government institutions?

Enduring Understandings The course content is developed from enduring understandings—statements that synthesize the important concepts in a discipline area and have lasting value even beyond that discipline area. For example, the College Board has articulated this enduring understanding derived from the big idea of constitutionalism:

A balance between governmental power and individual rights has been a hallmark of American political development.

Why is that an enduring understanding? It highlights a fundamental tension in American government between the individual liberties our culture cherishes and the recognition that to live in society, we must turn over some power to the government so that it can keep order and provide public safety. Exactly where the line should be drawn between government power and individual liberties has been debated and clarified over the centuries. Each unit in this book begins with a listing of the enduring understandings relevant to that unit.

Learning Objectives To help students fully develop those enduring understandings, the College Board has also articulated learning objectives—the expected outcomes of study that can be demonstrated through student action. For example, this is a learning objective related to the enduring understanding listed above:

Explain how democratic ideals are reflected in the Declaration of Independence and the U.S. Constitution.

This learning objective ties to the enduring understanding by providing specific examples for study—the Declaration of Independence and the U.S. Constitution—and then clearly identifies how a student can demonstrate this understanding: "Explain how democratic ideals are reflected . . . ." Each unit ends with a list of the unit's learning objectives and where you can find information in the book that helps you fulfill them.

Essential Knowledge Being able to fulfill the learning objectives requires content knowledge. The College Board has homed in on what it considers essential knowledge to achieve that purpose. Here is an example of essential knowledge tied to the above learning objective:

The U.S. government is based on ideas of limited government, including natural rights, popular sovereignty, republicanism, and social contract.

This essential knowledge statement outlines what you need to know to fulfill the learning objective, so you can focus your study on the truly relevant information. The essential knowledge has been boiled down to one concept, limited government, and the elements that contribute to it: natural rights, popular sovereignty (people's power), republicanism, and social contract. So the course description lays out exactly what you need to know to master the requirements of the course. This book provides all the essential knowledge you will need to fulfill the learning objectives and develop enduring understandings.

Understanding Historic Politics If you've already taken a high school U.S. history course, you will recognize some important eras and their relevance to politics. For example, the American founding included an intense dispute between the American colonists and Great Britain about a lack of democratic representation and liberty. This course focuses on the American Revolution's legal and political (not military) history, the ideas in the Declaration of Independence, and the creation and ratification of the Constitution.

Knowing something about a few leading presidents—their terms in office, impact, and accomplishments—will help you cement your understanding of key political events and forces. Other key historical personalities are also relevant to shaping the American government. Federalists James Madison and Alexander Hamilton promoted a strong national government. Chief Justice John Marshall became the father of the Supreme Court, serving during its formative era, 1801–1837. During the civil rights movement of the 1950s and 1960s, Thurgood Marshall, a civil rights attorney and later Supreme Court justice, helped forge the legal path for desegregating America. Individuals' names may appear on the exam, but they will not need to be recalled. However, knowing historical figures will provide you with strong examples to use as you answer the free-response questions.

Understanding Modern Politics This course focuses on the three branches of federal government outlined in the Constitution and how people and groups interact with these institutions to create public policy. However, the relationship between the federal and state governments is also a recurring theme in understanding the challenges of federalism.

Most high-level federal government decisions are made "inside the beltway"—the Washington, D.C., area encircled by Interstate 495. Congress convenes on Capitol Hill, the president lives and works in the White House, and the Supreme Court justices hear cases in their building nearby. These institutions and the vast federal bureaucracy are the policymaking bodies that create, shape, and carry out the law. The press, or media, report to citizens on the work of these branches. Interest groups and political parties try to influence all three branches in different ways. These different entities work together and at odds with one another to accomplish their separate goals.

In addition to the federal government, which includes hundreds of agencies and well over two million employees, each state has a legislature, a governor and state administration, and a court system. Countless municipal or city governments and school boards create a massive web of policies. This complex system is designed to address a variety of viewpoints while ultimately adopting only those few ideas on which the masses can largely agree. This is the basis of pluralism, a system of public policies resulting from compromise among competing groups. With pluralism, we create a consensus government to satisfy most participants most of the time.

Where Does the Power Lie? This course repeatedly asks that question. Officially, national political power and authority rests with "We the people" as introduced in the Preamble of the Constitution. To ensure the ideals of a government by the people, the Constitution defines the structure of delegated power from the people to Congress, the qualifications for president, and the jurisdiction of the courts. Actual government policies, however, depend on who holds these offices and how they approach their duties. In many instances, public policy is created after a competition between the political elites (upper-level politicians and policymakers) and the rank-and-file citizens (voters).

Those who subscribe to the elite theory of government claim that big businesses, political elites, and those with money and resources overly dominate the policymaking process. But pluralists counter that because such political resources and access to the media are so widely scattered, no single elite group has a monopoly on power. Pluralists also argue that the many levels of government and the officials within each branch bring a variety of views and divide the power to prevent one sector of society or one view from dominating.

The Design of This Book

This book explains American government in the most straightforward terms and with many memorable examples for understanding. It is the result of my experiences in teaching AP Government and Politics, serving as a Reader for the College Board, and engaging with real-world government and researching political history. I have also covered political campaigns for local newspapers and national publications, written for scholarly history and educational journals, profiled U.S. senators for magazines, and attended state-level political debates. All of these provide a real-world perspective for much of the explanation that follows.

I hope that I have provided a plainspoken yet colorful version of American government while aligning the presentation with the College Board's Course and Examination Description (CED).

The chapter sequence in this book corresponds to the order in the CED. However, the chapters' main points and concepts can be understood in isolation. As with other government books, there is overlap among the chapters, and we have included cross-references.

Five Units

This book contains 5 units and a total of 16 chapters.

Unit One: Foundations of American Democracy The first unit focuses on the historical creation of the United States government. It includes the struggle between the American colonists and the British government, the Revolutionary War, the infant U.S. government under the failed Articles of Confederation, and the creation of the Constitution and the Bill of Rights. A copy of the Constitution is provided in the back of this book, along with other foundational documents, in the Foundational Document Sourcebook. The second chapter covers how American federalism developed, largely after landmark Supreme Court rulings.

Unit Two: Interactions Among Branches of Government Unit Two covers the three branches (legislative, executive, and judicial) defined in Articles I, II, and III of the Constitution in four total chapters, each covering a major national governing institution—Congress, the presidency, the judiciary, and the bureaucracy of government agencies and departments that carry out the nation's laws. The bureaucracy is the president's administration, from cabinet-level advisors down to national park rangers. Government sub-institutions include the House and Senate, congressional committees, federal departments and agencies, and the lower U.S. courts. These chapters contain the legislative process, presidential decision-making, and how the Supreme Court accepts and decides cases. These institutions have relationships with one another, and these chapters look at their interactions.

Unit Three: Civil Liberties and Civil Rights This unit focuses on civil liberties—a person's political freedoms, such as the right to free speech, freedom of religion, fair trials, and basic privacy. This unit will help you understand the division of church and state, the limits of free speech in the public square, and the line between an individual's rights and society's responsibilities.

Civil rights generally refer to a person's basic rights to freedom and to equal treatment under the law. Civil rights quests usually involve the struggle for certain groups—African Americans, other ethnic minorities, women, or gays and lesbians—seeking equality under the law. Understanding civil rights and liberties requires solid knowledge of the Supreme Court's role and its many landmark decisions.

Unit Four: American Political Ideologies and Beliefs Unit Four examines why Americans hold different political ideologies and what forces or experiences cause people to develop their beliefs. Family, demographics, religion, school, geographic location, race, and countless other factors shape how a voter votes and affect the relationship between citizens and the federal government.

The science of polling and the art of using that data are discussed in this unit as well. Differing ideologies on the role of government in the economy and in social programs are also explored.

Unit Five: Political Participation The final unit focuses on the linkage institutions—political parties, campaigns, elections, interest groups, and the mass media— that connect voters to the government. The chapter on voting and voter behavior will help you master the constitutional amendments regarding voting rights and the factors that explain why people vote as they do. Political parties' structure, function, and impact on policy are also explained as are the way campaigns work and how elections are won. Interest groups, political action committees (PACs), and campaign financing are emphasized in Unit Five as well, as is the role of the media.

Updated Content

Besides covering every item in the College Board's materials and expected terms and concepts for any American Government course, this volume addresses an array of current and sometimes controversial topics, new voting trends, major news stories, and changes in modern communication. In determining what to include, the College Board's Content Outline and student interest played the biggest roles.

Legalizing Marijuana and Same-Sex Marriage Two major trends in government over the past decade are the quest to legalize marijuana and same-sex marriage. Both of these movements have existed for decades, but recently both have crossed new milestones. With administrations taking differing approaches to addressing and enforcing anti-marijuana laws at the federal level, the law has been in a state of flux for the past decade.

The gay rights movement and the quest for marriage equality has also crossed a new threshold. In 2015, the Supreme Court announced in its ruling in *Obergefell v. Hodges* that states could no longer prevent citizens of the same sex from marrying each other.

Challenges and Opportunities of the Digital Age The other phenomenon in politics lately has been the continually changing media landscape and how citizens are responding to it. Social media has taken on a major role in communications. Government officials are relying on innovative ways to communicate with citizens. People are examining how we receive news and how it is affecting democracy. The White House is operating under new media relations. And the federal government plans to regulate political advertising on social media platforms to prevent the ideological manipulation made possible by the use of social media data that targets people's personality types and political leanings.

Features to Support the Course and Exam Description from the College Board

To support the in-depth learning promoted by the College Board course, this book includes a number of special features. These features include Foundational Documents, Must-Know Supreme Court Decisions, Policy Matters, and a section on the civic connection project.

Foundational Documents You must be familiar with the nine foundational documents the College Board has selected. These include the charters of freedom that created the national republic, 4 of the 85 Federalist Papers, one Anti-Federalist essay, and Martin Luther King's "Letter from a Birmingham Jail." For each document, you will find a feature that formally introduces it, provides a selected passage or excerpt, and asks a few questions for understanding. The full text of these documents and additional questions are in the Foundational Documents Sourcebook. Through these documents, you can learn about the founding principles of government and the perspectives that helped shape it. By the end of the course and for the national exam, you should know these documents very well.

Must-Know Supreme Court Decisions Though you will read about a number of Supreme Court cases, the course requires you to know well 15 landmark decisions. These range from *Marbury v. Madison* (1803) through the more recent *Citizens United v. Federal Election Commission* (2010) decision. These cases cover an array of disputes, such as the limits of government action and the level of citizens' rights. For each Must-Know Decision, you will read an introduction and selected passages from the Court's majority, dissenting, and sometimes concurring opinions. Questions will follow each case for further analysis.

Policy Matters This book emphasizes the policymaking process and results throughout the book. The Policy Matters feature will highlight some of the recent attempts and occasional successes at making new law and policy. This feature also looks at the interactions among branches because more than one branch is normally involved in policymaking.

Think Tank: Making a Civic Connection In an effort to encourage political science research and civic engagement, the College Board requires that all students taking this course complete a project. This project can take several forms and is meant to show how you can affect, and how you are affected by, government and politics throughout your life. This must be a research-oriented or applied civics project tied to the AP US Government and Politics Course Framework. Your government teacher must be involved and likely has a project or options already planned. You can find more details about the project, the College Board's guidelines, and some examples on pages 592–596.

The Exam

You can earn college credit for your work in the course upon your successful performance on the national AP U.S. Government and Politics exam given in early May. This three-hour test consists of 55 four-option multiple-choice questions and 4 free-response questions. You will have 80 minutes (1:20) to complete the multiple-choice questions and then 100 minutes (1:40) for the free-response questions. Each section is worth half of the total test. A talented team of college faculty and experienced AP teachers draft the questions and create the exam each year. A parallel practice exam is included at the end of this book. On the test, you can earn a score of 1 through 5. The College Board considers a score of 3 as "qualified," but some colleges require a 4 or even a 5 for college credit. To learn more about how colleges regard the exam, check out this website:: https://apstudent.collegeboard.org/creditandplacement/search-credit-policies.

Multiple-Choice

The 55 multiple-choice questions take six different forms and always have four options, A through D. There will be one correct answer. Many of the multiple-choice questions require you to examine a graph, text passage, table, map, or political cartoon. Many questions compare governmental terms or concepts. Some parallel the classic multiple-choice questions that require deep conceptual understandings. Others are simple definitions to test your knowledge of terminology. In this book, you will find specific questions related to the content of the chapter at the end of each chapter, while questions covering a broader range of topics will be on the practice exam. Every question will require you to demonstrate an overarching knowledge or understanding of political science content.

As with most multiple-choice tests, determine what exactly the question is asking and then select the best answer. If an early option in (A) or (B) looks extremely obvious, continue to read and consider the remaining options to confirm or reconsider your first impressions. For questions you cannot immediately answer, use the process of elimination. Rule out and actually mark through the unlikely options to narrow your choices.

When you see a challenging or time-consuming question, remember time is limited. You have a little under a minute and a half per question. You should pass the midpoint of the exam, question No. 27, at about 40 minutes into the first portion of the test. Skip the occasional tough question (be sure to leave that spot blank on the answer form) and continue through the test. Return and answer those challenging questions after you have gone through all 55. Since there is no added penalty for guessing, if you do not know the answer, make your best guess.

If you're just beginning your preparation, the example questions that follow may be challenging. Don't worry if you do not know the correct answer; the following 16 chapters will teach you. These examples are to expose you to the formats of the questions. You could elect to revisit these questions as part of your review as exam day approaches.

Quantitative Analysis These questions will have a quantitative (numbers-based) presentation—chart, table, or graph—that measures some facet of government or politics, followed by two questions. The first question will call for you to recognize or identify data and trends. The second will dig deeper and ask you to demonstrate your understanding of an accurate comparison, conclusion, limitations, implication, or likely outcome based on the data. Your understanding of how the data implies or illustrates political principles, institutions, processes, and behaviors will also be tested with these questions. In other words, be ready to read, interpret, and explain the significance of a graph, table, or chart.

EXAMPLE

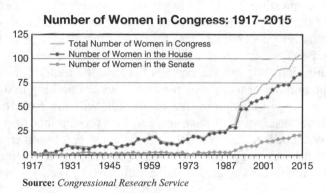

Number of Women in Congress: 1917–2015

Source: *Congressional Research Service*

Questions 1 and 2 refer to the graph.

1. Which of the following statements reflects the data in the chart?

    (A) The number of women serving in Congress is on the decline.

    (B) More women have served in the House than in the Senate.

    (C) About half of the members of the past two Congresses have been women.

    (D) There are more African Americans than women in Congress.

2. Which of the following might be a potential consequence of the trend illustrated in the chart?

    (A) More men will run for office in the upcoming election cycles.

    (B) Congress will have a greater number of members as democracy broadens.

    (C) Congress is more likely to address issues of health, education, and family.

    (D) The Republican Party will gain seats in both house of Congress.

The answer to question 1 is B. This question requires you to recognize the information a graphic conveys—the title, the symbols, and the key that explains them and, in this case, the meaning of the *x*- and *y-axis*. To answer the first question, you need to ask yourself exactly what information is represented in the graph. You can eliminate answer A because the trend is upward, not downward. You can eliminate answer C because the figures in the graph refer to numbers, not percentages, and they do not refer to men at all, so there is no way to know that women might make up 50 percent. You can eliminate D because there is likewise no mention of African Americans in the graph.

The answer to question 2 is C. To answer this question, you need to ask yourself, "Given that the number of women serving in the House and Senate has risen—the answer you chose in question 1— what might be a result of this trend?" You need to use critical reasoning processes to choose the correct answer to this question. You can eliminate A because the trend in the graphic clearly shows the number of women increasing—there is nothing in the graph to suggest that trend will change or that more men will run for office. You can eliminate B because you will have learned that the number of members of Congress was capped at 435 in 1929, and the number of women running does not affect that number. You can eliminate D because there's no indication that the women running for Congress are Republicans. In fact, you will learn that there are more Democratic women than Republican women in Congress. You can therefore confidently choose C as the correct answer, even though it is speculation. Women politicians, however, have traditionally initiated and supported legislation addressing health, education, and family.

The actual exam will have five quantitative stimuli, with two multiple-choice questions each, ten total questions (18 percent of the multiple-choice questions) going with a quantitative stimulus such as a line graph, bar chart, or pie graph.

Qualitative, Text-Based Analysis These questions require you to read a short passage and then analyze and apply what you have read. Expect a paragraph-length excerpt, about 100-200 words, from one of the Federalist Papers, a notable presidential speech, a government memo, or perhaps a news report. The passages, which you likely will not have seen before, could come from primary or secondary sources. They will be attributed with author, title, and year for context.

Three or four multiple-choice questions will follow, designed to test your ability to identify or describe the author's perspective, assumptions, claims, and reasoning. These questions will also focus on considering implications of the arguments and their effects on political principles, institutions, processes, and behaviors.

Both in this introduction and at the end of chapters, we offer only two questions after each text passage. On our practice exam on page 597 you will see three or four questions following the text-based stimulus questions.

EXAMPLE

Questions 3 and 4 refer to the passage below.

> The friends and adversaries of the plan of the convention, if they agree in nothing else, concur at least in the value they set upon the trial by jury . . . . the more the operation of the institution has fallen under my observation, [T]he more reason I have discovered for holding it in high estimation . . . as a defense against the oppressions of a hereditary monarch, . . . [and] a barrier to the tyranny of popular magistrates in a popular government. Discussions of this kind would be more curious than beneficial, as all are satisfied of the utility of the institution, and of its friendly aspect to liberty.

> —Alexander Hamilton, *Federalist No. 83*, 1788

3. Which of the following statements is most consistent with the author's argument in this passage?

   (A) Judicial panels in cases on appeal will assure fairness in the adjudication of laws.

   (B) A citizen-jury in our judicial branch will serve to prevent tyranny and safeguard liberty from other officials in government.

   (C) The jury system is about the only proposal in the Constitution that is worthy because both sides agree on it.

   (D) Juries are common in state courts and therefore unnecessary in federal courts.

4. Which governmental concept is the author most likely trying to protect or guarantee?

   (A) Sovereignty

   (B) Representative lawmaking

   (C) Equality

   (D) Rights of the accused

The answer for question 3 is B. A can be eliminated because there is no mention of appeals in the text. Answer C can be eliminated because it does not follow that other proposals in the Constitution are not worthy or not agreed on by both sides. Answer D can be eliminated both because state courts are not mentioned and, far from saying they are unnecessary in federal courts, Hamilton argues that they are necessary. Answer B is an accurate summary of the main idea of the text.

The correct answer for question 4 is D. A jury, Hamilton suggests, is a protector of liberty, assuring that accused defendants are not put away without this check on runaway prosecution. Of the four concepts listed as choices, only D is "the most likely" concept Hamilton is protecting.

The actual exam will have three or four questions with text passages, so six to eight questions of this type, or about 10-15 percent of the multiple-choice section.

Visual Analysis These multiple-choice questions call for you to analyze qualitative visual information. An image—a map, political cartoon, or information graphic (or "infographic")—will be followed by two questions. One will focus on identifying the topic and perspective that the image conveys. The second question will focus on explaining the elements of the image; relating the depiction to political principles, institutions, processes, and behaviors; or understanding what consequences may come based on arguments or depictions within the cartoon, map, or graphic.

EXAMPLE

Questions 5 and 6 refer to the political cartoon below.

Source: *CartoonStock*

5. Which of the following best describes the message in the political cartoon?

(A) Fundraisers and reception dinners are ineffective at influencing candidates.

(B) Candidates are influenced by big campaign donors more than by those who cannot afford to donate.

(C) Political fundraisers for all offices should be open to the general public.

(D) Political fundraising takes too much time away from officials' other duties.

6. Which of the following is a potential consequence of the message in the cartoon?

(A) Fundraisers will lose popularity.

(B) Third-party candidates will follow the fundraising conventions of the major party.

(C) Greater and greater amounts of money will be spent to influence candidates.

(D) Letter-writing campaigns by citizens will become more influential.

The answer to question 5 is B. Answer A can be eliminated because the words the woman says are expressing the opposite view—that politicians listen only to the big donors. Answer C can be eliminated because it is not logical—the woman represents someone who cannot make a big donation, so she or others like her would have no more influence even if they attended a fundraiser. Answer D, while it is likely true, can be eliminated because there is nothing in the cartoon that supports the idea.

The answer to question 6 is C. Nothing in the cartoon, not words or images, supports the idea that fundraisers will become less popular or that third-party candidates will follow suit. D can be eliminated because the woman has stated that candidates are not influenced by people's "two cents' worth," so letter writing is unlikely to have much of an effect. Answer C is a reasonable consequence because the woman says politicians won't listen for "less than $10,000," suggesting that the more money offered, the more carefully they will listen.

The actual exam will have three of these visuals, each with two questions, making a total of six questions accompanying a map, cartoon, or infographic, a little over 10 percent of the multiple-choice section.

Comparison Comparison questions will surface on the exam in different forms. One common format will test your understanding of two connected or related political concepts, institutions, groups, or policies via two lists in a table. A question will introduce the two terms. They will appear in the top row of the table. In each column under each term will appear four descriptions, each in its own row and each aligned with the letter answer option A–D. Where you see two true and accurate statements or descriptions that correspond with the item atop the table, you have your answer. These questions are likely to compare laws, documents, constitutional provisions and principles, Supreme Court decisions, and political terms.

EXAMPLE

7. Which of the following is an accurate comparison of the Declaration of Independence and the U.S. Constitution?

	DECLARATION OF INDEPENDENCE	CONSTITUTION
(A)	Reflects Enlightenment thought	Set up the framework for national government
(B)	Contains seven articles	Included a bill of rights as a priority
(C)	Justifies the need for an executive	Takes most powers from the state governments
(D)	Outlines the nation's first government	Was ratified with unanimous votes within states

The answer to question 7 is A. It is the only answer that makes an accurate statement about both the Declaration of Independence and the Constitution.

Knowledge The largest category of multiple-choice questions focuses on your acquisition of essential knowledge. These text-only, single questions require you to recall terms, concepts, functions, and processes. These questions will require you to classify concepts and identify stages in a process, such as how candidates get elected or how a bill becomes a law. These will require you to know how the three branches interact and to identify recent political trends. They will also test your recall of changes in policy and policymaking approaches over time, how the Supreme Court overturned a prior precedent, or how a particular voting bloc changed its loyalties from one political party to another. The questions will also test your knowledge of Supreme Court cases, notable laws, foundational documents, and terms.

Some of these are lengthy and could include complex definitions or even analysis within the question. Others are short with one-word answer choices. Common, too, in this type of question will be the real-world scenario question. A sentence or two will describe a situation that involves government officials, citizens, an issue, or an interaction, and you must determine the likely scenario to follow, the action one or more of the parties can take, or perhaps the cause(s) of the scenario.

EXAMPLES

8. Which of the following statements about the Electoral College is accurate?

   (A) The Electoral College votes for members of the House of Representatives.

   (B) The Electoral College votes for state governors.

   (C) The Electoral College votes for the president.

   (D) The Electoral College votes for senators.

9. Which of the following principles protects a citizen from imprisonment without fair procedures?

   (A) Due process

   (B) Separation of powers

   (C) Representative government

   (D) Checks and balances

10. Searching a person's car without a warrant or consent to search, a local police officer finds an illegal firearm. Which of the following concepts might prevent the firearm from being introduced as evidence at a trial?

    (A) Exclusionary rule

    (B) Probable cause

    (C) Freedom of speech

    (D) Right to remain silent

The answer to question 8 is C. The answer to question 9 is A and to question 10, A. The actual exam will have about 30 of these knowledge questions, a little over 50 percent of the multiple-choice questions.

Free-Response Questions

The free-response section of the exam consists of four questions you must answer in 100 minutes. These questions draw from multiple topics within the course. The College Board recommends you spend 20 minutes on the first three questions and 40 minutes on the fourth question, since it is more complex than the others.

There are four types of free-response questions on the exam.

Concept Application This type of free-response question will ask you to respond to a political scenario that often takes the form of a quoted passage from a news report or other document. The task is to explain how the scenario relates to political principles, institutions, process, policy, or behavior, using substantive examples to back up your answers.

EXAMPLE CONCEPT APPLICATION QUESTION

"Every day, more than 115 people in the United States die after overdosing on opioids. The misuse of and addiction to opioids—including prescription pain relievers, heroin, and synthetic opioids such as fentanyl—is a serious national crisis that affects public health as well as social and economic welfare. The Centers for Disease Control and Prevention estimates that the total "economic burden" of prescription opioid misuse alone in the United States is $78.5 billion a year, including the costs of healthcare, lost productivity, addiction treatment, and criminal justice involvement." —National Institute on Drug Abuse, March 2018

After reading the scenario, respond to A, B, and C below.

   (A) Describe a power Congress could use to address the issues outlined in the scenario.
   (B) In the context of the scenario, explain how the use of congressional power described in Part A can be affected by its interaction with special interest groups.
   (C) In the context of the scenario, explain how the interaction between Congress and special interest groups can be affected by the media.

The College Board has issued the following rubric for scoring this type of free-response question.

Scoring the Concept Application Question

A good response should:
   • Describe a political institution, behavior, or process connected with the scenario (0–1 point)
   • Explain how the response in part (A) affects or is affected by a political process, government entity, or citizen behavior as related to the scenario (0–1 point)
   • Explain how the scenario relates to a political institution, behavior, or process in the course (0–1 point)

As you can see, the maximum number of points you can earn on this free-response question is 3. A response earning 3 points might resemble the following:

SAMPLE ANSWER

The opioid crisis has been in the news for years now, and few solutions seem to have any lasting impact. However, it is within the power of Congress to pass legislation restricting the way opioids are prescribed and, through its power of the purse, appropriate more money for opioid education and addiction treatment. (This part addresses the first point, describing a process Congress could take to address the problem—1 point)

Unfortunately, these efforts may run into challenges. For example, special interest groups representing the pharmaceutical companies that make opioids tend to be large donors to officials' campaigns and to have a sizable number of well-connected lobbyists pressing the agendas of the pharmaceutical companies in Congress. (This part addresses the second point and is continued with elaboration—1 point.) These special interests develop long-term relationships known as iron triangles with elected officials as well as with employees of federal agencies that help carry out laws that try to balance the public interest with the demands of lobbyists and the corporations they represent and the reelection possibilities of officials. The reelection of officials requires both campaign contributions and the support of the public, so officials try to balance those needs in a reasonable way.

If the balance tends to tip too much in favor of the drug companies at the expense of public safety, the media can play a role to tip the balance back the other direction. Among the many roles media play is that of watchdog, keeping a close eye on government practices and investigating areas of concern and then bringing these matters out in public, where people can see for themselves what is taking place. (This part addresses the third point and continues with a substantive example.) An investigative report exposing corruption could be the catalyst for legal action and genuine change in policy, as it was in the days of the muckrakers in the Progressive Era when worker and consumer protections were put in place.

Quantitative Analysis A second type of free-response question resembles the type of multiple-choice question based on a table or graph. This type of question asks you to analyze data, identify trends or patterns, draw a conclusion from those trends, and then explain how the data relates to a political principle, institution, process, policy, or behavior.

EXAMPLE QUANTITATIVE ANALYSIS QUESTION

Use the information graphic on the next page to answer the questions.

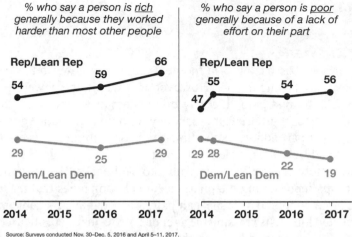

Differences between Republicans and Democrats on Why People are Rich or Poor

% who say a person is <u>rich</u> generally because they worked harder than most other people

Rep/Lean Rep
54   59   66

29   25   29
Dem/Lean Dem

2014   2015   2016   2017

% who say a person is <u>poor</u> generally because of a lack of effort on their part

Rep/Lean Rep
47   55   54   56

29 28   22   19
Dem/Lean Dem

2014   2015   2016   2017

Source: Surveys conducted Nov. 30–Dec. 5, 2016 and April 5–11, 2017.
PEW RESEARCH CENTER

(A) Identify the year in which Republicans/Lean Republican and Democrats/Lean Democrat were closest in their opinions on why people are poor.

(B) Describe a trend in the graph, and draw a conclusion about the possible causes of that trend.

(C) Explain how the attitudes shown in the information graphic demonstrate differences between Republicans and Democrats in Congress on social policy.

The College Board has issued the following rubric for scoring this type of free-response question.

Scoring the Quantitative Analysis Question

A good response should:

- Identify or describe the data in the quantitative visual (0–1 point)
- Describe a pattern, trend, or similarity/difference as prompted in the question (0–1 point) and draw a conclusion for that pattern, trend, or similarity/difference (0–1 point)
- Explain how specific data in the quantitative visual demonstrates a principle in the prompt (0–1 point)

The maximum number of points you can earn on this free-response question is 4. A response earning 4 points might resemble the following:

SAMPLE ANSWER

The graph shows how attitudes of Republicans and those leaning Republican differ from those of Democrats and those leaning Democratic on reasons people are rich or poor. The two groups were closest in their opinions about why people are poor in 2014, when 29 percent of Democrats and those leaning Democratic believed people are poor because of a lack of effort on their part, while 47 percent of Republicans and those leaning Republican held that view. The difference in opinions between the two groups widened after that. (This part of the answer addresses the first part of the prompt—1 point.)

One trend visible in the data is that attitudes about the reasons for poverty are moving in opposite directions for the two groups. In 2014, the percentage of Republican and Republican-leaning people who believed people were poor because of a lack of effort on their part was 47 percent. In 2017, that percentage had risen to 56 percent. In the same years, the views of Democrats and Democratic-leaning people moved from 29 percent to 19 percent. (The previous section identifies a trend—1 point.) One possible conclusion from this trend is that Americans are becoming more polarized, just as the Congress that represents them is. (This sentence offers a possible conclusion—1 point.)

These attitudes demonstrate a difference in how Republicans and Democrats in Congress approach social policy. Republicans are less supportive than Democrats of government-sponsored social programs, such as health care subsidies, welfare, and food stamps, believing that people are poor because they do not exert enough effort. Democrats, on the other hand, believing that poverty results from circumstances beyond people's control, tend to support programs that help people overcome some of the limitations of their environments to try to rise out of poverty. (This part shows how the attitudes demonstrate behavior of Congress members from different parties—1 point.)

SCOTUS Comparison This type of free-response question asks you to compare a non-required Supreme Court case to one of the 15 required cases. For this question you will need to explain how information from the required case relates to information in the non-required case.

EXAMPLE SCOTUS COMPARISON QUESTION

The 1942 Supreme Court case of *Betts v. Brady* centered on Smith Betts, a poor person indicted on burglary in Maryland. He had no money to hire a lawyer, so he requested that one be made available to him by the state. A previous case had concluded that defendants had the right to an attorney. However, the judge refused. Betts pleaded not guilty, served as his own counsel, and was found guilty. He held onto his conviction that he was entitled to a lawyer and appealed the case. When it reached the Supreme Court, the question the Court faced was, "Does refusing a poor person an attorney violate the Constitution?" The Supreme Court ruled that it did not, that the state could not prevent a defendant from using an attorney but it was not obligated to provide one.

(A) Identify the constitutional clause that is common to both *Betts v. Brady* and *Gideon v. Wainwright* (1963).

(B) Based on the constitutional clause identified in (A), explain why the facts of *Gideon v. Wainwright* led to a different holding than the holding in *Betts v. Brady.*

(C) Explain how the holding in *Betts v. Brady* relates to the process of selective incorporation.

The College Board provides the following scoring guide for the SCOTUS comparison question.

Scoring the SCOTUS Comparison Question

A good response should:

- Identify a similarity or difference between the two Supreme Court cases, as specified in the question (0–1 point)
- Provide prompted factual information from the specified required Supreme Court case (0-1 point) and explain how or why that information from the specified required Supreme Court case is relevant to the non-required Supreme Court case described in the question (0–1 point)
- Describe or explain an interaction between the holding in the non-required Supreme Court case and a relevant political institution, behavior, or process (0–1 point)

This type of question has a maximum of 4 points. A response earning 4 points might resemble the following.

SAMPLE ANSWER

The constitutional clause common to both *Betts v. Brady* and *Gideon v. Wainwright* is the Sixth Amendment's guarantee of an accused's right to counsel, specifically whether this right applies to state courts as well as federal courts and to felonies as well as more serious capital offences. (This earns 1 point.)

The facts of both cases are similar. Both defendants stood trial for a noncapital offence, and both made the same argument that under the Sixth Amendment, which provides the right to counsel in a federal court, they had the right to counsel in a state court as well and, as poor people, they should be provided counsel by the government. (This scores 1 point.) On just the facts of the cases, there is not much to explain the different holdings. A better explanation is that the makeup of the Supreme Court had changed. By the time Gideon's case came before the Court, the chief justice was Earl Warren, whose Court was known for taking a stand for individual liberties. (This scores 1 point.)

The holding in *Betts v. Brady* denied incorporation of the Sixth Amendment through the due process clause of the Fourteenth Amendment. The landmark case of *Gideon v. Wainwright* reversed that holding and incorporated the Sixth Amendment so that defendants in state courts had the same right to an attorney as defendants in federal courts and, further, that an attorney needed to be provided to people who could not afford one. (This scores 1 point.)

Argument Essay The final free-response question type, the argument essay, requires developing an argument in the form of an essay and using evidence from one or more foundational documents to back up your claim.

EXAMPLE ARGUMENT ESSAY QUESTION

Develop an argument that explains whether or not breaking the law in the course of civil disobedience is acceptable.
In your essay, you must:

- Articulate a defensible claim or thesis that responds to the prompt and establishes a line of reasoning
- Support your claim with at least TWO pieces of accurate and relevant information:
  - At least ONE piece of evidence must be from one of the following foundational documents:
    - Fourteenth Amendment
    - "Letter from a Birmingham Jail"
  - Use a second piece of evidence from the other foundational document above or from your study of civil rights
- Use reasoning to explain why your evidence supports your claim/ thesis
- Respond to an opposing or alternative perspective using refutation, concession, or rebuttal

The College Board provides this scoring guide for the argument essay.

The argument essay is worth 6 points. A response earning all six points might resemble the following.

SAMPLE ANSWER

As Americans, we value the rule of law. It is one of the principles that sets us apart from autocracies and dictatorships because it binds everyone, even those holding the highest offices in the nation, to the same legal limits. However, there are times when the importance of following the law may be outweighed by the importance of breaking it if breaking the law can help bring about a needed social change. The due process clause of the Fourteenth Amendment has motivated many social changes, and if groups of people are denied the protection of due process, civil disobedience may be the best way to bring the matter to the attention of the American people, who can then pressure their representatives in government for meaningful change. (The highlighted portion is a defensible claim, and the rest of the paragraph lays out a line of reasoning—1 point.)

The Fourteenth Amendment was developed to protect freed slaves. It made equal treatment under the law a fundamental governing principle. The ideal of the Fourteenth Amendment, however, is not always easy to achieve. The amendment, with its promises of life, liberty, and property and the equal protection of the laws, did not automatically enforce itself. (Description of one piece of evidence accurately linked to topic—1 point.) For example, African Americans, especially in the South, were routinely denied rights exercised by white citizens—the right to vote, the right to equal access to public accommodations, the right to nonsegregated schools, even in many cases the right to their lives. Without any reason to change, life in the South may have continued that way for another century, depriving more generations of African Americans the rights that many other Americans take for granted.

Dr. Martin Luther King Jr. recognized this possibility in his "Letter from a Birmingham Jail." He responded to the white clergy of Birmingham who criticized him for staging a protest over the Easter weekend by listing a long series of reasons African Americans have waited in the past based on promises from whites that never materialized. King knew that without a catalyst, change would never come. He recognized that negotiations were, as the white clergy stated, the best way to work toward progress, but King knew that no negotiations would actually happen unless they were forced. (One piece of specific and relevant evidence to support the argument—1 point.)

King also recognized that there were different types of laws and pointed out to his readers that for years, Jim Crow laws, fully legal, kept African Americans from equal protection of the laws. The law that Dr. King decided to break was not of that type. The law he broke was a court order not to hold a protest in the business district of Birmingham, where King had planned it because it would have the biggest economic effect on local businesses. It was a nonviolent protest, and when the police came to arrest him and Rev. Ralph Abernathy, they went to jail without resistance. (Another piece of specific and relevant evidence—1 point.)

Those who oppose civil disobedience, as the white clergy in Birmingham did, argue that civil disobedience will only increase hostilities and that with patience and good will progress can be made. As Dr. King points out, blaming nonviolent protesters for any violence that breaks out in response to it is like blaming the robbed man for having the money that led to the robbery. And the South had decades of good will and patience from African Americans with no progress to show for it. (Rebuttal consistent with the argument—1 point)

Both Dr. King's actions and his words in "A Letter from a Birmingham Jail" show the value and necessity of civil disobedience. While much remained to be done after the Birmingham protests, his actions there were no doubt an example of courage for others to follow—not just African Americans, but in later decades war protesters, women, members of the LGBT community, and people with disabilities. And his words laid out a careful argument for the necessity of civil disobedience tied to moral principles, tied to the growth that follows from tension over the injustice of laws when it is brought to light. (Explanation of how the evidence supports the argument—1 point)

Exam Day

Wake up in time to relax and eat a normal breakfast. Bring two #2 pencils for the multiple-choice section, two black or blue ink pens for the free-response section, and a watch. Wear comfortable clothing suitable for a cold or hot testing room. Do not bring any government books, laptops, cell phones, iWatches, or any other connective device. Follow the general advice below to make the most of your testing experience.

Overall Scoring and Credit

The exams are scored in early June and reported back to you and your high school in mid-summer. You can earn between 0 and 5 points.

Many colleges award credit for a score of 3 or better; some require a 5; and occasionally prestigious universities do not recognize the AP Government and Politics exam performance. The College Board equates a score of 5 to an A in a college-level class, a 4 to an A-, B+, or B, and a 3 to roughly a B-, C+, or C.

In 2017, just over 11 percent of those taking the exam earned a score of 5. More than 12 percent received a 4 and 26 percent earned a 3. About 25 percent earned a 2, and roughly another 25 percent earned a 1. So considering a score of 3 as passing (or "qualified"), just over half the students passed the exam. Many colleges consider a passing score on the AP exam to be equivalent to the introduction to American government course often called something like American Politics or Political Science 101. To help you plan for the exam, the College Board provides a site to connect with universities across the nation. Use it to find how your college regards the exam and what score they require (see www.collegeboard.com/ap/creditpolicy).

A Final Note

Large numbers of Americans, especially independents and young adults, mistrust politicians and the partisan talking heads on cable TV and are turned off by the political process. It is normal to feel this way. However, don't let an understandable irritation with polarizing partisans hamper your chances for success as a student or diminish your performance on the exam. You are primarily a student observer. As you begin your in-depth study of the course, though, you may find that as you learn more about the United States government, you can move from observer to participant.

UNIT 1: Foundations of American Democracy

Chapter 1 *The Constitution*

Chapter 2 *Federalism*

After suffering a decade of imposed tax laws and rights violations, in 1776 the British colonists presented the Declaration of Independence to the British Crown to break away from British control. The U.S. government at first operated under the Articles of Confederation, a weak form of government, until delegates convened in Philadelphia in 1787 to draft a new constitution. After a public debate between **Federalists**, who endorsed the plan, and Anti-Federalists, who opposed the plan, the states ultimately ratified the Constitution the following year.

The Constitution defined the three branches of government, relations among the states, national and state powers, and the process to alter, or amend, the document itself. Chief among its provisions are the checks and balances, which keep any one branch from becoming too powerful. Also, the amendment process allowed for a swift addition of the Bill of Rights in 1791 and, eventually, a total of 27 amendments.

The Constitution established **federalism**, a system of government that divides the power between the national and state governments. As new national concerns have surfaced, Congress has used its power to set policies to address these issues consistently throughout the states. The federal government has sometimes awarded large financial grants to encourage state action but has simply mandated others. Yet states use their power to maintain jurisdiction over schools, marriages and divorces, criminal law enforcement, wills, deeds, motor-vehicle law, and several other aspects of life. Through state referenda, citizens have recently made unique and varied changes on family leave, gambling, and the legalization of marijuana.

Enduring Understandings: Foundations of American Democracy

LOR-1: A balance between governmental power and individual rights has been a hallmark of American political development.

CON-1: The Constitution emerged from the debate about weaknesses in the Articles of Confederation as a blueprint for limited government.

PMI-1: The Constitution created a competitive policymaking process to ensure the people's will is represented and that freedom is preserved.

CON-2: Federalism reflects the dynamic distribution of power between national and state governments.

Source: *AP® United States Government and Politics Course and Exam Description*

The Constitution

"I doubt . . . whether any other Convention we can obtain, may be able to make a better Constitution . . . . From such an assembly can a perfect production be expected? It therefore astonishes me, Sir, to find this system approaching so near to perfection as it does . . . ."

—Ben Franklin on the proposed Constitution, 1787

Essential Question: How have theory, debate, and compromise influenced the United States' system of government that balances governmental power and individual rights?

The United States Constitution is the document that provides the guidelines for the national government. Drafted in Philadelphia in 1787 and officially ratified in 1788, the Constitution defines governing principles, national offices, functions, and limitations. It created the legislative, executive, and judicial branches; defined federalism and the relationship among the states; and provided for a method to alter, or amend, the document. In 1791, the states ratified the first ten amendments to the Constitution, known as the Bill of Rights. Seventeen amendments have been added since.

Because the Constitution is the blueprint for our government, knowing and understanding this document is essential to this course and to understanding American government. The full text of the Constitution is printed in the back of this book and available online at http://constitutioncenter.org/interactive-constitution. When reading about particular provisions or clauses, turn to it for reference. Keep good notes on key passages and their importance. These practices will help you master the content and overall structure of the document.

American Independence and Early National Government

The Constitution and the new government it defines did not come into being easily. It took a war with Great Britain, a governing experiment, and a three-year struggle to create a more perfect union.

In the 1770s, after a century of British rule in the American colonies, the colonists and Britain's King George III came to an impasse after Parliament passed a series of tax laws. Leaders from the 13 colonies challenged British authority. They were inspired by philosophers from the Enlightenment who had argued for natural,

God-given rights and for a **social contract** between a democratic government and the people. They argued that if a government violated the understood compact between the state and the governed, then the people could take that power back. After a successful military campaign, the leading American revolutionaries became the founding fathers of the new nation. After a failed attempt to govern themselves during the 1780s under the Articles of Confederation, a stronger framework—the Constitution—became necessary for the United States to transition from a loose collection of sovereign states into a united republic.

TIMELINE

1764 – Parliament passes Sugar Act

1765 – Parliament passes Stamp Act

1770 – Boston Massacre

1773 – Boston Tea Party

1774 – First Continental Congress

1775 – Battles of Lexington and Concord

1776 – Declaration of Independence

1781 – Articles of Confederation ratified

1783 – Treaty of Paris

1786 – Shays's Rebellion

1787 – Constitutional Convention

1789 – President Washington, Congress elected

1789 – Congress proposes Bill of Rights

1790 – Rhode Island, the 13th state, ratifies Constitution

1791 – Bill of Rights ratified

Source: *Allyn Cox, Architect of the Capitol*

The First Continental Congress

Source: *archive.org*

Shays's Rebellion

Source: *Library of Congress*

Constitution

The Road to Revolution

Britain's King George III and Parliament passed laws that restricted the colonists' freedoms and taxed them to help finance the Crown's empire. With plentiful land and resources, the North American colonies were among Britain's most financially successful properties in an otherwise financially challenging time. Decades of wars and imperial endeavors had ravaged the British treasury. The British empire controlled colonies throughout the world, and maintaining such a far-flung empire required revenue. The Sugar Act was Britain's first attempt at increasing revenue. Soon the Stamp Act, which taxed colonists who transacted legal documents, the Tea Act, and other acts followed.

The colonists organized to oppose the acts. Some colonists opposed the taxes on a practical, economic basis, but most outspoken American leaders took a principled position against the laws because Parliament created these without any colonial representation. No colonist expected the democratic representation Americans value today. At the time only white men with property could cast votes in English and in American elections, but colonists felt the Crown's complete disregard for any representation at all violated the Enlightenment philosophies they so revered.

"No taxation without representation!" demanded the colonists. The British government responded unapologetically and declared the colonists were "virtually represented." They reminded colonists that most citizens residing throughout the British Isles, about 90 percent, could not vote. Members of Parliament insisted they still considered the colonists' best interests.

Tensions increased as protesters refused to abide by the new laws and the British government doubled down to enforce them. Royal courts tried and convicted protesters unfairly. The British government violated the ideas of free speech, free assembly, and free press by exacting punishments when colonists spoke, gathered, or published in opposition. Colonial leaders attempted at first to negotiate a peaceful relationship through the Olive Branch Petition to King George, a symbolic act of peace in which they pledged loyalty but also made clear their grievances. The King rejected that petition, and the colonies mobilized for revolt.

Influence of Enlightenment Thought

The Sons of Liberty and other advocates for freedom drew on Enlightenment political theory. It had been developed when the principles of rationalism that had unlocked doors to the natural world during the Scientific Revolution were applied to the social world as well. Especially influential were the writings of English philosopher John Locke (1632–1704) and Swiss-born philosopher Jean-Jacques Rousseau (1712–1778).

John Locke and Natural Law Locke argued that **natural law** is the law of God and that this law is acknowledged through human sense and reason. He proposed that under natural law—in a state of nature—people were born free and equal. According to this law, Locke reasoned, "No one can be . . .

subjected to the political power of another, without his own consent." Locke argued further that natural law not only entitled but obligated people to rebel when the rule of kings did not respect the consent of the governed.

Jean-Jacques Rousseau and the Social Contract Rousseau was much influenced by Locke. He spoke for those "intending their minds" away from an irrational and oppressive political order, away from a governmental theory that rested in divine right of kings and clergy to rule and misrule. The opening sentence of his influential treatise, *The Social Contract,* dramatically lays out a key human problem: "Man was born free, and he is everywhere in chains." The social contract Rousseau describes is the agreement of free and equal people to abandon certain natural rights in order to find secure protections for society and to find freedom in a single body politic committed to the general good. He envisioned **popular sovereignty**—the people as the ultimate ruling authority—and a government of officials to carry out the laws.

French philosopher Montesquieu (1689–1755), like Rousseau, recognized both the sovereign and administrative aspects of governmental power. He argued for the separation of powers in the administrative government, comprised of the executive, legislative, and judicial branches.

Enlightenment thought was well known among English colonists in North America. According to historian Carl Becker, "Most Americans had absorbed Locke's works as a kind of political gospel." The American revolutionaries believed that men were entitled to "life, liberty, and property" and that these cannot be taken away except under laws created through the consent of the governed. These beliefs formed the bedrock of the political ideology known as **republicanism**. The lack of colonial representation in Parliament, taxation without consent, and subsequent infringements of liberty violated fundamental rights and the values of republicanism and would, in time, be remedied by an independent, limited, and representative government based on the ideas of natural rights, popular sovereignty, republicanism, and social contract.

Three Kinds of Representative Democracies

Representative democracies based on the values of republicanism can take at least three forms.

Participatory Democracy This form of democracy depends on direct participation of many, if not most, people in a society, not only in government but in public life as well. In a participatory democracy, people vote directly for laws and other matters that affect them instead of voting for people to represent their interests. The democracy in 5th-century Athens was participatory, though only adult male citizens could vote. More recently, a group of college students in the 1960s started a movement in participatory democracy. Protesting wars abroad and inequality at home, they formed Students for a Democratic Society. In 1962 some of the members met in Port Huron, Michigan. They modeled participatory decision-making as they collaboratively drafted their beliefs in the "Port Huron Statement." This document calls for the direct involvement of ordinary citizens, especially through civil disobedience. One of the founders of the organization and drafter of the statement, Tom Hayden, explained years later that "the concept arose . . . in response to the severe limitations of an undemocratic system that we saw as representing an oligarchy [a system in which a small number of people hold most of the power]."

In the 21st century, participants in the Occupy Wall Street movement, which spread to many locations in the United States partly through social media sharing, camped out in financial districts to protest wealth inequality, the corporate influence on government, and political corruption. Occupy Wall Street designed itself along the guidelines of participatory democracy, using a bottom-up rather than top-down approach to formalizing policy, encouraging each member to participate both in person and on social media. However, its participatory nature made decision-making difficult and slow and action agendas hard to develop.

A number of states use a form of participatory democracy when citizens who gather sufficient signatures place issues on the ballot for the people to decide. Twenty-six states allow some form of ballot measures. On Election Day 2016, some of the issues voters were deciding through ballot measures related to gun control, the death penalty, a minimum wage, and bilingual education. (See pages 487–488 for more on ballot measures.)

Pluralist Democracy In a **pluralist democracy**, nongovernmental groups organize to try to exert influence on political decision-making. *Interest groups*, as these groups are called, such as organized labor unions or gun advocates, are one of the most influential types of groups. They interact with government officials searching for consensus among competing interests. They raise and spend money in elections to ensure that people friendly to their ideas are elected. These groups send professional researchers and experts to testify at congressional committee hearings in hopes of shaping or stopping a bill. They monitor the government as it enforces existing law, and they buy advertisements and other media products to influence public opinion. (See Chapter 15 for more on interest groups.)

Pluralist theorists believe that the ideas and viewpoints in the United States are so scattered and so varied that no single view can control the shaping and administration of policy. We live in a world of so many policymakers putting into effect so many rules and procedures at the local, state, and federal levels that no single input shapes our body of law. We are a nation of immigrants, both ethnically and ideologically diverse, and the large variety of viewpoints results in public policy that is usually established and accepted by a consensus.

Elite Democracy In an **elite democracy**, elected representatives make decisions and act as trustees for the people who elected them. Elite democracy recognizes an inequity in the spread of power among the populace and that the elites—people with resources and influence—dominate. Dominating influence by the elites, a trait of the United States when it was founded, weakened somewhat in the Progressive Era (1890–1920) when the masses became more involved in politics. Yet in many ways, elite-dominated politics prevail today.

Individuals with the most time, education, money, and access to government will take more action than the less privileged, and because of their resources, they will be heard. People who serve in the leadership of a political party, whether on the local or national level, are usually of a higher socioeconomic level, better known, and better educated than the rank and file, the many members of a group who constitute the group's body.

Declaring Independence

Before Americans knew exactly what their representative democracy would look like, American-British tensions rose to new heights. By the summer of 1776, the Continental Congress commissioned a committee of five men—Thomas Jefferson, John Adams, Benjamin Franklin, Roger Sherman, and Robert Livingston—to draft an official statement to summarize the colonists' views. In that document, which became the **Declaration of Independence,** these men justified the break from Britain and proclaimed to the world the reasons for independence. The declaration, signed on July 4, 1776, created a moral and legal justification for the rebellion.

THE 13 ORIGINAL COLONIES

The Declaration of Independence drew from Locke and other Enlightenment philosophers, upholding popular sovereignty. It explained how abuses by the too powerful British Crown violated individual rights, justified the colonists' separation from Britain, and defined the newly independent states' relationship. Following are key excerpts from the declaration.

When in the Course of human events, it becomes necessary for one people to dissolve the political bands which have connected them with another . . . they should declare the causes which impel them to the separation. We hold these truths to be self-evident, that all men are created equal, that they are endowed by their Creator with certain unalienable Rights, that among these are Life, Liberty and the pursuit of Happiness.—That to secure these rights, Governments are instituted among Men, deriving their just powers from the consent of the governed, —That whenever any Form of Government becomes destructive of these ends, it is the Right of the People to alter or to abolish it . . . .

The history of the present King of Great Britain is a history of repeated injuries and usurpations . . . . He has refused his Assent to Laws, the most wholesome and necessary for the public good . . . . He has called together legislative bodies at places unusual, uncomfortable, and distant . . . . He has dissolved Representative Houses repeatedly, for opposing with manly firmness his invasions on the rights of the people . . . . He has plundered our seas, ravaged our Coasts, burnt our towns, and destroyed the lives of our people . . . .

[For these reasons], these United Colonies are, and of Right ought to be Free and Independent States . . . . And for the support of this Declaration, with a firm reliance on the protection of divine Providence, we mutually pledge to each other our Lives, our Fortunes and our sacred Honor.

Political Science Disciplinary Practices: Analyze the Declaration of Independence as Argument

The Declaration of Independence is widely regarded as an outstanding example of classic argument—a written or spoken effort to persuade people to adopt a certain point of view or take a certain action. When you analyze an argument, you take it apart to understand its elements. You identify the author's *claims*—statements asserted to be true—and the reasoning the author uses to support those claims. For example, the declaration asserts that governments derive their power from the consent of the governed, establishing the basis for popular sovereignty. The declaration also claims that people have the right to alter or abolish a government that is destructive to people's rights.

Apply: Explain how these claims relate to Enlightenment thought and republican ideals. Then read the full Declaration of Independence on pages 619–622, and answer the questions that follow it for an in-depth analysis of the argument in this founding document. You may also read it online.

The Declaration Committee (left to right: Thomas Jefferson, Roger Sherman, Benjamin Franklin, Robert R. Livingston, and John Adams)

During the war, Americans instituted the Continental Congress to govern the American states collectively, and they began to formalize their ideas for a permanent government. The war raged on until General George Washington's army defeated the British at Yorktown, Virginia, in 1781. An official peace was negotiated in 1783 with the Treaty of Paris.

The Articles of Confederation

As soon as the states declared independence, they realized a more formal relationship among them could only assist their cause. The Continental Congress created a committee of 13 men to draft the **Articles of Confederation,** a series of statements that defined the initial national government and redefined the former colonies as states. Though the Articles of Confederation were not officially ratified by the states until 1781, the Continental Congress legislated during wartime with a wide array of powers to adopt commercial codes, establish and maintain an army, define crimes against the United States, and negotiate foreign affairs abroad. This document defined "the firm league of friendship" that existed among the states, which had delegated a few powers to the national government.

How to apportion states' representation in the newly designed Confederation Congress was beset with controversy. Some leaders recognized the merits of giving greater representation to the more populated states, something the Virginia delegation advocated. Leaders from smaller states opposed representation based on population. After a furious debate, the authors of the Articles created an equal representation system—each state received one vote in the Congress.

The Confederation Congress continued to meet in New York. States appointed delegations of up to seven men that voted as a unit. National legislation required the votes of at least nine states to pass. A unanimous vote was required to alter or amend the Articles of Confederation. The Articles entitled the Congress to engage in international diplomacy, declare war, and acquire territory. They provided protection of religion and speech. They provided for **extradition**— that is, states were expected to extradite, or return, fugitives to states where they had committed crimes and runaway slaves to states they had fled. The document encouraged a free flow of commerce among the states. It required that states provide a public, fair government and that Congress could sit as a court in disputes between states.

The Articles of Confederation provide that "each state retains its sovereignty, freedom, and independence." This provision was essential, since the states were wary of a centralized power that might wield the same influence over them that the British government wielded. Following are some of the key provisions of the Articles of Confederation.

> Each state retains its sovereignty, freedom, and independence, and every Power, [not] . . . expressly delegated to the United States, in Congress assembled. . . .
>
> In determining questions in the United States, in Congress assembled, each State shall have one vote. . . .
>
> The United States in Congress assembled, shall have the sole and exclusive right and power of determining on peace and war. . . .
>
> Full faith and credit shall be given in each of these States to the records, acts, and judicial proceedings of the courts and magistrates of every other State. . . .
>
> Congress assembled shall also be the last resort on appeal in all disputes and differences now subsisting or that hereafter may arise between two or more States.

Political Science Disciplinary Practices: Relate the Articles of Confederation to Political Principles and Institutions

Apply: Review the three types of democracies described on pages 5–7. Based on the provisions above, identify the type of democracy that the Articles of Confederation created. Describe two provisions of the Articles of Confederation that demonstrate that type of democracy.

Then read the full Articles of Confederation on pages 622–628, and answer the questions that follow it. You may also read it online.

An Ineffective Confederation and a Call for New Government

The Articles of Confederation provided a weak system for the new United States and prevented leaders from making much domestic progress. The system had rendered the Confederation Congress ineffective. In fact, the stagnation and a degree of anarchy threatened the health of the nation. The country faced a high war debt, and foreign creditors lost faith in this new nation. States quarreled over boundary disputes. Interstate trade was chaotic.

The chart on the next page summarizes some of the weaknesses.

- The requirements that at least nine states must agree in order to enact national law and that all states must agree unanimously in order to amend the system of government proved daunting.
- The Congress could not tax the people directly.
- The national government could not raise or maintain an army.
- There was no national court system or national currency.
- The Congress encouraged but could not regulate commerce among the states.

Shays's Rebellion and Response

The lack of a centralized military power became a serious problem when a regional rebellion broke out. In western Massachusetts in 1786, a large group of impoverished farmers, including many Revolutionary War veterans, lost their farms to mortgage foreclosures and failure to pay taxes. Daniel Shays, a former captain in the Continental army, led the group, who demanded that the government ease financial pressures by printing more money, lightening taxes, and suspending mortgages. They grabbed their muskets and challenged the Massachusetts government. Massachusetts raised a small army with donations from the wealthy citizenry in an attempt to put down the uprising, but without a centralized military power, the Confederation could not muster a national army. Several skirmishes occurred, and three of Shays's men were killed. The movement soon collapsed, but Shays's Rebellion, along with irregularities in commerce, made leaders realize the need to revise government. A small group convened in Annapolis, Maryland, to discuss the concerns. This convention addressed trade and the untapped economic potential of the new United States. Little was accomplished, however, except to secure a recommendation for Congress to call a more comprehensive convention.

Congress scheduled the much larger convention for May of 1787 in Philadelphia. By then few Americans viewed the Articles of Confederation as sufficient. John Adams, who was serving in Congress, argued that a man's "country" was still his state and, for his Massachusetts delegation, the Congress was "our embassy." There was little sense of national unity.

Debate and Compromise at the Constitutional Convention

The Confederation Congress called the convention in Philadelphia "for the sole and express purpose of revising the Articles of Confederation." By the time the process was over, critics pointed to the extralegal manner—outside the law—in which the Articles were instead completely replaced by a new system of government. In May 1787, delegates from neighboring states began to arrive at Independence Hall (the Pennsylvania State House) to get an early start on improving national governance. Among the first to arrive was thirty-six-year-old Virginia lawyer **James Madison**, and he was well prepared for the deliberations. His friend Thomas Jefferson was serving in Paris as the U.S. ambassador to France, and he sent Madison books from Europe on ancient governments, both successful and failed examples. Though Madison was not the most vocal at the convention, he kept detailed records of the Convention, including debate speeches and the votes of the delegates present. His influence in creating the plan for the new government and his stalwart support of it during the ratification process (see pages 21–25) earned him the nickname Father of the Constitution.

Other noteworthy delegates included George Washington, who served as a cooling force during heated debate. In fact, Washington's participation alone elevated the validity of the meeting and the endeavor to enhance government. Another influential founder, Alexander Hamilton, Washington's aide-de-camp during the war, proved annoying at the meetings for his long-winded speeches. Benjamin Franklin, the elder statesman at age eighty-one, offered his experience as one who had participated in the drafting of the Declaration of Independence, the Articles of Confederation themselves, and the Treaty of Paris with Britain. He also held distinction in discovery, invention, and civic endeavors.

In addition to these leading statesmen, others in attendance included representatives with significant experience in public affairs, some of whom would become future Supreme Court justices, cabinet members, and notable congressmen. Nearly three-fourths of the delegates had served in the Continental Congress. Several had helped draft their state constitutions. Eight had also signed the Declaration of Independence. Twenty-one had fought in the Revolutionary War.

As soon as the quorum (enough present to conduct business) of seven states arrived, the convention established some basic ground rules. The delegates unanimously elected General Washington, the most revered man in

Source: *Thinkstock*
James Madison, the Father of the Constitution

the room, as president of the convention. All delegates had an opportunity to speak uninterrupted but then had to wait for any other delegates responding before speaking again. States would vote as units, and a simple majority would carry each state's vote. Perhaps the most controversial rule was that those attending the convention had to keep everything secret during the proceedings until the entire plan was ready to present to the public. The controversy and intense viewpoints had the potential to incite exaggerated rumors. Opponents of the convention would feed on any information, or misinformation, to dismantle this plan. To protect convention proceedings, and despite the heat and the annoyance of flies, the delegates kept the windows closed and the proceedings quiet for the duration of the convention.

The Virginia Plan Numerous plans were presented to the convention to improve the workings of the national government. Virginia's governor Edmund Randolph introduced what was later dubbed the **Virginia Plan**. Written largely by Madison, the plan created a three-branch system of government defined by 15 resolves. It called for a national executive to administer the business of state, a judiciary, and a **bicameral**, or two-house, legislature. The people would elect a lower house that would then elect members of an upper house. This plan became the blueprint for the Constitution. The Virginia Plan also made the national government supreme over the states and offered the ideas for a multitiered court system and the **separation of powers**, defining the distinct responsibilities and limits of each branch to keep any one branch from becoming too powerful. Delegates discussed and intensely debated the plan, as the smaller states began to fear the overwhelming representation larger states would have.

The New Jersey Plan William Paterson of New Jersey introduced a counterproposal for government. The **New Jersey Plan**, as it came to be known, differed from Randolph's proposal in important ways. It assured that states would retain sovereignty; it proposed that the national legislature would have only limited and defined powers; and it included no provision for national courts. Two other distinct differences between Paterson's plan and the Virginia Plan lay in how representation would be apportioned and whether or not the new government would be "federal," a collection of sovereign states gathered to govern, or "national," a unified authority with absolute sovereignty over the entire nation as well as the individual states.

The Great Compromise Representation had been the frustration of the Americans since they began seeking independence. The more populated states believed they deserved a stronger voice in making national policy decisions. The smaller states sought to retain an equal footing. The matter was referred to a committee made up of one delegate from each of the states represented at the convention, a committee that became known as the **Grand Committee**. George Mason, William Paterson, and Benjamin Franklin were among those on the Grand Committee. When Roger Sherman of Connecticut joined the committee, taking the place of Oliver Ellsworth who became ill, he took the lead in forging a compromise that became known as the **Great Compromise** (or the Connecticut Compromise). Sherman's proposal created a two-house Congress composed of a **House of Representatives** and a **Senate**. His plan satisfied both those wanting population as the criteria for awarding seats in a legislature, because House seats would be awarded based on population, and those wanting equal representation, because the Senate would receive two senators from each state, regardless of the state's size.

Slavery and the Three-Fifths Compromise Another compromise would be necessary before the question of representation was settled, however. Delegates from nonslave states questioned how slaves would be counted in determining representation. Since slaves did not have the right to vote, those who were able to vote in slave states would have more sway than voters in nonslave states if slaves were counted in the population. Roger Sherman once more put forward a compromise, this time with Pennsylvania delegate James Wilson. They introduced and the convention accepted the **Three-Fifths Compromise**: the northern and southern delegates agreed to count only three of every five slaves to determine representation in the House.

SUMMARY OF MAJOR COMPROMISES	
Virginia Plan	Three branches, bicameral legislature, supremacy of national government, separation of powers
New Jersey Plan	Sovereignty of states, limited and defined powers of national legislature
Great Compromise	Members of the House of Representatives apportioned by population; each state given two senators
Three-Fifths Compromise and Importation of Slaves	Only three of every five slaves would be counted for the purpose of representation in the House of Representatives Congress could not stop the importation of slaves for 20 years after ratification
Electoral College	States decide how their electors are chosen, with each state having the same number of electors as they had representatives in Congress

Two other issues regarding slavery were also debated then addressed in the Constitution, although the words "slave" and "slavery" do not appear in the document. Delegates questioned whether the states or the federal government should have the power to control or regulate slavery. They also debated how to handle slave insurrection, or runaways. Delegates resolved the first matter by prohibiting Congress from stopping the international slave trade for twenty years after ratification of the Constitution. They resolved the second debate with an extradition clause that addressed how states should handle runaway slaves.

Other compromises would be necessary during the summer-long convention in Philadelphia. For example, delegates debated whether or not the United States needed a president or chief executive and how such an officer should be elected. Some argued that the president should be elected by members of Congress. Others argued for the election of the president to be done by the state governors or state legislatures, and some thought the people themselves should directly elect the president. The **Electoral College** was the compromise solution. Under this plan, states could decide how their electors would be chosen. Each state would have the same number of electors that they had representatives in Congress, and the people would vote for the electors. Having electors rather than the popular vote choose the president represents one way in which the elite model of democracy helps shape government today.

Still other compromises were needed to resolve what powers the federal government would have and what powers the states would retain. This debate went back to the debates when the Articles of Confederation were drafted. The delegates who desired stronger states' rights and feared a national centralization of power wanted a limited list of powers granted to the national government. They wanted a confederal system—a loose collection of sovereign states gathered for a common purpose—the very relationship defined under the Articles of Confederation. A national government, however, would make the national lawmaking body supreme and create a stronger union instead of a loose collection of states. Delegates also considered what types of laws the Congress could make and what citizen rights to protect. What resulted from "a bundle of compromises" was the U.S. Constitution.

The table on the next page shows the relationship of key provisions of the Articles of Confederation to the debate over granting the federal government greater power formerly reserved to the states; it also shows how the debate was resolved in the new Constitution.

ARTICLES OF CONFEDERATION	DEBATE ABOUT STATE POWERS	RESOLUTION IN CONSTITUTION
"Each state retains its sovereignty, freedom, and independence, and every Power, [not] . . . expressly delegated to the United States, in Congress assembled."	After their struggle with the British government, members of the Confederation Congress were reluctant to turn over any but the most essential powers to the national government.	States retain sovereignty; the powers of national legislature are limited and defined. (New Jersey Plan)
"In determining questions in the United States, in Congress assembled, each State shall have one vote."	Leaders of populous states wanted representation based on population. Leaders from smaller states did not. One vote per state was a compromise. Representatives from more populous states would have to vote unanimously as one vote.	Members of the House of Representatives are apportioned by population; each state is given two senators. (The Great Compromise)
"Full faith and credit shall be given in each of these States to the records, acts, and judicial proceedings of the courts and magistrates of every other State."	The states were unsure how their records, laws, and judgments would be regarded in other states and how they would regard those of other states.	Article IV's "full faith and credit" clause guarantees that "the citizens of each state shall be entitled to all privileges and immunities of citizens in the several states."
"Congress assembled shall also be the last resort on appeal in all disputes and differences now subsisting or that hereafter may arise between two or more States."	To resolve differences among states, leaders at the Confederation Congress determined the federal government would have the final word.	Article VI's "supremacy clause" establishes the Constitution and the laws of the United States as the "supreme law of the land."

The Proposed Constitutional Structure

On September 17, 1787, 39 delegates put their signatures to the Constitution. Once the plan for national government was complete, the proposed Constitution contained seven articles with a host of provisions. The document opens with the **Preamble**, a sort of mission statement, that begins with "We the people" and outlines the purposes of the new government, such as "establishing justice" and providing for a "common defense."

BIG IDEA: The plan for government included three separate branches—legislative, executive, and judicial—each having unique powers and each able to block the other from gaining too much power. It included an executive president to serve as commander in chief and a Congress that could tax, borrow, and regulate commerce. It also called for a Supreme Court and a plan to create lower courts and the Electoral College system to elect the president.

Policy: How Government Business Gets Done The plan the framers created included a complex and competitive policymaking process to assure that the people's will would be well represented and freedom would be maintained. *Policy* means "the laws the government creates and the manner in which they are carried out." Under the framers' plan, Congress, as the most representative branch, writes and passes most laws. Those laws constitute the chief policies of the United States. The president and his or her administrative agencies, however, carry out and enforce those laws. There might be leeway or room for interpretation, and different presidents will carry out the law with different methods.

For example, the policy on marijuana held by the administration of President Barack Obama (2009–2017) differed from that of his predecessor, President George W. Bush (2001–2009). Bush's administration raided a California cannabis dispensary, even after medical marijuana had been legalized in the state. That raid resulted in a conviction, later upheld by the Supreme Court. A few years later, President Obama's attorney general signaled an easing of federal enforcement in states where the people had voted to legalize marijuana. The administration of President Donald Trump (2017–) supported the use of medical marijuana but in early 2018 ended a policy that provided legal shelter for businesses selling marijuana for recreational use in states where recreational marijuana had been legalized. (See pages 393–396.)

In another example, the way in which a president and the State Department interact with other countries and the treaties the United States enters help define foreign policy. Indeed, some of the agencies in the executive branch, such as the Food and Drug Administration or the Environmental Protection Agency, have authority to create and shape industry regulations. And of course when the Supreme Court interprets law and sets new precedents, it redefines what government can or cannot do, making law anew and shaping policy.

In this book, policy and the policymaking process will be explained in both the main text and in the Policy Matters features, where examples of policy set by the institutions of government will be explored.

The Constitution, written in the hot summer of 1787, emerged from the debate about the weak Articles of Confederation and created the legislative, executive, and judicial branches defined in the first three articles, a separation of powers among the branches, and the qualifications and terms for offices. It also included articles regarding the relations among the states, the amendment process, national supremacy, and the procedure for ratification. Below, key excerpts from each article are followed by explanatory text.

Article I

All legislative Powers herein granted shall be vested in a Congress of the United States, which shall consist of a Senate and House of Representatives . . . . Each House may determine the Rules of its Proceedings . . . .

Article I defines the basic setup and operation of Congress. House members are elected by the people every two years. In contrast, state legislatures would elect senators, who were then beholden to state governments (this provision was later changed by the Seventeenth Amendment). The House became the more representative, or more democratic, institution.

Article I has ten sections and is the longest article—about half of the entire Constitution—revealing the framers' concern for representative lawmaking and their reverence for the legislative branch. Sections 8, 9, and 10 detail the powers and limitations of Congress and the powers of the states. The framers identified a limited list of **enumerated powers**, named in Section 8, which include the powers to tax, borrow money, raise an army, create a postal system, address piracy on the seas, and define the immigration and naturalization process and a few others. The **commerce clause** empowers the Congress to "regulate commerce with other nations, and among the several states."

The final clause in Section 8 is the **necessary and proper clause**, or **elastic clause**. This provision states, "The Congress shall have power . . . to make all laws which shall be necessary and proper for carrying into execution the foregoing powers . . . ." Since this power goes beyond the explicitly enumerated powers, the elastic clause is said to grant *implicit* powers. After a fierce debate, the framers included this to assure the Congress some flexibility in legislating.

Section 9 lists what Congress *cannot* do. For example, the federal legislature cannot tax exported goods. Congress cannot take away the right of habeas corpus (the right to be formally charged after an arrest), cannot pass bills of attainder (legislative acts declaring one guilty of a crime) or ex post facto laws (making an act illegal after one has committed it). Nor can Congress grant any title of nobility. Section 10 lists powers the states are denied. States cannot, for example, enter into treaties with other countries, coin money, or tax exports.

Article II

The President shall be Commander in Chief of the Army and Navy . . . . He shall from time to time give to the Congress Information of the State of the Union . . . he shall take Care that the Laws be faithfully executed . . . .

How to create and define the office of president in Article II stirred one of the more heated discussions in Philadelphia. The rebellion against a monarch made the populace concerned about one-person rule. However, the lack of leadership under the Articles of Confederation and the need for an executive to take care of the nation's business made the creation of the presidency inevitable. Article II lays out the requirements to assume this office and the executive's role. As commander in chief, the president oversees and manages the U.S. military. As head of state, the president receives foreign ambassadors and sends U.S. ambassadors abroad.

Article III

The Judges, both of the supreme and inferior Courts, shall hold their Offices during good Behavior, and shall, at stated Times, receive for their Services a Compensation, which shall not be diminished during their Continuance in Office.

The need for national courts led to Article III, which defines the judiciary. The framers mentioned only one actual court, the Supreme Court, but they empowered Congress to create inferior courts. The federal courts have jurisdiction over cases involving federal law, disputes between states, and concerns that involve government officials. The president appoints Supreme Court justices and other federal judges, with approval of the Senate. These judges serve "during good behavior," which in practice means for life.

Article IV

Full Faith and Credit shall be given in each State to the public Acts, Records, and judicial Proceedings of every other State . . . . A Person charged in any . . . Crime, who shall flee from Justice, and be found in another State, shall . . . be delivered up, to be removed to the State having Jurisdiction of the Crime.

Article IV defines relations among the states. It includes the **full faith and credit clause** that requires states to be open about their laws and encourages states to respect one another's laws. It also requires that "the citizens of each state shall be entitled to all privileges and immunities of citizens in the several states." In other words, on most issues states cannot play favorites with their own citizens or exclude outsiders from basic privileges and immunities. For example, if a Nebraska police officer pulls over an Oklahoma driver, the Nebraska officer will honor the Oklahoma driver's license. If a California man is accused of a crime in Alabama, he'll get the same protections and immunities as an accused Alabama defendant. Article IV also guarantees that each state shall have a republican form of government, and it addresses the extradition process for fugitives who have committed state crimes.

Article V

[W]henever two thirds of both Houses shall deem it necessary, [they] shall propose Amendments to this Constitution . . . which . . . shall be valid to all Intents and Purposes, as Part of this Constitution, when ratified by the Legislatures of three fourths of the several States . . . .

Delegates in Philadelphia realized the Constitution would prove imperfect and that it would occasionally require some changes. That is why Article V defines the amendment process. There are two different ways to propose an amendment, and two different ways to ratify amendments. Congress can propose an amendment with a two-thirds vote in each house. Two-thirds of state legislatures can also vote to call a national convention to propose an amendment. To ratify the proposal, three-fourths of the state legislatures must agree to it, or three-fourths of state conventions. All successful amendments have been passed by Congress, and all but one, the Twenty-First Amendment to repeal prohibition of alcohol, were ratified by state legislatures. The framers included the alternative method to propose or ratify in case sitting governments refused the people's wishes.

Article VI

This Constitution, and the Laws of the United States which shall be made in Pursuance thereof . . . shall be the supreme Law of the Land . . . .

To avoid the lack of unification experienced under the Articles of Confederation and to unite the nation under stronger national policy, Article VI was included to establish **national supremacy**. The **supremacy clause** quoted above makes certain that all states must adhere to the Constitution. Article VI also states that no religious test will be required for a person to take a government office.

Article VII

> The Ratification of the Conventions of nine States, shall be sufficient for the Establishment of this Constitution . . . .

In this article, the framers outlined the process by which this new plan would be put into place. Rather than relying on existing state legislatures that might refrain from giving up power or delay the ratification process, Article VII declares the Constitution would go into effect when the ninth state convention approved it.

THE ORIGINAL U.S. CONSTITUTION	
Article I	The Legislative Branch
Article II	The Executive Branch
Article III	The Judiciary
Article IV	Relations Among States
Article V	Amendment Process
Article VI	National Supremacy
Article VII	Ratification Process

Political Science Reasoning Processes: Compare the Articles of Confederation with the U.S. Constitution

Often, comparing documents aids understanding the political concepts of each of them. When you compare, you look for similarities and differences.

Apply: Based on the information on the previous pages, write an essay in which you compare political principles as you identify and explain similarities and differences between the Articles of Confederation and the Constitution. To help you gather your thoughts, you may want to make a chart for the Articles of Confederation like the one above for the Constitution. Then read the full text of the Constitution on pages 628–644, and answer the questions within it. You may also read the Constitution online.

Ratification

When the framers finished the final draft of the Constitution, not all were present in Independence Hall. As most remaining men attached their names to the document, three stood by and refused to sign it. Edmund Randolph was one. He had watched as the convention altered the Virginia Plan he introduced in May. George Mason, the chief author of Virginia's Declaration of Rights, was another. He refused to sign because the Constitution had no federal bill of rights. The Constitution's lack of a detailed list of rights became the national debate over the following year.

The FŒDERALIST, No. 10.

To the People of the State of New-York.

AMONG the numerous advantages promifed by a well conftructed Union, none deferves to be more accurately developed than its tendency to break and control the violence of faction. The friend of popular governments, never finds himfelf fo much alarmed for their character and fate, as when he contemplates their propenfity to this dangerous vice. He will not fail therefore to fet a due value on any plan which, without violating the principles to which he is attached, provides a proper cure for it. The inftability, injuftice and confufion introduced into the public councils, have in truth been the mortal difeafes under which popular governments have every where perifhed; as they continue to be the favorite and fruitful topics from which the adverfaries to liberty derive their moft fpecious declamations. The valuable improvements made by the American Conftitutions on the popular models, both ancient and modern cannot certainly

The influence of factious leaders may kindle a flame within their particular States, but will be unable to fpread a general conflagration through the other States: A religious fect, may degenerate into a political faction in a part of the confederacy; but the variety of fects difperfed over the entire face of it, muft fecure the national Councils againft any danger from that fource: A rage for paper money, for an abolition of debts, for an equal divifion of property, or for any other improper or wicked project, will be lefs apt to pervade the whole body of the Union, than a particular member of it; in the fame proportion as fuch a malady is more likely to taint a particular county or diftrict, than an entire State.

In the extent and proper ftructure of the Union, therefore, we behold a republican remedy for the difeafes moft incident to republican Government. And according to the degree of pleafure and pride, we feel in being Republicans, ought to be our zeal in cherifhing the fpirit and fupporting the character of Fœderalifts.

PUBLIUS.

The Federalist Papers were published in three New York newspapers from 1787 to 1788.

Finally, Massachusetts delegate Elbridge Gerry did not agree to the new plan. The delegates departed Philadelphia wondering what the future held and if their months of work, debate, and detailed plans were for naught. Leaders and citizens fell into two camps: those for and those against the new plan.

James Madison headed for New York to serve in the Confederation Congress and immediately began working toward ratification, which looked promising early on. During December 1787, three states quickly voted to ratify. Two more states joined in January 1788. Of the first five state ratifying conventions, three approved the Constitution unanimously. The other two did so with strong majorities. Nonetheless, the future of the republic was uncertain. Massachusetts proved reluctant, and leading opponents of the Constitution criticized the plan in newspapers and in circulating pamphlets.

Support for the Constitution With the insistence of fellow pro-Constitution Virginians, Madison named himself a candidate for his state's ratifying convention to be held in Richmond. From New York, he began writing a series of essays for publication to argue in favor of this new plan. He soon joined fellow delegate Alexander Hamilton and New York governor John Jay in writing a series of essays that explained the framers' intentions. These authors, writing under the pen name Publius, published *The Federalist* to assure citizens that they had created a federal system and that states had not lost their importance (today these essays are called the **Federalist Papers**).The so-called Federalists also wanted to allay fears that their plan would subject people in the states to abuses by this new national government.

Of the 85 essays that Madison, Hamilton, and Jay penned, one of the most cited is *Federalist No. 10* because it addresses the concern over special interests. *Federalist No. 10* speaks of the "mischiefs of faction," or interest groups in government, whether a majority or a minority, "united and actuated by some common impulse of passion, or of interest, adversed to the rights of other citizens . . . ." Publius, the "voice" of the Federalist authors, stated that men of like mind might begin to dominate government for their own ends rather than for the public good. He explained how no plan for government can eliminate factions entirely but noted that the framers had created a system to stall and frustrate factions and thus limit their effects. They created not a pure, participatory democracy at the national level but rather a representative and pluralist republic that had to consider the interests of varied people from across many miles of land. America even at its birth was one of the most expansive countries in the world, and varied factions arriving from New England and from Georgia would neutralize one another. Following are some key quotes from *Federalist No. 10*.

> A zeal for different opinions concerning religion, concerning government, and many other points, . . . [and] an attachment to different leaders ambitiously contending for pre-eminence and power . . . have . . . divided mankind into parties, inflamed them with mutual animosity, and rendered them much more disposed to vex and oppress each other than to co-operate for their common good . . . .
>
> The inference to which we are brought is, that the causes of faction cannot be removed, and that relief is only to be sought in the means of controlling its effects. . . .
>
> Hence, it clearly appears, that the same advantage a republic has over a democracy, in controlling the effects of faction, is enjoyed by a large over a small republic, and is enjoyed by the Union over the States composing it.

Political Science Disciplinary Practices: Interpret *Federalist No. 10*
When you *interpret* a source, you explain how the *implications* within the text—conclusions conveyed even if they are not stated directly—may affect political principles (state vs. federal power, for example), processes (the best way to elect a president, for example), behaviors, and outcomes. (Implications are the mirror image of inferences. Implications are conveyed; inferences are received.) Further, you explain how the source you are interpreting relates to those same concepts—political principles, processes, behaviors, and outcomes.

Apply: Publius actually identifies an inference in the second quote above. Rewrite that inference in your own words, and explain how Publius uses it to advance the cause of adopting a republican government. Then read the full text of *Federalist No. 10* on pages 644–649, and answer the questions that follow it. You may also read *Federalist No. 10* online.

Opposition to the Constitution Opponents of the Constitution, including Virginia's Patrick Henry and George Mason, desired a federal government more like the one under the Articles. Madison and his colleagues' attaching the "Federalist" name to their cause preempted opponents from claiming the label. Opponents then became known as **Anti-Federalists** for lack of a better term. The irony was that the Anti-Federalists argued for a truly federal government as defined, while the Federalists advocated a national system with some loss of state sovereignty. The Anti-Federalist concerns came from the recent experience with an autocratic ruling country. Some feared a single executive might replicate a monarchical king, potentially limiting state and individual rights. Congress's power to tax, to control a standing army, and to do anything else it felt "necessary and proper" made the Anti-Federalists wary. The thick veil of secrecy in which designing men had conspired to draft the document made Anti-Federalists and much of the general public suspicious.

FOUNDATIONAL DOCUMENTS: *BRUTUS No. 1*

The Anti-Federalists had their spokespersons in the newspapers as well. The *New York Journal* and *Weekly Register* published a series of 16 articles written under the pseudonym Brutus and appearing at the same time as the Federalist Papers.

"Brutus" writes for the purpose of dissuading readers from supporting the new Constitution. He argues that the necessary and proper clause and the supremacy clause give the federal government unlimited power, risking personal liberty. He argues that in a free republic, people have confidence in their rulers because they know them, and the rulers are accountable to the people who have the power to displace them. He posits that "in a republic of the extent of this continent, the people . . . would be acquainted with very few of their rulers: [they] would know little of their proceedings, and it would be extremely difficult to change them." He also specifically counters Publius's view that a large country and government prevent the rise of controlling factions.

If respect is to be paid to the opinion of the greatest and wisest men who have ever thought or wrote on the science of government, we shall be constrained to conclude, that a free republic cannot succeed over a country of such immense extent, containing such a number of inhabitants, and these increasing in such rapid progression as that of the whole United States. . . .

In a republic, the manners, sentiments, and interests of the people should be similar. If this be not the case, there will be a constant clashing of opinions; and the representatives of one part will be continually striving against those of the other. This will retard the operations of government, and prevent such conclusions as will promote the public good. If we apply this remark to the condition of the United States, we shall be convinced that it forbids that we should be one government.

Newspapers published the text of the Constitution and essays for and against
it, such as the Federalist Papers and the articles by Brutus, giving citizens of
the newly independent nation the opportunity to read and digest views for
and against the ratification of the Constitution. Some state conventions had
remarkably close votes, but the Federalists won the day, with New Hampshire
becoming the ninth state to ratify. Yet most agreed that without New York and
Virginia, the new republic might stumble. Both of these states did ratify, but
only after contentious debate and close votes and after nine states had already
ratified. The government under the new Constitution was underway by 1789—
Congress began meeting and President Washington took office. North Carolina
and then Rhode Island ratified, resulting in ratification by all 13 states.

BY THE NUMBERS: RATIFYING THE CONSTITUTION			
State	**Date**	**For**	**Against**
Delaware	December 1787	30	0
Pennsylvania	December 1787	46	23
New Jersey	December 1787	38	0
Georgia	January 1788	26	0
Connecticut	January 1788	128	40
Massachusetts	February 1788	187	168
Maryland	April 1788	63	11
South Carolina	May 1788	149	73
New Hampshire	June 1788	57	47
Virginia	June 1788	89	79
New York	July 1788	30	27
North Carolina	November 1789	194	77
Rhode Island	May 1790	34	32

What do the numbers show? Which states ratified early, and which states took longer?
Which states ratified the Constitution by slim margins? Which were unanimous? Which
state's ratification put the Constitution into effect?

A Bill of Rights

George Mason's concern that the original Constitution had no bill of rights disturbed many others as well. Those who fought for independence argued that a bill of rights was necessary to secure the liberties earned through the revolution. The document framed in Philadelphia lacked a guarantee of free speech in Congress. There were no protections against aggressive prosecution and no promise against cruel and unusual punishments. The Constitution did, however, include a few basic rights.

RIGHTS IN THE ORIGINAL CONSTITUTION
• No religious tests to hold federal office
• Right to jury trials in criminal cases
• Neither Congress nor the states can pass a bill of attainder
• Neither Congress nor the states can pass ex post facto laws
• Congress cannot suspend habeas corpus rights except in wartime

The Anti-Federalists and some pro-Constitution leaders believed a list of rights was needed to complete the Philadelphia mission. There was opposition, however. One leading opponent was James Madison. He called bills of rights "parchment barriers," mere paper blocks to injustices and tyranny that could prevail if the government itself did not have provisions to prevent such tyranny. He offered as examples minorities who had suffered at the will of majorities in states that did, in fact, have bills of rights. He also believed that by listing all the rights the federal government could not take away, a right could be inadvertently overlooked and the new federal government *could* later take it away. He believed the Constitution never entitled the new federal government to take away any rights in the first place, so why was it necessary to list those that could not be taken away in the future?

The debate for or against adding a bill of rights overlapped the series of ratifying conventions that occurred throughout 1787–1790. With the efforts of the Federalists, as well as assurances that amendments protecting personal rights would be added, the large, later states ratified and joined the Union. Additionally, as the new Congress began meeting in 1789, delegates petitioned for these rights. Madison and the Congress compiled the many concerns into the amendments that became the **Bill of Rights**. The Bill of Rights was fully ratified by 1791.

SELECTED RIGHTS IN THE BILL OF RIGHTS	
Amendment I	Freedoms of religion, speech, press, assembly, and protest
Amendment II	Right to bear arms
Amendment III	No quartering of troops
Amendment IV	No unreasonable searches or seizures
Amendment V	Indictment, no double jeopardy, protection against self-incrimination, due process
Amendment VI	Speedy, public trial by jury of peers; cross-examination; right to defense counsel
Amendment VII	Lawsuits and juries
Amendment VIII	No cruel or unusual punishments, no excessive fines
Amendment IX	Listing rights in the Constitution doesn't deny others
Amendment X	Delegated and reserved powers

The Bill of Rights includes many essential rights, most of which were violated under the oppressive British regime. The First Amendment declares freedoms of religion, speech, press, and peaceable assembly and the right to petition the government. Congress and the people put a high priority on the right to express political ideas, even if unpopular. (For much more on the First Amendment, see Chapter 7.) Other amendments protect private property, due process, and fair trials and prevent cruel and unusual punishments. The Tenth Amendment prevents the federal government from taking any powers that are reserved to the states. The text of the Bill of Rights begins on page 637.

POLICY MATTERS: *INDIVIDUAL RIGHTS AND SEPTEMBER 11*

Like states' rights, the individual rights guaranteed by the Bill of Rights have sometimes seemed in conflict with federal law. Knowing where individual rights end and governmental authority begins has been the subject of many legal cases and will be covered in depth in Unit 3. One vivid example here—surveillance resulting from the federal government's response to the 9/11/2001 terrorist attacks that killed nearly 3,000 Americans and brought down the towering World Trade Center—will illuminate a key constitutional issue about democracy and governmental power.
BIG IDEA Government surveillance following 9/11 and the responses to it show how multiple political processes, actors, and institutions create solutions to address the concerns of citizens.

Not long after al-Qaeda terrorists hijacked four U.S. commercial aircraft to fly them into selected targets in New York and Washington, President George W. Bush addressed a joint session of Congress, stating, "Whether we bring our enemies to justice or bring justice to our enemies, justice will be done." Faced with an adversary that generally operated underground and not under the flag of any sovereign nation, the United States modified its laws and defense operations to create a series of federal policies to eradicate threats. These policies fueled an ongoing debate about proper recognition of the Bill of Rights.

USA PATRIOT Act Administration officials began to deliberate about how the United States might locate the perpetrators of the September 11 attacks and, further, how to prevent future attacks. By late October 2001, the Congress passed the **USA PATRIOT Act** (**U**niting and **S**trengthening **A**merica by **P**roviding **A**ppropriate **T**ools **R**equired to **I**ntercept and **O**bstruct **T**errorism). The law covered intelligence gathering and sharing by executive branch agencies, points of criminal procedure, and border protection. It allowed government agencies to share information about significant suspects, and it widened authority on tapping suspects' phones. Government can now share grand jury testimony and proceedings, detain illegal immigrants for longer periods, and monitor email communications. The new bipartisan law passed with strong majorities in both houses.

Soon after its passage, however, people began to question the law's constitutionality and its threat to civil liberties, especially the rights protected by the Fourth Amendment. Muslim communities were especially affected, but every American experienced a loss of some degree of privacy. Many communities and states passed resolutions opposing sections of the Act, but supporters argued that the ability to tap phones and seize information was critical to the prevention of future terrorist attacks.

Until 2013, when Edward Snowden leaked a document that proved the government was engaged in widespread collection of information, many Americans were unaware of the extent of the government's reach. Protests against what were believed to be incursions into rights guaranteed in the Bill of Rights kept the practice in the spotlight. In 2015, after evidence showed that the bulk call record collection was not necessary to prevent terrorist attacks, Congress passed the USA Freedom Act, which upheld certain portions of the USA PATRIOT Act but phased out bulk collection of phone and Internet data and set limits for its collection in certain circumstances.

You will read more about individual liberties in Unit 3. With the Bill of Rights in the Constitution, these liberties are as much a part of the nation's power structure as the federal and state governments and, like issues related to state and federal power, will no doubt continue to be matters for debate.

Constitutional Principles

The framers included several governing principles. They ensured a level of democracy by mandating elections for members of Congress and the president. Yet instead of creating a democracy, the Constitution creates a representative republic that limits government and tempers hasty, even if popular, ideas. Further, the framers called for a separation of powers, with each of the three branches responsible for different governmental functions. The separation of powers and the provisions for how laws are made and enacted establish a system of checks and balances that prevents one branch from becoming too powerful. Under federalism, the national and state governments divide and share power as well, though the principle of national supremacy gives the federal government the power to decide "the supreme law of the land." The Constitution's flexibility has empowered the government to face unforeseen circumstances.

A Democratic Republic

The framers wanted the citizen representation of a democracy, but on the national level, they created a **representative republic**, a collection of sovereign states gathered for the national interest, national needs, and national defense. To promote popular sovereignty, the framers required popular elections every two years for House members, but those were the only popular elections they put in the original Constitution. State legislatures elected their senators until 1913. The states name their electors to the Electoral College, and then the Electoral College elects the president.

Separation of Powers

The framers made the legislative, executive, and judicial branches distinct in their own powers and responsibilities to dilute power among the three branches. Earlier in school, you might have learned that "the legislature makes the law, the executive branch enforces the law, and the judicial branch interprets the law." This simplification overlooks the fact that all three branches can establish law and policy, but it does highlight the basic function of each branch. The legislature is the most numerous and representative branch, and it ultimately makes the public's will become public policy. The powers of Congress are further separated between the two chambers. Neither house can pass a bill into law without the consent of the other chamber. The president is ultimately the authority to enforce the law and to carry out Congress's policies, so the president and his administration shape policy in doing so. Members of the Supreme Court and the federal courts, appointed by the president and approved by the Senate, hear disputes and interpret laws and their application.

FOUNDATIONAL DOCUMENTS: *FEDERALIST No. 51*

In *Federalist No. 51,* Publius writes, "If men were angels, no government would be necessary." He points to the separation of powers outlined in the Constitution as a guard against tyranny. He also states that the best protection of the minority is that "the society itself will be broken into so many parts, interests, and classes of citizens, that the rights of individuals, or of the minority, will be in little danger from interested combinations of the majority."

The following excerpt addresses the separation of powers.

In order to lay a due foundation for that separate and distinct exercise of the different powers of Government . . . it is evident that each department should have a will of its own; and consequently should be so constituted, that the members of each should have as little agency as possible in the appointment of the members of the others. . . .

It is equally evident, that the members of each department should be as little dependent as possible on those of the others, for the emoluments [earnings] annexed to their offices. . . .

In framing a Government which is to be administered by men over men, the great difficulty lies in this: you must first enable the Government to control the governed; and in the next place oblige it to control itself. A dependence on the People is, no doubt, the primary control on the Government; but experience has taught mankind the necessity of auxiliary precautions. . . .

In republican Government, the Legislative authority necessarily predominates. The remedy for this inconveniency is to divide the Legislature into different branches; and to render them, by different modes of election and different principles of action, as little connected with each other as the nature of their common functions and their common dependence on the society will admit.

Political Science Disciplinary Practices: Explain How the Source Relates to Political Institutions

When you explain how a source relates to political institutions (or principles, processes, and behaviors), you test the degree to which the source accurately describes those features of government. When *Federalist No. 51* was published, the institutions referred to in this article—the executive, legislative, and judicial branches and the two chambers of Congress—had not yet been formed. Now, however, the nation has more than two centuries' experience with these institutions, and the ideas expressed in *Federalist No. 51* can be related to actual government institutions.

Apply: Research the 2017 efforts of members of the Republican Party to "repeal and replace" the Affordable Care Act, President Obama's signature accomplishment. Explain how *Federalist No. 51* relates to those efforts and the various institutions of government involved in them. Then read the full text of *Federalist No. 51* on pages 656–659, and answer the questions that follow it. You may also read the text online.

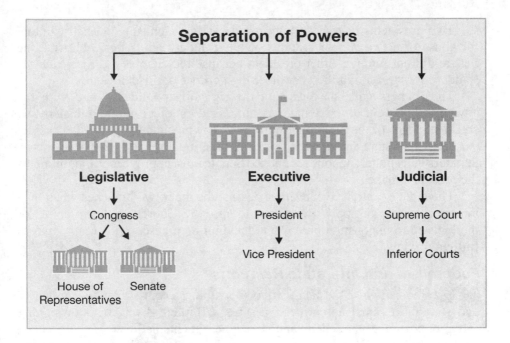

Separation of Powers

Legislative	Executive	Judicial
Congress	President	Supreme Court
House of Representatives Senate	Vice President	Inferior Courts

Checks and Balances

The limiting powers each branch can use on the others are known as **checks and balances**. They are especially clear in the lawmaking process. A bill (a proposed law) can originate in either the House or Senate and must pass both bodies with a simple majority (50 percent plus 1). Then the bill is presented to the president, who may sign it into law if he agrees with the proposal. Or, exercising executive checks and balances, the president may reject it with a **veto**. If after ten days (excluding Sundays) the president has done neither, the bill becomes law. If the president receives the bill at the end of a legislative session, however, refusal to sign is known as a **pocket veto** and kills the bill.

After the president consents to a law, it is entered into the United States Code, our body of federal statutes. If the president vetoes a bill, the Congress, each house acting separately, can reverse the veto with a **two-thirds override**, requiring a two-thirds super majority vote in each house.

The framers placed additional checks on power, such as the impeachment process and the Senate's right to provide **advice and consent**—formal approval—on presidential appointments. An **impeachment** is an accusation, an indictment of wrongdoing. Article I, Section II claims the House "shall have the sole power of impeachment" and can impeach the president, a federal judge, or another official of wrongdoing, The Senate then holds a trial for the accused official. The Chief Justice presides as the judge if the president is on trial. The Senate must vote by a two-thirds majority to find an official guilty or not guilty.

BIG IDEA: The system of checks and balances, including impeachment, is based on the rule of law (see page 352).

Two presidents have been impeached, Andrew Johnson and Bill Clinton, for abuse of office and accusations of lying under oath. After each trial, the Senate did not remove either president because the charges did not reach the standard for "treason, bribery, or other high crimes or misdemeanors."

The framers gave the president the right to appoint "by and with the advice and consent of the Senate . . . ambassadors, other public ministers and consuls, judges of the Supreme Court . . . ." The president appoints the cabinet (secretaries of state and defense, for example), judges, and heads of agencies. Senators will suggest appointees and the Senate must approve any appointments the president makes.

The federal courts have leverage against the other two branches when they interpret the law or apply it or refuse to apply it. Courts can deem an act of the legislature unconstitutional when deciding on a case, a process known as **judicial review.**

Federalism and Interstate Relations

`BIG IDEA:` **Federalism**—the balance of power among a central, national authority and state or regional authorities—assures a limited government. Assigning different powers to the federal and state governments had been a vital issue at the Constitutional Convention. Congress and the president have unique powers defining their responsibilities and limits. The states are denied certain powers. And the Tenth Amendment ensures that the states have delegated to the federal government only those powers listed in the document. All other powers are reserved to the states.

Flexibility

Limited government was important, but the framers had the foresight to ensure flexibility. These men had seen much change in their generation and suspected that unforeseen events and changes in society might require revolutionary changes in national policy and in the Constitution. That's why they included the necessary and proper clause and the amendment process. The first allows Congress to legislate on matters closely related to the expressed powers. The amendment process has allowed for the Bill of Rights, women's suffrage, a redefined presidency, and national income taxes, among other changes.

National Supremacy

To avoid the lack of unification experienced under the Articles of Confederation and to unite the nation under stronger national policy, Article VI was included to establish national supremacy, the authority of the federal government to be "the supreme law of the land." The Anti-Federalists heavily questioned this provision. Included to assure compliance with the acts of Congress and treaties with other nations, the supremacy clause has placed the national government in some respects above the states in the areas of law delegated to the federal government. For example, in coining or printing money, international diplomacy, or national defense, the federal government is the exclusive authority. Yet Congress cannot claim national supremacy on distinctly **reserved powers** (see pages 44–45).

Limited Government

The Constitution reveals the framers' commitment to limited government. The lawmaking process is slow and designed for gridlock among the branches to discuss, debate, and rewrite legislation before it is fully passed. Bicameralism ensures an extra step within the chief lawmaking branch. A president can veto popular ideas that may pass both houses too quickly without full consideration of the proposed law. The Bill of Rights serves as a broad limitation over an array of issues. Congress cannot establish a religion, abridge free speech, or arrest suspects without following a particular due process procedure. And the Tenth Amendment ultimately prevents Congress from actions beyond those limited in Article I, Section 8.

The Three Branches in Practice

The legislative, executive, and judicial branches operate mostly in the nation's capital and remain busy creating and refining national policy. A busy and divisive Congress, a president and his large administration, and a court system stretched across the land are all part of the policymaking process.

Legislative

Congress operates on Capitol Hill, where 435 House representatives and 100 senators make the nation's laws, determine how to fund government, and shape the nation's foreign policy. On opposite sides of the Capitol, the House and Senate operate in separate chambers and with different rules of procedure. Citizens elect these officials periodically and can contact them to express their views or to favor or oppose a bill. All Congress members have an office near the Capitol and multiple offices in their home districts. The two senators from each state represent the state at large and have staggered terms.

The two houses have differing age requirements, twenty-five years old for representatives and thirty for senators. That age difference, the size and scope of each body, and the number of citizens each represents create a unique dynamic in each house.

To carry out their duties, legislators in both houses have staffers— legislative research aides—and a communications chief. They have a budget to run their office, free use of the mail, and free travel back and forth to their home states. Experienced members have their areas of expertise in lawmaking, perhaps based on their careers before becoming a politician or a subject of law that is dear to them. Both the House and Senate have an array of committees, usually between 10 and 30 members on each, that oversee certain topics of law or policymaking. Congress has thousands of employees that write the bills, gather research data, take the pulse of the citizens in each district, and let the voters know about all the good things their Congress member has done, especially near election time.

In addition to contacting their legislators, citizens can gain understanding of proposed bills through the Congressional Research Service through the Library of Congress, where they can read synopses of bills. Also, the media reports on and analyzes proposed laws and critiques laws after they've taken effect. The House and Senate are aired live on C-SPAN television.

Executive

Article II lays out the requirements for office and the executive's role. The president must be thirty-five years old, a natural born citizen, and a resident of the United States for at least fourteen years. The president serves a four-year term and, since passage of the Twenty-Second Amendment, can serve only two full terms.

The presidency has grown in both scope and power. President George Washington had a four-person cabinet and no more than a few hundred government employees. Today, the cabinet has grown to about 20 members, and the federal executive branch has more than 2.7 million employees to carry out the nation's laws today.

The president's immediate staff in the West Wing of the White House advises the executive daily and provides the chief link to other institutions of government and to the public. Entire offices of aides shape the president's message and connect with Congress at the staff level. Large executive branch departments and agencies oversee entire wings of our government, such as the military, and govern entire national industries, such as the Federal Communications Commission, which regulates radio and television broadcasts and Internet communications. These offices and institutions below the president are part of the bureaucratic machinery that carries out the law or that defends the United States. Congress creates these entities, checks on their performance, determines their funding, and occasionally reshapes their mission. Congressional committees keep an eye on them.

Some agencies exist to protect citizens, who can file a complaint to assure enforcement of or fairness in the law. For example, the Equal Employment Opportunity Commission investigates complaints of discrimination in the workplace. Of course, citizens can report federal crimes to the FBI or the Drug Enforcement Administration. And a voter can find where a federal candidate's donations come from at the Federal Election Commission's website.

Judicial

Judicial review (see page 32) has often become a major step in determining and sometimes in finalizing law. The Supreme Court and lower courts have exercised judicial review to protect liberties and to properly initiate policy. Courts can use this power to check the legislature, the executive, or state actions in order to shape overall policy in the United States.

Citizens have often found the federal courts the place to challenge unfair government action, to appeal wrongful convictions, and to question actions of schools and state governments. Because of citizen lawsuits in these courts, Americans can now say and print unpopular and even antigovernment ideas, challenge convictions made in unfair trials, attend equal schools without limitations based on race, and marry whom they want regardless of gender. The Supreme Court is where such national policies have been established.

At least five of the nine justices who serve today must agree on a *majority opinion* for a decision to uphold (or overturn) law. Members who agree with the majority opinion but who have differing or additional reasons for reaching that conclusion can issue *concurring opinions*. Justices who disagree with the majority opinion issue *dissenting opinions*. As with concurring opinions, justices can dissent from the majority opinion for different reasons, so there may be several dissenting opinions. Throughout this book, you will encounter the Must-Know Decisions, those landmark Supreme Court cases that will likely be the basis of questions on the AP Government and Politics exam.

REFLECT ON THE ESSENTIAL QUESTION

Essential Question: *How have theory, debate, and compromise influenced the United States' system of government that balances governmental power and individual rights?* On separate paper, complete a chart like the one below to gather details to answer that question.

Political Philosophy of the Time	Example or Application

KEY TERMS AND NAMES

advice and consent/31

Anti-Federalists/24

Articles of Confederation/9

bicameral/13

Bill of Rights/26

checks and balances/31

commerce clause/18

Declaration of Independence/7

Electoral College/15

elite democracy/6

enumerated powers/18

extradition/9

Federalist Papers/22

federalism/1, 32

Federalists/1

full faith and credit clause/20

Grand Committee/13

Great Compromise/14

House of Representatives/14

impeachment/31

James Madison/11

judicial review/32

national supremacy/20

natural law/4

necessary and proper (elastic) clause/18

New Jersey Plan/13

participatory democracy/5

pluralist democracy/6

pocket veto/31

popular sovereignty/5

Preamble/17

representative republic/29

republicanism/5

reserved powers/32

Senate/14

separation of powers/13

social contract/3

supremacy clause/20

Three-Fifths Compromise/14

two-thirds override/31

USA PATRIOT Act/28

veto/31

Virginia Plan/13

1. Which is the most democratic institution of government that represents the framers' commitment to a limited republic?

(A) U.S. Senate

(B) Supreme Court

(C) House of Representatives

(D) Electoral College

2. Which of the following is a chief argument in James Madison's *Federalist No. 10*?

(A) A Bill of Rights is necessary to secure liberty.

(B) Free speech should be added to the Constitution.

(C) Judicial review will prevent harsh laws against the citizenry.

(D) A large, diverse republic will tame factions.

Questions 3 and 4 refer to the passage below.

The objection to the plan of the convention, which has met with most success in this State . . . is . . . the want of a constitutional provision for the trial by jury in civil cases. The disingenuous [insincere] form in which this objection is usually stated has been repeatedly [commented on] and exposed, but continues to be pursued . . . The mere silence of the Constitution in regard to civil causes, is represented as an abolition of the trial by jury [in an effort] to induce a persuasion that this pretended abolition is complete and universal, extending not only to every species of civil, but even to criminal causes. . . .

Every man of discernment must at once perceive the wide difference between silence and abolition. . . .

The maxims on which [the opponents' argument] rely are of this nature: "A specification of particulars is an exclusion of generals"; or, "The expression of one thing is the exclusion of another." Hence, say they, as the Constitution has established the trial by jury in criminal cases, and is silent in respect to civil, this silence is an implied prohibition of trial by jury in regard to the latter.

—Alexander Hamilton, *Federalist No. 83*, 1788

3. Which of the following statements is most consistent with Hamilton's argument in this passage?
   (A) Jury trials in civil cases are not as important as jury trials in criminal cases.
   (B) Silence and abolition have the same essential meaning and can be used interchangeably.
   (C) The lack of specific reference to something in the Constitution does not mean it is disallowed.
   (D) Trial by jury in civil cases is unacceptable because of jurors' lack of expertise.

4. Which governmental principle does the right to a jury trial support?
   (A) Sovereignty
   (B) Representative lawmaking
   (C) State rights
   (D) Individual liberties

5. "The Congress has the power . . . to create all laws that are necessary and proper . . . " can be found in which part of the Constitution?
   (A) Article I
   (B) Article II
   (C) Article III
   (D) The Bill of Rights

6. Shays's Rebellion highlighted which of the following weaknesses of the national government under the Articles of Confederation?
   (A) Lack of power to declare peace and war
   (B) Lack of power to tax the people directly
   (C) Lack of power to keep a standing army
   (D) Lack of power to regulate interstate commerce

7. Which statement about impeachment under the Constitution is true?
   (A) An impeachment is the removal of a president.
   (B) The Senate has the sole power of impeachment.
   (C) The House can impeach presidents but not other federal officials.
   (D) The House can impeach officials for "high crimes or misdemeanors."

Questions 8 and 9 refer to the infographic below.

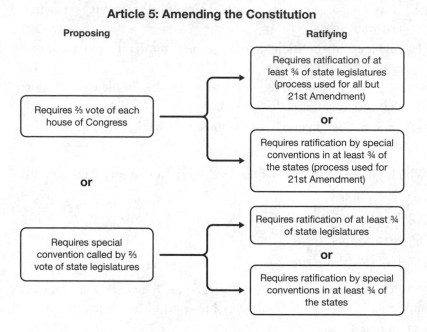

Article 5: Amending the Constitution

Proposing

Ratifying

Requires ⅔ vote of each house of Congress

Requires ratification of at least ¾ of state legislatures (process used for all but 21st Amendment)

or

Requires ratification by special conventions in at least ¾ of the states (process used for 21st Amendment)

or

Requires special convention called by ⅔ vote of state legislatures

Requires ratification of at least ¾ of state legislatures

or

Requires ratification by special conventions in at least ¾ of the states

8. Which of the following conclusions is best supported by the infographic above?
   (A) Once a proposed amendment passes the first round of approval, there are four ways it can be ratified.
   (B) Amendments are proposed more often by Congress than by special conventions.
   (C) Only a few amendments were ratified by special conventions in at least 34 of the states.
   (D) Amending the Constitution is a relatively easy process.

9. Which concern of the framers does the method illustrated in the infographic addresss?
   (A) National security
   (B) Individual rights
   (C) Flexibility
   (D) Fair representation

10. Which of the following is an accurate comparison of the New Jersey Plan and the Virginia Plan?

	NEW JERSEY PLAN	VIRGINIA PLAN
(A)	Included a layered system of national courts	Made the states supreme over the national government
(B)	Created a bicameral legislature	Assured states would retain sovereignty
(C)	Gave the national legislature only defined and limited powers	Included a three-branch system and a bicameral legislature
(D)	Made the national government supreme over the states	Allowed importation of slaves for 20 years after ratificaion

FREE-RESPONSE QUESTIONS

1. "I know the name of liberty is dear to . . . us; but have we not enjoyed liberty even under the English monarchy? Shall we . . . renounce that to go and seek it in I know not what form of republic, which will soon change into a licentious anarchy and popular tyranny? In the human body the head only sustains and governs all the members, directing them . . . to the same object, which is self-preservation and happiness; so the head of the body politic, that is the king, in concert with the Parliament, can alone maintain the union of the members of this Empire . . . and prevent civil war by obviating all the evils produced by variety of opinions and diversity of interests."
   —John Dickinson, July 1, 1776

   After reading the excerpt, respond to A, B, and C below:

   (A) Describe the political institution Dickinson wants to maintain.

   (B) In the context of the passage, explain how the political institution identified in part A affected the behavior of the colonists.

   (C) Explain how the passage relates to representative democracy.

RESULTS OF EARLY PRESIDENTIAL ELECTIONS			
Election Year	Top Candidates	Party	Electoral College Votes
1792	George Washington	Federalist	132
	John Adams	Federalist	77
	George Clinton	Democratic-Republican	50
1796	John Adams	Federalist	71
	Thomas Jefferson	Democratic-Republican	68
	Thomas Pinckney	Federalist	59
	Aaron Burr	Anti-Federalist	30
1800	Thomas Jefferson	Democratic-Republican	73
	Aaron Burr	Democratic-Republican	73
	John Adams	Federalist	65
	C. C. Pinckney	Federalist	64
1804	Thomas Jefferson	Democratic-Republican	162
	C. C. Pinckney	Federalist	14

2. Use the information graphic above to answer the questions.

   (A) Describe the information conveyed in the table.

   (B) Describe a trend in the information, and draw a conclusion about the reasons for that trend related to people's views on the policies of the Federalist Party.

   (C) Explain how the information in the table demonstrates a difference between the U.S. Constitution and the Articles of Confederation.

3. A student in your school has recently immigrated to the United States from a country run by an authoritarian government. He is afraid to speak his mind and worries that his new home country also runs the risk of becoming authoritarian.
   After reading the scenario, respond to A, B, and C below:

   (A) Describe a difference between the political institutions of your friend's home country and the political institutions of the United States.

   (B) In the context of the scenario, explain how one provision in the government of the United States protects your friend's freedoms.

   (C) In the context of the scenario, explain an action citizens could take if the U.S. government denied those freedoms.

4. Develop an argument that explains whether or not the Bill of Rights was a necessary addition to the U.S. Constitution. In your essay you must do the following:

- Articulate a defensible claim or thesis clearly stating your position
- Support your claim with at least TWO pieces of accurate and relevant information:
  - At least ONE piece of information must be from one of the following foundational documents:
    - The Declaration of Independence
    - *Brutus No. 1*
  - Use a second piece of evidence from the other document in the list above or from your study of the nation's constitutional foundation
- Use reasoning to organize and analyze evidence, explaining its significance to justify your claim or thesis
- Address opposing or alternative perspectives through refutation, concession, and rebuttal

WRITING: *ARTICULATE A DEFENSIBLE CLAIM*

A *claim* is a statement asserted to be true. It is not a fact, such as "The Constitution has a Bill of Rights." It is instead a debatable point, something about which people may reasonably disagree. You could assert a claim, for example, related to health care for Americans, such as "The federal government, state governments, and private companies should work together to provide health care." When you develop a claim, be sure that it goes beyond mere fact and asserts a viewpoint that you can defend with evidence.

2

Federalism

"The Government of the Union, though limited in its powers, is supreme within its sphere of action . . . ."
—Chief Justice John Marshall in *McCulloch v. Maryland*, 1819

Essential Question: How has federalism shaped the administration of public policy, and how do state, local, and national governments work within the federal framework today?

The framers of the U.S. Constitution had to balance the powers of Congress and the federal government at the national level with the powers held by the states. Where the power ultimately lies, however, has been a source of controversy since the U.S. Constitution was framed. The national legislature has stretched its powers in trying to address national needs, while states have tried to maintain their sovereignty. This chapter will explore how federalism evolved, how Congress's authority and modern function have blurred the line between state and national jurisdictions, and how modern leaders have tried to return much authority to the states.

Federalism Defined

In creating and empowering the new federal government, the framers of the Constitution debated where power should lie. The experience of having just defeated a tyrannical central government in London to secure liberty locally did not make the idea of centralizing power in the new United States very attractive. **BIG IDEA:** **Federalism**, the sharing of power between a central government and equally sovereign regional governments, became a key part of the framework to secure liberty while also dividing respective powers among multiple authorities.

Today, Canada, Australia, Germany, and other nations have a federal system. Some others have **unitary governments**, those with a single governing authority in a central capital with uniform law throughout the land. These include the United Kingdom, France, Italy, and Japan.

Under the original American federal system, the states had more authority than the nation. Recall that the Articles of Confederation (pages 9–11) merely created a firm league of friendship among the states. The revolutionaries created the Confederation government of the 1780s mainly for national defense and to engage in diplomatic relations with other countries. The Articles held that the national government derived all of its powers from the states.

By that time, every state had its own constitution, several with an attached bill of rights. All states had a legislature, defined crimes (such as murder and theft), and had courts for criminal trials. The framers focused on new national concerns, such as regulating commerce, building roads, coining money, defending the country, and defining immigration.

Provisions Defining Federalism

The foundation for federalism can be found in various parts of the original Constitution and the Bill of Rights. National needs require consistency across state lines, such as having uniform weights and measures and a national currency. To establish this consistency, Article I enables Congress to legislate on military and diplomatic affairs and international and interstate commerce. It also allows Congress to define such crimes as counterfeiting, mail fraud, immigration violations, and piracy. However, the framers also put limits on Congress with Article I, Section 9.

CONSTITUTIONAL PROVISIONS THAT GUIDE FEDERALISM	
Article I, Section 8	Enumerated powers of Congress, including the necessary and proper clause
Article I, Section 9	Powers denied Congress; no regulating slave trade before 1808; states to be treated uniformly
Article I, Section 10	Powers denied to the states, such as treaties; impairing contracts
Article IV	Full faith and credit; privileges and immunities; extradition
Article VI	Supremacy of the national government
Ninth Amendment	Rights not listed reserved by the people
Tenth Amendment	Powers not delegated to the federal government reserved by the states

Later provisions define the relations among the states and national supremacy. Article IV explains full faith and credit, protections of privileges and immunities, and extradition. The article requires each state to give **full faith and credit** "to the public acts, records, and judicial proceedings of every other state." In other words, states must regard and honor the laws in other states. The **privileges and immunities clause** declares "citizens of each state shall be entitled to all privileges and immunities of citizens in the several states." States have created laws to protect their own residents or to give them priority over nonresidents, but the Supreme Court has struck down most of them based on this clause. States can, however, charge different college tuition prices for in-state and out-of-state students, largely because in-state students and their families have paid into the state's tax system that supports state colleges. The **extradition** clause obligates states to deliver captured fugitive criminals back to the state where they committed the original crime.

Article VI, commonly called the *supremacy clause*, places national law above state authority. National law, however, is limited by the enumerated list of Congress's powers in Article I, Section 8. (See page 20.) But when a congressional act is enacted, even if the Supreme Court has not (or has not yet) determined its constitutionality, states cannot disregard it.

The States States already had prisons, state militias, and other services when the federal system was created. The framers left these concerns up to the states, along with the management of elections, marriage laws, and the maintenance of deeds and records. Skeptics and Anti-Federalists desired an expressed guarantee in the Constitution to assure the preservation of states' rights. It came in the form of the Tenth Amendment. "The powers not delegated to the United States . . . ," the amendment declares, "are reserved to the states . . . ."

States have **police powers**, or powers to create and enforce laws on health, safety, and morals. These concerns encompass much of state budgets today. States fund and operate hospitals and clinics. Law enforcement is predominantly composed of state personnel. States can set their own laws on speed limits, seat belts, and smoking in public places.

The terms of the **Tenth Amendment** distinguish the two governing spheres. The **delegated powers** (or expressed powers) are those the Constitution delegates to the federal government, listed in Article I, Section 8, and the job descriptions for the president and the courts in Articles II and III, respectively. The **reserved powers** are not specifically listed, and thus any powers not mentioned remain with the states. Some powers are held by authorities at both levels, state and federal. These are called **concurrent powers**. The states and the **nation** can both lay and collect taxes, define crimes, run court systems, and improve lands.

Federalism: A Sharing of Powers

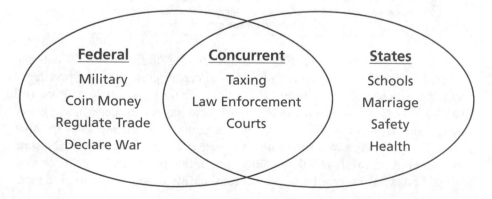

Federal	Concurrent	States
Military	Taxing	Schools
Coin Money	Law Enforcement	Marriage
Regulate Trade	Courts	Safety
Declare War		Health

Overlap and Uncertainty

States generally honored marriage licenses from other states, but the legalization of same-sex marriages in some states early in the 21st century caused other states to expressly refuse recognition of these marriages. Opposing states rewrote their marriage laws and added amendments to their state constitutions to define marriage as between a man and a woman only. This controversy put Article IV in direct conflict with the Tenth Amendment. The full faith and credit clause suggests that if Vermont sanctioned the marriage of two men, Missouri would have to honor it. Yet the reserved powers clause in the Tenth Amendment grants Missouri's right to define marriage within its borders. The Supreme Court settled this dispute in 2015 in *Obergefell v. Hodges*, ruling 5:4 that the right to same-sex marriage was guaranteed by the due process clause and the equal protection clause in the Fourteenth Amendment.

Federalism leaves schools, elections, and most law enforcement up to the states. Why, then, do we have a national Department of Education, the Federal Elections Commission, and a Federal Bureau of Investigation? These questions will be answered in the next section as you read about how the new nation began to walk a delicate line that divided state and federal power, how the Supreme Court has defined federalism, and how Congress became keenly interested in issues of education, political campaigns, and crime.

POWERS DELEGATED TO THE FEDERAL GOVERNMENT	POWERS RESERVED BY THE STATES
Declaring war	Regulating health and morals
Coining money	Safety regulations
Taxing	Incorporating cities and companies
Regulating interstate commerce	Defining legal relationships: marriage, divorce, wills
Defining immigration and naturalization	Operating schools

The New Republic to the New Deal

In 1788, in one of its final acts, the outgoing Confederation Congress directed states to choose presidential electors to vote for the nation's first president. With Virginia now in the Union, few doubted that George Washington was the best man for the job. He would oversee the birth of a federal system that would look drastically different after Franklin Roosevelt's New Deal went into effect.

Washington's Golden Age On February 4, 1789, electors unanimously elected Washington with their first ballot. His leadership at the Constitutional Convention, his endorsement of the new plan for government, and his alliance with Madison, Hamilton, and others made him a Federalist of the first order (though Washington would criticize the developing political parties). The same group that advocated ratification also pioneered establishing a strong national government. The first congressional elections resulted in sending mostly Federalist-minded men to the national legislature. Only 11 Anti-Federalists filled the 59 elected seats in the first House of Representatives, and only 2 Anti-Federalists served in the 20-member Senate. This dynamic in Congress and the leadership of Washington resulted in a mainly unified federal government that accomplished much during its first term. Congress designed the courts, declared the District of Columbia the new capital city, and created national financial institutions.

Beginning Divisions As Washington and his Federalist colleagues steered the new ship of state, national politics divided Americans into two camps. The familiar debate over national strength versus states' rights and individual liberties continued to shape the United States into a two-party nation. Though political parties as we know them did not yet exist, the Federalists faced off against the Democratic-Republicans led by Thomas Jefferson and later James Madison. Several showdowns between state and national authorities and between these two groups defined the era and shaped the interpretation of the Constitution.

One of the first pressing issues arose around Congress's creation of a national bank. Washington requested opinions on the bank idea from his secretaries, Jefferson and Hamilton, who clashed mightily on the bank question and on how to interpret the Constitution. Jefferson expressed that the bank was improper and that Congress had no power to create it. He was a **strict constructionist**, one who believes the Constitution should be interpreted literally, or strictly construed. He believed that what the Constitution did not expressly permit, it forbade. Hamilton, in contrast, generally believed that if the Constitution did not forbid something, then it permitted it. Washington and the Federalist Congress went with Hamilton and established the first Bank of the United States in 1791.

Whiskey Rebellion Another controversy brewed after a federal tax burdened whiskey distillers of the backcountry. Opponents sharply challenged the new national government and refused to pay federal tax collectors. President Washington summoned the militia of several states. About 13,000 soldiers rallied to Washington's call and easily put down the rebellion. But the incident strengthened the developing Jeffersonian faction. It also called the growing federal power into question. Numerous Federalist foes condemned the administration for its brutal display of force.

John Adams and the Jeffersonians

As Washington headed into retirement, Vice President John Adams barely defeated Jefferson in an electoral vote of 71 to 68, which, at the time, gave Jefferson the vice presidency. Adams continued to establish policies to strengthen the nation that also widened the gap between his followers and Jefferson's followers. In a time of nearly full-scale war against the French, Adams and the Federalist Congress passed the Alien and Sedition Acts. These laws empowered the federal government to jail any dissenters against the government's cause or deport foreigners who posed any threat to the United States. Many outspoken newspaper editors criticized Adams for this policy and were indicted under the law. In the minds of many, the Sedition Act, which set punishments for making false statements about the government, violated the First Amendment and sent many political converts over to Jefferson's camp.

States' Rights: Compact Theory and Nullification As Adams's administration jailed its detractors, Jefferson responded to the new laws while also developing a larger philosophy of the **compact theory**, which held that the 13 sovereign states, in creating the federal government, had entered into a compact, or contract, regarding its jurisdiction. The states created the national government and thus could judge whether federal authorities had broken the compact by overstepping the limited authority they granted in the first place. This theory challenged the authority of the federal judicial branch and the supremacy of national law. Jefferson and his supporters, however, believed that if the Federalists could stamp out free speech and free press with these harsh measures, they could soon violate other liberties in the compact. So, in secret to avoid prosecution, he penned a series of resolutions to address this violation, which became the bedrock ideas for the Jeffersonian movement and the Anti-Federalists' resurgence.

Ultimately, the resolutions declared the states' right to **nullification**, the right to declare null and void any federal law if a state thought the law violated the Constitution. The Alien and Sedition laws expired and Adams left office before opponents could challenge these in the courts. The South's reserved right to nullification—a right that has never been upheld in federal courts—continued over the ensuing decades, leading to the Civil War. Ever since the Union's victory in the conflict, the doctrine of nullification has disappeared.

The Supreme Court Shapes Federalism

"Has the government of the United States power to make laws on every subject?" delegate John Marshall asked at the Virginia ratifying convention in Richmond in 1788. Then he quickly asserted that the new federal judiciary "would declare it void" any law going against the Constitution. In 1801, outgoing president John Adams appointed Marshall as chief justice of the Supreme Court. Taking the seat as Jefferson became president, Marshall and Jefferson served as leading rivals in the Federalist-states' rights debate as the nation entered the 19th century. In 1819, the Supreme Court made a landmark decision in *McCulloch v. Maryland* addressing the balance of power between the states and the federal government.

Source: *thinkstock.com*

Chief Justice John Marshall

MUST-KNOW SUPREME COURT DECISIONS: *MCCULLOCH V. MARYLAND* (1819)

The Constitutional Question Before the Court: Does the federal government have implied powers and supremacy under the necessary and proper (elastic) clause and the supremacy clause?

Decision: Yes, for McCulloch, 6:0

Facts: The powers and supremacy of the federal government were the focus of a Supreme Court case when the U.S. bank controversy arose again. The state of Maryland, among others, questioned the legality of a congressionally created bank in Baltimore, where James McCulloch was the chief cashier. The Constitution does not explicitly mention that Congress has the power "to create a bank." So Maryland, recognizing the state's authority over everything within its borders, passed a law requiring all banks in Maryland not incorporated by the state to pay a $15,000 tax. The purpose of this law was to force the U.S. bank out of the state and to overcome the federal government's power. When McCulloch refused to pay the tax, the state brought the case to court. On appeal, the case of *McCulloch v. Maryland* (1819) landed in John Marshall's Supreme Court.

The dispute centered on two central questions. One, can Congress create a bank? And two, can a state levy a tax on federal institutions?

Reasoning: Article I, Section 8, was key to answering the first question. It contains no expressed power for Congress to create a bank, Maryland and strict constructionists had argued. But it did contain the phrases "coin money," "borrow money," "collect taxes," determine "laws on bankruptcies," and "punish counterfeiting." Banking was therefore very much the federal government's business, and supporters argued that a bank was therefore an appropriate endeavor under the necessary and proper clause of Article I, Section 8, also known as the elastic clause because it allows the federal government to stretch its powers to carry out its purpose. John Marshall's Court agreed unanimously. Marshall himself wrote the opinion.

Unanimous Opinion: We admit, as all must admit, that the powers of the Government are limited, and that its limits are not to be transcended. But we think the sound construction of the Constitution must allow to the national legislature that discretion with respect to the means by which the powers it confers are to be carried into execution which will enable that body to perform the high duties assigned to it in the manner most beneficial to the people. Let the end be legitimate, let it be within the scope of the Constitution, and all means which are appropriate, which are plainly adapted to that end, which are not prohibited, but consist with the letter and spirit of the Constitution, are Constitutional. . . .

The word "necessary" is considered as controlling the [elastic clause], and as limiting the right to pass laws for the execution of the granted powers to such as are indispensable, and without which the power would be nugatory [worthless].

To answer the second question—can a state tax a federal institution?—the Court in this landmark case invoked both the elastic clause and the supremacy clause (Article VI) for the first time, doubly strengthening the federal government. The Court strongly denounced the state's attempt to tax the national government, saying, "The power to tax involves the power to destroy . . . ." It broadened what Congress could do, denoting its **implied powers** in the Constitution (those not specifically listed in the Constitution but deriving from the elastic clause), and it declared that constitutional federal law will override state law.

The sovereignty of a State extends to everything which exists by its own authority or is introduced by its permission, but does it extend to those means which are employed by Congress to carry into execution powers conferred on that body by the people of the United States? We think it demonstrable that it does not. Those powers are not given by the people of a single State. They are given by the people of the United States, to a Government whose laws, made in pursuance of the Constitution, are declared to be supreme. Consequently, the people of a single State cannot confer a sovereignty which will extend over them.

Since _McCulloch v. Maryland_: The federal government has used its powers implied in the necessary and proper clause to play a role in other matters, such as education, health, welfare, disaster relief, and economic planning. In _Gibbons v. Ogden_ (1824), a dispute between New York and the federal government over navigation rights on the Hudson River, the Court looked to Article 1, Section 8, Clause 3—the **commerce clause**—to certify Congress's authority over most commercial activity as well. That interpretation of the commerce clause, as well as the interpretation of the necessary and proper clause and other enumerated and implied powers in _McCulloch v. Maryland,_ became the centerpiece of the debate over the balance of power between the national and state governments.

Political Science Disciplinary Practices: Analyze and Interpret Supreme Court Decisions

Apply: Write an essay in which you identify the two Constitutional questions addressed in _McCulloch v. Maryland_ and explain the reasoning for the answer to each question. Cite specific passages from the opinion and/or the Constitution to back up your explanation. Finally, explain how the opinion relates to political processes and behavior. For example, what impact did it have on the development of the growing nation?

Dual Federalism and Selective Exclusiveness Since the national government did not engage in too much legislation regarding commerce at the time, the *Gibbons* decision eventually led to a system of **dual federalism**, in which the national government is supreme in its sphere—having the authority given it in Article I—and the states are equally supreme in their own sphere. Article I entitled Congress to legislate on commerce "among the states" while it did not forbid the states from regulating commerce within their borders. Chief Justice Marshall did qualify that states still had some rights to commerce, rejecting an exclusive national authority over internal commercial activity. This became known as **selective exclusiveness**—a doctrine asserting that only Congress may regulate when the commodity requires a national uniform rule.

For years, this system worked because commerce and trade were mainly local, with fewer goods crossing state lines than they do today. Congress's relative inaction in regulating commerce until the Industrial Revolution during the mid-1700s to the mid-1800s allowed dual federalism to prevail. As the nation's business, manufacturing, transportation, and communication advanced, Congress became more and more interested in legislating business matters. Organized labor, reformers, and progressive leaders focused the national agenda on regulating railroads, factories, and banks and on breaking up monopolies. On some occasions, the federal government crossed into the states' domain on the strength of the commerce clause—the most frequently contested congressional power—and on some occasions lost.

National Concerns, State Obligations

State and federal governments generally followed dual federalism into the early 20th century. However, this practice gave way in response to changing societal needs as Congress's increased use of the commerce clause empowered it to legislate on a variety of state concerns.

The Progressive movement (1890–1920) brought much federal legislation that created a power play over commerce authority. In the early 1900s, democracy became stronger through a variety of government reforms. The Sixteenth Amendment, for example, created the **federal income tax** and expanded Congress's reach of regulation. The Seventeenth Amendment made senators accountable to the people instead of to the state governments. Voters then put reformers in office who wanted to clean up the railroads, factories, and corrupt government.

As the nation grew and citizens became more mobile, the nation's problems, much like its goods, began to travel across state borders. The police powers originally left up to the states now became national in scope, and Congress created the Federal Bureau of Investigation (FBI). Reformers pressured Congress to act on issues when states refused or could not act. Since the Constitution nowhere gave Congress the direct power to legislate to improve safety, health, and morals, it began to rely on its regulatory power over commerce to reach national goals of decreasing crime, making the workplace safer, and ensuring equality among citizens. The commerce clause served as the primary vehicle for such legislation. For example, the Mann Act of 1910 forbade the transportation of women across state lines for immoral purposes to crack down on prostitution. The Automobile Theft Act of 1915 made it a federal offense to knowingly drive a stolen car across state lines. Since then, Congress has made racketeering, drug dealing, and bank robbery federal crimes (though they remain illegal at the state level as well). The federal executive can enforce these laws even if the criminal activity is entirely contained in one state.

The Supreme Court Stretches the Commerce Clause

The Supreme Court, however, disappointed reformers and issued a few setbacks. The conservative Court declared that corporations as well as individuals were protected by the Constitution, and it questioned many health and safety regulations through the era. For example, when Congress passed a law prohibiting a company from hiring and forcing children to work in factories, the Supreme Court blocked it. In *Hammer v. Dagenhart* (1918), the Court ruled that the evils of child labor were entirely in the sphere of manufacturing, not commerce, and child labor was thus outside congressional authority. This ruling established a line between manufacturing as the creation of goods and commerce as the exchange of goods. By the 1920s, however, the Court relied on Justice Oliver Wendell Holmes's words, which said the shipment of cattle from one state to another for slaughter and sale constituted "a typical, constantly recurring course" and thus made both production and commerce subject to national authority.

After President Franklin Roosevelt initiated his New Deal programs during the Great Depression, a power play began between Congress and the Court that ultimately allowed the national legislature to assume broad powers under the interstate commerce authority. Specifically, the Court upheld Congress's right to create a national minimum wage law with the Fair Labor Standards Act of 1938. The act barred the shipment and transaction of commerce across state lines for firms failing to pay employees at least $0.25 per hour. The Court upheld the act and overturned the *Hammer* decision.

Two centuries of Court interpretations, a drastic turn by the Court to broaden the scope of the interstate commerce clause, changing societal needs, and prevailing attitudes of the last two generations have shaped American federalism into its current form. Congress has won more battles than the states in claiming authority on commerce-related legislation. But as you will see with the *Lopez* case later in this chapter (page 59), the Court does not always entitle Congress to legislate under the guise of regulating commerce.

Federal Grant Program

The overlap of federal and state authority in exclusive and concurrent powers is probably nowhere more obvious than in the federal grant program. In advancing the constitutional definition of federalism, Congress has dedicated itself to addressing national issues with federal dollars. Congress collects federal tax revenues and distributes these funds to the states to take care of particular national concerns. This process has different names, such as **revenue sharing**, **cooperative federalism**, or **fiscal federalism**. For decades, the federal government has encouraged, and at times required, states and localities to address safety, crime, education, and civil rights. Congress has largely done this by directing federal funds to states that qualify for aid. These **grants-in-aid** programs have developed over a two-hundred-year history and picked up steadily to meet the needs of society during the Progressive Era, with FDR's New Deal and then under President Lyndon Johnson's Great Society program of the 1960s. This financial aid helps states take care of basic state needs. Grants come in different forms with different requirements, and they sometimes stretch the limits of constitutionality. Political realities in Washington, D.C. and at the local level explain why these grants have gone through so many variations.

Grants Through the Mid-1900s After Americans earned independence and attained the vast lands west of the Appalachian Mountains, high-ranking soldiers received land grants for their service in the Revolution. The federal government later granted large sums of money to states so they could maintain militias. In 1862, Congress passed the Morrill Land-Grant Act. It allowed Congress to parcel out large tracts of land to encourage states to build colleges. Soon, colleges and universities grew in the Midwest and beyond. In more modern

Source: *Lewis Wickes Hine, Library of Congress*

The Court's decision in *Hammer v. Dagenhart* (1918) put children who worked in manufacturing, sometimes against their will, beyond the jurisdiction of the federal government. That decision was later overturned.

times, Congress has provided money to states to take care of improvements in the environment, education, unemployment, interstate highways, welfare, and health care.

In the early 1900s, most grants were grants-in-aid with conditions attached. These conditions suited the federal government because they made administration convenient. Congress used them to prod state governments to modernize. States had to match federal grants with state funds, secure statewide uniformity, and create agencies to report to the federal government. Congress started using grants heavily in 1916 to fund road construction as the automobile became central to American society and as roads became central to economic improvement.

The federal income tax caused the national treasury to grow exponentially. With these extra financial resources, Congress addressed concerns that were traditionally out of its jurisdiction. Additionally, larger numbers of people who had gained the right to vote pressed for more government reform and action. Women and other groups began voting and engaging in civic endeavors that resulted in the national government addressing more of society's concerns.

The economic crisis that followed, the Great Depression, caused the federal government to grow more, largely by implementing more grants. Traditionally, states, localities, and private charitable organizations provided relief for the poor. By 1935, most states had enacted laws to aid impoverished mothers and the aged. State funds did not always cover this effort, so President Franklin D. Roosevelt and Congress were pressured to address the issue.

Contemporary Federalism

Though state officials are well schooled in the reserved powers clause of the Tenth Amendment and can see the conflict of interest by accepting federal funds, they also find it challenging to turn away federal money to handle state concerns. States do not necessarily want to cede their authority, but at the same time, they want the funds to carry out state needs. The federal government has decided many times to pay the bill, as long as the states follow federal guidelines while taking care of the issue. Grants with particular congressional guidelines or requirements are known as **categorical grants**.

Societal Concerns of the 1960s and 1970s

During the 1960s and 1970s, several movements brought new federal initiatives. The fight for civil rights and school desegregation, the desire for clean air and clean water, and the concern for crime gained national interest. Once again, federal dollars spoke loudly to local officials. The 1964 Civil Rights Act, for example, withheld federal dollars from schools that did not fully desegregate their students. Under President Johnson, the federal government increased the number of grants to address poverty and health care.

Congress also began to redefine the grants process to give more decision-making power to local authorities. Some states felt grants had too many **strings**, or specific requirements, attached. In 1966, Congress introduced **block grants**. Block grants differ from categorical grants in that they offer larger sums of money to the states to take care of some large, overarching purpose, without the strings of the categorical grants. Democrats led the efforts for the early block grants, such as the Partnership for Health program approved in 1966 and the Safe Streets program created in 1968.

When Republican Richard Nixon became president in 1969, he wanted to return greater authority to local governments. A believer in clear boundaries between state and federal jurisdictions, Nixon desired a mix of block grants, revenue sharing, and welfare reform. Additionally, mayors and urban leaders saw a politicization of the grants process and the way the government awarded monies. They wanted the system revamped. Many other individuals in the field wanted to consolidate and decentralize the grant process and favored block grants over categorical grants. They believed federal agencies had little understanding of how local offices implemented particular programs.

In 1971, Nixon proposed to meld one-third of all federal programs into six loosely defined megagrants, an initiative called "special revenue sharing." He wanted to consolidate 129 different programs into six block grants in the fields of transportation, education, rural development, law enforcement, community development, and employment training. He didn't achieve this goal, but in 1972, general revenue sharing provided more than $6.1 billion annually in "no strings" grants to virtually all general-purpose governments. Congress passed two major block grants: the Comprehensive Employment and Training Act of 1973 (CETA) and the Community Development Block Grant program (CDBG) in 1974. By 1976, Congress had created three more large block grants.

Fiscal conservatives, who also favored local control, liked Nixon's plan. The result of his changes contributed to a phenomenon of mixing state and federal authority that had already begun. The classic explanation of our federal, state, and local governments often comes with a diagram of a layer cake with the federal government on top, the states in the middle, and the local government on the bottom. Everything is orderly and stacked. The flow of federal money to the various state and local governments, and even private charitable groups, however, has more recently created what is termed **marble cake federalism** because the lines are not straight and even. Federalism has become a hodgepodge of government authorities and has even mixed with the private sector. Federal grants are awarded to local nonprofits that help develop and clean up communities.

As soon as Nixon tried to steer federal money to states in larger, less restrictive ways, members of Congress realized the authority and benefits they would lose. Block grants took away Congress's role of oversight. Congress was losing control and individual members felt some responsibility to provide federal dollars to their districts in a more specific way. From a political standpoint, block grants denied individual representatives and senators the ability to claim credit. Chairs of relevant congressional committees, too, had suddenly lost control over the process.

"In Two Words, Yes And No"

Source: *Herblock*

Describe the characters, objects, and actions in this cartoon. How does the text help convey the message? What perspective about federalism is the cartoonist trying to convey? What is the implication of the cartoonist's perspective or argument?

What was the result? The number of categorical grants increased dramatically, while block grants subsided. Congress passed only five block grants between 1966 to 1980. Categorical grants with strings, or **conditions of aid**, became the norm again. In addition to the political benefits congressional members experienced, grant recipients at the state and local levels enjoyed categorical grants. Special interest groups could lobby Congress for funding their causes. State agencies, such as those that support state health care or road construction, depend on federal aid and appreciate these grants. Community groups and nonprofit agencies thrive on these as well.

THINK AS A POLITICAL SCIENTIST: *ANALYZE AND INTERPRET QUANTITATIVE DATA*

Often you will be interpreting and applying information presented in the form of charts, graphs, and tables. For an accurate understanding of that information, begin by reading the title, labels, and contents of the chart, graph, or table. Be sure you understand the exact purpose of the information and exactly what the numbers represent. For example, are they percentages or amounts? If they refer to money, are the amounts expressed in constant dollars (adjusted for inflation) or real (nominal) dollars? Are the numbers expressed in thousands, millions, or billions?

Once you are sure you understand the purpose, labels, and contents of the informational illustration, look for patterns and relationships. For example, do the numbers go up or down in a predictable pattern? If there is a sudden change in a pattern, how can you explain it? Is there a clear trend visible in the information? Draw a conclusion from the information to explain what it implies or illustrates about political principles, processes, behaviors, and outcomes.

Practice: Focusing on the table below, explain and draw conclusions from the table's information, trends, patterns, and variations. Answer these questions.

- When do you see increases or decreases?
- What events or priorities might explain these changes?

TOTAL FEDERAL OUTLAYS FOR STATE AND LOCAL GRANTS, 1955–1985		
Year	(in billions of constant dollars)	Percentage of Total Federal Outlays
1955	24.4	4.7
1960	45.3	7.6
1965	65.9	9.2
1970	123.7	12.3
1975	186.8	15.0
1980	227.0	15.5
1985	189.6	11.2

Source: *OMB Historical Tables, FY 2014*

Then discuss the following:

- What possible limitations of the data might there be? In other words, what might be missing or overrepresented?
- What possible limitations of the visual representation of the data might there be? In other words, if it were displayed another way, might you reach different conclusions?

Returning Authority to the States

The post-New Deal trend of fiscal federalism has experienced a mixed appreciation from state and local administrators. And conservatives have pushed to reduce federal taxes and return to state and local control over reserved powers. "It is my intention to curb the size and influence of the Federal establishment," President Ronald Reagan declared as he took the oath of office in 1981, "and to demand recognition of the distinction between the powers granted to the Federal Government and those reserved to the States or to the people." Reagan followed with initiatives meant to define a **New Federalism** that he had promised.

Grants in the 1980s and Beyond

The federal government has created a dilemma for the states because states have come to depend on these grants. The strings can also be costly. Building projects, which make up a large share of these programs, require the local government to pay prevailing wages to its construction workers. Recipients must be careful of their project's impact on the region, and they must follow federally imposed hiring guidelines. State officials all too often see the otherwise enticing funds as not so attractive.

The federal government offered states one notable categorical grant in the early 1980s as a way to both satisfy the upkeep of highways and to ease the national drunk driving problem. Congress offered large sums of money to states on the condition that states increase their drinking age to twenty-one. Studies showed that making twenty-one the legal drinking age would likely decrease the number of fatalities on the highways. Most states complied with the National Minimum Drinking Age Act of 1984 to secure these precious dollars. South Dakota, however, challenged these strings.

In *South Dakota v. Dole,* the Supreme Court ruled that Congress did have the power to set conditions of the drinking age for states to receive federal dollars for highway repair and construction. Congressional restrictions on grants to the states are constitutional if they meet certain requirements. They must be for the general welfare of the public and cannot be ambiguous. Conditions must be related to the federal interest in particular national projects or programs, and they must not run afoul of other constitutional provisions. That is, Congress cannot use a conditional grant to induce states to engage in unconstitutional activities. South Dakota lost and Congress continued creating and controlling strings.

Mandates With strings, states receive federal monies in exchange for following guidelines. Federal **mandates**, on the other hand, require states to comply with a federal directive, sometimes with the reward of funds and sometimes—in unfunded mandates—without. The legislative, executive, or judicial branches can issue mandates in various forms. Mandates often address civil rights, environmental concerns, and other societal needs. Federal statutes require state environmental agencies to meet national clean air and water requirements. Significant intergovernmental regulations in the late '80s and early '90s include the Clean Air Act Amendments, the Americans with Disabilities Act, the Civil Rights Restoration Act, the Family and Medical Leave Act, and the National Voter Registration Act (also known as the motor-voter law).

The **Clean Air Act**, originally passed in 1970, set requirements and timetables for dealing with urban smog, acid rain, and toxic pollutants. The **Americans with Disabilities Act** made public sector buildings and transportation systems accessible for disabled individuals. Cities and states had to make their buildings wheelchair accessible and install wheelchair lifts. The mandate imposed, according to the Congressional Budget Office's best estimates, as much as $1 billion in additional costs on states and localities. The Clean Air Act Amendments imposed $250 to $300 million annually, and the cost of the motor-voter law would reach $100 million over five years.

The federal courts have also issued mandates to ensure that state or local governing bodies act in certain ways. Judges have decreed that cities redefine their hiring practices to prevent discrimination. They have placed firm restrictions on federal housing projects. In the early 1970s, federal judges mandated that public schools arrange appropriate black-to-white enrollment ratios, essentially mandating busing for racial balance.

Devolution Americans generally agree that issues such as education and health care have become national in scope. In 1990, 75 percent of Americans believed the nation was spending too little on education and environmental protection; 72 percent said the same about health care. But people questioned whether the federal government in Washington could take care of these issues. They wanted Washington to pay, but they also wanted local control.

By 1994, the Republican Party, especially those in the House of Representatives, began a call for **devolution**—devolving some of the responsibilities assumed by the federal government over the years back onto the states. Prior to the 1994 elections, Minority House Whip Newt Gingrich led the House Republicans and congressional candidates in front of the Capitol building to push for a Contract with America, calling for "the end of government that is too big, too intrusive, and too easy with the public's money." An overwhelming Republican victory followed with a plan to return this power and those dollars to the states. With bipartisan support and President Bill Clinton's signature, they managed to pass the Unfunded Mandates Reform Act and the Personal Responsibility and Work Opportunity Reconciliation Act. The first denied Congress the ability to issue unfunded mandates, laws that were taking up some 30 percent of state budgets. The second restructured the welfare system to return much authority and distribution of welfare dollars—Medicaid, for example—to the states. As Clinton declared in a 1996 address, "The era of big government is over."

MUST-KNOW SUPREME COURT DECISIONS:
UNITED STATES V. LOPEZ (1995)

The Constitutional Question Before the Court: Does Congress have the authority under the commerce clause to outlaw guns near schools?

Decision: No, for Lopez, 5:4.

Before United States v. Lopez: Gibbons v. Ogden (1824) broadened the authority of the federal government to control commerce. (See page 49.)

Facts: Congress passed the Gun-Free School Zones Act in 1990 in hopes of preventing gun violence at or near schools. In 1992, senior Alfonso Lopez carried a .38 caliber handgun and bullets into a San Antonio high school. On an anonymous tip, school authorities confronted him, obtained the gun, and reported the infraction to the federal police. Lopez was indicted, tried, and sentenced in federal court for violating the statute. He challenged the ruling in the Supreme Court on the grounds that the federal government has no right to regulate specific behavior at a state-run school. The United States argued that the connections of guns and drug dealing put this area under federal jurisdiction and Congress's commerce power.

The Court sided with Lopez, refusing to let Congress invoke the commerce clause. "It is difficult to perceive any limitation on federal power," Chief Justice William Rehnquist wrote. "If we were to accept the Government's arguments, we are hard pressed to posit any activity by an individual that Congress is without power to regulate." Congress had stretched its commerce power too far. Most states have regulations on guns and where one can legally carry a firearm. That is where the Supreme Court said this authority should stay, ushering in a new phase of federalism that recognized the importance of state sovereignty and local control.

Reasoning: Chief Justice William Rehnquist, joined by justices O'Connor, Scalia, Kennedy, and Thomas, wrote the majority opinion arguing that a gun near school property does not have an impact on interstate commerce and is therefore not covered by the commerce clause.

Majority Opinion: The possession of a gun in a local school zone is in no sense an economic activity that might, through repetition elsewhere, substantially affect any sort of interstate commerce. Respondent was a local student at a local school; there is no indication that he had recently moved in interstate commerce, and there is no requirement that his possession of the firearm have any concrete tie to interstate commerce.

In addition to the majority opinion, there were two concurring and three dissenting opinions.

Concurring Opinions Justice Anthony Kennedy, joined by Justice Sandra Day O'Connor, focused on the nature of commerce, the obligation of the government not to tip the balance of power, and the state's control over education. Justice Clarence Thomas's concurring opinion argued that recent cases have drifted too far from the Constitution in their interpretation of the commerce clause and that if something "substantially affects interstate commerce," Congress could pass laws that regulated every aspect of human existence.

Dissenting Opinions Justice John Paul Stevens's dissent argued that the possession of guns is the result of commercial activity and is therefore under the authority of the commerce clause. Justice David Souter's dissent argued that the majority opinion is a throwback to earlier times and goes against precedent. Justice Breyer's dissent, with which Justice Stevens, Justice Souter, and Justice Ruth Bader Ginsburg joined, argued in part that given the effect of education upon interstate commerce, gun-related violence in and around schools is a commercial as well as human problem, since a decline in the quality of education has an adverse effect on commerce.

Since *United States v. Lopez:* Congress revised the federal Gun-Free School Zones Act in 1994 so that it would tie more clearly to interstate commerce. That law withholds federal funding for schools that do not adopt a zero-tolerance law for guns in school zones.

Political Science Disciplinary Practices: Analyze and Interpret Supreme Court Decisions
The full opinion of the divided court in the case of *United States v. Lopez* is available online. Refer to it as you work in small groups (or as your teacher directs) to understand the reasoning behind the various opinions. Different groups should study the reasoning behind the majority opinion, the concurring opinions, and the dissenting opinions and report a summary back to the class.

Apply: When studying your portion of the ruling, you may find the reading challenging. Take it slow, and make notes to yourself with any questions. Identify key passages in your portion of the ruling, and use them as evidence to explain your interpretation. Discuss your understanding with your group until each member is clear on the main ideas. Then decide on a way to present your summary to the class, and share the tasks in carrying that plan out.

After each group has made its presentation, discuss ways in which the concurring opinions and dissenting opinions are similar and different. Are there any points on which they all agree?

Related Case: How does the interpretation of the commerce clause in the majority opinion in *United States v. Lopez* compare to the interpretation of the commerce clause in *Gibbons v. Ogden* (page 49)?

Education: National Goals, State Management

The Constitution and the federal government left the creation and management of schools largely to the states until the 1960s. There has always been a national concern for an educated citizenry, but the racial desegregation of public schools and the Cold War competition with the Soviet Union in the 1950s caused education to move up the national agenda, and with that move came new debate about the roles of the central, state, and local governments. President Johnson (a former teacher) and Congress passed the Elementary and Secondary Education Act in 1965. The law was as much an assault on poverty as it was reform of education, ensuring that lesser-funded schools received adequate resources. State officials generally welcomed the law because of the federal government's hands-off approach to school management and the broad discretion it gave local authorities on how to spend federal monies.

By the end of Johnson's term, federal aid to education through the Department of Health, Education, and Welfare totaled $4 billion. By the late 1970s, Congress created a new seat for the secretary of education in the president's cabinet and an entire Department of Education. In the 1980s and 1990s, presidents and members of Congress found education a topic that almost all voters cared about and wanted to improve, though viewpoints on how to improve education varied widely.

The most sweeping changes in federal education law that caused tension between the states and the national government came in the form of the **No Child Left Behind Act (NCLB)**. After campaigning to end an "education recession," George W. Bush gained bipartisan support for NCLB and signed the bill in early 2002. The new law brought Republicans and Democrats together to improve the nation's education system. The law declared that every child can learn and that schools and states should be held accountable for student learning. The act called for "highly qualified" teachers in the core subjects in every classroom, the use of proven teaching methods, and the threat of sanctions on underperforming schools. No Child Left Behind pushed for classroom lessons and methods that research has proven effective, and it gave parents information and choices about their child's education.

With these requirements and rewards also came greater emphasis on testing and the cloud of federal intervention. NCLB required that students show annual yearly progress (AYP) through federally required and regulated tests. Underperforming schools could be reconstituted, replacing the administration and teaching staff.

Public support for the law was strong and widespread at its passage, but many teachers, administrators, and state governments came to criticize NCLB. Part of the frustration was that Congress provided only 8 percent of the total funding for education nationwide, while it had increased the Department of Education's power over the nation's schools. Some of its goals were just not realistic. Nearly 80 percent of U.S. schools would be labeled failures as they could not reach the idealistic goals and deadlines. One education professor at Harvard University called the bill the "single largest expansion of federal power over the nation's education system in history." Several states agreed. State and local officials complained of the law's restrictions and added management tasks.

President Obama's Race to the Top initiative, introduced in 2009, offered incentives for states to adopt new national standards or develop their own that require students to be college- and career-ready at graduation. As the federal government tried to revamp the law, traditionalists and those adhering to the Tenth Amendment argued that most of NCLB should disappear. Others, especially civil rights groups and advocates for the poor, saw a need to keep the federal government involved as a watchdog on the states.

In 2015, Congress passed and President Obama signed a new education law—the Every Student Succeeds Act (ESSA). Under this law, the challenging goals of NCLB have been eliminated, and states are free to determine their own standards for educational achievement while still upholding protections for disadvantaged students. However, the federal Department of Education must still approve each state's plan, assuring that the states live up to the requirements in the federal law.

State and federal governments continue to push and pull to determine who will ultimately govern and fund education and an array of other services. Federalism is designed so that government power is diluted while local control over police powers, the management of state prisons, and internal roads is assured. Yet Congress, taking care of citizens' concerns, will continue to act on national matters.

Source: *Florida Stop Common Core Coalition*

In response to the Race to the Top initiative, many states adopted the Common Core State Standards. Members of the Florida Stop Common Core Coalition and Florida Parents R.I.S.E., like citizens in many other states, protested these standards, believing their adoption weakened local control of education and allowed the federal government to overreach.

FEDERALISM TERMS	
Dual Federalism	The supremacy of the national and state governments in their own spheres, a Supreme Court doctrine common from the Civil War until the New Deal
Cooperative Federalism	The intermingled relationships among the national, state, and local governments to deliver services to citizens
Fiscal Federalism	The pattern of taxing, spending, and providing federal grants to state and local governments
New Federalism	A return to more distinct lines of responsibility for federal and state governments, begun by President Ronald Reagan
Revenue Sharing	A policy under fiscal federalism that requires both national and local funds for programs
Devolution	The continued effort to return original reserved powers to the states

POLICY MATTERS: *POLICYMAKING AND THE SHARING OF POWERS*

You may have heard people complain about how slow the national government is to get anything done. In fact, the sharing of powers between and among the three branches and the state governments does constrain national policymaking and slow it down, an outcome many framers of the new constitution sought in order to protect the nation from popular but possibly rash policies. **BIG IDEA** The competitive policymaking process built into the Constitution—drawing on checks and balances among the executive, legislative, and judicial branches of the federal government and the sharing of powers with the states—ensures that multiple stakeholders and institutions can influence public policy. Environmental policy provides a useful case in point for seeing how different stakeholders compete.

Background The executive branch provided the initial impetus for environmental policy. President Teddy Roosevelt (1901–1909) is known as "the conservationist president" because of his appreciation of and devotion to the natural beauty and resources of the United States. During his presidency, 230 million acres of land were set aside as public lands. One reason Roosevelt was able to achieve so much was that he believed the president was "the steward of the people" who could claim broad powers to advance the good of the American people. He had little patience with the slow pace of debate in Congress, many of whose members he regarded as "scoundrels and crooks." Congress was needed to establish national parks, but Roosevelt was able to hasten the protection of public lands by exercising his executive authority to establish national monuments. The Grand Canyon, now a national park, was originally established as a national monument by Teddy Roosevelt. National parks and forest preserves became mainstays on our American landscape.

Not until the 1960s and 1970s did the environmental movement take off among the public, and Congress itself began to strongly regulate industry to assist this effort. As Congress imposed environmental standards, the business community opposed regulations. Over the ensuing decades, environmental policy in the United States became a competition between environmental activists and conservative free-market thinkers. Today, millions of members of the Sierra Club, the National Wildlife Federation, Greenpeace, and the World Wildlife Fund push for greater regulations, while the manufacturing and construction sectors fight regulations that slow job development and cheer President Trump's rollback of some of these regulations.

Congress and Environmental Legislation The National Environmental Policy Act requires any government agency, state or federal, to file an environmental impact statement with the federal government every time the agency plans a policy that might harm the environment, dams, roads, or existing construction. The 1970 amendments to the Air Pollution Control Act, commonly known as the Clean Air Act, call for improved air quality and decreased contaminants. The act ultimately requires the Department of Transportation to reduce automobile emissions. The Clean Water Act of 1972 regulates the discharge of pollutants into the waters of the United States and monitors quality standards for surface waters. The Endangered Species Act established a program that empowers the National Fish and Wildlife Service to protect endangered species.

After the catastrophic Love Canal toxic waste disaster in western New York in the mid-1970s, the federal government forced industry to pay for the insurance necessary to manage their dangerous by-products. In that disaster, a company had dumped toxic chemicals in an area that later became a residential development. Heavy rains washed some of the chemicals out of the ground. Adults and children developed serious liver, kidney, and other health problems. The company responsible for this major environmental catastrophe had already gone out of business. In response, Congress created the Superfund. Essentially, industry pays into the Superfund as insurance so taxpayers do not have to pay the bill for waste cleanup. Under the law, the guilty polluter pays for the cleanup, but when the guilty party is unknown or bankrupt, the collective fund will cover these costs, not the taxpayers.

Clashes Between the Executive and Judicial Branches over Environmental Policy Over the years since the 1970 creation of the Environmental Protection Agency—an agency within the executive branch—it and the federal government in general have required states to set air quality standards, to reduce the damage done by automobiles, to measure city smog, and to set environmental guidelines. The EPA oversees the Superfund and toxic waste cleanup.

In 2012, the EPA established limits on how much mercury and other hazardous chemicals coal- and oil-fueled power plants could emit, asserting that although limiting these emissions would cost the plants nearly $10 billion dollars, the cost should not be a factor because the risk of the emissions to human health justified the regulation. Exercising a countervailing force, however, the Supreme Court overturned that regulation in 2015, arguing that the EPA had unreasonably neglected to consider the cost burden to the power plants and customers and exerting a check and balance to the EPA.

Clashes over Climate Change The burning of fossil fuels and the resulting greenhouse gases have heightened attention to global warming, an increase in average global temperatures. Melting polar ice caps, unusual flooding in certain areas, animal habitat destruction, and a damaged ozone layer have caused the scientific community, including the Intergovernmental Panel on Climate Change, to conclude that the use of these damaging fuels should be limited and regulated. One international attempt to combat this problem came with the 1997 Kyoto Protocol, a multicountry agreement that committed the signing nations to reduced greenhouse gas emissions. Most industrialized nations joined the treaty, and U.S. president Bill Clinton agreed to it. However, the conservative-leaning U.S. Senate at the time did not achieve the two-thirds support necessary for ratification, so the United States did not sign the treaty.

During President Obama's tenure, the Senate remained conservative-leaning, constraining the power of the government to join another international climate agreement, the 2015 Paris Agreement. President Obama sought to go around this constraint by making acceptance of membership in the agreement a matter of executive order, without the approval of the Senate. In 2017, President Trump used the same bypass method to withdraw from the Paris Agreement, though some argue that the United States was never officially a member of the Paris Agreement since the Senate did not have a voice in deciding.

State Initiatives In response to Trump's decision, a number of states decided to adhere to the guidelines in the Paris Agreement anyway, demonstrating yet another check and balance in the federal system. In 2017, for example, California passed legislation to extend its program to reduce carbon emissions, known as cap and trade, from its original expiration date of 2020 to 2030. Under this plan, companies must buy permits to release greenhouse gas emissions.

REFLECT ON THE ESSENTIAL QUESTION

Essential Question: *How has federalism shaped the administration of public policy, and how do state, local, and national governments work within the federal framework today?* On separate paper, complete a chart like the one below to gather details to answer that question.

Constitutional Approach to Federalism	Federalism in Practice

KEY TERMS AND NAMES

Americans with Disabilities Act/58

block grants/54

categorical grants/53

Clean Air Act (1970)/58

commerce clause/49

compact theory/47

concurrent powers/44

conditions of aid/strings/55

cooperative federalism/52

delegated powers/44

devolution/58

dual federalism/50

extradition/44

federal income tax/50

federalism/42

fiscal federalism/52

full faith and credit clause/43

grants-in-aid/52

implied powers/49

mandates/57

marble cake federalism/54

McCulloch v. Maryland (1819)/48

New Federalism/57

No Child Left Behind Act (2002)/61

nullification/47

police powers/44

privileges and immunities clause/43

reserved powers/44

revenue sharing/52

selective exclusiveness/50

strict constructionist/46

strings/53

Tenth Amendment/44

unitary government/42

United States v. Lopez (1995)/59

Whiskey Rebellion/46

MULTIPLE-CHOICE QUESTIONS

Questions 1 and 2 refer to the following passage:

> The Commerce Clause should be limited to its proper sphere. The current approach under the Commerce Clause requires courts to defer to congressional judgment that a regulated activity has an effect upon interstate commerce, provided that there is any rational basis for that judgment. This standard grants judicial power to the legislative branch and removes an important check on legislative power. Deference to the judgment of a coequal branch of government on a specific issue is only appropriate where the Constitution gives that branch the power to decide that issue. Here, the Constitution grants the Judicial Branch the power to decide whether Congress is acting within its enumerated powers, so no deference is due. Simply put, "The constitution is either a superior paramount law, unchangeable by ordinary means, or it is on a level with ordinary legislative acts, and, like other acts, is alterable when the legislature shall please to alter it." —Texas Justice Foundation, Amicus Brief filed in *United States v. Lopez* 1993

1. Which of the following statements best summarizes the argument in the Texas Justice Foundation's brief?
   (A) Judicial power should be granted to Congress in matters related to commerce.
   (B) The judicial branch can determine if Congress is operating within its enumerated powers and thus checks legislative power.
   (C) *Marbury v. Madison* confirms the coequal status of the branches of government.
   (D) The Court should uphold the process in place for determining the reach of the commerce clause.

2. This passage best aligns with which of the following opinions in *United States v. Lopez*?
   (A) We hold that the [Gun-Free School Zones] Act exceeds the authority of Congress "[t]o regulate Commerce . . . among the several States . . . ."—Justice Rehnquist
   (B) Congress's power to regulate commerce in firearms includes the power to prohibit possession of guns at any location because of their potentially harmful use. . . —Justice Stevens
   (C) A look at history's sequence will serve to show how today's decision tugs the Court off course.—Justice Souter
   (D) [T]he statute falls well within the scope of the commerce power as this Court has understood that power over the last half century.— Justice Breyer

3. Which of the following options represents the majority opinion in *United States v. Lopez*?

(A) Individuals have the right to own and carry guns.

(B) The power of the federal government in relation to state governments is limited in this case.

(C) The commerce clause gives Congress broad powers to determine the constitutionality of laws.

(D) Even small, local events ultimately have an effect on interstate commerce.

4. Which of the following statements accurately describes federalism?

(A) Federalism is a governing system that places a national authority above regional authority.

(B) Federalism ranks the sovereignty of the states over the power of the national government.

(C) Federalism is a balance of powers between state and local governments.

(D) Federalism is a sharing of powers between national and regional governments.

5. On which of the following issues did Federalists and Jeffersonians have most widely differing views?

(A) Declaring independence

(B) Writing the Constitution

(C) Ratifying the Constitution

(D) Creating a national bank

6. Most members of Congress believe the legal driving age should be 18, because statistics show that drivers under eighteen have many more accidents than those 18 and older. Which of the following is the most practical and lasting action Congress can take to address this issue?

(A) Urge the president to issue an executive order requiring drivers to be at least 18 years old.

(B) Mandate states to set the driving age at 18 and then withhold highway funds from any state that does not comply.

(C) Convince the Supreme Court that Congress, not the states, should regulate driving laws.

(D) Distribute educational materials on the issue to state legislatures.

7. Which of the following statements most closely conveys the main message in the cartoon below?

   (A) The federal government is like a king.

   (B) The framers foresaw the federal government becoming too powerful.

   (C) The framers tried to warn Americans the government might limit their right to vote.

   (D) Voters created a monster in the federal government.

Source: *CartoonStock*

8. Which of the following is an accurate comparison of federal block grants and categorical grants?

	BLOCK GRANTS	CATEGORICAL GRANTS
(A)	Let members of Congress control how to spend money in their districts	Give states control over how to spend federal money locally
(B)	Lead to loss of congressional oversight on spending grant money	Require states or localities to meet certain criteria
(C)	Are used primarily to combat terrorism at the local level	Are available to state governments but not city governments
(D)	Specify how the grant money is to be spent	Have declined in favor of block grants

FEDERAL GRANTS FROM THE TOP FIVE DEPARTMENTS FY 2011	
Department of Health and Human Services	$332 Billion
Department of Transportation	$25.7 Billion
Department of Agriculture	$23.3 Billion
Department of Education	$17.3 Billion
Department of Housing and Urban Development	$6.7 Billion

Source: www.usaspending.gov

9. Which of the following statements is reflected in the table above?

(A) More federal dollars go toward state education and farming than any other concern.

(B) The constitutional outline of federalism prevents the national government from assisting with state responsibilities.

(C) Grants appear to assist the inner-city interests, not rural interests.

(D) Medical and social needs receive the most federal grant money.

10. In the *McCulloch v. Maryland* (1819) decision, which two provisions in the Constitution were upheld and strengthened?

(A) Congress's power to regulate commerce and to levy taxes

(B) The necessary and proper clause and the supremacy clause

(C) The First and Tenth amendments

(D) The full faith and credit clause and the extradition clause

FREE-RESPONSE QUESTIONS

1. "In this present crisis, government is not the solution to our problem; government is the problem. From time to time we've been tempted to believe that society has become too complex to be managed by self-rule, that government by an elite group is superior to government for, by, and of the people. Well, if no one among us is capable of governing himself, then who among us has the capacity to govern someone else? All of us together, in and out of government, must bear the burden. The solutions we seek must be equitable, with no one group singled out to pay a higher price."

— President Ronald Reagan, First Inaugural Address, January 20, 1981

After reading the excerpt, respond to A, B, and C on the next page.

(A) Describe the political institution Reagan identifies as the problem.

(B) In the context of the scenario, explain how the power of the institution described in part A can be affected by its interaction with the U.S. Supreme Court.

(C) In the context of the excerpt, explain actions the public can take to influence the political institution described in part A.

"IF ONLY WE COULD HARVEST THE WIND COMING OUT OF THERE."

Source: *CartoonStock*

2. Use the political cartoon to answer the following questions.

(A) Describe the core message of the cartoon.

(B) Explain how the message described in part A relates to policymaking.

(C) Explain how states can respond to the issue described in part A.

3. In 1996, California voters passed the Compassionate Use Act that legalized the medical use of marijuana. However, that state law conflicted with the federal Controlled Substances Act, which made the possession of marijuana illegal. When federal agents from the Drug Enforcement Agency raided a medical marijuana user's home and confiscated the drug, a group of people prescribed marijuana for medical reasons sued the federal government. They argued that the Controlled Substances Act exceeded the government's authority since the use of medical marijuana was completely within the state of California, not between states. The case reached the Supreme Court in 2004 as *Gonzales v. Raich.* In a 6:3 ruling, the Court decided that the government did have authority to prohibit medical marijuana possession and use, even though it was legal in California. It reasoned

that since marijuana sales are part of a national market, marijuana possession can be controlled by the federal government.

(A) Identify the constitutional clause that is common to both *Gonzales v. Raich* (2004) and *United States v. Lopez* (1995).

(B) Based on the constitutional clause identified in part A, explain why the facts of *Gonzales v. Raich* led to a different holding than the holding in *United States v. Lopez*.

(C) Describe an action that California users of medical marijuana might take to limit the impact of the ruling in *Gonzales v. Raich*.

4. Develop an argument that explains how power over education should be shared in the U.S. federalist system. In your essay you must:

- Articulate a defensible claim or thesis clearly stating your position
- Support your claim with at least TWO pieces of accurate and relevant information.
  - At least ONE piece of information must be from one of the following foundational documents:
    - Article I, Section 8 of the Constitution
    - Article VI of the Constitution
    - The Tenth Amendment
  - Use a second piece of evidence from another foundational document from the list above or from your study of federalism
- Use reasoning to organize and analyze evidence, explaining its significance to justify your claim or thesis
- Address opposing or alternative perspectives through refutation, concession, and rebuttal

WRITING: *REFUTE CLAIMS*

Refute means "to contradict" or "disprove" an opposing or alternative view. A simple "I don't agree with you" is not an effective refutation or rebuttal. Instead, offer evidence and use solid reasoning to show why your position is stronger. However, if another view includes worthwhile ideas, acknowledge, or concede, those points, but then go on to show why your position is even stronger.

UNIT 1: Review

Revolutionaries and American leaders established the United States government, which culminated in the creation of the Constitution. The same concerns that brought independence—a lack of representation, an autocratic centralized government, and violations of liberties—coupled with powerful political theory from Enlightenment philosophers shaped the design of the U.S. government. After a failed experiment under the Articles of Confederation, leaders created a new federal government that was national in character.

The union of states assumed unique and limited powers, the individual states assumed others, and some powers were concurrent. The necessary and proper clause, Congress's right to regulate interstate commerce, the full faith and credit clause, and the Tenth Amendment guide federalism. Starting with *McCulloch v. Maryland,* the Supreme Court has more often emboldened Congress's commerce power and authority; and the federal government, through grants and mandates, has created and funded national initiatives in spite of some overlap with states' reserved powers. In more recent years, however, Congress has slowed this trend and devolved some powers back on the states.

Since 1789, the Constitution, its alterations, and its government have endured. The written, transparent guidelines for government have allowed the United States to operate largely uninterrupted on the same basic plan. Never has the country missed an election. Leaders have been democratically pushed out of office without bloodshed. And our courts have settled intense, divisive matters of law to solve national crises.

THINK AS A POLITICAL SCIENTIST: *CONSTRUCT A VISUAL AND FORMULATE AN ARGUMENT ABOUT FEDERALISM*

Construct a timeline that orders and explains key events that have defined American federalism. Be sure to include events before and after the drafting of the Constitution. Also, include acts of Congress, the president, and the Supreme Court that have shaped the Constitution and the practice of federalism. For each event, include the accurate year and add a brief note explaining the event's relevance.

When you have completed your timeline, use it to draft an argument that characterizes James Madison's vision for the new nation and that asserts and supports a claim on how closely contemporary federalism aligns with Madison's vision.

Review Learning Objectives

As you review Unit One, be sure you can complete the following learning objectives. Page numbers are provided to help you locate the necessary information to fulfill the learning objective.

UNIT ONE LEARNING OBJECTIVES	
LOR-1.A: Explain how democratic ideals are reflected in the Declaration of Independence and the U.S. Constitution.	Pages 4–5, 8. 18–27
LOR-1.B: Explain how models of representative democracy are visible in major institutions, policies, events, or debates in the U.S.	Pages 5–7 18–21, 28–35
CON-1.A: Explain how Federalist and Anti-Federalist views on central government and democracy are reflected in U.S. foundational documents.	Pages 22, 23–25, 29–30
CON-1.B: Explain the relationship between key provisions of the Articles of Confederation and the debate over granting the federal government greater power formerly reserved to the states.	Page 16
CON-1.C: Explain the ongoing impact of political negotiation and compromise at the Constitutional Convention on the development of the constitutional system.	Pages 11–16
PMI-1.A: Explain the constitutional principles of separation of powers and checks and balances.	Pages 29–32
PMI-1.B: Explain the implications of separation of powers and checks and balances for the U.S. political system.	Pages 29–35
CON-2.A: Explain how societal needs affect the constitutional allocation of power between the national and state governments.	Pages 50–62
CON-2.B: Explain how the appropriate balance of power between national and state governments has been interpreted differently over time.	Pages 47–62
CON-2.C: Explain how the distribution of powers among three federal branches and between national and state governments impacts policymaking.	Pages 31–35, 63–65

Review the following foundational documents, Supreme Court cases, and political science disciplinary practices as well.

UNIT ONE FOUNDATIONAL DOCUMENTS	
Declaration of Independence	Pages 8, 619–622
Articles of Confederation	Pages 10, 622–628
Constitution of the United States	Pages 18–21, 628–644
Federalist No. 10—Madison's idea that a large republic was well suited to controlling factions	Pages 23, 644–649
Brutus No. 1—Anti-Federalist view that a large, centralized government endangered personal liberty	Pages 24–25, 649–656

UNIT ONE FOUNDATIONAL DOCUMENTS	
Federalist No. 51—Madison's idea that the separation of powers and checks and balances would control abuses by the majority	Pages 29–30, 656–659

UNIT ONE SUPREME COURT CASES	
McCulloch v. Maryland (1819)—Declared that Congress has implied powers necessary to implement its enumerated powers and established supremacy of the U.S. Constitution and federal laws over state laws	Pages 48–49
United States v. Lopez (1995)—Ruled that Congress may not use the commerce clause to make possession of a gun in a school zone a federal crime. The ruling introduced a new phase of federalism that recognized the importance of state sovereignty and local control	Pages 59–60

UNIT ONE POLITICAL SCIENCE DISCIPLINARY PRACTICES AND REASONING PROCESSES	
Analyze and interpret text-based qualitative sources.	Pages 8, 10, 21, 23, 25, 29–30
Read, analyze, and interpret quantitative data to draw conclusions about political principles, processes, behaviors, and outcomes.	Pages 25, 56
Analyze and interpret visual information.	Page 55

UNIT ONE CONTEMPORARY ISSUES AND POLICY	
Policy Matters: The National Government and Individual Rights	Pages 27–28
Policy Matters: National Policymaking and Sharing of Powers	Pages 63–65

UNIT ONE WRITING	
Articulate a Defensible Claim	Page 41
Refute Claims	Page 68

UNIT 2: Interaction Among Branches of Government

The responsibilities of the three branches of government are carried out by four institutions: Congress, defined in Article I; the president and the executive branch's large bureaucracy, deriving from Article II; and the courts, more vaguely mentioned in Article III.

Congress is the most representative branch. Its 535 members, delegates, committees, and staffers determine policy in the areas of national defense, the economy, trade, and an array of government services. The House and Senate have developed unique leadership roles and legislative procedures to carry out their business.

The American presidency is an iconic and powerful institution that has become much more influential over time and that is visible on a world scale. Presidents administer the law through a large bureaucracy of law enforcement, military, trade, and financial agencies. Chief executives meet with world leaders, design the national budget, and campaign for their party's candidates.

The judicial branch settles federal disputes (criminal and civil), ensures justice, and interprets the law. A loosely defined branch at the founding, the judiciary has become a complex three-level court system with courthouses across the country and a nine-member Supreme Court in Washington, D.C. that shapes much U.S. law.

As you read these chapters, notice how each branch's unique customs and rules define it, and notice how the branches interact with one another.

Enduring Understandings: Interactions Among Branches

CON-3: The republican ideal in the U.S. is manifested in the structure and operation of the legislative branch.

CON-4: The presidency has been enhanced beyond its expressed constitutional powers.

CON-5: The design of the judicial branch protects the court's independence as a branch of government, and the emergence and use of judicial review remains a powerful judicial practice.

PMI-2: The federal bureaucracy is a powerful institution implementing federal policies with sometimes questionable accountability.

Source: *AP® United States Government and Politics Course and Exam Description*

The Legislative Branch

"I served with, not under, eight presidents."
—Sam Rayburn, Speaker of the House (D-TX, b.1882, d.1961)

Essential Question: How do the structure and operation of the legislative branch reflect the United States' republican ideal?

The United States Congress is one of the world's most democratic governing bodies. Defined in Article I of the Constitution, Congress consists of the Senate and the House of Representatives. These governing bodies meet in Washington, D.C., to craft legislation that sets out national policy. Congress creates statutes, or laws, that become part of the United States Code. Its 535 elected members and roughly 30,000 support staff operate under designated rules to carry out the legislative process, to build and enhance highways and other public works, and to protect American citizens. In January 2017, Speaker of the House Paul Ryan in the House of Representatives and Vice President Mike Pence in the Senate gaveled the 115th Congress to order for its new term.

The 535 voting members of Congress (with nonvoting House delegates from Washington, D.C., Guam, Puerto Rico, the Virgin Islands, and American Samoa) have become increasingly diverse and therefore increasingly representative of their constituents, but they by no means mirror the ethnic, gender, or socioeconomic divisions in America at large. At the start of the 115th Congress, 48 House members and three Senators were African American. There were almost as many Hispanics in the legislature as blacks, 46. Eighteen members were from the Asia-Pacific realm. Most all profess a religion; 56 percent are Protestant, 31 percent are Catholic, and about 6 percent are Jewish.

Men have dominated the seats in Congress since it opened in 1789, but female membership has grown since Jeannette Rankin of Montana became the first female representative in 1917. As of January 2018, 111 women serve in the Congress, 89 in the House and 22 in the Senate.

An overwhelming majority of members are college-educated and from households with above-average incomes. More than half of the members of Congress have a net worth of more than $1 million. The average age in the House is 58; in the Senate it is 62. The dominant professions prior to serving are law, public service, and business. Nearly 100 of the current members worked at some point as a staffer on Capitol Hill.

| BY THE NUMBERS | |
| Demographics of 115th Congress (2017–2019) | |
Classification	Total
Men	429
Women	111
African American	51
Protestant	299
Catholic	168
Jewish	30
Latino	46
Asian or Pacific Islander	18
Native American	2
Born outside U.S.	18
Service in military	102
With law degrees	222

(Statistics largely self-reported. Totals include delegates from U.S. territories and account for four vacancies.)

Structure of Congress

After a war with Britain over adequate citizen representation, developing a republican form of government—a representative system that reflected citizen views as well as those of an elite class—was of top concern for Americans at the Constitutional Convention. For that reason, the framers designed Congress as the most democratic branch and the chief policymaking branch. The First United States Congress opened in 1789 in New York City.

Source: *Thinkstock*
The Senate meets on the left side of the Capitol Building; the House meets on the right.

Bicameral Design

The **bicameral**, or two-house, legislature resulted from a dispute at the Constitutional Convention between small and large states, each desiring different forms of representation. The Great Compromise (page 14) dictated the number of House seats that would be allotted based on the number of inhabitants living within each state. Article I's provision for a census every 10 years assures states a proportional allotment of these seats. Together, the members in the House represent the entire citizenry. The Senate, in contrast, has two members from each state, so the states are represented equally in that chamber. With this structure, the framers created a republic that represented both the citizenry at large and the states.

The framers also designed each house to have a different character and separate responsibilities. Senators are somewhat insulated from public opinion by their longer terms (six years as opposed to two for members of the House), and they have more constitutional responsibilities than House members. Since each senator represents their whole state, senators typically face a more diverse electorate. In contrast, smaller congressional districts allow House members to have a more intimate constituent-representative relationship.

Originally, unlike House members, senators were elected by state legislators, but this practice changed with the **Seventeenth Amendment**, ratified in 1913, which broadened democracy by giving the people of the state the right to elect their senators.

The requirement that both chambers must approve legislation helps prevent the passage of rash laws. James Madison pointed out "a second house of the legislature, distinct from and dividing the power with the first, must always be a beneficial check on the government. It doubles the people's security by requiring the concurrence of two distinct bodies." BIG IDEA: The system of checks and balances in Congress helps keep an appropriate balance between majority rule and minority rights.

Size and Term Length The more representative House of Representatives is designed to reflect the will of the people and to prevent the kinds of abuses of power experienced in the colonial era. Most representatives are responsible for a relatively small geographic area. With their two-year terms, House members are forced to consider popular opinions lest the unsatisfied voters replace them. The entire House faces reelection at the same time.

Since 1913, the House has been composed of 435 members, with the temporary exception of adding two more for the annexation of Alaska and Hawaii. Each congressional district has more than 700,000 inhabitants. The Reapportionment Act of 1929 mandates the periodic **reapportionment**, or distribution, of U.S. congressional seats according to changes in the census figures. Each decade, the U.S. Census Bureau tabulates state populations and then awards the proportional number of seats to each state. Every state receives at least one seat. States gain, lose, or maintain the same number of seats based on the census figures.

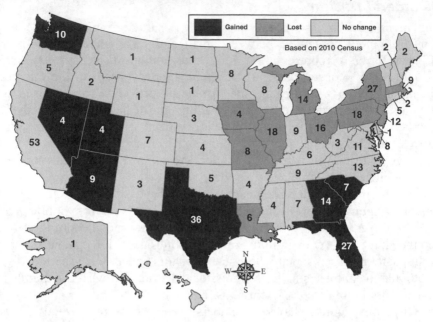

REAPPORTIONED HOUSE OF REPRESENTATIVES, 2012

What do the numbers show? In what regions of the country did states gain representatives? In what regions did states lose representatives? What conclusion can you draw about the population in those regions?

The Senate, in contrast, has 100 members. George Washington is said to have explained the character of the U.S. Senate through an analogy to cooling coffee so it can be consumed. "We pour our coffee into a saucer to cool it, we pour legislation into the senatorial saucer to cool it." The framers wanted a cautious, experienced group as yet another check in the lawmaking process. Only one-third of the Senate is up for reelection every two years, making it a continuous body. In *Federalist No. 64*, John Jay argued, "by leaving a considerable residue of the old ones (senators) in place, uniformity and order, as well as a constant succession of official information, will be preserved."

Senators' six-year terms—in contrast to the two-year terms of members of the House of Representatives—give Senators some ability to temper the popular ideas adopted by the House, since Senators do not have to worry about being voted out of office so soon.

Collectively, these two bodies pass legislation. Bills can originate in either chamber, except for those that raise revenue, or tax laws, which must originate in the House. To become law, bills must pass both houses by a simple majority vote and then be signed by the president.

Powers of Congress

The framers assigned Congress a limited number of specific powers, or **enumerated powers**. They are also known as **expressed powers** because they are expressly stated in Article I, Section 8 of the Constitution. Through the necessary and proper clause, the framers also assigned to Congress **implied powers**, those not directly stated but required to fulfill the obligations of the enumerated powers. These powers allow for the creation of *public policy*—the laws that govern the United States. Over the years, advancements in society, Supreme Court interpretations, and altered expectations of government have greatly expanded Congress's authority.

Power of the Purse

The congressional power enumerated first in the Constitution is the power to raise revenue—to tax. Article I also provides that no money can be drawn from the treasury without the approval of Congress. Congress appropriates, or allots, the public money it raises through taxes. Both chambers have committees for budgeting and appropriations. Congress also has the power to coin money.

The president proposes an annual budget while Congress members, who often differ on spending priorities, and their committees debate how much should be invested in certain areas. The budgeting process is complex and usually takes months to finalize. (See pages 96–101 and 542–544.)

Regulating Commerce

Congress also has the power "to regulate commerce among the states, with other nations, and with Indian tribes." In 1824 in *Gibbons v. Ogden*, a dispute about whether state or national government had authority over the regulation of navigable U.S. waterways, the Supreme Court sided with the national government and solidified Congress's commerce authority. (See page 49.) This case began a debate on the breadth of Congress's power over commerce that is ongoing even today. This congressional power has been contested in the Supreme Court more than any other. It came into contention when the Supreme Court struck down the National Recovery Act and the Agricultural Adjustment Act, two cornerstones of President Franklin Delano Roosevelt's New Deal program intended to address the problems of the Great Depression in the 1930s. Congress's authority over commerce was also the constitutional justification for the 1964 Civil Rights Act, as Congress required proprietors of lunch counters to accept customers of all races.

In recent years, Congress has assumed wide authority over nearly every type of both interstate and intrastate commerce. In an effort to protect the environment, for example, Congress has written regulations that apply to manufacturing and chemical plants to control the emissions these facilities might spew into our air. Congress can require gun manufacturers to package safety locks with the guns they sell. The commerce clause was the justification for the Patient Protection and Affordable Care Act, also known as Obamacare, which, among other things, requires citizens to purchase health insurance or pay a penalty.

However, there have been many legal challenges to wide-ranging Congressional authority based on the commerce clause. The landmark case of *United States v. Lopez* (1995) is one of a number of cases that has restricted this power (pages 59–60).

Foreign and Military Affairs

Congress is one of the key players in U.S. foreign policy, and it oversees the military. It can raise armies and navies, legislate or enact conscription procedures, mandate a military draft, and declare war. Congress determines how much money is spent on military bases and, through an independent commission, has authority over base closings. It sets the salary schedule for all military personnel.

Foreign and military policy are determined jointly by Congress and the president, but the Constitution grants Congress the ultimate authority to "declare war." The framers wanted a system that would send the United States to war only when deemed necessary by the most democratic branch, rather than by a potentially tyrannical or power-hungry executive making a solo decision to invade another country. Yet the framers also wanted a strong military leader who was responsible to the people, so they named the president the "commander in chief" of the armed forces. Congress does not have the power to deploy troops or receive ambassadors, leaving the primary influence on foreign policy to the executive branch.

FOREIGN AND MILITARY POWERS
Congress
• Congress has the power to declare war.
• Congress funds the military, foreign endeavors, and foreign aid.
• The Senate must approve appointed ambassadors and high-ranking military personnel.
• The Senate must ratify treaties with other nations by a two-thirds vote.
• Congress has oversight of the State and Defense Departments and relevant agencies.
• Congress can institute a mandatory military draft to staff the Armed Forces.
The President
• The president is commander in chief of the Armed Forces.
• The president appoints ambassadors and receives foreign ministers.
• The president negotiates treaties with other nations.
• The president issues executive orders that can impact foreign policy.
• The president makes executive agreements with other heads of state.
• The president commissions the military officers of the United States.

War Powers Act of 1973 The president and Congress have not always agreed on the balance of their military powers. In 1964, Congress gave the president wide latitude with the Gulf of Tonkin Resolution to stop the spread of communist control into South Vietnam. What resulted was America's longest war up to that point.

As the Vietnam War dragged on and public support for it dropped, Congress repealed this resolution and then passed the **War Powers Act** in 1973. This law tries to reign in the power the president gained in 1964 while still understanding the need for sudden, perhaps secret, emergency military action in the name of protecting the United States. The act gives the president 48 hours in which to engage in urgent combat without informing Congress. Congress, which had too quickly ceded its war authority to the president in 1964, had also abdicated the responsibility of checking the president. To correct this problem, the law mandates that within 60 days from the start of combat, with an optional 30-day extension, Congress must take positive action to continue funding the engagement if it is to continue. If Congress does not act, the combat cannot continue and the president's power is checked. This requirement forces Congress to take a position and guarantees the American people representation in military decisions.

The law strikes a balance between the framers' intended checks and balances and the need for quick action in the days of modern warfare. However, this relationship has been anything but clear since the law's passage. President Nixon vetoed the bill, only to be overridden. And no president has acknowledged the law's constitutional validity. In fact, most presidents have viewed it as an unconstitutional law that takes away powers the Constitution granted to them, yet some have followed it nonetheless.

Implied Powers

At the end of the list of enumerated powers in Article I is the necessary and proper clause. It gives Congress the power "to make all Laws which shall be necessary and proper for carrying into Execution the foregoing Powers." Also called the elastic clause, it implies that the national legislature can make additional laws intended to take care of the items in the enumerated list.

The elastic clause first came into contention in the case of *McCulloch v. Maryland* in 1819 over whether or not Congress could establish a bank. (See pages 48–49). The Supreme Court ruled that the enumerated list implied that Congress could create a bank. Since then, the *implied powers doctrine* has given Congress authority to enact legislation addressing a wide range of issues—economic, social, and environmental.

If those who served in the First Congress could take part in the modern legislature, "they would probably feel right at home," says historian Raymond Smock. Other observers disagree and point to burgeoning federal government responsibilities. Because of the elastic clause, Congress has created a Department of Education, defended marriage, and addressed various other modern issues outside the scope of Article I's enumerated powers.

Differing Powers for House and Senate

Certain powers are divided between the House and the Senate. The House has the power to create revenue (tax) laws. In fact, *only* the House can introduce a revenue bill. The House was given this power because it is the most representative body, and people who oppose their actions have to wait only two years to vote them out of office. The House also has the privilege to select the president if no candidate wins the Electoral College. When it has sufficient evidence of wrongdoing, the House also has the power to **impeach** federal officers. Impeaching an officer means charging a person with offenses so serious that they are determined to be "treason, bribery, and high crimes and misdemeanors."

The Senate, representing the interests of the states, also has several exclusive powers and responsibilities. Its **advice and consent** power allows Senators to recommend or reject major presidential appointees such as Cabinet secretaries and federal judges. Senators often recommend people for positions in the executive branch or as U.S. district judges to serve in their states. High-level presidential appointments must first clear a confirmation hearing, at which the appropriate Senate committee interviews the nominee. If the committee votes in favor of the nominee, then the entire Senate will take a vote. A simple majority is required for appointment. Over the years, the upper house has approved most appointees quickly, though there have been notable exceptions.

The Senate also has powers related to foreign affairs. The Senate must approve by a two-thirds vote any treaty the president enters into with a foreign nation before it becomes official.

While the House can level impeachment charges, only the Senate can try an official for wrongdoing, reach a judgment, and determine whether or not to remove the official from office.

Despite their different powers, both chambers have equal say in whether or not a bill becomes law, since both chambers must approve an identical bill before it is passed on to the president for signing.

Policymaking Structures and Processes

The design of Congress and the powers the framers bestowed on the two chambers within that institution have shaped how the legislative branch makes policy. Elected lawmakers work to improve America while representing people of unique views across the nation. Formal groups and informal factions operate differently in the House and Senate.

Congress is organized by house, party, leadership, and committee. The parties create leadership positions to coach their own party members, to move legislation, and to carry out party goals. Congress's formalized groups include both lawmaking committees and partisan or ideological groups. Some of the powerful committees are institutions unto themselves, since committees are where the real work of Congress is done, especially in the House.

Leadership

The only official congressional leaders mentioned in the Constitution are the Speaker of the House, the President of the Senate, and the President *Pro Tempore* of the Senate. The document states that the House and Senate "shall choose their other Officers." Both have done so.

At the start of each congressional term, the first order of business in each house is to elect leaders. The *party caucuses*—that is, the entire party membership within each house—gather privately days or weeks before to determine their choices for Speaker and the other leadership positions. The actual public vote for leadership positions takes place when Congress opens and is invariably a party-line vote. Once the leaders are elected, they oversee the organization of Congress, form committees, and proceed with the legislative agenda.

House Leaders At the top of the power pyramid in the House of Representatives is the **Speaker of the House**. In 2007, Nancy Pelosi, a Democrat from California, became the first female Speaker of the House when the Democrats were the majority party. Speaker Paul Ryan, a Republican from Wisconsin, began presiding over the Republican-controlled House in October 2015. The Speaker recognizes members for speaking, organizes members for conference committees, and has great influence in most matters of lawmaking.

On the next rung down in the House are the majority and minority leaders. These are the **floor leaders**; they lead debate among their party and guide the discussion from their side of the aisle. They are the first speakers recognized in debate. Party leaders have also become spokespersons for the party in press conferences and in interviews on Sunday talk shows.

The deputy floor leader, also known as the **whip**, is in charge of party discipline. The whip keeps the tally of votes among his or her party members, which aids in determining the optimum time for a vote. Whips have also strong-armed party members to vote with the party. Political favors or even party endorsements during an election can have a persuasive influence on representatives contemplating an independent vote. The whip also makes sure party members remain in good standing and act in an ethical and professional capacity. When scandals or missteps occur, the whip may ask a member to step down from a chair position or to leave Congress entirely.

Each party also has a **conference chair** below the whip. This chairperson takes care of party matters, such as heading the organization of party-centered groups in each house.

Senate Leaders In the Senate, a similar structure exists. The Constitution names the vice president of the United States as the nonvoting **President of the Senate**. In case of a tie, the vice president can vote to break it. The vice president is also meant to rule on procedure and to organize the Senate. For years, the vice president served a role like that of the Speaker, organizing committees and running floor debate. However, now the vice president is rarely in the Senate chamber and usually delegates the responsibility of moderating debate to other members. The Constitution also provided for the **president** *pro tempore*, or temporary president. The "pro tem" is traditionally the most senior member in the majority party. Often, however, even the pro tem assigns his or her role to junior members.

The **Senate majority leader** wields much more power in the Senate than the vice president and pro tem. The majority leader is, in reality, the chief legislator. As the first recognized in debate, the majority leader sets the legislative calendar, determining which bills reach the floor for debate and which ones do not. The majority leader also guides the party caucus on issues and party proposals. Senate leaders are not sovereign coaches of a party team; every member makes his or her own independent choice, and many members within the same party have different and specialized interests in framing legislation. Some former Senate leaders have expressed frustration over the effort to compromise even among party members. Senator Bob Dole (R-KS, 1974–1996), who served in a number of leadership positions in the Senate, once said the letter "P" was missing from his title, "Majority Pleader."

The Senate whips serve much the same purpose as their House counterparts. They keep a tally of party members' voting intentions and try to maintain party discipline. The conference chair also serves the same function in the Senate as in the House, overseeing party matters.

Committees

Committees are not mentioned in the Constitution, but they have been fixtures in Congress since it first met. Smaller groups can tackle tough issues and draft more precise laws than the entire House or Senate can. Committees allow lawmakers to put their expertise to use, and they make moving legislation manageable. The intricate committee system handles a vast amount of legislation. Committees dealing with finance, foreign relations, the judiciary, and other common topics have become permanent. The Democrats and

Leadership in Congress

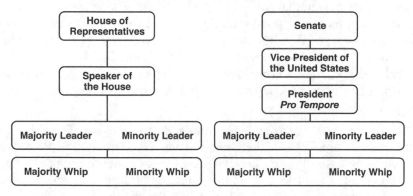

The Congressional leadership represented above results from a mix of party- and constitutionally defined positions. The Speaker is in charge in the House, while the majority leader has much control and influence in the Senate.

Republicans can create their own private committees, such as the House Democratic Congressional Campaign Committee or the National Republican Senatorial Committee, to further party goals and help elect party members to each house, especially through fundraising. Those two groups cannot, however, create law or policy. The committees discussed below, however, are public, lawmaking groups that play key roles in the legislative process in both houses.

Standing Committees Permanent committees focused on a particular subject and authorized under the rules of each house are called **standing committees**. Members of Congress can specialize on a few topics and become experts in these areas. For example, the House Energy and Commerce Committee has wide authority on utilities and gasoline, as well as almost any business matter. The Committee on Transportation and Infrastructure oversees the creation and maintenance of U.S. highways.

Standing committee members discuss and either polish or reject a variety of bills. The committees are chaired by a senior experienced member in the majority party or someone assigned for political, ideological, or diversity-related reasons. The vice chair or "ranking member" is the senior committee member in the minority party. The majority party always holds the majority of seats on each committee and therefore controls the flow of legislation, because a bill must first clear committee with a majority vote before it can move to the entire House or Senate for a vote. (See How a Bill Becomes Law on page 97.)

The Senate's committees often hold confirmation hearings for presidential appointments. For example, a nominated secretary of defense must appear before the Armed Services Committee to answer individual senators' questions. After this hearing, a majority can recommend the nominee to the full Senate for approval. The **House Judiciary Committee** drafts crime bills that define illegal behavior and outline appropriate punishments. It also handles impeachments. In 1974, the House Judiciary Committee voted 27 to 11 to recommend impeachment of President Richard Nixon. He resigned before the entire House took a vote.

Many representatives and senators want to be appointed to the powerful Ways and Means Committee in the House and the Budget Committee in the Senate. However, they also seek appointments to particular committees because they likely arrive in Congress with an expertise in a certain field, or they come from a state or district that has a high interest in certain congressional matters. For example, more than 100 members of Congress have served in the Armed Forces and likely want to shape Congress's military policy. Some lawmakers arrive with high-level business experience and therefore want to employ their experience in commerce or international trade law. Longtime members serve on a variety of committees and influence the decisions of some powerful ones.

The parties recommend certain members for committee assignments, but ultimately each full house votes to approve committee membership. The Democrats and Republicans each have a committee for the purpose of assigning members to standing committees to create favorable bills and to develop legislative strategy. The Democrats' **Steering and Policy Committee** and the Republicans' **Committee on Committees** both determine which of their members are assigned to the standing committees. "The campaign for committee assignments," recalls Senator Sherrod Brown (D-OH, 2007–), "is the most important task a new member performs between November and January."

Most standing committees are within one chamber, but a few permanent **joint committees** exist that unite members from the House and Senate, such as one to manage the Library of Congress and the Joint Committee on Taxation. Members of these committees do mostly routine research-based activities.

Temporary Committees In addition to the standing committees, both houses form **select committees** periodically for some particular and typically short-lived purpose. A select or special committee is established "for a limited time period to perform a particular study or investigation," according to the U.S. Senate's online glossary of terms. "These committees might be given or denied authority to report legislation to the Senate." Notable select committees have investigated major scandals and events, such as the 2012 terrorist attack on the U.S. Consulate in Benghazi, Libya. These groups also investigate issues to determine if further congressional action is necessary. Recently the House created a select committee on Energy Independence and Global Warming. Select committees can be exclusive to one house, or they can combine members from both.

Conference committees are created temporarily to iron out differences on bills that passed each house but in slightly different forms. When two similar bills pass each house, usually a compromise can be reached. Members from both houses gather in a conference committee for a **markup session**, a process by which the bill is altered. The final draft must pass both houses to go on to receive the president's signature.

In addition to creating bills and confirming presidential appointments, committees also oversee how the executive agencies administer the laws Congress creates. Congress authorizes entire departments and agencies to carry out the law. Congress authorized the State Department in 1789 and defined its diplomatic mission. In the early 1900s, Congress authorized the Federal Bureau of Investigation to arrest federal criminals. More recently, Congress authorized the Transportation Security Administration (TSA) to inspect airline passengers and their belongings before takeoff.

Therefore, Congress, through its committees, conducts **congressional oversight** to ensure that executive branch agencies, such as the FBI or the TSA, are carrying out the policy or program as defined by Congress. When corruption or a less than adequate job is suspected, committees call agency directors to testify. Other oversight hearings may simply be fact-finding exchanges between lawmakers and cabinet secretaries or agency directors about congressional funding, efficiency, or just general updates. (See pages 172–174 for more on congressional oversight.)

COMMITTEE TYPES		
Standing: Permanent committees that handle most of Congress's work		
Joint: Members of both houses that address a long-term issue or program		
Select or Special: Temporary committee that handles a particular issue or investigation		
Conference: House and Senate members who reconcile similar bills		

Caucuses In addition to formal, policymaking committees, Congress also contains nongovernmental groups of like-minded people organized into **caucuses**. These groups usually unite around a particular belief. Each party has a group in each house—the Democratic Caucus or the Republican Party Conference—which includes basically the entire party membership within that house. These groups gather to elect their respective leaders, to set legislative agendas, and to name their committee members. Many other smaller caucuses are organized around specific interests, even some that cross party lines, such as agriculture, business, or women's issues. Members can belong to multiple caucuses. Caucuses can have closed-door meetings and can draft legislation, but they are not officially part of the lawmaking process. Since legislators are members of both caucuses and committees, they can formulate ideas and legislative strategy in the caucuses, but any bill becoming a law would first go through the official, public committee system.

With their longer terms, Senators can build longer-lasting coalitions and working relationships. Although reelection rates tend to be high, House members with their shorter terms have more changeable coalition members.

Support Staff Today, each senator employs an average of 40 staffers, and each House member has about 17. Some of these assistants answer constituents' phone calls from a district office in their home state. Most work on Capitol Hill in a complex network that supports the legislative process. Senators and representatives can assign various titles and responsibilities to their staffers. Most will have a chief of staff (the lawmaker's chief aide), one or more communications experts, and constituent liaisons. Legislative assistants familiarize their boss with details on large bills. Press secretaries connect with the media and schedule interviews. Most Washington staffers are willing to work long hours for relatively low pay. Some staffers become so experienced in the legislative process that they become members of Congress themselves.

Committees and Rules Unique to the House

While the House and Senate have much in common in their overall structure, key differences influence the policymaking process in each chamber. For example, the difference in size and constituencies influences the formality of debate on bills in each chamber. Both chambers follow the parliamentary procedure outlined in Robert's Rules of Order, guidelines for conducting discussion and reaching decisions in a group. With so many members representing so many legislative districts, however, the House has rules that limit debate. A member may not speak for more than an hour. In certain situations, individual speaking time may be limited even more. In some cases, there is a limit set for debate on a measure by the entire membership. Further, speakers are required to offer only *germane* amendments to a bill, changes that relate specifically to the legislation under consideration.

The presiding officer—the Speaker of the House or someone he or she appoints—controls who speaks. House members address all their remarks to "Madam Speaker" or "Mister Speaker" and refer to their colleagues by the state they represent, as in "my distinguished colleague from Iowa." The control the presiding officer enjoys and other structural practices help make the large House of Representatives function with some efficiency.

Central to this efficiency are the House **Ways and Means Committee** and the **Rules Committee**. Ways and Means, a committee exclusive to the House, determines tax policy. The Ways and Means Committee is first to outline details when proposals are put forward to raise or lower income taxes.

The Rules Committee is also very powerful. It can easily dispose of a bill or define the guidelines for debate because it acts as a traffic cop to the House floor. Nothing reaches the floor for debate unless the Rules Committee allows it. The Rules Committee generally reflects the will and sentiment of House leadership and the majority caucus. The majority members on the Rules Committee typically outnumber the minority by two to one.

The House Rules Committee has an impact on every House bill because it assigns bills to the appropriate standing committees, schedules bills for debate, and decides when votes take place. It helps centralize the power in the House and establish a hierarchy that increases the efficiency of such a large body of lawmakers. The Rules Committee has the authority to alter standing rules of procedure. And because debate time is limited in the House, the Rules Committee decides for how much time a bill can be debated and how many, if any, amendments may be added to the bill. It can itself amend or rewrite a bill. The entire House must vote to make it law, but the Rules Committee is powerful in that this small group wields great power in determining what other members can or cannot vote on.

The **Committee of the Whole** is also unique to the House. It includes but does not require all the representatives. However, the Committee of the Whole is more of a state of operation in which the House rules are relaxed than an actual committee. It was created to allow longer debate among fewer people and allow members to vote as a group rather than in an individual roll call. Additionally, the otherwise nonvoting delegates from U.S. territories can vote when present during the Committee of the Whole. Only 100 members must be present for the Committee of the Whole to act. When it has finished examining or shaping a bill, the Committee "rises and reports" the bill to the House. At that point the more formal rules of procedure and voting resume, and, if a quorum is present, the entire House will vote on final passage of the bill.

A modern device that functions as a step toward transparency and democracy in the House is the **discharge petition.** The discharge petition can bring a bill out of a reluctant committee. The petition's required number of signatures has altered over the years. It now stands at a simple majority to discharge a bill out of committee and onto the House floor. Thus, if 218 members sign, no chair or reluctant committee can prevent the majority's desire to publicly discuss the bill. This measure may or may not lead to the bill's passage, but it prevents a minority from stopping a majority on advancing the bill and is a way to circumvent leadership.

Rules and Procedures Unique to the Senate

The Senate is much less centralized and hierarchical than the House. With its smaller size, the Senate does not have the same restrictions on debate as the House. Senators can speak for as long as they like if the presiding officer—the vice president, a senator chosen for the job, or even a Supreme Court Justice—gives them the floor to speak. However, the presiding officer has little control over who speaks when, since he or she must recognize anyone who stands to speak, giving priority to the leaders of the parties. Like representatives, senators are not allowed to directly address anyone but the presiding officer. They refer to other senators in the third person ("the senior senator from Illinois," for example).

Unlike House members, senators are not limited to proposing germane amendments. They can add amendments on any subject they want. Senators also have strategic ways to use their debate time. For example, they may try to stall or even kill a bill by speaking for an extremely long time, using the **filibuster,** to let the time run out on a deadline for voting for a bill or to wear down the opposition. In contrast, the only House members who are allowed to speak as long as they want are the Speaker of the House, the majority leader, and the minority leader. On February 6, 2018, House Minority Leader Nancy Pelosi spoke for eight hours straight in support of protections for people who were brought into the country illegally when they were children, the so called "DREAMers." (See page 171.) She could not take a seat or a bathroom break for the entire time or else she would have had to yield the floor.

The Senate also uses measures that require higher thresholds for action than the House and that slow it down or speed it up. These include **unanimous consent**—the approval of all Senators—and the **hold,** a measure to stall a bill. When the Senate takes action, unanimous consent is typically requested as a way to suspend the rules and limit debate. If anyone objects, the motion is put on hold or at least stalled for discussion, because an objection often signals the possibility of a filibuster. For years senators abused this privilege, since a few senators, even one, could stop popular legislation. Then and now, senators can place a hold on a motion or on a presidential appointment.

Delaying legislation in this way brought about changes in the rules. As the United States stepped closer to war in 1917, President Woodrow Wilson called for changes in Senate procedures so that a small minority of senators could not block U.S. action in arming merchant ships for military use. A filibuster had blocked his armed neutrality plan before America's entrance into World War I. President Wilson was enraged. The Senate, he said, "is the only legislative body in the world which cannot act when its majority is ready for action. A little group of willful men," Wilson went on, "have rendered the great government of the United States helpless."

Wilson called the Senate into special session and demanded the rules change. The Senate created Rule 22, or the **cloture rule**, which enabled and required a two-thirds supermajority to close up or stop debate on a bill and call for a vote. In 1975, the Senate lowered the standard to three-fifths, or 60 out of 100 senators. Cloture for breaking a filibuster on nominees to courts requires just a simple majority. Once cloture is reached, each senator has the privilege of speaking for up to one hour on that bill or topic.

Foreign Policy Functions While both houses have a foreign affairs committee, the Senate has more foreign relations duties than does the House. The framers gave the upper house the power to ratify or deny treaties with other countries. The Senate also approves U.S. ambassadors. In *Federalist No. 75*, Hamilton argued for the Senate, not the House, to handle treaties and foreign affairs due to its continuity. "Because of the fluctuating and . . . multitudinous composition of [the House, we can't] expect in it those qualities . . . essential to the proper execution of such a trust." The chairman of the Senate Foreign Relations Committee works with the president and secretary of state to forge U.S. foreign policy.

SELECTED CONGRESSIONAL COMMITTEES AND KEY POLICY FOCUS IN THE 115TH CONGRESS	
House	**Senate**
Ways & Means Determines tax policy	**Finance** Oversees spending and budgeting
Rules Determines House proceedings	**Armed Services** Oversees the military
Armed Services Oversees the military	**Foreign Relations** Guides U.S. foreign policy
Judiciary Drafts crime bills, impeachments	**Judiciary** Confirms judges, oversees courts
Energy & Commerce Regulates energy and business	**Agriculture, Nutrition, and Forestry** Addresses farming, food, and nature

In 2018, there were 21 standing committees in the House and 16 in the Senate.

The Legislative Process

In addition to the customs and procedures of the leadership structure, formal committees, and informal groups in Congress, there are designed differences in the two houses, defined leaders, and lawmaking procedures each house has developed that guide policymaking and legislative mores. Both bodies have defined additional leaders that guide floor debate, assure party discipline, and serve as liaisons to the opposing party, to the president, and to the media. The framers declared in Article I that each house would determine its own rules as further assurance of a bicameral system. The House and Senate have done just that over the years to shape how ideas become federal policy.

Introducing and Amending Bills

Only House or Senate members can introduce a bill. Today, however, the actual authors of legislation are more often staffers with expertise, lobbyists, White House liaisons, or outside professionals. When a bill's **sponsor** (the member who introduces it and typically assumes authorship) presents it, the bill is officially numbered. Numbering starts at S.1 in the Senate or H.R.1 in the House at the beginning of each biennial Congress. A bill can originate in either chamber (except for tax bills, which must originate in the House), but an identical bill must pass both houses and the president must sign it for the bill to become law. However, if the president vetoes a bill by not signing it within a certain time, Congress can override the veto and the bill can still become law. (See page 96 for more on the presidential veto and congressional override.)

Several events take place in the process, creating opportunities for a bill to drastically change along the way. Additional ideas and programs usually are attached to the original bill. How each house, the president, and the public view a bill will determine its fate. The rough-and-tumble path for legislation often leads to its death. In a typical two-year Congress, more than 10,000 bills are handled, introduced, and referred to committee, but only about 300 to 500 new laws are passed during that time.

In the House, amendments to bills typically must first be approved by the committee overseeing the bill. The amendments in the House must also be **germane**—directly related to the topic of the bill.

In the Senate, an individual senator can introduce an amendment to a bill on the floor. In the Senate, the additional points of a law may not even relate to the original. These are called **non-germane amendments**, or riders. These **riders**, additional bills that ride onto an often unrelated bill, are often added to benefit a member's own agenda or programs or to enhance the political chances of the bill. Morris ("Mo") Udall, a representative from Arizona from 1961 to 1991, once expressed frustration when he had to vote against his own "Udall bill," because with riders it had evolved into legislation he eventually opposed.

When a bill grows to mammoth size and takes care of several facets of law or addresses multiple programs, it is referred to as an **omnibus bill**. A long string of riders will earn the nickname "Christmas Tree bill," because it often delivers gifts in the form of special projects a legislator can take home, and, like the ornaments and tinsel on a Christmas tree, the "decorations" so many legislators added to the bill give it an entirely different look.

One product of these legislative add-ons is **pork barrel spending**. When funds are directed to a very specific purpose, such as building a senior citizen center in a legislator's district, the spending is called an **earmark**. Federal dollars are spent all across the nation to fund construction projects, highway repair, new bridges, national museums and parks, university research grants, and other programs. Members of Congress try to send federal dollars back to their district—which some people refer to as "bringing home the bacon." Riders are sometimes inserted onto bills literally in the dark of night by a powerful leader, sometimes within days or hours before a final vote to avoid debate on them.

Constituents who benefit from pork barrel spending obviously appreciate it. Yet, in recent years the competition for federal dollars has tarnished Congress's reputation. Citizens Against Government Waste reported an explosion of earmarks from 1994 to 2004. Congress passed more than five times as many earmark projects, and spending rose from $10 billion to $22.9 billion.

The most egregious example of pork barrel politics came when Alaska Senator Ted Stevens added a rider to a bill whose primary purpose was to fund and provide armor for U.S. troops in Iraq. The rider called for sending more than $400 million dollars to Stevens's state to build a bridge to connect the Alaska mainland to an island with 60 inhabitants. Critics dubbed the construction project "The Bridge to Nowhere."

In 2011, President Obama said he would veto any bill with earmarks, and soon after that the Senate Appropriations Committee instituted a ban on them. In 2018, President Trump suggested that bringing them back might help bills get passed, but many conservatives disagreed, expressing a desire to see a continued ban on the "pet projects" that have led to wasteful government spending.

Assigning Bills to Committee

The Senate majority leader and the House Rules Committee assign bills to committees in their respective chambers. Sometimes multiple committees have overlapping jurisdiction. A military spending bill may be examined by both the Armed Services Committee and the Appropriations Committee. In that case, the bill may be given **multiple referral** status, allowing both committees to address it simultaneously. Or it might have **sequential referral** status, giving one committee priority to review it before others. Frequently, subcommittees with a more narrow scope are involved.

In committee, a bill goes through three stages: hearings, markup, and reporting out. If the committee is "ordering the bill," the bill is under consideration. Hearings, expert testimony, and thorough discussion of the bill will take place. The chair will call for a published report, a summary, and analysis of the proposal with views of the other participants, such as the executive branch or interest groups, also included. Then the bill goes through markup, a process by which committee members amend the bill until they are satisfied. Once the bill passes the vote in the committee, the ratio of "yeas" to "nays" often speaks to the bill's chances when it is "reported out" on the House or Senate floor for debate. Further amendments are likely added. From this point, many factors can lead to passage, and many more can lead to the bill's failure.

The committee chair can also "pigeonhole" a bill—decide not to move it forward for debate until a later time, if at all.

Voting on Bills

Many legislators say one of their hardest jobs is voting. Determining exactly what most people want in their home state is nearly impossible. Legislators hold town hall meetings, examine public opinion polls, hold focus groups, and read stacks of mail and emails to get an idea of their constituents' desires. Members also consider a variety of other factors in deciding how to vote.

"Very often [lawmakers] are not voting for or against an issue for the reasons that seem apparent," historian David McCullough once explained. "They're voting for some other reason. Because they have a grudge against someone . . . or because they're doing a friend a favor, or because they're willing to risk their political skin and vote their conscience."

Source: *Department of Defense, Staff Sgt. Sean K. Harp*

Here the secretary of defense and another ranking Pentagon official testify before a House Appropriations subcommittee.

There are multiple views on what guides members' votes. Most members use a partisan model, following the general beliefs of their party. Party leaders encourage members to follow the party-line vote, especially if political favors are expected. Other members are ideologically aligned with certain groups who back them at election time. Those following the lead of their party or some other group are operating in an organizational way.

Logrolling—trading votes to gain support for a bill—is another factor affecting lawmaking. By agreeing to back someone else's bill, members can secure a vote in return for a bill of their own.

Those members trying to reflect the will of their constituency, especially in the House, follow the **delegate model**. At a town hall meeting in one member's district, an irritated and upset constituent shot down his representative's explanation for an unpopular vote. "We didn't send you to Washington to make intelligent decisions," the angry voter said, "we sent you to represent us." That representation can be *substantive*—that is, advocating on behalf of certain groups of constituents—or it can be *descriptive,* advocating not only for the views of constituents but also for the factors that make those constituents unique, such as geography, occupation, gender, and ethnicity.

Some members, especially in the Senate, use the **trustee model**. Representatives believe they are entrusted by their constituency to use their best judgment, regardless of how constituents may view an issue. This approach sidesteps any concern over an uniformed constituency reacting from emotion rather than reason and knowledge.

The **politico model** attempts to blend the delegate and trustee models. That is, they consider a variety of factors and decide their action or vote for whatever political calculations make the most sense to them at the time, especially when there seems to be a low degree of public opinion. On matters generating strong public opinion, the politico model would have representatives take those opinions strongly into account.

Overriding a Presidential Veto

Once both chambers of Congress have secured a majority vote on an identical bill, it goes to the president for signing. As part of the system of checks and balances, the president can veto (or reject) the bill by refusing to sign it within 10 days of receiving it (excluding Sundays). Congress can override a presidential veto if two-thirds of each house approve the bill. (For more on the presidential veto power, see page 129.)

Generating a Budget

One of the most important votes congressional members take is on the question of how to pay government costs. The budgeting process is a complicated, multistep, and often year-long process that begins with a budget proposal from the executive branch and includes both houses of Congress, a handful of agencies, and interest groups. (See pages 542–544 for how competing actors influence the national budget.)

How a Bill Becomes a Law

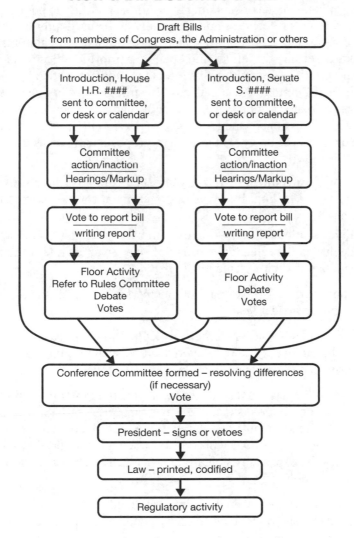

In the 1970s, Congress created the Office of Management and Budget (OMB) and established the budgeting process with the Congressional Budget and Impoundment Control Act (1974). The OMB is the president's budgeting arm. Headed by a director who is essentially the president's accountant, the OMB considers the needs and wants of all the federal departments and agencies, the fiscal and economic philosophy of the president, federal revenues, and other factors to arrange the annual budget. This spending plan is for the fiscal year (FY), the time frame from October 1 through September 30. For example, FY 2018 began on October 1, 2017, and ended on September 30, 2018. The president typically makes the budget plan public and sends it to Congress in early February so it can be finalized by the time the new fiscal year begins on October 1.

The 1974 act also defines the stages in *reconciling* the budget—passing changes to either revenue or spending by a simple majority in both houses with only limited time for debate—a process that can be used only once a year. It calls for Congress to set overall levels of revenues and expenditures, the size of the budget surplus or deficit, and spending priorities. Each chamber also has an appropriations committee that allots the money to federal projects. The Senate Finance Committee is a particularly strong entity in federal spending. Congress also created a congressional agency made of nonpartisan accountants called the Congressional Budget Office (CBO). This professional staff of experts examines and analyzes the budget proposal and serves as a check on the president's OMB.

Sources of Revenue For fiscal year 2019, the government expected to take in about $3.4 trillion. Every year, government revenue comes from five main sources:

- **Individual income taxes**—taxes paid by workers on the income they made during the calendar year. People pay different rates of taxes depending on their income level.

- **Corporate taxes**—taxes paid by businesses on the profits they made during the calendar year

- **Social insurance taxes (sometimes called payroll taxes)**—taxes paid by both employees and employers to fund such programs as Social Security, Medicare, and unemployment insurance

- **Tariffs and excise taxes**—taxes paid on certain imports or products. The tariff on imports is meant to raise their price so U.S.-made goods will be more affordable and competitive. Excise taxes are levied on specific products—luxury products, for example, or products associated with health risks, such as cigarettes—as well as on certain activities, such as gambling.

- **Other sources**—these include interest on government holdings or investments and estate taxes paid by people who inherit a very large amount of money.

The table on the next page shows the percentage of revenue from each category between 1950 and 2020.

CATEGORIES OF GOVERNMENT REVENUE					
FY	Individual Income Tax	Corp. Income Tax	Social Insurance and Retirement (Payroll taxes)	Excise	Other
	% of total revenue	% of total revenue	% of total revenue	% of total revenue	% of total revenue
1950	39.9	26.5	11	19.1	3.4
1960	44	23.2	15.9	12.6	4.2
1970	46.9	17	23	9.2	5
1980	47.2	12.5	30.5	4.0	4.8
1990	45.2	9.1	36.8	3.4	5.4
2000	49.6	10.2	32.2	3.4	4.5
2010	41.5	8.9	40	3.1	6.5
2020 (est)	49.6	7.3	35.7	3.1	4.2

Source: *US Government Publishing Office, 2019 Budget*

As you can see, the highest percent of government revenue comes from individual income taxes.

Government Spending The budget for fiscal year 2019 called for spending $4.4 trillion. Each year spending falls into three categories: mandatory spending, interest on debt, and discretionary spending.

Mandatory spending is expenditures required by law, or mandated, for certain programs. These programs include Social Security, Medicare, Medicaid, unemployment insurance, and other special funds for people in temporary need of help. Congress has passed laws determining the eligibility for these programs and the level of payments, so on the basis of those laws mandatory spending happens automatically. Of the $4.4 trillion, mandatory spending for 2019 was expected to be $2.7 trillion, more than 60% of the federal budget.

You may have noticed that the expected revenue for 2019 was $3.4 trillion, while the expected outlay was $4.4 trillion. The difference between spending and revenue, close to a trillion dollars in 2019, is the **deficit**. As in previous years, the government has to borrow money to pay that deficit, and each year's loans add to the already large national debt of $20 trillion. The interest payments on that huge debt, $363 billion in 2019, must also be paid out of each year's revenue. Some consider interest on debt as mandatory spending, since the government must pay its creditors or risk default, which would result in a serious financial crisis.

Discretionary spending—about 38 percent of the 2019 budget—pays for everything else. These are the funds that congressional committees debate and decide how to divide up. The chart on the next page shows the percentage of government spending from 1950 to 2020 in various categories.

CATEGORIES OF GOVERNMENT SPENDING						
FY	Defense (Military)	Human Resources*	Physical Resources**	Interest on Debt	Other Functions***	Undistributed offsetting receipts****
	% of total revenue	% of total revenue	% of total revenue	% of total revenue	% of total revenue	% of total revenue
1950	32.2	33.4	8.6	11.3	18.7	−4.3
1960	52.2	28.4	8.7	7.5	8.4	−5.2
1970	41.8	38.5	8.0	7.4	8.8	−4.4
1980	22.7	53	11.2	8.9	7.6	−3.4
1990	23.9	49.4	10.1	14.7	4.8	−2.9
2000	16.5	62.4	4.7	12.5	6.4	−2.4
2010	20.1	69	2.6	5.7	5.0	−2.4
2020 (est)	15.9	69.8	3.0	9.7	3.6	−2.0

Source: *US Government Publishing Office, 2019 Budget*

* Includes Education, Health and Human Services, Housing and Urban Development, and mandatory spending on Social Security, Medicare, Income Security, and Veterans Benefits and Services

** Includes Energy, Natural Resources and Environment, Commerce and Housing Credit, Transportation, Community and Regional Development

*** Includes International Affairs; Science, Space, and Technology; Agriculture; Administration of Justice; General Government

**** Includes government earnings on oil and gas leases and collection of funds from government agencies for their employees' retirement and other benefits

In 2013, Senator Ted Cruz (R-TX) presented a flag in Austin, Texas, to the oldest living World War II veteran. Veterans' benefits are part of the Human Resources spending category in the government budget.

Source: *U.S. Department of Veterans Affairs*

As the chart shows, military spending is the largest category of discretionary spending. In 2019 it accounted for more than half of discretionary spending. All the rest of discretionary spending needs must be met by what remains.

Between 1950 and 2020, government spending in the Human Resources category, most of which is mandatory, has grown from about 30 percent of revenue to about 70 percent. That increase needs to be balanced with a decrease in discretionary spending (a trend you can see in the chart in the Defense, Physical Resources, and Other Functions categories) or an increase in revenue or national debt. Conservatives tend to argue that people's tax burden is already significant and that instead of raising taxes or increasing debt, the government should pass laws that reduce the social programs that are responsible for most mandatory spending. Liberals tend to argue that rich people can bear a burden of higher taxes—historically the rich have paid taxes at a higher rate than they do today—and that the mandated social programs serve a vital function in an economy with a vastly unequal distribution of wealth. These principles, as well as pressures from a variety of interest groups (see pages 542–544), are behind the annual push and pull of budget negotiations in Congress.

THINK AS A POLITICAL SCIENTIST: *EXPLAINING CAUSES AND EFFECTS*

Political scientists use their knowledge of political processes and institutions along with data available each year to understand changes in the patterns of government revenue and spending. They identify trends and then look for causes for these trends, reasons for the causes and/or effects, the significance of the causes and/or effects, and the implications of the changes over time. Being able to explain causes and effects is necessary for devising solutions to the many challenges facing government.

Practice: Complete the following activities.

1. Study the table of revenue over time on page 99 and identify one downward trend and one upward trend.

2. Use your knowledge of governmental budgeting to explain the cause for each of those trends.

3. Study the table of government spending over time on page 100 and identify the only spending category that has consistently risen.

4. Explain why the other categories of spending decreased.

5. Explain the significance of the changes over time in federal spending and their effect on possible directions the federal budget might take in the future.

DIFFERENCES BETWEEN HOUSE AND SENATE		
	House of Representatives	**Senate**
Qualifications	• At least 25 years old • Citizen for past 7 years • Resident of state they represent when elected	• At least 30 years old • Citizen for past 9 years • Resident of state they represent when elected
Powers	• Originates revenue bills • Impeachment	• Provides "advice and consent" on treaties and presidential appointments • Handles trial of impeached officials
Members and Terms	• 435 members • 2-year terms	• 100 members • 6-year terms
Structures and Processes	• Centralized and hierarchical • Rules Committee (majority party) controls agenda • Limited debate time • Powerful Speaker of the House • Focus on revenue and spending	• Less centralized • Committees do not have as much authority • Looser debate (filibuster allowed but limited by cloture vote) • Focus on foreign policy • Leaders less powerful except for the powerful majority leader

Influences on Congress

The effectiveness of Congress is determined by an array of factors. Some of the most important are the ideological division of its members, the changing nature of the job, the citizens lawmakers represent, and the way lawmakers represent them. Intensifying partisanship has caused **gridlock**—so much "congestion" of opposing forces that nothing can move forward—within each house and between the Congress and the president. Also, the reshaping of House voting districts has created one-party rule in several regions, making winning legislative seats too easy for some members and unreachable for those from the opposite party. Bitter election contests and longer campaign periods have put Republican and Democratic members at further odds. And legislators' differing approaches in determining their congressional votes has shaped the institution and influenced how Congress acts.

Partisanship and Polarization

The legislature has developed into a partisan and sometimes uncivil institution. A variety of factors has driven a wedge between liberal and conservative members and has placed them at points farther from the middle on each end of the ideological spectrum. From the 1950s into the 1970s, political scientists complained that on many issues it was difficult to tell the parties apart. As Republicans retired, more conservative Republicans replaced them. Southern Democrats, once a moderating force in the Congress, have all but disappeared. Party-line voting is much more common than it once was, and straying from party positions has become dangerous for those interested in reelection.

Reduced Member Interaction Changes in the law have enhanced members' ability to connect with their constituents, especially with regular taxpayer-funded flights from Washington back to their home states or districts. This allowance has discouraged elected members from moving families to the nation's capital. It takes lawmakers away from Washington and from colleagues in the opposite party on weekends. The constant travel allows for few bipartisan friendships to develop. Also, the need to constantly campaign has resulted in a hectic workweek, which ends with a weekend exodus from D.C. A generation ago, representatives and senators overlooked ideological difference in their personal encounters. "Despite our various disagreements in the House," Speaker Tip O'Neill once reflected, "we were always friends after six o'clock and on weekends."

Redistricting One phenomenon that affects House membership is the reshaping of congressional districts every ten years. State legislatures must alter congressional district maps to reflect population changes determined by the U.S. Census. The **redistricting** process in each state can be competitive and contentious and has increased partisanship and decreased accountabilities. The party in power in the state legislature ultimately determines the new statewide map of congressional districts and does so to benefit the party in the following election.

How district boundaries are drawn has an enormous impact on levels of democratic participation and the makeup of the House of Representatives, which in turn has an enormous impact on public policy. Until the 1960s, legislative districting was regarded as having too much political and partisan conflict for the Supreme Court to get involved, since the Court's reputation of neutrality is vital to its authority. However, a landmark decision in 1962 opened the door for the Supreme Court to play a role in making legislative districts as democratic as possible.

MUST-KNOW SUPREME COURT DECISIONS: *BAKER V. CARR* (1962)

The Constitutional Question Before the Court: Can the Supreme Court render judgment on the constitutionality of legislative districts?

Decision: Yes, for Baker, 6:2

Before *Baker*: In 1946, the Court decided in *Colegrove v. Green* that if a state legislature wasn't dividing up congressional districts fairly, it was the people's duty to force the legislature's hand or to vote the legislators out of office. Political scientist Kenneth Colegrove of Northwestern University had brought suit against Illinois officials to stop the upcoming election, because the congressional districts, Colegrove said, lacked "compactness of territory and approximate equality of population." The Supreme Court held that the districts were constitutional, since no law required districts to be compact and equal in population. Justice Frankfurter went further, stating the redistricting process was an issue that would take the court into the "political thicket," a place it shouldn't go.

The Facts: A Tennessee law from 1901 laid out guidelines for redrawing state legislative boundaries, and the state constitution required redistricting every 10 years based on census reports. However, the legislature had failed to redraw the state's 95 voting districts since the census of 1900 and instead had continued to apply the apportionment guidelines from the 1901 law. Over the years, the cities of Nashville, Memphis, Chattanooga, and Knoxville grew, while rural areas developed much more slowly. As a result, the rural areas kept much lower constituent-to-lawmaker ratios. This disparity strengthened some rural citizens' votes and diluted those of some urban voters. For example, one-third of the voters living in the rural areas were electing two-thirds of the state's legislators, so citizens in these districts had a stronger voice on Election Day than voters in the urban districts. In the most extreme cases, some voters had one-twentieth the voting power of other citizens. This practice resulted in minority rule, an outcome in conflict with democratic principles of majority rule and fair representation, since a minority of voters had the majority of voting power. Yet legislators were dissuaded from voting for new maps because they could lose power in the redistricting.

In 1959, Charles Baker and several other litigants sued the Tennessee secretary of state—typically a state's chief election official—because the populations in various state legislative districts varied greatly. The fact that one person's vote was not necessarily equal to another person's vote, Baker said, violated the equal protection clause of the Fourteenth Amendment.

Reasoning: Based on this political inequality, the petitioner wanted the question for the Court to be, "Do Tennessee's outdated and disproportionally populated legislative districts violate the equal protection clause of the Fourteenth Amendment?" But the Court, having decided in *Colegrove*, had to first address the question of its jurisdiction. Was the issue a *political* question, one for the legislature and ultimately the people to decide, or was it a *justiciable* question, a question capable of being answered with legal reasoning and therefore within the Court's jurisdiction?

The Court decided the matter was justiciable and ruled that the Court can intervene when states do not follow constitutional principles in defining political borders, since those practices undermine the democratic ideal of an equal voice for all voters. The Court also developed a set of six criteria for determining when a question is political and therefore outside of the realm of the Court. But it gave no judgment on the uneven districts and let the lower courts then determine if in fact an inequality existed.

Chief Justice Earl Warren served from 1953–1969, overseeing a number of dramatic landmark cases that protected civil liberties and promoted civil rights.

Yet he said after he retired that *Baker v. Carr* was the most important case during his tenure. It helped established the "one person-one vote" principle that greatly expanded democratic participation and the voting rights of minorities.

The Court's Majority Opinion by Mr. Justice William Brennan:
. . . [W]e hold today only (a) that the court possessed jurisdiction of the subject matter; (b) that a justiciable cause of action is stated upon which appellants would be entitled to appropriate relief, and (c) because appellees raise the issue before this Court, that the appellants have standing to challenge the Tennessee apportionment statutes. Beyond noting that we have no cause at this stage to doubt the District Court will be able to fashion relief if violations of constitutional rights are found, it is improper now to consider what remedy would be most appropriate if appellants prevail at the trial . . .

. . . the 1901 statute constitutes arbitrary and capricious state action, offensive to the Fourteenth Amendment in its irrational disregard of the standard of apportionment prescribed by the State's Constitution or of any standard, effecting a gross disproportion of representation to voting population. The injury which appellants assert is that this classification disfavors the voters in the counties in which they reside, placing them in a position of constitutionally unjustifiable inequality vis-a-vis voters in irrationally favored counties. A citizen's right to a vote free of arbitrary impairment by state action has been judicially recognized as a right secured by the Constitution when such impairment resulted from dilution by a false tally, or by a refusal to count votes from arbitrarily selected precincts, or by a stuffing of the ballot box . . .

We conclude that the complaint's allegations of a denial of equal protection present a justiciable constitutional cause of action upon which appellants are entitled to a trial and a decision.

Justice Felix Frankfurter and Justice John Marshall Harlan II dissented pointedly, arguing that the decision overturned well established precedents and overstepped the separation of powers between Congress and the Court.

Dissenting Opinion by Mr. Justice Felix Frankfurter with which Justice John Marshall Harlan II joined: The Court today reverses a uniform course of decision established by a dozen cases, including one by which the very claim now sustained was unanimously rejected only five years ago [in *Colegrove*] . . . Such a massive repudiation of the experience of our whole past in asserting destructively novel judicial power demands a detailed analysis of the role of this Court in our constitutional scheme. Disregard of inherent limits in the effective exercise of the Court's "judicial Power" . . . presages the futility of judicial intervention in the essentially political conflict of forces by which the relation between population and representation has time out of mind been, and now is, determined . . . The Court's authority—possessed of neither the purse nor the sword—ultimately rests on sustained public confidence in its moral sanction. Such feeling must be nourished by the Court's complete detachment, in fact and in appearance, from political entanglements and by abstention from injecting itself into the clash of political forces in political settlements. . . .

To charge courts with the task of accommodating the incommensurable factors of policy that underlie these mathematical puzzles is to attribute, however flatteringly, omnicompetence to judges. The Framers of the Constitution persistently rejected a proposal that embodied this assumption, and Thomas Jefferson never entertained it.

Since *Baker*: The effect of the Court's decision in *Baker v. Carr* was widespread, since not only Tennessee but all states had to redraw legislative boundaries as a result because each person's vote had to be weighted equally. In the 1964 case of *Reynolds v. Sims,* the Court reaffirmed its role in apportionment issues.

Political Science Disciplinary Practices: Analyze, Interpret, and Apply the Decision

Apply: Complete the following tasks.

1. Identify the constitutional principle at issue in this case.

2. Explain how the Court's reasoning in the majority opinion supported the opinion.

3. Explain Justice Frankfurter's concerns in his dissent.

4. Explain differences between the opinion in *Colegrove v. Green* and the opinion in *Baker v. Carr*.

5. Predict what followed after the Court ruled on the principle that all votes must be weighted equally.

6. Research the California Citizens Redistricting Commission's proposals. Evaluate their effectiveness as a remedy for legislative boundaries that disadvantage some voters and give other voters a stronger political voice.

Gerrymandering Too often, there are illogical district lines drawn to give the advantage to one party, a process called **gerrymandering**. Districts in which a party consistently wins by more than 55 percent of the vote are considered **safe seats**; those districts with closer elections are referred to as **marginal seats** or **swing districts**. Countless districts across the United States have been carved out to guarantee safe seats and one-party rule through a process known as *partisan gerrymandering*. Each party has more than 180 safe seats in Congress, meaning there are only about 75 marginal seats up for grabs. Certain victory for incumbents or for candidates of the majority party of districts with safe seats lowers the incentive to compromise and raises the incentive to stick with party doctrine. As a result of the large number of safe seats, a vast proportion of Congress members fall far to the left or far to the right on the ideological spectrum. Partly because of that divide, at the end of a legislative session, fewer policies that address and appease the middle—the vast majority of America—will ever get beyond a committee hearing.

This gerrymandering of safe-seat congressional districts has sometimes made the primary election the determining race and made the general election in November a mere formality. "Getting primaried" has become the new term explaining how an ideologically more extreme challenger can expose an incumbent's record of compromise or tilt away from party positions in order to defeat him or her when the party faithful make that decision. Such challengers are often backed by special interests.

The result is a system of nominating the more conservative Republicans or more liberal Democratic candidates who will ultimately win the primary and face off with their extreme counterparts in their respective legislative chambers. This system has shrunk the number of moderates in Congress. To counter this tactic, several states through citizen ballot initiatives and state laws have created independent commissions to remove the parties' dominance in the process of drawing the maps.

Racial gerrymandering—intentionally drawing legislative districts on the basis of race—has also been the subject of scrutiny for conflicting reasons. First, it has been used to dilute the votes of African Americans and therefore has been found to violate their Fifteenth Amendment voting rights. Second, in well-intentioned overcorrections of this problem, racial gerrymandering was found to violate other voters' rights to equal protection under the Fourteenth Amendment. This latter issue was the focus of another landmark redistricting decision from the Supreme Court, *Shaw v. Reno* (1993).

MUST-KNOW SUPREME COURT DECISIONS: *SHAW V. RENO* (1993)

The Constitutional Question Before the Court: Does a congressional district, designed for the purposes of assuring a majority black population, violate the Fourteenth Amendment's equal protection clause?

The Answer: Yes, for Shaw, 5:4

Before *Shaw*: In the late 1950s, as greater numbers of African Americans registered and voted in Alabama, the case of *Gomillion v. Lightfoot* came to the Supreme Court. The city of Tuskegee contained a large black population and was on a path to constituting the majority of voters in the city. In response to this trend and fearing an African American-dominated government, the state legislature passed special legislation to alter the city's borders. What resulted was a 28-sided city border that placed black neighborhoods beyond the new city lines. Tuskegee Institute professor Charles Gomillion sued Tuskegee Mayor Phil Lightfoot. The Supreme Court decided the state, in its purposeful redesign of the city, had violated the litigants' Fifteenth Amendment right to vote.

Facts: After the 1990 census, and in compliance with the 1965 Voting Rights Act (see page 315), North Carolina submitted to the federal Justice Department its new map of congressional districts for review. Decades of racial gerrymandering in the era before the Gomillion decision had effectively disfranchised black voters and kept them from serving in the halls of government. To correct that problem, the Court had ruled that using race as a basis in creating legislative districts, including so-called majority-minority districts that contained more black than white residents, was permissible in the interest of fairness. In the North Carolina map submitted for review, only one district was a majority-minority district. Federal directives and goals encouraged U.S. Attorney General Janet Reno to send the map back to the state and insist it redraw the map with a second black-majority district. North Carolina complied and created some oddly shaped districts in the process.

Early court filings and editorials commenting on the illogical districts compared them to a Rorschach ink-blot test and "a bug splattered on a windshield." North Carolina's serpent-like 12th district stretched and curved from inner city neighborhood to inner city neighborhood to accumulate a majority black population. At some points it was no wider than the Interstate it straddled. Dubbed the "I-85 District," this district and another resulted in two African American candidates— Mel Watt and Eva Clayton—winning seats in Congress. The map called into question the degree to which race can or should be used as a factor in drawing congressional districts. North Carolina's Republican Party and five white individual

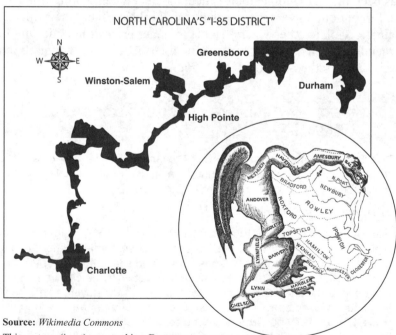

NORTH CAROLINA'S "I-85 DISTRICT"

Source: *Wikimedia Commons*

This cartoon (inset) appeared in a Boston newspaper
in 1812 in response to a redistricting in Massachusetts created
to favor the party of then-Governor Elbridge Gerry. The oddly shaped district
resembled a salamander but in "honor" of the governor was dubbed the
"Gerry-mander."

voters brought suit—Ruth Shaw among them—suggesting the effort came as a result of separating citizens into classes by race in order to form the districts.

Reasoning: In a close vote, the Court ruled for Shaw, not because race was used as a factor in drawing district boundaries but rather that *only* race as a factor could explain the highly irregular district shape and its lack of other characteristics, including geography, usually considered when drawing boundaries. Using race as the only factor in drawing lines opposed the "colorblind" ideal of United States law, separating citizens into different classes without the justification of a compelling state interest and violating the Fourteenth Amendment.

The Court's Majority Opinion by Mrs. Justice Sandra Day O'Connor:
Our focus is on appellants' claim that the State engaged in unconstitutional racial gerrymandering. That argument strikes a powerful historical chord: It is unsettling how closely the North Carolina plan resembles the most egregious racial gerrymanders of the past . . .

This Court never has held that race-conscious state decision making is impermissible in all circumstances. What appellants object to is redistricting legislation that is so extremely irregular on its face that it rationally can be viewed only as an effort to segregate the races for purposes of voting, without regard for traditional districting principles and without sufficiently compelling justification. For the reasons that follow, we conclude that appellants have stated a claim upon which relief can be granted under the Equal Protection Clause . . .

Accordingly, we have held that the Fourteenth Amendment requires state legislation that expressly distinguishes among citizens because of their race to be narrowly tailored to further a compelling governmental interest . . .

The message that such districting sends to elected representatives is equally pernicious. When a district obviously is created solely to effectuate the perceived common interests of one racial group, elected officials are more likely to believe that their primary obligation is to represent only the members of that group, rather than their constituency as a whole.

Each of the four dissenting justices filed a dissenting opinion. The dissent focused in part on the idea that the 12th district did not dilute the votes of citizens in other districts, a consideration on which previous gerrymandering cases had relied for their resolution. Justice Stevens also dissented on the grounds that since minorities benefited from the redistricting, there were no constitutional conflicts. Justice White, joined by Justices Blackmun and Stevens, stressed that even with the oddly shaped 12th district, whites remained a majority in a disproportionate number of districts.

Dissenting Opinion by Mr. Justice Byron White:
The Court today chooses not to overrule, but rather to sidestep [prior precedents]. It does so by glossing over the striking similarities, focusing on surface differences, most notably the (admittedly unusual) shape of

the newly created district, and imagining an entirely new cause of action. Because the holding is limited to such anomalous circumstances, it perhaps will not substantially hamper a State's legitimate efforts to redistrict in favor of racial minorities. Nonetheless, the notion that North Carolina's plan, under which whites remain a voting majority in a disproportionate number of congressional districts, and pursuant to which the State has sent its first black representatives since Reconstruction to the United States Congress, might have violated appellants' constitutional rights is both a fiction and a departure from settled equal protection principles. Seeing no good reason to engage in either, I dissent.

Political Science Disciplinary Practices: Analyze, Interpret, and Apply the Decision

Apply: Complete the following tasks.

1. Identify two potentially conflicting constitutional principles at issue in this case.

2. Explain how the Court justified its reasoning in the majority opinion.

3. Explain Justice White's concerns in his dissent.

4. Describe a similarity and a difference between the opinion in *Shaw v. Reno* and the opinion in *Gomillion v. Lightfoot*.

5. Describe a similarity and a difference between the opinion in *Shaw v. Reno* and the opinion in *Baker v. Carr*.

Divided Government and Senate Showdowns Polarization is also a product of divided government. Government is divided when the president is from one party and the House and/or Senate is dominated by the other. Divided government can cause an inordinate amount of gridlock. Conflict in a divided government has become apparent, especially with judicial nominations. As the Supreme Court has become the arbiter of law on affirmative action, abortion, marriage equality, and gun rights, the fight between the parties about who sits on the Court has intensified.

In 2016, after the death of Associate Justice Antonin Scalia, Democratic President Barack Obama nominated Merrick Garland, Chief Judge of the United States Court of Appeals for the District of Columbia Circuit, to replace him. However, the Republican-majority Senate, in a rare though not unprecedented move, refused to consider his nomination during Obama's last year in office—his so-called "lame duck" year—highlighting the partisan divide in government. President Trump then nominated conservative judge Neil Gorsuch, who was quickly confirmed by a Republican-dominated Senate. (For more on the lame-duck year, see page 126.)

In both chambers, real floor debate has been replaced by carefully orchestrated speeches, while combative media-hungry lawmakers face off in head-to-head confrontations on cable TV news. As historian Lewis Gould put it, "In this hectic atmosphere of perpetual campaigning, the older values of collegiality and comity, though rarer than senatorial memory had it, eroded to the point of virtual disappearance."

Congress's Public Image

When people asked humorist Will Rogers where he got his jokes, he replied, "Why I just watch Congress and report the facts." Critics from Mark Twain to comedian Jon Stewart have cast Congress in a bad light. The media have also contributed to its tarnished reputation. Controversial battles in the legislature receive prime coverage, while routine compromises do not. Members' conflicts of interest and an increased number of scandals have given the institution a black eye. Finally, the lawmaking process is simply slower and more complicated than what most citizens expect, despite its design to move cautiously. All of these factors help to create an image of an uncaring, "do nothing" Congress. The branch's approval rating, as measured by Gallup, hovered in the mid-30 percent range in the early 1970s. Over the past few terms, it has generally fallen below 15 percent.

Yet most individual members of Congress enjoy about a 60 percent approval rating from their constituents. Citizens view Congress as a faceless, bumbling, hyper-partisan institution, but they see their individual representative as a respectable official trying his or her best. This dynamic causes challengers to point to the "mess in Washington," but the composition of Congress changes very little every two years.

With enhanced technology, more people are watching Congress, and more constituents have access to their legislators. Congress now receives well over 50 million email messages and 200 million pieces of mail annually, whereas it received about 10 million letters in the late 1960s. Meanwhile the average population of House districts has risen 40 percent. Interest groups and political action committees have brought more participants into the policymaking arena. There is simply more pressure on members. This increased interest and visibility has made the race for reelection a never-ending battle.

The number of scheduled days in Washington and number of votes on the House and Senate floors has dropped. During the 1960s and 1970s, the average Congress (two-year term) was in session 323 days. Now Congress meets about 250 days per two-year period. But this change is largely due to the other business a member of Congress must take care of and the expectation of spending time in home districts. Veteran Congressman Lee Hamilton (D-IN, 1965–1999) once suggested this help-wanted ad to better define the job description: "Wanted: A person with wide-ranging knowledge of scores of complex policy issues. Must be willing to work long hours in Washington, then fly home to attend an unending string of community events. Applicant should expect that work and travel demands will strain family life, and that every facet of public and private life will be subject to intense scrutiny and criticism."

REFLECT ON THE ESSENTIAL QUESTION

Essential Question: *How do the structure and operation of the legislative branch reflect the United States' republican ideal?* On separate paper, complete a chart like the one below to gather details to answer that question.

Republican Ideals	House of Representatives	Senate

KEY TERMS AND NAMES

advice and consent/84

Baker v. Carr (1962)/105

bicameral/79

caucuses/89

cloture rule/92

Committee of the Whole/90

Committee on Committees (Republican)/88

conference chair/85

conference committees/85

congressional oversight/88

deficit/99

delegate model/96

discharge petition/91

discretionary spending/99

earmark/94

enumerated powers/81

estate taxes/98

expressed powers/81

filibuster/91

floor leaders/85

germane/93

gerrymandering/106

gridlock/102

hold/91

House Judiciary Committee/87

impeach/84

implied powers,/81

interest/98

joint committees/88

logrolling/96

mandatory spending/99

marginal seats/106

markup session/88

multiple referral/94

non-germane amendments/93

omnibus bill/93

politico model/96

pork barrel spending/94

President of the Senate/85

president *pro tempore*/86

reapportionment/79

redistricting/103

riders/93

Rules Committee/90

safe seats/106

select committees/88

Senate majority leader/86

sequential referral/94

Seventeenth Amendment/79

Shaw v. Reno (1993)/107

Speaker of the House/85

sponsor/93

standing committees/87

Steering and Policy Committee (Democratic)/88

swing districts/106

trustee model/96

unanimous consent/91

War Powers Act/83

Ways and Means Committee/90

whip/85

Questions 1–3 refer to the passage below.

> We have before us one of the most important duties of the U.S. Senate and of the U.S. Congress, and that is to decide whether or not we will be involved in war. I think it is inexcusable that the debate over whether we involve the country in war, in another country's civil war, that this would be debated as part of a spending bill, and not as part of an independent, free-standing bill . . . . I think it is a sad day for the U.S. Senate. It goes against our history. It goes against the history of the country.

> —Senator Rand Paul, Senate Floor Speech, September 18, 2014

1. Which of the following statements best summarizes this excerpt from Senator Paul's speech?
   (A) The United States should not become involved in another country's civil war.
   (B) The president should not have war-making authority except in an emergency.
   (C) The military intervention the United States is considering needs a spending appropriation.
   (D) The U.S. Senate should decide on war-like action on its merits, not along with other legislation.

2. Which power of Congress is Senator Paul probably most concerned about based on this passage?
   (A) Congress's power to tax and spend
   (B) The Senate's power to ratify treaties
   (C) The expressed power to declare war
   (D) The power to regulate interstate commerce

3. Which foreign policy reality might limit what the Senate can do in this scenario?
   (A) The reserved powers clause requires House approval for military intervention.
   (B) The president's power to declare war on foreign nations overrides the Senate's power to declare war.
   (C) The Senate requires advice and consent power from the president to act in war.
   (D) The War Powers Act gives the president freedom to act with the military for a limited time.

4. In what way did the Seventeenth Amendment broaden democracy?

   (A) It extended voting rights to women.

   (B) It allowed citizens to alter the Electoral College.

   (C) It gave citizens greater impact on lawmaking in the U.S. Senate.

   (D) It extended voting rights to African Americans.

5. When the Senate Judiciary Committee passes a proposed crime bill by a vote of 11 to 10, which of the following scenarios is most likely to follow?

   (A) The Supreme Court will review the bill for constitutionality.

   (B) The full Senate will consider the bill.

   (C) The House of Representatives will take up the bill.

   (D) The president will sign the bill.

Questions 6 and 7 refer to the table below.

HOUSE AND SENATE MEMBERS' AVERAGE AGE, 2011–2018				
Congress	Representatives	Newly Elected Representatives	Senators	Newly Elected Senators
112th	56.7 years	48.2 years	62.2 years	52.1 years
113th	57.0 years	49.2 years	62.0 years	53.0 years
114th	57.0 years	52.3 years	61.0 years	50.7 years
115th	57.8 years	50.8 years	61.8 years	54.8 years

6. Which of the following statements is reflected in the table above?

   (A) Newly elected members are older than the other members.

   (B) Senators, on average, are younger than representatives.

   (C) The 115th Congress had the youngest newly elected Senators.

   (D) Newly elected senators were on average older than newly elected House members.

7. Which of the following is an accurate conclusion based on the data in the table above?

   (A) Older people vote more frequently, and they want older people serving them.

   (B) It takes years to get through law school before one can run for Congress.

   (C) Levels of reelection in both the House and Senate are high.

   (D) The Constitution requires these lawmakers to be 50 or older.

8. A senator realizes a Senate vote on an immigration bill is coming up. The senator examines public opinion polls on the issue and carefully reads her inbox for constituents' views on the bill and the issue. This senator is following which model of representation?

(A) Trustee

(B) Politico

(C) Delegate

(D) Partisan

9. Which of the following is an accurate comparison of the U.S. House of Representatives and the U.S. Senate?

	HOUSE	SENATE
(A)	Allows filibusters until a majority vote defeats the filibuster	Is a 101-member body, as the vice-president can vote on all bills
(B)	Has committees chaired by members in the minority	Is first in the lawmaking process when it comes to tax law
(C)	Has more rules of procedure to guide its lawmaking process	Has authority over the ratification of treaties with other nations
(D)	Is solely in charge of declaring war	Has the sole power of impeachment

10. Which of the following statements about congressional reapportionment and redistricting is true?

(A) The federal government redraws district maps every 10 years after each census.

(B) Districts must be drawn so that, within a state, every person's vote is roughly equal to every other person's vote.

(C) The Senate, unlike the House, is reapportioned every 20 years.

(D) States that have no major increase or decrease in population do not draw new district lines every ten years.

1. "Across the country, heroin and opioid abuse are growing at rapid rates, especially in New Hampshire. In schools, kids are learning to administer anti-overdose medication. That's how bad the problem is: Police and firefighters, even family and friends, must carry medication like Narcan and know how to use it at a moment's notice. We must protect them from liability laws that could interfere with emergency treatment. I'm grateful to the Judiciary Committee for helping to remove legal barriers."

> — Representative Frank Guinta (R-NH), author of House of Representatives Bill No. 5048 (H.R. 5048), April 27, 2016

After reading the scenario, respond to A, B, and C below:

(A) Describe the power the House Judiciary Committee used to address the concerns outlined by Representative Frank Guinta.

(B) In the context of the scenario, explain how the House of Representatives followed legislative processes to approach the problem.

(C) In the context of the scenario, explain how the interactions between the House of Representatives and the Senate would be required to move H.R.5048 into law.

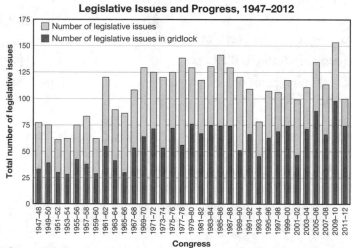

Legislative Issues and Progress, 1947–2012

☐ Number of legislative issues
■ Number of legislative issues in gridlock

Total number of legislative issues

Congress

Source: *Brookings*

2. The number of legislative issues in the graph on the previous page was derived from the topics mentioned in unsigned *New York Times* editorials during 33 sessions of Congress. Gridlock was determined by following progress on the issues to see if Congress and/or the president took action. Use the graph to answer the questions.

   (A) Describe the information the data conveys.

   (B) Describe a trend illustrated in the graphic, and draw a conclusion about the causes of that trend.

   (C) Explain how gridlock demonstrates a key characteristic of the U.S. government as envisioned by the framers.

3. After the 2000 census, a federal judge drew legislative districts in Texas because Democrats and Republicans could not agree on a map. After gaining power in the elections of 2002, Republicans in the Texas legislature redrew the map in 2003. Plaintiffs sued, arguing that the plan was an unconstitutional partisan gerrymander and violated the equal protection clause and the Voting Rights Act of 1965 by diluting racial minority voting strength. They also believed the mid-decade redistricting was illegal. A three-judge panel ruled that the new map was not unconstitutional, and the case was appealed to the Supreme Court as *League of United Latin American Citizens v. Perry* (2006). The Court ruled that only one of the new districts, District 23, was drawn in violation of Section 2 of the Voting Rights Act, because under the previous redistricting it was a protected majority-minority district of Latinos, but Latinos became a minority of voting age citizens in the newly drawn district. However, the Court also ruled that the legislature could redraw the map at any time as long as they did it at least every ten years. It also ruled that the map was not unconstitutional on the basis of partisan gerrymandering.

   (A) Identify a difference between *League of United Latin American Citizens v. Perry* (2003) and *Shaw v. Reno* (1993).

   (B) Based on the difference in part A, explain why the ruling on District 23 in *League of United Latin American Citizens v. Perry* is different from the ruling on the "I-85" district in *Shaw v. Reno* (1993).

   (C) Describe the concern of the Supreme Court about getting into the "political thicket" in relation to the foundational principle of separation of powers.

4. Develop an argument that explains whether term limits for members of Congress would be beneficial or harmful.

In your essay, you must:

- Articulate a defensible claim or thesis that responds to the prompt and establishes a line of reasoning
- Support your claim with at least TWO pieces of accurate and relevant information:
    - At least ONE piece of evidence must be from one of the following foundational documents:
        - *Federalist No. 51*
        - The Constitution
    - Use a second piece of evidence from a document from the list above or from your study of Congress
- Use reasoning to explain why your evidence supports your claim/thesis
- Respond to an opposing or alternative perspective using refutation, concession, or rebuttal

WRITING: *SUPPORT THE ARGUMENT WITH RELEVANT EVIDENCE*

Relevant evidence has a direct connection with the claim. If you can explain how evidence relates to a claim, it is likely relevant. Sometimes evidence that seems relevant on first examination turns out not to be, however. Suppose, for example, you are developing your argument on term limits for members of Congress and you remember that the state of Florida has term limits for its legislature. Is that relevant evidence? Just the fact of it is not. For it to be relevant evidence, you would have to be able to explain what effect the term limits have had on the governance of Florida and how likely those effects would apply to the national government as well.

4

The Executive Branch

*"The office of the President requires the constitution of
an athlete, the patience of a mother, and the
endurance of an early Christian....
The President is a superior kind of slave."*

—Woodrow Wilson, President 1913–1921

Essential Question: *How does the president use the powers of the
executive branch and interact with Congress to
implement a policy agenda?*

With the American presidency comes ceremony, custom, and expectation. Presidential institutions, such as the White House, *Air Force One*, and the State of the Union address, are likely familiar to you. Signing ceremonies and photo opportunities with foreign dignitaries are common images. The Constitution lays out the president's job description. He has both formal and informal powers and functions to accomplish a policy agenda. The president interacts with Congress in the lawmaking process, in appointing his administration and filling the judiciary, and in interacting with other countries. Yet since the creation of the office, American citizens have come to expect more and more from the president, while there is a constant push and pull on the office in ultimately defining what a president can do. For example, not long after Donald J. Trump was sworn into office in January 2017, the debate about his powers intensified, and as he tried to move his policy agenda forward, he met with resistance and tension from Congress, the courts, and media, and some protesting citizens. This chapter explores the design of the executive branch, the expansion of the presidency, the process the president uses to choose advisers, and the way he communicates to accomplish goals and the daily responsibilities of the president.

An Enhanced Presidency

The presidency is shaped by Article II, Article I (which covers vetoes), five constitutional amendments, federal law, Supreme Court decisions, customs, and precedents. The framers designed a limited executive office meant to carry out the ideas put into law by Congress. The office, however, has become the seat for a powerful captain of the ship of state, buoyed by support institutions and American expectation.

Framers' Vision

The delegates in Philadelphia in 1787 voted to make the presidency an executive office for one person. Fears arose because skeptics saw this office as a potential "fetus of monarchy." One delegate tried to allay such fears, explaining "it will not be too strong to say that the station will probably be filled by men preeminent for their ability and virtue."

FOUNDATIONAL DOCUMENTS: *FEDERALIST No. 70*

Critics of the proposed Constitution questioned Article II and the creation of the presidency. A single person, the Anti-Federalists argued, in charge of the administration of government and the executive branch would be dangerous. In the 85 essays the Federalists penned, 25 of them address Article II, and 42 different passages across the collection of these essays make points about the chief executive, his powers, term, relationship to the other branches, and the method of elections. In *Federalist No. 70*, Alexander Hamilton, writing as Publius, foreshadows the "ingredients" of the presidency, "first, unity; secondly, duration; thirdly, an adequate provision for its support; fourthly, competent powers." In No. 70, he addresses his first point (he goes on to address the others in the following essays). *Federalist No. 70* focuses on the value of the unity in a single executive to avoid conflicts and to ensure accountability.

[The framers] have declared in favor of a single Executive, and a numerous legislature. They have, with great propriety, considered energy as the most necessary qualification of the former, and have regarded this as most applicable to power in a single hand . . . Wherever two or more persons are engaged in any common enterprise or pursuit, there is always danger of difference of opinion . . . And what is still worse, they might split the community into the most violent and irreconcilable factions, adhering differently to the different individuals who composed the Magistracy . . .

But the multiplication of the Executive adds to the difficulty of detection in either case. It often becomes impossible, amidst mutual accusations, to determine on whom the blame or the punishment of a pernicious measure, or series of pernicious measures, ought really to fall. It is shifted from one to another with so much dexterity, and under such plausible appearances, that the public opinion is left in suspense about the real author . . .

When power, therefore, is placed in the hands of so small a number of men, as to admit of their interests and views being easily combined in a common enterprise, by an artful leader, it becomes more liable to abuse, and more dangerous when abused, than if it be lodged in the hands of one man; who, from the very circumstance of his being alone, will be more narrowly watched and more readily suspected, and who cannot unite so great a mass of influence as when he is associated with others.

Political Science Disciplinary Practices: Analyze and Interpret
Federalist No. 70

When Publius wrote the Federalist articles, the authors were trying to convince those in the Anti-Federalist camp to support ratification of the Constitution. For this reason, the arguments Hamilton presented reflected the concerns of the Anti-Federalists, those who feared the "fetus of monarchy" because of their recent experience with the British monarch. With this in mind, consider the perspective of each side of the debate.

Apply: Complete the activities below.

1. Describe the author's central claim about a chief executive.

2. Explain how the author's argument for that claim ensures a better government.

3. Explain how the implications of the author's argument may affect the behavior of the chief executive.

Then read the full text on page 660 and answer the questions that follow it.

Article II The Constitution requires the president to be a natural-born citizen, at least 35 years old, and a U.S. resident for at least 14 years before taking office. The president is the commander in chief and also has the power to issue pardons and reprieves and appoint ambassadors, judges, and other public ministers. The president can recommend legislative measures to Congress, veto or approve proposed bills, and convene or adjourn the houses of Congress. The framers also created a system by which the Electoral College chooses the president every four years.

Article II: Qualifications, Duties, and Limits of the Presidency

- Must receive a majority of Electoral College votes to win the office
- Shall hold office for a four-year term
- Must be a natural-born citizen, at least 35 years old, and have lived in the United States for 14 years
- Shall be the commander in chief of the Army and Navy
- May require opinions of advisers and department heads
- Shall have the power to pardon convicted persons for federal offenses
- Shall appoint ambassadors and judges, and make treaties with Senate approval
- May recommend measures he finds necessary
- May convene or adjourn Congress

Checks on Presidential Powers The framers took seriously the concerns of the Anti-Federalists and included specific roles and several provisions to limit the powers of the future strong, singular leader. BIG IDEA There are several constitutional checks on a president—the Senate has the power to provide advice and consent on appointments, for example, and the presidential salary cannot increase or decrease during the elected term.

The framers also expressly made the president subject to **impeachment**. The president "shall be removed from office on impeachment for and conviction of, treason, bribery, or other high crimes and misdemeanors." The impeachment process, outlined in Article I, gives the House the sole power of impeachment (accusation), which it can declare with a simple majority. The impeached official then receives a trial in front of the Senate, with the Chief Justice of the Supreme Court presiding. After sitting as the jury, the Senate can vote to convict (and thus remove) or acquit the president. A two-thirds vote is required to remove the president. An impeached president cannot be pardoned.

Only two presidents have been impeached—Andrew Johnson for violating the Tenure of Office Act (1867) after the Civil War and Bill Clinton for perjury and obstruction of justice in 1998. Johnson escaped removal by one vote. When the Senate voted to remove Clinton, the votes did not reach the required two thirds to do so. The House nearly voted on an impeachment bill during Richard Nixon's presidency in response to the Watergate affair. The measure cleared the House Judiciary Committee, but Nixon resigned before it reached the full House. To date, no president has ever been removed from office.

While some presidential powers, such serving as commander in chief, appointing judges and ambassadors, and vetoing legislation, are explicit, presidents and scholars have argued about the gray areas of a president's job description. Most presidents have claimed **inherent powers**, those that may not be explicitly listed but are nonetheless within the jurisdiction of the executive. This debate has taken place during nearly every administration. Presidents have fought battles for expanded powers, winning some and losing others. The debate continues today.

Washington's Example For first President George Washington, the Constitution provided a mere five-paragraph job description. He took on the role with modesty and accepted being addressed as "Mr. President" as a title though some suggested more lofty labels.

Washington had some key accomplishments, primarily in instilling public confidence in the nation's constitutional experiment. Though he surely would have won a third term, Washington chose to leave government after his second term to allow others to serve and to allay any fears of an overbearing executive.

The presidents that followed Washington had moments of questionable initiative and international confrontation, but most of the early presidents faithfully carried out congressional acts, exercised the veto minimally, and followed Washington's precedent to serve no more than two terms. Thomas Jefferson purchased the Louisiana Territory without congressional approval, and James Madison led the nation in a second war against Great Britain. And

Monroe established a foreign policy, the Monroe Doctrine, by which the United States dominated the Western Hemisphere. For the most part, however, these powerful men let Congress fill its role as the main policymaking institution while the presidents executed Congress's laws.

The Imperial Presidency

Yielding to Congress, however, began to fade as stronger presidents came to office. The president's strength relative to that of Congress has grown steadily, with occasional setbacks, to create a kind of **imperial presidency**, a powerful executive position guided by a weaker Congress. *Webster's Dictionary* defines an imperial presidency as "a U.S. presidency that is characterized by greater powers than the Constitution allows." Historian Arthur Schlesinger Jr. popularized the term with his 1973 book of the same name. The book was published in the shadow of an overreaching Nixon presidency.

Reasons for Expanded Powers A century before the U.S. founding, John Locke argued that in emergencies reasonable rulers should be able to resort to exceptional power. Legislatures were too big, too unwieldy, and too slow to cope with crisis. On occasion, "a strict and rigid observation of the laws may do harm," Locke said. Every president, once in office, has agreed with this assessment. War and international conflict have necessitated the commander in chief's strong, rapid, and sometimes unilateral response to enemies and hostile nations. Economic and other domestic crises have raised popular expectations for strong leadership and new ideas. Sometimes a president's personality and popularity have also helped to expand executive powers.

Source: *Library of Congress*

President Andrew Jackson's critics often questioned if he had stepped outside his authority. What symbols does the cartoonist use to signal this accusation? What is at Jackson's feet? What does he hold in his hand?

Personality and Popularity The dominating personality and popularity of the headstrong **Andrew Jackson** brought about a noticeable shift in presidential power during his presidency (1829–1837). Jackson was a forceful military general who had led the Southern expedition that evacuated the Native Americans. As president, he blazed a path of executive dominance. He used the veto 12 times, more than any president had before. Jackson's opposition to a national bank, combined with his headstrong demeanor, created a rift between the president and other branches, while his popularity among farmers and workers in an age of expanded suffrage and increased political participation enhanced his power even more.

Under the presidency of chief executives who served after Andrew Jackson and before Abraham Lincoln, the powers of the presidency contracted. None of the eight presidents served more than one term, and two died in office. It was a time of relative peace, with the exception of the Mexican-American War. Franklin Pierce and James Buchanan, who preceded Lincoln, are noted for their lack of presidential leadership and clear policy agenda and for allowing the nation to drift toward Civil War. Historians rank Buchanan and Pierce at the bottom of the list of effective presidents.

National Crisis After the Southern states seceded, **Abraham Lincoln** (1861–1865) once again expanded the presidency as he assumed sweeping presidential powers to save the Union and to limit slavery. During the four years of the conflict, writes historian Arthur Schlesinger: "Lincoln ignored one constitutional provision after another. He assembled the militia, enlarged the Army and Navy beyond the congressional appropriation, suspended habeas corpus, arrested 'disloyal' people, asserted the right to proclaim martial law behind the lines, to arrest people without warrant, to seize property, and to suppress newspapers." Lincoln is generally excused for these constitutional violations because he stretched the powers of his office in the name of saving the United States and emancipating the slaves.

On the World Stage Through Reconstruction and after, a host of Union officers, mostly Republicans, served as chief executives. In the late 1800s, the United States began to compete on an international stage with the industrial and imperial powers of Europe. President **William McKinley**, for example, sent 5,000 American troops to China to help put down the Boxer Rebellion.

As the United States became a world military and industrial power, **Theodore Roosevelt** (1901–1909) and **Woodrow Wilson** (1913–1921) stretched presidential power in the name of advancing the nation and serving the people. Roosevelt's gallant Rough Rider background from the Spanish-American War and his brash, forward manner made people respect his strong persona. His progressive actions for environmental conservation against corporate giants contributed greatly to both his reputation and his legacy. He strengthened the Monroe Doctrine with his foreign policy motto that the United States would "speak softly and carry a big stick." During his tenure, he sent troops to Cuba and the Philippines, and he sent the U.S. Navy around the world. He acquired property from Panama to build a canal. (See pages 133–135.)

Roosevelt's so-called **stewardship theory** approach to governing presumed that presidential powers are only strictly limited by the actual limits listed in the Constitution. Like a good steward, Roosevelt insisted, the president should exercise as much authority as possible to take care of the American people, as Lincoln had done before him. "I have used every ounce of power there was in the office," he wrote.

Democrat Woodrow Wilson became a strong leader with an international voice. When he delivered the **State of the Union** address to the Congress, the first such in-person delivery of the report since John Adams had done it, Wilson created for himself a platform from which to present and gain popularity for his ideas. His involvement in international affairs became inevitable as the United States entered World War I. Within two years, he led a successful American mission and became a world leader. His celebrity in Paris for the war-ending Treaty of Versailles elevated his stature in the United States and around the world. "We can never hide our President again as a mere domestic officer," he wrote. "We can never again see him the mere executive he was in the [past]. He must stand always at the front of our affairs, and the office will be as big and as influential as the man who occupies it." However, Wilson failed to use his powers of persuasion with Congress, and the Treaty of Versailles was never ratified, mainly over objections to United States membership in the League of Nations, of which Wilson was the founder.

The Turning Point In a discussion of presidents who expanded the reach of the office, there is perhaps no better example than Theodore Roosevelt's cousin, **Franklin Delano Roosevelt** (FDR) (1933–1945). He became president during the Great Depression (1929–1941), the most severe economic crisis in history. The large coalition that rallied behind him included people from nearly every walk of life who had been harmed by the Depression. His New Deal programs promised to bring the nation out of despair.

FDR arrived in Washington with revolutionary ideas that fundamentally changed not only the role of presidency but also the role of the whole federal government. He recommended and Congress passed laws that required employers to pay a minimum wage, created the Social Security system, and started a series of public works programs to stimulate the economy. These measures greatly expanded the role of government and required vast new additions to the bureaucracy that supports the executive branch in order to carry out the new policies. In trying to prevent a conservative Supreme Court from striking down his self-described liberal legislation, he moved to increase the number of seats on the Court with plans to place judges favorable to his proposals on the bench. His plan failed, but it illustrates Roosevelt's imperial tendencies. He ran for and won an unprecedented third term as the United States moved closer to entering World War II.

The foreign policy dilemma that resulted in war with Germany and Japan only strengthened his leadership and America's reliance on him as the federal government took on a greater role. As Roosevelt mobilized the nation for an overseas war, he overpowered civil liberties in the name of national security by authorizing the creation of "military areas" that paved the way for relocating Japanese-Americans to internment camps. At the time, FDR acted as a wartime commander in chief, not as an administrator concerned about constitutional rights. (See page 290 on *Korematsu v. United States*, a 1944 Supreme Court case that arose from the internment.) What would have seemed autocratic in peacetime was accepted as an appropriate measure during wartime. Americans rallied behind their commander in chief and accepted most of his measures, electing him to a fourth term, but he died just months after the election.

In the post World War II era, the presidency has grown even stronger. Cold War tensions, military engagements abroad, and greater expectation to protect Americans in the age of terrorism has also further imperialized the American presidency. Since that time, the **Twenty-Second Amendment**, ratified in 1951, prevents any president from serving more than two consecutive terms or a total of 10 years. If a person becomes president by filling a vacancy (see next page), that person can still serve two consecutive terms—hence the 10-year limit.

Continuity, Transition, and Succession

Despite sometimes widely differing views on governance and the role of the president, the United States has never experienced any bloodshed resulting directly from a disputed election or a major problem during a transfer of presidential power. Presidents have smoothly transitioned, whether at the dawn of the Civil War, at the end of World War II, after Nixon's resignation, or after the disputed election of 2000. Such presidential transitions are a result of both a reverence for constitutional provisions and a focus on the rule of law.

The **Twentieth Amendment** moved the presidential inauguration date from March 4 to January 20 in 1933. An outgoing president, especially an unpopular one, is sometimes referred to as a "lame duck"—that is, a duck that can't fly—because by that point in the term the president's power and ability to get things done have greatly diminished. The **lame duck period** typically begins after the nation has elected a new president and before the exit of the old one. The Twentieth Amendment shrank this period because the country no longer required as much time for presidential transition.

Transition The president begins his term by agreeing to the oath of office word for word from the Constitution before the chief justice of the Supreme Court at noon on January 20. The early days of the president's first term are known as the **honeymoon period** as the people get to know their new president. Typical news stories at this time include how the new president plans to fulfill campaign promises, appoint his Cabinet, and how the first family will decorate the White House. The honeymoon period also represents a period of good feeling and typically high rates of legislative success during the first 100 days.

Presidents who win with large margins claim the electorate gave them a mandate to fulfill their campaign promises and carry out their policy agendas. They begin by naming their chief administration officials, such as Cabinet secretaries and agency directors. They also create an inner circle of close advisers to help them form policies and programs to achieve their goals. Much depends on how they set up their White House and administration, as well as their relationship to Congress and the public.

Succession If a problem should arise—illness, impeachment, death— and the office of the presidency becomes vacant, the 1947 **Presidential Succession Act** prevents any doubt about who will assume the presidency. In fact, the law assigns a succession order to 18 positions beyond the president. The succession order goes from the vice president, to the congressional leaders, and then to the 15 Cabinet secretaries in the chronological order of each department's creation. The **Twenty-Fifth Amendment**, passed in 1967, provides for the vice president to assume presidential duties if the president is incapacitated or disabled. The amendment also provides for the president to officially hand over temporary decision-making authority to the vice president. This provision has been needed only three times, all for medical procedures.

PRESIDENTIAL SUCCESSION
Vice President
Speaker of the House
President Pro Tempore of the Senate
Secretary of State
Secretary of the Treasury
Secretary of Defense
Attorney General
Remaining Cabinet Secretaries

Based on the Presidential Succession Act of 1947, in the event of presidential vacancy, the next office assumes the presidency. All vacancies except the presidency are filled in the normal routine of such vacancies.

Presidential Powers, Functions, and Policy Agenda

The president of the United States has many powers and functions that enable him to carry out the policy agenda he laid out during the campaign. He exercises the **formal powers** of his office, those defined in Article II, as well the political power he wields with **informal powers**, those interpreted to be inherent in the office, to achieve his policy goals. Congress, too, has bestowed additional duties and limits on the presidency.

Formal and Informal Powers

A president cannot introduce legislation on the House or Senate floor but in many ways still serves as the nation's chief lawmaker. Article II also gives the president the option to convene or adjourn Congress at times. As the head of state, the president becomes the nation's chief ambassador and the public face of the country. As commander in chief, the president manages the military. Running a federal bureaucracy that resembles a corporation with nearly three million employees, the president is a CEO. And finally, as the de facto head of the party, the president becomes the most identifiable Republican or Democrat.

Chief Legislator The Constitution provides that the president "may recommend [to Congress] such measures as he shall judge necessary and expedient." Presidents may recommend new laws in public appearances and in their State of the Union address or at other events, pushing Congress to pass their proposals.

Presidents have asked Congress to pass laws to clean up air and water, amend the Constitution, create a national health care system, and declare war. A president with a strong personality can serve as the point person and carry out a vision for the country more easily than any or all of the 535 members of

Congress. FDR, for example, was the key architect of the New Deal legislation, using his informal powers of persuasion to ensure that Congress enacted the measures. The media's attention on the president provides a **bully pulpit**—a brightly lit stage to pitch ideas to the American people. FDR used the popular radio medium to address Americans during his "fireside chats." He reassured a worried populace and articulated his solutions in a persuasive way. After each "chat," letters from listeners poured in urging their Congress members to support the president's ideas.

Staff The president meets with the leaders of Congress on occasion to discuss pending bills or to compromise on proposals. But bringing ideas in congruence with those of lawmakers on Capitol Hill can be tricky. Modern presidents realize they need a staff to research, draft, and manage legislation, and most presidents have appointed liaisons with Congress to carry out those tasks. The current White House Office of Legislative Affairs works with senators and representatives and their staffs to promote the president's legislative priorities. This office is part of the vast bureaucracy that is under the control of the executive to help carry out laws and the presidential agenda. (Chapter 5 covers the bureaucracy in depth.) The Office of Legislative Affairs differs in approach with each president—sometimes it delivers completely drafted bills to Capitol Hill; sometimes it takes Congress's desires to the president.

President Obama's legislative affairs team had his full confidence. The people he put in charge of guiding the Patient Protection and Affordable Care Act through the House and Senate succeeded by bargaining and accepting input from both legislative houses. Obama was savvy enough to realize several members of Congress had been working toward a health care policy long before he arrived in Washington.

Powers of Persuasion President Trump's only notable bill to pass Congress in his first year was a major tax overhaul that reduced corporate taxes from 35 to 21 percent and changed federal income tax rates, lowering them, at least temporarily, for a vast majority of citizens. The Tax Cuts and Jobs Act passed only after Trump use his skills as a salesman to push for it. As *Politico* reported, "He has spent weeks wooing, prodding, cajoling and personally calling Republican lawmakers to pass sweeping tax legislation in time for Christmas." He closed on this tax bill as he would have closed on a real estate deal decades ago, with a hard and convincing sell. Using his informal political powers, Trump personally called the moderate members of the Senate who were wavering. The White House organized a speech and presentation in the closing efforts, showcasing how the changes would impact some average families, personalizing the promised effects of the bill.

Veto The president has the final stamp of approval of congressional bills and also a chance to reject them with the executive **veto**. After a bill passes both the House and the Senate, the president has 10 days (not including Sundays) to sign it into law. If vetoed, "He shall return it," the Constitution states, "with his objections to the House in which it shall have originated." This provision creates a dialogue between the two branches and encourages Congress to consider the president's critique. This procedure requires some accountability on the part of the executive, and it also encourages consensus policies.

At times, a president will *threaten* a veto, exercising an informal power that may supersede the formal process. Congressional proponents of a bill will work cooperatively to pass it, reshaping it if necessary to avoid the veto. The use of the veto has fluctuated over presidential history. When there is a divided government—one party dominating Congress and another controlling the presidency—there is usually a corresponding increase in the use of the veto.

The president can also opt to neither sign nor veto. Any bill not signed or vetoed becomes law after the 10-day approval period. However, if a president receives a bill in the final 10 days of a congressional session and does nothing, the bill dies, an outcome known as a **pocket veto**. Since much legislation arrives at the end of a session, the president can eliminate congressional plans with a pocket veto. Presidents George W. Bush and Barack Obama both vetoed 12 bills. One of Bush's was a pocket veto. Of the 12 bills Obama nixed, Congress overrode only one. Congress overrode four of Bush's vetoes.

Line-Item Veto Since the founding, presidents have argued for the right to a **line-item veto**, a measure that empowers an executive to eliminate a line of spending from an appropriations bill or a budgeting measure, allowing the president to veto part, but not all, of the bill. Many state governors have the line-item veto power. In 1996, Congress granted that right to the president for appropriations, new direct spending, and limited tax benefits. As the chief representative of the nation, and unlike a Congressional member, the president has no loyalties to a particular district, except in swing states, and can thus sometimes make politically difficult local spending cuts without concern for losing regional support.

Under the new act, President Clinton cut proposed federal monies earmarked for New York City. The city sued, arguing that the Constitution gave Congress the power of the purse as an enumerated power, and New York City believed this new law suddenly shifted that power to the president. The Court agreed and struck down the act in *Clinton v. City of New York* (1998). Presidents and fiscal conservatives continue to call for a line-item veto to reduce spending. There is little doubt that such power would reduce at least some federal spending. However, it is difficult to convince lawmakers (who can currently send pork barrel funds to their own districts) to provide the president with the authority to take away that perk.

Commander in Chief

The framers named the president the **commander in chief** with much control over the military. The Constitution, however, left the decision of declaring war solely to the Congress. The question of what constitutes a war, though, is not always clear.

Senator Barry Goldwater proclaimed in the waning days of the Vietnam conflict, "We have only been in five declared wars out of over 150 that we have fought." His point was fair, if his estimate was high. The issue remains: Should all troop landings be considered wars that require congressional declarations?

When a military operation is defensive, in response to a threat to or attack on the United States, the executive can act quickly. FDR ordered U.S. troops to Greenland in 1940 after the Nazis marched into Denmark but before any U.S. declaration of war. President Clinton bombed Iraq after finding out about the failed assassination attempt on his predecessor, the elder President Bush. President Obama authorized the U.S. mission in 2011 to capture or kill Osama bin Laden, the founder of al-Qaeda, the organization responsible for the 9/11/2001 attacks on the World Trade Towers and the Pentagon. A U.S. Navy Seal team was on the ground in Pakistan for only about 40 minutes. Some believe that actions such as these stretch the meaning of "defensive" too far. Yet how successful would this mission have been if Congress had to vote in advance on whether or not to invade the unwilling country that harbored bin Laden?

The Cold War era greatly expanded the president's authority as commander in chief. In the early 1960s, one senator conceded that the president must have some war powers because "the difference between safety and cataclysm can be a matter of hours or even minutes." The theory of a strong defense against "imminent" attack has obliterated the distinction the framers set and has added an elastic theory of defensive war to the president's arsenal. As recent presidents tried to assume more power, they argued the world was figuratively much larger in 1789, meaning that travel and communication were much slower. This situation, some have argued, allowed the commander in chief time to react to perceived aggressors and to consult with Congress. Today, with so many U.S. interests abroad, an attack on American interests or an ally far from U.S. shores can directly and immediately impact national security.

War Powers Act President Johnson mobilized the U.S. Army into Southeast Asia in 1964. After reports of a naval skirmish off the coast of Vietnam in the Tonkin Gulf (which were later found to be untrue), Congress yielded some of its war-making authority with the Tonkin Gulf Resolution, allowing the president "to take all necessary measures to repel any armed attack against the forces of the United States to prevent further aggression." Congressional leaders rushed through the resolution in a stampede of misinformation and misunderstanding. This rapid reaction to aggressive Communists led to a long and unpopular war.

In 1973, Congress decided to fix this political mistake and passed the **War Powers Act.** The law maintains the president's need for urgent action and defense of the United States while preserving the war-declaring authority of Congress. The president can order the military into combat 48 hours before informing Congress. In turn, Congress can vote to approve or disapprove any presidential military action at any time, with the stipulation that the vote must take place within 60 days, although the president may take a 30-day extension if he wants.

The commander in chief's authority often shifts with the president. In the recent war on terrorism, President Obama developed his own policy for targeting top al-Qaeda enemies and operatives. On a somewhat regular basis, intelligence and military officers presented the president with a portfolio of names of these leaders in what one report said looked like a few pages in a high school yearbook, with profiles for each operative of their lives, families, and contributions to terrorism against the United States and their allies. In certain situations, taking into account knowledge of their whereabouts and calculations of "collateral damage," or innocent victims, Obama would give the order as commander in chief to carry out this micro war policy. Scores of terrorists were eliminated by armed drones with this policy.

Chief Diplomat

The Constitution says the president shall have the power "to make treaties," and "he shall receive ambassadors and other public ministers" from other countries. **Ambassadors** are official diplomatic representatives of other countries. The framers argued that the executive, a liaison with appointed ambassadors, should have the primary role in foreign affairs. The U.S. secretary of state has become the president's main diplomat, overseeing U.S. ambassadors to foreign countries. The State Department, headed by the secretary of state, is one of 15 presidential cabinet departments (see page 139). Yet the president also remains active in diplomatic relationships, using informal interpersonal powers to advance U.S. interests with other nations. Nearing the end of his presidency, George W. Bush reportedly had more than 750 phone conversations with other chiefs or world leaders, participated in more than 675 face-to-face meetings, and conducted 15 video teleconferences.

The balance of power between the president and Congress on foreign relations, however, is sometimes uncertain. For example, Congress can fund or refuse to fund a diplomatic endeavor, such as aid for a country hit by a natural disaster. The Senate can also reject a president's appointed U.S. ambassadors and can ratify (by two-thirds) or reject the president's treaties.

Treaties vs. Executive Agreements Through treaties, presidents can facilitate trade, provide for mutual defense, help set international environmental standards, or prevent weapons testing, as long as the Senate approves. President Woodrow Wilson wanted the United States to join the League of Nations after World War I, but the Senate refused to ratify Wilson's Treaty of Versailles that established the plan.

An **executive agreement** resembles a treaty yet does not require the Senate's two-thirds vote. It is a simple contract between two heads of state: the president and a prime minister, king, or president of another nation. Like any agreement, such a contract is only as binding as each side's ability and willingness to keep the promise. And, to carry it out, presidents will likely need cooperation from other people and institutions in the government. These compacts cannot violate prior treaties or congressional acts, and they are not binding on successive presidents.

Presidents have come to appreciate the power of the executive agreement. President Washington found conferring with the Senate during each step of a delicate negotiation extremely cumbersome and perhaps dangerous. It compromised confidentiality and created delays.

Executive agreements are a preferred diplomatic path to ensure secrecy or speed or to avoid senatorial egos. During the Cuban Missile Crisis in October 1962, President Kennedy discovered the Soviet Union's plan to install nuclear missiles in Cuba. Intelligence reports estimated these weapons would soon be operational. After days of contemplation, negotiation, and a naval standoff in the Caribbean, the United States and the USSR made a deal. The agreement stated that the Soviets would remove their offensive missiles from Cuba if the United States would later remove its own missiles from Turkey. Had Kennedy relied on two-thirds of the Senate to help him solve the crisis, a different outcome could very well have occurred. Time, strong words on the Senate floor, or an ultimate refusal could have drastically reversed this historic outcome.

POLICY MATTERS: *PRESIDENTS, POLITICS, AND THE PANAMA CANAL*

The policies of two presidents toward the Panama Canal show two very different ways of using the powers of the executive to advance a policy agenda and interact with Congress.

Acquiring the Panama Canal Zone "Speak softly and carry a big stick." These words of President Theodore Roosevelt describe his foreign policy in relation to Latin America, where he wanted to assert U.S. power. However, the words might also describe his approach to Congress.

Shortly after he became president in 1901, Roosevelt spoke to Congress of the importance of building the Panama Canal, using his powers of persuasion. "No single great material work which remains to be undertaken on this continent," he said, "is as of such consequence to the American people." Roosevelt's secretary of state, John Hay, drew up a treaty to acquire the canal zone from Colombia, the colonial power ruling Panama at the time, so the United States could build a canal to connect the Pacific and the Atlantic Oceans, providing a time- and money-saving shortcut for shippers who would no longer have to go all the way around the southern tip of South America. The Senate approved the treaty, but the government of Colombia balked.

Panamanians had long wanted their independence from Colombia, and a deal was struck with the United States: If American forces would support their independence effort, Panama would grant the U.S. the acquisition of the Panama Canal Zone it had sought from Colombia. Some Americans with a business interest in the canal then helped stage a revolt. Panamanian soldiers were bribed to lay down their guns so the rebels could prevail, and

Roosevelt sent the naval ship *USS Nashville* in a show of support. Secretary of State Hay negotiated an agreement with the newly independent nation of Panama in 1903 to acquire control over the Isthmus of Panama to create the canal. Roosevelt's handling of Panama independence is sometimes used as an example of his "gunboat diplomacy"—foreign policy influenced by a show of naval force.

Some in the United States saw Roosevelt's participation in the rebellion as an act of piracy or worse. But Roosevelt defended his actions and use of executive powers, saying years later, "If I had followed traditional, conservative methods, I should have submitted a dignified state paper of probably two hundred pages to Congress, and the debate would have been going on yet. But I took the Canal Zone, and let Congress debate, and while the debate goes on, the Canal does also!" The treaty was finally ratified in 1904; the canal opened in 1914.

Returning the Canal Zone to Panama While favorable to the United States and its allies for shipping and military strategy, over the years the canal put a strain on relations between the United States and Panama. The canal cut Panama into two sections, with the Canal Zone under the control of the United States. Foreign policy attitudes changed over the decades as well. Roosevelt's big stick diplomacy, by which the United States justified its intervention in foreign countries in the Western Hemisphere to protect its interests, was replaced with softer diplomatic efforts and an interest in supporting independent democracies.

On January 9, 1964, violence erupted in the Canal Zone when a Panama flag flying next to an American flag was torn. A number of protesting students overwhelmed Canal Zone police and U.S. troops were brought in. Twenty Panamanians were killed. In Panama, that day has since become known as Martyrs Day. Panama broke off diplomatic relations with the United States and demanded a new treaty.

When Jimmy Carter became president, he articulated his approach to foreign policy, with an emphasis on morality. "Our policy is based on a historical vision of America's role. Our policy is derived from a larger view of global change. Our policy is rooted in our moral values, which never change. Our policy is reinforced by our material wealth and by our military power. Our policy is designed to serve [hu]mankind."

Returning the Canal Zone to Panamanian control was high on Carter's foreign policy objectives, for several reasons. First, he saw the control of the Canal Zone as a holdover from an imperial past and wanted to remove any symbolic representation of imperialism, believing it affected U.S. relations with all Latin American countries. On a more practical basis, he was also concerned about sabotage to the canal. Since the 1964 Martyrs Day, there had been concerns about protesters disrupting the operations of the canal. Finally, he believed it was the nation's moral responsibility to respect the complete self-governance of Panama.

However, he faced strong opposition in the Senate and among the American people who believed that the United States paid for the canal and should keep it. In contrast to Teddy Roosevelt's big stick approach, Carter set in motion a carefully planned effort to win support in the Congress, relying on powers of persuasion and personal relationships to achieve his goals. Specifically, he and his legislative team provided extensive briefings and education to members of Congress and sent them to the region to gather information firsthand, and Carter got personally involved in discussions. His team was also meticulous about learning exactly which votes they could count on and which votes they needed to nurture. They developed an extensive public relations campaign to educate the American people on the issue and made visits to congressional districts where pressure from constituents might sway a member's vote.

Carter's patient diplomacy with Congress paid off, and in 1978 new treaties that allowed Panama to regain control of the Canal Zone on December 31, 1999, were ratified by a Senate vote of 68-32.

Chief Executive and Administrator

How the president implements or enforces a new law, the approach appointees take to implement that law, and their understanding of policies will all shape the administration's policy agenda. Executive orders, signing statements, and running the machinery of the vast executive branch mark how a president carries out his powers and functions as the chief executive. The Supreme Court has defined some of the gray areas associated with the president's largely confidential decision-making process. For example, the president can fire subordinates that have been approved by the Senate.

Executive Orders An **executive order** empowers the president to carry out the law or to administer the government. Unlike a criminal law or monetary appropriation, which requires Congress to act, a presidential directive falls within executive authority. For example, the president can define how the military and other departments operate.

Executive orders have the effect of law and address issues ranging from security clearances for government employees to smoking in the federal workplace. In 1942, for example, FDR issued the infamous Executive Order 9066, which allowed persons identified by the Secretary of War to be excluded from certain areas. This executive order was the basis for the internment of Japanese-Americans in West Coast camps during World War II. In 1948, through an executive order, President Harry Truman directed the military to racially integrate. More recently, President Trump issued an executive order outlining an immigration policy that limited travelers to the United States from six Muslim-dominated countries. Executive orders cannot address matters that have exclusive congressional jurisdiction, such as altering the tax code, creating new interstate commerce regulations, or redesigning the currency. Executive orders can also be challenged in court.

Signing Statements Though the president cannot change the wording of a bill, several presidents have offered **signing statements** when signing a bill into law. These statements explain their interpretation of a bill, their understanding of what is expected of them to carry it out, or just a commentary on the law. A signing statement allows a president to say, in effect, "Here's how I understand what I'm signing and here's how I plan to enforce it." Critics of the signing statement argue that it violates the basic lawmaking design and overly enhances a president's last-minute input on a bill.

Executive Privilege Presidents have at times asserted **executive privilege,** the right to withhold information or their decision-making process from another branch, especially Congress. They have particularly asserted that they need not make public any advice they received from their subordinates. Sometimes staff input is offered confidentially, which presents a problem for a president if he is asked to reveal the source. Some presidents have declined to identify a source, claiming that the information is privileged. They argue that their right to executive privilege comes from the separation of powers, and they point out that nothing in the Constitution requires the president to reveal any part of the decision-making process en route to an official act. If controversial input from subordinates can simply be demanded by another branch, presidents argue further, then subordinates may refuse to give worthy advice and thereby weaken a president's ability to lead.

The right to assert executive privilege, however, has its limits. In the early 1970s, as the Watergate scandal developed, investigators subpoenaed the White House tapes that contained President Richard Nixon's confidential conversations. Nixon refused to hand over the tapes, claiming through executive privilege that his conversations were confidential. The Court disagreed. In a unanimous vote, the Court acknowledged a president's right to confidentiality in decision making, but declared that there is no absolute, unqualified presidential privilege of immunity from handing over prosecutorial evidence. Allowing a president to assert such a right in this instance would have thwarted law enforcement. Presidents can still withhold some information, but they cannot do so when it involves a criminal investigation.

Judicial Powers

The president has some judicial powers and can shape the courts. In addition to appointing federal judges (see page 145), the Constitution gives the president the power "to grant reprieves and pardons for offenses against the United States." These checks on the courts make the president the last resort for those convicted of federal criminal offenses. On occasion, a president will issue an act of clemency through pardon, commutation (lessening sentences), or amnesty (pardoning a large group). President Ford pardoned Nixon after the ouster to put the Watergate scandal in the past. President Carter issued a general amnesty for Vietnam draft dodgers. On his final day in office, President Bill Clinton granted 140 pardons, including one for his brother Roger Clinton, who had been convicted of drug charges and other crimes. This additional role makes a president the "chief magistrate."

Source: *Harper's Weekly October 14, 1865*

A number of higher-ranking ex-Confederates were excluded from the general amnesty extended by both President Abraham Lincoln and President Andrew Johnson. Thousands applied for a special pardon during Johnson's term, signing an oath of allegiance in order to have full citizenship restored.

As presidents take on new roles, additional contemporary role titles surface. "Salesman in chief" might be a fair label when the president travels about the country pushing for one of his new initiatives. "Healer in chief" might apply when he visits a disaster-ridden area after a flood, hurricane, or mass shooting. The president is also the face of his political party, the "chief of party." During election season, the president campaigns for fellow party members, because such contests can have a direct effect on the success or failure of enacting presidential policy.

The President's Team

The president's formal powers enable him to appoint a team to execute the laws and to accomplish his policy agenda. Some of those administrators are in positions as old as the Republic. Many more subordinate positions exist because Congress has since created them or has allotted funds for offices to support the president. A typical president will appoint about 2,000 executive branch officials during each Congress. Atop that list are the Cabinet officials, then the agency directors, military leaders and commissioned officers, and the support staff that works directly for the president. Most of these employees serve at the pleasure of the president and some are kept on when a new president is elected. Other positions are protected by statute or Supreme Court decisions.

Because the founders did not anticipate that Congress would convene as frequently as it does in modern times, they provided for **recess appointments**. If the Senate is not in session when a vacancy arises, the president can appoint a replacement who will serve until the Senate reconvenes and votes on that official. This recess appointment is particularly necessary if the appointee is to handle urgent or sensitive work.

The Vice President

Unofficially, a president's first named assistant is the vice president because that decision and announcement are made before the president has been elected. To many, the vice presidency seems the second most powerful governmental officer in America, but in reality the vice president is an assistant to the president with little influence and a somewhat undefined job description. Different presidents have given their vice presidents differing degrees of authority and roles.

The Constitution names the vice president as the president of the Senate, a nonvoting member except in cases of a tie. Article II declares that in case of presidential removal, death, resignation, or inability, the president's duties and powers "shall devolve on the vice president."

Other than those constitutional duties, a vice president's role and influence are determined by the president. Some vice presidents have been leaders on both domestic and international causes. Others have kept their distance and had cool relations with the chief executive. The office is described as a "heartbeat away from the presidency" yet is actually relatively weak unless that unfortunate moment arrives.

Shaping and Supporting Policy In recent years, the position has been especially influential on presidential policy. Many saw George W. Bush's vice president Dick Cheney, a hawkish former defense secretary, as overly influential, at least in Bush's first term, in promoting a tough stance not only on terrorists but also on the nations that harbor them and in pushing for the 2003 invasion of Iraq to eliminate "weapons of mass destruction" that turned out not to exist. Others have questioned the reality of Cheney's influence, which appeared to diminish in the second term.

Vice President Joe Biden, serving under Obama, sustained his high influence for eight years. Obama attained several policy goals by assigning them to the affable former senator who had served in Washington since the mid-1970s. With Biden, he wrapped up the mission in Iraq, had what most economists praise as success with the economic stimulus in the opening months of his first term, and gained various budget deals with Republican congressional leaders. Biden was also the point man on other foreign policy matters. Insiders have reported on the friendship between these men and on Obama's forgiving attitude after Biden's public gaffes, such as the time he endorsed gay marriage before the president did and another time when he cursed on a hot mic at the signing of Obama's health care bill. Their casual exchanges proved their trust with each other and common policy beliefs. One reporter called their relationship a "mind-meld." The president gave "Uncle Joe" a presidential medal of freedom and called him "the best vice president America has ever had."

Before he was named the Republican presidential nominee, Donald Trump chose Indiana Governor Mike Pence to be his running mate. Vice President Pence has taken an active role supporting issues of concern to evangelical Christians.

The Cabinet and Bureaucracy

Article II refers to a **Cabinet** when it mentions "the principal officers in each of the executive departments." Today, 15 Cabinet secretaries, such as the secretary of defense and secretary of transportation, advise the president, but they spend even more time running large governmental departments that take care of a wide range of national concerns. Presidents can add additional members to the Cabinet. President Trump has included the vice president, his chief of staff, and seven others beyond the 15 department heads to this formal group.

Secretaries When appointing Cabinet secretaries, modern presidents create some balance based on geography, gender, ethnicity, and even party membership. As James King and James Riddlesperger posit in their study of diversity and Cabinet appointments, "a public feeling underrepresented by an administration is less likely to support that administration's broader policy agenda." Therefore, presidents have found showcasing token minority appointments and stocking their team with a visible, diverse staff to be in the interest of accomplishing their agenda.

FDR appointed the first woman to the Cabinet, Secretary of Labor Francis Perkins, and Lyndon Johnson appointed the first African American, Secretary of Housing and Urban Development Robert Weaver. This tokenism to the Cabinet continued until President Jimmy Carter appointed substantial numbers of blacks

Source: *Lyndon Baines Johnson Library and Museum*

Robert Clifton Weaver was the first Secretary of Housing and Urban Development, serving from 1966–1968 under President Lyndon Johnson. Weaver was also the first person of color appointed to a cabinet-level position.

and women to his senior executive positions—16 percent women and 11 percent ethnic minorities. The Cabinet has since included Latinos, Asian Americans, and nontraditional appointees to inner Cabinet positions, and 53 percent of Obama's first-term Cabinet appointees were either women or minority.

State Department The first department Congress created was the Department of State, headed by Thomas Jefferson. The State Department is the president's main diplomatic body. Deputy secretaries oversee U.S. relations in designated regions or continents. For each nation that the U.S. recognizes (nearly every nation in the world), the State Department employs an ambassador and operates an embassy in that country, and that country has an embassy in Washington. About two-thirds of U.S. ambassadors come from careers in foreign affairs or are international experts. About one-third are political appointees—former senators or celebrities the host country will receive well.

Defense Department The Defense Department is headquartered at the Pentagon, just outside the nation's capital. Secretaries of defense are civilian officers who serve the president and have not served in the uniformed military service for at least seven years. The Constitution and American tradition dictate that the leadership and policy-making apparatus of the military be distinct and separate from the uniformed divisions that carry out military missions. Ultimately, the people run the military through their elected and constitutional civil officers, in contrast to many dictatorships where a strong military leader takes over the military first and the government second.

The Defense Department includes the Army, Navy, Air Force, and Marines—all of the nation's military branches under one command. A council made up of the chiefs of staff of those organizations heads up the department. Defense comprises about one-fifth of the overall federal budget and the largest portion of the nation's discretionary spending, expenditures that are not fixed by law.

Federal Agencies Federal agencies are subcabinet entities that carry out specific government functions. Many fall within the larger departments. The Federal Bureau of Investigation (FBI)—a crime fighting organization—falls in the Justice Department. The Coast Guard falls in the Department of Homeland Security. Other agencies include the Food and Drug Administration (FDA), the Internal Revenue Service (IRS), the Central Intelligence Agency (CIA), and the Postal Service. Thousands of people in Washington and across the country staff these agencies. They carry out laws Congress has passed with funds Congress has allotted. The *Federal Register* currently lists 441 agencies working in the federal government.

President's Immediate Staff

In 2008, there were 74 separate policy offices and 6,574 total employees (most not working in the White House). Ideally, all of the offices and agencies play a part in implementing the president's policy agenda.

EOP The **Executive Office of the President (EOP)**, an office that coordinates several independent agencies, carries out most constitutional duties, with a large group of advisers and supporting agencies that handle the budget, the economy, and staffing across the bureaucracy. Created in 1939 when FDR needed an expanded presidential staff, the EOP now includes the Office of Management and Budget, the Central Intelligence Agency, the Council of Economic Advisers, and other agencies.

White House Staff The president's immediate staff of specialists runs the White House Office. These staffers require no Senate approval and tend to come from the president's inner circle or campaign team. They generally operate in the West Wing of the building. Presidents sometimes come to rely on their staffs more than their Cabinets or agency heads because staff members serve the president directly. White House staffers, unlike secretaries, do not have loyalties to departments or agencies and do not compete for funding. The staff interacts and travels with the president daily and often has worked with the president in the past. A staffer's individual relationship and access to the president will determine his or her influence.

In the 1950s, President Eisenhower's **chief of staff** became his gatekeeper, responsible for the smooth operation of the White House and the swift and accurate flow of business, paper, and information. Though the chief of staff has no official policymaking power, a president seeks the chief of staff's opinion on many issues, giving the position a great deal of influence. Chiefs of staff tend to be tough, punctual, detail-oriented managers, and these qualities allow the president to concentrate on big-picture decisions.

Beyond the chief of staff, the president has an inner circle that includes the top communicator to the people, the White House press secretary; the president's lawyer, or chief counsel; and his point person on any issue of international safety, the national security adviser. This assistant coordinates information coming to the president from the CIA, the military, and the State Department to assess any security threat to the United States.

National Security Council The National Security Council is a statutorily defined group that includes the president, vice president, secretaries of defense, state, the head of the CIA, the president's national security advisor, the top uniformed military leaders, and a few other major principals of the executive branch. The group is defined in a 1947 law that ensures the president is adequately and regularly informed as to the dangers that America may face. It is an advisory group, but the president chairs this council and still remains the commander in chief who would make any wartime executive decisions.

Interactions with Other Branches

Since Congress is the branch that authors most law, the cashier of the federal purse, and the interview committee for presidential appointments, presidents must stay in good graces with the members—representatives and senators—of that branch. The president's agenda is not always Congress's

Executive Hierarchy
Selected Cabinet Level Departments and Agencies

Executive Office of the President	President Vice President	White House Office
Council on Economic Advisors Office of Management & Budget Central Intelligence Agency National Security Council Others	15 Cabinet Secretaries	White House Staff Chief of Staff Press Secretary Legal Counsel

State	Treasury	Defense	Justice	Labor	Homeland Security
Regional Offices, Economic & Business Affairs Ambassadors United States Agency for International Development	IRS, Comptroller of Currency, Engraving & Printing, U.S. Mint Financial Crimes Enforcement Network	Joint Chiefs of Staff Army, Navy, Air Force, Marine Corp, National Guard, Defense Intelligence Agency NSA	Solicitor General FBI, DEA, ATF, Civil Rights Division, Bureau of Prisons, U.S. Attorneys, Marshals	Bureau of Labor Statistics Mine Safety & Health Disability Employment	FEMA, TSA, Customs & Border Protection Coast Guard Secret Service USCIS

Independent Agencies and Government Corporations	Independent Regulatory Agencies
NASA Post Office AMTRAK Corporation for Public Broadcasting Tennessee Valley Authority Others	FCC: Federal Communications Commission FEC: Federal Elections Commission FDA: Food & Drug Administration EPA: Environmental Protection Agency SEC: Securities & Exchanges Commission

agenda, however, and tensions often arise between the branches. As chief legislator, the president directs the Office of Legislative Affairs to draft bills and assist the legislative process. (See page 129.) Sometimes the aides employ techniques to push public opinion in a lawmaker's home district in the direction of a desired presidential policy so that lawmaker's constituency can apply pressure. As the president enforces or administers the law, the courts determine if laws are broken, misapplied, or entirely unjust. For these reasons, a president regularly interacts with the legislative and judicial branches.

The Senate and Presidential Appointees

In addition to the more visible Cabinet appointees, a president will appoint approximately 65,000 military leaders and about 2,000 civilian officials per two-year congressional term, most of whom are confirmed routinely, many times approved *en bloc*, hundreds at a time. But each year, hundreds of high-level appointments are regularly subjected to Senate investigation and public hearing. Most are still approved, while a few will receive intense scrutiny and media attention, and some confirmations will fail.

The Senate invariably accepts presidential Cabinet nominations. The upper house swiftly confirmed every Cabinet-level secretary until 1834, when it rejected Andrew Jackson's appointee, Roger Taney, as secretary of the treasury over his opposition to a national bank. The makeup of the Senate changed with the next elections and Jackson appointed Taney as chief justice of the Supreme Court, who was confirmed for the position by a slim margin. Senator John Tyler soon became President Tyler and faced some opposition when forming his own Cabinet. To date, the Senate has rejected only nine department secretaries; four of those occurred during the Tyler administration.

The typical acceptance of Cabinet appointees results from the custom of the Senate to let the president form his own team. The president won a democratic election and should therefore have the prerogative of shaping his administration. Presidents commonly choose senators to move over to the executive branch and serve in their Cabinet. In recent years, the president has selected one or more members of the opposite party. President Obama named three Republicans to serve as secretaries (though one declined the offer). Presidents and their transition teams do a considerable amount of vetting of potential nominees and connecting with senators to evaluate their chances before making official nominations. Though only nine nominations have been voted down, 13 Cabinet appointees have withdrawn their nominations (or the president did so) anticipating a losing vote. Many more officials were considered, their names floated about to test their viability among senators, and never officially nominated.

Senate Standoffs The two most recent standoffs on Cabinet appointments came in 1989 and in 2017. President George H.W. Bush named former Senator John Tower as secretary of defense, and President Donald J. Trump nominated Betsy DeVos as secretary of education. Senator Tower represented Texas in the Senate since Lyndon Johnson had vacated his seat to become vice president. Tower had the resume and experience to serve as defense secretary. He served in World War II and as the chairman of the Senate Armed Services Committee. Upon his nomination, even Democrat leaders anticipated his nomination would sail through. However, allegations of heavy drinking surfaced, as did his reputation as a playboy and "womanizer." With more scrutiny, Tower was found to own stock in corporations with potential future defense contracts, an obvious conflict of interest. President Bush stuck by his old congressional colleague (Bush had represented Texas in the House when Tower was in the Senate). In the end, the Senate voted Tower down in a 53 to 47 vote.

In 2017, President Trump nominated Betsy DeVos as education secretary. Her views tended to coincide with those of many Republicans, including Trump, who are interested in privatizing education, so her confirmation would help further that agenda goal. DeVos has much experience in the education world as a private school advocate, but she has never worked in any public school in any capacity, including as a teacher, and along with her billionaire husband she had invested in for-profit charter schools and pushed for online education. The educational community was generally against her nomination, with some exceptions. At her public confirmation hearing, many senators expressed concern about her priorities, her experience, and her high-dollar donations to Republican candidates. As she fielded questions before the Senate Health, Education, Labor, and Pensions Committee, her competence in the field seemed shaky. Exchanges on school choice, guns in schools, students with disabilities, and private or online school accountability raised eyebrows on Capitol Hill and in news reports that followed. In the end, two Republican senators voted against her, leaving the Senate in a dead tie. Vice President Pence's tie-breaking vote was the first time in U.S. history that a vice president cast the tie vote on a Cabinet secretary confirmation.

Ambassadors The Senate is also likely to confirm ambassador appointments, although those positions are often awarded to people who helped fund the president's campaign rather than people well qualified for the job. On one of the "Nixon Tapes" from 1971, Nixon tells his chief of staff, "anybody who wants to be an ambassador must at least give $250,000." About 30 percent of ambassadors are political appointees. Some may have little or no experience to qualify them, though they are rarely rejected by the Senate. Hotel magnate George Tsunis, appointed by President Obama as ambassador to Norway, was questioned critically by Senator John McCain (R-AZ) in 2014 and shown to have limited understanding of Norwegian political issues; he withdrew his nomination after a year when confirmation seemed unlikely.

Removal The president can remove upper-level executive branch officials at will, except those that head independent regulatory agencies. (These will be discussed in the next chapter). A president's power of removal has been the subject of debate since the founding. Alexander Hamilton argued that the Senate should, under its advice and consent power, have a role in the removal of appointed officials. James Madison, however, argued that to effectively administer the government the president must retain full control of his subordinates. The Article II phrase that grants the president the power to "take care that the laws be faithfully executed" suggests the president has a hierarchical authority over secretaries, ambassadors, and other administrators.

This issue brought Congress and the president to a major conflict in the aftermath of the Civil War. President Andrew Johnson dismissed Secretary of War Edwin Stanton, congressional Republicans argued, in violation of the Tenure of Office Act. This act led to Johnson's impeachment.

The question of removal resurfaced in 1926—this time with regard to President Wilson's earlier removal of a postmaster in violation of an 1876 law. The Supreme Court concluded that presidential appointees serve at the pleasure of the president. The Court tightened this view a few years later when it looked at a case in which the president had fired a regulatory agency director. The Court ruled in that case that a president can dismiss the head of a regulatory bureau or commission but only upon showing cause, explaining the reason for the dismissal. The two decisions collectively define the president's authority: executive branch appointees serve at the pleasure of the president, except regulatory heads, for which the president must show cause if he wants to remove them.

Judicial Interactions

Presidents interact with the judiciary in a few ways. As the head of the executive branch, presidents enforce judicial orders. For example, when the Supreme Court ruled in 1957 that Central High had to admit nine African American students into the school, President Eisenhower ordered the 101st Airborne Division into Little Rock, Arkansas, to ensure the school followed the court order. The branches also interact when courts check the executive if they find presidential action unconstitutional. For example, in 1952 the Supreme Court overturned President Truman's nationalizing of the steel industry during the Korean War. Truman had taken that step to mobilize resources for the Korean War and also to prevent a strike by steelworkers. The Court ruled, however, that the president lacked authority to seize private property.

A more frequent encounter of the two branches comes when presidents appoint federal judges. All federal judges serve for life terms, so only a fraction of the federal courts will have openings during a president's time in office, yet presidents see this opportunity as a way to put like-minded men and women on federal benches across the country. In fact, no presidential appointment has more influence than the appointment of lifetime judges who have the power to shape policy for years to come. Of course, like appointments in the executive branch, the Senate must approve these nominees.

While standoffs about Cabinet appointees are rare, judicial nominations are another story. The president appoints scores of federal judges during each four-year term, because in addition to the nine justices that serve on the Supreme Court, more than 650 serve on the 94 U.S. district courts across the country, and more than 170 serve on the U.S. appeals courts. Federal judges, especially those at the Supreme Court level, have a great impact on the nature of U.S. law, and with lifetime appointments, they serve a much longer time than do the heads of executive departments. Thirty Supreme Court nominees have been rejected by a Senate vote on their first try. Countless other lower court nominees have also been rejected or delayed to the point of their giving up on the job.

The interaction between the branches on these judicial nominees is complicated and sometimes contentious. Senate rules and traditions govern the process. Senators, especially those on the Judiciary Committee, expect to give advice to presidents on selecting these nominees and are slow to consent to the president's choices for a variety of reasons. They, too, realize the longevity of a federal judge's service. If the president appoints like-minded judges, senators on the opposite end of the ideological spectrum are unlikely to welcome the judges, since their future decisions could define controversial or unclear law.

As you read in Chapter 3, the Senate has some unique rules and customs that result in slow-moving action and require voting thresholds above the simple majority of 51 senators. As the divided electorate has caused majority control of the body to shift from one party to the other after congressional elections, the cloture motion has served a somewhat stabilizing function. (See page 92.) If a senator wants to block a judicial nomination, 60 or more senators would be required to prevent that. The cloture rule prevents the majority party from overrunning the minority party. Although the majority party may control the Senate, it is rare for one party to hold 60 or more seats. Senators in the majority party recognize that they may be in the minority after the next election.

Communicator in Chief

In a democracy, the president's need to communicate with the citizenry and keep good relations with Americans is essential for success. To pass legislation, the constituents of individual Congress members must like the president's proposed bills and foreign policy plans—if they don't, they will pressure their representative or senator not to support it. The executive branch must publicize its reasons for proposed legislation and the benefits it will provide to people in the United States. Another function the president assumes, then, is "communicator in chief." Meanwhile, a free press in the United States entitles citizen-journalists to tell their readers, listeners, and viewers about the government. Among the government entities they are most interested in is the executive branch of the United States and its head, the president.

Relationship with the Press

In the early 1900s, as national newspapers grew, Theodore Roosevelt developed a unique relationship with the press. He referred to the presidency as a bully pulpit, from which he could speak to the people using his powers of persuasion, and the people would in turn persuade Congress. He sometimes spoke with reporters while getting his morning shave. With his colorful remarks, unique ideas, and vibrant persona, Roosevelt always provided a good story. He and his Cabinet officials distributed speeches and photos to journalists to use in their reports, and he saved the richest pieces of information for his favorite journalists.

State of the Union Address The Constitution requires the president to report to Congress from time to time on the state of the Union. The president explains the economic, military, and social state of the nation, proposes new policies or acts Congress should pass, and explains how he is administering government programs. George Washington and John Adams drafted their first reports and delivered these in person as a speech. Thomas Jefferson broke that pattern, declaring a speech looked too much like a British monarch opening Parliament, so he delivered his report on how the nation was doing in writing, a practice that endured for a century after that.

In 1913, Woodrow Wilson delivered the address in person, thus redefining the report as an event. Since then all presidents have followed suit, taking advantage of the opportunity through the expanding media to reach millions of Americans who listen on the radio, watch on television, or, more recently, stream online. The State of the Union address has become an annual tradition;

both houses of Congress convene in the more-roomy House chamber and receive the president, his Cabinet, and his prepared words for about an hour, typically in late January or early February. Presidents realize they can command a large audience and a few news cycles to follow. Carefully crafted speeches include statistics and sound bites that will help propel presidents' initiatives. Presidents often follow the speech with some appearances in carefully chosen locations in the country. In these appearances, he sells ideas or takes credit for progress his administration has made.

Communications Staff Contemporary presidents have an entire communications office that includes speechwriters and public relations experts. Since the 1930s, the White House has had a day-to-day challenge responding to the 50 or more assigned journalists clamoring for the president's attention.

The expansion of the media has redefined the communications office and role. In the 1930s, Franklin Roosevelt pioneered the radio message with his fireside chats and John F. Kennedy did the first live televised press conferences in the early 1960s. In the White House, speechwriters and wordsmiths are nearly always hard at work. They work to control information coming out of the White House and try to shape the president's message that will ultimately define his policy agenda and its success or failure.

Spin and Manipulation The press conference is in many ways a staged event. Press secretaries and presidents anticipate questions and rehearse in advance with planned answers. President George W. Bush's critics complained that his press relations were an affront to the media. Reporter and media expert Eric Alterman and others reported how the Bush Administration was caught manipulating the news process. The president's administration distributed government-prepared "news reports" to local TV stations across the country to promote his programs, planted a fake reporter in the briefing room to throw softball questions at the president's press secretary, and paid large sums of public money to writers to promote their programs. The most notable example was a payment of $240,000 that went to conservative columnist and radio host Armstrong Williams to promote Bush's No Child Left Behind initiatives.

Modern Technology and a Social Media President

From advances in the printing press to the advent of Twitter, presidents have had to keep pace with technology. From Eisenhower to Clinton, the president could cut into the big three television networks with an announced speech. Now, with the exception of the State of the Union address, many public addresses are aired only by lesser-watched cable TV channels. The 24-hour news cycle is always hungry for headlines. The recent explosion of immediate electronic communication, social media use, push notifications, and the reliance on the Internet for information has transformed how the president communicates with the people to accomplish his policy agenda.

Obama Embraces New Media On his way to the White House, President Obama forecasted his media presence when he hired a 30-year-old "new media director," introduced a Twitter feed, and employed a videographer to upload segments on YouTube and, later, on WhiteHouse.gov. As president, Obama had a 14-member staff on the new White House Office of Digital Strategy, a crew slightly larger than George W. Bush's press secretary's office. By his second term, President Obama had essentially created his own news service, digitally transmitting a stream of photo images, videos, blog posts, and interviews for social media sites for his fans and skeptics alike. Twitter, Facebook, Snapchat, Instagram, and Flickr quickly became standard platforms to broadcast his message.

The Obama team found this digital bully pulpit useful in the constant effort to persuade the citizenry, who could then apply pressure on their representatives in Congress to accomplish the Obama agenda. His White House generated close to 300 infographics supplied with quick and digestible data. They worked hard to successfully compress complex ideas and goals into Twitter bites. They found it useful and easy to target certain audiences with certain messages. In his quest for a health care law and amid the GOP's efforts to stop it, the White House established a "Reality Check" website which debunked rumors about the drawbacks of the health care plan that his opponents were spreading. (For more on Obama's use of digital data, see page 459.)

Image Control Presidents for some decades have employed a taxpayer-funded photographer. Congress has allotted the money for this purpose for the good of the office, to create a record, and to connect people with government. Obama's photographer, Pete Souza, and the new media team used photography in a way to legitimize his presidency, picture him as a man of the people, promote policy programs, and generally chronicle his presidency.

Social media lets presidents communicate directly with the public, daily and inexpensively, in ways that bypass unpredictable decisions of news outlets. Presidents have always tried to streamline, control, or shape information coming out of the White House. Prepared statements, packaged videos, and an avoidance of the press in times of scandal are nothing new. Much like Teddy Roosevelt's efforts of shaping his image with expensive photography more than a century ago, Obama's publicly distributed photos were carefully curated to show the president in a particular light. As photography has become affordable and common among media outlets, independent photojournalists want to show the presidency with their own original images and to tell the full story of the president, not the controlled story.

"Obama [took] unprecedented advantage of the digital revolution in photography," says expert Cara Finnegan in an Illinois News Bureau interview. By the end of his administration, his Flickr feed had more than 6,500 quality and well-chosen images. The public had access to these, and more importantly, they and the news media picked these up and circulated them further. Meanwhile, the White House took steps to prevent independent journalistic photographs, hoping that a greater share of White House-released photos would dominate news websites. The press corps' response revealed a unique relationship between the president and the press. An Associated Press photographer issued an op-ed criticizing the "Orwellian Practice," claiming that the White House "has systematically tried to bypass the media by releasing a sanitized visual record of his activities through official photographs and videos, at the expense of independent journalistic access." The president's press secretary, Jay Carney, found himself bombarded with complaints at his next press conference. "Our problem is access," said correspondent Ann Compton. "You can put out a million pictures a day from the White House photographer, but you bar photos [from Air Force One]." Correspondent Brianna Kieler declared, "Anyone here can tell you, that there's less access than under the Bush Administration." Journalists were chafed because the practice resembles the media strategies of dictators in countries with no free press, ultra cautious and even controlling about how their leaders are portrayed. This issue raised serious concerns for transparency.

In addition to embracing the Internet and new media, Obama made efforts to appear as a guest on late night comedy shows and unique Internet broadcasts. Obama's grand attempts to shape his image and get the citizenry to know him led the *New York Times* to call him "Obama the Omnipresent."

Tweeter in Chief Within his first year in office, President Trump became well known for the use of his Twitter feed to speak directly to the nation. Shortly before taking office, Trump tweeted: "I use Social Media not because I like to, but because it is the only way to fight a VERY dishonest and unfair "press," now often referred to as Fake News Media. Phony and non-existent "sources" are being used more often than ever. Many stories & reports a pure fiction!"

All presidents have a somewhat adversarial relationship with the press, but Trump goes further than most presidents have by disparaging journalists and referring to mainstream media outlets as "fake news." He has broken established presidential communication norms repeatedly, publicly questioned the legitimacy of judges, publicly denounced his own justice department, and tweeted his views on foreign policy without consulting with his advisors.

THINK AS A POLITICAL SCIENTIST: *EVALUATE THE PRESIDENT'S CABINET*

Presidents—and all officials—face big questions every day. Before they can begin to answer such questions, they need to establish *how* to answer them. What are the possible methods and techniques for gathering information and evidence necessary to answer a question? Are there existing studies to research, or should a new study be undertaken? If a new study, how can it be set up to yield appropriate and accurate information? Or should expert opinion be sought? After identifying the various ways to pursue an inquiry, decision-makers must then evaluate those approaches to determine which method or combination of methods will yield the best results.

Students of political science follow the same general approach for identifying and evaluating methods, techniques, and evidence for the inquiries they pursue.

Practice: Suppose you have identified the following inquiry for research: What does the current president's Cabinet reveal about the policy agenda of the president's administration? Before you can begin to answer that, you need to determine the best methods and techniques for finding answers to that question. Begin with some preliminary research by going to the web page of the president's Cabinet at www.whitehouse. gov/administration/cabinet. Select two or three Cabinet secretaries and follow the links to their respective departments. Read their biographies and ask yourself some basic questions: When were they appointed? What line of work were they in before serving the president and heading a department? Did they serve in government or in the private sector? What recent actions have they taken?

Then ask yourself what else you need to know to answer your research inquiry: What do these leaders reveal about the president's administration? Identify several paths to pursue to answer that question. Evaluate them and determine the best approach for gathering the information you need. In a paragraph, summarize the research plan you believe would be most appropriate for addressing your inquiry.

Source: *White House Flickr Feed*

On May 1, 2011, in the White House Situation Room, President Obama (second from left) and Vice President Joe Biden (far left), along with members of the president's cabinet, including Secretary of State Hillary Rodham Clinton (second from right, seated), Secretary of Defense Robert Gates (far right), and members of the national security team, watched a live feed from Navy SEAL helmet cameras as the mission to kill or capture al-Qaeda founder Osama bin Laden unfolded. Bin Laden was killed in the mission.

REFLECT ON THE ESSENTIAL QUESTION

Essential Question: *How does the president use the powers of the executive branch and interact with Congress to implement a policy agenda?* On a separate paper, complete a chart like the one below to gather details to answer that question.

Formal and Informal Powers	Interactions with Congress

KEY TERMS AND NAMES

ambassadors/132

bully pulpit/129

Cabinet/139

chief of staff/141

commander in chief,/130

executive agreement/132

Executive Office of the President (EOP)/141

executive order/135

executive privilege/136

honeymoon period/126

impeachment/122

imperial presidency/123

inherent powers/122

lame duck period/126

line-item veto/130

National Security Council/141

pocket veto/130

Presidential Succession Act (1947)/127

recess appointments/138

signing statements/136

State of the Union/125

stewardship theory/125

Twelfth Amendment/128

Twentieth Amendment/126

Twenty-Second Amendment/126

Twenty-Third Amendment/128

Twenty-Fifth Amendment/127

veto/129

War Powers Act (1973)/131

White House staff/141

Questions 1 and 2 refer to the graph below.

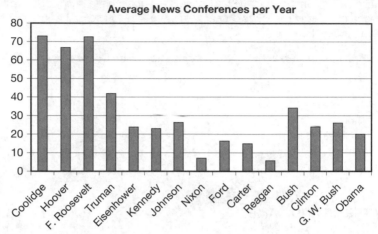

Average News Conferences per Year

Source: *The American Presidency Project*

1. Which of the following statements is supported by the data in the chart?

   (A) Coolidge, Hoover, and Roosevelt were the first to take advantage of televised news conferences.

   (B) The average number of press conferences per year varies from administration to administration.

   (C) Among presidents depicted in the graph, Presidents Nixon and Reagan were the harshest on reporters and the press.

   (D) Presidents who gave more press conferences had higher approval ratings.

2. Which of the following is a potential cause of the trend illustrated in the bar graph with the presidents after Truman?

   (A) As more media platforms have become common, presidents have steadily increased their number of news conferences.

   (B) Recent presidents may be trying to control the information people receive so they have limited press conferences.

   (C) Presidents Nixon and Reagan held fewer press conferences because they were both elected to only one term.

   (D) Press conferences are a product of the television era.

Questions 3 and 4 refer to the following passage.

> The President will be elected to four years and is re-eligible as often as the people of the United States think him worthy of their confidence . . . we must conclude that the permanency of the President's four-year term is less dangerous than a three-year term for the top official in a single state. The president of the United States can be impeached, tried, and, on conviction of bribery, or other high crimes or misdemeanors, removed from office. Afterwards he would be liable to prosecution and punishment in the ordinary course of law.
>
> —Alexander Hamilton, *Federalist No. 69*, 1788

3. Which of the following statements best summarizes the author's argument?
   (A) A president's potential danger is limited because he can serve only a limited number of terms.
   (B) People are protected from a dangerous president by elections every four years and a process the legislature can undertake.
   (C) Congress can imprison the president as any other citizen for crimes.
   (D) An impeached president is forcibly removed from office.

4. Which amendment to the Constitution has made some of the argument in the passage above moot?
   (A) Twenty-Second Amendment
   (B) Twelfth Amendment
   (C) Twentieth Amendment
   (D) Twenty-Fifth Amendment

5. Which of the following is true regarding the impeachment process?
   (A) The House can impeach, but the Supreme Court determines if the impeachment is warranted.
   (B) The vice president and a majority of the Cabinet can impeach a president.
   (C) Impeachment requires such serious wrongdoing that no president has been impeached.
   (D) The House can impeach a president and the Senate can remove a president on conviction of bribery or other high crimes and misdemeanors.

6. Which of the following may the president do to limit the power of Congress?

(A) The president can veto particular items or language in a bill while passing the remainder of the bill.

(B) The president can veto a congressional bill that has passed the House and Senate.

(C) The president can refuse to spend money that Congress has appropriated.

(D) The president can impeach selected members of Congress.

Questions 7 through 9 refer to the passage below.

> . . . Some of those who have entered the United States through our immigration system have proved to be threats to our national security. Since 2001, hundreds of persons born abroad have been convicted of terrorism-related crimes in the United States. . . . the unrestricted entry into the United States of nationals of Iran, Libya, Somalia, Sudan, Syria, and Yemen would be detrimental to the interests of the United States. I therefore direct that the entry into the United States of nationals of those six countries be suspended for 90 days from the effective date of this order, subject to the limitations, waivers, and exceptions set forth . . .
>
> —President Donald Trump, Executive Order, March 6, 2017

7. Which type of power did President Trump exert in issuing this executive order?

(A) Reserved

(B) Formal

(C) Informal

(D) Constitutional

8. Which of the following describes President Trump's perspective in the executive order?

(A) The talents immigrants bring to the United States outweigh the risk of terrorism.

(B) Foreign nationals of all religions may enter the United States.

(C) People who have already immigrated from the named countries may be untrustworthy.

(D) A person's nationality is just one of many influences on behavior.

9. With which statement would supporters of this executive order most likely agree?

(A) The president should signal that refugees are welcome in the United States.

(B) The president should make developing world alliances his top foreign policy priority.

(C) The president should make protecting the nation from foreign terrorism a top priority.

(D) The president should limit immigration regardless of any immigrant's religious identity.

10. Which of the following is an accurate comparison of changes in the scope of the presidency?

	Earlier Presidents	Later Presidents
(A)	Early presidents tended to execute the laws passed by the legislature and serve no more than two terms.	Abraham Lincoln stayed within traditional bounds of the presidency to avoid fomenting regional tensions.
(B)	Teddy Roosevelt's stewardship theory greatly expanded the scope of the presidency.	Modern presidents have scaled back since Teddy Roosevelt to a scope more like that of Washington.
(C)	Times of national stability led to a contraction in presidential scope under James Buchanan.	Times of crisis such as during the Great Depression led to the expansion of the president's powers under Franklin D. Roosevelt.
(D)	The imperial presidency started with James Madison.	The imperial presidency reached its peak with Andrew Jackson.

FREE-RESPONSE QUESTIONS

1. "This morning [Homeland Security] Secretary Napolitano announced new actions my administration will take to mend our Nation's immigration policy to make it more fair, more efficient, and more just, specifically for [young people. These] young people . . . study in our schools, they play in our neighborhoods, they're friends with our kids, they pledge allegiance to our flag. They are Americans in their heart, in their minds, in every single way but one: on paper. They were brought to this country by their parents . . . and often have no idea that they're undocumented . . . Over the next few months, eligible individuals who do not present a risk to national security or public safety will be able to request temporary relief from deportation proceedings and apply for work authorization."

—President Barack Obama, June 15, 2012

After reading the above passage, respond to A, B, and C on the next page:

(A) Describe the presidential power exhibited in the announced policy.

(B) In the context of the scenario, explain how the use of the power described in part A can be affected by interactions between the president and Congress.

(C) In the context of the scenario, explain how the interaction between the president and Congress can be affected by the media.

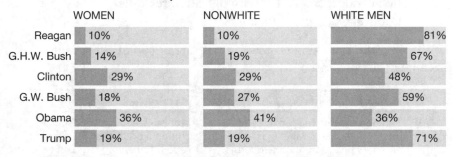

Makeup of Recent Presidential Cabinets

	WOMEN	NONWHITE	WHITE MEN
Reagan	10%	10%	81%
G.H.W. Bush	14%	19%	67%
Clinton	29%	29%	48%
G.W. Bush	18%	27%	59%
Obama	36%	41%	36%
Trump	19%	19%	71%

Notes

— The 22 Cabinet-level positions in the Obama administration (not counting the Vice President) are held constant across all five administrations, except for the Department of Homeland Security, which wasn't established until 2002. We have counted Tom Ridge, the first DHS secretary, as an initial pick for George W. Bush.

— Census Bureau classifications were used for race. Hispanics are counted as nonwhite.

Credit: Meg Anderson, Danielle Kurtzleben and Alejandra Salazar/NPR

2. Use the information graphic to answer the following questions.

(A) Identify the demographic most represented in presidential cabinets.

(B) Describe a difference in the demographic makeup of presidential cabinets, as illustrated in the information graphic, and draw a conclusion about that difference.

(C) Explain how the makeup of the presidential cabinet as shown in the information graphic demonstrates the principle of presidential leadership of the executive branch.

3. When Menachem Zivotofsky was born in Jerusalem in 2002 to U.S. citizen parents, the United States regarded Jerusalem as neutral territory. In its effort to treat Jerusalem as part of Israel, President George W. Bush signed the Foreign Relations Authorization Act (FRRA) in 2002. Part of that Act specified that the birth certificate and passport of U.S. citizens born in Jerusalem could list Israel as their place of birth, if desired. Menachem's parents asked that their son's place of birth be listed as "Jerusalem, Israel" but the State Department refused and would only agree to the neutral "Jerusalem" as the birth

location. Zivotofsky's family sued the State Department in response. After a series of lower court decisions, the case reached the U.S. Supreme Court as *Zivotofsky v. John Kerry, Secretary of State.* The question the Court considered was whether that part of the FRRA that recognized Jerusalem as part of Israel took away the power of the president to decide if and how to recognize foreign nations. The Court held that the clause in Article II that empowers the president to receive foreign ambassadors and implies the power to recognize nations conflicts with that part of the FRRA requiring that Jerusalem be treated as part of Israel and was therefore unconstitutional.

(A) Identify the constitutional principle that is common to both *Zivotofsky v. Kerry* and *Marbury v. Madison* (1803).
(See page 199.)

(B) Based on the constitutional principle identified in part A, explain a difference in the impact on interactions between the branches of government in *Zivotofsky v. Kerry* and *Marbury v. Madison.*

(C) Describe an action the president could have taken to limit Congress from assuming a foreign relations power constitutionally granted to the president.

4. Develop an argument that explains whether or not the powers of the presidency as executed since the Great Depression have made the presidency a dangerous office.

In your essay, you must:

- Articulate a defensible claim or thesis that responds to the prompt and establishes a line of reasoning
- Support your claim with at least TWO pieces of accurate and relevant information:
  - At least ONE piece of evidence must be from one of the following foundational documents:
    - *Federalist No. 70*
    - Article II of the Constitution
  - Use a second piece of evidence from another foundational document from the list above or from your study of the presidency
- Use reasoning to explain why your evidence supports your claim/thesis
- Respond to an opposing or alternative perspective using refutation, concession, or rebuttal

Use the style conventions of political science when answering your questions. For example, Supreme Court cases are italicized when they appear in print. If you are writing by hand, underline them. Use a small v. with a period for "versus." When citing a constitutional provision, name the parts in order (Article I, Section 8, for example), or describe it in enough detail so it will be easily understood (the Fourteenth Amendment's equal protection clause, for example, or the Fourteenth Amendment's due process clause).

Source: *Official White House Photo by Shealah Craighead*

President Donald Trump delivered his first State of the Union address in January 2018.

5

The Bureaucracy

*"Are you laboring under the impression that I read
these memoranda of yours? I can't even lift them."*

—attributed to President Franklin Delano Roosevelt to an appointed bureaucrat

Essential Question: How does the bureaucracy carry out laws, implement
policy, and interact with the executive, legislative, and
judicial branches?

The federal government provides many services, such as maintaining interstate
highways, coordinating air traffic at airports, protecting borders, enforcing laws,
and delivering mail. For each of these services, Congress has passed a law and
created one or more executive branch departments or agencies to carry out the
responsibilities of government. The federal bureaucracy is the vast, hierarchical
organization of executive branch employees—close to 3 million people ranging
from members of the president's Cabinet to accountants at the Internal Revenue
Service—that takes care of the federal government's business. Within the
bureaucracy are the men and women who serve the U.S. military, the largest group
in the executive branch. Currently, the *Federal Register*—the federal government's
official journal of regulations, proposed regulations, and public notices—lists 441
total executive branch entities that carry out the nation's business.

Sometimes referred to as the "fourth branch of government," the bureaucracy
is composed of experts with specialized roles and some with unique authority.
These include soldiers, tax collectors, and letter carriers. Others are regulators and
policymakers with unique authority but with questionable accountability. Additional
personnel support the federal system from the private sector or as employees of
state and local governments who are paid with federal funds and guided by federal
directives.

The bureaucracy has grown from a four-man council and a few hundred
employees at the nation's founding to a massive administration of expansive
programs. (See page 162.) George Washington established the first Cabinet
by appointing an attorney general and secretaries of state, treasury, and war.
Congress created a military, a coast guard, and a postal system, thereby creating
many quality federal jobs for President Washington to fill. As the nation has
grown, so have its responsibilities. The bureaucracy has transitioned from an old-
boy network system of political patronage to a professionalized institution with
traits of specialization and some political neutrality.

Makeup and Tasks of the Bureaucracy

Today's bureaucracy is a product of 200 years of increased public expectation and increased federal responsibilities. The professionals who head the departments and agencies, and their many subordinates, carry out the tasks and responsibilities of government. They assure the executive agenda and congressional mandates are implemented or followed. These bureaucrats and their government structures touch every issue involving the nation and provide countless services to U.S. citizens. Like all bureaucracies, such as those in large corporations and financial institutions, the federal bureaucracy is characterized by hierarchies, a distinct division of labor or specialization, and highly tailored rules.

A Hierarchy of Bureaucrats

Federal bureaucrats include anyone in the executive branch carrying out some decision or applying some law. Bureaucrats sit on the president's Cabinet, and they work in regional offices throughout the country. In fact, only 10 percent of federal workers are employed in Washington, D.C. Some bureaucrats are upper-level problem solvers and administrators. Others are lawyers, doctors, and educators. Still others are plumbers, carpenters, and drivers. Many lower-level bureaucrats must follow heavily scripted routines to assure consistency in government's application of the law.

Cabinet Secretaries and Deputies Although employment in the federal bureaucracy uses a merit system (see page 168), presidents still name friends and campaign managers to upper-level White House jobs as well as to Cabinet and subcabinet positions that require Senate confirmation. President John F. Kennedy named his brother, Robert, as the nation's attorney general. Barack Obama brought with him from Chicago the city superintendent of schools to serve as his secretary of education. President Donald Trump named fellow New York financiers and Wall Street moguls to direct economic agencies.

Most presidents appoint more than 2,000 upper-level management positions, deputy secretaries, and bureau chiefs who are the leaders and spokespeople for the executive branch. Many of these people tend to be in the president's party and have experience in a relevant field of government or the private sector.

The Cabinet historically has been a place for political appointees. Former senators, governors, and other elected officials accepted Cabinet posts when they lost re-election. Since the mid 1900s, the Cabinet has become a place for academics, university presidents, and other experts. For example, President John Kennedy appointed Ford Motor Company CEO Robert McNamara as his secretary of defense.

An "old boy" network of federal officers, mostly white males, dominates these upper level posts. They tend to go in and out of government depending on which party controls the White House.

President Nixon's administration had sizable numbers of African-American appointees, especially in the more liberal agencies in which Nixon allowed directors to select subcabinet appointees. However, only three percent of Nixon appointees were women. Nearly 20 years later, roughly 27 percent of the appointees of George H. W. Bush (1989–1993) were women.

The upper-level executives tend to come from privileged backgrounds. It is no mystery, then, that top-level appointees come from prestigious universities. Most fathers of presidential appointees had worked in managerial or professional jobs. Roughly 72 percent of appointees have some postgraduate training and advanced degrees.

Comparisons of top-appointed federal officials with those in the top ranks of the private sector reveal that officials in government earn considerably lower salaries. Private sector leaders earned 15 to 16 times as much as their government counterparts. Department and agency leaders are 50 percent more likely to have attended graduate school than top corporate executives, and they are three times as likely to have a Ph.D.

When a new position is created, bureaucrats recommend and recruit some of their own people who have experience in that area. This is called a name-request job, a job for which those doing the hiring already have someone in mind. Additionally, members of Congress will contribute to this process by recommending a colleague who can fit this position.

According to the U.S. **Office of Personnel Management (OPM)**, "The federal workforce is diverse, and the demographics are similar to that of the overall labor force." However, as of 2014, there were about 14 percent more men than women. About a third of federal employees were minorities, with African-Americans making up the largest portion (18 percent) of these minority workers. And nearly 9 percent of federal workers have a disability.

Competitive Service The **competitive service** includes those merit-based jobs that require some type of exam or competitive hiring process. Foreign Service officers, the State Department workers who represent the United States abroad, for example, must pass a challenging and competitive test. The **excepted service** includes the non-tested jobs, providing hiring options when the competitive service is not practical. The ratio of competitive versus excepted positions in the civilian bureaucracy has fluctuated with different laws and different presidents. In recent years, the two groups have been about even.

Organizations

The executive hierarchy is a vast structure of governing bodies headed by these professional bureaucrats. They include departments, agencies, commissions, and a handful of private-public organizations known as government corporations.

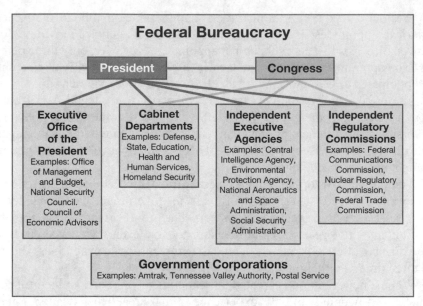

Federal Bureaucracy

President — **Congress**

Executive Office of the President
Examples: Office of Management and Budget, National Security Council, Council of Economic Advisors

Cabinet Departments
Examples: Defense, State, Education, Health and Human Services, Homeland Security

Independent Executive Agencies
Examples: Central Intelligence Agency, Environmental Protection Agency, National Aeronautics and Space Administration, Social Security Administration

Independent Regulatory Commissions
Examples: Federal Communications Commission, Nuclear Regulatory Commission, Federal Trade Commission

Government Corporations
Examples: Amtrak, Tennessee Valley Authority, Postal Service

Congress creates the various elements within the federal bureaucracy, but they are administered through the executive branch. However, parts of the executive bureaucracy—independent executive agencies, independent regulatory commissions, and government corporations— are not directly supervised by the president.

Departments The president oversees the executive branch through a structured system of 15 departments. Newer departments include Energy, Veterans Affairs, and Homeland Security. Departments have been renamed and divided into multiple departments. The largest department is by far the Department of Defense.

Each Cabinet secretary directs a department. At formal Cabinet meetings, the secretaries sit in seats based on the age of their department, with the oldest departments seated closest to the president. Though different secretaries handle different issues, and surely have different pressures and workloads, they are all paid the same salary.

Agencies The departments contain agencies that divide the departments' goals and workload. In addition to the term *agency*, these subunits may be referred to as divisions, bureaus, offices, services, administrations, and boards. The Department of Homeland Security houses the Immigration and Customs Enforcement (ICE), the Coast Guard, and the Transportation Security Administration (TSA). These agencies deal with protecting the country and its citizens. There are hundreds of agencies, many of which have headquarters in Washington, D.C., and regional offices in large U.S. cities. The president appoints the head of each agency, typically referred to as the "director." Most directors serve under a president during a four or eight year term. Some serve longer terms as defined in the statute that creates the agency.

FEDERAL DEPARTMENTS	
Department	Established
Department of State	1789
Department of Treasury	1789
Department of Defense	1789
Department of Interior	1849
Department of Agriculture	1862
Department of Justice	1870
Department of Commerce	1903
Department of Labor	1913
Department of Veterans Affairs	1930
Department of Health, Education, and Welfare, later divided into Department of Education (1979) and Department of Health and Human Services (1980)	1953
Department of Housing and Urban Development	1965
Department of Transportation	1967
Department of Energy	1979
Department of Homeland Security	2002

One of the most notable agencies is the FBI—the **Federal Bureau of Investigation**. This Justice Department law enforcement agency first dealt with immigration violations, national banking, and antitrust violations. Then interstate crimes—transporting stolen property, bank robbery, and fraudulent schemes—became federal crimes. Today, the FBI also works with state and local law enforcement to find America's most wanted criminals. The bureau also helps to track and uncover terrorist organizations that threaten the United States.

After Congress began to tax individual incomes, it then established an agency to collect the taxes. Originally named the Bureau of Internal Revenue, the Internal Revenue Service is the nation's tax collector within the Treasury Department. Its mission is to help Americans understand and fulfill their tax responsibilities and to enforce the tax code fairly. With its Criminal Investigation Division, the IRS also prosecutes those who evade their taxes. The statutes that create these bodies require that they are staffed fairly with members of both major parties.

EXECUTIVE BRANCH ORGANIZATION
• **Cabinet-Level Departments:** 15 departments, plus others the president names to the Cabinet
• **Agencies Within Departments** (selected): Coast Guard in Homeland Security; FBI in the Justice Department
• **Independent Agencies** (selected): NASA and the Postal Service
• **Independent Agencies and Regulatory Commissions** (selected): EPA, FCC, FEC
• **Government Corporations** (selected): Amtrak and Federal Deposit Insurance Corporation (FDIC)

Independent Agencies and Commissions Cabinet agencies and purely executive agencies have one head. Independent agencies have a body (board or commission) that consists of five to seven members. Members of these boards and commissions have staggered terms to ensure that a president cannot completely replace them with his own cronies. Such an action would make the agencies and commissions political rather than neutral.

SELECTED INDEPENDENT REGULATORY AGENCIES AND COMMISSIONS	
Organization	**Established**
Interstate Commerce Commission	1887
Federal Reserve System	1913
Federal Trade Commission	1914
Federal Communications Commission	1934
Securities and Exchange Commission	1934
Federal Aviation Administration	1948
Environmental Protection Agency	1970

Government corporations are a hybrid of a government agency and a private company. These started to appear in the 1930s, and they usually come into being when the government wants to overlap with the private sector. Some examples of these government corporations are listed on the next page.

Source: *David Gubler*

The California Zephyr, once run by private railroads, is an Amtrak train now. After President Dwight Eisenhower enacted the Interstate Highway System in 1956, travel by car became very popular and the railroad decline worsened.

Tasks

When Congress creates the departments and agencies in the executive branch, it defines the organization's mission and empowers it to carry out that mission. The legislature gives the departments broad goals, as they administer several agencies and a large number of bureaucrats within those departments. Agencies have more specific goals while the independent regulatory agencies have an even more unique responsibility in their law-enforcement mission and are protected by their bureaucratic structure and several notable Supreme Court decisions, including *Chevron v. Natural Resources Defense Council* (page 178).

Writing and Enforcing Regulations The legislation that creates and defines the departments and agencies often gives wide latitude as to how they administer the law. Though all executive branch organizations have a degree of discretion in how they carry out the law, the independent regulatory agencies and commissions have even greater leeway and power to shape and enforce national policies. The laws that create and define these agencies are often vague, and the directors of these agencies and the appointed officials who sit on their boards or commissions are more removed from political pressures than the heads of the departments and the agencies that fall within the departments.

Take, for example, the chief passage from the 1970 Clean Water Act that charged the Environmental Protection Agency (EPA) to enforce it:

> "The nation's waters should be free of pollutants in order to protect the health of our citizens and preserve natural habitats. Individuals or companies shall not pollute the nation's water. If they do, they will be fined or jailed in accordance with the law. The EPA shall set pollution standards and shall have the authority to make rules necessary to carry out this Act."

Few of the 535 legislators who helped pass this act are experts in the environmental sciences. So they delegated this authority to the EPA and keep in contact with the agency to assure that this mission is accomplished.

Many additional independent agencies have a regulatory capacity. Congress has vested regulatory authority in agencies, commissions, and boards to oversee or regulate certain industries or concerns. They can make narrow, industry-specific regulations, and they can adjudicate (process and punish) violators. In a sense, these executive branch bodies have powers normally held by the legislature and the judiciary.

Enforcement and Fines Like a court, the agencies, commission, and boards within the bureaucracy can impose fines or other punishments. This administrative adjudication targets industries or companies, not individual citizens. For example, the federal government collected civil penalties paid in connection with the 2010 Deepwater Horizon oil spill ranging from about $400 million in fiscal year 2013 to about $160 million in fiscal year 2016.

One key aspect of enforcement is **compliance monitoring**, making sure the firms and companies that are subject to industry regulations are following those standards and provisions. The Environmental Protection Agency monitors for compliance in several ways. It assesses and documents compliance, requiring permits for certain activities. It collects measurable scientific evidence by taking water or air samples near a factory to measure the amount of pollutants or emissions coming from the factory. After an EPA decision or ruling, the agency checks whether those subject to the ruling are following it. Officials and regulators of the EPA also go back to the rule writers about the successes or failures of the rules and procedures to either assure fairness in future rules or to tighten them up.

Testifying Before Congress Federal employees in the many departments, agencies, commissions, and boards within the bureaucracy are often experts in their field. For this reason, they frequently appear before congressional committees to provide expert testimony. For example, former FBI Director James Comey testified before the Senate Intelligence Committee in June of 2017 about matters related to his bureau's investigation into Russian interference in the presidential election of 2016. In September of 2017, Deputy Secretary of State John L. Sullivan testified before the House Committee on Foreign Affairs to discuss a redesign of the State Department. The Secretary of Veterans Affairs, the Honorable David J. Shulkin, M.D., testified before the Senate Veterans Affairs Committee in the same month to address the problem of suicide among veterans.

Iron Triangles and Issue Networks Over time, congressional committees and agencies become well acquainted. Lawmakers and leaders in the executive branch may have worked together in the past. At the same time, interest groups target agencies for pressing their agendas. Industry, especially, creates political action committees (PACs) to impact policy and its success. These special interests meet with and make donations to members of Congress as elections near. They also meet with bureaucrats during the rule-making process (see page 170) in an ongoing effort to shape rules that affect them.

The relationship among these three entities—an agency, a congressional committee, and an interest group—is called an **iron triangle** because the three-way interdependent relationships are so strong. The three points of the triangle join forces to create policy. Iron triangles establish tight relationships that are collectively beneficial. Bureaucrats have an incentive to cooperate with congressional members who fund and direct them. Committee members have an incentive to pay attention to interest groups that reward them with PAC donations. Interest groups and agencies generally are out to advance similar goals from the start.

More recently, scholars have observed the power and influence of **issue networks**. Issue networks include committee staffers (often the experts and authors of legislation), academics, think tanks, advocates, interest groups, and/or members of the media. These experts and stakeholders—sometimes at odds with one another on matters unrelated to the issue they are addressing—collaborate to create specific policy on one issue. The policymaking web has grown because of so many overlapping issues, the proliferation of interest groups, and the influence of industry. **BIG IDEA:** Multiple actors and institutions interact to produce and implement possible policies.

From Spoils to Merit

For the bureaucracy to do its job well, federal employees need to be professional, specialized, and politically neutral. Reforms over the years have helped create an environment in which those goals can be achieved.

In the early days of the nation, the bureaucracy became a place to reward loyal party leaders with federal jobs, a practice known as **patronage**. When Jefferson took office in 1801 atop a developing party organization, for example, he filled every vacancy with a member of his party until achieving a balance of Federalists and Jeffersonians.

The growing impact of political parties caused a "rotation system" of appointments regardless of merit or performance. The outgoing president's appointees left with him. On Andrew Jackson's Inauguration Day in 1829, job-hungry mobs pushed into the White House, snatching refreshments as aggressively as they sought patronage jobs. Congressmen began recommending fellow party members, and senators—with advice and consent power—asserted their influence on the process.

The U.S. Post Office became the main agency for the president to run party machinery. Nearly every city had a branch office, creating an established organizational hierarchy across the United States. Presidents appointed regional and local postmasters based on their efforts to help elect the presidents and with an expectation of loyalty after the appointment. This patronage system became known as the **spoils system**.

The Civil War and its aftermath brought an even greater need for bureaucracy, an enlarged federal staff, and, ultimately, an opportunity for corruption in government. By the 1870s, the spoils system, including a high degree of nepotism, was thoroughly entrenched in state and federal politics.

Considering Merit

The desire for the best government rather than a government of friends and family became a chief concern among certain groups and associations. Moral-based movements such as emancipation, temperance, and women's suffrage also encouraged taming or dismantling the spoils system. Reformers called for candidate appointments based on merit, skill, and experience.

In 1870, Congress passed a law that authorized the president to create rules and regulations for a civil service. The system, the law said, would "best promote the efficiency thereof, and ascertain the fitness of each candidate in respect to age, health, character, knowledge, and ability."

Reformers' efforts temporarily faded, however, until a murder of national consequence brought attention back to the issue. Soon after James Garfield was sworn in as president in 1881, an eccentric named Charles Guiteau began insisting Garfield appoint him to a political office. Garfield denied his requests. On July 2, only three months into the president's term, Guiteau shot Garfield twice as he was about to board a train. Garfield lay wounded for months before he finally died.

Garfield's assassination brought attention to the extreme cases of patronage and encouraged more comprehensive legislation. Congress passed the **Pendleton Civil Service Act** in 1883 to prevent the constant reward to loyal party members. The law ultimately created the **merit system**, which included competitive, written exams for many job applicants. The law also created a bipartisan **Civil Service Commission** to oversee the process and prevented officers from requiring federal employees to contribute to political campaigns.

The establishment of the civil service and an attempt by the U.S. government during the Industrial Era (1876–1900) to regulate the economy and care for the needy brought about the modern administrative state. The bureaucratic system became stocked with qualified experts dedicated to their federal jobs. These workers served across administrations to create continuity and expertise that professionalized the institution.

The federal government began more frequently to legislate on business and corporations. In 1887, the government created its first regulatory commission, the Interstate Commerce Commission, to enforce federal law regarding train travel and products traveling across state lines. As the Industrial Age became the Progressive Era (1890–1920), the departments of Commerce and Labor were developed, ostensibly at cross-purposes. The Pure Food and Drug Act (1906) brought attention to the meatpacking industry and other industries producing consumable goods, and thus agencies were created to address these concerns. The Sixteenth Amendment (1913), which gave Congress the power to collect taxes on income, put more money into Treasury coffers, which helped the federal bureaucracy expand.

Over the next several decades, the United States survived two world wars and an economic depression that resulted in an entirely new view of government's administrative role. New Deal programs of the 1930s gave the government more responsibility and worked to strengthen the Democratic Party in ways the Pendleton Act was meant to prevent. The Pendleton Act placed only a segment of the federal civilian workforce under an examination system. Leading federal officeholders across the country were still wrapped up in politics. At the 1936 Democratic National Convention, a majority of the delegates were postmasters, U.S. marshals, revenue collectors, or close relatives.

Republicans joined reform-minded Democrats to create another regulation meant to curb the overlap of politics and profession. Congress passed statutes in 1939 and 1940 that are collectively referred to as the **Hatch Act.** Sponsored by Democratic Senator Carl Hatch of New Mexico, the law distanced federal employees, as well as state employees paid with federal funds, from politics. It prohibits federal workers from becoming directly involved in federal political campaigns. The law, however, interfered with the First Amendment rights of free speech and free association. The Hatch Act was criticized on these grounds and was eventually softened by the Federal Employees Political Activities Act of 1993. Today, federal employees cannot use their official position to influence or interfere in an election. They cannot engage in political activity while on duty, while using a government vehicle, or while in official uniform. They can, however, express opinions about candidates, contribute to a campaign fund, join political parties, and attend political functions after hours.

Movements and Modernizing

In the 1960s laws that ensured the equal rights of minorities and women brought on the need for new offices to guarantee them. The Justice Department established the Office of Civil Rights and later the Equal Employment Opportunity Commission. A push for consumer rights and product safety led Congress to create the Consumer Product Safety Commission. Concerns for clean air and water brought about the establishment of the Environmental Protection Agency.

President Jimmy Carter ran for office in 1976 promising to change Washington and to reform the bureaucracy. With experience as an engineer and as a governor, he spent much time analyzing systems. He tinkered with the structure of the federal government as much as any other president. What became the **Civil Service Reform Act (**1978) altered how a bureaucrat is dismissed, limited preferences for veterans in hopes of balancing the genders in federal employment, and put upper-level appointments back into the president's hands.

The law also created the **Senior Executive Service,** a system that placed more emphasis on a bureaucrat's skills and experiences than on the job. The administration paid the recruited and incoming senior executives a standard salary, but the president had the right to move these officials laterally or put them in a lesser job with no loss of pay. Carter's reforms increased managerial flexibility and gave political leaders the tools to carve and mold the Senior Executive Service.

Office of Personnel Management The Civil Service Commission established by the Pendleton Act operated until the 1978 reforms replaced it with the **Office of Personnel Management (OPM)**. The OPM runs the merit system and coordinates the federal application process for jobs and hiring. The OPM's goals include promoting the ideals of public service, finding the best people for federal jobs, and preserving merit system principles. Many of the larger, more established agencies do their own hiring.

Delegated Discretionary Authority

Much as a local police chief might instruct her officers on how to enforce speed limits or jaywalking, federal executive branch officers can shape the enforcement of policy through instruction, directives, and personal interpretation of the laws. They have this power through the delegation of **discretionary authority**: Congress has granted departments, agencies, bureaus, and commissions—staffed with experts in their field—varying degrees of discretion in developing rules and interpreting legislation.

Rule Making

The constitutional basis for bureaucratic departments or agencies stems from Congress's power to create and empower them. Congress also guides and funds them. The legislative branch decides on the broad principles for law; the details emerge during debate over policies. However, Congress leaves the specific regulations for implementing the policy up to the members of the bureaucracy.

Depending on its discretionary authority, any executive branch agency may have the power or influence to make decisions and to take, or not take, courses of action. Congress has given the executive branch significant authority in three ways, by (1) creating agencies to pay subsidies to groups, such as farmers or Social Security recipients; (2) creating a system to distribute federal dollars going to the states, such as grant programs (page 51); and (3) giving many federal offices the ability to devise and enforce regulations for various industries or issues. This quasi-legislative power enables the Federal Communications Commission, for example, to determine what is indecent for televised broadcasts and enables the EPA to define factory emission standards.

As laws are made in a public manner, the agency rule making process and schedule must also be available to the public in advance to allow relevant players to participate in the process. Company representatives or concerned citizens can submit arguments or appear and testify before a commission, much as an expert might appear before a congressional committee.

EXAMPLES OF DISCRETIONARY AUTHORITY IN SELECT DEPARTMENTS	
Homeland Security	Allowing certain exemptions for immigrants
Transportation	Determining which highway projects get special grants
Veterans Affairs	Deciding how to administer a health program for veterans
Education	Cancelling or lowering student debt
Environmental Protection Agency	Intervening in state environmental issues
Securities and Exchange Commission	Determining if financial firms should be disqualified from raising money because of illegal conduct

Perhaps more familiar are the rules established by the Transportation Security Administration, the agency in the Department of Homeland Security that monitors passengers boarding airplanes. Who will be searched and how? These procedures change from time to time as the government finds new reasons to ban certain items from flights or to soften an overly strict list. The chief lawmaking body, Congress, with its complex lawmaking procedures and necessary debates, cannot keep up with the day-to-day changes in policies and procedures so it entrusts the TSA to monitor the airlines and empowers it to make rules to keep passengers safe.

Interpreting Policy

In addition to rule making, departments and agencies in the federal bureaucracy have latitude in interpreting policy. For example, Secretary of Homeland Security Janet Napolitano (2009–2013) issued a directive declaring that agencies in her department would neither arrest nor deport illegal immigrants who had come into the United States as children, those covered under the proposed (but not enacted) **D**evelopment, **R**elief, and **E**ducation of **A**lien **M**inors (DREAM) Act. She issued the directive with the full support of her boss, President Obama, yet her declaration brought a firestorm of controversy. Was this in violation of basic law—aren't undocumented immigrants illegal regardless of how old they were upon entering the U.S.? Like the local police chief who suggested not ticketing motorists driving a mere two miles over the speed limit, the president and his departments can enforce the law with some discretion, as Napolitano and Obama demonstrated with the DREAMers.

In a similar way, in 2013, Attorney General Eric Holder announced the Obama administration's revised approach to enforcing marijuana violations. In doing so, he did not rewrite the law. Holder did, however, declare that the Justice Department would not use federal resources to crack down on selling or using the drug in states where voters had democratically deemed marijuana legal.

During the Trump Administration, the Department of Justice under Attorney General Jeff Sessions declared that local U.S. attorneys—those presidentially appointed prosecutors who bring federal crime cases to court in their districts across the country—shall be the local determiners of how federal marijuana policy is handled. In fact, the Justice Department attorneys and the FBI deal with a variety of federal crimes on a daily basis and decide whether to prosecute and which crimes are higher on their priority list. This inconsistency from administration to administration may be confusing and destabilizing to some, but it is an inevitable element of administrative discretion.

Holding the Bureaucracy Accountable

It is often difficult to determine who is ultimately responsible for any bureaucratic decision. Congress creates the big-picture laws and some of the regulations. The president shapes the departments and agencies when appointing Cabinet secretaries and agency directors, who have discretionary authority. Challenges to department directives and agency rulings come in the courts, which may uphold or overrule the executive branch body while interest groups and industry try to influence regulations and their enforcement. With so many players interacting with these executive branch sub-units, it is difficult to tell to whom the bureaus, administrations, and offices are beholden.

Also, in trying to follow prescribed law, these executive branch bodies still face political constraints and challenges despite their discretionary latitude. Cabinet secretaries serve at the pleasure of the president but have to please many people, including, to some degree, their subordinates and staff in the field carrying out the law. These secretaries and their employees report to Congress and thus must please legislative members, especially for funds.

Congressional Oversight

The bureaucracy's discretion in rule-making authority raises many questions. Does it violate the separation of powers doctrine? How democratic is it for a handful of experts to create rules that entire industries must follow? Is due process followed when an agency fines an individual or company for violating a policy for which no elected representative voted and on which no American court ruled?

In part to address these questions, Congress passed the Administrative Procedures Act (APA) in 1946 to better guide agencies in developing their policies. The APA assures that those who will be governed by a policy can have input into shaping it. There must be a notice-and-comment opportunity for citizens to voice concerns about proposed regulations.

Committee Hearings Congress also has a responsibility to assure that the agencies and departments charged with carrying out the ideas in the law are in fact doing so, and doing so fairly. Congressional oversight is essentially a check and balance on the agencies themselves and over the president's influence of them. With some regularity, House and Senate committees hold oversight hearings to address agency action, inaction, or their relationship with the agency.

The list of standing House and Senate committees parallels a list of notable agencies. For example, the House Committee on Homeland Security has jurisdiction over the department of the same name. The Senate Committee on Agriculture, Nutrition, and Forestry oversees the National Parks Service, which is part of the Department of the Interior. Committees and subcommittees receive reports from directors and call the directors to testify. Cabinet secretaries, agency directors, and other ranking bureaucrats testify before the relevant committee. Sometimes these are routine and collegial encounters that allow for the agency or department to update Congress on how it is doing, what goals it has accomplished, or what plans it may have. At other times, the committee with authority will call a hearing to get to the bottom of a thorny issue. A few years ago, for example, the Veterans Affairs Department showed some serious mismanagement and failures in its quest to serve U.S. military

Nuclear Regulatory Commission (NRC) Chair Allison Macfarlane, far left, and (left to right) Commissioners Kristine Svinicki, William Magwood and William Ostendorf appear before the joint House Energy and Commerce subcommittees on July 24, 2012, to answer questions ranging from commission voting procedures to various aspects of safe disposal of nuclear waste.

veterans. Primary among the allegations were long wait times at VA hospitals to get medical attention and bureaucrats falsifying records. One report alleged that the average wait time for an appointment was 115 days. The poorly organized operation resulted in a congressional investigation of the department and the resignation of the Veterans Affairs secretary.

Power of the Purse In addition to general oversight, Congress determines how much funding these organizations receive, asks top-level bureaucrats how they can improve their goals, and sometimes tries to constrain agencies. With the power of the purse, Congress can determine the financial state of an agency and its success when it allocates money. The agency cannot spend public funds until a committee or subcommittee first passes **authorization of spending** measures. These measures state the maximum amount the agency can spend on certain programs. The distribution of money defined in such an authorization may be a one-time allotment of funds, or it could be a recurring annual allotment. The agency will not receive the actual funds until each house's appropriations committee and the full chamber also approve the spending. These **appropriations** are typically made annually as part of the federal budget.

A few agencies do not require a congressional appropriation. The Federal Reserve Board actually makes money through its system of charging interest to commercial banks. The Postal Service is also self-sufficient. Others charge fees and fines that supplement their operating costs. These agencies are a little less beholden to Congress, at least when it comes to asking for money.

The Final Say Congress and agencies share a good deal of authority. This sharing has created an unclear area of jurisdiction. One procedure that has developed to sort out any overlap is *committee clearance*. Some congressional committees have secured the authority to review and approve certain agency actions in advance. Few executive branch leaders will ignore the actions the congressional committee requests, knowing the same committee determines its funding.

Congress established the legislative veto in the 1930s to control executive agencies. The **legislative veto** is a requirement that certain agency decisions must wait for a defined period of either 30 or 90 days. During the conflict in Vietnam, Congress used the legislative veto to put some limits on the deployment of military activity. But the public interest groups that had fought to create regulatory agencies in the 1960s watched agencies' lawful decisions being stopped by one or the other house of Congress.

So when the opportunity arose for a case challenging the constitutionality of the legislative veto, Public Citizen, a group advocating for citizen protections and the separation of powers, used its litigation services to eventually bring it before the Supreme Court. The case centered on Jagdish Chadha, born in British-controlled Kenya, who immigrated to the United States in the 1960s to study. When his U.S. visa expired, neither Britain nor Kenya, which had gained independence from Britain in 1963, would accept him, so he applied for permanent residency in the United States. The Immigration and Naturalization Service (INS) approved his application. Two years later, the House rejected it through a legislative veto.

Chadha sued to retain his U.S. residency. Chadha's fight to remain in the United States became a power play between the president and Congress over the constitutionality of the legislative veto. In *INS v. Chadha* (1983), the Supreme Court sided with Chadha and against Congress's use of this procedure. The veto was intended only for the president, not the legislative branch. The Court stated that when the House rejected Chadha's application, it exercised a judicial function by expressing its opinion on the application of a law, something reserved for the courts. The Court ruled against Congress's use of the legislative veto as a violation of separation of powers. Since then, informal compromises between agencies and congressional committees have proven successful in working out differences.

The President and the Bureaucracy

Departments and agencies must compete with others for funding and for the president's ear. Similar departments and agencies have overlapping goals. They all contend that with more money they could better complete their missions.

At the same time, the president exerts authority and influence to make sure the executive ideology is carried out in policy. Through the regulatory review process, administered through the **Office of Information and Regulatory**

Affairs (OIRA), all regulations that have a significant effect on the economy, public health, and other major aspects of policy undergo close review. Any regulations that conflict with the president's agenda may be questioned, revised, and even eliminated.

In 2017, during the Trump administration, the Federal Communications Commission rolled back the regulations covering oversight of Internet providers, often referred to as "net neutrality." This rollback lifted regulations from the Obama Administration that required cable and telecommunications companies to treat all web traffic equally. The deregulation was part of President Trump's ideology—as in other areas, he called for the government to reduce regulation on business so that businesses could grow and prosper in a freer marketplace.

Competition The different beliefs or approaches of executive departments can create friction between them when the United States must state a position or make a decision. The departments of State and Defense, for example, have had differences on foreign policy. The Department of State is the diplomatic wing of the government; the Department of Defense trains the military and prepares the country for armed conflict. These differing perspectives can make the development of coherent goals challenging.

Law enforcement agencies sometimes cooperate to find criminals, but they are also protective of their methods and desire credit in a way that breeds dissension. The lack of information sharing among the government's many intelligence agencies before September 11 likely increased the terrorists' chances of a successful and unexpected attack.

Sometimes upper-level bureaucrats get caught between their boss and the many people who work for them. The president's policy goals may not take into account some of the practical constraints of the bureaucracy and as a result may be too difficult to achieve. An appointed bureaucrat may therefore "go native" by siding with his or her own department or agency instead of with the president. Going native is a risky proposition, and many who have publicly disagreed with the president have been replaced. Presidents have at times rotated appointees from agency to agency to assure loyalty to the administration.

Federal employees sometimes see corruption or inefficiency in their offices but are tempted to keep quiet. Exposing illegal or improper government activities can lead to reprisals from those in the organization or retaliation that can lead to their termination. However, citizens in a democracy want transparency in government and often encourage such exposure. That is why Congress passed the **Whistleblower Protection Act** in 1989, which prohibits a federal agency from retaliating or threatening an employee for disclosing acts that he or she believes were illegal or dishonest.

Presidential Goals and Streamlining The bureaucracy can be either an impediment or a vehicle for fulfilling presidential goals. When the bureaucracy works against or impedes the administration's ideas and goals, presidents are encouraged to shake up or restructure the system. Presidents have used both their formal powers, such as the power to appoint officials, and their informal powers, such as persuasion and leadership, to make the bureaucracy work for their executive agenda.

Presidents have also tried to curb bureaucratic waste. President Ronald Reagan, who arrived in Washington in 1981, stated in his inaugural address, "Government is not the solution to our problem; government is the problem." To gain greater control over departments and agencies, he put people who agreed with the Reagan agenda into top positions. He sought officials who would show loyalty to the White House and reduce administrative personnel.

President Clinton promised early in his administration to address government inefficiency. However, he used a more careful tone than his predecessors did, conveying that problems in a large administration came not from bureaucrats but rather from the outdated systems and inefficient institutions. His vice president, Al Gore, headed the effort to investigate and revamp the administration. The Clinton-Gore team signaled that the administration was doing something to make government work better and cost less. The president ultimately promised to "reinvent" rather than dismantle the bureaucracy system.

In 1993, Clinton announced a six-month review of the federal government. The **National Performance Review (NPR)** became Clinton's key document in assessing the federal bureaucracy. The review was organized to identify problems and offer solutions and ideas for government savings. The group focused on diminishing the paperwork burden and placing more discretionary responsibility with the agencies. The report made almost 400 recommendations designed to cut red tape, put customers first, empower employees, and produce better and less-expensive government. One report, "From Red Tape to Results," characterized the federal government as an industrial-era structure operating in an information age. The bureaucracy had become so inundated with rules and procedures, so constrained by red tape, that it could not perform the way Congress had intended.

The review differed from prior ones that had sought to increase efficiency, accountability, and consistency. The NPR review pushed for greater customer satisfaction and a more businesslike manner of running government. Clinton, by way of executive order, also told heads of executive agencies to expand flex options so federal workers could better balance the demands of job and family.

The Courts and the Bureaucracy

Bureaucratic agencies interact with courts in a variety of ways. The implementation of some rules can result in a prosecution of an offender in a criminal trial. Agency fines and punishments can be appealed in federal court. And the U.S. Supreme Court has shaped how Congress can interact with agencies and has generally empowered the agencies with wider latitude to enact their missions—some would say at the expense of democratically developed policy and the rights of industry.

Courts and Accountability The courts are involved when citizens challenge federal bureaucratic decisions. Because agency actions are not always constitutional, fair, or practical, individuals have the right of due process and review of the law. This judicial review, writes one scholar, serves as a "check on lawlessness, a check on administrative agents making choices based on convenient personal or political preferences without substantial concern for matters of inconvenient principle."

Before an individual may claim harm by a departmental action, or a company claim adverse effects by a regulatory agency, the complainants must first go through a required, multi-step review process. The Administrative Procedures Act defines the procedure, but it differs by agency across the federal hierarchy, including the relevant review boards and adjudication processes.

Once the appeals process is fully exhausted, a court might consider a challenge by the allegedly injured party. A detailed record of the agency action and the review process up to this point will reveal the substance of the policy and most relevant facts. The court uses this record to determine whether the law has been followed and whether the agency acted within reason.

U.S. Circuit Courts of Appeals Most judicial hearings challenging agency decisions and regulatory punishments are looking for a complicated interpretation of a law, its application, or its constitutionality. These are concerns for appeals courts. When Justin Timberlake accidentally exposed Janet Jackson's breast during the 2004 Super Bowl halftime show on a live CBS television broadcast, the Federal Communications Commission got involved because of concerns that broadcast decency rules had been violated. The FCC punished Viacom, the CBS parent company, the standard indecency fine of this type, $27,500, times the number of affiliates that broadcast the show. It added up to $550,000. The network's lawyers challenged the ruling in the Third Circuit Court of Appeals. The federal court overruled the FCC and sided with CBS-Viacom.

However, over the last few decades, although these appeals courts have had the power to hold bureaucratic agencies accountable, they have acted as less as a check on executive authority and more as an enabler of it. U.S. Courts of Appeals have increased the number of cases they take, as the bureaucracy has generally grown in size and authority. The Supreme Court simply doesn't take many cases when appealed from the circuit courts, so the Courts of Appeals have largely become the final arbiter of agency decisions. These court decisions, and most of the rare cases the Supreme Court hears, tend to uphold the idea that unless agency discretion is blatantly unlawful or abusive, deference should go to the agency.

Two principles, the substantial evidence doctrine and the arbitrary and capricious test, have governed their rulings. That is, unless the appealing party can provide substantial evidence that the agency has gone far afield of the law or damaged the party outside of this law, the agency should be permitted to govern under its enabling statute. And, if the agency is applying the law equally and consistently, it should be allowed to do so. The fundamental support for this approach is that the people's branch—Congress—has enabled the agency and that the bureaucrats making the decisions are experts in the field. And when federal courts examine these disputes, they focus more on the decision-making procedures than the substance of the rules or decisions.

When the Third Circuit Court overruled the FCC in the Super Bowl controversy, it did so in part by following standards of consistency. The FCC had ruled that "fleeting indecency," that is, accidental and unintentional indecency, usually in the form of verbal slips, had not been punished in the past. How could the FCC now instate an ex post facto policy that, when compared with prior decisions, went the other way?

Trends Appeals courts are more likely to protect and uphold independent regulatory agency decisions than general executive branch department and agency decisions. One study found that lower federal courts uphold the agencies' decisions and punishments about 76 percent of the time. Another found the Supreme Court upheld challenges to these executive branch decisions 91 percent of the time.

The Standard The Supreme Court has yielded to bureaucratic authority when the language in the statute that defines their authority is vague. In other words, when Congress bestows power on an entity it creates but has perhaps failed to explicitly define scenarios or rulings that the agency might make, the Court recommends erring on the side of the bureaucracy. The preeminent case that governs this approach is *Chevron v. National Resources Defense Council* (NRDC), decided in 1984. The case pitted Chevron Oil against an environmental protection group. But the real question was to what degree an agency can set industry standards when the law governing that power is incomplete or vague.

The Clean Air Act of 1970 required states to create permit programs for any new or modified plants that might affect air pollution. The EPA passed a regulation that grouped these plants into a geographic bubble-area for pollution measurement, creating the possibility that some plants would not need a permit if the modification would not affect their overall impact on the defined bubble. The NRDC challenged the EPA procedure in order to protect the air. The District of Columbia Circuit Court of Appeals set aside the EPA regulation, and Chevron appealed.

The Supreme Court overruled the D.C. Circuit Court and established the Chevron doctrine under which courts are supposed to defer to agencies when laws defining their responsibilities are vague or ambiguous. Under the *Chevron* concept, agencies can not only determine what the law is, they can also change that interpretation at any time.

Inefficiency

"The only thing that saves us from the bureaucracy is inefficiency," said Eugene McCarthy, a Minnesota Democrat who served in the House and Senate from 1949 to 1971. Indeed, the structures, rules, and overlapping jurisdictions seem an inevitable by-product of government. These qualities of bureaucracy have led to some cumbersome challenges for citizens, policymakers, and bureaucrats themselves.

Duplication

Congress has a tough time establishing clear laws and clear goals; as a result, it creates multiple entities to manage or oversee important activities with only marginal differences. It is a rare agency that has exclusive authority over a particular responsibility. For example, both the FBI and the Drug Enforcement Administration seek to apprehend drug dealers. Both the Army and the Navy provide military protection while the CIA and the National Security Agency seek foreign intelligence. This kind of duplication creates competition among agencies and causes jurisdictional issues. This also creates redundancy that expands government cost and frustrates taxpayers because two or more agencies that overlap responsibilities might handle matters differently. The very specific rules of dealing with government can slow things down.

Red Tape

The most common complaint among U.S. citizens about government is **red tape**. Red tape is the vast amount of paperwork, procedures, forms, and formal steps citizens must take to accomplish a government-mandated task. Any driver who has stood in a long line at the local state bureau of motor vehicles with proof of insurance, an emissions check, and other paperwork to receive a driver's license can understand red tape.

IT'S THE LATEST GOVERNMENT GUIDANCE ON 'MANAGING
PAPERWORK FOR SMALL BUSINESSES'

Source: *Cartoonstock*

Explain the artist's attitude toward the bureaucracy and an
assumption on which that attitude is based.

Governmental restrictions on agency decisions and purchases contribute
to slowing down bureaucratic decision making. In many cases, agencies must
meet contingencies before they can move ahead with projects. For example,
Congress mandates that government contracts must be with American
firms. The federal government institutes targets and guidelines to encourage
companies to work with minority-owned businesses. Agreements dictate
that the federal government hire firms supporting unions and pay prevailing
wages. Major construction firms require environmental and economic impact
studies to determine the project's effect on the location.

Accountability Another concern for the operation of the bureaucracy is
accountability. Presidents and their subordinates have ordered performance
reviews and assessments for decades. Trying to enhance responsiveness and
effectiveness while also seeking to boost efficiency can be counterproductive.
A government of laws is one that avoids arbitrary or capricious rule, but the
more an agency is held accountable, the more forms, guidelines, and systems
are required. Accountability, therefore, increases red tape and decreases
responsiveness.

For example, the Paperwork Reduction Act of 1979, one of President
Jimmy Carter's reforms, sounded like a good idea when it was proposed. To
enforce it, Congress created the Office of Internal Regulatory Affairs, which
created numerous obstacles for agencies issuing regulations. It decreased the
flow of paper by increasing regulations on the federal bureaucracy itself.

Public Impression

Bashing bureaucrats has been fashionable for decades. Outspoken Alabama Governor George Wallace, who served in the 1960s, 1970s, and 1980s, was known for attacking the "pointy-headed bureaucrats." Presidents Nixon, Carter, and Reagan taught the American populace to distrust them. The bureaucracy has become a favorite scapegoat of politicians promising to reform government, largely because so many people have had negative experiences with red tape. Politicians and commentators have primed citizens to focus their resentments on this amorphous, faceless entity, despite the fact that most citizens desire the government services that agencies offer and tend to speak positively about individual bureaucrats they have encountered.

REFLECT ON THE ESSENTIAL QUESTION

Essential Question: *How does the bureaucracy carry out laws, implement policy, and interact with the executive, legislative, and judicial branches?*
On separate paper, complete a chart like the one below to gather details to answer that question.

Functions of the Bureaucracy	
Interactions with Executive Branch	
Interactions with Legislative Branch	
Interactions with Judicial Branch	

KEY TERMS AND NAMES

appropriations/173

authorization of spending/173

Civil Service Commission/168

Civil Service Reform Act (1978)/169

competitive service/161

compliance monitoring/166

discretionary authority/170

excepted service/161

Federal Bureau of Investigation/163

Freedom of Information Act (1966)/177

Hatch Act (1939)/169

iron triangle/166

issue networks/167

legislative veto/174

merit system/168

National Performance Review (NPR)/176

Office of Information and Regulatory Affairs (OIRA)/174

Office of Personnel Management (OPM)/161

patronage/167

Pendleton Civil Service Act (1883)/168

red tape/179

Senior Executive Service/169

spoils system/167

Sunshine Act (1976)/177

Whistleblower Protection Act (1989)/175

Questions 1 and 2 refer to the passage below.

> First, always, is the question whether Congress has directly spoken to the precise question at issue. If the intent of Congress is clear, that is the end of the matter; for the court, as well as the agency, must give effect to the unambiguously expressed intent of Congress. If, however, the court determines Congress has not directly addressed the precise question at issue, the court does not simply impose its own construction on the statute, as would be necessary in the absence of an administrative interpretation. Rather if the statute is silent or ambiguous with respect to the specific issue, the question for the court is whether the agency's answer is based on a permissible construction of the statute.
>
> —Justice John Paul Stevens, Majority Opinion, *Chevron v. Natural Resources Defense Council* (1984)

1. Which of the following statements in relation to the bureaucracy would Stevens most likely support?
   - (A) A strict construction of the Constitution and the laws that govern bureaucratic agencies is necessary.
   - (B) A degree of discretion is necessary when bureaucratic agencies must apply laws that are imperfectly written.
   - (C) More congressional oversight of bureaucratic agencies is needed to prevent any misapplication of vague laws.
   - (D) The courts need to exert more strength to stop the bureaucratic agencies from implementing vague law.

2. Those who disagree with the above Supreme Court's opinion would likely point to which facts?
   - (A) Experts in the bureaucracy have the knowledge to make the best clarifications.
   - (B) Bureaucratic agencies need to be more diligent in doing their jobs.
   - (C) The courts have no say in interpreting this kind of executive branch law.
   - (D) The lawmaking process becomes less democratic when bureaucratic agencies can regulate beyond their defined jurisdiction.

3. A federal agency has been accused of not enforcing laws it is charged with enforcing. Which is the most likely action the relevant House committee will first take?

   (A) Fire and replace the director of the agency

   (B) Repeal the law that creates and governs the agency

   (C) Call for an oversight hearing to understand the problem

   (D) Increase the federal appropriation for the agency

Questions 4 and 5 refer to the table below.

FEDERAL EXECUTIVE BRANCH EMPLOYMENT BY DEPARTMENT (Selected Departments)			
Department	FY 2012	FY 2014	FY 2016
Education	3,899	3,815	3,973
State	9,761	10,068	10,500
Commerce	35,013	34,857	35,661
Homeland Security	169,166	167,422	169,547
Justice	113,358	110,427	112,900

Source: *Office of Personnel Management*

4. Which of the following accurately describes the data presented in the table?

   (A) The number of employees increased in all the selected departments during the period shown.

   (B) The Justice Department is the largest department because most crime fighting is done at the federal level.

   (C) Homeland Security was a high federal priority requiring many workers during these years.

   (D) The number of employees in each of the selected departments usually declined from 2012 to 2016.

5. What conclusion can you draw from the patterns of change represented in the table?

   (A) Retiring bureaucrats are not being replaced with new hires.

   (B) The size of the federal bureaucracy is fairly stable.

   (C) An economic downturn reduced employment levels in 2014.

   (D) The Education Department employs the largest number of workers.

6. Which of the following is an accurate comparison of Cabinet-level departments and regulatory agencies?

	CABINET-LEVEL DEPARTMENTS	REGULATORY AGENCIES
(A)	Fifteen Cabinet departments, each with a secretary or head that serves on the president's Cabinet	Created and empowered by Congress to monitor particular industries and enforce unique laws
(B)	Cabinet Secretaries can run their department in their own way and cannot be removed without Senate approval.	Regulatory agencies are usually larger than departments in both employees and funding.
(C)	Include the Federal Election Commission and the Securities and Exchange Commission	Senior level agency directors get an automatic seat on the president's Cabinet.
(D)	Nine federal organizations that carry out the nation's business	Are usually within a department and work under the direction of a White House staff member

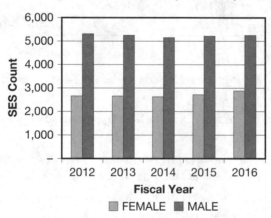

Senior Executive Service (SES) Gender Trends (2012–2016)

Source: *United States Office of Personnel Management*

7. Which of the following statements can be determined from the data in the chart?

(A) The contemporary imbalance between men and women results from a ban on women in the Army or Navy.

(B) Fewer women than men apply for senior executive positions.

(C) The change reflected in the chart is a result of the women's movement in the 1970s.

(D) The ratio of men to women working in the Senior Executive Service has stayed similar over the years depicted in the chart.

Questions 8–10 refer to the passage below.

> [W]e find that the licensees of the CBS Network Stations . . . aired program material . . . during the halftime entertainment show of the National Football League's Super Bowl XXXVIII, that apparently violates the federal restrictions regarding the broadcast of indecent material. Based upon our review of the facts and circumstances of this case, Viacom Inc. ("Viacom"), as the licensee or ultimate parent of the licensees of the Viacom Stations, is apparently liable for a monetary forfeiture in the aggregate amount of Five Hundred Fifty Thousand Dollars ($550,000.00), which represents the statutory maximum of $27,500 for each Viacom Station that broadcast the material.
>
> —Federal Communications Commission, Notice of
> Apparent Liability, 2004

8. Which of the following statements best reflects the role of the Federal Communications Commission in this instance?

   (A) The FCC is acting to uphold the First Amendment and endorse what was broadcast during the Super Bowl.

   (B) The FCC is fining Viacom for the actions of one of its companies that violated broadcast regulations.

   (C) The FCC is punishing Viacom and CBS, but the courts determine the amount of the fines.

   (D) The FCC does not require television broadcasters to be responsible for what performers might do on their broadcasts.

9. Which bureaucratic authority is illustrated with this allegation?

   (A) Enforcement

   (B) Logrolling

   (C) Legislative veto

   (D) Red tape

10. If Viacom disagrees with this notice, what is the most likely step it will take?

    (A) Appeal the ruling to the appropriate Circuit Court of Appeals

    (B) Make campaign contributions to congressional candidates that will strike down the ruling

    (C) Convince its viewers to ask their Congress members to overrule the decision

    (D) Pressure the president to fire the chair of the FCC

1. "Under *Chevron* the people . . . are required to guess whether the statute will be declared 'ambiguous' (courts often disagree on what qualifies); and required to guess (again) whether an agency's interpretation will be deemed 'reasonable'. . . . Even if the people somehow manage to make it through this far unscathed, they must always remain alert to the possibility that the agency will reverse its current view 180 degrees anytime based merely on the shift of political winds and *still* prevail."

–U.S. Circuit Court Judge Neal Gorsuch,
Guitierez-Brizueala v. Lynch, 2016

Based on the above scenario, respond to A, B, and C below.

(A) Describe the power the circuit court asserted in the *Chevron* case.

(B) In the context of this scenario, explain how the *Chevron* decision to which Judge Gorsuch refers affected the federal bureaucracy.

(C) In the context of this scenario, explain how federal bureaucracy rule making relates to the separation of powers.

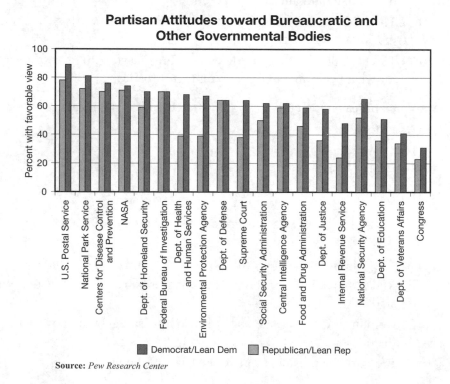

Partisan Attitudes toward Bureaucratic and Other Governmental Bodies

Source: *Pew Research Center*

2. Use the information graphic above to answer the questions on the next page.

(A) Identify a body within the bureaucracy that has lower than 50 percent unfavorable ratings from both parties.

(B) Describe the difference between Republican/Lean Republican and Democrat/Lean Democrat respondents in their rating of the Environmental Protection Agency, and draw a conclusion about the cause of this disparity.

(C) Explain how areas of agreement as shown in the graphic demonstrate values common to both parties.

3. In 2005, the Supreme Court heard the case of *National Cable & Telecommunications Association v. Brand X Internet Services*. The case centered on how the Telecommunications Act, interpreted and enforced by the FCC, defined "information service" and "telecommunication service." The difference in designation mattered because if cable Internet were classified as a telecommunication service, cable companies would be considered "common carriers" like phone companies and would have to make their cable networks available for competitors to use as well. Brand X, a small Internet provider, argued that cable Internet was a telecommunication service, not an information service, and Brand X should have access to the cables to be able to deliver faster Internet service. The Court found the designation in the Telecommunications Act vague, and by a 6:3 margin ruled that the FCC, as a congressionally enabled commission, had the authority to determine the designation of cable Internet as an information service.

(A) Identify the constitutional principle at issue in *National Cable & Telecommunications Association v. Brand X Internet Services* (2005) and in *Marbury v. Madison* (1803). (See page 199.)

(B) Based on the constitutional principle identified in part A, explain why the facts of *Marbury v. Madison* (1803) led to a different holding than the holding in *National Cable & Telecommunications Association v. Brand X Internet Services*.

(C) Describe an action that members of the public who disagree with the holding in *National Cable & Telecommunications Association v. Brand X Internet Services* could take to limit its impact.

4. Develop an argument that explains whether the federal bureaucracy operates with sufficient checks and balances or whether it has too much discretionary authority to be a fully democratic element of government.

In your essay, you must:

- Articulate a defensible claim or thesis that responds to the prompt and establishes a line of reasoning
- Support your claim with at least TWO pieces of accurate and relevant information:
  - At least ONE piece of evidence must be from one of the following foundational documents:
    - *Federalist No. 51*
    - *Federalist No. 70*
    - Article I of the Constitution
    - Article II of the Constitution
  - Use a second piece of evidence from another foundational document from the list above or from your study of the federal bureaucracy
- Use reasoning to explain why your evidence supports your claim/ thesis
- Respond to an opposing or alternative perspective using refutation, concession, or rebuttal

WRITING: *RESPOND TO ALTERNATIVE PERSPECTIVES*

As you plan your argumentative essay, be aware of alternative perspectives from the beginning. Use them to help you choose the position you believe you are best able to defend with your evidence. You may even incorporate one of the stronger alternative perspectives into your claim, so your readers will know to anticipate your rebuttal to it later. For example, your claim might read:

Although there are some good reasons why discretionary authority is necessary in the federal bureaucracy, in more cases than not that authority goes too far and the bureaucracy operates with insufficient accountability.

Readers will expect you to address the "good reasons" and to show why, despite them, you argue for a different position.

6

The Judicial Branch

"It is emphatically the province and duty of the judicial department to say what the law is."

—John Marshall for the Supreme Court in *Marbury v. Madison*, 1803

Essential Question: How do the nation's courts compete and cooperate with the other branches to settle legal controversies and to shape public policy?

Most of us have some understanding of trials where accused criminals are innocent until proven guilty and where one party sues another. Courtroom drama has been popular since Perry Mason—a 1950s television defense attorney who lost only one case in a nine-year series run. More recently, TV has stereotyped small claims courts with the feisty, tell-it-like-it-is judge, a beefy courtroom bailiff, and litigants who rudely yell at each other.

The true picture of the judiciary shows a revered institution shaped by Article III of the Constitution, the Bill of Rights, and federal and state laws. The courts handle everything from speeding tickets to death penalty cases. State courts handle most disputes, whether criminal or civil. Federal courts handle crimes against the United States, high-dollar lawsuits involving citizens of different states, and constitutional questions. The U.S. Supreme Court is the nation's highest appeals court.

Constitutional Authority of the Federal Courts

Today's three-level federal court system consists of the **U.S. District Courts** on the lowest tier, the **U.S. Circuit Courts of Appeals** on the middle tier, and the **U.S. Supreme Court** alone on the top. These three types of courts are known as "constitutional courts" because they are either directly or indirectly mentioned in the Constitution. All judges serving in these courts are appointed by presidents and confirmed by the Senate to hold life terms.

No national court system existed under the Articles of Confederation, so the framers decided to create a national judiciary while empowering Congress to expand and define it. Because states had existing courts, many delegates saw no reason to create an entirely new, costly judicial system to serve essentially the same purpose. Others disagreed and argued that a national judicial system with a top court for uniformity was necessary. "Thirteen independent [state] courts of final jurisdiction over the same cases, arising out of the same laws," *Federalist No. 80* argued, "will produce nothing but contradiction and confusion."

Article III

The only court directly mentioned in the Constitution is the Supreme Court, though Article III empowered Congress to create "inferior" courts. Article III establishes the terms for judges, the jurisdiction of the Supreme Court, the definition of treason, and the right of a defendant to a jury trial.

Judge's Terms All federal judges "shall hold their offices during good behavior," the Constitution states. Although this term of office is now generally called a "life term," judges can be and have been impeached and removed. This key provision empowers federal judges to make unpopular but necessary decisions. The life term assures that judges can operate independently from the other branches, since the executive and legislative branches have no power to remove justices over disagreements in ideology. The life term also allows for a consistency over time in interpreting the law. Of course, most federal judges take senior status at age 65 or fully retire. So, short of the challenging standard of an impeachment charge by the House and a two-thirds removal vote by the Senate, federal judges and their jobs are protected for life. Additionally, Congress cannot diminish judges' salaries during their terms in office. This way, Congress cannot use its power of the purse to leverage power against this independent branch. These are the chief ways that Article III protects the independence of the Supreme Court and lower courts, as well as the independence of the judiciary branch of government.

Jurisdiction The Supreme Court has **original jurisdiction**—the authority to hear a case for the first time—in cases affecting ambassadors and public ministers and those in which a state is a party. For the most part, however, the Supreme Court acts as an appeals court with **appellate jurisdiction**.

Treason Article III also defines *treason* as "levying war" or giving "aid or comfort" to the enemy. Treason is the only crime mentioned or defined in the Constitution. Because English kings had used the accusation of treason as a political tool in unfair trials to quiet dissent against the government, the founders wanted to ensure that the new government could not easily prosecute that charge just to silence alternative voices. At least two witnesses must testify in open court to the treasonous act in order to convict the accused.

Right to Jury Trial This article also mentions a criminal defendant's right to a jury trial. Many more rights of the accused were included later in the Bill of Rights, but the right to a jury trial was a priority to the framers as a citizen-check on accusation by the government and was thus included in Article III.

Anti-Federalists were concerned about establishing an independent judiciary. In England, Parliament could vote to remove judges from office, and it could pass laws overriding judicial decisions. Brutus, the mouthpiece for the Anti-Federalists, expressed concern that there was no similar checking power on the Supreme Court. "Men placed in this situation," he wrote in *Brutus No. 15*, "will generally soon feel themselves independent of heaven itself."

Alexander Hamilton and other Federalists did not share this concern. In *Federalist No. 78*, Hamilton affirms that the independent judicial branch has the power of judicial review to examine acts of legislatures to see if they comport with the proposed Constitution. He also emphasizes that as long as judges are acting properly, they shall remain on the bench. This "permanency" shall protect them from the other branches when they make unpopular but constitutional decisions. He believed an independent judiciary posed no threat.

[The Judiciary] will always be the least dangerous to the political rights of the Constitution; because it will be least in a capacity to annoy or injure them. . . . [since it] has no influence over either the sword or the purse. . . .
[F]rom the natural feebleness of the judiciary, it is in continual jeopardy of being overpowered, awed, or influenced by its co-ordinate branches; and that as nothing can contribute so much to its firmness and independence as permanency in office . . .

No legislative act . . . contrary to the Constitution, can be valid. To deny this, would be to affirm, that the deputy is greater than his principal; that the servant is above his master; that the representatives of the people are superior to the people themselves . . . A constitution is, in fact, and must be regarded by the judges, as a fundamental law. It therefore belongs to them [the judges] to ascertain its meaning, as well as the meaning of any particular act proceeding from the legislative body. . . .

[T]he independence of the judges may be an essential safeguard against the effects of occasional ill humors in the society. These sometimes extend no farther than to the injury of the private rights of particular classes of citizens, by unjust and partial laws. . . . That inflexible and uniform adherence to the rights of the Constitution, and of individuals, which we perceive to be indispensable in the courts of justice, can certainly not be expected from judges who hold their offices by a temporary commission.

However, the establishment of judicial review was not settled by Hamilton's writing. As you will read, the landmark decision in *Marbury v. Madison* (1803) established that principle. Nonetheless, it is still debated today.

A Three-Level System

The first Congress quickly defined a three-tier federal court system with the Judiciary Act of 1789 to clear up the vague and brief Article III. The law established one district court in each of the 13 states, plus one each for the soon-to-be states of Vermont and Kentucky. The law also defined the size of the Supreme Court with six justices, or judges. President Washington then appointed judges to fill these judgeships. In addition to the district courts, Congress initially created three regional circuit courts designated to take cases on appeal from the district courts. Two Supreme Court justices were assigned to each of the "circuits" and were required to hold court twice per year in every state. The presiding district judge joined them to make a three-judge intermediate panel. In a given period, the Supreme Court justices would hold one court after another in a circular path, an act that became known as "riding circuit."

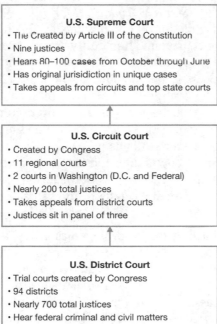

Federal Court System

U.S. Supreme Court
- The Created by Article III of the Constitution
- Nine justices
- Hears 80–100 cases from October through June
- Has original jurisidiction in unique cases
- Takes appeals from circuits and top state courts

U.S. Circuit Court
- Created by Congress
- 11 regional courts
- 2 courts in Washington (D.C. and Federal)
- Nearly 200 total justices
- Takes appeals from district courts
- Justices sit in panel of three

U.S. District Court
- Trial courts created by Congress
- 94 districts
- Nearly 700 total justices
- Hear federal criminal and civil matters

U.S. District Courts

There are 94 district courts in the United States—at least one in each state, and for many western states, the district lines are the same as the state lines. Each district may contain several courthouses served by several federal district judges. Nearly 700 district judges nationwide preside over trials concerning federal crimes, lawsuits, and disputes over constitutional issues. Annually, the district courts receive close to 300,000 case filings nationwide, most of a civil nature.

A Trial Court U.S. district courts are trial courts with original jurisdiction over federal cases. The litigants in a trial court are the **plaintiff**—the party initiating the action—and the **defendant**, the party answering the action. In a criminal trial, the government is the plaintiff, usually referred to as the "prosecution." In civil trials, a citizen-plaintiff brings suit against another, the defendant, who allegedly injured him or her. Others who may be part of a trial court are witnesses, jury members, and a presiding judge. Trial courts are finders of fact; that is, these courts determine if an accused defendant did in fact commit a crime, or if a civil defendant is indeed responsible for some mistake or wrongdoing.

Federal Crimes The U.S. district courts try federal crimes, such as counterfeiting, mail fraud, or evading federal income taxes—crimes that fall under the enumerated powers in Article I, Section 8 of the Constitution. Most violent crimes, and indeed most crimes overall, are tried in state courts.

Congress has outlawed some violent crime and interstate actions, such as drug trafficking, bank robbery, terrorism, and acts of violence on federal property. For example, in *United States v. Timothy McVeigh* (1998), the government argued that McVeigh exploded an Oklahoma City federal building and killed 168 victims. A federal court found him guilty and sentenced him to death.

Defendants have a constitutional right to a jury and defense lawyer and several other due process rights included in the Bill of Rights. The judge or jury must find the defendant guilty "beyond a reasonable doubt" in order to convict and issue a sentence. Many cases are disposed of when a defendant pleads guilty before the trial. This **plea bargain** allows the government and the defendant to agree to a lesser sentence in exchange for the defendant's guilty plea. A plea bargain saves courts time and taxpayers money, and it guarantees a conviction. For example, FBI agent Robert Hanson was discovered to have sold government secrets to the Russians for years. He was charged with espionage crimes and pleaded guilty in order to avoid the death penalty.

U.S. Attorneys Each of the 94 districts has a U.S. attorney, appointed by the president and approved by the Senate, who represents the federal government in federal courts. These attorneys are executive branch employees who work in the Department of Justice under the **attorney general**. They serve as federal prosecutors, and with assistance from the FBI and other federal law enforcement agencies they prosecute federal crimes committed within their districts. Nationally, they try close to 80,000 federal crimes per year. Of those, immigration crimes and drug offenses take up much of the courts' criminal docket. Fraud is third.

Civil Cases Citizens can also bring civil disputes to court to settle a business or personal conflict. Some plaintiffs sue over torts, civil wrongs that have damaged them. In a lawsuit, the plaintiff files a complaint (a brief that explains the damages and argues why the defendant should be held responsible). The party bringing suit must prove the defendant's liability or negligence with a "preponderance of evidence" for the court to award damages. Most civil disputes, even million-dollar lawsuits, are handled in state courts. Congress has empowered the U.S. district courts to have jurisdiction over disputes involving more than $75,000 with *diversity citizenship*—cases in which the two parties reside in different states.

Disputes involving constitutional questions also land in this court. In these cases, a federal judge, not a jury, determines the outcome because these cases involve a deeper interpretation of the law than more general cases do. Sometimes a large group of plaintiffs claim common damage by one party and will file a **class action suit**. After a decision, courts may issue an **injunction**, or court order, to the losing party in a civil suit, making them act or refrain from acting to redress a wrong.

Suing the Government Sometimes a citizen or group sues the government. Technically, the United States operates under the doctrine of sovereign immunity—the government is protected from suit unless it permits such a claim. Over the years, Congress has made so many exceptions that it even established the U.S. Court of Claims to allow citizens to bring complaints against the United States. Citizens and groups also regularly bring constitutional arguments before the courts. One can sue government officials acting in a personal capacity. For example, the secretary of defense could be personally sued for causing a traffic accident that caused thousands of dollars in damage to another's car. But the secretary of defense or Congress cannot be sued for the loss of a loved one in a government-sanctioned military battle.

Special Legislative Courts In addition to the constitutional trial courts that make up our U.S. district courts, Congress has created a handful of unique courts to hear matters of expert concern. These are known as the special legislative courts because they are created by the legislature as opposed to the Constitution. Presidents appoint these judges and the Senate must approve them, typically for a 15-year fixed term. These courts deal with specific issues, and therefore an experienced judge in that area of law is desired for a defined period of time. Special courts include the court of federal claims mentioned above, as well as courts that determine matters of taxation; international trade; spying and surveillance; and military matters. (See page 219.)

U.S. Circuit Courts of Appeals

Directly above the district court is the U.S. Circuit Courts of Appeals. The circuit courts have appellate jurisdiction, taking cases on appeal. In 1891, Congress made the circuit court of appeals a permanent body. The country had expanded to the Pacific Coast, and Supreme Court justices still had to travel across the now distant and expansive circuits. The increasing caseload, too, made this task unmanageable for justices based in Washington.

Appellate Courts Appeals courts are especially influential because they don't determine facts; instead, they shape the law. The losing party in a trial can appeal based on the concept of *certiorari*, Latin for "to make more certain." Thousands more cases are appealed than accepted by higher courts. The appellant must offer some violation of established law or procedure that led to the incorrect verdict in the trial court. Appeals courts look different and operate differently from trial courts. Appeals courts have a panel of judges sitting at the bench. There is no witness stand or jury box since the court does not entertain new facts but decides instead on some narrow question or point of law.

The **petitioner** appeals the case, and the **respondent** responds, claiming why and how the lower court ruled correctly. The hearing lasts about an hour as each side makes oral arguments before the judges. Appeals courts don't declare guilt or innocence when dealing with criminal matters, but they may order new trials for defendants. After years of deciding legal principles, appeals courts have shaped the body of U.S. law.

The U.S. Courts of Appeals consist of 11 geographic circuits across the country, each with one court in major cities such as Atlanta, New Orleans, and Chicago. Nearly 200 circuit court justices sit in panels of three to hear appeals from both criminal and civil trials. Occasionally in important matters, an entire circuit court will sit *en banc;* that is, every judge on the court will hear and decide a case. Appeals court rulings stand within their geographic circuits.

In addition to the 11 circuits, two other appeals courts are worthy of note. The Circuit Court for the Federal Circuit hears appeals dealing with patents, contracts, and financial claims against the United States. The Circuit Court of Appeals for the District of Columbia, among other responsibilities, handles appeals from those fined or punished by executive branch regulatory agencies. The D.C. Circuit might be the second most important court in the nation and has become a feeder for Supreme Court justices.

The United States Supreme Court

Atop this hierarchy is the U.S. Supreme Court, with the chief justice and eight associate justices. The Supreme Court mostly hears cases on appeal from the circuit courts and from the state supreme courts. The nine members determine which appeals to accept, they sit *en banc* for attorneys' oral arguments, and they vote to decide whether or not to overturn the lower court's ruling. The Court overturns about 70 percent of the cases it takes. Once the Supreme Court makes a ruling, it becomes the law of the land. Contrary to what many believe, the Supreme Court doesn't hear trials of serial murders or billion-dollar lawsuits. However, they decide on technicalities of constitutional law that have a national and sometimes historic impact.

Common Law and Precedence

Courts follow a judicial tradition begun centuries ago in England. The **common law** refers to the body of court decisions that make up part of the law. Court rulings often establish a **precedent**—a ruling that firmly establishes

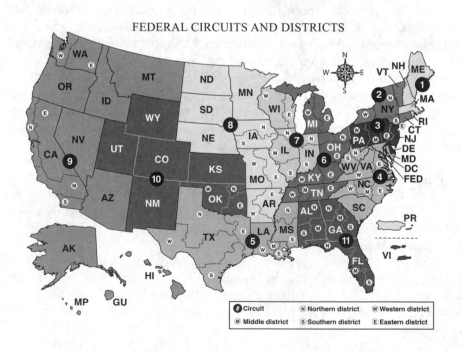

FEDERAL CIRCUITS AND DISTRICTS

a legal principle. These precedents are generally followed later as other courts consider the same legal logic in similar cases. The concept of **stare decisis**, or "let the decision stand," governs common law.

Lower courts must follow higher court rulings. Following precedence establishes continuity and consistency in law. Therefore, when a U.S. district court receives a case that parallels an already decided case from the circuit level, the district court is obliged to rule in the same way, a practice called **binding precedent**. Even an independent-minded judge who disagrees with the higher court's precedent is guided by the fact that an appeal of her uniquely different decision will likely be overruled by the court above. That's why all courts in the land are bound by U.S. Supreme Court decisions. Judges also rely on **persuasive precedent**. That is, they can consider past decisions made in other districts or rulings in other circuits as a guiding basis for their decision. Precedents can of course be overturned. No two cases are absolutely identical, and for this reason differing considerations come into play. Attitudes and interpretations differ and evolve over time in different courts.

POLICY MATTERS: *SUPREME COURT PRECEDENTS ESTABLISH POLICY*

The Supreme Court's authority of binding precedent combined with its power of **judicial review**—the ability to declare a legislative act or an executive branch action void—makes it a powerful institution and often the final arbiter of national law. With these two powers, the Court has had a strong hand in establishing national policy. Early on, it addressed national supremacy and states' rights. Later, it defined the relationship between government and industry. Most recently, the Court has ruled on individual rights and liberties.

Defining Federalism The Supreme Court in its early years was a nondescript, fledgling institution that saw little action and was held in low esteem. President Washington appointed Federalist John Jay as the first chief justice. For its first year the Court was given a second-floor room in a New York building and convened for only a two-hour session. Several early justices didn't stay on the Court long. Jay resigned in 1795 to serve as governor of New York. The Court's reputation and role would soon change.

Once President John Adams appointed Federalist **John Marshall** as chief justice, the Court began to assert itself under a strong, influential leader. Marshall remained on the Court from 1801 until his death in 1835, establishing customs and norms and strengthening national powers. Marshall was a Virginian who acquired a strong sense of nationalism and respect for authority and discipline during his service in the Revolutionary War. After independence, he became an ardent Federalist and attended the Virginia ratifying convention to vote in favor of ratification.

Some consider John Marshall the father of the Supreme Court, since the Marshall Court established its customs and solidified the nation under the framers' plan. Throughout his 34 years as chief justice, he and his colleagues lived in a convivial atmosphere at a boarding house in Washington. Most who knew Marshall liked him. The Supreme Court, seven members at the time, simply shared a small room in the old Capitol with Congress. It held hearings in a designated committee room on the first floor for seven years until it was given more spacious quarters. It did not have its own building until the 1930s.

Marshall created a united court that spoke with one voice. When he arrived, he found the Supreme Court functioning like an English court in that multiple judges issued separate opinions. Marshall insisted that this brotherhood of justices agree and unite in their rulings to shape national law. The Court delivered mostly unanimous opinions written

Source: *: Library of Congress*

The Supreme Court is the only federal court named in Article III of the Constitution, yet it did not operate in its own building—shown here in a drawing before it was built—until 1935.

by one judge. In virtually every important case during his time, that one judge was Marshall. "He left the Court," Chief Justice William Rehnquist wrote years later, "a genuinely coequal branch of a tripartite national government . . . the final arbiter of the meaning of the United States Constitution." He fortified the Union and the powers of the federal government with rulings that strengthened national supremacy and Congress's commerce power.

Shaping a Strong Nation Marshall developed a legacy of siding with Congress when controversies regarding federalism arose, strengthening the national government and expanding Congress's powers more than Jeffersonian Republicans wanted. The *McCulloch v. Maryland* and *Gibbons v. Ogden* rulings empowered Congress to create a bank and to regulate interstate commerce.

The Marshall Court also established the principle of **judicial review**—the right of the Court to determine the constitutionality of a law or executive order—in one of its first landmark cases, *Marbury v. Madison* (1803). In deciding the case, the Court struck down part of the Judiciary Act and thereby exercised judicial review.

MUST-KNOW SUPREME COURT DECISIONS:
MARBURY V. MADISON (1803)

The Constitutional Question Before the Court: Can an appointed judge sue for his appointment, and does the Supreme Court have the authority to hear and implement this request?

Decision: Yes and No. Unanimous, 5:0

Facts: This controversy started as a dispute regarding the procedures of appointments during a presidential transition. Outgoing President John Adams had lost reelection to Thomas Jefferson and, in one of his final acts as president, appointed several members of his own Federalist Party to the newly created judgeships. The Senate had confirmed these "midnight judges," so-called because their appointment was made so late in the tenure of President Adams. Secretary of State John Marshall, who had just been named chief justice of the Supreme Court, had prepared the commissions, the official notices of appointment, and had most of them delivered. William Marbury was among 17 appointees who did not receive official notice. Marshall simply left these to be delivered by the next administration.

Once President Thomas Jefferson, a Democratic-Republican, took office, he instructed his new secretary of state, James Madison, to hold the commissions. Jefferson did reappoint several of those appointees, but he refused others on partisan grounds. Marbury wanted the Supreme Court to issue a court order known as a writ of mandamus forcing Madison and the executive branch to deliver the appointment to him and, thus, his job.

Marbury brought the case to the Supreme Court because of language in the relatively new Judiciary Act of 1789 that defined the Supreme Court's jurisdiction in cases like his.

Reasoning: Marshall's Supreme Court took the case and determined that an appointed judge with a signed commission could sue if denied the job. (That is the yes vote.) However, they also ruled that the law entitling Marbury to the commission and the job, Section 13 of the Judiciary Act, ran contrary to Article III of the Constitution when it decided that the Court had original rather than appellate jurisdiction in such cases. (That is the no vote.) Congress could not, Marshall's Court said, define the Court's authority outside the bounds of the Constitution.

The Court unanimously ruled that it had no jurisdiction in the matter, and in so ruling cancelled Marbury's claim. It simultaneously instituted the practice of judicial review. The Court had asserted its powers and checked Congress.

The Court's Unanimous Opinion by Mr. Justice John Marshall:

> If it had been intended to leave it in the discretion of the legislature to apportion the judicial power between the supreme and inferior courts according to the will of that body, it would certainly have been useless to have proceeded further than to have defined the judicial power, and the tribunals in which it should be vested . . . If Congress remains at liberty to give this court appellate jurisdiction, where the Constitution has

declared their jurisdiction shall be original and original jurisdiction where the Constitution has declared it shall be appellate; the distribution of jurisdiction, made in the Constitution, is form without substance . . .

The authority, therefore, given to the Supreme Court, by the act establishing the judicial courts of the United States [the Judiciary Act of 1789], to issue writs of mandamus to public officers, appears not to be warranted by the Constitution . . .

The act to establish the judicial courts of the United States authorizes the Supreme Court "to issue writs of mandamus, in cases warranted by the principles and usages of law, to any courts appointed, or persons holding office, under the authority of the United States." The secretary of state, being a person, holding an office under the authority of the United States, is precisely within the letter of the description; and if this court is not authorized to issue a writ of mandamus to such an officer, it must be because the law is unconstitutional. . . .

It is emphatically the province and duty of the judicial department to say what the law is. Those who apply the rule to particular cases, must of necessity expound and interpret that rule. If two laws conflict with each other the courts must decide on the operation of each . . .

So if a law be in opposition to the Constitution; if both the law and the Constitution apply to a particular case, so that the Court must either decide that case conformably to the law, disregarding the Constitution; or conformably to the Constitution, disregarding the law; the Court must determine which of these conflicting rules governs the case. This is of the very essence of judicial duty . . .

Since *Marbury*: Marbury is a landmark for its initiation of judicial review in American jurisprudence and in defining common law. Marshall had declared at the Virginian Ratifying Convention—a Federalist allaying fears of opponents to the proposed Constitution—that Congress would not have power to make law on any subject it wanted. A new federal judiciary, he said, "would declare void" any such congressional act repugnant to the Constitution. Marshall became the first judge to do just that.

Judicial review or striking down acts of Congress came as a rarity after Marbury. Not until the infamous Dred Scott case in 1857 (page 201) did the Court again strike down a law, this time one that outlawed slavery north of the Missouri Compromise line. During the Industrial Era (1874–1920) and into the 20th century, the Court used its power of judicial review to strike down laws with greater frequency.

Political Science Disciplinary Practices: Analyze and Interpret Supreme Court Decisions

1. Describe the facts in the *Marbury v. Madison* case.

2. Describe the controversy in the *Marbury v. Madison* case.

3. Explain the Court's reasoning from the majority opinion.

4. Explain how the ruling in *Marbury* relates to the U.S. Constitution.

5. Explain how the ruling in *Marbury* relates to *Federalist No. 78.*

An Evolving Court

Since the Marshall Court, the Supreme Court has reflected the changes in the composition of the Court—the individual justices who have come and gone and the perspectives each of them brought—as well as changes in society. Yet the Supreme Court is known more for continuity than for change. Membership is small and justices serve long tenures. The Court's customs are established through consensus and remain over generations.

Early Courts to the New Deal

Chief Justice Roger Taney replaced John Marshall. The Court's operation changed somewhat with new leadership and new members. In 1837, Congress increased its membership to nine justices to ease the workload and created additional circuits. It also took up questions regarding slavery during the antebellum period. Taney and his fellow justices were determined to protect slavery as a state's right and upheld a congressional fugitive slave act.

In 1857, as the North and the South grew further apart, the Court decided the Dred Scott case. The slave Dred Scott had traveled with his master into free territory and claimed, with the help of abolitionist lawyers, that having lived in free northern territory, he should have his freedom. Taney and the Court's majority shocked abolitionists with their decision and left one of the Court's worst legacies. The *Dred Scott v. Sandford* ruling held that Scott wasn't even a citizen and thus had no legal right to be a party in federal court, much less the country's top tribunal. The Court went further, stating that a slave owner's constitutional right to due process and property prevented depriving him of that property, regardless of where he traveled. Abolitionists and anti-slavery advocates in the territories challenged the Court's legitimacy.

Corporations and the State In the late 1800s, the Court examined concerns over business, trade, and workplace regulations. The nation had expanded manufacturing power, factories, railroads, and interstate trade. Workers were subjected to long hours in unsafe conditions for modest pay. Congress tried to address these issues under its power to regulate interstate commerce. State legislatures also devised laws creating safety bureaus, barring payment in company scrip, setting maximum working hours, and preventing women and children from working in certain industries. While lawmakers tried to satisfy workers' groups and labor unions, their counterparts—typically strong businesses dominant in the northeastern United States—argued that minimal government interference and a *laissez-faire* approach to governance was the constitutionally correct path. When pressed by corporations to toss out such laws, the Court had to decide two principles: what the Constitution permitted government to do, and which government—state or federal—could do it.

The Court began to overturn various state health, safety, and civil rights laws, and in so doing shaped social policy. It threw out a congressional act that addressed monopolies. It also ruled Congress's income tax statute null and void. By the turn of the century, the Court had developed a conservative reputation as it questioned business regulation and progressive ideas. In *Lochner v. New York* (1905), the Court overturned a New York state law that prevented bakers from working more than 10 hours per day. The law was meant to counter the pressures from the boss that mandated long hours in an era before overtime pay. In *Lochner,* the Court ruled that liberty of contract—a worker's right to freely enter into an agreement—superseded the state's police powers over safety and health. The Court later considered research and sociological data submitted by noted attorney Louis Brandeis, who eventually became a justice on the Court. The Brandeis brief persuaded the Court to uphold a maximum-hours law for women working in laundries. The consequence of protective work laws for women was that they could not effectively compete with men.

During the Progressive Era, the Court made additional exceptions but quickly returned to a conservative, strict constructionist view of business regulation. A **strict constructionist** interprets the Constitution in its original context, while a **liberal constructionist** sees the Constitution as a living document and takes into account changes and social conditions since ratification. The Court held that Congress could not use its commerce power to suppress child labor. The Court's conservative viewpoint turned further to the right, taking social policy with it, when former president William Howard Taft became chief justice. It ruled that minimum wage law for women also violated liberty of contract.

The New Deal and Roosevelt's Plan During the Depression, the Court transformed. Charles Evans Hughes replaced Taft as chief justice in 1929. Hughes managed a mixed group with a strong conservative four, nicknamed the "Four Horsemen," who overturned several New Deal programs. The Court struck down business regulations, invalidated the National Recovery Act (1933), ruled out New York's minimum wage law, and restricted the president's powers to remove commissioners on regulatory boards.

Congress raised the Court's status with a new building in Washington that represented its authority, ceremony, and independence. In 1935, the justices moved into their current building with its majestic façade and familiar red-curtained courtroom. The Court also went through another transformation as it changed ideologically to solidify New Deal laws for the next generation.

After his 1936 landslide reelection, Franklin Delano Roosevelt (FDR) responded to the rebuffs of the conservative Court by devising a plan to "pack the Court." He proposed legislation to add one justice for every justice then over the age of 70, which would have allowed him to appoint up to six new members. FDR claimed this would relieve the Court's overloaded docket, but in reality he wanted to dilute the power of the conservative majority who had been unreceptive to his New Deal proposals. The sitting Court denied any need for more justices. Conservatives and liberals alike believed such a plan amounted to an attack on the Court's independence. Many consider FDR's plan an example of an imperial presidency (pages 123–126).

The Court changed ideologically, however, when one of the conservatives took an about-face in *West Coast Hotel v. Parrish* (1937), which sustained a Washington state minimum wage law. Justice Owen Roberts became "the switch in time that saved nine," meaning that there was no longer any need to try to pack the Court with additional justices. After the *West Coast Hotel* decision, the Court upheld every New Deal measure that came before it. Roosevelt pressed ahead with more legislation, including a national minimum wage that has withstood constitutional scrutiny ever since. Winning four elections, he was able to appoint nine new justices to the Court friendly to his policies before his death in 1944.

A Court Dedicated to Individual Liberties

In the post-World War II years, the Court protected and extended individual liberties. It delivered mixed messages on civil liberties up to this point—holding states to First Amendment protections while allowing government infringements in times of national security threats. For example, it upheld FDR's executive order that placed Japanese Americans in internment camps after the Japanese attack in 1941 of the U.S. naval base in Pearl Harbor, in what was then Hawaii Territory (*Korematsu v. United States*, 1944). After that, however, the Court began a fairly consistent effort to protect individual liberties and the rights of accused criminals. The trend crested in 1973 when the Court upheld a woman's right to an abortion in *Roe v. Wade*.

The Warren Court The Court extended many liberties under Chief Justice **Earl Warren** after President Dwight Eisenhower appointed him in 1953. As attorney general for California during the war, Warren oversaw the internment of Japanese Americans, and in 1948 he was the Republican's vice presidential nominee. But any expectations that Warren would act as a conservative judge were lost soon after he took the bench.

Civil Rights and Civil Liberties Warren's first major case was *Brown v. Board of Education* decided in 1954 (pages 305–307). When the National Association for the Advancement of Colored People Legal Defense Fund argued that the "separate but equal" standard set by the Court in the 1896 *Plessy v. Ferguson* decision was outdated and violated the Fourteenth Amendment's equal protection clause in public education, Warren rallied his fellow justices to a unanimous opinion in favor of Brown. As the district courts worked out the particulars of the integration process, the High Court issued several subsequent unanimous pro-integration rulings over the next decade.

Warren was flanked by civil libertarians Hugo Black and William O. Douglas. With them, the Court set several precedents to guarantee rights to accused defendants that ultimately created a national criminal justice system. They declared that courts could throw out evidence obtained unlawfully by the police. States soon had to provide defense attorneys for indigent (poor) defendants at state expense. And arrested suspects had to be formally informed of their rights with the so-called *Miranda* ruling.

The Supreme Court also placed a high priority on the First Amendment's protection against a government-established religion and protection for citizens' free speech. It outlawed school-sponsored prayer (*Engel v. Vitale,*

1962—page 254) and upheld students' rights to nondisruptive symbolic speech in schools (*Tinker v. Des Moines Public Schools*, 1969—page 243). The Court upheld the press's protection against charges of libel. The Warren Court legacy is that of an activist, liberal court that upheld the individual rights of minorities and the accused.

Warren's legacy did not please traditionalists because his Court overturned state policies created by democratically elected legislatures. The controversial or unpopular decisions led some people to challenge the Court's legitimacy. Several Warren Court decisions seemed to insult states' political cultures and threaten to drain state treasuries. Some argued that Earl Warren should be impeached. The Warren Court had made unpopular decisions, but it had not committed impeachable acts—such as taking bribes or failing to carry out the job—so there wasn't political support in the House for Warren's impeachment. Then, as now, the only surefire way to alter the Court's membership is to await justices' retirements or deaths so a president can replace them with different nominees.

The Burger Court President Richard Nixon won the 1968 election, in part by painting Warren's Court as an affront to law enforcement and local control. When Warren announced his retirement, Nixon replaced him with U.S. appeals court justice Warren Burger. But Burger by no means satisfied Nixon's quest to instill a conservative philosophy, and he largely failed in judicial leadership. While lacking Warren's leadership skills, Burger continued American law on a path similar to the one Warren had begun.

Burger had a difficult time leading discussions "in conference"—the Court's closed-chamber discussions. Some suspected that Burger at times switched his opinion toward the end of the process in order to gain control and to draft or assign the writing of the opinion. The chief often couldn't round up enough agreement to get a five-justice majority. Thus cases went undecided while the Court took on additional ones. The justices became overworked and took as many as 150 appeals in a year.

In *Roe v. Wade*, Burger joined six others on the Court to outlaw or modify state anti-abortion laws as a violation of due process. With this ruling, a woman could now obtain an abortion, unconditionally, through the first trimester of pregnancy. He also penned a unanimous opinion to uphold school busing for racial enrollment balance.

Supreme Court historian and former clerk Edward Lazarus refers to Burger as "an intellectual lightweight" who had "alienated his colleagues and even his natural allies." By 1986, Burger had proven pretentious and chafing to his colleagues, and he had simply become tired. At the press conference where he announced his retirement, a reporter asked him what he would miss most on the Court. Burger stalled, sighed, and said, "Nothing."

The Rehnquist Court At the same press conference, President Reagan elevated Associate Justice William Rehnquist to the chief position. Rehnquist had attended Stanford Law School and clerked for Supreme Court Justice

Robert Jackson in the 1950s. Based on Rehnquist's strict constructionist views, President Nixon had nominated Rehnquist for the High Court. The Senate did not confirm him easily and accused him of racism, as he had recommended upholding the "separate but equal" doctrine when clerking for a justice in the early 1950s en route to the *Brown* ruling. This same controversy arose in 1986 as he accepted the chief's position.

Initially, Rehnquist found himself in dissent and all alone on several cases, earning him the nickname "the Lone Ranger." When Rehnquist took over for Burger, however, additional strict constructionists soon joined him. He improved the conference procedures and decreased the Court's caseload. All the justices, liberals and conservatives alike, welcomed the changes. In the 1990s, the Rehnquist Court upheld state rights to place limitations on access to abortions and limited Congress's commerce clause authority. In addition to efficiency, Rehnquist had ushered in another ideological shift.

The Supreme Court Today

When President George W. Bush replaced Chief Justice Rehnquist after his death with John Roberts (2005), the Court's membership had not changed for about 12 years. President Barack Obama appointed two justices during his first term, circuit judge Sonia Sotomayor (2009), who became the first justice of Hispanic descent and the first Latina, and U.S. Solicitor General Elena Kagan (2010). In 2017, President Trump nominated Neil Gorsuch as the Court's newest member.

Diversity Originally, the Court was a white, Protestant man's institution. Some diversity came when presidents appointed Catholics and Jews. In 1967, President Lyndon Johnson appointed the first African American, Thurgood Marshall. Ronald Reagan appointed the first woman, Sandra Day O'Connor, in 1981.

The current Court is as diverse and as experienced as it has ever been. One African American, Clarence Thomas, and three females serve on the Court. There are five Catholics, three Jews, and one Protestant. Historically, many Supreme Court justices had never served as judges before their nomination. Presidents from FDR through Nixon tended to nominate highly experienced political figures and presidential allies. Since 1969, however, that trend has changed to naming lesser-known jurists who have served on other federal courts and therefore bring considerable judicial experience to the Court.

Ideology The Rehnquist Court and the current Roberts Court have been difficult to predict. The conservative and liberal wings have been balanced by the swing votes of O'Connor and now Justice Anthony Kennedy. **Swing votes** are those often tie-breaking votes cast by justices whose opinions cannot always be easily predicted. For the past decade or so, most experts have been quick to characterize the Court as leaning conservative. However, the Court has limited states' use of the death penalty and upheld government's eminent domain authority for economic development.

Chief Justice **John Roberts** has guided the Court with judicial minimalism. "Judges and justices are servants of the law, not the other way around. Judges are like umpires," he said during his confirmation hearing. "Umpires don't make rules; they apply them . . . nobody ever went to a ball game to see the umpire." Robert's operation takes fewer cases, while the conversations and conferences go longer. He has achieved more unanimity in decisions than some previous chief justices and has written more narrow opinions to address the questions before the Court.

CURRENT AND RECENT SUPREME COURT JUSTICES				
Current Justices	**President**	**Senate vote**	**Prior Job**	**Law school**
John Roberts, Chief	G.W. Bush	78—22	DC Circuit	Harvard
Anthony Kennedy	Reagan	97—0	Ninth Circuit	Harvard
Clarence Thomas	G.H.W. Bush	52—48	DC Circuit	Yale
Ruth Bader Ginsburg	Clinton	96—3	DC Circuit	Harvard
Stephen Breyer	Clinton	87—9	First Circuit	Harvard
Samuel Alito	G.W. Bush	58—42	Third Circuit	Yale
Sonia Sotomayor	Obama	68—31	Second Circuit	Yale
Elena Kagan	Obama	63—37	Solicitor General	Harvard
Neil Gorsuch	Trump	54-45	Tenth Circuit	Harvard
Recent Justices				
William Rehnquist	Nixon	68—26	Justice Dept.	Stanford
Antonin Scalia	Reagan	98—0	DC Circuit	Harvard
John Paul Stevens	Ford	98—0	Seventh Circuit	Northwestern
David Souter	G.H.W. Bush	90—9	First Circuit	Harvard
Byron White	Kennedy	Voice vote	Justice Dept.	Yale
Sandra Day O'Connor	Reagan	99—0	Arizona Court of Appeals	Stanford
Harry Blackmun	Nixon	94—0	Eighth Circuit	Harvard
Lewis Powell	Nixon	89—1	ABA President	Harvard
Warren Burger	Nixon	74—3	DC Circuit	St. Paul

Continuity and Change Over Time

The Supreme Court is known more for continuity than for change. Membership is small and justices serve long tenures. The Court's customs are established through consensus and remain over generations. The contemporary group operates in many ways as the earlier Courts did. Debate about the Court focuses on some of the same issues as in earlier times as well.

The combination of the lifetime tenure of justices and the Court's exercise of judicial review has given rise to debates over the legitimacy of the Supreme Court. Some people believe, as Brutus expressed more than 200 years ago, that with no power to hold them accountable, the justices on the Supreme Court are too separated from the real sources of power—the people and the legislature—to be legitimate arbiters of democratic law. Brutus believed the Supreme Court justices would "be placed in a situation altogether unprecedented in a free country. They are to be rendered totally independent, both of the people and the legislature, both with respect to their offices and salaries. No errors they may commit can be corrected by any power above them, if any such power there be, nor can they be removed from office for making ever so many erroneous adjudications."

Furthermore, as you read, the composition of the Court changes as seats become vacant, and the presidential appointments to fill them can lead to shifts in the ideology of the Court. These changes can result in the overturning of some precedents, calling into question the reliability and therefore legitimacy of Supreme Court decisions. Controversial and unpopular decisions can face a number of challenges.

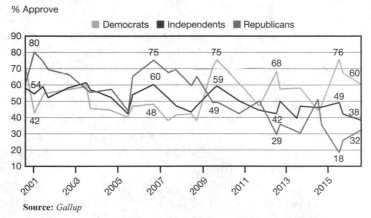

Supreme Court Job Approval, by Political Party

Source: *Gallup*

Democrats tend to have higher approval of the Supreme Court than Republicans. Two controversial rulings widened the partisan gap. In 2012, the Court upheld a key provision in the Patient Protection and Affordable Care Act ("Obamacare"), an act much disliked by Republicans. In 2015, the Court ruled in *Obergefell v. Hodges* that same-sex couples have a fundamental right to marry. The partisan gap in the view of the Supreme Court after that decision was the widest ever recorded.

Stare Decisis and Constitutional Application

Precedent plays an important role in judicial decision-making. Rulings by higher courts bind lower courts to the same ruling. However, in 1932 Justice Brandeis wrote in a dissenting opinion in *Burnet v. Coronado Oil & Gas Co.,* "Stare decisis is usually the wise policy, because in most matters it is more important that the applicable law be settled than it be settled right." This was especially true about rulings related to legislation, he argued, because errors in the Court's decision could be corrected by Congress. However, on matters related to the application of the Constitution, which the legislature has no power to change, Brandeis noted that the Court has often reconsidered and overturned its own previous ruling if an earlier one was made in error.

Consider the 1944 case of *Smith v. Allwright*. The Court had ruled in 1935 in *Grovey v. Townsend* that the Democratic Party of Texas, as a private, voluntary organization, could determine its own membership rules even if those rules banned African Americans from membership and therefore prevented them from voting in the primary. In 1944, Lonnie E. Smith, an African American denied the right to vote in a Texas primary, brought suit, arguing that his rights under the Fifteenth Amendment were being violated. Mr. Justice Reed delivered the majority opinion in *Smith v. Allwright* and furthered the discussion of stare decisis vs. overturning a previous decision.

"The privilege of membership in a party may be, as this Court said in *Grovey v. Townsend,* no concern of a state. But when, as here, that privilege is also the essential qualification for voting in a primary to select nominees for a general election, the state makes the action of the party the action of the state. In reaching this conclusion, we are not unmindful of the desirability of continuity of decision in constitutional questions. However, when convinced of former error, this Court has never felt constrained to follow precedent. In constitutional questions, where correction depends upon amendment, and not upon legislative action, this Court throughout its history has freely exercised its power to reexamine the basis of its constitutional decisions. . . This is particularly true when the decision believed erroneous is the application of a constitutional principle, rather than an interpretation of the Constitution to extract the principle itself. Here, we are applying, contrary to the recent decision in *Grovey v. Townsend,* the well established principle of the Fifteenth Amendment, forbidding the abridgement by a state of a citizen's right to vote. *Grovey v. Townsend* is overruled."

Why in only nine years was the opinion of the Court changed so dramatically? First, the composition of the Court had changed significantly. The conservative "Four Horsemen" had retired, and FDR had appointed more liberal judges to replace them. Second, the social context was very different. The United States was at war, and African Americans in the military served in segregated divisions, fighting to overturn fascism and establish democratic rule. Many in the United States noticed the gap between the ideals of the war, supported by 2.5 million African Americans who volunteered for duty, and the realities of African American disenfranchisement in the South. As an independent body, the Supreme Court is not accountable to public opinion; nonetheless, the liberal justices no doubt reflected the changing social context as they overturned *Grovey*.

Judicial Activism vs. Judicial Restraint

After the Supreme Court first exercised judicial review in *Marbury*, it checked the legislature only one more time in the Republic's first full century, in the Dred Scott case. Other courts have since reserved the right to rule on government action in violation of constitutional principles, whether by the legislature or the executive. Judicial review has placed the Supreme Court, as Brutus predicted, above the other branches, making it the final arbiter on controversies of federalism that typically have made the federal government supreme while defining what states, Congress, and the president can or cannot do.

When judges strike down laws or reverse public policy, they are said to be exercising **judicial activism**. (To remember this concept, think *judges acting* to create the law.) Activism can be liberal or conservative, depending on the nature of the law that is struck down. When the Court threw out the New York maximum-hours law in 1905 in *Lochner*, it acted conservatively because it rejected an established liberal statute. In *Roe v. Wade*, the Court acted liberally to remove a conservative anti-abortion policy in Texas. Courts at multiple levels in both the state and federal systems have struck down statutes as well as executive branch decisions.

The Court's power to strike down parts of or entire laws has encouraged litigation and changes in policy. Gun owners and the National Rifle Association (NRA) supported an effort to overturn a ban on handguns in Washington, D.C. and got a victory in the *Heller* decision (page 263). Several state attorneys general who opposed the Affordable Care Act sued to overturn it. In a 5:4 decision, in *National Federation of Independent Business v. Sebelius*, the Court upheld the key element of the Affordable Care Act, the individual mandate. That mandate is the federal requirement that all citizens must purchase health insurance or pay a penalty. In striking down limits on when a corporation can advertise during a campaign season, it struck down parts of Congress's Bipartisan Campaign Reform Act (2002) in *Citizens United v. FEC* (2010) (page 508).

Critics of judicial activism tend to point out that, in a democracy, elected representative legislatures should create policy. These critics advocate for **judicial self-restraint**. Chief Justice Harlan Fiske Stone first used the term in his 1936 dissent when the majority outlawed a New Deal program. The Court should not, say these critics, decide a dispute in that manner unless there is a concrete injury to be relieved by the decision. Conservative strict constructionist Antonin Scalia once claimed, "A 'living' Constitution judge [is] a happy fellow who comes home at night to his wife and says, 'The Constitution means exactly what I think it ought to mean!'" Justices should not declare a law unconstitutional, strict constructionists say today, when it merely violates their own idea of what the Constitution means in a contemporary context, but only when the law clearly and directly contradicts the document. To do otherwise is "legislating from the bench," say strict constructionists. This ongoing debate about judicial activism and restraint has coincided with discussions about the Court's role in shaping national policy

Still other critics argue that judicial policymaking is ineffective as well as undemocratic. Wise judges have a firm understanding of the Constitution and citizens' rights, but they don't always study issues over time. Most judges don't have special expertise on matters of environmental protection, operating schools, or other administrative matters. They don't have the support systems of lawmakers, such as committee staffers and researchers, to fully engage an issue to find a solution. So when courts rule, the outcome is not always practical or manageable for those meant to implement it. Additionally, many such court rulings are just unpopular.

How Cases Reach the Supreme Court

The Supreme Court is guided by Article III, congressional acts, and its own rules. Congress is the authority on the Court's size and funding. The Court began creating rules in 1790 and now has 48 formal rules. These guide the submission of briefs, the Court's calendar, deadlines, fees, paperwork requirements, jurisdiction, and the handling of different types of cases. Less formal customs and traditions it has developed also guide the Court's operation.

As you read, the Court has both original and appellate jurisdiction. It serves as a trial court in rare cases, typically when one state sues another over a border dispute or to settle some type of interstate compact. It also accepts *in forma pauperis* briefs, filings by prisoners (in the form of a pauper) seeking a new trial.

As the nation's highest appeals court, the Court takes cases from the 13 circuits and the 50 states. Two-thirds or more of appeals come through the federal system. The Supreme Court has a more direct jurisdiction over cases starting in U.S. district courts.

Like the circuit courts, the Supreme Court accepts appeals each year from among thousands filed. The petitioner files a **petition for certiorari**, a brief arguing why the lower court erred. The Supreme Court reviews these to determine if the claim is worthy and if it should grant the appeal. To be more efficient, the justices share their clerks, who review the petitions for certiorari and determine which are worthy. This "cert pool" becomes a gatekeeper at the Supreme Court. If an appeal is deemed worthy, the justices add the claim to their "discuss list." On a regular basis, all nine justices gather in conference to discuss these claims. They consider past precedents and the real impact on the petitioner and respondent. The Supreme Court does not consider hypothetical or theoretical damages; the claimant must show actual damage. Finally, the justices consider the wider national and societal impact if they take and rule on the case. Once four of the nine justices agree to accept the case, the appeal is granted. This **rule of four**, a standard less than a majority, reflects courts' commitments to claims by minorities.

The Court then issues a **writ of certiorari** to the lower court, informing it of the Court's decision and to request the full trial transcript. The justices spend much time reading the case record. Then a date is set for oral arguments. When the Court opens on the first Monday in October, the nine justices enter to hear the petitioner and respondent make their cases, each having 30 minutes for argument. A Supreme Court hearing is not a trial but a chance for each side to persuade justices on one or more narrow points of law. Justices will ask questions, pose hypothetical scenarios, and at times boldly signal their viewpoints. Sometime after the hearing, the justices will reconvene in conference to discuss the arguments and make a decision. A simple majority rules.

Opinions and Caseload

Chief Justice John Marshall's legacy of unanimity has vanished. The Court comes to a unanimous decision only about 30 to 40 percent of the time. Therefore, it issues varying opinions on the law. Once the Court comes to a majority, the chief justice, or the most senior justice in the majority, either writes the Court's opinion or assigns it to another justice in the majority. In making that decision, the assigning justice considers who has expertise on the topic, who is passionate about the issue, and what the nature of the discussions were that took place in conference. The **majority opinion** is the Court's opinion. It is the judicial branch's law much as a statute is Congress's law or an executive order is law created by a president. The majority opinion sums up the case, the Court's decision, and its rationale.

Front row, left to right: Associate Justice Ruth Bader Ginsburg, Associate Justice Anthony M. Kennedy, Chief Justice John G. Roberts, Jr., Associate Justice Clarence Thomas, Associate Justice Stephen G. Breyer. Back row: Associate Justice Elena Kagan, Associate Justice Samuel A. Alito, Jr., Associate Justice Sonia Sotomayor, Associate Justice Neil M. Gorsuch. Credit: Franz Jantzen, Collection of the Supreme Court of the United States

Justices who find themselves differing from the majority can draft and issue differing opinions. Some may agree with the majority and join that vote but have reservations about the majority's legal reasoning. They might write a **concurring opinion**. Those who vote against the majority often write a **dissenting opinion**. The dissenting opinion has no force of law but allows a justice to explain his disagreements with his colleagues. While these have no immediate legal bearing, dissenting opinions send a message to the legal community or to America at large and are often referenced in later cases when the Court might revisit the issue or reverse the precedent. On occasion, the Court will issue a decision without the full explanation. This is known as a *per curium* **opinion**.

Each justice typically employs four law clerks to assist them with handling briefs and analyzing important cases. These bright young attorneys typically graduate high in their classes at Ivy League law schools and have a prosperous legal career ahead of them. In fact, several Supreme Court justices of the modern era served as clerks in their earlier days. They preview cases for their bosses and assist them with writing the opinions.

Interactions with Other Branches of Government

Congress and the president interact with the judiciary in many ways. From the creation of various courts to the appointment of judges to implementation of a judicial decision, the judiciary often crosses paths with the other two branches. Despite the concern of some Anti-Federalists, the other branches of government do have ways to limit the power of the Supreme Court. BIG IDEA: The Constitution built in checks and balances to keep any branch from becoming too powerful.

Presidential Appointments and Senate Confirmation

With hundreds of judgeships in the lower courts, presidents will have a chance to appoint several judges to the federal bench over their four or eight years in office. When a vacancy occurs, or when Congress creates a new seat on an overloaded court, the president carefully selects a qualified judge because that person can shape law and will likely do so until late in his or her life.

Since John Adams's appointment of the Federalist "midnight judges" in 1801 (page 199), presidents have shaped the judiciary with jurists who reflect their political and judicial philosophy. District and circuit appointments receive less news coverage and have less impact than Supreme Court nominees but are influential nonetheless. Presidents tend to consider candidates from the same or nearby areas in which they will serve. Law school deans, high-level state judges, and successful lawyers in private practice make excellent candidates. The president's White House legal team and the Department of Justice, in conjunction with the Senate, seek out good candidates to find experienced, favorable nominees.

BY THE NUMBERS SUPREME COURT'S RECENT CASELOAD		
Term	**Cases Filed**	**Cases Argued**
2004	7,496	87
2005	8,521	87
2006	8, 857	78
2007	8,241	75
2008	7, 738	87
2009	8,159	82
2010	7,857	86
2011	7,713	79
2012	7,509	77
2013	7,376	79
2014	7,033	75
2015	6,575	82

What do the numbers show? Roughly how many cases are appealed to the Supreme Court each year? How many cases does the Court generally accept? What fraction or percent of cases appealed does the Court take? Recall the reasons the Supreme Court will or will not accept an appeal.

Source: *U.S. Supreme Court*

Not all confirmed judges follow the philosophy the appointing president expected. Once confirmed, judges are independent from the executive. Several have disappointed the presidents who appointed them. Eisenhower did not bring Earl Warren to the Supreme Court to make liberal, activist decisions. Warren Burger disappointed Nixon when he voted to legalize abortion and to promote school busing for racial balance. Justice David Souter, appointed by Republican George H.W. Bush in 1990, proved to be a reliably liberal vote until he retired in 2009.

Senate's Advice and Consent The Senate Judiciary Committee looks over all the president's judicial appointments. Sometimes nominees appear before the committee to answer senators' questions about their experience or their views on the law. Less controversial district judges are confirmed without notice based largely on the recommendation of the senators from the nominee's state. The more controversial, polarizing Supreme Court nominees will receive greater attention during sometimes contentious and dramatic hearings.

The quick determination of an appointee's political philosophy has become known as a **litmus test**. Much like quickly testing a solution for its pH in chemistry class, someone trying to determine a judicial nominee's ideology on the political spectrum will ask a pointed question on a controversial issue, or look at one of his or her prior opinions from a lower court. Presidents, senators, or pundits can conduct such a "test." The very term has a built in criticism, as a judge's complex judicial philosophy should not be determined as quickly as a black-and-white scientific measure.

Senatorial Courtesy The Senate firmly reserves its right of advice and consent. "In practical terms," said George W. Bush administration attorney Rachel Brand, "the home state senators are almost as important as—and sometimes more important than—the president in determining who will be nominated to a particular lower-court judgeship." This practice of **senatorial courtesy** is especially routine with district judge appointments, as districts are entirely within a given state. When vacancies occur, senators typically recommend judges to the White House.

Senate procedure and tradition give individual senators veto power over nominees located within their respective states. For U.S. district court nominations, each of the two senators receives a blue slip—a blue piece of paper they return to the Judiciary Committee to allow the process to move forward. To derail the process, a senator can return the slip with a negative indication or never return it at all. The committee chairman will usually not hold a hearing on the nominee's confirmation until both senators have consented. This custom has encouraged presidents to consult with the home-state senators early in the process.

All senators embrace this influence. They are the guardians and representatives for their states. The other 98 senators tend to follow the home state senators' lead, especially if they are in the same party, and vote for or against the nominated judge based on the senators' views. This custom is somewhat followed with appeals court judges as well. Appeals courts never encompass only one state, so the privilege and power of senatorial courtesy is less likely.

Confirmation When a Supreme Court vacancy occurs, a president has a unique opportunity to shape American jurisprudence. Of the 161 nominations to the Supreme Court over U.S. history, 36 were not confirmed. Eleven were rejected by a vote of the full Senate. The others were either never acted on by the Judiciary Committee or withdrawn by the nominee or by the president. Few confirmations brought rancor or public spectacle until the Senate rejected two of President Nixon's nominees. Since then, the Court's influence on controversial topics, intense partisanship, the public nature of the confirmation process, and contentious hearings have highlighted the divides between the parties.

Interest Groups The increasingly publicized confirmation process has also involved interest groups. Confirmation hearings were not public until 1929. In recent years, they have become a spectacle and may include a long list of witnesses testifying about the nominee's qualifications. The most active and reputable interest group to testify about judicial nominees is the American Bar Association (ABA). This powerful group represents the national interest of attorneys and the legal profession. Since the 1950s, the ABA has been involved in the process. They rate nominees as "highly qualified," "qualified," and "not qualified." More recently, additional groups weigh in on the process, especially when they see their interests threatened or enhanced. Interest groups also target a senator's home state when they feel strongly about a nominee, urging voters to contact their senators in support or in opposition to the nominee. Indeed, interest groups sometimes suggest or even draft questions for senators to assist them at the confirmation hearings.

Getting "Borked" The confirmation process began to focus on ideology during the Reagan and first Bush administrations. The process took this turn when Reagan chose U.S. Appeals Court Justice Robert Bork in 1987. Bork was the conservatives' leading intellectual in the legal community. At 60 years old, he had been a professor at Yale Law School, U.S. solicitor general, and a successful corporate lawyer. He was an advocate of original intent, seeking to uphold the Constitution as intended by the framers. He made clear that he despised the rulings of the activist Warren Court. He spoke against decisions that mandated legislative reapportionment, upheld affirmative action, and placed citizen privacy over state authority.

When asked about his nomination, then-Senator Joe Biden, chair of the Senate Judiciary Committee, warned the White House that choosing Bork would likely result in a confirmation fight. Within hours of Reagan's nomination, Senator Edward Kennedy drew a line in the sand at a Senate press conference. "Robert Bork's America," Kennedy said, "is a land in which women would be forced into back alley abortions, blacks would sit at segregated lunch counters, rogue police could break down citizen's doors in midnight raids, and school children could not be taught evolution."

Kennedy's warning brought attention to Judge Bork's extreme views that threatened to turn back a generation of civil rights and civil liberties decisions. What followed was a raucous, lengthy confirmation hearing. Bork himself jousted with Senator Biden for hours. This contest drew attention as it was a pivotal moment for the Court when every liberal and conservative onlooker in the country had chosen sides as well as a clear illustration of the power of the Senate to influence the direction of the judiciary. After hearings with the committee, the full Senate, which had unanimously confirmed Bork as an appeals court judge in 1981, rejected him by a vote of 58 to 42. The term "to bork" entered the American political lexicon, defined more recently by the *New York Times*: "to destroy a judicial nominee through a concerted attack on his character, background, and philosophy."

Clarence Thomas In 1991, Justice Thurgood Marshall, the first African American on the Court, retired. President George H.W. Bush and his advisors introduced Marshall's replacement, conservative African-American judge Clarence Thomas. Thomas's controversial confirmation process centered on ideology, experience, and sexual harassment.

By naming Thomas, Bush satisfied the left's penchant for diversity, while also satisfying his conservative base with a strict constructionist. As Jeffrey Toobin, author of *The Nine*, says, "The list of plausible candidates that fit both qualifications pretty much began and ended with Clarence Thomas." After onlookers expressed concern about Thomas's ideology, they then pointed at his lack of experience. He had never argued a single case in any federal appeals court, much less the Supreme Court. He had never written a book, an article, or legal brief of any consequence. He had served as an appeals judge on the D.C. Circuit for about one year. The ABA gave him only a "qualified" rating, a rarity among nominees to the High Court.

Then Anita Hill came forward. Hill had some years earlier worked on Thomas's staff in the Department of Education and the Equal Employment Opportunity Commission and accused him of an array of sexually suggestive office behavior. The Judiciary Committee then invited her to testify. In a highly televised carnival atmosphere, Hill testified for seven hours about the harassing comments Thomas had made and the pornographic films he discussed. Thomas denied all the allegations and called the hearing a "high-tech lynching." After a tie vote in committee, the full Senate barely confirmed him.

"The Nuclear Option" During George W. Bush's first term, Democrats did not allow a vote on 10 of the 52 appeals court nominees that had cleared committee. Conservative nominees were delayed by Senate procedure. The Democrats, in the minority at the time, invoked the right to filibuster votes on judges. One Bush nominee waited four years.

Bush declared in his State of the Union message, "Every judicial nominee deserves an up or down vote." Senate Republicans threatened to change the rules to disallow the filibuster, which could be done with a simple majority vote. The threat to the filibuster became known as a drastic "nuclear option." The nuclear option was averted when a bipartisan group of senators dubbed the "Gang of 14" joined forces to create a compromise that kept the Senate rules the same while confirming most appointees.

President Obama had a lower confirmation rate than Bush. Late in his first term, about 76 percent of Obama's nominees had been confirmed, while nearly 87 percent of Bush's nominees were confirmed. Bush nominees waited, on average 46 days to be confirmed; Obama's waited an average of 115 days.

Denying Garland In February 2016, Associate Justice Antonin Scalia died. Republican presidential candidates in the primary race agreed on one thing: the next president should appoint Scalia's replacement. With Democratic President Obama in his final year on the job, Republican Senate Majority Leader Mitch McConnell announced that the Senate would not hold a vote on any nominee until the voters elected a new president. A month later, with 10 months remaining until a new president would be sworn in, Obama nominated Judge Merrick Garland to replace Scalia. Garland was a judicial pick from the D.C. Circuit with a unanimous "well-qualified" rating from the ABA. Senator

McConnell's decision was strategic if unusual, and he kept his promise to the dismay of many. Vacancies on the Supreme Court of course occur and the Court can operate temporarily with eight members, but to assure the vacancy for that period was unprecedented.

Constitutionally, nothing mandates a timeline on the Senate's confirmation process. Pundits and onlookers alike wondered about the propriety of this decision. Democrats saw the drastic move as a power grab by the Republican Senate. Some Republicans questioned McConnell's strategy, especially considering Democrat Hillary Clinton was the odds-on favorite to win the presidential election and might nominate a judge more liberal than Garland. On the day Americans would elect a new president, they would also elect several new senators. Who knew whether Republicans would have any say in the process after this election?

In the end, Donald Trump won the presidency, Republicans retained control of the Senate, and Trump nominated Tenth Circuit Justice Neil Gorsuch within two weeks of his inauguration. The Senate confirmed Gorsuch by a vote of 54 to 45.

BY THE NUMBERS RECENT PRESIDENTS' JUDICIAL APPOINTMENTS				
President	Supreme Court	Appeals Courts	District Courts	Total
Nixon (1969–1974)	4	45	182	231
Ford (1974–1977)	1	12	52	65
Carter (1977–1981)	0	56	206	262
Reagan (1981–1989)	3	78	292	373
G.H.W.Bush (1989–1993)	2	37	149	188
Clinton (1993–2001)	2	62	306	370
G.W. Bush (2001–2009)	2	61	261	324
Obama (2009–2017)	2	49	268	319

Source: *U.S. Courts. Excludes Court of International Trade*

What do the numbers show? What presidents appointed more judges than others? On average, how many Supreme Court judges does a president appoint? How many lower court judges? Which president of recent years appointed the most? How do a president's judicial appointees impact law and government in the United States?

Reforming Judicial Confirmation With all the interested parties focused on the potential impact of a new Supreme Court justice, confirmation has become a public and hotly debated event for an otherwise private, venerable institution. Joyce Baugh of Central Michigan University offers a solution to tame the confirmation process: Limit the number of participants at the hearings, prevent nominees from testifying, prevent senators from offering specific hypotheticals to conduct a litmus test, and base confirmation solely on nominees' written records and testimony from legal experts. Chief John Roberts spoke to the persistent problem of filling judicial vacancies in an age of partisanship. In his annual report on the judiciary, he declared, "Each party has found it easy to turn on a dime from decrying to defending the blocking of judicial nominations, depending on their changing political fortunes."

Executive and Legislative Influence on the Courts' Power

In addition to strategically choosing judicial nominees and selectively approving them, the president and Congress interact with lower courts and the Supreme Court in additional ways. The first two branches have the powers to bring matters and crimes to court, impeach and remove judges, use the power of the purse to affect the Judiciary and judicial decisions, partially redefine courts' jurisdiction, and implement court rulings in their own way.

The Justice Department In addition to appointing the judiciary, the executive branch enters the federal courts to enforce criminal law and to weigh in on legal questions. The president's Department of Justice, headed by the attorney general, investigates federal crimes with the Federal Bureau of Investigation (FBI) or the Drug Enforcement Administration (DEA), and U.S. attorneys prosecute the accused criminals. These attorneys are also the legal authority for federal civil law on a more local basis. When a party sues the federal government, it is the U.S. attorneys who defend the United States. In appealed criminal cases, these attorneys present the oral arguments in the circuit courts.

Another high-ranking figure in the Department of Justice is the **solicitor general,** who works in the Washington office. Appointed by the president and approved by the Senate, the solicitor general determines which cases to appeal to the U.S. Supreme Court and represents the United States in the Supreme Court room. When you see a Supreme Court case entitled the *United States v. John Doe*, it means the United States lost in one of the circuit courts and the solicitor general sought an appeal.

The solicitor general may also submit an *amicus curiae* **brief** (friend of the court brief) to the Supreme Court in cases where the United States is not a party. An amicus brief argues for a particular ruling in the case. Several solicitors general have later been appointed to the High Court, notably Stanley Reed, Thurgood Marshall, and Elena Kagan.

Impeachment Federal judges who have acted improperly can be removed by the same process for accusing and removing a president. In 1804, John Pickering became the first judge to be impeached. He was an abusive, partisan drunkard on his way to insanity. Pickering refused to resign, so the House impeached him and the Senate convicted him on the charges of drunkenness and unlawful rulings. Almost immediately, Thomas Jefferson's party, the Democratic-Republicans, moved to impeach Supreme Court Justice Samuel Chase. In an age of partisan attacks, Jefferson's party wanted to weaken the remaining presence of Federalists on the federal bench. Chase had vigorously supported convictions under the Sedition Acts.

However, Jefferson wanted to avoid making the impeachment process a political tool to rid the third branch of opponents, so he withdrew his support for the endeavor, and Chase survived the Senate vote. Impeachment has served as Congress's check on the so-called life terms.

The House has impeached a total of 15 federal judges. The most recent was the 2010 impeachment of U.S. District Judge Thomas Porteous, whom the Senate later found guilty of corruption and perjury and voted to remove.

Congressional Oversight and Influence Congress sets and pays judges' salaries. Congress budgets for the construction and maintenance of federal courthouses. It has passed an entire body of law that helps govern the judiciary. This includes regulations about courtroom procedures to judicial recusal—judges withdrawing from a case if they have a conflict of interest. Occasionally Congress creates new seats in the 94 district courts and on the 13 appeals courts. Congress has more than doubled the number of circuit and district judges over the last 50 years.

SELECTED U.S. COURTS OF SPECIAL JURISDICTION
• U.S. Court of Appeals for the Armed Services
• U.S. Court of Federal Claims
• U.S. Court of International Trade
• U.S. Tax Court
• U.S. Court of Appeals for Veterans Claims

Some federal courts have only a limited, or special, jurisdiction. They are authorized to hear only those cases that fall within their limited jurisdiction.

Defining Jurisdiction Article III includes the power to consider all cases arising under the Constitution, federal law or treaty, and admiralty or maritime jurisdiction. It also addresses the types of cases that the judicial branch and specifically the "Supreme Court shall have . . . under such Regulations as the Congress shall make."

Since the initial Judiciary Act of 1789, Congress has periodically defined and reshaped the courts' jurisdiction. The most convenient and unquestioned power involves the legislature's power to define what types of cases are heard by which federal courts and which types of cases are left to the state courts. Article III also empowers Congress to define the types of parties that can go to the various courts, thereby defining **standing**, the requirements for bringing a case to court. Congress cannot create state courts, but it can endow them with concurrent power to hear certain cases concerning federal law.

Congress occasionally delves into "court-stripping," or jurisdiction stripping, when it wants to limit the judicial branch's power in hearing cases on particular topics. For example, in the 108th Congress of 2003–2005, in an effort to protect the Pledge of Allegiance which was under fire for its "under God" phrase, the House voted to take away the courts' power to hear such cases. It also voted to deny funds in order to implement any such decisions. The same House voted to prevent federal courts from hearing cases regarding the Defense of Marriage Act. Conservative representatives were reacting to court filings, lower federal court decisions, or the coming strategy of using the courts to legalize same-sex marriage. The Senate failed to vote for the law, and thus courts have ruled on these matters.

Legislating after Unfavorable Decisions Many people believe the Supreme Court's decision is final, but sometimes it is not. In many precedent-setting decisions, the High Court is interpreting language in the Constitution. That language can be changed through constitutional amendments. Among Congress's earliest reactions to unfavorable judicial decisions was the passage and ratification of the obscure Eleventh Amendment in response to the 1794 ruling in *Chisolm v. Georgia*.

Anti-Federalists and states' rights advocates had warned that the new federal courts might overpower the state courts, and they saw the decision in *Chisolm v. Georgia* as such an encroachment. The case involved South Carolina residents seeking to recoup war debts from Georgia's government. Georgia denied that such a suit could take place in federal court and refused to show up. The Supreme Court ruled in *Chisolm* that federal courts had jurisdiction over such cases and opened the door for additional pending suits against other states. In response, Congress members, especially from the states involved in the lawsuits, proposed the Eleventh Amendment. The Amendment prohibits the federal courts from considering certain lawsuits against states. It is also understood to mean that state courts do not have to hear certain suits against the state, if they are based on federal law. The Eleventh Amendment altered the judicial branch's jurisdiction at the highest level and is the only amendment to do so.

However, additional amendments that addressed the substance of law have been proposed and ratified as reactions to unfavorable Supreme Court decisions. For example, following the Civil War, the passage of the Fourteenth Amendment effectively overturned the decision in the Dred Scott case by guaranteeing citizenship to those born in the United State and requiring states to afford their citizens "equal protection."

In the late 1800s, on the basis of the Fourteenth Amendment, the National Women's Suffrage Association brought suit looking to give women the right to vote. The Supreme Court ruled in *Minor v. Happersett* (1875) that citizenship conferred "membership of a nation and nothing more," thus declaring states did not have to give women the franchise even though they were citizens. Progressive-minded officials were outraged and began attempts to change the Constitution. It took some time, but eventually Congress proposed and the states ratified the Nineteenth Amendment to override the decision.

Also in the late 1800s, Congress passed a national tax on individual incomes. Because the language in Article I, Section 8 is unclear on the types of taxes Congress can create and the manner in which these are to be applied, the Court struck down the law. However, later in the Progressive Era, enough support for such a tax enabled Congress to propose and the states to ratify the Sixteenth Amendment (1913) to assure this power to create the national income tax.

Amending the Constitution is the surest way to trump a Supreme Court decision, but it is a high hurdle to clear. In recent years, movements have surfaced to amend the document to stop abortions, to prevent same-sex marriage, and to enable legislatures to criminalize flag burning—all reactions to unpopular Supreme Court decisions, and all failed attempts.

A more practical path is for Congress or state legislatures to pass laws that the Supreme Court has declared unconstitutional in a slightly different form.

Implementation Courts decide principles and order citizens or government entities to take action or refrain from action. The executive branch enforces the law. In the same way, on a basic, local level, a state judge may issue a restraining order, but the police must do any necessary restraining.

When a court orders, decrees, or enjoins a party, it can do so only from the courtroom. Putting a decision into effect is another matter. Judges alone cannot implement the verdicts and opinions made in their courts. Nine robed justices in Washington simply cannot put their own decisions into effect. They require at least one of several other potential governing authorities— the president, U.S. marshals, regulatory agencies, or other government agencies—to carry out their decisions. Legislatures may have to rewrite or pass new laws or finance the enforcement endeavor. The implementing population, those charged with putting a court's decision into effect, doesn't always cooperate with or follow court orders.

When the Supreme Court makes decisions it assesses potential enforcement and cooperation. When John Marshall's Court deemed that Georgia could not regulate Cherokee Indian lands in its state because such regulation was exclusive to the federal government, President Andrew Jackson strongly disagreed and allegedly said, "John Marshall has made his decision, now let him enforce it." In the late 1950s, after the Court ruled that a Little Rock high school had to integrate, the executive branch sent federal troops to escort the claimants into the formerly all-white school.

REFLECT ON THE ESSENTIAL QUESTION

Essential Question: *How do the nation's courts compete and cooperate with the other branches to settle legal controversies and to shape public policy?* On separate paper, complete a chart like the one below to gather details to answer that question.

Interactions with Executive Branch	Interactions with Legislative Branch

KEY TERMS AND NAMES

amicus curiae brief/218

appellate jurisdiction/190

attorney general/194

binding precedent/197

certiorari/195

class action suit/194

common law/196

concurring opinion/212

defendant/193

dissenting opinion/212

Dred Scott v. Sandford/201

injunction/194

judicial activism/209

judicial review/197

judicial self-restraint/209

liberal constructionist/202

litmus test/213

majority opinion/211

Marbury v. Madison (1803)/199

Marshall, John/197

original jurisdiction/190

per curium opinion/212

persuasive precedent/197

petition for certiorari/210

petitioner/195

plaintiff/193

plea bargain/194

precedent/196

respondent/195

Roberts, John/206

rule of four/210

senatorial courtesy/214

solicitor general/218

stare decisis/197

strict constructionist/202

Supreme Court/189

U.S. Circuit Court of Appeals/189

U.S. District Courts/189

Warren, Earl/203

writ of certiorari/211

MULTIPLE-CHOICE QUESTIONS

Questions 1 and 2 refer to the graphs.

Supreme Court Overturning Precedents and Laws, 1953–2010

Average number of precedents overturned per term, by chief justice, 1953–2010

Warren (1953–69) 1.2
Burger (1969–85) 1.2
Rehnquist (1985–2005) 1.7
Roberts (2005–2010) 1.2

Average number of federal laws found unconstitutional per term, by chief justice, 1953–2010

Warren (1953–69) 2.6
Burger (1969–85) 2.7
Rehnquist (1985–2005) 2.4
Roberts (2005–2010) 1.3

Average percent of precedents overturned by conservative-leaning rulings, 1953–2010

Warren (1953–69) 10%
Burger (1969–85) 46%
Rehnquist (1985–2005) 60%
Roberts (2005–2010) 88%

Percentage of federal laws found unconstitutional by conservative-leaning rulings, 1953–2010

Warren (1953–69) 0%
Burger (1969–85) 14%
Rehnquist (1985–2005) 44%
Roberts (2005–2010) 29%

Includes only rulings in cases with oral arguments. Source: Supreme Court Database

1. Which of the following accurately describes the data in these graphs?

   (A) The Warren Court tended to act conservatively when it overturned prior Court precedents.

   (B) The Supreme Court overturns more federal laws each year than it overturns prior Supreme Court precedents.

   (C) The Burger Court struck down a greater number of precedents annually than the Rehnquist Court did.

   (D) The Roberts Court struck down more laws than its predecessors.

2. Based on the information in the charts, which of the following conclusions can you draw?

   (A) The Court by its actions is creating more law than the Congress.

   (B) The results in the graphs stem from the Senate's reluctance to confirm judicial nominees.

   (C) The Court overturns laws more often than it follows stare decisis.

   (D) The Court has issued more conservative rulings when it overturns prior Court precedents.

3. Which of the following is an accurate comparison of judicial activism and judicial restraint?

	JUDICIAL ACTIVISM	JUDICIAL RESTRAINT
(A)	Can result in shaping federal, but not state, policies	Is practiced when an appeals court agrees to grant an appeal
(B)	Was established with the Judiciary Act of 1789	Was practiced in the Court's ruling in *Roe v. Wade*
(C)	Is a democratic way to assure popular polices in a representative government	Is practiced when courts restrain the legislative or executive branches
(D)	Is practiced when courts overrule legislative acts or shape policy	Is exercised when courts refrain from interfering with policies created by elected bodies

Questions 4–5 refer to the passage below.

If there are such things as political axioms, the propriety of the judicial power of a government being coextensive with its legislative, may be ranked among the number. The mere necessity of uniformity in the interpretation of the national laws, decides the question. Thirteen independent courts of final jurisdiction over the same causes, arising upon the same laws, is a hydra in government, from which nothing but contradiction and confusion can proceed.

—Alexander Hamilton, *Federalist No. 80, 1788*

4. Which of the following statements best summarizes Hamilton's argument?

(A) The thirteen states should retain their courts and have independence from national law.

(B) The proposed federal courts and the Supreme Court will provide national consistency in law.

(C) Because the national court system will have multiple judges, differing decisions will cause confusion.

(D) The judicial branch should be the superior branch of government.

5. Which of the following principles does Hamilton suggest the new federal judiciary will establish?

(A) Advice and consent

(B) Judicial activism

(C) Stability in the law

(D) Freedom and liberty

6. A U.S. district judge in Alabama has a dispute in his court in which an employee is suing her employer over improper termination. The Ninth Circuit Court of Appeals and the U.S. District Court of Kansas have both ruled on highly similar cases under the same law and sided with the employee. Which of the following is the likely action this federal judge will take?

(A) The judge must rule in the same way because of binding precedent.

(B) The judge will read the other two courts' opinions and consider them before making a ruling.

(C) The judge will ask the Justice Department for guidance.

(D) The judge will refuse to hear the case because the federal courts have no jurisdiction in this matter.

7. Which of the following methods is the most certain way to override a Supreme Court decision?

(A) Passing legislation the Court declared unconstitutional in a slightly different form

(B) Appealing the decision

(C) Proposing and ratifying a constitutional amendment that counters the decision

(D) Convincing the president to veto the decision

Questions 8 and 9 refer to the cartoon below.

Source: *Jimmy Margulies, Politicalcartoons.com*

8. Which of the following best describes the message of the cartoon?

(A) One judge shows judicial restraint; one shows judicial activism.

(B) There are too many applicants for the Supreme Court.

(C) The Court is tied up in bureaucratic matters.

(D) One president's appointment was replaced by another president's.

9. Which of the following constitutional principles allowed the events shown in the cartoon?

(A) The legislative process

(B) The Senate's advice and consent role

(C) Congress's role in determining the number of justices

(D) Original jurisdiction

10. Which of the following statements is true regarding the Court's decision in *Marbury v. Madison* (1803)?

(A) It resolved a dispute about Congress's commerce power.

(B) It estabished the principle of stare decisis.

(C) It overturned part of an act of Congress.

(D) It established the supremacy of federal law.

FREE-RESPONSE QUESTIONS

1. "The Supreme Court closed out its 2011–12 term today in dramatic fashion, upholding the Affordable Care Act by a sharply divided vote [in *National Federation of Independent Business v. Sebelius*]. The Court's bottom line, reasoning and lineup of justices all came as a shock to many. . . . I don't think anyone predicted that the law would be upheld *without* the support of Justice Anthony Kennedy, almost always the Court's crucial swing vote. And while most of the legal debate focused on Congress's power under the Commerce Clause, the Court ultimately upheld the law as an exercise of the taxing power . . . .The most surprising thing of all, though, is that in the end, this ultraconservative Court decided the case, much as it did in many other cases this term, by siding with the liberals."

—David Cole, *The Nation*, June 28, 2012

After reading the scenario above, respond to A, B, and C below.

(A) Describe the process that led to the Supreme Court's ruling on the challenge to the Affordable Care Act.

(B) In the context of this scenario, explain how the process described in part A can be affected by the executive branch.

(C) In the context of this scenario, explain how the ruling relates to enumerated powers.

Supreme Court Justices' Voting Relationships, 2017

Justice Agreement in full, in part, or in judgment

	AMK	CT	RBG	SGB	SAA	SMS	EK	NMG
JGR	87.5%	75%	81.25%	81.25%	75%	81.25%	85.71%	93.75%
AMK		87.5%	68.75%	68.75%	87.5%	68.75%	71.43%	93.75%
CT			68.75%	68.75%	100%	68.75%	71.43%	81.25%
RBG				100%	68.75%	100%	100%	81.25%
SGB					68.75%	100%	100%	75%
SAA						68.75%	71.43%	81.25%
SMS							100%	75%
EK								78.57%
NMG								

Justices' Initials, Full Names, and President Who Appointed Them

JGR: Chief Justice John G. Roberts, appointed by Republican George W. Bush
AMK: Anthony Kennedy, appointed by Republican Ronald Reagan
CT: Clarence Thomas, appointed by Republican George H.W. Bush
RBG: Ruth Bader Ginsburg, appointed by Democrat Bill Clinton
SGB: Stephen G. Breyer, appointed by Democrat Bill Clinton
SAA: Samuel Anthony Alito Jr., appointed by Republican George W. Bush
SMS: Sonia Sotomayor, appointed by Democrat Barack Obama
EK: Elena Kagan, appointed by Democrat Barack Obama
NMG: Neil Gorsuch, appointed by Republican Donald Trump

Source: *SCOTUSblog*

2. Use the information in the graphic to answer the questions below.

   (A) Describe the data presented in the table.

   (B) Identify the justices with the highest percentage of agreement with one another, and draw a conclusion about why they agree so often.

   (C) Explain how the information in the table demonstrates the independence of the justices from the ideology of the executives who appointed them.

3. During the Watergate investigation in the early 1970s, the special prosecutor wanted information discussed on President Nixon's White House audio tapes as evidence in the investigation. When the lower court issued a subpoena for the tapes, the president refused to hand them over, claiming executive privilege (his right to keep his discussions confidential) as part of the separation of powers, because some were of delicate national security interests and not the business of the court. Only by guaranteeing confidentiality, he argued, could he preserve the candor of advisors. In *United States v. Nixon* (1974), the Supreme Court ruled in a unanimous decision that, in the fair administration of justice, a court could compel even the president with its power of subpoena during an investigation. Nixon had to comply by handing over the tapes as evidence in the investigation.

(A) Identify a similarity or difference between the rulings in *United States v. Nixon* (1974) and *Marbury v. Madison* (1803).

(B) Based on the similarity or difference identified in A, explain how *United States v. Nixon* relates to the interactions between branches.

(C) Describe an action the executive branch might take to limit the impact of *United States v. Nixon*.

4. Develop an argument that explains whether the Supreme Court should take seriously the public's concerns about its legitimacy.

In your essay, you must:

- Articulate a defensible claim or thesis that responds to the prompt and establishes a line of reasoning

- Support your claim with at least TWO pieces of accurate and relevant information:

  ◆ At least ONE piece of evidence must be from one of the following foundational documents

    – *Federalist No. 78*

    – Article III of the Constitution

  ◆ Use a second piece of evidence from another foundational document from the list above or from your study of the federal judiciary

- Use reasoning to explain why your evidence supports your claim/thesis

- Respond to an opposing or alternative perspective using refutation, concession, or rebuttal

WRITING: *ORGANIZE YOUR ESSAY*

A well-organized essay will help get your points across clearly.

- In your introduction, assert your claim and let the reader know what line of reasoning you will use.

- In the body of your essay, present your evidence, taking care to clearly connect each piece of evidence to your claim. What about the evidence supports your claim?

- Respond to other viewpoints after you have developed your own.

- Be sure to keep each paragraph in the body focused on one main idea.

- Write a conclusion that follows from your claim and evidence.

UNIT 2: Review

Our national institutions govern the United States through constitutional designs, historic customs, and practical relationships. Congress's bicameral set-up provides an additional check within the legislature to assure the legitimacy and popularity of most legislation. The many committees in the House and Senate determine particulars of our national laws and handle the day-to-day business on Capitol Hill. Congress has become less a white man's institution and more a democratic and inclusive body with the Seventeenth Amendment, the one-person, one-vote rule, and legislative measures such as the discharge petition and the decreased threshold to break a filibuster.

The Executive Branch carries out Congress's laws. Presidents have become stronger with increased media attention, international face-offs, and their handling of domestic crises. The president is the chief executive of government and the chief of military and foreign policy as well as a manager of the nation's funds. Able and experienced advisors help the president develop policies and manage large departments and agencies. These sub-units range from the mammoth Department of Defense to the Federal Communications Commission.

The Judiciary adjudicates federal crimes and high-dollar civil disputes between citizens of different states. The Circuit Courts hear appeals and interpret law in their respective circuits. Special legislative courts hear cases dealing with specialized areas of law. The less visible, nine-judge Supreme Court hears about 80 cases a year to rule on constitutionality and national policy.

Together these institutions govern the United States.

THINK AS A POLITICAL SCIENTIST: *TRACE INTERACTIONS*

The three branches of government and the bureaucracy interact in many and varied ways to implement law and policy and uphold the principles outlined in the Constitution. Though the interactions can be complex, they do follow a process that can be traced. Being able to describe the steps in the process, how the steps relate to one another, challenges faced during the process, and the implications of the process will help you work through the maze of interactions with the eye of a political scientist. Create a visual or written description of the stages in the process.

Practice: Trace the process of a controversial bill on its way to becoming law. Answer these questions. Be as specific and detailed as you can be.

- What process does a bill go through in both houses of the legislature?
- What happens to a bill in the executive branch?
- How does the bureaucracy get involved in the process?
- What process occurs if the constitutionality of the law is challenged?

Review Learning Objectives

As you review Unit Two, be sure you can complete the following learning objectives. Page numbers are provided to help you locate the necessary information to fulfill the learning objective.

UNIT TWO LEARNING OBJECTIVES	
CON-3.A: Describe the different structures, powers, and functions of each house of Congress.	Pages 79–80, 84–92, 102
CON-3.B: Explain how the structure, powers, and functions of both houses of Congress affect the policymaking process.	Pages 84–96
CON-3.C: Explain how congressional behavior is influenced by election processes, partisanship, and divided government.	Pages 102–110
CON-4.A: Explain how the president can implement a policy agenda.	Pages 128–141
CON-4.B: Explain how the president's agenda can create tension and frequent confrontations with Congress.	Pages 141–144
CON-4.C: Explain how presidents have interpreted and justified their use of formal and informal powers.	Pages 122–126, 128–137
CON-4.D: Explain how communication technology has changed the president's relationship with the national constituency and the other branches.	Pages 146–149
CON-5.A: Explain the principle of judicial review and how it checks the power of other institutions and state governments.	Pages 198–200
CON-5.B: Explain how the exercise of judicial review in conjunction with life tenure can lead to debate about the legitimacy of the Supreme Court's power.	Pages 207–210
CON-5.C: Explain how other branches in the government can limit the Supreme Court's power.	Pages 212–221
PMI-2.A: Explain how the bureaucracy carries out the responsibilities of the federal government.	Pages 160–167
PMI-2.B: Explain how the federal bureaucracy uses delegated discretionary authority for rule making and implementation.	Pages 170–171
PMI-2.C: Explain how Congress uses its oversight power in its relationship with the executive branch.	Pages 88, 171–174
PMI-2.D: Explain how the president ensures that executive branch agencies and departments carry out their responsibilities in concert with the goals of the administration.	Pages 174–177
PMI-2.E: Explain the extent to which governmental branches can hold the bureaucracy accountable given the competing interests of Congress, the president, and the federal courts.	Pages 171–179

Review the following foundational documents, Supreme Court cases, and political science disciplinary practices and reasoning processes as well.

UNIT TWO FOUNDATIONAL DOCUMENTS

Federalist No. 70—argues for a single president for unity and accountability	Pages 120–121, 660–664
Twenty-Second Amendment—sets limits on presidential terms	Pages 126, 128, 642
Article III of the Constitution—establishes the court system	Pages 634–635
Federalist No. 78—Hamilton's argument for judicial review	Page 191, 665

UNIT TWO SUPREME COURT CASES

Baker v. Carr (1962)—determined redistricting was a justiciable matter, not political, and established the one-person, one-vote principle	Pages 103–106
Shaw v. Reno (1993)—ruled that redistricting based on race had to meet a strict scrutiny test	Pages 107–110
Marbury v. Madison (1803)—set the precedent for judicial review	Pages 199–200

UNIT TWO POLITICAL SCIENCE DISCIPLINARY PRACTICES AND REASONING PROCESSES

Explaining Causes and Effects	Pages 99–101
Analyze, Interpret, and Apply Supreme Court Decisions Baker v. Carr (1962) *Shaw v. Reno* (1993) *Marbury v. Madison* (1803)	Page 106 Page 110 Page 200
Analyze and Interpret *Federalist No. 70*	Page 121
Evaluate the President's Cabinet	Page 149–150
Analyzing Visuals	Page 180
Trace Interactions	Page 229

UNIT TWO CONTEMPORARY ISSUES AND POLICY

Policy Matters: Presidents, Politics, and the Panama Canal	Pages 133–135
Policy Matters: Supreme Court Precedents Establish Policy	Pages 197–198

UNIT TWO WRITING

Support the Argument with Relevant Evidence	Page 118
Use Disciplinary Conventions	Page 158
Respond to Alternative Perspectives	Page 188
Organize Your Writing	Page 228

UNIT 3: Civil Liberties and Civil Rights

Chapter 7 *Individual Liberties*

Chapter 8 *Due Process and Rights of the Accused*

Chapter 9 *Civil Rights*

In a diverse America, people have used the institutions of government to seek individual liberties and equality. The Bill of Rights guarantees fundamental freedoms and prevents government from denying citizens free speech, free religion, privacy, a fair trial, and other essential liberties. The American Civil Liberties Union and other rights groups have fought to prevent government from squelching these freedoms. For both equal treatment and due process, advocates have emphasized the Fourteenth Amendment and turned to the courts as the most useful institution to secure these rights. The Supreme Court has ordered that states, too, must refrain from infringing on most of the same rights.

African Americans overcame the notorious legacy of slavery and persevered through a century of discrimination before experiencing legal equality and fair representation. The National Association for the Advancement of Colored People has led the charge for racial equality, due process for black defendants, school desegregation, and voting rights for more than 100 years. By lobbying Congress, organizing public protests and voter registration drives, and pressing their cases in the courts, the NAACP and other civil rights groups dismantled laws that denied equality to African Americans in the South. Women, Asian Americans, Latinos, members of the LGBT community, people with disabilities, and other minorities have also taken a path toward equality via congressional laws, presidential directives, and court decisions.

Enduring Understandings: Civil Liberties and Civil Rights

LOR-2: Provisions of the U.S. Constitution's Bill of Rights are continually being interpreted to balance the power of government and the civil liberties of individuals.

LOR-3: Protections of the Bill of Rights have been selectively incorporated by way of the Fourteenth Amendment's due process clause to prevent state infringement of basic liberties.

PRD-1: The Fourteenth Amendment's equal protection clause as well as other constitutional provisions have often been used to support the advancement of equality.

PMI-3: Public policy promoting civil rights is influenced by citizen-state interactions and constitutional interpretation over time.

CON-6: The Court's interpretation of the U.S. Constitution is influenced by the composition of the Court and citizen-state interactions. At times, it has restricted minority rights and, at others, protected them.

Source: *AP®United States Government and Politics Course and Exam Description*

7

Individual Liberties

"If there is any principle of the Constitution that more imperatively calls for attachment than any other, it is the principle of free thought—not free thought for those who agree with us but freedom for the thought that we hate."
—Justice Oliver Wendell Holmes's dissent in *United States v. Schwimmer,* 1929

Essential Question: How do Supreme Court decisions on the First and Second Amendments and the relationship of those amendments to the Fourteenth Amendment reflect a commitment to individual liberties?

Americans have held liberty in high regard since lost liberties initiated the break from Great Britain. The original Constitution includes a few basic protections from government—Congress can pass no bill of attainder and no ex post facto law, and *habeas corpus* cannot be suspended in peacetime. Article III guarantees a defendant the right to trial by jury. However, the original Constitution lacked many fundamental protections, so critics and Anti-Federalists pushed for a bill of rights to protect **civil liberties**—those personal freedoms protected from arbitrary governmental interference or deprivations. The United States has struggled to fully interpret and define phrases such as "free speech," "unreasonable searches," and "cruel and unusual punishments."

Citizens and governmental officials often differ on where the line should be drawn between government's pursuit of order and the individual's right to freedom. When this conflict occurs, citizens can challenge government in court—appeal a conviction or criminal procedure ruling or sue the government to stop or reverse a state action that violates provisions in the Constitution.

As you read in Chapter 6, it's a somewhat complicated path from the initial challenge in court up to the highest court in the land. When the Supreme Court makes a civil liberties ruling—that flag burning cannot be criminalized or that an all-out ban on citizen-owned handguns is unreasonable—it sets a general standard, or precedent, shaping policy. In making such rulings, the Court articulates its reasoning in its majority opinion, written by a chosen justice, or judge, after deciding the case. And for the more complicated decisions, the Court will develop "tests" so government can consider what state action is acceptable and when it crosses a constitutional line. Lower courts, too, can use these precedents as guidance when citizens challenge similar, future cases.

BIG IDEA: Governmental laws and policies balancing order and liberty are based on the U.S. Constitution and have been interpreted over time. As you read this chapter, pay close attention to the balance the Court found between order and individual liberties as it interpreted the First and Second Amendments.

Protections in the Bill of Rights

As you read in Chapter 1, the Constitution includes a Bill of Rights—the first ten amendments—designed specifically to guarantee individual liberties and rights. These civil liberties include protections of individuals, protections of their opinions and the right to express them, and protections of their property. Specifically, individuals were protected *from the government*, from the "misconstruction or abuse of its powers," according to the Preamble to the Bill of Rights that was sent out to the states for ratification in 1789.

Over the years, the provisions in the Bill of Rights have been interpreted by the Supreme Court in an effort to balance individual rights and public safety and order. Eight of the fifteen Supreme Court cases that you need to know for the AP exam are tied to the Bill of Rights, as the chart below shows, as well as to the Fourteenth Amendment. You will read about each of the cases in depth in this chapter and the next.

MUST-KNOW SUPREME COURT CASES AND RELEVANT AMENDMENTS		
Must-Know Supreme Court Cases	**Ruling**	**Amendment**
Schenck v. United States (1919)	Speech representing "a clear and present danger" is not protected. (See page 240.)	First
Tinker v. Des Moines Independent Community School District (1969)	Students in public schools are allowed to wear armbands as symbolic speech. (See page 243.)	First
New York Times Co. v. United States (1971)	The government cannot exercise prior restraint (forbid publication ahead of time). (See page 250.)	First
Engel v. Vitale (1962)	School-sponsored religious activities violate the establishment clause. (See page 254.)	First
Wisconsin v. Yoder (1972)	Requirements that Amish students attend school past the eighth grade violate the free exercise clause. (See page 257.)	First

McDonald v. Chicago (2010)	The right to keep and bear arms for self-defense in one's home applies to the states. (See page 264.)	Second
Gideon v. Wainwright (1963	States must provide poor defendants an attorney to guarantee a fair trial. (See page 284.)	Sixth
Roe v. Wade (1973)	The right of privacy extends to a woman's decision to have an abortion, though the state has a legitimate interest in protecting the unborn after a certain point and protecting a mother's health. (See page 287.)	The First, Third, Fourth, Fifth, and Ninth amendments have been interpreted as creating "zones of privacy."

A Culture of Civil Liberties

The freedoms Americans enjoy are about as comprehensive as those in any Western democracy. Anyone can practice or create nearly any kind of religion. Expressing opinions in public forums or in print is nearly always protected. Just outside the Capitol building, the White House, and the Supreme Court, ever-present protestors criticize law, presidential action, and alleged miscarriages of justice without fear of punishment or retribution. Nearly all people enjoy a great degree of privacy in their homes. Unless the police have "probable cause" to suspect criminal behavior, individuals can trust that government will not enter unannounced. When civil liberties violations have occurred, individuals and groups such as the American Civil Liberties Union (ACLU) have challenged them in court. Both liberals and conservatives hold civil liberties dear, although they view them somewhat differently.

At the same time, however, civil liberties are limited when they impinge on the public interest, another cherished democratic ideal. **Public interest** is the welfare or well-being of the general public. For example, for the sake of public interest, the liberties of minors are limited. Their right to drive is restricted until they are teenagers (between 14 and 17 years old, depending on their state), both for their safety and the safety of the general public. And although people generally have the right to free speech, what they say cannot seriously threaten public safety or ruin a person's reputation with untruthful claims. In the culture of civil liberties in the United States, then, personal liberties have limits out of concern for the public interest.

Selective Incorporation

All levels of government adhere to most elements of the Bill of Rights, but that wasn't always the case. The Bill of Rights was ratified to protect the people from the *federal* government. The First Amendment states, "Congress shall make no law" that violates freedoms of religion, speech, press, and assembly. The document then goes on to address additional liberties Congress cannot take away. Most states had already developed bills of rights with similar provisions, but states did not originally have to follow the national Bill of Rights because it was understood that the federal Constitution referred only to federal laws, not state laws. Through a process known as **selective incorporation**, the Supreme Court has ruled in landmark cases that state laws must also adhere to selective Bill of Rights provisions through the Fourteenth Amendment's due process clause.

Due Process The right to **due process** dates back to England's Magna Carta (1215), when nobles limited the king's ability to ignore their liberties. Due process ensures fair procedures when the government burdens or deprives an individual. It prevents arbitrary government decisions to avoid mistaken or abusive taking of life, liberty, or property (including money) from individuals without legal cause. Due process also ensures accused persons a fair trial. Due process is a fundamental fairness concept that ensures a legitimate government in a democracy. The due process clause in the **Fifth Amendment** establishes that no person shall be "deprived of life, liberty, or property, without due process of law; nor shall private property be taken for public use, without just compensation."

Fourteenth Amendment The ratification of the **Fourteenth Amendment** (1868) in the aftermath of the Civil War strengthened due process. Before the war, Southern states had made it a crime to speak out against slavery or to publish antislavery materials. Union leaders questioned the legality of these statutes. During Reconstruction, Union leaders complained that Southerners denied African Americans, Unionists, and Republicans basic liberties of free speech, criminal procedure rights, and the right to bear arms. They questioned whether the losing rebel state governments would willingly follow the widely understood principles of due process, especially toward freed slaves. Would an accused black man receive a fair and impartial jury at his trial? Could an African American defendant refuse to testify in court, as whites could? Could the Southern states inflict the same cruel and unusual punishments on freed men that they had inflicted on slaves? To ensure the states followed these commonly accepted principles in the federal Bill of Rights and in most state constitutions, the House Republicans drafted the most important and far-reaching of the Reconstruction Amendments, the Fourteenth, which declares that "all persons born or naturalized in the United States ... are citizens" and that no state can "deprive any person of life, liberty, or property, without due process of law. . . ."

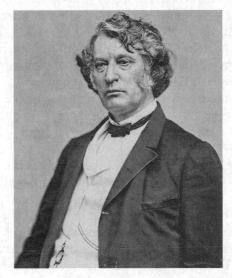

Speaker of the House Thaddeus Stevens (left) and Massachusetts Senator Charles Sumner crafted and led passage of the Fourteenth Amendment to, in part, ensure newly freed African Americans due process of law.

Early Incorporation The first incorporation case used due process to evaluate issues of property seizure. In the 1880s, a Chicago rail line sued the city, which had constructed a street across its tracks. In an 1897 decision, the Court held that the newer due process clause compelled Chicago to award just compensation when taking private property for public use. This ruling incorporated the "just compensation" provision of the Fifth Amendment, requiring that the states adhere to it as well.

Later, the Supreme Court declared that the First Amendment prevents states from infringing on free thought and free expression. In a series of cases that addressed state laws designed to crush radical ideas and sensational journalism, the Court began to hold states to First Amendment standards. Benjamin Gitlow, a New York Socialist, was arrested and prosecuted for violating the state's criminal anarchy law. The law prevented advocating a violent overthrow of the government. Gitlow was arrested for writing, publishing, and distributing thousands of copies of pamphlets called the *Left Wing Manifesto* that called for strikes and "class action … in any form."

In one of its first cases, the ACLU appealed his case and argued that the due process clause of the Fourteenth Amendment compelled states to follow the same free speech and free press ideas in the First Amendment as the federal government. In *Gitlow v. New York* (1925), however, the Court actually enhanced the state's power by upholding the state's criminal anarchy law and

Gitlow's conviction because Gitlow's activities represented a threat to public safety. Nonetheless, the Court did address the question of whether or not the Bill of Rights did or could apply to the states. In the majority opinion, the Court said, "For present purposes, we may and do assume that freedom of speech and of the press . . .are among the fundamental personal rights and 'liberties' protected by the due process clause of the Fourteenth Amendment from impairment by the States." In other words, Gitlow's free speech was not protected because it was a threat to public safety, but the Court did put the states on notice.

The Court applied that warning in 1931. Minnesota had attempted to bring outrageous newspapers under control with a public nuisance law, informally dubbed the Minnesota Gag Law. This statute permitted a judge to stop obscene, malicious, scandalous, and defamatory material. A hard-hitting paper published by the unsavory J.M. Near printed anti-Catholic, anti-Semitic, anti-Black, and anti-labor stories. Both the ACLU and Chicago newspaper mogul Robert McCormick came to Near's aid on anti-censorship principles. The Court did too. In *Near v. Minnesota* it declared that the Minnesota statute "raises questions of grave importance . . . . It is no longer open to doubt that the liberty of the press . . . is within the liberty safeguarded by the due process clause of the Fourteenth Amendment. . . ." In this ruling, through the doctrine of selective incorporation, the Court imposed limitations on state regulation of civil rights and liberties. (For another case demonstrating limitations on state regulations, see *McDonald v. Chicago* on pages 264-266.)

It is appropriate that the Court emphasized the First Amendment freedoms early on in the incorporation process. The basic American idea that free religion, speech, and press should be protected from all governments dates back to the founding. In creating the Bill of Rights in 1789, James Madison and others had strongly supported an early draft that stated, "No state shall infringe on the equal rights of conscience, nor the freedom of speech, or of the press." It was the only proposed amendment directly limiting states' authority. As biographer Richard Labunski reveals, Madison called it the most valuable amendment on the list because it was "equally necessary that [these rights] should be secured against the state governments."

In case after case, the Court has required states to guarantee free speech, freedom of religion, fair and impartial juries, and rights against self-incrimination. Though states have incorporated nearly all rights in the document, a few rights in the Bill of Rights remain denied exclusively to the federal government but not yet denied to the states.

RIGHTS NOT YET INCORPORATED
• Third Amendment protections against quartering troops in homes
• Fifth Amendment right to a grand jury indictment in misdemeanor cases
• Seventh Amendment right to jury trials in civil cases
• Eighth Amendment protection against excessive bail

The First Amendment: Free Speech and Free Press

Once the Court, through the incorporation doctrine, had required states and localities to follow the First Amendment, it took two generations of cases to define "free speech" and "free press." When does one person's right to free expression violate others' right to peace, safety, or decency? Free speech is not absolute, but both federal and state governments have to show substantial or **compelling governmental interest**—a purpose important enough to justify the infringement of personal liberties—to curb it.

The creators of the First Amendment meant to prevent government censorship. Many revolutionary leaders came to despise the accusation of seditious libel—a charge that resulted in fines and/or jail time for anyone who criticized public officials or government policies. Because expressing dissent in assemblies and in print during the colonial era led to independence and increased freedoms, the members of the first Congress preserved this right as the very first of the amendments.

The Court has not made much distinction between "speech" and "press" and ordinarily provides the same protective standards for both rights. "Speech" includes an array of expressions—actual words, the lack of words, pictures, and actions. An average citizen has as much right to free press as does a professional journalist. The First Amendment does not protect all speech, however, especially speech that invites danger, that is obscene, or that violates an existing law.

The government also has no prerogative of **prior restraint**—the right to stop spoken or printed expression in advance—first declared in *Near* and later reaffirmed in *New York Times v. United States* (see page 250). Governments cannot suppress a thought from entering the marketplace of ideas just because most people see the idea as repugnant or offensive. A government that can squelch ideas is one that violates the very essence of a free democracy. The Court, however, has never suggested that its reverence for free expression means that all expression should be tolerated at all times under all conditions. In addition to what the federal government prevents on the airwaves (see Chapter 16), there are exceptions that allow state and federal governments to limit or punish additional forms of speech.

Balancing National Security and Individual Freedoms

The Supreme Court continually interprets provisions of the Bill of Rights to balance the power of government and the civil liberties of individuals, sometimes recognizing that individual freedoms are of primary importance, other times finding that limitations to free speech can be justified, especially when they are needed to maintain social order. (For more on national security and other individual freedoms protected in the Bill of Rights, see page 28.)

Clear and Present Danger The first time the Court examined a federal conviction on a free speech claim was in *Schenck v. United States* (1919). This case helped establish that limitations on free speech may be warranted during wartime.

The Constitutional Question Before the Court: Does the government's prosecution and punishment for expressing opposition to the military draft during wartime violate the First Amendment's free speech clause?

Decision: No, for *United States*, 9:0.

Facts: As the United States entered World War I against the Central Powers, including Germany, the 1917 Sedition and Espionage Acts prevented publications that criticized the government, that advocated treason or insurrection, or that incited disloyal behavior in the military. A U.S. district court tried and convicted Charles Schenck, the secretary of the Socialist Party, when he printed 15,000 anti-draft leaflets intended for Philadelphia-area draftees. In an effort to dissuade people from complying with the draft, he argued in his pamphlet that a mandatory military draft, or conscription, amounted to involuntary servitude, which is denied by the Thirteenth Amendment. The government was very concerned at the time about the Socialist Party, German Americans, and those who questioned America's military draft and war effort.

Schenck appealed the guilty verdict from the district court. On hearing the case, the Supreme Court drew a distinction between speech that communicated honest opinion and speech that incited unlawful action and thereby represented a "clear and present danger." In a unanimous opinion delivered after the war's end, the Court upheld the government's right to convict citizens for certain speech. Schenck went to prison, as did defendants in five similar cases. The **clear and present danger test** became the balancing act between competing demands of free expression and a government needing to protect a free society.

Reasoning: The Court arrived at its opinion through recognizing that the context of an expression needs to be considered to determine its constitutionality. At other times, under other circumstances, the pamphlet or circular might have been allowed. But during wartime and because of the immediate actions the pamphlet could lead to, the harm from the circular overrode Schenck's right to publish and distribute it.

The Court's Majority Opinion by Mr. Justice Oliver Wendell Holmes:
In impassioned language, [the pamphlet] intimated that conscription was despotism in its worst form, and a monstrous wrong against humanity in the interest of Wall Street's chosen few . . . . It described the arguments on the other side as coming from cunning politicians and a mercenary capitalist press, and even silent consent to the conscription law as helping to support an infamous conspiracy . . . . Of course, the document would not have been sent unless it had been intended to have some effect, and we do not see what effect it could be expected to have upon persons subject to the draft except to influence them to obstruct the carrying of it out . . . .

We admit that, in many places and in ordinary times, the defendants, in saying all that was said in the circular, would have been within their constitutional rights. But the character of every act depends upon the circumstances in which it is done . . . . The most stringent protection of free speech would not protect a man in falsely shouting fire in a theatre and causing a panic. It does not even protect a man from an injunction against uttering words that may have all the effect of force . . . . The question in every case is whether the words used are used in such circumstances and are of such a nature as to create a clear and present danger that they will bring about the substantive evils that Congress has a right to prevent. It is a question of proximity and degree. When a nation is at war, many things that might be said in time of peace are such a hindrance to its effort that their utterance will not be endured so long as men fight, and that no Court could regard them as protected by any constitutional right.

Since Schenck: Justice Holmes famously reconsidered and redefined his views in a similar case that arrived in the Court soon after *Schenck*. In *Abrams v. United States*, an appeal by Russian immigrants convicted under the same law as Schenck had been, the Court decided once again—mainly for the same reason—to uphold convictions. Holmes, however, voted this time to overturn the conviction and wrote a dissenting opinion declaring the Court should uphold such convictions only if the speech "produces or is intended to produce clear and imminent danger that it will bring about . . . substantive evils." Decades later, the Court ruled in *Brandenburg v. Ohio*—an appeal of a convicted Klansman accused of inciting lawlessness at a rally—that such speech could be punished only if it is meant to incite or produce "imminent lawless action and is likely to . . . produce such action." The clear and present danger standard did not prevent all forms of speech nor was the claim always a justification for criminal charges.

Political Science Disciplinary Practices: Explain Reasoning, Similarities, and Differences

A number of Supreme Court cases have established a "test"—a set of criteria to determine whether speech is protected or not. Like other Supreme Court opinions, however, the tests are always being interpreted and reinterpreted over time.

Apply: Complete the following activities focusing on *Schenck v. United States*.

1. Explain the reasoning behind the Supreme Court's decision. Take into account the context in which the pamphlet was published.

2. Describe the "clear and present danger" the pamphlet was seen to create. What practical effect on the United States would that danger have had if it were realized?

3. Explain how later Court decisions reinterpreted or refined the "clear and present danger" test for protected or unprotected speech. In other words, how were the opinions in *Schenck* similar to and different from those in *Abrams* and *Brandenburg*?

Free Speech and the Cold War Congress's attempts to suppress speech temporarily subsided but rose again during Cold War threats. In 1949, President Truman's justice department convicted 11 Communist Party leaders under the 1940 Smith Act—a law that made advocating the overthrow of any government in the United States a criminal act. After a nine-month trial, the jury convicted the Communists. But later the Court drew a line between advocating a government change in the abstract versus calling for actual illegal action to cause an overthrow. The Court did not toss out the Smith Act, but it overturned these convictions and weakened the Justice Department's efforts to prosecute Communists for expressing unpopular ideas.

Vietnam War Era As the Court softened its restrictions on free speech, Americans became more willing to protest. The 1960s witnessed a revolution in free expression. As support for the Vietnam War waned, young men burned their draft cards to protest the military draft. Congress quickly passed a law to prevent the destruction of these government-issued documents.

David O'Brien burned his Selective Service registration card in front of a Boston courthouse and was convicted for that action under the Selective Service Act, which prohibited willful destruction of draft cards. He appealed to the Supreme Court, arguing that his protest was a symbolic act of speech that government could not infringe. The Court, however, upheld his conviction and sided with the government's right to prevent this behavior in order to protect Congress's authority to raise and support an army. O'Brien was disrupting the draft effort and publicly encouraging others to do the same. Others continued to burn draft cards, but after *United States v. O'Brien* (1968), this symbolic act was not protected.

Symbolic Speech

As David O'Brien learned, people cannot invoke **symbolic speech** to defend an act that might otherwise be illegal. For example, a nude citizen cannot walk through the town square and claim a right to symbolically protest textile sweatshops after his arrest for indecent exposure. Symbolic speech per se is not an absolute defense in a free speech conflict. That said, the Court has protected a number of symbolic acts or expressions.

In April 1968, Paul Robert Cohen wore a jacket bearing the words "F — the Draft" while walking into a Los Angeles courthouse. Local authorities arrested and convicted him for "disturbing the peace . . . by offensive conduct." The Supreme Court later overturned the conviction in *Cohen v. California* (1971). As opposed to its stance on the act of burning a draft card in *O'Brien*, the Court declared the state could not prosecute Cohen for this expression. The phrase on the jacket in no way incited an illegal action. "One man's vulgarity is another's lyric," the majority opinion stated.

Along similar reasoning, the Court struck down both state and federal statutes meant to prevent desecrating or burning the U.S. flag in *Texas v. Johnson* (1989) and *United States v. Eichman* (1990), respectively. The Court found that these laws serve no purpose other than ensuring a government-imposed political idea—reverence for the flag.

Time, Place, and Manner Regulations In evaluating regulations of symbolic expression, the Court looks primarily at whether the regulation suppresses the content of the message or simply regulates the accompanying conduct. Is the government ultimately suppressing what was being said, or the time, place, or manner in which it was expressed? Compare the *Cohen* and *O'Brien* rulings. In both cases, someone expressed opposition to the Vietnam-era draft. O'Brien burned a government-issued draft card. The Court didn't protect the defendant's speech but rather upheld a law to assist Congress in its conscription powers. Cohen publicly expressed dislike for the draft with an ugly phrase printed on his jacket, but he did nothing to incite public protest and did not actually refuse to enlist, so the Court protected the speech.

Time, place, and manner regulations must be tested against a set of four criteria.

TIME, PLACE, AND MANNER TEST

1. The restriction must be *content-neutral*. That is, it must not suppress the content of the expression.

2. The restriction must serve a *significant government interest*. In the *O'Brien* case, the Court ruled that the burning of a draft card was disrupting the government's interest of raising an army.

3. The restriction must be *narrowly tailored*. That is, the law must be designed in the most specific, targeted way possible, avoiding spillover into other areas. For example, the law upheld in *O'Brien* was specifically about burning draft cards, not other items, such as flags, whose burning might express a similar message.

4. There must be adequate *alternative ways of expression*. The court can suppress expression on the basis of time, place, and manner if there are other times, places, and manners in which the idea can be expressed.

The question of "place" and "manner" became key aspects of a landmark case involving free speech in schools.

 MUST-KNOW SUPREME COURT DECISIONS: *TINKER V. DES MOINES INDEPENDENT COMMUNITY SCHOOL DISTRICT* (1969)

The Constitutional Question Before the Court: Does a public school ban on students wearing armbands in symbolic, political protest violate a student's First Amendment freedom of speech?

Decision: Yes, for Tinker, 7:2

Facts: In December of 1965 in Des Moines, Iowa, Mary Beth Tinker, her brother

John F. Tinker, their friend Christopher Eckhardt, and others developed a plan for an organized protest of the U.S. conflict underway in Vietnam. They planned to wear black armbands for a period of time as well as have two days of fasting. The school administrators learned of the organized protest and predicted it would become a distraction in the learning environment they had to maintain. They also believed it might be taken as disrespectful by some students and become, at minimum, a potential problem. School principals met and developed a policy to address their concerns. When the Tinkers and other students arrived to school wearing the armbands, principals instructed the students to remove them. The students, with support from their parents, refused. The school then suspended the students until they were willing to return without wearing the bands. The Tinkers and the others sued in U.S. district court on free speech grounds and eventually appealed to the Supreme Court.

Reasoning: Noting that the record or facts showed no disruption took place, the Court ruled in favor of the students who challenged the suspension, declaring that the students' right to political, symbolic speech based on the First Amendment overrode the school administrators' concern for *potential* disorder. The decision protected this speech because the suspension failed the content-neutral criterion of the time, place, and manner test: it was intended to quiet the students' anti-war message to avoid possible disruptions.

The Court's Majority Opinion by Mr. Justice Abe Fortas: First Amendment rights, applied in light of the special characteristics of the school environment, are available to teachers and students. It can hardly be argued that either students or teachers shed their constitutional rights to freedom of speech or expression at the schoolhouse gate. This has been the unmistakable holding of this Court for almost 50 years . . . .

Our problem involves direct, primary First Amendment rights akin to "pure speech" . . . .

The school officials banned and sought to punish petitioners for a silent, passive expression of opinion, unaccompanied by any disorder or disturbance on the part of petitioners. There is here no evidence whatever of petitioners' interference, actual or nascent, with the schools' work or of collision with the rights of other students to be secure and to be let alone. Accordingly, this case does not concern speech or action that intrudes upon the work of the schools or the rights of other students. . . .

Clearly, the prohibition of expression of one particular opinion, at least without evidence that it is necessary to avoid material and substantial interference with schoolwork or discipline, is not constitutionally permissible.

In our system, state-operated schools may not be enclaves of totalitarianism. School officials do not possess absolute authority over their students. Students in school, as well as out of school, are "persons" under our Constitution . . . In the absence of a specific showing of constitutionally valid reasons to regulate their speech, students are entitled to freedom of expression of their views.

Concurring opinions separated themselves from some parts of the majority opinion. Justice Potter Stewart questioned the assumption that children's First Amendment rights are equal to those of adults. Justice Byron White noted the distinction between words and behaviors and the effect of expression on a valid government interest.

Concurring Opinion by Mr. Justice Potter Stewart: Although I agree with much of what is said in the Court's opinion, and with its judgment in this case, I cannot share the Court's uncritical assumption that, school discipline aside, the First Amendment rights of children are coextensive with those of adults.

Concurring Opinion by Mr. Justice Byron White: While I join the Court's opinion, I deem it appropriate to note, first, that the Court continues to recognize a distinction between communicating by words and communicating by acts or conduct which sufficiently impinges on some valid state interest; and, second, that I do not subscribe to everything the Court of Appeals said about free speech in its opinion in *Burnside v. Byars* . . . a case relied upon by the Court in the matter now before us.

Justice Hugo Black issued a strong dissent, questioning the authority of courts to decide how students will spend their time in school and worrying about how the Court might be fostering an era of permissiveness. Justice John Marshall Harlan II also dissented, noting that he would rather the burden of proof be on the complainants to prove that the school was trying to prevent expression of an unpopular opinion while allowing the expression of a more popular one.

Dissenting Opinion by Mr. Justice Hugo Black: The crucial remaining questions are whether students and teachers may use the schools at their whim as a platform for the exercise of free speech—"symbolic" or "pure"—and whether the courts will allocate to themselves the function of deciding how the pupils' school day will be spent. While I have always believed that, under the First and Fourteenth Amendments, neither the State nor the Federal Government has any authority to regulate or censor the content of speech, I have never believed that any person has a right to give speeches or engage in demonstrations where he pleases and when he pleases . . . .

If the time has come when pupils of state-supported schools, kindergartens, grammar schools, or high schools, can defy and flout orders of school officials to keep their minds on their own schoolwork, it is the beginning of a new revolutionary era of permissiveness in this country fostered by the judiciary."

Since *Tinker*: The Tinkers' war protest was a brand of political speech. A different brand of speech was at the center of another case involving a school suspension, settled in 1986. High school student Matt Fraser gave a speech to a student assembly at his Bethel, Washington, school that showcased student government candidates. In introducing his friend, Fraser delivered a speech riddled with sexual innuendo that caused a roaring reaction and led the school to suspend him. Fraser challenged his suspension. The Court, after fully analyzing Fraser's sexually suggestive language, upheld the school's punishment (*Bethel School District v. Fraser*, 1986). The Court considered the *Tinker* precedent, but unlike the speech in *Tinker*, the speech in this case had no real political value and was designed to entertain an audience of high school students. Students still do not shed their rights at the schoolhouse gates, but neither are they entitled to lewd or offensive speech.

A similar case reached the Court in 2007 *(Morse v. Frederick)*. In Alaska, a student body gathered outside a school to witness and cheer on the Olympic torch as runners carried it by. In a quest for attention, one student flashed a homemade sign that read "BONG HITS 4 JESUS" as the torch passed the school. The student was suspended, and he lost his appeal challenging the suspension. The Court ruled that even though the event took place off of school grounds, it was school-sponsored and therefore a matter for school officials to decide, and the school was reasonable to see his sign as promoting illegal drug use.

Political Science Disciplinary Practices and Reasoning Processes: Explain Complex Similarities and Differences

Concurring and dissenting opinions clearly show that cases are not black and white, that there are more than two possible positions on a controversial matter. Concurring opinions show that while a justice voted with the majority, he or she did so for reasons other than or in addition to those articulated in the majority opinion. More than one dissenting opinion shows that there are different grounds on which to disagree with the majority opinion. When you are developing your own arguments, be aware of the multitude of possible positions on your topic and be ready to address them.

Apply: Complete the following activities.

1. Explain the facts, majority decision, and reasoning in the *Tinker* case.

2. Explain the constitutional principle under consideration in this case.

3. Explain three points Justice Fortas made in the majority opinion.

4. Identify unique points Justices White and Black made in their opinions.

5. Justice White mentions one case on which the *Tinker* case was decided, *Burnside v. Byars*. Explain the role of precedents in determining the Court's opinions. What similar kinds of evidence can you use as you develop your own arguments?

6. Explain what the Supreme Court defined as the line between individual freedom and public order in *Tinker*.

7. Explain the similarities and differences of the outcome in *Tinker* with the outcomes of *Bethel School District v. Fraser* and *Morse v. Frederick*.

Writing the majority opinion in the *Tinker* case, Justice Abe Fortas stated that schools could forbid conduct that would "materially and substantially interfere with the requirements of appropriate discipline" but not activities that merely create "the discomfort and unpleasantness that always accompany an unpopular viewpoint."

Obscenity

Some language and images are so offensive to the average citizen that governments have banned them. Though obscenity is difficult to define, two trends prevail regarding **obscene speech**: the First Amendment does not protect it, and no national standard defines what it is.

In the 19th century, some states and later the national government outlawed obscenity. Reacting to published birth control literature, postal inspector and moral crusader Anthony Comstock pushed for the first national anti-obscenity law in 1873, which banned the circulation and importation of obscene materials through the U.S. mail. Yet the legal debate since has generally been over state and local ordinances brought before the Supreme Court on a case-by-case basis. The Court has tried to square an individual's right to free speech or press and a community's right to ban filthy and offensive material.

A Transformational Time From the late 1950s until the early 1970s, the Supreme Court heard several appeals by those convicted for obscenity. In *Roth v. United States* (1957), Samuel Roth, a long-time publisher of questionable books, was prosecuted under the Comstock Act. He published and sent through the mail his *Good Times* magazine, which contained partially airbrushed nude photographs. On the same day, the Court heard a case examining a California obscenity law. The Court upheld the long-standing view that both state and federal obscenity laws were constitutionally permissible because obscenity is "utterly without redeeming social importance." In *Roth*, the Court defined speech as obscene and unprotected when "the average person, applying contemporary community standards," finds that it "appeals to the prurient interest" (having lustful or lewd thoughts or wishes).

The new rule created a swamp of ambiguity that the Court tried to clear during the next 15 years. Before Roth finished his prison term, the law was on his side. The pornography industry grew apace during the sexual revolution of the 1960s and 1970s. States reacted, creating a battle between those declaring a constitutional right to create or consume risqué materials and local governments seeking to ban smut. The Court struggled to determine this balance. In his frequently quoted phrase from a 1964 case regarding how to distinguish acceptable versus unacceptable pornographic expression, Justice Potter Stewart said, "I know it when I see it." Although the Court could not reach a solid consensus on obscenity, from 1967 to 1971 it overturned 31 obscenity convictions.

Defining Obscenity The conflict continued in *Miller v. California* **(1973)**. After a mass mailing from Marvin Miller promoting adult materials, a number of recipients complained to the police. California authorities prosecuted Miller under the state's obscenity laws. On appeal, the justices reaffirmed that obscene material was not constitutionally protected, but they modified the *Roth* decision saying in effect that a local judge or jury should define obscenity by applying local community standards. Obscenity is not necessarily the same as pornography, and pornography may or may not be obscene. The following year, the Court overturned Georgia's conviction of a theater owner for showing the film *Carnal Knowledge*. The Court has heard subsequent cases dealing with obscene speech, but the Miller test—a set of three criteria that resulted from the *Miller* case—has served as the standard in obscenity cases.

THE MILLER TEST

- The average person applying contemporary community standards finds it appeals to the prurient interest.
- It depicts or describes, in a patently offensive way, sexual conduct specifically defined by state law.
- It lacks serious literary, artistic, political, or scientific value.

Free Press

"Our liberty depends on the freedom of the press," Thomas Jefferson wrote, "and that cannot be limited without being lost." Centuries later, President Donald Trump often referred to the press as "the enemy of the people." A free press had become an important topic during Trump's presidential campaign. He repeatedly complained about "fake news," and at a campaign rally in February 2016 he said, "I'm going to open up our libel laws so when they [the press] write purposely negative and horrible and false articles, we can sue them and win lots of money." Could he win those lawsuits? His past efforts, as well as the standards for freedom of the press, say no.

Libelous or Defamatory Language A charge of **libel** refers to false statements in print that defame someone, hurting their reputation. Much negativity can be printed about someone of a critical, opinionated, or even speculative nature before it qualifies as libel. American courts have typically allowed for a rather high standard of defamation before rewarding a suing party. The main decision that defined the First Amendment's protection of printed speech against the charge of libel was *New York Times v. Sullivan* (1964). In 1960, a civil rights group, including Martin Luther King Jr., put an ad in the *New York Times* entitled "Heed their Rising Voices," which included some inaccuracies and false information about a Montgomery, Alabama, city commissioner, L. B. Sullivan. Sullivan sued for libel in an Alabama court and won $500,000 in damages. The *Times* appealed, arguing that the First Amendment protected against slight mistakes and these should differ from an intentional defamation. The Supreme Court sided with the newspaper. Uninhibited debate "may well include vehement, caustic, and sometimes unpleasantly sharp attacks on government and public officials," the Court noted. The fear of an easy libel suit would stifle robust debate and hard reporting. Even false statements, therefore, must be protected "if the freedoms of expression are to have the 'breathing space' that they need . . . to survive."

The standard to prove libel is therefore high. The suing party must prove that they were damaged and that the offending party knowingly printed the falsehood and did so maliciously with intent to defame. Public officials are less protected than lay people and cannot recover damages for defamatory falsehoods relating to their official conduct unless they can prove actual malice—that is, reckless disregard for the truth. The Court later broadened the category of "public figure" to include celebrities such as movie stars, top athletes, and business leaders.

New York Times v. Sullivan and subsequent decisions have generally ruled that to win a libel suit in a civil court, the suing party must prove that the offending writer either knowingly lied or presented information with a reckless disregard for the truth, that the writer did so with malicious intent to defame, and that actual damages were sustained.

Prior Restraint Though the special circumstances of a school environment were a key factor in the *Tinker* decision, the Court also ruled that the school

Source: *Thinkstock*

The *New York Times*, founded in 1851, has the largest circulation of any newspaper in the United States and is considered authoritative for its journalistic standards.

administration could not ban armbands protesting the war in Vietnam on the grounds that they could *possibly* cause a disruption. In a similar way, neither can the government prevent something true from being published, even if it was obtained illegally and conveys government secrets that could *possibly* endanger national security.

MUST-KNOW SUPREME COURT CASES: *NEW YORK TIMES V. UNITED STATES* (1971)

The Constitutional Question Before the Court: Can the executive branch block the printing of reporter-obtained classified government information in an effort to protect national secrets without violating the First Amendment's free press clause?

Decision: No, for *New York Times*, 6:3.

Before *New York Times v. United States*: In the selective incorporation case of *Near v. Minnesota* (1931), the Supreme Court ruled that a state law preventing the printing of radical propaganda violated freedom of the press.

Facts: Daniel Ellsberg, a high-level Pentagon analyst, became disillusioned with the war in Vietnam and in June of 1971 released a massive report known as the Pentagon Papers to the *New York Times*. (The case also included the *Washington Post* since it, too, had been given the document.) The seven-thousand-page top-secret document— which unlike today's easily released digital content had to be photocopied—told the backstory of America's entry into the Vietnam conflict and revealed government deception. These papers put the government's credibility on the line and, President Nixon claimed, hampered the president's ability to manage the war. Nixon's lawyers petitioned a U.S. district court to order the *Times* to refrain from printing in the name of national security. "I think it is time in this country," Nixon said of Ellsberg and the *Times*, "to quit making national heroes out of those who steal secrets and publish them in the newspaper." The lower court obliged and issued the injunction (order), and armed guards arrived at the newspaper's office to enforce the injunction.

The *Times* appealed, and the Supreme Court ruled in its favor. The ruling assured that the hasty cry of national security does not justify censorship in advance and that the government does not have the power of prior restraint of publications. Even Nixon's solicitor general, the man who argued his side in the Supreme Court, later said the decision "came out exactly as it should." This decision was "a declaration of independence," claimed *Times* reporter Hedrick Smith, "and it really changed the relationship between the government and the media ever since."

The Court ruled on the newspaper's right to print these documents, not on Ellsberg's right to leak them. In fact, Ellsberg was later indicted under the 1917 Espionage Act in his own trial.

Reasoning: In a rare instance, the Court in this case did not fully explain its ruling with a typical majority opinion. Instead, it issued a *per curiam* opinion, which is a judgment issued on behalf of a unanimous court or the court's majority without attribution to a specific justice. It relied heavily on the reasoning in previous cases. The judgment overruled the lower court's injunction and prevented the executive branch from stopping the printing.

Per Curiam Opinion: "Any system of prior restraints of expression comes to this Court bearing a heavy presumption against its constitutional validity." *Bantam Books, Inc. v. Sullivan* . . . (1963); *see also Near v. Minnesota* (1931). The Government "thus carries a heavy burden of showing justification for the imposition of such a restraint." *Organization for a Better Austin v. Keefe* (1971). The District Court for the Southern District of New York, in the *New York Times* case, and the District Court for the District of Columbia and the Court of Appeals for the District of Columbia Circuit, in the *Washington Post* case, held that the Government had not met that burden. We agree.

Several justices issued separate opinions, both concurring and dissenting.

Concurring Opinions: Justices issuing or joining with concurring opinions stressed the absolute nature of the First Amendment and the vague nature of the term "security." Justice Hugo Black, for example, in an opinion with which Justice William O. Douglas joined, wrote the following:

Mr. Justice Black: Now, for the first time in the 182 years since the founding of the Republic, the federal courts are asked to hold that the First Amendment does not mean what it says, but rather means that the Government can halt the publication of current news of vital importance to the people of this country. In seeking injunctions against these newspapers, and in its presentation to the Court, the Executive Branch seems to have forgotten the essential purpose and history of the First Amendment. . . . . The word "security" is a broad, vague generality whose contours should not be invoked to abrogate the fundamental law embodied in the First Amendment. The guarding of military and diplomatic secrets at the expense of informed representative government provides no real security for our Republic.

Dissenting Opinions: Chief Justice Warren Burger wrote a dissenting opinion with which Justices John Harlan and Harry Blackmun joined. The dissent focused in part on the hurried nature of the proceedings, making it difficult to assess the security risk the Pentagon Papers really posed. They also supported the idea that there were exceptions to the absolute superiority of the First Amendment, though they did not argue that this case qualified as one those exceptions.

Mr. Justice Warren Burger: In these cases, the imperative of a free and unfettered press comes into collision with another imperative, the effective functioning of a complex modern government, and, specifically, the effective exercise of certain constitutional powers of the Executive. Only those who view the First Amendment as an absolute in all circumstances—a view I respect, but reject—can find such cases as these to be simple or easy . . . . Of course, the First Amendment right itself is not an absolute, as Justice Holmes so long ago pointed out In his aphorism concerning the right to shout "fire" in a crowded theater if there was no fire.

Political Science Disciplinary Practices and Reasoning Processes: Explain Reasoning, Similarities, and Differences

In another concurring opinion, Justice William Brennan noted that the executive branch "is endowed with enormous power in the two related areas of national defense and international relations." Given this relatively unchecked power, he reasoned that in these areas "the only effective restraint upon executive policy and power . . . may lie in an enlightened citizenry—in an informed and critical public opinion which alone can here protect the values of democratic government. For this reason, it is perhaps here that a press that is alert, aware, and free most vitally serves the basic purpose of the First Amendment. For, without an informed and free press, there cannot be an enlightened people."

Apply: Complete the following activities.

1. Explain the reasoning behind Justice Brennan's views that an "enlightened citizenry" can protect the democratic values of our government.

2. Explain the role of the press in creating that citizenry.

3. Explain how the judgment in *New York Times v. The United States* balances claims for individual freedom with concerns for national security.

4. Read about the case *Near v. Minnesota* (1931) and the Court's decision at Oyez.com or supremecourt.gov, and then explain the similarities and differences between the opinions in *Near* and those in the *New York Times* case.

5. Explain the ways in which Justice Burger and those who joined his dissent differ from the other justices on the nature of the First Amendment.

6. Explain the impact that this decision might have had on (1) the credibility of the government, (2) the outcome of the Vietnam War, and (3) the legal standing of whistleblowers today. Do research if necessary.

The First Amendment: Church and State

The First Amendment also guarantees freedom of religion. The founders wanted to stamp out religious intolerance and outlaw a nationally sanctioned religion. The Supreme Court did not address congressional action on religion for most of its first century, and it did not examine state policies that affected religion for another generation after that. As the nation became more diverse and more secular over the years, the Supreme Court constructed what Thomas Jefferson had called a **"wall of separation"** between church and state. In this nation of varied religions and countless government institutions, however, it is easy for church and state to encroach on each other. Like other interpretations of civil liberties, those addressing freedom of religion are nuanced and sometimes confusing. More recently, the Court has addressed laws that regulate the teaching of evolution, the use of school vouchers, and the public display of religious symbols.

Freedom of Religion

Both James Madison and Thomas Jefferson led a fight to oppose a Virginia tax to fund an established state church in 1785. Madison argued that no law should support any true religion nor should any government tax anyone, believer or nonbeliever, to fund a church. During the ratification battle in 1787, Jefferson wrote Madison from Paris and expressed regret that the proposed Constitution lacked a Bill of Rights, especially an expressed freedom of religion. The First Amendment allayed these concerns because it reads in part, "Congress shall make no law respecting an *establishment* of religion, or prohibiting the *free exercise* thereof." In 1802, President Jefferson popularized the phrase "separation of church and state" after assuring Baptists in Danbury, Connecticut, that the First Amendment builds a "wall of separation between church and state." Today some citizens want a stronger separation; others want none.

Members of the First Congress included the **establishment clause** to prevent the federal government from establishing a national religion. More recently, the clause has come to mean that governing institutions—federal, state, and local—cannot sanction, recognize, favor, or disregard any religion. The **free exercise clause** prevents governments from stopping religious practices. This clause is generally upheld, unless an unusual religious act is illegal or deeply opposes the interests of the community. Today, these two clauses collectively mean people can practice any religion they want, provided it doesn't violate established law or harm others, and the state cannot endorse or advance one religion over another. The Supreme Court's interpretation and application of the establishment clause and free exercise clause show a commitment to individual liberties and an effort to balance the religious practice of majorities with the right to the free exercise of minority religious practice.

Mormons brought the first freedom of religious exercise issue to the Supreme Court in 1879. Under President Ulysses S. Grant, the federal government pushed to end Mormon polygamy common in the Utah Territory. U.S. marshals rounded up hundreds of Mormons who had violated a congressional anti-polygamy law. George Reynolds, secretary to Mormon leader Brigham Young, brought a test case that argued the free exercise clause prevented such law. The Mormons lost, and the Court said the federal government could limit religious practices that impaired the public interest.

The Court Erects a Wall In the 1940s, New Jersey allowed public school boards to reimburse parents for transporting their children to school, even if the children attended parochial schools—those maintained by a church or religious organization. Some argued this constituted an establishment of religion, but in *Everson v. Board of Education* (1947), the Court upheld the law. State law is not meant to favor or handicap any religion. This law gave no money to parochial schools but instead provided funds evenly to parents who transported their children to the state's accredited schools. Preventing payments to parochial students' parents would handicap them. Much like fire stations, police, and utilities, school transportation is a nonreligious service available to all taxpayers.

Though nothing changed with *Everson*, the Court did signal that the religion clauses of the First Amendment applied to the states via the Fourteenth Amendment in the incorporation process. The Court also used Jefferson's phrase in its opinion and began erecting the modern wall of separation.

Prayer in Public Schools In their early development, public schools were largely Protestant institutions; as such, many began their day with a prayer. But the Court outlawed the practice in the early 1960s in its landmark case, *Engel v. Vitale* **(1962)**. A year later, in *School District of Abington Township, Pennsylvania* v. *Schempp,* the Court outlawed a daily Bible reading in the Abington schools in Pennsylvania and thus in all public schools. In both cases, the school had projected or promoted religion, which constituted an establishment.

MUST-KNOW SUPREME COURT CASES: *ENGEL V. VITALE* (1962)

The Constitutional Question Before the Court: Does allowing a state-created, nondenominational prayer to be recited voluntarily in public schools violate the First Amendment's establishment clause?

Decision: Yes, for Engel et al., 6:1

Before *Engel*: Since the days of one-room schools, many public schools across the United States started the school day with a prayer. In the 1950s, the state of New York tried to standardize prayer in its public schools by coming up with a common, nondenominational prayer that would satisfy most religions. The State Board of Regents, the government body that oversees the schools, did so: "Almighty God, we acknowledge our dependence upon Thee, and we beg Thy blessings upon us, our parents, our teachers and our Country." Each school day, classes recited the Pledge of Allegiance followed by this prayer, which teachers were required to recite. Students were allowed to stand mute or, with written permission, to depart the room during the exercise.

Facts: In 1959, the parents of ten pupils organized and filed suit against the local school board because this official prayer was contrary to the beliefs, religions, or religious practices of both themselves and their children. Lead plaintiff Stephen Engel and the others argued the prayer—created by a state actor and recited at a state-funded institution where attendance was required by state law—violated the establishment clause. The respondent, William Vitale, was the chairman of the local Hyde Park, New York, school board.

Reasoning: The majority reasoned that since a public institution developed the prayer and since it was to be used in a public school setting with mandatory attendance, the Regents Board had made religion its business, a violation of the establishment clause. Because of the Fourteenth Amendment and incorporation, states as well as the federal government are forbidden from officially backing any religious activity. They also noted that including the word "God" was denominational—not all religions believe in God. Further, they explained that even though participation was voluntary, students would likely feel reluctant not to take part in a teacher-led activity.

The Court's Majority Opinion by Mr. Justice Black: We think that, by using its public school system to encourage recitation of the Regents' prayer, the State of New York has adopted a practice wholly inconsistent with the Establishment Clause. . . .

The petitioners contend . . . the State's use of the Regents' prayer in its public school system breaches the constitutional wall of separation between Church and State. We agree with that contention, since we think that the constitutional prohibition against laws respecting an establishment of religion must at least mean that, in this country, it is no part of the business of government to compose official prayers for any group of the American people to recite as a part of a religious program carried on by government . . . .

One of the greatest dangers to the freedom of the individual to worship in his own way lay in the Government's placing its official stamp of approval upon one particular kind of prayer or one particular form of religious services. . . .

It is true that New York's establishment of its Regents' prayer as an officially approved religious doctrine of that State does not amount to a total establishment of one particular religious sect to the exclusion of all others—that, indeed, the governmental endorsement of that prayer seems relatively insignificant when compared to the governmental encroachments upon religion which were commonplace 200 years ago. To those who may subscribe to the view that, because the Regents' official prayer is so brief and general there can be no danger to religious freedom in its governmental establishment, however, it may be appropriate to say in the words of James Madison, the author of the First Amendment:

"[I]t is proper to take alarm at the first experiment on our liberties. . . ."

Justice Douglas agreed with the majority but made the point that children may feel like a "captive" audience, even though they were technically free to leave the room.

Concurring Opinion by Mr. Justice Douglas: The point for decision is whether the Government can constitutionally finance a religious exercise. Our system at the federal and state levels is presently honeycombed with such financing [with government-paid clergymen for the House and Senate and a Supreme Court Crier, all who offer prayers at the opening of each session]. Nevertheless, I think it is an unconstitutional undertaking whatever form it takes . . . for, in each of the instances given, the person praying is a public official on the public payroll, performing a religious exercise in a governmental institution . . . .

It is said that the element of coercion is inherent in the giving of this prayer. . . . Few adults, let alone children, would leave our courtroom or the Senate or the House while those prayers are being given. Every such audience is in a sense a "captive" audience . . . A religion is not established in the usual sense merely by letting those who choose to do so say the prayer that the public school teacher leads. Yet once government finances a religious exercise, it inserts a divisive influence into our communities.

Justice Stewart dissented, noting Mr. Douglas's point that the Supreme Court itself begins with a pronouncement of "God save the United States and this Honorable Court" and that Congress opens with a prayer as well. He disagreed that the Regents' prayer established a preferred religion, arguing that it provided students the opportunity to share "in the spiritual heritage of our Nation . . . ."

> **Dissenting Opinion by Mr. Justice Stewart:** The Court today decides that, in permitting this brief nondenominational prayer, the school board has violated the Constitution of the United States. I think this decision is wrong . . . . With all respect, I think the Court has misapplied a great constitutional principle. I cannot see how an "official religion" is established by letting those who want to say a prayer say it. On the contrary, I think that to deny the wish of these school children to join in reciting this prayer is to deny them the opportunity of sharing in the spiritual heritage of our Nation . . .
>
> I do not believe the State of New York has [established an "official religion"] in this case. What [it] has done has been to recognize and to follow the deeply entrenched and highly cherished spiritual traditions of our Nation.

Since *Engel*: The Court has since ruled against student-led prayer at official public school events. In the 1980s, Alabama created a policy to satisfy community wishes without violating the 1960s' precedents. The state provided that schools give a moment of silence at the beginning of the school day to facilitate prayer or meditation. In a 1985 ruling, however, the Court said this constituted an establishment of religion. The Court left open the possibility that an undefined, occasional moment of silence might pass constitutional muster.

Political Science Disciplinary Practices and Reasoning Processes: Explain Reasoning, Similarities, and Differences

Justice Black quoted James Madison, the author of the First Amendment, in the majority opinion: "[I]t is proper to take alarm at the first experiment on our liberties." Madison's words following that quote help explain why: "We hold this prudent jealousy to be the first duty of Citizens, and one of the noblest characteristics of the late Revolution. The free men of America did not wait till usurped power had strengthened itself by exercise, and entangled the question in precedents. They saw all the consequences in the principle, and they avoided the consequences by denying the principle."

Apply: Complete the following tasks.

1. Explain the point Justice Black made in the Court's majority opinion when he quoted Madison's admonition to be alarmed.

2. Explain Justice Douglas's elaboration of the majority opinion, especially the role of public money.

3. Explain how Justice Stewart in his dissent justified an intermingling of religion and government. What did he mean by "the spiritual heritage of our Nation"?

The Lemon Test In 1971, the Court created a measure of whether or not the state violated the establishment clause in ***Lemon v. Kurtzman***. Both Rhode Island and Pennsylvania passed laws to pay teachers of secular subjects in religious schools with state funds. The state mandated such subjects as English and math and reasoned that it should assist the parochial schools in carrying out a state requirement. In trying to determine the constitutionality of this statute, the Court decided these laws created an "excessive entanglement" between the state and the church because teachers in these parochial schools may improperly involve faith in their teaching. In the unanimous opinion, Chief Justice Warren Burger further articulated Jefferson's "wall of separation" concept, and "far from being a 'wall,'" the policy made a "blurred, indistinct, and variable barrier." To guide lower court decisions and future controversies that might reach the High Court, the justices in the case of *Lemon v. Kurtzman* developed the Lemon test to determine excessive entanglement.

THE LEMON TEST
To avoid an excessive entanglement, a policy must
• have a secular purpose that neither endorses nor disapproves of religion
• have an effect that neither advances nor prohibits religion
• avoid creating a relationship between religion and government that entangles either in the internal affairs of the other

Education and the Free Exercise Clause In 1972, the Court ruled that a Wisconsin high school attendance law violated Amish parents' right to teach their own children under the free exercise clause. The Court found that the Amish's alternative mode of informal vocational training paralleled the state's objectives. Requiring these children to attend high school violated the basic tenets of the Amish faith because it forced their children into unwanted environments.

MUST-KNOW SUPREME COURT DECISIONS: *WISCONSIN V. YODER* (1972)

The Constitutional Question Before the Court: Does a state's compulsory school law for children aged 16 and younger violate the First Amendment's free exercise clause for parents whose religious beliefs and customs dictate they keep their children out of school after a certain age?

Decision: Yes, for Yoder, 7:0

Facts: A Wisconsin statute required parents of children aged 16 and under to send their children to a formal school. Three parents in the New Glarus,

Wisconsin, school system—Jonas Yoder, Wallace Miller, and Adin Yutzy—had teenagers they did not send to school. Yoder and the others were charged, tried in a state criminal court, found guilty, and fined $5.00 each. The parents appealed the case to the state supreme court, arguing their religion prevented them from sending their children to public schools at their age. That court agreed. The state then appealed to the Supreme Court, hoping to preserve the law and its authority to regulate compulsory school attendance.

These same children had attended a public school through eighth grade. Their parents felt an elementary education suitable and necessary, but they refused to enroll their 14- and 15-year-olds in the public schools. Amish teens are meant to develop the skills for a trade, not continue learning subjects that do not have a practical application. Also, the parents did not want their children exposed to divergent values and practices at a public high school. The parents argued that the free exercise clause entitled them to this practice and this decision.

The state invoked the legal claim of *parens patriae*—parental authority— claiming it had a legal responsibility to oversee public safety and health and to educate children to age 16. Those who skipped this education would become burdens on society.

Reasoning: The Court found making the Amish attend schools would expose them to attitudes and values that ran counter to their beliefs. In fact, the Court also said that forcing the Amish teens to attend would interfere with their religious development and integration into Amish society. Further, the Court realized that stopping schooling a couple of years early and continuing informal vocational education did not make members of this community burdens on society.

The Court declared in this case that the free exercise clause overrode the state's efforts to promote health and safety through ensuring a full, formal education. In a rare instance, Justice William O. Douglas voted with the majority but wrote a partial dissenting opinion, excerpted below. Justices William Rehnquist and Lewis Powell did not participate.

The Court's Majority Opinion by Mr. Justice Burger: Formal high school education beyond the eighth grade is contrary to Amish beliefs not only because it places Amish children in an environment hostile to Amish beliefs, with increasing emphasis on competition in class work and sports and with pressure to conform to the styles, manners, and ways of the peer group, but also because it takes them away from their community, physically and emotionally, during the crucial and formative adolescent period of life. During this period, the children must acquire Amish attitudes favoring manual work and self-reliance and the specific skills needed to perform the adult role of an Amish farmer or housewife. They must learn to enjoy physical labor. Once a child has learned basic reading, writing, and elementary mathematics, these traits, skills, and attitudes admittedly fall within the category of those best learned through example and "doing," rather than in a classroom. And, at this time in life, the Amish child must also grow in his faith and his relationship to the Amish community if he is to be prepared to accept the heavy obligations imposed by adult baptism. In short, high school attendance with teachers who are not of the Amish faith— and may even be hostile to it—interposes a serious barrier to the integration of the Amish child into the Amish religious community. Dr. John Hostetler, one of the experts on Amish society, testified that the modern high school is not equipped, in curriculum or social environment, to impart the values promoted by Amish society.

Justice Douglas, while agreeing with the majority, believed the views of a mature 16-year-old should be taken into account.

A Partial Dissenting Opinion by Mr. Justice Douglas: If the parents in this case are allowed a religious exemption, the inevitable effect is to impose the parents' notions of religious duty upon their children. Where the child is mature enough to express potentially conflicting desires, it would be an invasion of the child's rights to permit such an imposition without canvassing his views. . . . As the child has no other effective forum, it is in this litigation that his rights should be considered. And if an Amish child desires to attend high school, and is mature enough to have that desire respected, the State may well be able to override the parents' religiously motivated objections.

Political Science Disciplinary Practices: Understanding Opposing Views

While the majority opinion becomes the lasting legacy of a Supreme Court case, knowing the arguments the opposing side made can help clarify the Court's decision. Here is how the Court summarized the state's position.

The State advances two primary arguments in support of its system of compulsory education. It notes, as Thomas Jefferson pointed out early in our history, that some degree of education is necessary to prepare citizens to participate effectively and intelligently in our open political system if we are to preserve freedom and independence. Further, education prepares individuals to be self-reliant and self-sufficient participants in society. We accept these propositions.

However, the evidence adduced [cited] by the Amish in this case is persuasively to the effect that an additional one or two years of formal high school for Amish children in place of their long-established program of informal vocational education would do little to serve those interests. Respondents' experts testified at trial, without challenge, that the value of all education must be assessed in terms of its capacity to prepare the child for life. It is one thing to say that compulsory education for a year or two beyond the eighth grade may be necessary when its goal is the preparation of the child for life in modern society as the majority live, but it is quite another if the goal of education be viewed as the preparation of the child for life in the separated agrarian community that is the keystone of the Amish faith. . . . The State attacks respondents' position as one fostering "ignorance" from which the child must be protected by the State. No one can question the State's duty to protect children from ignorance, but this argument does not square with the facts disclosed in the record. Whatever their idiosyncrasies as seen by the majority, this record strongly shows that the Amish community has been a highly successful social unit within our society, even if apart from the conventional "mainstream." Its members are productive and very law-abiding members of society; they reject public welfare in any of its usual modern forms. The Congress itself recognized their self-sufficiency by authorizing exemption of such groups as the Amish from the obligation to pay social security taxes.

Apply: Complete the following tasks.

1. Explain the First Amendment principle at issue in this case.

2. Identify the public policy or law the citizens challenged in this case.

3. Explain the Court's reasoning described in the majority opinion.

4. Interpret the Court's response to the state's two primary arguments by identifying the kind of evidence the Court relied on to address the state's arguments.

5. Explain the unique point Justice Douglas made in his partial dissent.

Source: Shutterstock

Amish families, such as this one in Pennsylvania, wear simple clothing, use horses and buggies rather than cars, and value manual labor. The Amish parents involved in *Wisconsin v. Yoder* believed that sending their children to high school would endanger their families' salvation.

Contemporary First Amendment Issues

Real and perceived excessive entanglements between church and state have continued in issues that make the news today. Can government funding go to private schools or universities at all? Does a display of religious symbols on public grounds constitute an establishment of religion? As with so many cases, it depends.

Public Funding of Religious Institutions Many establishment cases address whether or not state governments can contribute funds to religious institutions, especially Roman Catholic schools. Virtually every one has been struck down, except those secular endeavors that aid higher education in religious colleges, perhaps because state laws do not require education beyond the twelfth grade and older students are not as impressionable.

Vouchers Supporters of private parochial schools and parents who pay tuition argue that the government should issue vouchers to ease their costs. Parents of parochial students pay the same taxes as public school parents while they also ease the expenses at public schools. A Cleveland, Ohio, program offered as much as $2,250 in tuition reimbursements for low-income families and $1,875 for any families sending their children to private schools. The Court upheld the program largely because the policy did not make a distinction between religious or nonreligious private schools, even though 96 percent of private school students attended a religious-based school. This money did not go directly to the religious schools but rather to the parents for educating their children.

Religion in Public Schools Since the *Engel* and *Abington* decisions, any formal prayer in public schools and even a daily, routine moment of silence are violations of the establishment clause. The Court has even ruled against student-led prayer at official public school events. However, popular opinion has never endorsed these stances. Gallup consistently found that strong majorities of American citizens still approved of a form of daily prayer in public schools, though the size of that majority is shrinking. In 2014, Gallup found that 61 percent of Americans supported allowing daily prayer, down from 70 percent in 1999.

Students can still operate extracurricular activities of a religious nature provided these take place outside the school day and without tax dollars. The free exercise clause guarantees students' rights to say private prayers, wear religious T-shirts, and discuss religion. Public teachers' actions are more restricted because they are employed by the state.

Religious Symbols in the Public Square A Rhode Island town annually adorned its shopping district with Christmas decor, including a Christmas tree, a Santa's house, and a nativity scene. Plaintiffs sued, arguing that the nativity scene created government establishment of Christianity. In *Lynch v. Donnelly* (1984), the Court upheld the city's right to include this emblem because it served a legitimate secular purpose of depicting the historical origins of the Christmas holiday. In another case in 1989, the Court found the display of a crèche (manger scene) on public property, when standing alone without other Christmas decor, a violation because it was seen as a Christian-centered display. "Endorsement sends a message to non-adherents that they are outsiders, not full members of the political community," the Court wrote, while it signals that adherents are favored insiders.

Ten Commandments In 2005, the Court ruled two different ways on the issue of displaying the Ten Commandments on government property. One case involved a large outdoor display at the Texas state capitol. Among 17 other monuments sat a six-foot-tall rendering of the Ten Commandments.

The other case involved the Ten Commandments hanging in two Kentucky courthouses, accompanied by several historical American documents. The Court said the Texas display was acceptable because of the monument's religious and historical function. It was not in a location that anyone would be compelled to be in, such as a school or a courtroom. And it was a passive use of the religious text in that only occasional passersby would see it. The Kentucky courtroom case brought the opposite conclusion because an objective observer would perceive the displays as having a predominantly religious purpose in state courtrooms—places where some citizens must attend and places meant to be free from any prejudice.

SELECTED SUPREME COURT FIRST AMENDMENT RULINGS (NON-REQUIRED CASES)	
Case	Ruling
Reynolds v. United States (1879)	Government can limit religious practices that impair the public interest.
Gitlow v. New York (1925)	Upheld New York's criminal anarchy law but put states on notice that some rights in the Bill of Rights could protect citizens from state action.
Near v. Minnesota (1931)	Court followed through on Gitlow, preventing states from violating free press rights against printing obnoxious material and thus beginning the incorporation process.
New York Times v. Sullivan (1964)	To win a libel lawsuit, the accusing party must prove defendant issued intentional falsehoods, with malicious intent, and caused actual damage.
Lemon v. Kurtzman (1971)	States cannot have an excessive entanglement of church and state.
Miller v. California (1973)	States can prohibit obscene speech that lacks literary, artistic, political, or scientific value.
Bethel v. Fraser (1986)	Schools can punish speech that administrators find lewd or offensive.

The Second Amendment

Interpretations of the Second Amendment, like those of the First Amendment, represent a commitment to individual liberties. The Second Amendment is strongly tied to the gun debate. A careful reading of the provision—"A well regulated militia, being necessary to the security of a free State, the right of the people to keep and bear arms, shall not be infringed"—sheds light on why the policy has been so controversial. The precise meaning is difficult to ascertain in today's world. Was the amendment written to protect the state's right to maintain a militia or the citizen's unfettered right to own a firearm? Gun control advocates might point out these state militias were "well regulated" and thus subject to state requirements such as training, occasional military exercises, and limitations on the type of gun possessed. The concern at the time was about the federal government imposing its will on or overthrowing a state government with a standing federal army. The original concern was not with the general citizenry's right to gun ownership. Today's gun advocates, however, supported by recent Supreme Court decisions, argue that the amendment guarantees the personal right to own and bear arms because each citizen's right to own a firearm guaranteed the state's ability to have a militia. Similarly, gun rights proponents argue that the "right of the people" clause means the same as it does with other parts of the Bill of Rights.

Federalism and Gun Policy

Recall that the Bill of Rights was originally created to limit the federal government. States made their own gun-related laws for years and still do today. A handful of national gun laws exist based on the commerce clause. However, as you will read in the *McDonald* case, states must follow the Second Amendment because of selective incorporation.

Federal Policy Gun laws, such as defining where people can carry, fall within the police powers of the state as explained in Chapter 2. Not until 1934, in an era of bootleggers and gangsters, did Congress pass a national statute about possession of guns. The National Firearms Act required registration of certain weapons, imposed a tax on the sale and manufacture of certain guns, and restricted the sale and ownership of high-risk weapons such as sawed-off shotguns and automatic machine guns. The law was challenged not long after Congress passed the bill. The Supreme Court upheld the law because the Second Amendment did not protect ownership of sawed-off shotguns because such weapons were never common in a "well-regulated militia."

Increased urban crime, protest, and assassinations in the 1960s influenced the passage of the Gun Control Act of 1968. Along with other anti-crime bills that year, the act sought safer streets. It ended mail-order sales of all firearms and ammunition and banned the sale of guns to felons, fugitives from justice, illegal drug users, people with mental illness, and those dishonorably discharged from the military. In reality, the law's effect was to punish those who owned a gun or used it illegally more than prevent the purchase or possession of guns.

The gun debate came to the forefront again after a mentally disturbed John Hinckley shot President Ronald Reagan in 1981. Reagan survived as did his press secretary James Brady, but Brady suffered a paralyzing head wound. His wife and a coalition organized to prevent handgun violence pushed for legislation that became the Brady Handgun Violence Prevention Act in 1993. This law established a five-day waiting period for purchases of handguns to allow for a background check and for a potential cooling-off period for any buyer motivated by immediate impulse, anger, or revenge. The law expired in 1998, but a similar policy that establishes the National Instant Criminal Background Check System has gone into effect. The Brady Campaign to Prevent Gun Violence reported that the initial Brady law prevented the sale of guns to more than two million people.

The law, however, has several loopholes. Private gun collectors can avoid the background check when purchasing firearms at private gun shows, and some guns can be purchased via the Internet without a background check. Federal law and 28 states still allow juveniles to purchase long guns (rifles and shotguns) from unlicensed dealers, and the national check system has an insufficient database of non-felon criminals, domestic violence offenders, and mental health patients.

States and Localities Meanwhile, states have increasingly passed laws to allow for ease in gun possession. The National Rifle Association (NRA) and Republican-controlled legislatures have worked to pass a number of state laws to enable citizens to carry guns, some concealed, some openly. The NRA has also fought in the courts against laws restricting gun ownership. Among the two most noted cases are *District of Columbia v. Heller* (2008) and *McDonald v. Chicago* (2010).

MUST-KNOW SUPREME COURT DECISIONS: *MCDONALD V. CHICAGO* (2010)

The Constitutional Question Before the Court: Does the Second Amendment apply to the states, by way of the Fourteenth Amendment, and thus prevent states or their political subdivisions from banning citizen ownership of handguns?

Decision: Yes, for McDonald, 5:4

Before *McDonald*: The Second Amendment prevents the federal government from forbidding people to keep and bear arms. In 2008, gun rights advocates and the National Rifle Association challenged a law in the District of Columbia, the seat of the federal government, which effectively banned all handguns, except those for law enforcement officers and other rare exceptions. In the case of *District of Columbia v. Heller*, the Court ruled that the Second Amendment applied and that the district's handgun ban violated this right. Because the Bill of Rights was intended to restrain Congress and the federal government, not the states, this ruling applied only to the federal government and did not incorporate the Second Amendment to state governments. Any existing state laws preventing handguns were not altered by this precedent—until Otis McDonald came to court.

Facts: Citizens in both Chicago and in the nearby suburb of Oak Park challenged policies in their cities that were similar to the ones struck down in Washington. Chicago required all gun owners to register guns, yet the city invariably refused to allow citizens to register handguns, creating an effective ban. The lead plaintiff, Otis McDonald, pointed to the dangers of his crime-ridden neighborhood and how the city's ban had rendered him without self-defense, and he argued that the Second Amendment should have prevented this vulnerability. His attorneys also attempted to take the *Heller* decision further, extending its holding to the state governments via the Fourteenth Amendment's due process clause.

Reasoning: In a close vote, the Court applied the Second Amendment to the states via the Fourteenth Amendment's due process clause, arguing that, based on *Heller,* the right to individual self-defense is at the heart of the Second Amendment. The majority also noted the historical context for the Fourteenth Amendment and asserted that the amendment sought to provide a constitutional foundation for the Civil Rights Act of 1866. The selective incorporation doctrine has encouraged the Court to require state governments and their political subdivisions to follow most parts of the Bill of Rights. The ruling in *McDonald* highlighted yet another right that the states and their municipalities could not deny citizens.

Justice Samuel Alito wrote the Court's majority opinion; Justices Antonin Scalia and Clarence Thomas wrote concurring opinions.

Majority Opinion by Mr. Justice Alito: Self-defense is a basic right, recognized by many legal systems from ancient times to the present, and the *Heller* Court held that individual self-defense is "the central component" of the Second Amendment right . . . .[T]he Court found that this right applies to handguns because they are "the most preferred firearm in the nation to 'keep' and use for protection of one's home and family." . . . It thus concluded that citizens must be permitted "to use [handguns] for the core lawful purpose of self-defense.". . . *Heller* also clarifies that this right is "deeply rooted in this Nation's history and traditions. . . ."

A survey of the contemporaneous history also demonstrates clearly that the Fourteenth Amendment's Framers and ratifiers counted the right to keep and bear arms among those fundamental rights necessary to the Nation's system of ordered liberty . . . .

After the Civil War, the Southern States engaged in systematic efforts to disarm and injure African Americans. . . .These injustices prompted the 39th Congress to pass the Freedmen's Bureau Act of 1866 and the Civil Rights Act of 1866 to protect the right to keep and bear arms. Congress, however, ultimately deemed these legislative remedies insufficient, and approved the Fourteenth Amendment. Today, it is generally accepted that that Amendment was understood to provide a constitutional basis for protecting the rights set out in the Civil Rights Act. . . . In Congressional debates on the proposed Amendment, its legislative proponents in the 39th Congress referred to the right to keep and bear arms as a fundamental right deserving of protection. Evidence from the period immediately following the Amendment's ratification confirms that that right was considered fundamental.

Justice Stephen Breyer wrote a dissent with which Justices Ruth Bader Ginsburg and Sonia Sotomayor joined. Associate Justice John Paul Stevens also wrote a dissent.

Dissenting Opinion by Mr. Justice Stevens: I do not mean to deny that there can be significant practical, as well as esthetic, benefits from treating rights symmetrically with regard to the State and Federal Governments . . . In a federalist system such as ours, however, this approach can carry substantial costs. When a federal court insists that state and local authorities follow its dictates on a matter not critical to personal liberty or procedural justice, the latter may be prevented from engaging in the kind of beneficent "experimentation in things social and economic" that ultimately redounds to the benefit of all Americans. . . . The costs of federal courts' imposing a uniform national standard may be especially high when the relevant regulatory interests vary significantly across localities, and when the ruling implicates the States' core police powers.

Furthermore, there is a real risk that, by demanding the provisions of the Bill of Rights apply identically to the States, federal courts will cause those provisions to "be watered down in the needless pursuit of uniformity . . ." When one legal standard must prevail across dozens of jurisdictions with disparate needs and customs, courts will often settle on a relaxed standard. This watering-down risk is particularly acute when we move beyond the narrow realm of criminal procedure and into the relatively vast domain of substantive rights. So long as the requirements of fundamental fairness are always and everywhere respected, it is not clear that greater liberty results from the jot-for-jot application of a provision of the Bill of Rights to the States. Indeed, it is far from clear that proponents of an individual right to keep and bear arms ought to celebrate today's decision.

Political Science Disciplinary Practices: Understanding Opposing Views

Later in his dissent, Justice Breyer succinctly stated a key controversy in this case.

[I]n evaluating an asserted right to be free from particular gun-control regulations, liberty is on both sides of the equation. Guns may be useful for self-defense, as well as for hunting and sport, but they also have a unique potential to facilitate death and destruction and thereby to destabilize ordered liberty. *Your* interest in keeping and bearing a certain firearm may diminish *my* interest in being and feeling safe from armed violence. And while granting you the right to own a handgun might make you safer on any given day . . . it may make you and the community you live in less safe overall, owing to the increased number of handguns in circulation. It is at least reasonable for a democratically elected legislature to take such concerns into account in considering what sorts of regulations would best serve the public welfare.

Apply: Complete the following tasks.

1. Explain how the majority in *District of Columbia v. Heller* balanced the equation to which Justice Breyer referred in his dissent.

2. Explain the similarities and differences of the *Heller* and *McDonald* cases.

3. Identify the historic period to which Justice Alito referred in the majority opinion, and explain the reasoning behind referring to this period.

4. Explain the impact of the *McDonald* ruling on the selective incorporation doctrine.

5. Explain how, according to Justice Stevens in his dissent, a uniform, nation-wide application of the Second Amendment might "water down" the right to bear arms.

After *Heller* and *McDonald* The *Heller* and *McDonald* decisions partially govern gun policy in the United States, but the Court has done little to define gun rights and limits since. It declined to hear cases on assault weapons bans from Maryland and from a Chicago-area municipality. The Court has also declined to rule on a restrictive California limitation on who may carry concealed guns.

Congress is typically at loggerheads in both a bipartisan and bicameral manner when it comes to gun policy. After each nationally notable homicide or massacre, the discussion about the Second Amendment becomes loud and intense, but little national law changes. Republicans tend to fiercely defend citizens' rights to own and carry guns, while Democrats tend to seek stronger restrictions on sale, ownership, and public possession. The U.S. House of Representatives has recently been friendly to pro-gun legislation—bills supporting concealed carry reciprocity (the right for a legally registered gun-owner to carry a concealed gun in another state that allows concealed carry) and protecting veterans' rights to carry—while the Senate, even with Republicans in the majority, has been reluctant to pass such legislation. Presidential policy has shifted with changes in office. After a deranged young man shot and killed 20 schoolchildren and 6 adults in Newtown, Connecticut, President Barack Obama issued an executive order to keep guns out of the hands of mentally disabled Social Security recipients. In other words, those tagged as mentally unstable by the Social Security Administration would be flagged and seen on the national background registry. President Donald Trump, a pro-gun advocate, reversed the order in 2017.

POLICY MATTERS: *RECENT STATE POLICY AND SECOND AMENDMENT RIGHTS*

Though attempts to hone gun policy continue with little success at the federal level, most gun policy and efforts to balance order and freedom with respect to the Second Amendment are scattered among varying state laws and occasional lower court decisions.

About 33,000 American deaths result from handguns each year; roughly one-third are homicides and two-thirds are suicides. In 2014, about 11,000 of the nearly 16,000 homicides in the United States involved a firearm. In addition to the thousands of single deaths, an uptick in mass shootings has brought attention to the issue of accessibility to weapons. With shootings at Virginia Tech (2007), Newtown (2012), Charleston (2015), Orlando (2016), San Bernardino (2017), Las Vegas (2017), and Parkland (2018), activists and experts on both sides of the gun debate push for new legislation at the state level in hopes of solving a crisis and preventing and protecting future would-be victims.

According to a count by the Law Center to Prevent Gun Violence, located in San Francisco, more than 160 laws that restrict gun use or ownership were passed in 42 states and D.C. after the Newtown massacre. These include broadening the legal definition of assault weapons, banning sales of magazines that hold more than seven rounds of ammunition, and including additional dangerous people on the no-purchase list. By another expert's estimate, as G. M. Filisko reports in the *American Bar Association Journal*, about 9 states have made more restrictive laws, and about 30 have passed more pro-Second Amendment legislation. Those laws include widening open-carry and increasing the number of states that have reciprocity in respecting out-of-state permits. In 2009, only two states had permit-less carry. North Dakota became the twelfth state to pass an open-carry law in 2017, sometimes called "constitutional carry" by its advocates.

One study found that mass shootings—defined as those in which four or more people died—account for only about 0.13 percent of gun deaths, but a single mass shooting leads to a 15-percent increase in the number of state firearms bills introduced the following year. The type of laws passed depends on the party in power. Republican pro-Second Amendment civil liberties bills increased more permissive laws by 75 percent in states where Republicans dominate, but in Democrat-controlled states researchers found no significant increase in new restrictive laws enacted.

After the Las Vegas shooting in 2017, which resulted in a new record number of deaths in such modern shootings, many people have focused on banning bump stocks, a device that essentially turns a semiautomatic rifle into an automatic one. New policies on both sides of the gun argument will continue to come and go with public concern over the issue, as legislatures design and pass them, and as courts determine whether they infringe on citizens' civil liberties.

REFLECT ON THE ESSENTIAL QUESTION

Essential Question: *How do Supreme Court decisions on the First and Second Amendments and the relationship of those amendments to the Fourteenth Amendment reflect a commitment to individual liberties?*

On separate paper, complete a chart like the one below to gather details to answer that question.

Cases that protect civil liberties	Cases that protect national security and social order

THINK AS A POLITICAL SCIENTIST: *INTERPRET* SNYDER V. PHELPS

When you interpret information, you attempt to understand and explain the meaning of an idea or event in context. You consider the time period in which the author created the work and the place where it was created. You use critical thinking skills and prior information to help you interpret and understand the overall meaning of the work. Similarly, to understand an event, you analyze the facts as you understand them and interpret them according to such factors as the politics and social trends of the day, as well as other related events that may have happened around the same time or that may have engendered or resulted from the event you are studying.

In legal proceedings, courts analyze events and claims to interpret the law. Supreme Court justices must be able to examine the facts of each case—time, place, and extenuating circumstances—and interpret them in the context of existing law to reach complex decisions on how a given law is or should be carried out.

Practice: In 2006, a young U.S. Marine named Matthew Snyder was killed in a noncombat-related accident in Iraq. Later, Westboro Baptist Church of Topeka, Kansas, picketed Snyder's funeral as part of the church's ongoing protest of the U.S. military's increasing tolerance of homosexuality among its personnel. Matthew Snyder's father, Albert Snyder, sued the church, its pastor Fred Phelps, and two members of Phelps's family for, among other things, defamation and intentional infliction of emotional distress. Use the Internet to research the events and decisions involved in this case since it first went to trial in 2007. Then write an interpretation of the Supreme Court's ruling in *Snyder v. Phelps*.

KEY TERMS AND NAMES

civil liberties/233

clear and present danger test/240

compelling governmental interest/239

due process/236

Engel v. Vitale (1962)/254

establishment clause/253

Fifth Amendment/236

Fourteenth Amendment/236

free exercise clause/253

Lemon v. Kurtzman (1971)/257

libel/248

McDonald v. Chicago (2010)/264

Miller v. California (1973)/248

New York Times v. United States (1971)/250

obscene speech/247

prior restraint/239

public interest/235

Schenck v. United States (1919)/240

selective incorporation/236

symbolic speech/242

Tinker v. Des Moines Independent Schools (1969)/243

wall of separation/252

Wisconsin v. Yoder (1972)/257

1. Which of the constitutional provisions is at issue in *Schenck v. United States*?

   (A) The necessary and proper clause in Article I

   (B) First Amendment free speech and free press rights

   (C) Congress's power to declare war in Article I

   (D) Fourteenth Amendment due process clause

2. What was the effect of the opinion in *Schenck v. United States?*

   (A) People can say or express anything as long as the nation is not at war.

   (B) During wartime, no person can criticize the U.S. government.

   (C) Free speech in the United States was expanded.

   (D) As long as speech does not present a clear and present danger, it is allowed.

3. Those who disagree with the views in the majority opinion in *Schenck* would likely celebrate the shaping of the Constitution in which free-speech ruling?

   (A) *Tinker v. Des Moines*

   (B) *Engel v. Vitale*

   (C) *United States v. Lopez*

   (D) *New York Times Co. v. United States*

4. With the variety of religious denominations and religions represented at a public high school, the administration has decided to bar students from wearing any religious symbols or garb that reflect a particular religious faith. Which of the following would be the best legal advice for school administrators?

   (A) This is a sound policy because of the decision in *Engel v. Vitale.*

   (B) This is an unsound policy based on the Constitution's free exercise clause unless the practice causes disruption.

   (C) This is an unsound policy because of the decision in *Wisconsin v. Yoder.*

   (D) This is an unsound policy based on the Constitution's reserved powers clause.

Question 5 refers to the cartoon below.

5. With which of the following statements would the cartoonist most likely agree?

(A) The government should be able to impose religion on its citizens.

(B) Elected officials cannot be religious.

(C) There is a constant struggle to define the separation of church and state.

(D) The government should provide more help to churches.

6. In what way do the decisions in *Engel v. Vitale* and *Wisconsin v. Yoder* differ?

(A) One suggests a public policy creates an establishment of religion, while the other suggests a public policy denies a free exercise of religion.

(B) One was decided on free speech grounds and one was decided on free press grounds.

(C) One preserved the governmental policy and the other struck down a governmental policy.

(D) One decision resulted from judicial activism and one resulted from judicial restraint.

7. What must a suing party prove to win a libel lawsuit?

(A) A factual mistake was made in reporting.

(B) The offending party acted maliciously and caused damages.

(C) An unfair criticism of public officials was made.

(D) His or her reputation was tarnished.

8. Which of the following is the most complete summary of the selective incorporation doctrine?

(A) The selective incorporation process and resulting law represent the primary intent of the framers of the Fourteenth Amendment.

(B) The Supreme Court has required states to apply certain rights in the Bill of Rights through the Fourteenth Amendment's due process clause.

(C) The Supreme Court has determined that citizens have the right to own firearms.

(D) A separation of church and state is required even in states where large majorities of the population are strongly religious.

Questions 9 and 10 refer to the graphic below.

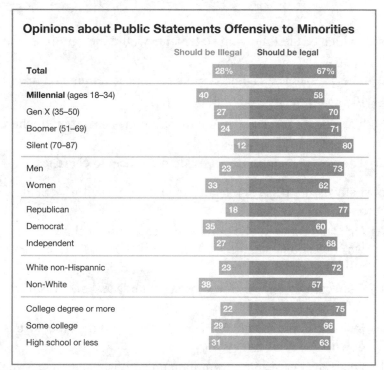

Opinions about Public Statements Offensive to Minorities

	Should be Illegal	Should be legal
Total	28%	67%
Millennial (ages 18–34)	40	58
Gen X (35–50)	27	70
Boomer (51–69)	24	71
Silent (70–87)	12	80
Men	23	73
Women	33	62
Republican	18	77
Democrat	35	60
Independent	27	68
White non-Hispannic	23	72
Non-White	38	57
College degree or more	22	75
Some college	29	66
High school or less	31	63

Source: *Pew Research Center, 2015*

9. Which of the following constitutional issues is represented in the graphic?

(A) Prior restraint

(B) Clear and present danger

(C) Free speech

(D) Free exercise

10. Which of the following consequences may occur based on the data in the graph?

(A) Restrictions on offensive school speech will likely be eased.

(B) Americans are likely open to limits on speech in the future.

(C) Republicans will be more open to limits on speech than Democrats.

(D) Men will be more likely than women to make offensive statements about minorities.

FREE-RESPONSE QUESTIONS

1. Read the following statement about the 2010 publication by WikiLeaks, under the direction of Julian Assange, of leaked information on State Department diplomacy efforts and intelligence. After reading it, respond to A, B, and C below.

> [S]everal members of Congress and the Obama Administration suggested that Assange should indeed face criminal prosecution for posting and disseminating to the media thousands of secret diplomatic cables containing candid—and often extremely embarrassing—assessments from American diplomats. Senate Minority Leader Mitch McConnell went so far as to label Assange a high-tech terrorist. "He has done enormous damage to our country and I think he needs to be prosecuted to the fullest extent of the law. And if that becomes a problem, we need to change the law," McConnell said on NBC's *Meet the Press* Sunday. Attorney General Eric Holder on Monday vowed to examine every statute possible to bring charges against Assange, including some that have never before been used to prosecute a publisher. And in the Senate, some members are already readying a bill that could lower the current legal threshold for when revealing state secrets is considered a crime.
>
> —Michael Lindenberger, *Time*, December 2010

(A) Describe the constitutional principle at issue in this event and how the Supreme Court helped shape it.

(B) In the context of this scenario, explain how the principle described in part A affects the behavior of the press.

(C) In the context of this scenario, explain how the interactions among the three branches relate to the tension between public order and individual rights.

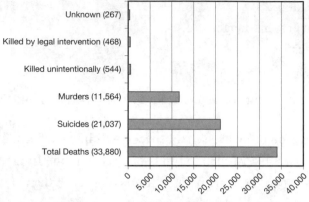

Average Number of U.S. Deaths Per Year from Gun Violence (2011–2015)

Sourse: *Brady Campaign*

2. Use the information in the graphic to answer the questions below.

(A) Based on the data in the graph, identify the most common type of death from guns.

(B) Describe a similarity or difference in the data presented in the chart, and draw a conclusion about how a gun-control interest group might use this information to promote its cause.

(C) Explain how those protecting Second Amendment liberties might respond to this information.

3. On January 24, 2002, the Juneau [Alaska] School District sanctioned an outdoor event across the street from the high school—watching the Olympic torch as it passed by on its journey to Salt Lake City, where the winter games were going to be held. Just as the torch and camera crews passed by, student Joseph Frederick unfurled a 14-foot banner that said "BONG HITS 4 Jesus." Principal Deborah Morse confiscated the banner and suspended Frederick for ten days. Although he appealed his suspension, the Juneau School District upheld the suspension, arguing that the sign promoted illegal drug use and the school had a policy against displaying messages that promoted drug use. Frederick sued. A district court decided in favor of the principal. On appeal the Ninth Circuit Court decided that Frederick's constitutional right to free speech was abridged because the school had not shown the message was disruptive. The case reached the Supreme Court, which ruled 5:4 in *Morse v. Frederick* in 2007 that the school was within its rights to remove the banner and suspend Frederick. In the majority opinion, Justice Roberts argued that students' right to free speech in schools does not extend to pro-drug messages, because an important objective of the school was to discourage drug use.

(A) Identify a similarity between *Morse v. Frederick* (2002) and *Tinker v. Des Moines Independent School District* (1969).

(B) Based on the similarity identified in part A, explain why the facts of the *Morse v. Frederick* case led to a different holding than the holding in *Tinker*.

(C) Describe how the holding in *Morse v. Frederick* might affect (or not affect) the effort of high school students to hold an assembly on school grounds supporting the decriminalization of marijuana.

4. Develop an argument that explains whether or not hate speech—speech that offends or insults groups based on race, religion, sexual orientation, or disabilities—should be illegal in the United States.

In your essay, you must:

- Articulate a defensible claim or thesis that responds to the prompt and establishes a line of reasoning
- Support your claim with at least TWO pieces of accurate and relevant information:
  - At least ONE piece of evidence must be from one of the following foundational documents:
    - The First Amendment of the Constitution
    - The Fourteenth Amendment of the Constitution
  - Use a second piece of evidence from another foundational document from the list above or from your study of civil liberties
- Use reasoning to explain why your evidence supports your claim/thesis
- Respond to an opposing or alternative perspective using refutation, concession, or rebuttal

WRITING: *USE CONCESSION*

As you develop an argument, recognize opposing views that have been well reasoned. Doing so is called *conceding a point*, or *making a concession*. When you make a concession, you actually strengthen your own argument, because you not only show your fair-mindedness, but you also are ready to provide reasons why, despite a well-reasoned opposing view, you still believe your own position is more sound. You may find that using the words *although, though*, and *while* are especially useful in conceding a point. For example, you may write, "Although supporters of a hate speech ban point to other countries where the policy does not appear to significantly diminish individual rights, the Court has made clear that in the United States only certain classes of speech can be suppressed, and hate speech does not fall in those categories." The use of *although* puts the opposing view in a position subordinate to your view.

8

Due Process and Rights of the Accused

Ways someday may be developed by which the government . . . will be enabled to expose to a jury the most intimate occurrences in the home."

—Justice Louis Brandeis's dissent in *Olmstead v. United States*, 1928

Essential Question: How have the provisions in the Bill of Rights and the Fourteenth Amendment been interpreted to balance due process and the rights of the accused with public safety and national security?

Whise the First and Second Amendments focus on guaranteeing individual liberties in relation to speech, religion, assembly, and gun ownership, other amendments in the Bill of Rights focus on protections of vulnerable populations—those suspected or accused of crimes, the poor and indigent, and the unborn—through the due process clause of the Fifth and Fourteenth Amendments. Constitutional provisions also help guide conflicts between individual liberties and national security concerns.

The United States has struggled to fully interpret and define phrases such as "unreasonable searches" and "cruel and unusual punishments." Citizens, leaders, and courts have interpreted these ideas differently over time. Justice Louis Brandeis's quote above—from his dissent in *Olmstead v. United States*, an early FBI wiretapping case—speaks to his concern for citizens' rights to privacy and protection from government intrusion into the home as basic wiretapping technology enabled the government to create a surveillance state. Brandeis, as spot on as his prediction was, could not have conceived the technological possibilities of invading citizen's dwellings, personal information, and everyday routines. In the past few years, the Supreme Court has ruled on when the government can or cannot look into your cell phone, when a drug-sniffing dog can step onto a citizen's porch, and whether police can use GPS devices to monitor suspects. **BIG IDEA:** Governmental laws and policies balancing order and liberty are based on the U.S. Constitution and have been interpreted differently over time.

Due Process

There are two types of due process: procedural and substantive. **Procedural due process** addresses the manner in which the law is carried out. **Substantive due process** addresses the essence of a law—whether the point of the law violates a basic right to life, liberty, or property. Both types of due process apply to the federal and state governments through the Fifth and Fourteenth Amendments. These measures prevent government from unfairly depriving citizens of their freedoms or possessions without being heard or receiving fair treatment under the authority of law. The concept ensures that government does not act arbitrarily on unstable whims and is consistently fair. The government *can* take away life, liberty, and property, but only in a highly specific, prescribed manner. Democratically elected legislatures must define criminal offenses before they are committed, and the government must follow prescribed procedures to ensure defendants' rights en route to a legitimate prosecution. As one Supreme Court justice wrote in an early decision, "The fundamental requisite of due process of law is the opportunity to be heard." As the Court interpreted and defined due process in various cases, it also selectively required states to follow additional rights from the Bill of Rights, thus expanding the incorporation doctrine discussed earlier in this chapter.

Procedural Due Process and the Fourth Amendment

Procedural due process refers to the way in which a law is carried out. For example, did the local court give the defendant a fair trial? Did the zoning board accurately appraise the value of the citizen's house before seizing it under its legal powers? Were the suspended students given a chance to explain

Source: © *Bettman/CORBIS*

The Warren Court, shown here in 1953, extended individual liberties and limited states' authority in the areas of search and seizure, the right to counsel, and self-incrimination.

their side of the story? Such questions arise in cases that have defined the concept of due process nationally. Under the leadership of Chief Justice Earl Warren (1953–1969), the Court extended liberties and limited state authority in areas of **search and seizure**, the right to legal counsel, and the right against self-incrimination during police interrogations.

The Fourth Amendment prevents law enforcement from conducting unreasonable searches and seizures. Before American independence, Great Britain cracked down on smugglers who tried to avoid taxes. To do so, it used writs of assistance—blanket search warrants—that empowered British soldiers to search any warehouse, vessel, or home at any time. This practice violated any sense of privacy or respect for personal property. The Fourth Amendment seeks to prevent the emergence of such an overpowering police state and requires courts to issue search warrants and arrest warrants only "upon probable cause" supported by a witness on record and under oath. The warrant, if issued, must list the place(s) to be searched and the persons or items to be seized. There are exceptions to the warrant requirement, however, especially when police see or quickly respond to crimes.

Exclusionary Rule In 1914, in *Weeks v. United States*, the Court established the **exclusionary rule**, which states that evidence the government finds or takes in violation of the Fourth Amendment can be excluded from trial. This decision protected the citizenry from aggressive federal police by reducing the chances of conviction. The justice system rejects evidence that resembles the "fruit of the poisonous tree," as Justice Felix Frankfurter called evidence tainted by acquisition through illegal means.

In 1961, the Court incorporated the exclusionary rule to state law enforcement. Seven police officers broke into Dollree Mapp's Cleveland house in search of a fugitive suspect and gambling paraphernalia. The police found no person or evidence related to either suspect or paraphernalia, but they did find some obscene books and pictures. Mapp was convicted on obscenity charges and sent to prison. When her case arrived in the Supreme Court, the justices ruled the police had violated her rights and should never have discovered the illegal contraband. *Mapp v. Ohio* (1961) became the selective incorporation case for the Fourth Amendment. Since that ruling state laws must abide by the Fourth Amendment.

Exceptions Law enforcement can still conduct searches without warrants, but they need to establish probable cause. Other exceptions to the warrant requirement include the consent of the person being searched and searches in airports and at U.S. borders.

Chief Justice Burger's Court refined the exclusionary rule to include the "inevitable discovery" and "good faith" exceptions. The inevitable discovery exception is when police find evidence in an unlawful search but would have eventually made the same discovery in a later, lawful search. The good faith exception addresses police searches under a court-issued warrant that is proven unconstitutional or erroneous later. In such instances, the police conducted the search under the good faith that they were following the law and thus have not abused or violated the Fourth Amendment. Evidence discovered under these exceptions will likely be admitted at trial.

Searches in Schools As the *Tinker* decision upheld, students' constitutional rights do not stop at the schoolhouse gate. However, students in school have fewer protections against searches that may violate the public interest than do average citizens in public or in their home because, within the public school context, the public interest argument outweighs concerns for individual liberties.

This issue was decided in ***New Jersey v. TLO*** (1985). After a student informed a school administrator that another student, TLO (the Court used only initials to protect this minor's identity), had been smoking in the restroom, an assistant principal searched TLO's purse. He found cigarettes, as well as marijuana, rolling papers, plastic bags, a list of students who owed her money, and a large amount of cash. The administrator turned this evidence over to the police, who prosecuted the student. She appealed her conviction on exclusionary rule grounds. The Court ruled that although the Fourth Amendment does protect students from searches by school officials, in this case the search was reasonable. School officials are not required to have the same level of probable cause as police. Students are entitled to a "legitimate expectation of privacy," the Court said, but this must be weighed against the interests of teachers, administrators, and the school's responsibility and mission. The *New Jersey v. TLO* ruling gave administrators a greater degree of leeway than police in conducting searches, requiring that they have reasonable cause or suspicion.

What if a student leaves a backpack behind on the bus? Can school officials search it, knowing or not knowing who the owner is? That was recently answered in Ohio after a bus driver discovered a backpack left behind in his bus. He handed it over to the school security officer, who reached not-too-deeply into the bag to find a paper with the rightful owner's name on it. He then recalled a rumor that this student was a gang member. Then, with the principal, he emptied the bag and found bullets. They then summoned the student and searched a second bag and found a gun. Were these discovered items found lawfully or in violation of the Fourth Amendment? On appeal the Ohio Supreme Court found both the initial and secondary searches were reasonable. The school's public duty to act on unattended bags, and the student's relinquishing his expectation of privacy by leaving the bag behind, enhanced the school's ability to search. If the bag were just unattended while the owner went to the bathroom, of course, a high expectation of privacy would have remained. The Ohio court gave the administrators wide latitude on searching that bag, even if the administrators had no belief of imminent threat. Once the bullets were discovered, searching the second bag was within the school officials' scope.

Source: *GettyImages*

What is the current national legal standard for a school official to conduct a search of a student's locker, backpack, or person?

Erring on the Side of Warrants In other recent Fourth Amendment rulings the U.S. Supreme Court has extended protections regarding cell phones, GPS locators, and narcotics-sniffing dogs at a person's front door. In one case after a constitutional arrest in California, the police, in clearing a commandeered vehicle, discovered the arrestee's cell phone. They searched it and found video evidence of his membership in a gang. The challenge in the High Court questioned whether, after the arrest, law enforcement can search a suspect's phone for any general information. The Court ruled unanimously that, though police are allowed to search immediate items in the name of protecting other officers or preserving evidence, searching such comprehensive items as a cell phone and all the suspect's digital data—that which can be preserved without a search and does not pose an immediate threat—is only reasonable after a court-ordered warrant.

In a separate case, the Court ruled that attaching a GPS tracker to monitor a suspected drug dealer's movements and daily interactions was unconstitutional. When the challenge arrived at the Supreme Court, the government argued that a motorist moving about on the public streets does not have an expectation of privacy and their monitoring his movements did not even amount to a search. The Court, however, asserted that the government invades a reasonable expectation of privacy when it violates a subjective expectation of privacy. All motorists realize they might be seen, but few assume all their movements are monitored for 24-hour cycles. So this was indeed a search—an unreasonable search that would have been reasonable had the police secured a warrant ahead of time.

As a final example, a case from Florida, in which an officer walked a drug-sniffing dog up onto a citizen's front porch, arrived before the Court. The dog communicated to the officer that marijuana was inside the home. The officer secured a warrant, came into the home, and found 25 pounds of marijuana. Appealing the conviction, the suspect and his lawyer claimed that the search had taken place on the porch long before a warrant was obtained. Law enforcement cannot search willy-nilly along citizens' front porches in hopes of having their dogs smell incriminating evidence that the police can then pursue. The Court was divided on this case, but for now, police cannot take drug dogs onto a resident's porch without obtaining a warrant.

The Fourth Amendment in the Digital Age Two major changes in the past two decades have shaped government's relationship with its citizens and have disrupted the balance between American freedoms and national security. At the same time the United States and other developed countries moved from traditional to electronic and cellular communication, the concern for terrorism spiked when al-Qaeda terrorists attacked the United States on September 11, 2001 and killed about 3,000 people. In a drastic response to find these terrorists and prevent future attacks, the U.S. government capitalized on modern forms of investigation and electronic surveillance. (See pages 27–28 on the USA PATRIOT Act.) Not long after the attack, President George W. Bush initiated a program by executive order that secretly allowed the executive branch to connect with third parties—Verizon and other telecommunications companies—to acquire and examine cell phone data. This third-party relationship excused the government from obtaining warrants as long as the third party was willing to give up the information. In essence, this relationship was similar to the police asking a cocaine user where he purchased his stash, or asking a suspect's friend what the suspect had told him. No warrant is required for these questions.

As governmental security organizations, especially the National Security Agency (NSA), increased their surveillance efforts, they instituted a program code-named PRISM that compels Internet service providers to give up information related to Internet activity and communications. Also, as revealed by NSA contractor and now U.S. fugitive Edward Snowden, a program that processed overwhelming amounts of data allowed the United States and its intelligence apparatus to collect telephone metadata. **Metadata** is all the cell phone communication information minus the actual conversation; that is, who is calling whom, when, and for how long. The constitutional acceptance for such collection parallels an earlier Court ruling that allowed police to monitor calls made, though not the content of the conversation, if disclosed by a third party. The government's motivation here is to determine who might be connected to terror suspects in the United States and abroad and to what degree.

The government contends that since its activities do not spy on the actual conversation, the actions are non-intrusive and in compliance with the Fourth Amendment. But as David Cole of *The Nation* points out, "We are in danger of seeing our privacy go the way of the eight-track player." Metadata "can reveal whether a person called a rape-crisis center, a suicide or drug-treatment hotline, a bookie, or a particular political organization." Should the government be privy to such information without probable cause or securing a particular warrant?

As David Gray sums up in his 2017 book *The Fourth Amendment in an Age of Surveillance*, investigative journalists report that "every major domestic telecommunications company provided telephonic metadata to the NSA under this program," and that the agency has gathered and stored metadata associated with a substantial proportion of calls made since 2006. In the wake of Snowden's blowing the whistle on the program while criminally violating his security agreement with the U.S. government (he is still in Russia under the protection of the Russian government), civil libertarians, privacy activists, Fourth Amendment attorneys, and ordinary citizens immediately sought to end the program. The 2015 USA FREEDOM Act has at least altered it. The new law does not completely eliminate the collection and storage of this metadata by cell-phone operators, but it does prevent the government easy access to it. The new law requires the Executive Branch to acquire a warrant to examine the metadata.

Procedural Due Process and the Rights of the Accused

Procedural due process also guarantees that the accused are treated fairly and according to the law. The Fifth, Sixth, and Eighth Amendments have been mostly incorporated so they apply to the states as well.

Self-Incrimination "You have the right to remain silent . . . ." goes the famed Miranda warning. This statement also reminds arrested suspects that "anything you say can and will be used against you." Since 1966, this statement has become familiar, mostly through TV crime dramas. The warning resulted from an overturned conviction of a rapist who confessed to his crime in *Miranda v. Arizona*.

For years, the Court handled a heavy appellate caseload addressing the problem of police-coerced confessions. Many losing defendants claimed during appeal that they had confessed only under duress, while police typically insisted the confessions were voluntary. The **Fifth Amendment** states, "nor shall [anyone] be compelled in any criminal case to be a witness against himself." Since a number of related cases about police procedures were reaching the Court, the justices took Miranda's case and created a new standard.

Ernesto Miranda, an indigent man who never completed the ninth grade, was arrested for the kidnapping and rape of a girl in Arizona. The police questioned Miranda for two hours until they finally emerged from the interrogation room with a signed confession. The confession was a crucial piece of evidence at Miranda's trial.

There had been some question as to when the Fifth Amendment right against self-incrimination begins. It clearly meant no defendant was compelled to take the witness stand at trial. In *Miranda*, the Court declared the right applies once a suspect is in custody by the state. It declared that custodial interrogation carries with it a badge of intimidation. If such pressures from the state are going to occur, the police must inform the suspect of his or her rights.

Civil libertarians hailed the *Miranda* ruling, while conservatives and law enforcement saw it as tying the hands of the police. Miranda received a new trial that did not use his confession. Additional proof, it turned out, was enough to convict this rapist. He went to prison while changing the national and state due process law.

There is, however, one exception to the *Miranda* rule, the **public safety exception**. A number of cases starting in the 1980s have allowed statements obtained before a suspect was warned of his or her rights to be admitted as evidence on the basis of protecting the public safety. In the first such case, *New York v. Quarles*, police chased Benjamin Quarles, who had been identified as assaulting a woman and carrying a gun, into a grocery store. When he was surrounded by police officers, he was searched and the police found an empty gun holster. The police asked Quarles where the gun was, and Quarles indicated it was in an empty milk carton. In the original case, the suspect's attorneys tried to have Quarles's statement on the location of the gun and the gun itself suppressed from evidence because he had not been warned of his rights against self-incrimination. When the case reached the Supreme Court, however, the Court reasoned that although the suspect was surrounded by police, he was not otherwise coerced to answer the question, and the question was necessary to protect the public from the danger of a loaded gun. Later cases upheld the public safety exception. If the questioning is for the purpose of neutralizing a dangerous situation, and a suspect responds voluntarily, the statement can be used as evidence even though it was made before the *Miranda* rights were read.

Right to Counsel "If you cannot afford an attorney, one will be appointed for you," the Miranda warning continues. This wasn't always the case. Though the Sixth Amendment's right to counsel has been in place since the ratification of the Bill of Rights, it was first merely the right to have a lawyer present at trial, and, as with the rest of the Bill of Rights, it originally applied only to defendants in federal court. In a series of cases starting in the 1930s, the Supreme Court developed its view of right to counsel in state criminal cases. The first established that when the death penalty was possible, the absence of counsel amounted to a denial of fundamental fairness. In 1942, the Court ruled in *Betts v. Brady* that refusal to appoint defense counsel in noncapital cases did not violate the amendment, but that the state did have to provide counsel when defendants had special circumstances, like incompetency or illiteracy. These precedents were shaped further with *Gideon v. Wainwright*.

MUST-KNOW SUPREME COURT DECISIONS:
GIDEON V. WAINWRIGHT (1963)

The Constitutional Question Before the Court: Does a state's prosecution of a criminal defendant without counsel constitute a violation of the Sixth Amendment's right to counsel?

Decision: Yes, for Gideon, 9:0

Facts: Clarence Earl Gideon, a drifter who had served jail time in four previous instances, was arrested for breaking and entering a Florida pool hall and stealing some packaged drinks and coins from a cigarette machine. He came to his trial expecting the local court to appoint him a lawyer because he had been provided one in other states in previous trials. The Supreme Court had already ruled that states must provide counsel in the case of an indigent defendant facing the death penalty, or in a case in which the defendant has special circumstances, such as illiteracy or psychological incapacity. At the time of Gideon's trial, 45 states appointed attorneys to all indigent defendants. Florida, however, did not.

Gideon was convicted and sent away to Florida's state prison in Raiford. From the prison, Gideon filed an *in forma pauperis* brief with the Supreme Court, a procedure "in the form of a pauper" available to those who believe they were wrongly convicted and do not have the means to appeal through the typical channels. The Court receives thousands of these each year, and every now and then it deems one worthy. The Court appointed an attorney for Gideon to argue this case. His attorney argued that the Fourteenth Amendment's due process clause required states to follow the Sixth Amendment provision. Since this decision in *Gideon v. Wainwright*, all states must pay for a public defender when a defendant cannot afford one

The Court voted 9:0 for Gideon and ruled that Florida had to provide defense attorneys to all indigent defendants regardless of the severity of the crime.

Reasoning: The Court reasoned that a basic principle of the American system of government is that every defendant should have an equal chance at a fair trial, and that without an attorney, a defendant does not have that equal chance. In the majority opinion, Justice Black quoted from a number of previous cases that supported the appointment of an attorney for indigent persons and argued that the 1942 case of *Betts v. Brady* went against the Court's own precedents. Further, the Court reasoned that there was no logical basis to the distinction between a capital offense, which would allow the appointment of an attorney for an indigent person, and a noncapital offense, which

Source: *Public Domain/State of Florida*
Clarence Earl Gideon

until the Gideon decision would not have allowed free legal representation to indigent persons.

The Court's Majority Opinion by Mr. Justice Hugo Black: In returning to these old precedents, we . . . restore constitutional principles established to achieve a fair system of justice. Not only these precedents, but also reason and reflection, require us to recognize that, in our adversary system of criminal justice, any person hauled into court, who is too poor to hire a lawyer, cannot be assured a fair trial unless counsel is provided for him. This seems to us to be an obvious truth. Governments, both state and federal, quite properly spend vast sums of money to establish machinery to try defendants accused of crime. Lawyers to prosecute are everywhere deemed essential to protect the public's interest in an orderly society. Similarly, there are few defendants charged with crime, few indeed, who fail to hire the best lawyers they can get to prepare and present their defenses. That government hires lawyers to prosecute and defendants who have the money hire lawyers to defend are the strongest indications of the widespread belief that lawyers in criminal courts are necessities, not luxuries. The right of one charged with crime to counsel may not be deemed fundamental and essential to fair trials in some countries, but it is in ours. From the very beginning, our state and national constitutions and laws have laid great emphasis on procedural and substantive safeguards designed to assure fair trials before impartial tribunals in which every defendant stands equal before the law. This noble ideal cannot be realized if the poor man charged with crime has to face his accusers without a lawyer to assist him.

Three other justices filed concurring opinions with different reasons for supporting the ruling. In his concurring opinion, Justice Tom C. Clark focused on due process.

Concurring Opinion by Mr. Justice Tom Clark: That the Sixth Amendment requires appointment of counsel in "all criminal prosecutions" is clear both from the language of the Amendment and from this Court's interpretation. It is equally clear . . . that the Fourteenth Amendment requires such appointment in all prosecutions for capital crimes. The Court's decision today, then, does no more than erase a distinction which has no basis in logic and an increasingly eroded basis in authority . . . I must conclude here . . . that the Constitution makes no distinction between capital and noncapital cases. The Fourteenth Amendment requires due process of law for the deprival of "liberty," just as for deprival of "life," and there cannot constitutionally be a difference in the quality of the process based merely upon a supposed difference in the sanction involved. How can the Fourteenth Amendment tolerate a procedure which it condemns in capital cases on the ground that deprival of liberty may be less onerous than deprival of life—a value judgment not universally accepted—or that only the latter deprival is irrevocable? I can find no acceptable rationalization for such a result, and I therefore concur in the judgment of the Court.

Death Penalty The Eighth Amendment prevents cruel and unusual punishments and excessive bail. Capital punishment, or the death penalty, has been in use for most of U.S. history. A handful of states, as well as most Western and developed countries, have banned the practice. States can use a variety of methods of execution; lethal injection is the most common. From 1930 through the 1960s, 87 percent of death penalty sentences were for murder, and 12 percent were for rape. The remaining 1 percent included treasonous charges and other offenses. In the United States, strong majorities have long favored the death penalty for premeditated murders.

The Court put the death penalty on hold nationally with the decision in *Furman v. Georgia* in 1972. In a complex 5:4 decision, only two justices called the death penalty itself a violation of the Constitution. The Court was mostly addressing the randomness of the death penalty. Some justices pointed out the disproportionate application of the death penalty to the socially disadvantaged, the poor, and racial minorities.

With the decision of *Gregg v. Georgia* in 1976, the Court began reinstating the death penalty as states restructured their sentencing guidelines. No state can make the death penalty mandatory by law. Rather, aggravating and mitigating circumstances must be taken into account in the penalty phase, a second phase of trial following a guilty verdict. Character witnesses may testify in the defendant's favor to affect the issuance of the death penalty. In recent years, in cases of murder, the Court has outlawed the death penalty for mentally handicapped defendants and those defendants who were under 18 years of age at the time of the murder.

Substantive Due Process

Substantive due process places substantive limits on what laws can actually be created. If the substance of the law—the very point of the law—violates some basic right, even one not listed in the Constitution, then a court can declare it unconstitutional. State policies that might violate substantive due process rights must meet some valid interest to promote the police powers of regulating health, welfare, or morals. The right to substantive due process protects people from policies for which no legitimate interest exists.

These policies became a thorny issue as labor unions and corporations debated the Constitution and while legislatures tried to promote the health and safety of citizens. The 1873 *Slaughterhouse Cases* forced a decision on the privileges or immunities clause of the recently ratified Fourteenth Amendment. The *Slaughterhouse Cases* were a group of cases relating to the state of Louisiana's consolidation of slaughterhouses into one government-run operation outside of New Orleans, requiring butchers in other locations to close up shop and thereby infringing on their right to pursue lawful employment. The majority opinion ruled that the Fourteenth Amendment's privileges or immunities clause protected only those rights related to national citizenship and did not apply to the states, even though the state law in this case limited the butchers' basic right to pursue lawful employment. In a dissenting opinion, Justice Joseph Bradley asserted that "the right of any citizen to follow whatever lawful employment he chooses to adopt . . . is one of his most valuable rights and one which the legislature of a State cannot invade," so a law that violates such a fundamental, inalienable right cannot be constitutional. The Court majority, however, interpreted the law on a procedural basis rather than addressing the substance of the right involved. In later years, when the Court addressed business regulation in the industrial period, it developed the substantive due process doctrine in relation to state and federal regulations in the workplace.

Right to Privacy In the 1960s a new class of substantive due process suits came to the Court. These suits sought to protect individual rights, especially those of privacy and lifestyle. In *Griswold v. Connecticut* (1965), the Court ruled an old anti–birth control state statute in violation of the Constitution. The overturned law had even barred married couples from receiving birth control literature. The Court for the first time emphasized an inherent **right to privacy** that, though not expressly mentioned in the Bill of Rights, could be found in the penumbras (shadows) of the First, Third, Fourth, and Ninth Amendments.

The Court further bolstered the right to privacy in the *Roe v. Wade* (1973) decision. Primarily a question of whether Texas or other states could prevent a woman from aborting her fetus, the decision rested on a substantive due process right against such a law. Whether a pregnant woman was to have or abort her baby was a private decision between her and her doctor and outside the reach of the government. These two cases together revived the substantive due process doctrine first laid down a century earlier.

MUST-KNOW SUPREME COURT DECISIONS: *ROE V. WADE* (1973)

The Constitutional Question Before the Court: Does Texas's anti-abortion statute violate the due process clause of the Fourteenth Amendment and a woman's constitutional right to an abortion?

Decision: Yes, for Roe, 7:2

Facts: In 1971, when Texas resident Norma McCorvey, a single circus worker, became pregnant for the third time at age 19, she sought an abortion. States had developed anti-abortion laws since the early 1900s, and this case reached the Court as the national debate about morality, responsibility, freedom, and women's rights had peaked. At the time, only four states allowed abortions as in this case, and Texas was not one of them (Texas did allow abortions in cases when the mother's life was at stake).

With Attorney Sarah Weddington of the American Civil Liberties Union (ACLU), McCorvey filed suit against local District Attorney Henry Wade. To protect her identity the Court dubbed the plaintiff "Jane Roe" and the case became known as *Roe v. Wade*.

Reasoning: The legal principle on which the case rests was new and somewhat revolutionary. Weddington and her team argued that Texas had violated Roe's "right to privacy" and that it was not the government's decision to determine a pregnant woman's medical decision. Though there is no expressed right to privacy in the Constitution, the Court had decided in *Griswold v. Connecticut* in 1965 that the right to privacy was present in the penumbras of the Bill of Rights. Meanwhile, the state stood by its legal authority to regulate health, morals, and welfare under the police powers doctrine, while much of the public argued the procedure violated a moral code. Roe relied largely on the Fourteenth Amendment's due process clause, arguing that the state violated her broadly understood liberty by denying the abortion. However, the majority opinion recognized that the "potentiality of human life" represented by the unborn child is also of interest to the state.

> **The Court's Majority Opinion by Mr. Justice Harry Blackmun, with which Justices Douglas, Brennan, Stewart, Marshall, Powell, and Chief Justice Burger joined:** State criminal abortion laws, like those involved here . . . violate the Due Process Clause of the Fourteenth Amendment, which protects against state action the right to privacy, including a woman's qualified right to terminate her pregnancy. Though the State cannot override that right, it has legitimate interests in protecting both the pregnant woman's health and the potentiality of human life, each of which interests grows and reaches a "compelling" point at various stages of the woman's approach to term . . . .
>
> (a) For the stage prior to approximately the end of the first trimester, the abortion decision and its effectuation must be left to the medical judgment of the pregnant woman's attending physician.
>
> (b) For the stage subsequent to approximately the end of the first trimester, the State, in promoting its interest in the health of the mother, may, if it chooses, regulate the abortion procedure in ways that are reasonably related to maternal health.

> (c) For the stage subsequent to viability the State, in promoting its interest in the potentiality of human life, may, if it chooses, regulate, and even proscribe, abortion except where necessary, in appropriate medical judgment, for the preservation of the life or health of the mother.

Justice Stewart wrote a concurring opinion that stressed the foundational role of substantive due process and the Fourteenth Amendment in arriving at the majority opinion, arguing that the liberty to which the Fourteenth Amendment refers must be understood broadly.

In dissenting opinions, Justice Rehnquist raised a technical question about the legal standing of the case, questioning whether Roe, who already gave birth to her baby (and had given the baby up for adoption), could file a complaint on behalf of others who might find themselves in her position. He wrote that plaintiffs "may not seek vindications for the rights of others." Justice White addressed substantial disagreement with the interpretation of the majority.

Dissenting Opinion written by Justice Byron White with which Justice William Rehnquist joins: At the heart of the controversy in these cases are those recurring pregnancies that pose no danger whatsoever to the life or health of the mother but are, nevertheless, unwanted for any one or more of a variety of reasons— convenience, family planning, economics, dislike of children, the embarrassment of illegitimacy, etc. . . . The Court, for the most part, sustains this position: during the period prior to the time the fetus becomes viable, the Constitution of the United States values the convenience, whim, or caprice of the putative mother more than the life or potential life of the fetus; the Constitution, therefore, guarantees the right to an abortion as against any state law or policy seeking to protect the fetus from an abortion not prompted by more compelling reasons of the mother. . . .With all due respect, I dissent. I find nothing in the language or history of the Constitution to support the Court's judgment.

Since Roe: The Court has addressed a series of cases on abortion since Roe and the abortion issue inevitably comes up at election time and during Supreme Court nominees' confirmation hearings. In Planned Parenthood v. Casey, the Court outlawed a Pennsylvania law designed to discourage women from getting an abortion or expose abortion patients via public records. It also did not uphold the "informed consent" portion of the law that required the aborting woman (mother), married or unmarried, to inform and secure consent from the father. However, the Casey decision did uphold such state requirements as a waiting period, providing information on abortion alternatives, and requiring parental (or judge's) consent for pregnant teens.

Political Science Disciplinary Practices: Explain the Court's Reasoning

The Roe case against the Texas law forbidding abortion came to the Supreme Court on appeal after a decision by the United States District Court for the Northern District of Texas. That decision struck down the Texas law on the basis of the Ninth Amendment, relying in part on the decision in Griswold. The Supreme Court, however, based its decision on the due process clause of the Fourteenth Amendment, reinforcing substantive due process.

Apply: Complete the following tasks.

1. Analyze the wording in the due process clause of the Fourteenth Amendment that supports the privacy right of a woman to decide whether or not to carry her unborn child to term. (See page 639 for the Fourteenth Amendment.) Explain your answer.

2. Explain how the Court distinguished different legal standards throughout a woman's pregnancy.

3. Explain the competing interests the Court had to consider and how it balanced those interests.

4. Explain Justice White's concern about the impact of the Court's decision.

5. Explain the issues related to federalism in this decision.

6. Explain the similarities and differences in the *Roe* and *Planned Parenthood* rulings.

Roe **and Later Abortion Rulings** Before 1973, abortion on demand was legal in only four states. The *Roe* decision made it unconstitutional for a state to ban abortion for a woman during the first trimester, the first three months of her pregnancy. An array of other state regulations developed in response. States passed statutes to prevent abortion at state-funded hospitals and clinics. They adjusted their laws to prevent late-term abortions. In 1976, Congress passed the Hyde Amendment (named for Illinois Congressman Henry Hyde) to prevent federal funding that might contribute to an abortion.

Civil Liberties and National Security

The Court has typically sided with governmental restrictions on liberties that protect national security during times of war or international threat. (See *Schenck v. United States* on page 240.) Two months after the Japanese bombed Pearl Harbor, the federal government created internment camps to relocate Japanese immigrants and Japanese Americans for the remainder of the war. Internee Fred Korematsu challenged this practice in the Supreme Court on the grounds that the government had exceeded its proper war powers and that the practice violated the equal protection clause of the Fourteenth Amendment because it targeted only Japanese Americans. Korematsu lost—the Court applied strict scrutiny and found the government's interest during wartime sufficiently compelling to limit individual liberties even of a selected group of people. Although the internees were compensated in the 1980s for their treatment, the ruling has never been officially overturned. Congress curtailed First Amendment liberties during the Cold War and during the Vietnam War. Since the September 11th attacks in 2001, the United States has wrestled with the issue of protecting the nation from terrorism while also maintaining constitutional rights.

September 11

In Chapter 1 you read about the USA PATRIOT Act in response to the terrorist attacks on September 11, 2001, and the civil liberties questions raised when government surveillance efforts intensified. (See pages 27–28.) Additional issues related to the "war on terror" also drew attention to civil liberties.

Executive Branch Initiatives U.S. armed forces quickly invaded Afghanistan, where al-Qaeda operated under the ruling Taliban regime. The terrorist network, however, also operated in cells throughout the Middle East and beyond. Some members were in the United States. President Bush issued an executive order authorizing trials of captured terrorists to take place via military tribunals rather than civilian courts.

A debate about handling terrorists created controversy. Should the United States seek out these terrorists as criminals who violated federal law under the established criminal justice system, or should the federal government treat this as a war against an outside adversary? In other words, does the Bill of Rights apply to these people? In both cases, the government must follow established laws. If done through law enforcement, the government arrests terrorists and tries them in U.S. district courts to put them away in prison if convicted. This approach requires the government to follow standard criminal justice due process rights. If done as part of a war effort, the federal government has fewer restrictions but still must recognize U.S. law and international treaties. Depending on the circumstance, the government currently acts in both ways and employs tactics that critics declare violate the Constitution and international law.

When President Bush declared a "war on terror," questions arose. For example, does the 1949 Geneva Convention, the international treaty that governs the basic rules of war, apply? Al-Qaeda is not a nation-state and is not a signatory (signer) of the Geneva Convention or any international treaty. In that case, does the United States have to honor Geneva provisions when acting against al-Qaeda? And does the Constitution apply to U.S. action beyond U.S. soil (especially when acting against enemies)? The Bush administration categorized those captured on the terror battlefield— meaning basically anywhere—as "enemy combatants" and treated their legal condition differently than either an arrested criminal or a conventional prisoner of war.

Guantanamo Bay and Interrogations The U.S. military set up a detention camp at its naval base in Guantanamo Bay, Cuba, to hold terror suspects. Placing the camp at this base provided stronger security, minimal press contact, and less prisoner access to legal aid than if it had been within U.S. borders. Administration officials believed that the location of the camp and interrogations outside the United States allowed a loosening of constitutional restrictions.

Soon after 9/11, administration officials signaled that unconventional tactics would be necessary to prevent another devastating attack. In trying to determine the legal limits of an intense interrogation, President Bush's lawyers issued the now infamous "torture memo." In August of 2002, President George

W. Bush's Office of Legal Counsel offered the legal definition of torture, calling it "severe physical pain or suffering." The memo claimed such pain "must be equivalent in intensity to the pain accompanying serious physical injury, such as organ failure, impairment of bodily function, or even death." One of the notorious techniques employed to gather information from reluctant detainees that fit this description was waterboarding—an ancient method that simulates drowning.

As these policies developed and became public, some people became outraged. Civil libertarians in the United States questioned the disregard for both *habeas corpus* rights and the Eighth Amendment's prohibition of cruel and unusual punishment. The international community, too, was aghast.

In the Courts

These legal complications and competing views on how to apply international law and the Bill of Rights in a war against an enemy with no flag have caused detainees and their advocates to challenge the government in court. A lower court has declared part of the USA PATRIOT Act unconstitutional. The Supreme Court has addressed *habeas corpus* rights.

The right of *habeas corpus* guarantees that the government cannot arbitrarily imprison or detain someone without formal charges. Could detainees at Guantanamo Bay question their detention? The president said no, but the Court said yes. *Rasul v. Bush* (2004) stated that because the United States exercises complete authority over the base in Cuba, it must follow the Constitution. Fred Korematsu, who lost his own *habeas corpus* claim in 1944, submitted an *amicus curiae* brief in support of Rasul. "It is during our most challenging and uncertain moments that our nation's commitment to due process is most severely tested," Justice Sandra Day O'Connor wrote, "and it is in those times that we must preserve our commitment at home to the principles for which we fight abroad."

In *Hamdi v. Rumsfeld* (2004), the Court overruled the executive branch's unchecked discretion in determining the status of detainees. After this, the United States could not detain a U.S. citizen without a minimal hearing to determine the suspect's charge. In a separate case, *Hamdan v. Rumsfeld* (2006), the Court found that Bush's declaration that these detainees should be tried in military tribunals violated the United States Code of Military Justice. The commissions themselves, wrote Associate Justice John Paul Stevens, violated part of the Geneva Convention that governed noninternational armed conflicts before a "regularly constituted court ... affording judicial guarantees ... by civilized peoples." As summed up in *Hamdi*, "We have long since made clear that a state of war is not a blank check for the president when it comes to the rights of the nation's citizens.

Source: *Rena Schild / Shutterstock*

Citizens rally to protest mass surveillance policies.

BY THE NUMBERS SUPREME COURT VOTES IN DUE PROCESS DECISIONS		
Mapp v. Ohio (1961)	States must follow the exclusionary rule.	6 : 3
Gideon v. Wainwright (1963)	States must supply defense attorneys to indigent defendants.	9 : 0
Miranda v. Arizona (1966)	States must inform the accused of their rights.	5 : 4
Griswold v. Connecticut (1965)	Privacy rights prevent state anti–birth control law.	7 : 2
Roe v. Wade (1973)	States cannot outlaw abortion in first trimester and must adhere to the trimester standard established by the Court.	7 : 2
Hamdi v. Rumsfeld (2004)	The U.S. cannot hold terror suspects without following *habeas corpus* rights.	6 : 3
Hamdan v. Rumsfeld (2006)	The U.S. must follow Geneva Convention and cannot rely strictly on military commissions in prosecuting terror suspects.	5 : 3

What do the numbers show? In which decisions did the Court have stronger majorities or unanimous opinions? Which cases brought narrow decisions? What do the narrow decisions say about the view of civil liberties? Which cases altered or shaped law enforcement? Which ones dealt with privacy? Which amendments were at issue in each case?

REFLECT ON THE ESSENTIAL QUESTION

Essential Question: *How have the provisions in the Bill of Rights and the Fourteenth Amendment been interpreted to protect civil liberties, and how has the government responded to questions when there are conflicts between security and liberty?*

On separate paper, complete a chart like the one below to gather details to answer that question.

Cases that protect civil liberties	Cases that protect national security and social order

KEY TERMS AND NAMES

exclusionary rule/278

Fifth Amendment/282

Gideon v. Wainwright (1963)/283

Griswold v. Connecticut (1965)/287

Mapp v. Ohio (1961)/278

metadata/281

Miranda v. Arizona (1966)/282

New Jersey v. TLO (1985)/279

procedural due process/277

public safety exception/283

right to privacy/287

Roe v. Wade (1973)/287

search and seizure/278

substantive due process/277

MULTIPLE-CHOICE QUESTIONS

1. The Bill of Rights guarantees which of the following rights to a person arrested and charged with a crime?

   (A) The right to participate in elections

   (B) The right to negotiate a plea bargain

   (C) The right to an appeal if convicted

   (D) The right to legal representation

2. Which of the following principles is meant to discourage government from conducting unlawful searches and to protect citizens when unlawful searches occur?

(A) Clear and present danger

(B) Police powers

(C) Exclusionary rule

(D) Prior restraint

3. Which of the following statements best describes how the balance of liberties and safety has been interpreted over time?

(A) The balance has been interpreted consistently over time.

(B) The balance leans more toward liberties than safety.

(C) Different courts in different times have found different balances.

(D) Stare decisis requires similar findings in similar cases.

4. Which statement best describes the Supreme Court's interpretation of the Fourteenth Amendment?

(A) The Fourteenth Amendment has restricted the application of judicial review.

(B) The Fourteenth Amendment prevents states from taxing agencies of the federal government.

(C) The Fourteenth Amendment's due process clause makes most rights contained in the Bill of Rights applicable to the states.

(D) The Fourteenth Amendment's equal protection clause defines certain classes of people who are not eligible for equal protection.

5. What is the key difference between the due process clause in the Fifth Amendment and the due process clause in the Fourteenth Amendment?

(A) The Fifth Amendment prevents government from depriving persons of liberty, while the Fourteenth Amendment prevents a deprivation of life.

(B) The Fifth Amendment sets limits on the private sector, while the Fourteenth Amendment restrains governmental institutions.

(C) The Fifth Amendment protects citizens against the federal government, while the Fourteenth protects citizens against the states.

(D) The Fifth Amendment protects citizens against criminal charges, while the Fourteenth Amendment protects citizens against civil lawsuits.

6. Which statement accurately describes the Supreme Court's contemporary interpretation of the death penalty?

   (A) States may not use the death penalty.

   (B) The interpretation focuses on the method of execution.

   (C) The Court has found the practice unconstitutional because it is cruel and unusual.

   (D) The Court has interpreted the execution of minors and the mentally handicapped as unconstitutional.

7. Under what circumstance can police conduct searches?

   (A) Only if a court issues a warrant

   (B) If they have slight suspicion of wrongdoing

   (C) As long as they have probable cause of criminal activity

   (D) If they have been tipped off by a reliable source

8. Which statement is accurate regarding the law and government surveillance of persons in the United States?

   (A) Police and FBI can listen to private phone conversations when they see fit.

   (B) U.S. law enforcement first began to watch or surveil U.S. persons after the September 11th attacks.

   (C) The Constitution and Bill of Rights protect only U.S. citizens from arbitrary surveillance.

   (D) Policies have changed over time as people debate the balance between security needs and individual liberties.

9. Which of the following is an accurate comparison of substantive and procedural due process?

	SUBSTANTIVE DUE PROCESS	PROCEDURAL DUE PROCESS
(A)	Deals with "the how" of the law, or steps in carrying out the law	Must be followed by the states, not the federal government
(B)	Followed when the ideas or points of the law are fundamentally fair and just	Focuses on the manner in which government acts towards its citizens
(C)	Applicable because of the Fifth Amendment, not the Fourteenth Amendment	Was violated in the *Roe v. Wade* case according to the Supreme Court
(D)	Must be followed by the federal government, not state governments	Is followed when Congress follows the legislative process in lawmaking

10. The Miranda rule stems from rights protected by which of the following amendments?

(A) Fourth and Fifth amendments

(B) Fifth and Sixth amendments

(C) Seventh and Eighth amendments

(D) Ninth and Tenth amendments

FREE-RESPONSE QUESTIONS

1. Many homes today are equipped with "smart" devices, sometimes called "always on" devices. One such type of device will take orders from an owner's voice after a "wake" word. The wake word sets in motion a process of responding to the owner's order and starting a recording, which is then stored on a cloud computer. Suppose a crime took place in the home of a person with such a smart device. If police have a warrant to search that home, do they also have a right to seize the device and obtain information stored in the cloud that might help in solving the case? Tech companies and the Electronic Freedom Frontier say no. They argue that people have a reasonable expectation of privacy in their homes, and tech companies have refused to comply with the order to provide users' personal information even under warrant. To support its position, Amazon has quoted an opinion in a 2010 court case that was decided in its favor when the tech giant refused such compliance: "[t]he fear of government tracking and censoring one's reading, listening and viewing choices chills the exercise of First Amendment rights."

After reading the scenario, respond to A, B, and C below.

(A) Describe the constitutional principle at issue in this scenario.

(B) In the context of the scenario, explain how the principle described in part A affects law enforcement.

(C) In the context of the scenario, explain how the principle in part A demonstrates a tension between individual liberties and public safety.

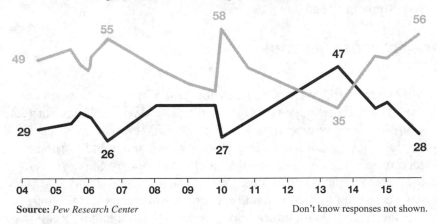

Public's Shifting Concerns on Security and Civil Liberties (2004–2015)

——— Percent of people believing the government has not gone far enough to protect country

——— Percent of people believing the government has gone too far restricting civil liberties

58

55

56

49

47

29

35

26

27

28

04   05   06   07   08   09   10   11   12   13   14   15

Source: *Pew Research Center*   Don't know responses not shown.

2. Use the information graphic to answer the questions below.

(A) Describe the tension expressed in the graph.

(B) Describe the relationship between the issues in tension, and draw a conclusion about the reason for the relationship.

(C) Explain how the information graphic demonstrates a principle in the Fourth Amendment.

3. In *Planned Parenthood v. Casey* (1992), the Supreme Court ruled on a case that challenged a Pennsylvania law that placed certain requirements on women seeking an abortion. These were: (1) a doctor had to provide information on the procedure to the woman at least 24 hours before the procedure; (2) in most cases, a married woman had to notify her husband of the planned procedure; (3) minors had to obtain informed consent from a parent or guardian or let the court assume a parental role; (4) if a doctor determined the pregnancy was a medical emergency endangering the mother, an abortion could be performed; (5) facilities providing abortions were held to reporting and record-keeping standards. A divided Court upheld the essential ruling in *Roe v. Wade* but said that the state could not interfere with a woman's right to an abortion until the fetus reached viability—the condition that would allow it to survive outside the womb—which could happen as early as 22 weeks. The ruling also set an "undue burden" test for state abortion laws—those that presented an undue burden on the mother seeking an abortion were unconstitutional. The only one of the five provisions explained above that failed that test was the notification of the husband.

(A) Identify the assumed protection that is common to both *Planned Parenthood v. Casey* (1992) and *Roe v. Wade* (1973).

(B) Based on the assumed protection identified in part A, explain why the facts of the case in *Planned Parenthood v. Casey* led to a modification of the holding in *Roe v. Wade*.

(C) Explain how the holdings in *Planned Parenthood v. Casey* and *Roe v. Wade* demonstrate change over time in the law.

4. Develop an argument that explains whether or not the death penalty should be determined as unconstitutional in all circumstances.

In your essay, you must:

- Articulate a defensible claim or thesis that responds to the prompt and establishes a line of reasoning
- Support your claim with at least TWO pieces of accurate and relevant information:
  - At least ONE piece of evidence must be from one of the following foundational documents:
    - The Eighth Amendment of the Constitution
    - The Tenth Amendment of the Constitution
    - The Fourteenth Amendment of the Constitution
  - Use a second piece of evidence from another foundational document from the list above or from your study of the rights of the accused
- Use reasoning to explain why your evidence supports your claim/ thesis
- Respond to an opposing or alternative perspective using refutation, concession, or rebuttal

WRITING: *BUDGET YOUR TIME*

All four of the free-response questions will be weighted equally when the exams are scored—each accounts for 12.5 percent of your score. However, the College Board recommends that you spend 20 minutes on each of the first three free-response questions and leave 40 minutes to devote to the argumentative essay.

9

Civil Rights

"Our Constitution is colorblind, and neither knows nor tolerates classes among citizens. In respect of civil rights, all citizens are equal before the law."

—Justice John Marshall Harlan's dissent in
Plessy v. Ferguson, 1896

Essential Question: How have constitutional provisions, the Supreme Court, and citizen-state interactions led to laws and policies that promote equality?

United States political culture places a high priority on freedom and equality and on **civil rights,** protections from discrimination based on such characteristics as race, national origin, religion, and sex. These principles are evident in the Declaration of Independence, the Constitution, the Bill of Rights, and later constitutional amendments. They are guaranteed to all citizens under the due process and equal protection clauses in the Constitution and according to acts of Congress. Civil rights organizations representing African Americans and women have pushed for governments to deliver on the promises these documents laid out. In more recent years, other groups—Latinos, people with disabilities, and gays, lesbians, and transgender individuals—have petitioned the government for fundamental fairness and equality. All three branches have responded in varying degrees to address civil rights issues. Even so, racism, sexism, and other forms of bigotry have not disappeared. Today, a complex body of law shaped by constitutional provisions, Supreme Court decisions, federal statutes, executive directives, and citizen-state interactions defines civil rights in America.

Constitutional Provisions Supporting Equality

In the United States, federal and state governments generally ignored civil rights policy before the Civil War. The framers of the Constitution left the legal question of slavery up to the states, allowing the South to strengthen its plantation system and relegate slaves and free blacks to subservience. The North had a sparse black population and little regard for fairness to African Americans. Abolitionists, religious leaders, and progressives sought to outlaw slavery and advocated for African Americans in the mid-1800s.

A major setback for the antislavery movement came with the Supreme Court's Dred Scott decision, also known as *Dred Scott v. Sandford*. (See page 201.) Scott, a slave living in free territory, sued for his freedom, but the Court did not recognize Scott as a citizen and ruled that he had no legal grounds to bring a case. Ruling on the Fifth Amendment, the Court declared that property—including slaves—cannot be taken away without just compensation through due process.

This blow ignited support for abolition on a national level and helped to bring about the Civil War and the Reconstruction Era following the South's defeat. Throughout the 19th and 20th centuries, the Supreme Court, because of its changing makeup, sometimes protected and sometimes restricted the civil rights of African Americans and other minority groups as it interpreted constitutional provisions regarding equality.

The Fourteenth Amendment and Other Reconstruction Amendments

During the Civil War, a Republican-dominated Congress outlawed slavery in the capital city, and President Abraham Lincoln issued the Emancipation Proclamation. After the Confederacy surrendered, Radical Republicans took the lead. The House and Senate passed legislation, including proposals for three constitutional amendments, to reconstruct the Union and to protect the freed slaves. The amendments were ratified by the states, sometimes as a condition of Southern states resuming their delegations in Congress.

The **Thirteenth Amendment** outlawed slavery across the United States, trumping the Tenth Amendment's reserved power that before had enabled states to have slavery. The **Fifteenth Amendment** prohibited states from denying the vote to anyone "on account of race, color, or previous condition of servitude." It was the **Fourteenth Amendment,** however, that became the foundation for policy and social movements for equality.

The Fourteenth Amendment had a host of provisions to protect freed slaves. It promised U.S. citizenship to anyone born or naturalized in the United States. The Fourteenth Amendment required states to guarantee privileges and immunities to its own citizens as well as those from other states. The due process clause (see page 236) ensured all citizens would be afforded due process in court as criminal defendants or in other areas of law. The amendment's **equal protection clause** prohibited state governments from denying persons within their jurisdiction equal protection of the laws.

Section 1 of the Fourteenth Amendment is the section used most often in legal cases. It reads: "All persons born or naturalized in the United States, and subject to the jurisdiction thereof, are citizens of the United States and of the state wherein they reside. No state shall make or enforce any law which shall abridge the privileges or immunities of citizens of the United States; nor shall any state deprive any person of life, liberty, or property, without due process of law; nor deny to any person within its jurisdiction the equal protection of the laws."

As with the other Reconstruction amendments, the Fourteenth Amendment was obviously directed at protecting the freed slaves, making them citizens and ensuring equal treatment from the states. But since neither slaves nor African Americans are specifically mentioned in the amendment, several other groups—women; ethnic minorities; people in the lesbian, gay, bisexual, transgender (LGBT) community—have benefitted from it in their search for equality. Criminal defendants have made claims against states to establish new legal standards. As with native-born U.S. citizens, immigrants, documented or undocumented, who bear children in the United States will see their offspring become U.S. citizens because of the Fourteenth Amendment.

RECONSTRUCTION AMENDMENTS

- The **Thirteenth Amendment** (1865) abolished slavery.
- The **Fourteenth Amendment** (1868) guaranteed citizenship, privileges and immunities, due process, and equal protection.
- The **Fifteenth Amendment** (1870) prevented state denial of suffrage on account of race.

Another expansion of civil rights looked imminent after the **Civil Rights Act of 1875** made it illegal for privately owned places of public accommodation—trains, hotels, and taverns—to make distinctions between black and white patrons. The law also outlawed discrimination in jury selection, public schools, churches, cemeteries, and transportation. These measures created a relative equality for the emancipated slave. The franchise (the right to vote) greatly expanded black men's rights. African Americans elected men from their own ranks to represent them in state capitals and in Washington. Virginia had at least some black representation in the state assembly every year from 1869 to 1891. Between 1876 and 1894, North Carolina elected 52 black representatives to its state legislature. Ten black men were sent to Congress during Reconstruction; ten others were elected afterward.

Restrictions from the Supreme Court The black presence in elected bodies and federal protections, however, soon disappeared after federal troops departed from the South and after a conservative Supreme Court took away Congress's authority over civil rights. When Union troops departed, so did the freed slaves' protection. Additionally, the Supreme Court reviewed the civil rights law. In a series of decisions collectively dubbed the *Civil Rights Cases* **(1883)**, the Court ruled that the equal protection clause was meant to protect African Americans against unfair state action and not to guide a shopkeeper's service policy.

Disenfranchisement, economic reprisals, and discrimination against blacks followed. States created a body of law that segregated the races in the public sphere. These **Jim Crow laws**—named after a disrespected character in a minstrel show in which whites performed in "blackface"—separated blacks and whites on trains, in theaters, in public restrooms, and in public schools.

Circumventing the Fifteenth Amendment As former Confederates returned to power, the Southern states circumvented the Fifteenth Amendment. Disenfranchising African Americans, Southern whites believed, would return them to second-class status. The South began requiring property or literacy qualifications to vote. Several states elevated the **literacy test**—a test of reading skills required before one could vote—into their state constitutions. The **poll taxes**—a simple fee required of voters—became one of the most effective ways to discourage the potential black voter. And the **grandfather clause**, which allowed states to recognize a registering voter as it would have recognized his grandfather, prevented thousands of blacks from voting while it allowed illiterate and poor whites to be exempt from the literacy test and poll tax. The **white primary**, too—a primary in which only white men could vote—became a popular method for states to keep African Americans out of the political process. Though primary elections empowered greater numbers of rank and file voters, primaries in the South became another method used to disenfranchise blacks early in the electoral process.

These state-level loopholes did not violate the absolute letter of the Constitution because they never prevented blacks from voting "on account of race, color, or previous condition of servitude," as the Fifteenth Amendment prohibits.

"Separate but Equal" Policymakers continued to draw lines between the races. They separated white and black citizens on public carriers, in public restrooms, in theaters, and in public schools. This institutionalized separation was tested in *Plessy v. Ferguson* **(1896)**. Challenging Louisiana's separate coach law, Homer Adolph Plessy, a man with one-eighth African blood and thus subject to the statute, sat in the white section of a train. He was arrested and convicted and then appealed his conviction to the Supreme Court. His lawyers argued that separation of the races violated the Fourteenth Amendment's equal protection clause. The Supreme Court saw it differently, however, and sided with the state's right to segregate the races in public places, claiming **"separate but equal"** facilities satisfied the amendment. One lone dissenter, Justice John Marshall Harlan, decried the decision (as he had in the *Civil Rights Cases*) as a basic violation to the freed African Americans. Unfortunately, Harlan's dissent was only a minority opinion. Segregation and Jim Crow continued for two more generations.

The Fourteenth Amendment and the Social Movement for Equality

The Fourteenth Amendment's equal protection clause also spurred citizens to take action. One organization, the NAACP, stood apart from the others in promoting equal rights for African Americans.

State-sponsored discrimination and a violent race riot in Springfield, Illinois, led civil rights leaders to create the **National Association for the Advancement of Colored People (NAACP)** in 1909. On Abraham Lincoln's birthday, a handful of academics, philanthropists, and journalists sent out a call for a national conference. Harvard graduate and Atlanta University professor Dr. W.E.B. DuBois was among those elected as the association's first leaders. By 1919, the organization had more than 90,000 members.

Citizen Action

Before World War I, the citizen group and its leaders pressed President Woodrow Wilson to overturn segregation in federal agencies and departments. The NAACP had also hired two men as full-time lobbyists in Washington, one for the House and one for the Senate. The association joined in filing a case to challenge the grandfather clause. The Supreme Court ruled the practice a violation of the Fifteenth Amendment. Two years later, the Court again sided with the NAACP when it ruled government-imposed residential segregation a constitutional violation.

Legal Defense Fund The NAACP regularly argued cases in the Supreme Court. It added a legal team led by Charles Hamilton Houston, a Howard University law professor, and his assistant, Baltimore native Thurgood Marshall. The association's Legal Defense Fund's lawyers argued for the Scottsboro Nine—nine black youths falsely accused of rape—to have the right to counsel in a death penalty case. They defended helpless and mostly innocent black defendants across the South in front of racist judges and juries. Finally, they successfully convinced the Supreme Court to outlaw the **white primary**—a primary in which only white men could vote. The white primary, in suppressing African American voters, had essentially extinguished the Republican Party—the party of Lincoln—in the South, allowing Southern Democrats to stay in power and pass discriminatory laws.

Desegregating Schools The NAACP next developed a legal strategy to chip away at state school segregation. The federal judiciary was the ideal place to start since federal judges served life terms and could issue an unpopular decision in the South without fear of losing their jobs. Thurgood Marshall and other attorneys would prove that states and local school boards did not follow the Fourteenth Amendment's equal protection clause while creating segregated schools. Marshall argued that the *Plessy v. Ferguson* principle of "separate but equal" simply did not result in equal education.

The NAACP filed suits to integrate college and graduate schools first and then K-12 schools. Early success came with the case of *Missouri ex. Rel. Gaines v. Canada* (1938), with which the NAACP won Lloyd Gaines's entrance into the University of Missouri's Law School. The state had offered to pay his out-of-state tuition at a neighboring law school, but the Fourteenth Amendment specifically requires states to treat the races equally, and failing to provide the "separate but equal" law school, the Court claimed, violated the Constitution. The state created an all-black law school within the University of Missouri campus.

In 1950, the NAACP won decisions against graduate and law schools in Oklahoma and Texas. Beyond the obvious differences in the facilities and tangible materials, the Court recognized stark differences in discourse and the professional connections essential to success in the field after graduation. The Supreme Court ruled that separate schools were not equal and that states had to admit blacks seeking advanced degrees.

As the Supreme Court delivered these decisions, the NAACP had already filed several suits in U.S. district courts to overturn *Plessy v. Ferguson*, which had provided the justification for K-12 segregation. With assistance from sociologists Kenneth and Mamie Clark, two academics from New York, the NAACP improved its strategy. In addition to arguing that segregation was morally wrong, they argued that separate schools were psychologically damaging to black children. In experiments run by the Clarks, when black children were shown two dolls identical except for their skin color and asked to choose the "nice doll," they chose the white doll. When asked to choose the doll that "looks bad," they chose the dark-skinned doll. With these results, the Clarks argued that the segregation system caused feelings of inferiority in the black child. Armed with this scientific data, attorneys sought strong, reliable plaintiffs who could withstand the racist intimidation and reprisals that followed the filing of a lawsuit.

MUST-KNOW SUPREME COURT DECISIONS: *BROWN V. BOARD OF EDUCATION OF TOPEKA, KANSAS* **(1954)**

The Constitutional Question Before the Court: Do state school segregation laws violate the equal protection clause of the Fourteenth Amendment?

The Decision: Yes, 9:0 for Brown

Before *Brown*: In 1896, the case of *Plessy v. Ferguson* reached the Supreme Court. In this effort, civil rights activists and progressive attorneys argued that Louisiana's state law segregating train passengers by race violated the Fourteenth Amendment's equal protection clause. In a 7:1 decision, the Court ruled that as long as states provided separate but equal facilities, they were in compliance with the Constitution.

Facts: Topeka, Kansas, student Linda Brown's parents and several other African American parents similarly situated filed suit against the local school board in hopes of overturning the state's segregation law. In fact, the NAACP had filed similar cases in three other states and against the segregated schools of the District of Columbia. The Supreme Court took all these cases at once, and they were together called *Brown v. Board of Education*.

Reasoning: The petitioners, led by Thurgood Marshall, put forth arguments found in social science research that the racially segregated system did damage to the black child's psyche and instilled feelings of inferiority. The inevitably unequal schools—unequal financially, unequal in convenience of location—created significant differences between them. Marshall and the NAACP argued that even in the rare cases where black and white facilities and education were the same tangibly, the separation itself was inherently unequal. In fact, part of this strategy resulted in Southern governments and school boards increasing spending, late in the game, so black and white educational systems would appear equal during the coming court battles. Black leaders felt true integration was the only way to ever truly reach equality.

Chief Justice Earl Warren and all eight associate justices agreed and ruled in favor of striking down segregation and overturning *Plessy* to satisfy the equal protection clause of the Fourteenth Amendment. *Brown's* unanimous ruling came in part as a result of former politician Earl Warren, now chief justice, pacing the halls and shaping his majority opinion as he tried to bring the questionable or reluctant justices over to the majority.

Majority (Unanimous) Opinion by Mr. Justice Warren: Here, unlike *Sweatt v. Painter* [a case in which the Court ordered the University of Texas Law School to admit a black applicant because the planned "law school for Negroes" would have been grossly inferior], there are findings below that the Negro and white schools involved have been equalized, or are being equalized, with respect to buildings, curricula, qualifications and salaries of teachers, and other "tangible" factors. Our decision, therefore, cannot turn on merely a comparison of these tangible factors in the Negro and white schools involved in each of the cases. We must look instead to the effect of segregation itself on public education.

In approaching this problem, we cannot turn the clock back to 1868, when the Amendment was adopted, or even to 1896, when *Plessy v. Ferguson* was written. We must consider public education in the light of its full development and its present place in American life throughout the Nation. Only in this way can it be determined if segregation in public schools deprives these plaintiffs of the equal protection of the laws . . .

We conclude that, in the field of public education, the doctrine of "separate but equal" has no place. Separate educational facilities are inherently unequal. Therefore, we hold that the plaintiffs and others similarly situated for whom the actions have been brought are, by reason of the segregation complained of, deprived of the equal protection of the laws guaranteed by the Fourteenth Amendment. This disposition makes unnecessary any discussion whether such segregation also violates the Due Process Clause of the Fourteenth Amendment.

Since *Brown*: The *Brown* decision of May 17, 1954, decided the principle of segregation but did not determine a timeline for when this drastic societal change would happen or how it would happen. So the Court invited litigants to return and present arguments. In *Brown II*, the Court determined that segregated school systems should desegregate "with all deliberate speed," and that the lower federal courts would serve as venues to determine if that standard was met. That is, black parents could take local districts to U.S. district courts to press for integration.

It took a decade before any substantial integration occurred in the Deep South and a generation before black-to-white enrollments were proportional to the populations of their respective school districts. A generation of litigation followed *Brown* that chipped away at unreasonable desegregation plans, brought racial enrollment targets, and tried to counter **white flight**—the movement of white people from racially mixed neighborhoods to neighborhoods with little, if any, diversity. Nearly every Supreme Court ruling on this issue throughout the era was in favor of integration, and most were unanimous opinions.

Political Science Disciplinary Practices: Analyze and Interpret Supreme Court Decisions

As you read, Chief Justice Warren wanted to make certain this ruling was unanimous. He also wanted to make sure that the wording in the ruling was in plain language so that everyone reading it could understand the rationale. The opinion is also relatively brief. You may want to read the entire opinion, which you can do online at Oyez or other sites.

Apply: Complete the following activities.

1. Explain why the Court had to base its decision on factors other than "the tangible factors in the Negro and white schools."

2. Describe the type of evidence on which the NAACP relied to make its case.

3. Identify the clause in the Fourteenth Amendment on which this case was founded.

4. Explain the reasoning of the unanimous opinion.

5. Describe the differences between the opinion in *Brown* and the opinion in *Plessy.*

6. Explain how this case can be considered a turning point in civil rights.

Source: *Granger, NYC*

The great-grandson of a slave, Thurgood Marshall was a leader in shaping civil rights law well before he became the first African American justice on the Supreme Court in 1967.

The Southern response to the decision in *Brown* ranged from civil dissent to violent massive resistance. Southerners began a campaign to impeach members of the Supreme Court and quickly promised to defy the order. A total of 101 Southern members of Congress, attempting to sidestep the Supreme Court ruling, signed the Southern Manifesto, a document denouncing the ruling and promising to use all legal means to maintain "separate but equal" as the status quo. Racist organizations such as the Ku Klux Klan revived, and the White Citizens Council—sometimes referred to as "the white-collar Klan"—was born. Most school administrators across the segregated South stalled while a few brave African Americans enrolled in token, compliant school districts. Although these Congressional and citizen pressures succeeded in delaying integration, they did not succeed in defying the law of the land.

Over the next decade, against strong Southern opposition and in response to pressure from citizen groups committed to civil rights, Congress struggled but succeeded in passing legislation to fulfill the promise of the Fifteenth Amendment, to prevent discrimination in employment, and to enforce the school integration order. The NAACP had more than 300,000 members in the late 1950s, and other grassroots movements were visibly pushing for equality. The Urban League, the Congress on Racial Equality (CORE), and the Southern Christian Leadership Conference (SCLC) headed by Dr. Martin Luther King Jr. also petitioned Congress to enact laws to bring equality to African Americans. In the spring of 1956, more than 2,000 delegates from various civil rights organizations traveled to Washington for a national convention on civil rights.

President Dwight D. Eisenhower (1953–1961) had a less-than-aggressive record on civil rights, and the NAACP did not see him as an ally. In his January 1957 State of the Union address, he failed to note that four Montgomery, Alabama, churches had been bombed the night before. Though many may recall Eisenhower's order on September 24, 1957, to send the 101st Airborne into Little Rock to enforce a desegregation order, he is also remembered for criticizing Chief Justice Warren's *Brown* ruling.

In his second term, however, the president advocated for a civil rights bill. The proposal would create a civil rights commission to investigate voter discrimination, establish a civil rights division within the U.S. Justice Department, empower the attorney general to sue noncompliant school districts refusing to desegregate, and protect African Americans' right to vote in federal elections. After some debate, the House passed a modified version that accomplished three of Eisenhower's four goals; not until passage of a later, more comprehensive law would the attorney general be able to sue noncompliant school districts.

Passing the bill in the Senate was a much more difficult task. With Mississippi's James Eastland chairing the Senate Judiciary Committee, the bill had little chance of making it out of committee. However, a handful of Southern senators—Lyndon Johnson of Texas among them—maneuvered the bill to passage.

Passage in the Senate required enduring a 24-hour filibuster by South Carolina Senator Strom Thurmond, a strong advocate of segregation. A *filibuster* is a strategy allowed by Senate rules that permits senators to talk as long as they want on any subject. Its purpose is to delay or sometimes even kill legislative efforts, a strategy known as "talking a bill to death." But rather than adjourn without voting, some senators brought in cots for sleeping, and on August 29, the **1957 Civil Rights Act** passed the Senate by a vote of 72–18. The passage of this act proved Northern Democrats and Republicans could work together to overcome southern obstructionism. Over the next few years, a series of organized citizen protests, along with the rise and fall of a presidential ally and national media attention to white-on-black violence in the South, brought the most sweeping civil rights package in American legislative history.

Outlawing Discrimination

The civil rights movement had a pivotal year in 1963, with both glorious and horrific consequences. On the one hand, Martin Luther King Jr. assisted the grassroots protests in Birmingham, and more than 200,000 people gathered in the nation's capital for the March on Washington. On the other hand, Mississippi NAACP leader Medgar Evers was shot and killed. In Birmingham, brutal police Chief Bull Connor turned fire hoses and police dogs on peaceful African American protesters.

FOUNDATIONAL DOCUMENTS: *LETTER FROM A BIRMINGHAM JAIL*

Motivated by the Fourteenth Amendment's equal protection clause, on April 12, 1963—Good Friday, the Friday before Easter—the Alabama Christian Movement for Human Rights and the Southern Christian Leadership Conference sponsored a parade down the streets of Birmingham, Alabama, to protest the continued segregation of the city's businesses, public spaces, and other institutions. Three key leaders headed the march of about 50 participants: the Revs. Fred Shuttlesworth and Ralph Abernathy, and Dr. Martin Luther King Jr. Because the city feared disruption from the march, the protesters had been denied a parade permit, and on those grounds, Dr. King and Ralph Abernathy were arrested and put in jail.

On the day of the march, "A Call for Unity," written by eight white clergymen from Birmingham and published in a Birmingham newspaper, called on the protesters to abandon their plans, arguing that the proper way to obtain equal rights was to be patient and let those in a position to negotiate do their job. While serving 11 days in solitary confinement in a Birmingham jail, Dr. King composed a response to that entreaty and in so doing laid out the foundations for the nonviolent resistance to segregation that guided the civil rights movement.

Source: *Birmingham, Ala. Public Library Archives*
Fred Shuttlesworth, Ralph Abernathy, and Martin Luther King Jr. leading the Good Friday March.

In any nonviolent campaign there are four basic steps: 1) Collection of the facts to determine whether injustices are alive. 2) Negotiation. 3) Self-purification and 4) Direct Action. We have gone through all of these steps in Birmingham. . . . Birmingham is probably the most thoroughly segregated city in the United States. Its ugly record of police brutality is known in every section of this country. Its unjust treatment of Negroes in the courts is a notorious reality. There have been more unsolved bombings of Negro homes and churches in Birmingham than any city in the nation. These are the hard, brutal and unbelievable facts. On the basis of these conditions Negro leaders sought to negotiate with the city fathers. But the political leaders consistently refused to engage in good faith negotiation. . . .we had no alternative except that of preparing for direct action, whereby we would present our very bodies as a means of laying our case before the conscience of the local and the national community. We were not unmindful of the difficulties involved. So we decided to go through a process of self purification. We started having workshops on nonviolence and repeatedly asked ourselves the questions, "Are you able to accept blows without retaliating?" "Are you able to endure the ordeals of jail?"

Dr. King also expressed disappointment in the white clergy, in whom he had hoped and expected to find allies. Yet he tried to understand their call for patience.

> We know through painful experience that freedom is never voluntarily given by the oppressor; it must be demanded by the oppressed. . . . For years now I have heard the word "Wait!" . . . .I guess it is easy for those who have never felt the stinging darts of segregation to say, "Wait." But when you have seen vicious mobs lynch your mothers and fathers at will and drown your sisters and brothers at whim; when you have seen hate filled policemen curse, kick, brutalize and even kill your black brothers and sisters with impunity; when you see the vast majority of your twenty million Negro brothers smothering in an air tight cage of poverty in the midst of an affluent society; . . . when you are forever fighting a degenerating sense of "nobodiness;" then you will understand why we find it difficult to wait. There comes a time when the cup of endurance runs over, and men are no longer willing to be plunged into an abyss of injustice where they experience the bleakness of corroding despair. I hope, Sirs, you can understand our legitimate and unavoidable impatience.

Political Science Disciplinary Practices: Explain How Argument Influences Behaviors

Dr. King's "Letter from a Birmingham Jail" is an argument—or more precisely, a counterargument. King addresses each of the points the white clergy make in "A Call for Unity" to make a clear case for the need for nonviolent direct action. Think about the implications of that argument on the political behaviors of African Americans and whites.

Apply: Complete the following activities.

1. Explain how the four basic steps of a nonviolent campaign were carried out in Birmingham before the Good Friday demonstration.

2. Explain the implications of Dr. King's argument on breaking or upholding the law.

3. Compare the lawbreaking of the protestors marching without a permit to the lawbreaking King refers to by mobs.

4. Explain how the civil rights movement was motivated by constitutional provisions.

Then read the full "Letter from a Birmingham Jail" on pages 670–680 and answer the questions that accompany it. You may also read it online.

Presidential Leadership As the events of the early 1960s unfolded, President John F. Kennedy (JFK) became a strong ally for civil rights leaders. He had avoided the topic in the 1960 campaign and let Cold War concerns push civil rights to the bottom of his agenda. However, the president's brother, Robert Kennedy, the nation's attorney general, witnessed violent, ugly confrontations between southern civil rights leaders and brutal state authorities. It was Robert who persuaded President Kennedy to alter his views. JFK began hosting black leaders at the White House and embraced victims of the violence. By mid-1963, Kennedy buckled down to battle for a comprehensive civil rights bill. Kennedy's empathy for the plight of blacks, later followed by President Johnson's commitment to the civil rights cause, proved crucial to the enforcement of ideas written into the Reconstruction amendments a century earlier.

President Kennedy addressed Congress on June 11, 1963, informing the nation of the legal remedies of his proposal. "They involve," he stated, "every American's right to vote, to go to school, to get a job, and to be served in a public place without arbitrary discrimination." Kennedy's bill became the center of controversy over the next year and became the most sweeping piece of civil rights legislation to date. The proposal barred unequal voter registration requirements and prevented discrimination in public accommodations. It empowered the attorney general to file suits against discriminating institutions, such as schools, and to withhold federal funds from noncompliant programs. Finally, it outlawed discriminatory employment practices.

As Kennedy began to push for this omnibus bill, he faced several dilemmas. How strong should it be? The president had served in both the House and the Senate and knew the difficult path for such a revolutionary bill becoming a law. Should he put forth a fairly moderate bill that had better chances of passage, or should he push forward with a stronger civil rights proposal that the NAACP, Urban League, and Dr. King's SCLC desired? Should the process begin in the House or the Senate? And where exactly was the nation on civil rights?

Civil Rights Act of 1964

By this point, nationwide popular opinion favored action for civil rights. In one poll, 72 percent of the nation believed in residential integration, and a full 75 percent believed in school integration. Kennedy's popularity, however, was dropping; his 66 percent approval rating had sunk below 50 percent. The main controversy in his plan was the bill's public accommodations provision. Many Americans—even those opposed to segregation in the public sphere— still believed in a white shop owner's legal right to refuse service to a black patron. But Kennedy held fast to what became known as Title II of the law and sent the bill to Capitol Hill on June 19, 1963.

Days later, Attorney General Robert Kennedy arrived at the House Judiciary Committee's hearing. The House was the preferred starting ground for this controversial measure, largely because the Senate Judiciary Committee was known as the "graveyard for civil rights proposals."

Public Opinion By mid-1963, the national media had vividly presented the civil rights struggle to otherwise unaffected people. Shocking images of racial violence published in the *New York Times* and national newsweeklies such as *Time* and *Life* were eye-opening. Television news broadcasts that showed violence at Little Rock, standoffs at southern colleges, slain civil rights workers, and Bull Connor's aggressive Birmingham police persuaded Northerners to care more about the movement. (For more on the role of media as a linkage institution, connecting citizens and government, see Chapter 16.)

Suddenly the harsh, unfair conditions of the South were very real to the nation. In a White House meeting with black labor leader A. Phillip Randolph and Martin Luther King Jr., President Kennedy reportedly joked when someone criticized Connor: "I don't think you should be totally harsh on Bull Connor. After all, Bull Connor has done more for civil rights than anyone in this room."

Johnson Takes Over Soon after Kennedy had championed the cause of civil rights, he was slain by a gunman in Dallas on November 22, 1963. Within an hour, Lyndon Baines Johnson (LBJ) was sworn in as the 36th president. Onlookers and black leaders wondered how the presidential agenda might change. Johnson had supported the 1957 Civil Rights Act but only after he moderated it. Civil rights leaders hadn't forgotten Johnson's Southern roots or the fact that he and Kennedy had not seen eye to eye.

Fortunately, President Johnson took the helm and privately told two of his top aides that the first priority would be passage of Kennedy's bill. As Johnson and other Democratic leaders drafted his speech for his first televised presidential address, they paid tribute to Kennedy by supporting his civil rights package. "No memorial oration or eulogy could more eloquently honor President Kennedy's memory," Johnson stated to the nation, "than the earliest passage of the civil rights bill for which he fought so long." Days later, on Thanksgiving, Johnson promoted the bill again: "For God made all of us, not some of us, in His image. All of us, not just some of us, are His children."

Johnson was a much better shepherd for this bill than Kennedy. Johnson, having been a leader in Congress, was skilled at both negotiation and compromise. He had a better chance as the folksy, towering Texan than Kennedy had as the elite, overly polished, and often arrogant patriarch. Johnson was notorious for "the treatment," an up close and personal technique of muscling lawmakers into seeing things his way. Johnson beckoned lawmakers to the White House for close face-to-face persuasion that some termed "nostril examinations."

With LBJ's support, the bill had a favorable outlook in the House, which was more representative of popular opinion and more dominated by Northerners than the Senate. On February 10, after the House had debated for less than two weeks and with a handful of amendments, the House passed the bill 290 to 130.

The fight in the Senate was much more difficult. A total of 42 senators added their names as sponsors of the bill. Northern Democrats, Republicans, and the Senate leadership formed a coalition behind the bill which made passage of this law possible. After a 14-hour filibuster by West Virginia's Robert C. Byrd, a cloture vote was finally taken. A *cloture vote*, which must pass by a three-fifths majority, limits further debate on a subject to 30 hours. (For more on cloture, see page 92.) The final vote came on June 19 when the civil rights bill passed by 73 to 27, with 21 Democrats and six Republicans in dissent.

The ink from Johnson's signature was hardly dry when a Georgia motel owner refused service to African Americans and challenged the law. He claimed it exceeded Congress's authority and violated his constitutional right to operate his private property as he saw fit. In debating the bill, Congress had asserted that its power over interstate commerce granted it the right to legislate in this area. Most of this motel's customers had come across state lines. By a vote of 9:0, the Court in *Heart of Atlanta Motel v. United States* (1964) agreed with Congress.

KEY PROVISIONS OF THE CIVIL RIGHTS ACT OF 1964
• Required equal application of voter registration rules (Title I)
• Banned discrimination in public accommodations and public facilities (Titles II and III)
• Empowered the Attorney General to initiate suits against noncompliant schools (Title IV)
• Cut off federal funding for discriminating government agencies (Title VI)
• Outlawed discrimination in hiring based on race, color, religion, sex, or national origin (Title VII)

Impact of the Civil Rights Act of 1964

In April 2014, President Barack Obama gave a speech at a ceremony in Austin, Texas, in honor of the 50th anniversary of LBJ's signing of the Civil Rights Act of 1964. Obama reminded listeners that LBJ himself had grown up in poverty, that he had seen the struggles of Latino students in the schools where he taught, and that he pulled those experiences and his prodigious skills as a politician together to pass this landmark law. "Because of the civil rights movement," Obama said, "because of the laws President Johnson signed, new doors of opportunity and education swung open for everybody, not all at once, but they swung open. Not just blacks and whites, but also women and Latinos and Asians and Native Americans and gay Americans and Americans with a disability. They swung open for you and they swung open for me. And that's why I'm standing here today, because of those efforts, because of that legacy. . . . Half a century later, the laws LBJ passed are now as fundamental to our conception of ourselves and our democracy as the Constitution and the Bill of Rights. They are a foundation, an essential piece of the American character."

As you will read in the following pages, the Civil Rights Act of 1964 had far-reaching effects. It laid the foundation for a new era of equal opportunity, not just for African Americans but for the other groups Obama listed as well. The Civil Rights Act of 1964 helped set the stage for passage of an immigration reform bill in 1965, which did away with national-origin quotas and increased the diversity of the U.S. population. Vice President Hubert Humphrey said before the bill's passage: "We have removed all elements of second-class citizenship from our laws by the Civil Rights Act. We must in 1965 remove all elements in our immigration law which suggest there are second-class people." Instruction in schools for students whose first language is not English relates back to the Civil Rights Act of 1964, which prohibits discrimination on the basis of national origin. The Americans with Disabilities Act, passed in 1990, was modeled on the Civil Rights Act of 1964 and forbade discrimination in public accommodation on the basis of disability. Cases in the news today— from transgender use of bathrooms to baking a wedding cake for a same-sex couple—relate back to the bedrock provisions of the Civil Rights Act of 1964.

Focus on the Franchise

The 1964 Civil Rights Act addressed discrimination in voting registration but lacked the necessary provisions to fully guarantee African Americans the vote. Before World War II, about 150,000 black voters were registered throughout the South, about 3 percent of the region's black voting-age population. In 1964, African American registration in the Southern states varied from 6 to 66 percent but averaged 36 percent.

Twenty-Fourth Amendment Congress passed a proposal for the **Twenty-Fourth Amendment**, which outlaws the poll tax in any federal, primary, or general election, in 1962. At the time, only five states still charged such a tax. By January 1964, the required number of states had ratified the amendment. It did not address any taxes for voting at the state or local levels, but the Supreme Court ruled those unconstitutional in 1966.

Citizen Protest in Selma Many loopholes to the Fifteenth Amendment had been dismantled, yet intimidation and literacy tests still limited the number of registered African American voters. King had focused attention on Selma, Alabama, a town where blacks made up about 50 percent of the population but only 1 percent of registered voters. Roughly 9,700 whites voted in the town compared to only 325 blacks. To protest this inequity, King organized a march from Selma to Alabama's capital, Montgomery. Alabama state troopers violently blocked the mostly black marchers at the Edmund Pettus Bridge as they tried to cross the Alabama River. Mounted police beat these activists and fired tear gas into the crowd. Two Northerners died in the incident.

Again the media offered vivid images that brought great attention to the issue of civil rights. President Johnson had handily won the 1964 presidential election, and the Democratic Party again dominated Congress. In a televised speech before Congress, Johnson introduced his voting rights bill, ending with a line that defined the movement: "We shall overcome."

Voting Rights Act of 1965 The **Voting Rights Act** was signed into law on August 6, 1965, 100 years after the Civil War. It passed with greater ease than the 1964 Civil Rights Act. The law empowered Congress and the federal government to oversee state elections in Southern states. It addressed or "covered" states that used a "test or device" to determine voter qualifications or any state or voting district with less than 50 percent of its voting-age population actually registered to vote. The law effectively ended the literacy test.

BY THE NUMBERS REGISTERED AFRICAN AMERICAN VOTERS BEFORE AND AFTER THE 1965 VOTING RIGHTS ACT		
	1964	1971
Alabama	18%	54%
Arkansas	42%	81%
Florida	51%	54%
Georgia	28%	64%
Louisiana	32%	56%
Mississippi	6%	60%
North Carolina	44%	43%
South Carolina	33%	45%
Tennessee	66%	65%
Virginia	38%	52%

What do the numbers show? What impact did the 1965 Voting Rights Act have on black voter registration? Which states had the lowest voter registration before the law? Which states experienced the greatest increases in registration? Is there a regional trend regarding registration among these Southern states?

The law also required these states to ask for **preclearance** from the U.S. Justice Department before they could enact new registration policies. If Southern states attempted to invent new, creative loopholes to diminish black suffrage, the federal government could stop them.

Section 2 of the Voting Rights Act further requires that voting districts not be drawn in such a way as to "improperly dilute minorities' voting power." The Supreme Court in *Thornburg v. Gingles* (1982) determined that recently drawn districts in North Carolina "discriminated against blacks by diluting the power of their collective vote," and the Court established criteria for determining whether vote dilution has occurred. The Court also ruled that **majority-minority districts**— voting districts in which a minority or group of minorities make up a majority—can be created to redress situations in which African Americans were not allowed to participate fully in elections, a right secured by the Voting Rights Act.

Over time, as the makeup of the Court changed, the Court has revised its position. The Court ruled in 1993 in *Shaw v. Reno* that if redistricting is done on the basis of race, the actions must be held to strict scrutiny in order to meet the requirement of the equal protection clause, yet race must also be considered to satisfy the requirements of the Voting Rights Act, bringing into question the "colorblind" nature of the Constitution. **Strict scrutiny** is the highest standard of judicial review. It requires that laws infringing on a fundamental right must meet two tests: 1) there must be a compelling state interest for the law; and 2) the law is necessary to protect that interest and designed to be as narrow as possible. Most laws examined under strict scrutiny are overturned. (See page 325 for other levels of scrutiny.) Justice Blackmun in his dissent to *Shaw v. Reno* noted that "[i] t is particularly ironic that the case in which today's majority chooses to abandon settled law . . . is a challenge by white voters to the plan under which North Carolina has sent black representatives to Congress for the first time since Reconstruction."

The Court once again interpreted the law, upholding the rights of the majority, in its 2017 ruling on *Cooper v. Harris*, determining that districts in North Carolina were unconstitutionally drawn because they relied on race as the dominant factor.

The Voting Rights Act was the single greatest improvement for African Americans in terms of access to the ballot box. The law shifted the registration burden from the victims to the perpetrators. By 1967, black voter registration in six Southern states increased from about 30 to more than 50 percent. African Americans soon held office in greater numbers. Within five years of the law's passage, several states saw marked increases in their numbers of registered voters. The original law expired in 1971, but Congress has renewed the Voting Rights Act several times, most recently in 2006.

THINK AS A POLITICAL SCIENTIST: *ANALYZE AND INTERPRET QUANTITATIVE DATA ON AFRICAN AMERICAN SUFFRAGE*

Analysis and interpretation of quantitative (numbers-based) sources require that you first understand the purpose, labels, and contents of an informational illustration and then look for patterns and relationships. For example, do the numbers go up or down in a predictable pattern? If there is a sudden change in a pattern, how can you explain it? Is there a clear trend visible in the information? Draw a conclusion from the information to explain what it implies or illustrates about political principles, processes, behaviors, and outcomes.

Practice: Describe the data in the table and the trends, patterns, and variations they represent. Referring to this information, describe and explain in a brief essay the change in Southern African American voter registration during the period shown in the table. Explain how the data relate to each of the following: 1) political principles, 2) processes, 3) institutions, and 4) behavior.

AFRICAN AMERICAN VOTER REGISTRATION IN SOUTHERN STATES			
State	**1960**	**1964**	**1968**
Alabama	14%	23%	57%
Arkansas	38%	54%	68%
Florida	39%	64%	62%
Georgia	n/a	39%	56%
Louisiana	40%	32%	59%
Mississippi	6%	7%	59%
North Carolina	38%	47%	55%
South Carolina	n/a	39%	51%
Tennessee	64%	69%	73%
Texas	34%	58%	83%
Virginia	23%	46%	58%

Source: *Piven, et al. Keeping Down the Black Vote, 2009*

Voting Rights Today More recent, racially charged voting rights controversies have arisen around a Supreme Court decision on part of the Voting Rights Act and the fairness of voter identification laws. Seeking to reclaim local control and to end the preclearance procedure, Shelby County, Alabama, sued. In a 5:4 ruling in *Shelby County v. Holder* (2013), the Court struck down the formula that determines which districts are covered for preclearance, stating that it imposes burdens that "must be justified by current needs."

State laws requiring voters to present identification at the voting booth have also brought criticism and constitutional challenges. Since 2011, 13 mostly Republican-dominated states have introduced voter ID laws. Conservative supporters of voter ID laws cite very rare instances of voter fraud and the goal of restoring integrity in elections. Liberal opponents say these laws create another voting impediment and unfairly disenfranchise lower socioeconomic groups—minorities, workers, the poor, immigrants—who also typically vote for Democrats. They point out that very little coordinated voter fraud actually goes on in the United States. A 2007 Justice Department study found virtually no proof of organized skewing of elections. A 2014 Loyola Law School study of elections since 2000 found just 31 examples of voter impersonation.

Are these voter ID requirements suppressing the vote? The Brennan Center for Justice says about 25 percent of eligible black voters and 16 percent of Hispanics do not have IDs compared to 9 percent of whites. It's likely that

VOTER ID LAWS IN EFFECT IN 2018

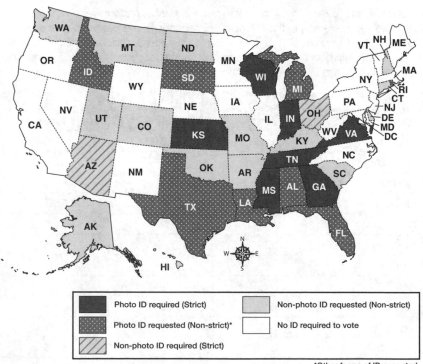

Photo ID required (Strict)

Photo ID requested (Non-strict)*

Non-photo ID required (Strict)

Non-photo ID requested (Non-strict)

No ID required to vote

*Other forms of ID accepted

Source: *National Conference of State Legislatures*

at least some of the 33 to 35 percent of eligible African American voters who did not participate before the voter ID requirements are among those without IDs. Participation among these groups has generally grown during that period, and voter ID laws could interfere with that growth. At the same time, voter ID laws seem to serve as a rallying cry against voter suppression and actually help increase turnout. *The National Council of State Legislatures* reports that as of 2018, 34 states have some variation of a voter ID law on the books.

Fulfilling the Spirit of *Brown*

After gaining civil rights protections and increasing black voting via Congress throughout the 1960s, interest groups and civil rights activists questioned the effectiveness of the *Brown* decision on schools across the nation. The ruling met with varying degrees of compliance from state to state and from school district to school district. A great degree of segregation still existed in both the North and the South.

The *Brown* ruling and the *Brown II* clarification spelled out the Court's interpretation of practical integration, but a variety of reactions followed. To avoid the Court's ruling, school officials created measures such as **freedom-of-choice plans** that placed the transfer burden on black students seeking a move to more modern white schools. Intimidation too often prevented otherwise willing students to ask for a transfer.

In short, "all deliberate speed" had resulted in a deliberate delay. In 1964, only about one-fifth of the school districts in the previously segregated Southern states taught whites and blacks in the same buildings. In the Deep South, only 2 percent of the black student population had entered white schools. And in many of those instances, there were only one or two token black students willing to stand up to an unwelcoming school board and face intimidation from bigoted whites. Rarely did a white student request a transfer to a historically black school. Clearly, the intention of the *Brown* ruling had been thwarted.

Bearing the Burden of Brown

Activists and civil rights lawyers took additional cases to the Supreme Court to ensure both the letter and the spirit of the *Brown* ruling. From 1958 until the mid-1970s, a series of lawsuits—most filed by the NAACP and most resulting in unanimous pro-integration decisions—brought greater levels of integration in the South and North.

The Little Rock Nine faced violent confrontations as they entered school on their first day at Central High School in 1957. School officials and the state government asked for a delay until tempers could settle and until a safer atmosphere would allow for smoother integration. The NAACP countered in court and appealed this case to the high bench. In *Cooper v. Aaron*, the Court ruled potential violence was not a legal justification to delay compliance with *Brown*.

Source: *A. Y. Owen / Getty Images*

President Dwight Eisenhower dispatched the 101st Airborne division to Arkansas to escort African American students into Little Rock's Central High School, executing a court order to desegregate.

By the late 1960s, the transfer option had yielded few integration results. In 1968, the Court ruled the freedom-of-choice plans, by themselves, were not a satisfactory remedy for integration.

BY THE NUMBERS DESEGREGATED DISTRICTS 1964		
Percent of African Americans Attending Schools with Whites		
South	Alabama	0.03
	Arkansas	0.81
	Florida	2.65
	Georgia	0.37
	Louisiana	1.12
	Mississippi	0.02
	North Carolina	1.41
	South Carolina	0.10
	Tennessee	5.33
	Texas	7.26
	Virginia	5.07

BY THE NUMBERS DESEGREGATED DISTRICTS 1964		
Percent of African Americans Attending Schools with Whites		
Border	Delaware	57.8
	D.C.	86.0
	Kentucky	62.5
	Maryland	51.7
	Missouri	44.1
	Oklahoma	31.7
	West Virginia	88.1

What do the numbers show? What percentage of African American students attended with whites? How effective was the *Brown* ruling in integrating previously segregated schools? What states reached the highest integration levels? Describe the factors that kept the percentage of African Americans in traditionally white schools low.

Balancing Enrollments Three years later, in *Swann v. Charlotte-Mecklenburg* **(1971),** the Supreme Court addressed a federal district judge's solution to integrate a North Carolina school district. The judge had set a mathematical ratio as a goal to achieve higher levels of integration. The district's overall white-to-black population was roughly 71 to 29 percent. The district judge ordered the school district to assign students to school buildings across town to reflect roughly the same proportion of black to white students in each building. The Supreme Court later approved his decision and thus sanctioned mathematical ratios to achieve school integration in another unanimous decision.

Busing The *Swann* opinion ended a generation of litigation necessary to achieve integration, but it did not end the controversy. A popular movement against busing for racial balance sprang up as protesters questioned the placement of students at distant schools based on race. Ironically, though the constitutionality of busing grew out of a Southern case, cases from Indianapolis, Dayton, Buffalo, Detroit, and Denver brought much protest. Those protests included efforts to sabotage buses as well as seek legal means to stop this ruling. The antibusing movement grew strong enough to encourage the U.S. House of Representatives to propose a constitutional amendment to outlaw busing for racial balance, though the Senate never passed it. White parents in scores of cities transferred their children from public schools subject to similar rulings or relocated their families to adjacent, suburban districts to avoid rulings. This situation, known as white flight, became commonplace as inner cities became blacker and the surrounding suburbs became whiter.

In one of the final attempts in this busing saga, the NAACP tried to convince the Supreme Court to approve a multi-school district integration order that assigned racial enrollments and interdistrict busing (busing across district lines) of students for racial balance and to combat white flight. The Court stopped short of approving this plan (by a close vote of 5:4) in its 1974 ruling in the Detroit case of *Milliken v. Bradley*, noting that if the district boundaries were not drawn for the purpose of racial segregation, interdistrict busing is not justified by the *Brown* decision. Such a plan would have meant that parents electing school boards in their home district would not have had a say in the school board in the district where their children were assigned to attend. In his dissent, Justice Thurgood Marshall wrote, "School district lines, however innocently drawn, will surely be perceived as fences to separate the races when, under a Detroit-only decree, white parents withdraw their children from the Detroit city schools and move to the suburbs in order to continue them in all-white schools." At the time, the Detroit public schools were, in fact, 99 percent black.

Women's Rights

Women's quest for equal rights began formally at the Seneca Falls Convention in 1848, was enhanced with a suffrage amendment, and reached new levels when Congress passed legislation that mandated equal pay, fairness in property and family law, and a more even playing field in education.

The western states, beginning with Wyoming, allowed women to vote in some or all elections. In the late 1800s, women entered the workplace, and they became a valued part of the workforce during World War I. After the war's end, women secured the right to vote. It wasn't until the 1950s and 1960s, however, that women organized to gain full independence, equal protection, and civil rights.

Seeking Women's Suffrage

Obtaining the franchise was key to altering public policy toward women, and Susan B. Anthony led the way. In 1872, in direct violation of New York law, she walked into a polling place and cast a vote. An all-male jury later convicted her. She authored the passage that would eventually make it into the Constitution decades later as the Nineteenth Amendment.

Women and Industry At the end of the 1800s, industrialization brought large numbers of women into the workplace. They took jobs in urban factories for considerably lower pay than men. Oregon passed a law that set a maximum number of work hours for women, but not for men. The law was largely to prevent harsh supervisors from overworking female employees who needed to be healthy to bear children. In 1908, noted attorney Louis Brandeis, representing Oregon's right to enact such a law, presented social science findings that proved a woman's physical makeup made her less suited to work lengthy days in rough conditions. The Court decided the state had a right to establish such a law that allowed it to treat women differently from men. This was a bittersweet victory for women. On the one hand, progressives sought to protect the health and safety of women; on the other, this double standard gave lawmakers ammunition to treat women differently.

Suffragists still pressed on. By 1914, 11 states allowed women to vote. In the 1916 election, both major political parties endorsed the concept of women's suffrage in their platforms, and Jeanette Rankin of Montana became the first woman elected to Congress. The following year, however, World War I completely consumed Congress and the nation, and the issue of women's suffrage drifted into the background.

Organized groups pressured President Woodrow Wilson. Suffrage leader Alice Paul had organized public picket lines in the nation's capital. Women were arrested and jailed—usually for minor charges such as disturbing the peace—in the name of seeking a stronger political voice. The perpetual picket lasted for more than a year until President Wilson, after pardoning the arrested suffragists, spoke in favor of the amendment, influencing its vote in Congress. The measure passed both houses in 1919 and was ratified as the **Nineteenth Amendment** in 1920.

From Suffrage to Action

What impact did the amendment have on voter turnout for women, how did it impact elections after 1920, and what did it do for the overall quest for women's rights? An in-depth study of a Chicago election from the early 1920s found that 65 percent of potential women voters stayed home, many responding that it wasn't a woman's place to engage in politics or that the act would offend their husbands. Men outvoted women by roughly 30 percent.

Voting laws were not the states' only unfair practice. The Supreme Court had ruled in 1948 that states could prevent women from tending bar unless the establishment was owned by a close male relative, and states were allowed to seat all-male juries. The 1960s, however, witnessed advancements for women in the workplace. In 1963, Congress passed the **Equal Pay Act** that required employers to pay men and women the same wage for the same job. It was still legal, even after the Equal Pay Act, to deny women job opportunities. Thus, equal pay applied only when women were hired to do the same jobs that men were hired to do. The 1964 Civil Rights Act protected women from discrimination in employment.

In addition, Betty Friedan, the author of *The Feminine Mystique*, encouraged women to speak their minds, to apply for male-dominated jobs, and to organize for equality in the public sphere. Friedan went on to cofound the **National Organization for Women (NOW)** in 1966.

Women and Equality

In the 1970s, Congress passed legislation to give equal opportunities to women in schools and on college campuses. Pro-equality groups pressed the Court to apply strict scrutiny standards to policies that treated genders differently. However, the women's movement fell short of some of its goals. The Court never declared that legal gender classification deserves the same level of strict scrutiny as policies that differentiated classes based on race or national origin, but instead could be determined with intermediate or heightened scrutiny (see page 325). Additionally, women were unable to amend the Constitution to declare absolute equality of the sexes. All in all, though, the 1970s was a successful decade for women gaining legal rights and elevating their political and legal status.

Title IX of the Education Amendments Act of 1972, which amended the 1964 Civil Rights Act, guaranteed that women have the same educational opportunities as men in programs receiving federal government funding. Two congresswomen, Patsy Mink (D-HI) and Edith Green (D- OR), introduced the bill, which passed with relative ease. The law states, "No person in the United States shall, on the basis of sex, be excluded from participation in, be denied the benefits of, or be subjected to discrimination under any education program or activity receiving federal financial assistance." This means colleges must offer comparable opportunities to women. Schools don't have to allow females to join football and wrestling teams—though some have—nor must schools have precisely the same number of student athletes from each gender. However, any school receiving federal dollars must be cognizant of the pursuits of women in the classroom and on the field and maintain gender equity.

To be compliant with Title IX, colleges must make opportunities available for male and female college students in substantially proportionate numbers based on their respective full-time undergraduate enrollment. Additionally, schools must try to expand opportunities and accommodate the interests of the underrepresented sex.

The controversy over equality, especially in college sports, has created a conundrum for many that work in the field of athletics. Fair budgeting and maintaining programs for men and women that satisfy the law has at times been difficult. Some critics of Title IX claim female interest in sports simply does not equal that of young men, and therefore a school should not be required to create a balance. In 2005, the Office of Civil Rights began allowing colleges to conduct surveys to assess student interest among the sexes. Title IX advocates, however, compare procedures like these to the burden of the freedom-of-choice option in the early days of racial integration. Federal lawsuits have resulted in courts forcing Louisiana State University to create women's soccer and softball teams and requiring Brown University to maintain school-funded varsity programs for girls.

In 1972, about 30,000 women competed in college varsity-level athletics. Today, more than five times that many do. When the USA women's soccer team won the World Cup championship in 1999, President Clinton referred to them as the "Daughters of Title IX."

Pro-Choice vs. Pro-Life The year after Title IX passed, the Supreme Court made its landmark *Roe v. Wade* (1973) decision. Many women's groups and the ACLU felt state restrictions on abortion denied a pregnant woman and her doctor the right to make a highly personal and private medical choice. In Texas, where abortion was a crime, pro-choice attorneys provided assistance to a pregnant young woman, given the alias of Jane Roe, who sought an abortion.

The Court in *Roe v. Wade* decided that a state cannot deny a pregnant woman the right to an abortion during the first trimester of the pregnancy.

In a 7:2 decision, the *Roe* opinion erased or modified statutes in most states, effectively legalizing abortion (see page 288).

Since then, however, the battle over abortion has continued. States can still regulate abortion by requiring brief waiting periods and other restrictions. Anti-abortion or pro-life groups continue to press for legal rights for the unborn, many believing that life begins at conception and for that reason even a zygote—a fertilized egg—is entitled to legal protection.

Strict Scrutiny and the Equal Protection Clause Also during the 1970s, women pressed the Supreme Court to give gender-based laws the same level of scrutiny it required of laws that distinguish classes of citizens based on race or national origin. In 1971, activists looked on as the Supreme Court heard an Idaho case in which both the mother and the father of their deceased child wanted to administer the child's estate. Idaho law gave preference to the father when both parents made equal claims. Then-ACLU attorney Ruth Bader Ginsburg, who was appointed to the U.S. Supreme Court in 1993, argued that the law arbitrarily favored men over women and thus created a legal inequity. The Court agreed and struck down this law because it "establishes a classification subject to scrutiny under the equal protection clause." For the first time, the Court concluded sex-based differences of policy were entitled to some degree of scrutiny. Ginsburg's brief devoted 46 pages to applying the strict scrutiny standard. However, only four of the eight in the majority wanted to make gender a classification deserving of strict scrutiny. Although feminists won this case, they also felt somewhat of a loss because the Court did not conclude that gender classifications deserved "strict scrutiny."

Five years later, an Oklahoma law that prevented the sale of beer to men under 20 and women under 18 was at issue. Under this law, young women could purchase beer two years before young men could. The Court ruled that this violated the equal protection of the law and that the state would have to set the same drinking age for both men and women. But more importantly, the Court established what has become known as the intermediate or **heightened scrutiny test**.

To this day, the Court has not given the same kind of deference to laws that create classes of gender as it has to those that distinguish people of different races and has instead offered a **reasonableness standard** for treating the sexes differently—for allowing gender bias. For example, it is deemed reasonable for the federal government to require men, but not women, to register for the military draft—in fact, women cannot register for the draft—and to assign men, but not women, to combat roles in the armed services (though women serve in combat roles today).

Equal Rights Amendment Feminists and their supporters also fell short of adding the **Equal Rights Amendment** to the Constitution. Alice Paul, the suffragist mentioned earlier and founder of the National Woman's Party, actually managed to get the Equal Rights Amendment introduced into Congress in 1923. The proposed amendment stated, "Equality of rights under the law shall not be denied on account of sex" and gave Congress power to enforce this. The amendment was introduced in every session of Congress with various degrees of support until 1972, when it passed both the House and the Senate. Both major parties supported the amendment. Thirty of the 38 states necessary to ratify the amendment approved the ERA within one year. At its peak, 35 states had ratified the proposal, but when the chance for full ratification expired in 1982, the ERA failed.

Why would anyone vote against the idea of equality of the sexes? Several reasons might explain their reluctance. Though it was easy for Congress to reach the two-thirds requirement, it was hard to overcome traditionalists' concerns about the military draft, coed bunking of men with women, and other potentially delicate matters that might arise from the ERA. The *Roe v. Wade* decision, though seen as a victory among feminists, was not approved by masses of people in the 1970s. The *Roe* decision likely harmed the credibility of the ERA's allies, such as NOW and the ACLU. Finally, the proposition of absolute equality caused opponents to argue the amendment might hurt women, especially in cases involving assault, alimony, and child custody.

Gay Rights and Equality

Like African Americans and women, those who identify as LGBT have been discriminated against and have sought and earned legal equality and rights to intimacy, military service, and marriage.

The state and federal governments had long set policies that limited the freedoms and liberties of these citizens. One historian notes that in the 1950s, Senator Joseph McCarthy railed against gays and lesbians, much as he did against communists, and claimed they "lacked emotional stability of normal persons." President Eisenhower signed an executive order banning any type of "sexual perversion" as it was defined in the order in any sector of the federal government. And Congress enacted an oath of allegiance for immigrants to assure that they were neither communist nor gay. State and local authorities closed gay bars. Meanwhile, the military intensified its exclusion of homosexuals.

The first magazine cover story suggesting "homophile" marriage was printed in *One*, a publication targeted at gay readers. It made the case for the public and legal same-sex relationship not just on equality terms but also to remove the stereotype of promiscuity. The first known public gay rights protest outside the White House took place in 1965. In 1973, psychiatrists removed homosexuality as a mental disorder from their chief diagnostic manual.

Throughout the 1970s and 1980s, in part to seek legal protections and gain a political voice, homosexuals "came out" and began publicly proclaiming their sexual identity. Governments make a host of policies and thus legal definitions regarding sexual behaviors, relationships, and family law in which the LGBT community has an interest, as do people who believe in traditional marriage. When states had to define and regulate marriage, morality, public health, adoption, and wills, controversy over to whom these laws pertained and how they would be applied to straight and LGBT citizens followed.

Debates regarding these issues are complex, with a wide array of overlapping constitutional principles. The states' police powers, privacy, and equal protection are all at stake. Federalism and geographic mobility create additional complexities. To what degree should the federal government intervene in governing marriage, a reserved power of the states? When gays and lesbians moved from one state to another, differing state laws concerning marriage, adoption, and inheritance brought legal standoffs as the Constitution's full-faith-and-credit clause (Article IV) and the states' reserved powers principle (Tenth Amendment) clashed.

Seeking Legal Intimacy

Traditionalists responded to the growing visibility of gays by passing laws that criminalized homosexual behavior. Though so-called anti-sodomy laws had been around for more than a century, it was not until the 1970s when state laws were passed that specifically criminalized same-sex relations and behaviors. Can a state regulate such behavior as part of its police powers? The Supreme Court ruled in *Bowers v. Hardwick* (1986) that it could.

The Court heard the issue again and reversed itself in the case of *Lawrence v. Texas* (2003). Law enforcement officers had entered John Lawrence's home based on a reported weapons disturbance only to discover homosexual activity. The Texas law declared, "a person commits an offense if he engages in deviate sexual intercourse with another individual of the same sex." Lawrence's attorneys argued that the equal protection clause voided this law because the statute specifically singled out gays and lesbians. The Court agreed. Writing for the majority, Justice Anthony Kennedy stated, the Court "was not correct when it was decided, and it is not correct today."

Culture Wars of the 1990s

The battle between the religious right—those social conservatives who coalesced in the early 1980s around an anti-*Roe*, pro-family values platform—and the social liberals of the Democratic Party created major friction. Republican presidential primary candidate Pat Buchanan got only a fraction of the Republican vote, but he spoke for much of the religious right at the party's 1992 convention when he declared, "we stand with [George H.W. Bush] against the amoral idea that gay and lesbian couples should have the same standing in law as married men and women." Into the 1990s, these competing interests battled over who should serve in the military, to what degree gays and lesbians should be protected, and which organizations can lawfully exclude gays.

Military The U.S. Armed Forces has addressed the issue of gays within its ranks since the creation of the United States. In 1917, the Articles of War passed by Congress in 1916 were implemented, making sodomy illegal. In 1949, the military banned any "homosexual personnel" and began discharging known homosexuals from service. More recently, high-ranking officers and the civilian personnel in the Pentagon debated the impact—real or perceived—that homosexuals would have on the military's morale, unit cohesion, discipline, and combat readiness.

In the 1992 presidential campaign, Democratic candidate Bill Clinton promised to end the ban on gays in the military. Clinton won the election but soon discovered that neither commanders nor the rank and file welcomed reversing the ban. In a controversy that mired the first few months of his presidency, Clinton compromised as the Congress passed the **"don't ask, don't tell"** policy. This rule prevented the military from asking about the private sexual status of its personnel but also prevented gays and lesbians from acknowledging or revealing it. In short, "don't ask, don't tell" was meant to cause both sides to ignore the issue and focus on defending the country.

The debate continued for 17 years. Surveys conducted among military personnel and leadership began to show a favorable response to allowing gays to serve openly. In December 2010, with President Obama's support, the House and Senate voted to remove the "don't ask, don't tell" policy so all service members can serve their country openly.

DOMA Not long after Hawaii's state supreme court became the first statewide governing institution to legalize same-sex marriage in 1993, lawmakers elsewhere reacted to prevent such a policy change in their backyards. Utah was the first state to pass a law prohibiting the recognition of same-sex marriage. In a presidential election year at a time when public opinion was still decidedly against gay marriages, national lawmakers jumped to define and defend marriage in the halls of Congress. The 1996 **Defense of Marriage Act (DOMA)** defined marriage at the national level and declared that states did not have to accept same-sex marriages recognized in other states. The law also barred federal recognition of same-sex marriage for purposes of Social Security, federal income tax filings, and federal employee benefits. This was a Republican-sponsored bill that earned nearly every Republican vote. Democrats, however were divided on it. Civil rights pioneer and Congressman John Lewis declared: "I have known racism. I have known bigotry. This bill stinks of the same fear, hatred, and intolerance." The sole Republican vote against the law came from openly gay member Steve Gunderson who asked on the House floor, "Why shouldn't my partner of 13 years be entitled to the same health insurance and survivor's benefits that individuals around here, my colleagues with second and third wives, are able to give them?" The bill passed in the House 342 to 67, and in the Senate, 85 to 14. Republicans supported it nearly unanimously, while Democrats supported with majorities in both chambers. By 2000, 30 states had enacted laws refusing to recognize same-sex marriages in their states or those coming from elsewhere.

Discrimination Gays have faced discrimination in the workforce and in the private sector as well. During the 1960s civil rights movement, outlawing racial discrimination in the private sector was difficult because the Fourteenth Amendment's equal protection clause does not require states to prohibit nongovernmental discrimination. In the 1970s and 1980s, states and cities began passing laws to prevent discrimination against homosexuals. These policies surfaced in urban areas and in states with higher numbers of LGBT residents. Conservatives argued that these policies created a special class for the LGBT community and were thus unequal and unconstitutional.

The Supreme Court, however, did not stop private organizations from discriminating against gays. In 1990 when Scoutmaster James Dale was outed as gay, the Boy Scouts of America quickly invoked its policy and dismissed Dale. He sued, arguing that the Boy Scouts, though nongovernmental, amounted to a public accommodation under state civil rights law. Dale won at the state level, but after the Boy Scouts appealed, the U.S. Supreme Court disagreed. In a ruling in 2000, it upheld the Boy Scouts' right to create and enforce its own policies with regard to membership under free speech and free association ideals.

Same-Sex Marriage

While Dale failed to secure equal treatment from the Boy Scouts, other activists pursued gaining the right to marry. Even before the *Lawrence* decision, few states enforced their anti-sodomy statutes. Thus, same-sex partners lived with one another yet lacked formal legal recognition and the legal benefits that came with a state-sanctioned marriage. Since their founding, states have defined and regulated marriage. The states set age limits, marriage license requirements, divorce law, and other policies. If members of the LGBT community could legally marry, not only could they publicly enjoy the principled expressions and relationships that go with marriage, they could also begin to enjoy the practical and tangible benefits granted to heterosexual couples: purchasing a home together, inheriting a deceased partner's estate, and qualifying for spousal employee benefits. In order for these benefits to accrue, states would have to change their marriage statutes.

Initial Legalization The first notable litigation occurred in 1971 when Minnesota's highest court heard a challenge to the state's refusal to issue a marriage license to a same-sex couple. The state court dismissed the plaintiff's argument that preventing gays from marrying paralleled state laws preventing interracial marriage, which the Supreme Court had struck down. "In common sense and constitutional sense," the state court said, "there is a clear distinction between a marital restriction based merely on race and one based upon the fundamental difference in sex." This opinion also relied on the simple definitions from *Webster's Dictionary* and *Black's Law Dictionary* to uphold the Minnesota legislature's marriage definition.

These may seem like simple sources for courts to consult, but the issue is very basic: Should the state legally recognize same-sex partnerships, and if so, should the state refer to it as "marriage"? In the past two decades, the United States battled over these two questions, as advocates sought for legal equality and as public opinion on these questions shifted dramatically.

Vermont was an early state to legally recognize same-sex relationships and did so via the Vermont Supreme Court. The legislature then passed

Vermont's "civil unions" law, which declared that same-sex couples have "all the same benefits, protections and responsibilities under law … as are granted to spouses in a civil marriage," but stopped short of calling the new legal union a "marriage." Massachusetts's high court also declared its traditional marriage statute out of line, which encouraged the state to legalize same-sex marriage there. What followed was a decade-long battle between conservative opposition and LGBT advocates, first in the courts and then at the ballot box, ending much of the controversy at the U.S. Supreme Court in 2015.

The 2004 Ballot Initiatives After gay marriage became legal in New England, conservatives in 11 states countered with ballot measures in November 2004. Most of these statewide initiatives added to their respective state constitutions a distinct definition of traditional marriage to prevent state courts from overturning traditional marriage statutes. President George W. Bush supported the movement and, in his pursuit of a second term, called for a national constitutional amendment to do the same. Conservatives turned out on Election Day to pass these various ballot issues and to re-elect Bush.

The Push and Pull for Marriage Equality After the 2004 elections, however, a patchwork of marriage law was sewn across the United States mostly by the hands of courts, then by legislatures and ballot initiatives, in a trajectory toward legalizing same-sex marriage that culminated in the Supreme Court 2015 decision in *Obergefell v. Hodges*.

In that decade before the landmark ruling, a coalition of gay rights advocates and legal teams sought to overturn "traditional marriage" laws. Occasional successful policy geared toward protecting heterosexual marriage passed and some court cases were lost. While pro-gay lawyers articulated and won most legal arguments, public opinion moved in a direction that would eventually make it practical to campaign for marriage rights in the political arena as well as the legal arena.

Additional statewide initiatives affirmed traditional marriage and conservative groups campaigned to oust state judges who ruled in favor of same-sex marriage. The legal arguments centered on the equal protection, full-faith-and-credit, and reserved powers clauses. Meanwhile, public opinion "solidified" on the issue, according to Gallup. The year 2011 marks the point when more than half of the public consistently favored legalizing same-sex marriage, and it has grown since.

President Obama had publicly opposed same-sex marriage during the 2008 campaign and after. He stood on the side of gay rights generally and was preferred by the gay community tenfold over the Republican candidate, but he stopped short of advocating for same-sex marriage. However, in May 2012, he publicly supported same-sex marriage. What followed was a surge in public opinion among the African American community for marriage equality. An endorsement from the NAACP followed. Black support for same-sex marriage went from 41 to 59 percent.

That November, for the first time, pro-same-sex marriage initiatives passed in all four states where they were on the ballot. This outcome broke a 31-state losing streak at the actual polls. Political pundits suggest that Obama's public switch likely turned out greater numbers of voters passionate about the issue and contributed largely to his reelection win on the same day.

Two Supreme Court rulings secured same-sex marriage nationally. The first was filed by New York state resident Edith Windsor, legally married in Canada to a woman named Thea Spyer. Spyer died in 2009. Under New York state law, Windsor's same-sex marriage was recognized, but it was not recognized under federal law, which governed federal inheritance taxes. Windsor thus owed taxes in excess of $350,000. A widow from a traditional marriage in the same situation would have saved that amount. The Court saw the injustice and ruled that DOMA created "a disadvantage, a separate status, and so a stigma" on same-sex marriage that was legally recognized by New York.

The ruling saved Windsor the unfair tax, chipped away at DOMA, and encouraged the legal teams that were already going after the remaining state marriage laws that prevented members of the LGBT community from entering into same-sex marriages. After separate rulings in similar cases at the sixth and ninth circuit courts of appeals, the Supreme Court decided to hear *Obergefell v. Hodges* **(2015).** By the time both sides arrived for arguments, Alabama had become the thirty-seventh state to have same-sex marriage rights.

Fourteenth Amendment Foundation The Court was being asked two questions: Does the Fourteenth Amendment require a state to issue a marriage license to two people of the same sex?" and "Does the Fourteenth Amendment require a state to recognize a marriage between two people of the same sex when their marriage was lawfully licensed and performed out-of-state?" If the answer to the first question is "yes," then the second question becomes moot. On June 26, 2015, the Court ruled 5:4 that states preventing same-sex marriage violated the Constitution. Justice Anthony Kennedy wrote the opinion, his fourth pro-gay rights opinion in nearly 20 years.

Contemporary Issues Since **Obergefell**

Within a year of the same-sex marriage ruling, the percent of cohabiting married same-sex couples rose from about 38 percent to 49 percent, according to *Congressional Quarterly*. In making law and policy, it's never really "over." For practical purposes, we can conclude that public schools will never return to a pre-*Brown* segregated status, not simply because the Court ruled against it, but because a generation of subsequent litigation settled the law and citizen views on public school segregation changed. This wasn't the case in the years immediately following *Brown*. Now the Court has ruled that states cannot deny gays the right to marry, but not all Americans have accepted the ruling. Some public officials refused to carry out their duties to issue marriage licenses, claiming that doing so violated their personal or religious views of marriage. In 2016, about 200 state-level anti-LGBT bills were introduced (only four became law). Though the *Obergefell* decision was recent and was determined by a close vote on the Court, public opinion is moving in such a direction that the ruling is on its way to becoming settled law. Yet controversies around other public policies—such as hiring or firing people because they are transgender, refusing to rent housing to same-sex couples, or refusing business services, such as catering, for same-sex weddings—affect the LGBT community and have brought debates and changes in the law.

Workplace Discrimination When the 1964 Civil Rights Act prevented employers from refusing employment or firing employees for reasons of race, color, sex, nationality, or religion, it did not include homosexuality or gender identity. No federal statute has come to pass that would protect LGBT groups. Twenty-two states and the District of Columbia bar such a practice and afford a method for victims of such discrimination to take action against the employer. In several of the remaining states, efforts are being made to create similar legislation. Localities can sometimes pass ordinances that govern or regulate such commercial behavior, however; states can also make statewide rules to guide or prevent cities from doing so. Three states have a law that limits localities from enacting LGBT protections. Yet, the Seventh Circuit Court of Appeals recently ruled that discrimination against gays is covered by the 1964 law. For up-to-date information on the status of these ordinances, the

EMPLOYMENT PROTECTIONS FOR LGBT PEOPLE, 2018

Employment Protections for LGBT Population

Employment non-discrimination law covers sexual orientation and gender identity

Employment non-discrimination law covers sexual orientation, though federal law offers some protection

No employment non-discrimination law covering sexual orientation or gender identity, though federal law offers some protections

Source: *Movement Advancement Project*

Movement Advancement Project (MAP) shows the progress of policy changes in LGBT law, in a "mapped" state-by-state fashion. Go to www.lgbtmap.org.

One aspect of workplace discrimination is sexual harassment. In the 1986 case *Meritor Savings Bank v. Vinson*, the Supreme Court ruled that sexual harassment creates unlawful discrimination against women by fostering a hostile work environment and is a violation of Title VI of the 1964 Civil Rights Act. Sexual harassment became a major issue in 2017 when a number of women came forward to accuse men in prominent positions in government, entertainment, and the media of sexual harassment. In a number of the high-profile cases, the accused men lost their jobs and the victims received financial compensation. In a show of solidarity and to demonstrate how widespread the problem of sexual harassment is, the #MeToo movement went viral. Anyone who had experienced sexual harassment or assault was asked to write #MeToo on a social media platform. Millions of women took part. A 2016 report by the Equal Employment Opportunity Commission found that between 25 and 85 percent of women experience sexual harassment at work, but most are afraid to report it for fear of losing their jobs. The "Time's Up" movement, also started in 2017, is an effort to raise money to provide funding for legal support for victims of sexual harassment and to lobby for laws that impose consequences on employers who engage in sexual harassment.

Refusal to Serve and Religious Freedom The 1964 law did not include LGBT persons when it defined the reasons merchants could not refuse service, the so-called public accommodations section of the law. So, depending on the state, businesses might have the legal right to refuse service, especially products or services directly tied to a lesbian wedding. In reaction to *Obergefell*, a movement sprang up to enshrine in state constitutions wording that would protect merchants or employees for this refusal, particularly if it is based on the merchant's religious views. How can the First Amendment promise a freedom of religion if the state can mandate participation in some event or ceremony that violates the individual's religious beliefs? About 45 of these bills were introduced in 22 states in the first half of 2017.

Transgender Issues One more unresolved issue is how schools and other government institutions handle where transgender citizens go to the restroom or what locker room they use. In education, this controversy is often handled on a local level. But not all citizens have been satisfied with how it has been handled. Several "bathroom bills" have surfaced at statehouses across the country. In other scenarios, the issue has been solved at a school board meeting or in a federal court. President Obama's Department of Education issued a directive after interpreting language from Title IX that would guarantee transgendered students the right to use whatever bathroom matched their gender identity. President Donald Trump's administration has rescinded that interpretation. The reversal won't change policy everywhere, but it returns to the states and localities the prerogative to shape policy on student bathroom use, at least for now as courts are also examining and ruling on the issue.

Affirmative Action

Affirmative action is the label placed on institutional efforts to diversify by race or gender. Presidents Kennedy and Johnson helped define the term as they developed policy in the hope of creating an equal environment for the races. Both men knew that merely overturning "separate but equal" would not bring true equality. Kennedy issued an executive order to create the Committee on Equal Employment Opportunity and mandated that federal projects "take affirmative action" to ensure hiring free of racial bias. Johnson went a step further in his own executive order requiring federal contractors to "take affirmative action" in hiring prospective minority contractors and employees. President Johnson also said in a speech at Howard University, "You do not take a man who for years has been hobbled by chains, liberate him, bring him to the starting line of a race, saying, 'you are free to compete with all the others,' and still justly believe you have been completely fair."

Seeking Diversity

Civil rights organizations, progressives, and various institutions agree with Kennedy's ideas and Johnson's statements. The federal government, states, colleges, and private companies have echoed these sentiments in their hiring and admissions practices. Yet, affirmative action has been mired in controversy since the term was coined.

Two current schools of thought generally follow a pro- or anti-affirmative action line, though neither willingly accepts those labels. One group believes that our government institutions and society should follow *Brown* and later decisions and be blind to issues of race and gender. Another group, influenced by feminists and civil rights organizations, asks government and the private sector to develop policies that will create parity by elevating those individuals and groups who have been discriminated against in the past. The debate on affirmative action includes Supreme Court justices who insist that the Constitution is colorblind and justices who maintain that it forbids racial classifications only when they are designed to harm minorities, not help them.

These two groups have divergent views on college admissions and hiring practices. Colleges and companies have set aside spots for applicants with efforts to accept or hire roughly the same percent of minorities that exist in a locality or in the nation. Institutions that use such numeric standards refer to these as **targets**, while those opposed call them **quotas**.

Supreme Court and Affirmative Action The issue of affirmative action came to a head in the decision in *Regents of the University of California v. Bakke* (1978). This case addressed the UC-Davis medical school and its admission policy. The school took in 100 applicants annually and had reserved 16 spots for minorities and women. Allan Bakke, a white applicant, was denied admission and sued to contest the policy. He and his lawyers discovered that his test scores and application in general were better than some of the minorities and women who were admitted ahead of him. He argued that the university violated the equal protection clause and denied his admission because of his race.

In this reverse-discrimination case, the Court sided with Bakke in a narrow 5:4 ruling, leaving the public and policymakers wondering what was constitutional and what was not. As far as mandatory quotas are concerned, this case made them unconstitutional. Yet the Court, through its nine different opinions (all justices gave an interpretation), made it clear that the concept of affirmative action was permitted, provided the assisted group had suffered past discrimination and the state has a compelling governmental interest in assisting this group. Clearly, recruitment of particular groups could continue, but government institutions could not be bound by hard and fast numeric quotas.

The ruling was a victory for those who believed in equality of opportunity, but it by no means ended the debate. Since *Bakke*, the Court has upheld a law that set aside 10 percent of federal construction contracts for minority-owned firms. It overturned a similar locally sponsored set-aside policy. Then it upheld a federal policy that guaranteed a preference to minorities applying for broadcast licenses.

Legal scholars and government students alike are confused by this body of law. Quotas have a hard time passing the strict scrutiny test that is applied to them. To give preference, a pattern of discriminatory practices must be proven.

The Court heard two more cases regarding admissions policies from the University of Michigan. The Michigan application process worked on a complex numeric point system that instantly awarded 20 extra points for ethnic minorities including African Americans, Hispanics, and Native Americans. By contrast, an excellent essay was awarded only one point. Though the school did not use a quota system per se, the point breakdown resembled something rather close to what *Bakke* banned. The Court reaffirmed its 1978 stance and made it plain by rejecting the University of Michigan's use of fixed quotas for individual undergraduate applicants, though it upheld the practice for admission to the university's law school. In 2016, the Court ruled race-based admissions at the University of Texas were permissible only under a standard of strict judicial scrutiny.

REFLECT ON THE ESSENTIAL QUESTION

Essential Question: *How have constitutional provisions, the Supreme Court, and citizen-state interactions led to laws and policies that promote equality?* On separate paper, complete a chart like the one below to gather details to answer that question.

Groups Seeking Equality	Constitutional Provisions	Supreme Court	Laws and Policies

affirmative action/334

Brown v. Board of Education of Topeka, Kansas (1954)/305

Civil Rights Act (1875)/302

Civil Rights Act (1957)/309

Civil Rights Act (1964)/312

Civil Rights Cases (1883)/302

Defense of Marriage Act (DOMA)/328

"don't ask, don't tell"/328

Equal Pay Act (1963)/323

equal protection clause/301

Equal Rights Amendment/325

Fifteenth Amendment/301

Fourteenth Amendment/301

freedom-of-choice plans/319

grandfather clause/303

heightened scrutiny test/325

Jim Crow laws/302

Lawrence v. Texas (2003)/327

literacy test/303

majority-minority districts/316

National Association for the Advancement of Colored People (NAACP)/303

National Organization for Women (NOW)/323

Nineteenth Amendment/323

Obergefell v. Hodges (2015)/331

Plessy v. Ferguson (1896)/303

poll taxes/303

preclearance/316

quotas/334

reasonableness standard/325

Regents of the University of California v. Bakke (1978)/334

"separate but equal"/303

strict scrutiny/316

Swann v. Charlotte-Mecklenburg (1971)/321

Thirteenth Amendment/301

Title IX/324

Twenty-Fourth Amendment/315

Voting Rights Act (1965)/315

white flight/306

white primary/303

MULTIPLE-CHOICE QUESTIONS

Questions 1–3 are based on the table on the next page, which comes from the study on racial identification and preference by Kenneth B. Clark and Mamie P. Clark that helped provide support for the *Brown* decision. Among the eight requests made to the African American child participants in the study, this table reports on responses to (1) Give me the doll that you like to play with (or like best); (2) Give me the doll that is a nice doll; (3) Give me the doll that looks bad; and (4) Give me the doll that is a nice color. Review the table and then answer the questions that follow it.

CHOICES OF SUBJECTS AT EACH AGE LEVEL*										
	3 yr.		4 yr.		5 yr.		6 yr.		7 yr.	
Choice	No.	%	No.	%	No.	%	No.	%	No.	%
Request 1 (play with) colored doll	13	42	7	24	12	26	21	29	30	40
white doll	17	55	22	76	34	74	51	71	45	60
Request 2 (nice doll) colored doll	11	36	7	24	13	28	33	46	33	44
white doll	18	58	22	76	33	72	38	53	39	52
Request 3 (looks bad) colored doll	21	68	15	52	36	78	45	63	32	43
white doll	6	19	7	24	5	11	11	15	13	17
Request 4 (nice color) colored doll	12	39	8	28	9	20	31	43	36	48
white doll	18	58	21	72	36	78	40	56	36	48

*Individuals failing to make either choice not included; hence some percentages add to less than 100.

1. Which of the following statements reflects a trend represented in the table?

   (A) When asked which doll looks bad, the older children are more likely to say the colored doll than the younger children.

   (B) In response to most requests, preference for the black doll increases between ages 3 and 4 and then steadily declines.

   (C) In response to most requests, preference for the white doll increases between ages 3 and 4 and then steadily declines.

   (D) When asked which doll they wanted to play with, a higher percentage of 7-year-olds chose the white doll than did the 3-year-olds.

2. Which of the following expresses a reasonable interpretation of a trend in the table?

(A) Seven-year-olds in the study have lower self-esteem than three-year-olds.

(B) Four- and five-year-olds appear to be sensitive to cultural attitudes toward race.

(C) Preschool programs would help African American students integrate well with whites.

(D) Separate black schools might boost the self-esteem of African American students.

3. Which of the following statements from the *Brown* opinion ties most directly to the table?

(A) "Under [*Plessy v. Ferguson*], equality of treatment is accorded when the races are provided substantially equal facilities, even though these facilities be separate."

(B) "The plaintiffs contend that segregated public schools are not 'equal' and cannot be made 'equal,' and that hence they are deprived of the equal protection of the laws.

(C) "The question presented in these cases must be determined, not on the basis of conditions existing when the Fourteenth Amendment was adopted, but in the light of the full development of public education and its present place in American life throughout the Nation."

(D) "To separate [African American children] from others of similar age and qualifications solely because of their race generates a feeling of inferiority as to their status in the community that may affect their hearts and minds in a way unlikely ever to be undone."

Questions 4 and 5 refer to the cartoon below.

Source: Mike Keefe, InToon.com

4. Which of the following best describes the message in the political cartoon?
   (A) Affirmative action should not be allowed in the United States.
   (B) The Supreme Court has limited the way colleges can recruit minorities.
   (C) Republicans practice affirmative action policy, while Democrats do not.
   (D) The Supreme Court refuses to consider the constitutionality of affirmative action policies.

5. Which of the following best explains why the figure holding the scales of justice is blindfolded?
   (A) To show that justice is turning a blind eye to racial discrimination
   (B) To show that justice should be colorblind
   (C) To show that the Court has blinded justice with restrictions
   (D) To show that affirmative actions laws are blindsided by the Court

6. Which of the following is an accurate comparison of the two court cases?

	Brown v. Board of Education	**Roe v. Wade**
(A)	Required all-black schools to have facilities and faculties of the same quality as all-white schools	Brought vocal opposition to abortion and encouraged legislatures to reshape abortion policy
(B)	Required students to be bused	Made abortion illegal in all states
(C)	Concluded that "separate but equal" schools are impossible	Assured a pregnant woman's right to have an abortion in the first trimester
(D)	Upheld the separation of races in public accommodations	Upheld states' police powers to regulate safety, health, and morals.

7. Which of the following comparisons of the 1964 Civil Rights Act and the 1965 Voting Rights Act are accurate?
   (A) One applied to white citizens and one applied to African American citizens.
   (B) One outlawed discrimination in hiring and the other increased African American voter registration and participation.
   (C) One allowed discrimination in certain government agencies and the other made literacy tests easier to pass.
   (D) One has been entirely struck down by the Supreme Court and one has not.

Questions 8–10 refer to the passage below.

> It is now clear that the challenged laws burden the liberty of same-sex couples, and it must be further acknowledged that they abridge central precepts of equality. Here the marriage laws enforced by the respondents are in essence unequal: same-sex couples are denied all the benefits afforded to opposite-sex couples and are barred from exercising a fundamental right. Especially against a long history of disapproval of their relationships, this denial to same-sex couples of the right to marry works a grave and continuing harm. The imposition of this disability on gays and lesbians serves to disrespect and subordinate them.
>
> —Justice Anthony Kennedy, Majority Opinion in
> *Obergefell v. Hodges* (2015)

8. Which statement best summarizes Justice Kennedy's opinion?

(A) Some level of burden on the liberty of same-sex couples is acceptable.

(B) The framers of the Constitution did not support legal marriage of gays and lesbians.

(C) Same-sex couples are unfairly harmed by states' denial of their legal marriage.

(D) Gay couples have the right to all tangible benefits under civil unions but not in marriage.

9. Which of the following constitutional provisions would the author cite to support the opinion?

(A) The equal protection clause of the Fourteenth Amendment

(B) The establishment clause of the First Amendment

(C) The reserved powers clause of the Tenth Amendment

(D) The due process clause of the Fifth Amendment

10. With which of the following statements would supporters of Kennedy's position above be most likely to agree?

(A) Marriage laws are rightfully left to the states to decide.

(B) Gays and lesbians are equal to other people under the law.

(C) Congress should pass a law to protect traditional marriage.

(D) Government should stay out of personal matters.

FREE-RESPONSE QUESTIONS

1. "The white man can lynch and burn and bomb and beat Negroes—that's all right: 'Have patience' . . . 'The customs are entrenched' . . .

'Things are getting better.' . . . .Well, I believe it's a crime for anyone who is being brutalized to continue to accept that brutality without doing something to defend himself. . . .

I tried in every speech I made to clarify my new position regarding white people—I don't speak against the sincere, well-meaning, good white people. . . . I am speaking against and my fight is against the white racists. I firmly believe that Negroes have the right to fight against these racists, by any means that are necessary. . . .

I am for violence if non-violence means we continue postponing a solution to the American black man's problem—just to avoid violence. I don't go for non-violence if it also means a delayed solution. To me a delayed solution is a non-solution."—Malcolm X, from *The Autobiography of Malcolm X* (1965)

After reading the above quotation, respond to A, B, and C below.

(A) Describe an action by a citizen organization that would address the concerns of Malcolm X without the use of violence.

(B) In the context of this passage, explain how the action described in Part A would be affected by the actions Malcolm X recommends.

(C) Explain how Malcolm X's approach reflects the relationship between political behavior and the rule of law.

2. Use the information in the graphic below to respond to A, B, and C below it.

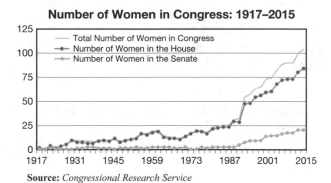

Number of Women in Congress: 1917–2015

Source: *Congressional Research Service*

(A) Describe the data conveyed in the graphic.

(B) Describe a trend conveyed in the graphic, and draw a conclusion about the cause of that trend.

(C) Explain how the information in the graphic demonstrates the impact of the Nineteenth Amendment.

3. In 2013, the Supreme Court ruled on a case involving a white student, Abigail Fisher, who was denied undergraduate admission to the University of Texas. The University of Texas accepts all in-state students who graduate in the upper 10 percent of their class, but for the remainder of the admissions, the university considers race as one factor among many in an effort to reflect the diversity of the population. Fisher was not in the upper 10 percent of her class, and when she was denied admission, she sued the school on the grounds that her constitutional rights were violated because the university used race to consider applicants. The district and circuit courts affirmed the university's policy, so she appealed to the Supreme Court. In *Fisher v. University of Texas* (2013), the Court found that the circuit court had not exercised strict scrutiny and remanded the case. In 2015, the Court heard the case again (*Fisher v. University of Texas II,* 2016) after the lower court, applying strict scrutiny, once again sided with the university. This time the Court upheld the right of the university to use race as one factor in considering admission under strict judicial scrutiny.

   (A) Identify the constitutional provision that is common to both *Brown v. Board of Education* (1954) and *Fisher v. University of Texas II* (2016).

   (B) Based on the constitutional provision identified in part A, explain a difference in the facts of the case between *Fisher v. University of Texas II* and *Brown v. Board of Education* (1954).

   (C) Explain how the ruling in *Fisher v. University of Texas II* relates to the principle of a colorblind Constitution.

4. Develop an argument that explains whether citizen engagement in civil rights matters is a worthwhile effort.

   In your essay you must

   - Articulate a defensible claim or thesis that responds to the prompt and establishes a line of reasoning

   - Support your claim with at least TWO pieces of accurate and relevant information:

     ⬧ At least ONE piece of evidence must come from one of the following foundational documents
       - "Letter from a Birmingham Jail"
       - The Fourteenth Amendment of the Constitution

- Use a second piece of evidence from another foundational document from the list above or from your study of civil rights
- Use reasoning to explain why your evidence supports your claim/thesis
- Respond to an opposing or alternative perspective using refutation, concession, or rebuttal

WRITING: *USE SUBSTANTIVE EXAMPLES*

In your argument essay, use strong, specific examples and put them clearly to use in supporting the claim you assert. For example, if you use "Letter from a Birmingham Jail" as one of your documents, pull from it as many relevant points as you can to make your point. Refer specifically to the parts of the letter that support your argument. Quoting key words from the foundational documents may also add strength to your examples and evidence. You might note, for example, that Dr. King wrote about the "self-purification" necessary to participate in civil disobedience and argue that that process alone adds worth to citizen engagement in civil rights issues.

Source: *Library of Congress*

With the March on Washington, more than 200,000 activists petitioned their government to address injustices and inequalities. In the photo, individuals and organizations surround the Reflecting Pool at the Washington Monument, August 28, 1963.

UNIT 3: Review

Noted groups and individuals have pushed for the civil liberties promised in the Bill of Rights. Though at times states have infringed on free speech, free religion, and rights of the accused, the Supreme Court has generally restored these liberties. This process has occurred on a case-by-case basis via the selective incorporation doctrine. The Court has prevented government censorship, protected people from aggressive police and overzealous school administrators, set standards to allow localities to define public obscenity, and prevented excessive entanglements of church and state.

Women, African Americans, and other ethnic and political minorities have pushed for fairness and equality because they were overlooked at the U.S. founding and by state and federal governments during the decades that followed. The Bill of Rights, later amendments, and subsequent laws were meant to afford these groups and individuals real justice and freedoms. Brave, principled leaders and organized groups had to press the government to fully deliver these.

The Supreme Court's evolving interpretation of the Fourteenth Amendment's equal protection clause eventually required states to treat citizens equally. From *Brown v. Board of Education* to the current debate about affirmative action, civil rights have been on the front burner of public policy. Women's rights came partially with the ratification of the Nineteenth Amendment in 1920 but more fully after Congress mandated equal pay and a fair footing in college. Gays have successfully sought to serve openly in the military and have won the right to marry.

THINK AS A POLITICAL SCIENTIST: *APPLY DISCIPLINARY THEORIES AND CONCEPTS IN RESEARCHING A CIVIL RIGHTS ORGANIZATION*

Select a notable civil rights or civil liberties organization.

- Find the organization's official website. Read the "About" and/ or "History" pages. What issues are front and center on its agenda today?

- Find historic or recent primary sources about your organization. Use digital databases and national online newspapers.

- Consider your sources and analyze the evidence. How does the organization gather and mobilize members? How does the organization interact with Congress, state legislatures, and elected officials? What court cases, if any, did you learn about?

- Present your findings in a short paper that explains the group's activity, assesses its effectiveness, and shows your understanding of government and politics.

Review Learning Objectives

As you review Unit Three, be sure you can complete the following learning objectives. Page numbers are provided to help you locate the necessary information to fulfill the learning objective.

UNIT THREE LEARNING OBJECTIVES	
LOR-2.A: Explain how the U.S. Constitution protects individual liberties and rights.	Pages 234–238
LOR-2.B: Describe the rights protected in the Bill of Rights.	Pages 27, 234–235
LOR-2.C: Explain the extent to which the Supreme Court's interpretation of the First and Second Amendments reflects a commitment to individual liberty.	Pages 239–268
LOR-2.D: Explain how the Supreme Court has attempted to balance claims of individual freedom with laws and enforcement procedures that promote public order and safety.	Pages 239–242, 248–252, 290–293
LOR-3.A: Explain the implications of the doctrine of selective incorporation.	Pages 236–238
LOR-3.B: Explain the extent to which states are limited by the due process clause from infringing upon individual rights.	Pages 276–290
PRD-1.A: Explain how constitutional provisions have supported and motivated social movements.	Pages 300–302, 303-312, 323
PMI-3.A: Explain how the government has responded to social movements.	Pages 311–322, 323–324
CON-6.A: Explain how the Supreme Court has at times allowed the restriction of the civil rights of minority groups and at other times has protected those rights.	Pages 303–307, 334–335

Review the following foundational documents, Supreme Court cases, and political science disciplinary practices and reasoning processes as well.

UNIT THREE FOUNDATIONAL DOCUMENTS	
Fourteenth Amendment of the Constitution—This amendment helped motivate social change and was the basis for civil rights and incorporation of some amendments from the Bill of Rights.	Pages 236-238, 300–303, 639
"Letter from a Birmingham Jail"—Dr. King's reply to the white clergy of Birmingham, which makes the case for civil disobedience	Pages 309–311, 670–680

UNIT THREE SUPREME COURT CASES	
Engel v. Vitale (1962)—School-sponsored religious activities violate the establishment clause.	Pages 254–256
Wisconsin v. Yoder (1972)—Requirements that Amish students attend school past eighth grade violate the free exercise clause.	Pages 257–260
Tinker v. Des Moines Independent Community School District (1969)—Students in public schools are allowed symbolic speech.	Pages 243–246

UNIT THREE SUPREME COURT CASES	
Schenck v. United States (1919)—Speech representing "a clear and present danger" is not protected.	Pages 240–241
New York Times Co. v. United States (1971)—The government cannot exercise prior restraint.	Pages 250–252
McDonald v. Chicago (2010)—The Second Amendment's right to bear arms applies to the states as well through the Fourteenth Amendment.	Pages 264–266
Roe v. Wade (1973)—The right of privacy extends to a woman's decision to have an abortion depending on the state of the pregnancy and health considerations.	Pages 288–290
Gideon v. Wainwright (1963)—Poor people are guaranteed the right to an attorney.	Pages 284–286
Brown v. Board of Education of Topeka, Kansas (1954)—Race-based school segregation violate the Fourteenth Amendment's equal protection clause.	Pages 305–307

UNIT THREE POLITICAL SCIENCE DISCIPLINARY PRACTICES AND REASONING PROCESSES	
Explain Reasoning, Similarities, and Differences in Supreme Court Cases —*Schenck v. United States* —*New York Times v. United States* —*Engel v. Vitale* —*Roe v. Wade*	Page 241 Page 252 Page 256 Page 290
Explain Complex Similarities and Differences—*Tinker v. Des Moines Independent Community School District*	Page 246
Understanding Opposing Views —*Wisconsin v. Yoder* —*McDonald v. Chicago*	Page 260 Page 266
Interpret Supreme Court Cases —*Snyder v. Phelps* —*Brown v. Board of Education of Topeka, Kansas*	Page 259 Page 307
Analyze and Interpret Quantitative Data on African American Suffrage	Page 317

UNIT THREE CONTEMPORARY ISSUES AND POLICY	
Policy Matters: Recent State Policy and Second Amendment Rights	Pages 267–268
Policy Matters: Policy and Citizen-State Interactions	Pages 308–309

UNIT THREE WRITING	
Use Concession	Page 275
Budget Your Time	Page 299
Use Substantive Examples	Page 343

UNIT 4: American Political Ideologies and Beliefs

Chapter 10 *Citizen Beliefs and Public Opinion Polls*

Chapter 11 *Political Ideologies and Policy*

What the public thinks and how that thinking is conveyed to government officials are factors in shaping public policies. Professionals try to measure public opinion for a variety of reasons, using a method that makes the results as accurate as possible. Analysts and citizens alike should consider the legitimacy of a poll as much as its general finding, because if its method is faulty, its findings will be as well.

Public opinion changes, but the factors that help determine public opinion remain fairly constant. Voters' backgrounds, professions, and a range of demographic traits all have an impact on their political opinions. The family has the largest impact, since it is an early source of political information and understanding.

Public opinion and diverse political ideologies all have an influence on policy debates and choices. Liberal, conservative, and other political ideologies compete in such areas as monetary and fiscal policy, social equality and opportunity, and civil liberties to shape policy. **BIG IDEA:** Using various types of analyses, political scientists measure how U.S. political behavior, attitudes, ideologies, and institutions are shaped by a number of factors over time.

Enduring Understandings: American Political Ideologies and Beliefs

MPA-1: Citizen beliefs about government are shaped by the intersection of demographics, political culture, and dynamic social change.

MPA-2: Public opinion is measured through scientific polling, and the results of public opinion polls influence public policies and institutions.

PMI-4: Widely held political ideologies shape policy debates and choices in American policies.

Source: *AP® United States Government and Politics Course and Exam Description*

10

Citizen Beliefs and Public Opinion Polls

"Without common ideas, there is no common action, and without common action men still exist, but a social body does not. Thus in order that there be society, and all the more, that this society prosper, it is necessary that all the minds of the citizens always be brought together and held together by some principle ideas."

—Alexis de Tocqueville, *Democracy in America,* 1835

Essential Question: How do demographics, political culture, and dynamic social change shape citizen beliefs about government, and how are those beliefs measured?

Citizen beliefs include a range of opinions that help guide political actions and shape public policy. Some views amount to a clear consensus. For example, nearly everyone agrees children should be educated and that the government should punish violent criminals. However, Americans also disagree on aspects related to those issues. For example, exactly what topics should children learn? What is the appropriate punishment for premeditated murder? Policymakers try to answer these questions in a society of diverse and constantly shifting views. The framers built processes into the Constitution so that different interpretations of the core values Americans share can be debated and shaped into policy that represents the divergent views of Americans. The most effective way to reach consensus on these issues is for citizens to put forth and debate their ideas in a civil and respectful way.

Core Values and Attitudes

Citizens' attitudes toward government and toward one another are influenced by the way citizens interpret core American values. American citizens, coming from a range of backgrounds and experiences, have widely different views of how government ought to govern. Even when citizens generally agree on the basic premise of a governing value, they often disagree on how public officials should address it, how to define the terms of the debate, and how government should fund it. For example, most citizens believe that government should provide an economic safety net for citizens, some kind of welfare system that will help those unfortunate people who have lost their jobs, fallen to ill health, or found themselves without shelter. Yet citizens differ greatly on what defines "poor," at what point the government should reach out and help people, and what type of help that recipients should be given.

In a similar way, nearly all Americans oppose murder, and all want to correctly identify the killer before punishment is administered. In other words, we agree that murder should be criminal and all defendants should receive a fair trial. But we differ noticeably on how government might prosecute the accused and what punishment a guilty defendant will receive.

You'll notice an "either or," or maybe even a linear spectrum, to the ideological views outlined above. From the perspective of some citizens, the threshold below which people will qualify for welfare is lower than what others may define. Many of these same people favor hard punishment for criminals. People at this end of the spectrum are usually known as **conservative**.

In contrast, other groups may want government to provide welfare to people at a higher, though still impoverished, income level. These same people may desire leniency from the government on punishments. People at this other end of the spectrum are usually known as **liberal**. (See pages 353–355 for more on the political spectrum.)

Relying on this linear scale to discuss citizens' views oversimplifies the array of viewpoints, but the scale can be useful for discussion. No matter where on the scale people's views might lie, Americans also have strongly held common views that form the country's *political culture*—the set of attitudes that shape political behavior. The cornerstones of this political culture are individualism, equal opportunity, free enterprise, and the rule of law.

Individualism

From the days of self-reliant colonists and rugged settlers in the West to today's competitive entrepreneurs, **individualism**—a belief in the fundamental worth and importance of the individual—has been a value of American social and political life. It is rooted in the Enlightenment philosophy that helped shape American government—the "inalienable rights" of individuals precede government; they are not bestowed by government. Individual liberties are enshrined in and protected by the Bill of Rights. Individualism is the value that encourages people to pursue their own best interest.

Individualism, however, is in tension with other social values Americans share, such as respect for the common good and protection of the public interest. Alexis de Tocqueville warned about the dangers of individualism in his treatise on the early United States. He wrote that individualism "disposes each citizen to isolate himself from the mass of his fellows and withdraw into the circle of family and friends." If everyone sought only his or her best interest, society as a whole would become fractured.

The principle of *enlightened* self-interest, the belief that one's own interests are best served when the good of the group is also considered, balances the drive of individualism with the realities of social life. American individualism seeks the freedom to fulfill one's own promise while also enjoying the benefits and protections of living in society.

Different interpretations of individualism create a spectrum of views between self-centered individualism, which places the individual's interest above the group's interest and wants little interference from the government, to enlightened self-interest, which sacrifices some individual freedom for the greater good and expects the government to help promote the public good.

Equality of Opportunity

Thomas Jefferson included the line "all men are created equal" in the Declaration of Independence. The purpose of the line was not to suggest that every person was an absolute equal to every other in ability or character, or any other subjective measure. Rather, the purpose of the line was to emphasize the equal rights of people to pursue life, liberty, and happiness. Yet not until the ratification of the Fourteenth Amendment in 1868 was there a national constitutional demand for the state governments to guarantee the equal protection of citizens. In the Progressive Era (1890–1920), as government began to act to make things fair and to protect citizens from the harmful effects of industrialization and unfair business practices, President Theodore Roosevelt spoke of practical equality for all and declared, "[E]very man will have a fair chance to make of himself all that in him lies; to reach the highest point to which his capacities . . . can carry him." He also pointed out the practical result that would enhance our nation, "[E]quality of opportunity means that the commonwealth will get from every citizen the highest service of which he is capable."

The equal protection clause of the Fourteenth Amendment (in bold) guarantees that people in similar conditions in every state will be treated equally under the law.

All persons born or naturalized in the United States, and subject to the jurisdiction thereof, are citizens of the United States and of the State wherein they reside. No State shall make or enforce any law which shall abridge the privileges or immunities of citizens of the United States; **nor shall any State** deprive any person of life, liberty, or property, without due process of law; nor **deny to any person within its jurisdiction the equal protection of the laws.**

Unequal treatment, however, was not limited to the states. The federal government also had discriminatory practices at one time. The federal government provided remedies to redress these and state laws that resulted in unequal treatment. Title VII of the Civil Rights Act of 1964, for example, prohibits employment discrimination based on race, sex, national origin, color and religion. In the 1960s, Congress created an agency to combat discrimination in hiring or firing of employees. The Equal Employment Opportunity Commission investigates complaints of discrimination in job termination or refusal to hire, based on race, sex, and other Title VII criteria.

Citizens who debate the practical side of equality of opportunity may ask, "Doesn't every person born these days have the same chance at greatness and wealth in America if he or she makes the right decisions?" Others will agree that the occasional rags-to-riches story is impressive but not always possible without some level of government support for advancement. Still others will argue that it is fine for the government to step in and, by law and policy, influence or redirect the natural forces of society and the market. Despite these different viewpoints, however, nearly all agree that equality of opportunity is a shared value.

Free Enterprise

Most colonists came to America for economic reasons: jobs, opportunity, or a greater distance from a government that might inhibit economic success. The same year the colonists declared independence, Scottish economist and philosopher Adam Smith wrote *The Wealth of Nations*, an examination of government's role in the economy. Smith posited that the state (meaning government in general) should be primarily concerned with protecting its people from invasion and with maintaining law and order and should only intervene in the natural flow of human economic interaction to protect the people. Businesses and merchants would succeed or fail based on their decisions and those of the consumer. Government should take a *laissez-faire* ("let it be") approach, and an "invisible hand"—guided by the interactions of producers and consumers—would regulate over time. This approach to the economy is called **free enterprise**. Those who adhere to this approach are known as free-market advocates.

Smith would no doubt take issue with today's government-required overtime pay and limits on factory emissions. But times have changed. Today, even most strict free-market advocates believe in a minimum wage and some controls to keep the air we breathe clean.

Through the Progressive Era (1890–1920) and New Deal (1933–1937), the state and federal governments began to regulate industry, minimum wage, child labor, and fairness in the workplace. Labor unions organized to press companies and the government to address their concerns. Free-market advocates challenged those plans and suggested that the invisible hand of supply, demand, and independent citizen decisions should work things out.

In the last 100 years, while free enterprise is still a driving ideal, government involvement in the marketplace has increased to protect workers or guarantee economic successes overall. The U.S. Supreme Court, too, has shaped much law that governs corporations and how they act, as well as legal expectations and freedoms in the workplace. But each time government debates a new business or economic regulation, strong voices on both sides suggest a move in one direction or the other.

Conservatives tend to want government to stay out of the way and want fewer burdensome regulations on businesses. For these reasons, small businesses owners and corporate leaders tend to vote with the Republican Party. Republican President Donald Trump issued a number of executive orders rolling back regulation on business, and in 2017, the Republican-dominated Congress passed a tax bill that greatly reduced corporate taxes. In contrast, liberals tend to see government regulation as necessary to assure fairness and safety, and labor union leaders and hourly workers tend to side with the Democratic Party. The Republican-backed tax law of 2017 passed without a single Democratic vote.

Rule of Law

Every four years, the newly elected (or reelected) president is required to make the following promise before taking office: "I do solemnly swear (or affirm) that I will faithfully execute the Office of President of the United States, and will to the best of my Ability, preserve, protect and defend the Constitution of the United States." In fact it is the Constitution itself that spells out this requirement (Article II, Section 1, Clause 8). This oath assures that even the president, the highest office holder in the land, must obey and protect the laws of the nation. **Rule of law**—the principle of a government that establishes laws that apply equally to all members of society and prevents the rule and whims of leaders who see themselves as above the law—was a cornerstone of Enlightenment political thought. John Adams cited Enlightenment philosophers when pointing to the British injustices leading to the Revolution: "They [the philosophers] define a republic to be a government of laws, and not of men."

The rule of law assures stability and certainty. In many foreign governments today, whatever dictator happens to be in charge will make most decisions in the government, regardless of prior policy, including when and even if there will be elections. In contrast, the U.S. Constitution dictates a presidential election every four years under the rule of law, and thus the United States has never missed an election and has never had a serious problem with the transfer of power.

At times, however, government officials disregard the rule of law for personal gain, corruption, or power. Fortunately, there are systems in place to address or reverse such disregard for law. Public records of government spending, regular auditing of the public purse, independent law enforcement, a free press, and public opinion all preserve the rule of law.

Sometimes the law is not followed for the sake of leniency. A traffic cop might let a young motorist go without a speeding ticket because the infraction was small. A president might provide a new interpretation for how the government treats immigrants brought as young children into the United States illegally versus adults who entered the United States illegally. Our laws are written in language that has evolving meaning and interpretation.

Limited Government

American individuality and the story of the nation's birth after a battle with an over-reaching government have ingrained in citizens a desire to have a **limited government**—one kept under control by law and by checks and balances and the separation of powers. The Constitution is filled with as many devices and designs to prevent government action as to empower it. The Bill of Rights is nothing more than a list of rights the national government cannot take away. Citizens of all political viewpoints agree that none should suffer from the heavy hand of government.

Both parties have embraced the idea of a limited government. The Democrats for nearly a century represented the party of limited government. After a transformation through the Progressive Era and New Deal and a tipping point with President Lyndon Johnson's Great Society (1964–1965), Democrats became more accepting of liberal government action for the greater good. Republicans, once the party that used the federal government to free the slaves, to build railroads, and to create state colleges, now desire less government involvement in business and other matters.

Limited government is key to civil liberties, another arena in which public opinion is divided. Limited government is at issue when people grapple with such questions as "When can government come into your home? When can it regulate affairs related to church and morality?" among others.

Political Ideologies

People take positions on public issues and develop a political viewpoint on how government should act in line with their ideology. An **ideology** is a comprehensive and mutually consistent set of ideas. When there are two or more sides to an issue, voters tend to fall into different camps, either a conservative or a liberal ideology or philosophy. However, this diverse nation has a variety of ideologies that overlap one another. (You will read more about political ideologies in Chapter 11.)

Regardless of ideology, for example, most Americans agree that the government should regulate dangerous industries, educate children at public expense, and protect free speech, at least to a degree. Everyone wants a strong economy and national security. These are **valence issues**—concerns or policies that are viewed in the same way by people with a variety of ideologies. When political candidates debate valence issues, "the dialogue can be like a debate between the nearly identical Tweedledee and Tweedledum," says congressional elections expert Paul Herrnson.

Wedge issues, in contrast, sharply divide the public. These include the issues of abortion and the 2003 invasion and later occupation of Iraq. The more divisive issues tend to hold a high **saliency**, or importance, to an individual or a group. For senior citizens, for example, questions about reform of the Social Security system hold high saliency. For people eighteen to twenty years old, the relative lack of job opportunities may have high saliency, since their unemployment rate is higher than that of older age groups.

The Liberal-Conservative Spectrum

Political scientists use the terms *liberal* and *conservative*, as well as "left" and "right," to label each end of an ideological spectrum. Most Americans are **moderate** and never fall fully into one camp or the other. Many others may think conservatively on some issues and have liberal beliefs on others.

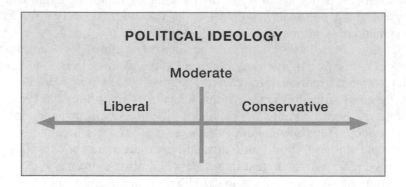

POLITICAL IDEOLOGY

Moderate

Liberal   Conservative

The two major political parties—Democrats and Republicans—tend to embody the liberal and the conservative ideology, respectively. Yet labeling the two parties as liberal or conservative is an oversimplification. Some self-described conservatives want nothing to do with the Republican Party, and many Democrats dislike the "liberal" label.

The meaning of the terms *liberal* and *conservative* has changed over history. In early America, a "liberal" government was one that did little. Thomas Jefferson believed in a high degree of liberty, declaring that a government that governs best is one that governs least. With this statement, Jefferson described the government's liberal approach toward the people, allowing citizen freedom, a free flow of ideas, free markets, fewer laws, and fewer restrictions. This understanding of the word continued into the late nineteenth century.

In the Progressive Era, the federal government expanded its activity, going outside the confines of traditional government. In the 1930s, Democratic President Franklin Delano Roosevelt (FDR) proposed a "liberal" plan for emergency legislation. His New Deal agenda was new and revolutionary. The government took on new responsibilities in ways it never had. The government acted in a liberal way, less constrained by tradition or limitations that guided earlier governments. Since the 1930s, the term *liberal* has usually meant being open to allowing the government to flexibly expand beyond established constraints.

The term *conservative* describes those who believe in following tradition and having reverence for authority. Modern-day conservatives often invoke Jefferson and argue that government should do less and thus allow people more freedom. Arizona Senator Barry Goldwater, the 1964 Republican presidential nominee, embraced the conservative label and published a book, *The Conscience of a Conservative*, in 1960. He and much of his party believed that Roosevelt's party had unwisely altered the role of government. Goldwater and his party wanted less economic regulation and more responsibility on the citizenry. Many conservatives call themselves "fiscal conservatives" because they want to see less taxation and less government spending overall.

Since FDR's presidency and Goldwater's nomination, these political terms have further evolved, and now it is difficult to know exactly what they mean. Roosevelt would likely not support some of the more liberal goals of the Democratic Party today, and Goldwater, in retirement, supported Democratic President Bill Clinton's initiatives to open the door for members of the LGBT community in the military. Additionally, an array of cultural and social issues that came to the forefront in the 1960s and 1970s changed the dynamic between those who consider themselves conservative and those who consider themselves liberal, and thus also changed the meaning of the terms.

Traditional Christian voters, family values groups, and others who oppose abortion and same-sex marriage and support prayer in school have adopted the conservative label and have aligned themselves with the Republican Party. However, policies that restrict abortion, censor controversial material in books or magazines, or seek to more tightly define marriage actually require more, not less, law and regulation. For supporters of these policies, then, the conservative label is not necessarily accurate. People who believe in more regulation on industry, stronger gun control, and the value of diversity are generally seen as liberal. But when government acts to establish these goals, Jefferson might say, it is not necessarily acting liberally in relation to the rights of the people.

Off the Line

If you have trouble finding the precise line between liberal and conservative, you are not alone. Cleavages, or gaps, in public opinion make understanding where the public stands on issues even more difficult. Few people, even regular party members, agree with every conservative or every liberal idea. Many people simply do not fall on the linear continuum diagrammed on page 354 but rather align themselves with one of several other notable political philosophies: **libertarian, populist**, or **progressive**.

Libertarians Libertarian voters generally oppose government intervention or regulation. As their name suggests, they have a high regard for civil liberties, those rights outlined in the Bill of Rights. They oppose censorship, want lower taxes, and dislike government-imposed morality. Though a small Libertarian Party exists, more citizens claim the libertarian (small "l") label than formally belong to the party. Libertarian-minded citizens can be found in both the Republican and Democratic parties. In short, libertarians are conservative on fiscal or economic issues, such as government spending or raising the minimum wage, while they tend to be liberal on moral or social issues. Most libertarians are pro-choice on abortion and support the equal treatment of LGBT persons. As Nick Gillespie and Matt Welch write of libertarians in their book, *Declaration of Independents*, "We believe that you should be able to think what you want, live where you want, trade for what you want, eat what you want, smoke what you want, and wed whom you want."

Populists Populists have a very different profile. They generally attend a Protestant church and follow fundamental Christian ideas: love thy neighbor, contribute to charity, and follow a strict moral code. More populists can be found in the South and Midwest than along each American coast. They tend to come from working-class families.

Many saw Donald Trump as a populist candidate. Although Trump promised as a candidate to "Make America Great Again" for the hard-working middle class and to "drain the swamp" of Washington insiders, many believe his 2017 tax plan and other polices in his agenda may in fact have helped the rich at the expense of poor.

Progressives The Progressive Movement emerged in cities from roots in the Republican Party. It peaked in the United States in the early 1900s when reformers challenged government corruption that ran counter to the values of equality, individualism, democracy, and advancement. At that time, the Republican Party split into its two wings: conservative and progressive. Progressives criticized traditional political establishments that concentrated too much power in one place, such as government and business. Modern progressives are aligned with labor unions. They believe in workers' rights over corporate rights, and they believe the wealthier classes should pay a much larger percentage of taxes than they currently do.

With some variation, about 40 to 50 percent of America consider themselves moderate, nearly 30 percent consider themselves conservative, and about 20 percent consider themselves liberal. A poll that asks voters if they are "moderate," "conservative," or "liberal" have starkly different responses from one that asks if respondents are "Democrat," "Republican," or "independent."

A 2016 Pew Research survey found that 32 percent claimed to be Democrats, 32 percent called themselves Republicans, and 34 percent considered themselves independent. In answering a parallel question, only 34 percent considered themselves "strongly partisan." Many people's views fall between these ideologies and between the two major political parties

Cultural Factors, Political Socialization, and Attitudes

If you try to pinpoint yourself with an X on the ideological spectrum shown on page 354, where would you fall? Would you be on the continuum at all, or would you fall into one of the other ideologies you read about? If you are not sure, think of someone you know, maybe a parent or good friend, and decide where that person might fall. Just how did you or the person you chose arrive at that point on the continuum? What influences or factors caused you, or anyone, to think about politics and policy in particular ways?

Political socialization is the process by which one develops political beliefs. The process begins as soon as one is old enough to start forming opinions on public matters, and it never really ends. Attending college, getting married, purchasing a home, and having children can have an enormous impact on one's thinking. Even career politicians whose positions are well

Source: *Getty Images*
Family is a key influence in shaping political development.

known modify or switch somewhat due to an evolving world with countless circumstances. Every constituent and political participant is affected by a variety of influences that assist in political development.

Family

Family has long been regarded as the biggest influence on one's political socialization. As children begin to inquire about world events or local issues, parents begin to explain these. Most moms or dads have some degree of opinion that will likely influence their children. At the dinner table, families discuss "kitchen table politics," considering events currently happening and what impact they might have on the family.

Children can differ from their parents in political opinions. Teenagers who strongly differ from their parents in nonpolitical ways may find themselves adopting far different political views as well. Moms and dads may differ from each other. Younger voters vote less frequently than older voters and, not surprisingly, have less consistent views. Citizens aged 18–24 are not solidly aligned with their parents in great numbers, yet those who hold strong opinions do not veer far from their parents. Studies show that among high school seniors, only about 10 percent identified with the party opposite one or both of their parents.

The children's magazine *Weekly Reader* conducted an unscientific poll on presidential elections from 1956 through 2008. Responding children generally answered as one or both of their parents would have, and thus the massive sample became reflective of the parent population at large. The *Weekly Reader* presidential poll failed to accurately predict the outcome just one time in its history.

How do these children differ from their elders once they reach adulthood or after they have voted in a few elections? About 50 percent of adults reject or misperceive their mothers' and fathers' **party identification.** Most who differ from their parents proclaim political independence instead of aligning with the opposite party.

School and College

Both teachers and peer groups can have a large impact on student beliefs. In school, topics come up in classes that may allow a teacher to influence students politically, intentionally or not. There is no solid evidence that the K–12 experience makes one more conservative or liberal.

College campuses are places where professional scholars and students can discuss new ideas and explore revolutionary theories. Colleges have more flexible rules than the average high school. College deans and professors encourage a free flow of ideas in classroom discussion. Nonetheless business, economics, and engineering majors tend to be Republican while students majoring in English and humanities tend to be Democrats.

From the 1950s to the early 1980s, fewer high school graduates attended college than do so today. In fact, in 1968 only about 13 percent of Americans had a four-year college degree. In 2012, more than 33 percent of Americans aged 24–29 had attended college and earned a degree. Because such large numbers of people attend college and because so many post-college forces impact one's beliefs, it is not possible to say that people with an undergraduate degree tend to adhere to one particular ideology.

Graduate school, however, is a different story. When researchers examine voters with advanced degrees—people with master's and doctoral degrees— they find they more frequently vote Democratic and hold more liberal attitudes, although the highest percentage (46.1%) consider themselves moderate, according to a 2007 study by academics Neil Gross and Solon Simmons.

Peers

Race and ethnic heritage are other factors that play a major role in determining one's outlook on the world and how one votes. African Americans have closely aligned with the Democratic Party since 1932 and even more strongly since the Civil Rights Movement of the 1960s. Hispanics, in recent years, have cast more Democratic than Republican votes, usually by 55 to 65 percent. Asian Americans vote more often with the conservative Republican Party, though exit polls in 2016 showed Asian American support for Hillary Clinton. New American citizens or voters with strong ties to a foreign country will consider their votes in the context of their culture or how an issue might affect the relationship between the United States and their country of origin.

Media

As they have spread to so many aspects of daily life, the media have a significant influence on political socialization. In fact, young people spend so much time in front of a screen—on their computers, phones, and other digital devices—that they spend less time with their family members, and for this reason the influence of the family on political socialization may be weakening somewhat. Young people are exposed to a great deal of political information and opinion through their exposure to media. Engaging with that content helps young people form their political identity. They follow politicians they admire and join groups that plan citizen events. As in face-to-face experiences, peer influence is strong in social media, and through online discussions with their friends and family, young people develop their viewpoints.

Media are also influential in political socialization because of the way they depict politics and politicians through both news coverage and fictional television shows that are politically oriented. Even nonpolitical figures in the media—fictional characters with a strong sense of individualism, for example, or real-life people whose acts of bravery or self-sacrifice (or cowardice and greed, on the other side of the coin)—both reflect and help shape political and social views. (For more on the media as a linkage institution, see Chapter 16.)

Social Environments

A person's social environments beyond family and schools also influence political socialization. Two types of environments are especially important: religious institutions and civic institutions.

Religious Institutions Churches and other places of worship influence individuals' political thought. The National Election Study estimates that 33 percent of Americans attend church on a weekly or near-weekly basis. Churches are more ideological and convey a more coherent philosophy than does a typical school. There are so many different churches, religions, and sects in this nation that there is no way to say how religion in general influences where the average voter lies on the political spectrum. However, people who attend church are more likely than those who don't to vote or participate in politics in other ways.

Specific religious affiliations, though, can be directly tied to a political stance. Fundamentalists and Evangelical Christians have a strong political presence in the South and somewhat in the Midwest. Fundamentalists believe in a literal interpretation of the Holy Bible. Evangelicals promote the Christian faith. Both tend to take conservative positions and vote Republican. Catholics have traditionally voted with the Democratic Party, though their vote is less attached to Democratic candidates today than it was in earlier years. Jews make up a small part of the national electorate and tend to vote for Democrats.

Civic Institutions If you are a Girl Scout, Boy Scout, an athlete on a neighborhood team, or a volunteer at a hospital, you are part of a civic institution. Civic institutions make up civil society—the nongovernmental, non-business, and voluntary sector of social life. Some civic institutions—such as groups with extreme political views—bring only like-minded people together, while other civic institutions bring together people from a variety of backgrounds and viewpoints and help them learn how to bridge or work around their differences. Both types influence political socialization: one reinforces already held beliefs while the other socializes a person to accept diversity.

Location

Geographic location plays a key role in the way people think or approach certain issues. For example, for a century after the Civil War, the most identifiable Democratic region was the South. The party went through a long- term metamorphosis that shifted that affiliation (see page 468). A close look at Electoral College results from a recent election will give you some indication where the two parties, and thus the two ideologies, are strong or weak. The candidate with the most votes in each state received the electoral votes for that state.

THINK AS A POLITICAL SCIENTIST: *ANALYZE AND INTERPRET VISUAL INFORMATION*

When you analyze visual information, begin by identifying the topic. In certain visuals, you may also need to identify the perspective. Political cartoons, for example, will always convey the cartoonists' point of view. Maps, on the other hand, tend to be informational. Understanding the information in a map requires understanding the map's key. The key includes visual symbols—colors, bars, and icons, for example—and an explanation of what they represent on the map. Analyzing information on a political map requires explaining how the elements of the map illustrate or relate to political principles, institutions, processes, and behavior.

Once you can explain those ideas, you can then take a closer look to interpret the information. When you interpret a political map, you explain the *implications* of the map's information in relation to political principles, institutions, processes, and behaviors. Identifying trends and patterns will often help you see those implications.

ELECTORAL COLLEGE 2016

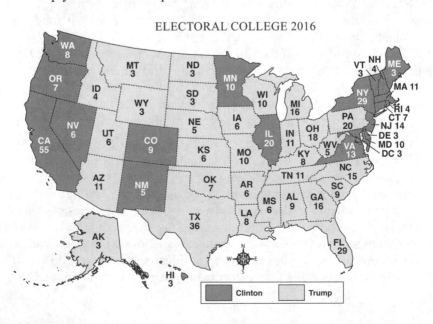

In the Northeast, Democrats dominate and more liberal policies prevail: higher tax rates, for example, fund more services, such as public transportation. Vermont and Massachusetts were among the first states to legalize civil unions and same-sex marriage. New York has followed. Democrats dominate the congressional delegations from New England, New York, and New Jersey. California and other western states also lean Democratic with liberal philosophies, having a strong concern for the environment and a tolerance for diverse lifestyles.

The South is more influenced by conservative Christian values than are the Northeast and West. Southern states contain higher percentages of gun ownership than in other regions and are less friendly to organized labor. The South is more religious than other parts of the country. Church attendance is higher, and voters are decidedly more Protestant. Roughly 76 percent of the South is Protestant versus 49 percent for the remainder of the nation. There is also a high concern for issues related to farming and agriculture.

Republicans have enjoyed southern majorities in the last several national elections, but there are still many southern voters who remain Democrat, reflecting generations of party loyalty and the growth of southern cities. The working-class southerner may side with the Democratic Party on economic issues such as worker pay and employee benefits, but these same working-class voters want tighter immigration enforcement, and they tend to vote with traditional values in mind.

Shifting Influences on Political Socialization

Culture and demographics are fairly stable influences on political socialization. Changes, however, can also have an influence on political socialization. These changes can be in society as a whole as a result of dynamic social change brought on by major political or social events, and they can also be within a person as an individual grows and changes through the lifecycle.

Influence of Major Political Events

"Where were you when you heard that President Kennedy had been shot?" is a question most people of school age or older in 1963 can answer without a second thought. Such an event has a lasting impact on a person's absorption of political culture. Kennedy's assassination was one of an unfortunate number of assassinations during the 1960s: presidential candidate Robert Kennedy, brother of the slain President Kennedy; civil rights leaders Medgar Evers, Malcolm X, and Martin Luther King Jr. were also gunned down. The same decade became known for protests—of racial segregation and discrimination and also of the United States involvement in the conflict in Vietnam and the draft that forced young men to defend the United States. Mass protests—marches on Washington and around the country—were a feature of the political culture of the time and influenced the political socialization of both participants and observers as an active democracy engaged members of society over life and death matters. Challenging the government became a political norm, and people tended to feel they had the power to bring about social changes through their actions.

In contrast, those who endured the economic hardships of the Great Depression (1929–1939) lived in an era in which many people had a favorable attitude toward government involvement in social life. President Franklin D. Roosevelt's New Deal put people back to work by creating government jobs related to infrastructure (roads, canals, railroads) and even the arts. Social Security provided support for seniors and lifted many members of that age group out of poverty. These events influenced political socialization—in this case advancing trust in the government and support for the role of government in providing a social safety net.

Each generation has its own political events that bring about dynamic social change. As the Depression waned, the United States became involved in World War II. The war brought the nation together against fascism, creating a sense of united purpose and a belief in the reliability of the government. Women entered the workforce to help industrial output of needed war materials and in so doing redefined the role of women in society and helped shape political attitudes about gender.

Influence of Globalization

Globalization is the process of an ever-expanding and increasingly interactive world economy. However, globalization has an impact beyond the economy. The political culture of the United States has both influenced and been influenced by the values of other countries as a result of globalization.

U.S. Influence on Other Countries The United States is the dominant economic power affecting globalization, with U.S. businesses and products spread throughout the world. For example, American film, television, commercials, streaming content, music, and video games are popular throughout the world. These products reflect American values, such as individualism and equality of opportunity, and consumers in foreign countries, even those with political cultures very different from that of the United States, can be influenced by these values. That influence may heighten tension between the American values and local values. For example, in countries where women do not have social or legal equality, American movies and television shows portraying women as equals clash with local values. In some places, that clash has led to the weakening of certain cultural values and the adoption of more Western values. In other cases, however, that clash has led to a strengthening of local cultures that do not want to see their cultural ideals become subsumed into a dominant world culture.

In general, however, U.S. influence in the world is seen as "democratizing." The more people in other countries are exposed to the United States political culture, the more they may wish to have a democratic political culture themselves.

100 Largest Companies in the World By Country

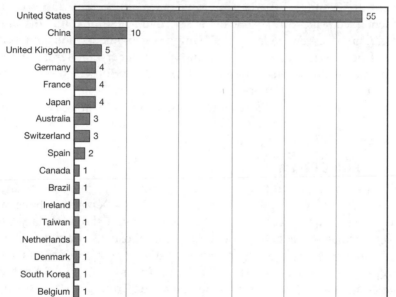

Source: *Bloomberg and PwC analysis*

As you analyze and interpret this graph, consider its possible limitations. What other information might help put these figures into perspective?

Influence of Other Countries on the United States Although most of the globalization influence flows from the United States to other countries, through globalization and the immigration it encourages, the United States also is exposed to values from other parts of the world. The nation's diversity has increased as a result of globalization. Professionals and other workers from all parts of the world bring their political and cultural ideas with them, and as they engage with American society, they exert influence. People from Asian countries, for example, tend to put the needs of the community above individual needs. For this reason, these cultures are called collectivistic, while the culture of the United States is called individualistic. Collectivistic values have had an influence on American culture, especially in the workplace, where collaboration, a collectivistic ideal, has been shown to lead to better results than those of individuals working in isolation.

Global Identification Globalization has also created a political culture in which people think beyond national borders for their identity. For example, the European Union (EU) is a group of sovereign European nations that function as an economic and political unit, somewhat like the early confederation of states under the Articles of Confederation. Many people within the EU, while not abandoning their national identity, also feel a political and cultural kinship with other members of the Union.

The global reach of news coverage can also foster a sense of global citizenship. Just as TV images of Bull Connor's violence against peaceful protesters in Birmingham, Alabama, awakened support for the civil rights movement (see page 309), so can news coverage of natural disasters or humanitarian crises engender global support—volunteers and donations of money—from a sense of shared humanity. A number of international, non-governmental organizations, such as Doctors without Borders, provide services wherever they are needed, many on a volunteer basis.

Pressures on the world's resources, especially global warming, remind people that they share their fate with other people around the world and can promote a sense of global citizenship.

Generational Effects

Many polls show the differing voting patterns for people in different generations. In the past few presidential elections, Democrats have won a majority of the younger vote. The 2016 CNN exit poll shows Hillary Clinton won voters under 45 years old, and Trump won those 45 and older. Clinton's share of younger voters was larger than Trump's share of older voters. Clinton won 56 percent of voters age 18 to 24, while Trump took only 34 percent of that age group. For those 65 years of age and over, Trump won 52–45 percent.

Yet when we examine generations as voting blocs, we examine millions of people who come from all parts of the United States, each influenced not only by their age but also by additional demographic characteristics discussed earlier in this chapter. In fact, there is more variation in political attitudes within a given generation or age bloc than between generations. As you have seen, notable events can have different effects on liberal- or conservative-leaning citizens. Citizens in different generations can learn different lessons from the same events.

The impressionable-age hypothesis posits that most persons forge most of their political attitudes during the critical period between ages 14 and 24. Political and perhaps personal events occurring at age 18 are about three times as likely to impact partisan voting preferences as similar events occurring at age 40.

Political scientists, psychologists, and pollsters typically place Americans into four generational categories to measure attitudes and compare where they might stand on a political continuum. They include from youngest to oldest: **Millennials, Generation X, Baby Boomers**, and the **Silent Generation**. Different authorities define the cutoffs at slightly different years. The Silent Generation, those born before 1945, are senior citizens born during the Great Depression or as late as the aftermath of World War II. Baby Boomers (those born between 1946–1964) lived during an era of economic prosperity after World War II and through the turbulent 1960s. Generation X includes those Americans born after the Baby Boomers (between about 1962–1982), and Millennials came of voting age at or after the new millennium. A look at two of the age groups on this timeline will show the role of generational effects on political socialization.

Millennials This under-35 population tends to be more accepting of interracial and same-sex marriage, legalization of marijuana, and second chances in the criminal justice system than their elders. They are also more ethnically and racially diverse than previous generations. About 12 percent of millennials are first generation Americans. They tend to be tech-centered, generally supportive of government action to solve problems, and highly educated. They have a high level of social connectedness and great opportunities for news consumption. By any measure, they are more liberal than previous generations. Gallup researcher Jeffrey Jones says that Millennials will remain more liberal and the United States will become more liberal as this group ages.

On Foreign Policy As Millennials began reading their news online, they encountered a world characterized by a complex distribution of power, a network of state and non-state actors shaping the foreign policy process and international relations. Millenials' frequent interactions with people not exactly like them and at great distances have led them to be more willing to promote cooperation over the use of force in foreign policy compared with other generations. Although they are hopeful about the future of the country, only about 70 percent of Millenials regard themselves as patriotic, a lower percentage than older Americans.

The two seminal events in Millennials' formative years were the September 11, 2001 attacks orchestrated by al-Qaeda (see pages 27–28) and the conflicts in Afghanistan and Iraq that followed. Two schools of thought prevail in how Millennials view the 9/11 attacks. One is that the attack on U.S. soil calls for aggressive homeland security and counterterrorism measures. Another is that the event should serve as a wake-up call that the United States should be less involved and present in the Middle East. Some studies report that 53 percent of Millennials believe the United States provoked the attacks.

The U.S. and North Atlantic Treaty Organization (NATO) military attacks on Afghanistan following 9/11 and the 2003 Iraq invasion and subsequent occupation have also helped shape Millennials' views. Afghanistan eventually surpassed Vietnam as America's longest military conflict, and the chief premise for invading Iraq, a search for weapons of mass destruction, turned up empty. This younger generation will likely compare future conflicts to the war in Iraq, predisposing this cohort to be more reluctant to intervene or use military force than older generations. A 2014 study by the Chicago Council on Global Affairs found that almost 50 percent of Millennials say the United States should stay out of world affairs, the largest percentage since the Council began the survey in 1974.

Economic Views Millennials tend to follow a similar "stay out" mindset in regard to social questions and some economic questions, yet their lines separating government from the economy are not easy to draw. They are business friendly but not opposed to regulation. They want citizens to earn their way. But they want to protect the consumer, the environment, and society at large. Their coming of age in a post-Earth Day world has caused them to see the reasons to protect the environment including recycling and other measures. They often acknowledge government waste and are disgusted by it, but they believe in a higher degree of regulation than do conservatives. Nearly four out of five Millennials believe Americans should adopt a sustainable lifestyle by conserving energy and consuming fewer goods.

Millennials are more conservative on free trade and in allowing citizens more control over their Social Security retirement savings. They are not big supporters of labor unions because labor unions do not hold the sway or respect they once had, and Millennials see unions as part of the problem. They also believe in a meritocracy, with 48 percent saying that government programs for the poor undermine initiative and responsibility, while 29 percent disagree with that statement.

Many in this generation became politically aware around the time of the Great Recession (2007–2012). Studies show that growing up in an economic recession can greatly shape attitudes toward government redistribution of wealth—welfare and Social Security. Nearly 70 percent of Millennials accept the idea of government intervention in a failing economy, 10 percent more than the next older cohort. Pessimistic views formed during a sudden economic downturn tend to be long-lasting. Such experiences could increase the chances these citizens vote for a Democratic presidential candidate by 15 percent.

Voting Though Millennials' views are somewhat nuanced, their voting habits on Election Day are not. The Pew Research Center found in a 2016 study that 55 percent of 18- to 35-year-olds identified as Democrats or leaning Democrat, and 27 percent called themselves "liberal Democrats." More than two out of three young Americans has a progressive tilt on energy, climate change, government efforts to assist people and the economy, and fighting inequality. In the 2016 presidential election, Millennials favored the Democratic Party by 43 percent, while only 26 percent of that group favored the Republican Party. About 10 percent of Millennials voted for someone other than Trump or Clinton, while those 40 and older voted for minor candidates only about 4 percent of the time.

Silent Generation On the opposite end of the age spectrum, senior citizens are defined as those over 65 years old. The Silent Generation and Baby Boomers overlap in this age group, but we focus here on the older generation.

Unique times and political events shaped this generation's thinking. They are the last group to remember the era before the 1960s counterculture movement and before the Vietnam War. They grew up hating communism, and many of them supported America's nine-year involvement in Southeast Asia until the U.S. departure from the region in the mid-1970s. American prosperity, patriotism, and a Christian-Judeo moral code were foremost in shaping their views during their impressionable years.

On Foreign Policy After World War II, the Russians (Soviets at the time) replaced the Axis powers as the new enemy, and the United States stood up to totalitarianism and the Soviet annexation of or influence on vulnerable nations. The Vietnam War was one of the final major efforts that placed large numbers of American GIs on the battlefield to defeat communism. The basic motives behind the Vietnam mission were stopping the spread of communism while assuring democracy and freedoms in those friendly nations that were susceptible to communist takeover. As the mission in Vietnam proved to be a failure and as a rising number of Americans disagreed with U.S. involvement, many of those over 35 years old, especially blue collar workers and those in rural communities, differed from the Baby Boomers. They had trusted and supported their government on the way into Vietnam, and they refrained from criticizing their government as failure became imminent. They were more forgiving of their government in the aftermath of the conflict.

On Social Issues The same generation gave religious values high priority and opposed the cultural changes that came during the 1960s and 1970s. Racial integration led to more interracial marriage and societal acceptance of racial equality, but that acceptance came more slowly to those who grew up under segregated societies in the South and the North. The women's movement changed the traditional roles of the family and eventually legalized abortion. Casual drug use and a counterculture movement caused many who had come of age in the 1950s and early 1960s to question the order of things, yet many of those who started voting in the 1970s stood with the old guard, influenced by their parents' choices. Many still held conservative beliefs and questioned changing American values.

As Molly Ball of *The Atlantic* explained while on the campaign trail in 2016, this cohort "has fought through the culture wars, has watched God and prayer leave the public square, and has watched immigration infiltrate U.S. society and culture." The same group today wants government to be tougher on criminal defendants and terror suspects than do younger groups, they more often oppose gay marriage, and they are bewildered that states are legalizing marijuana. A 2016 PRRI-Brookings survey showed that a majority of those over 65 believe America's "culture and way of life" have changed for the worse.

Voting Seniors are the most reliable voters. Consistently, the retired and elderly show up to vote in the highest percentages. According to a 2015 study by the U.S. Census Bureau, in the 2014 midterm elections, 59 percent of those over 65 voted. National averages in most midterm elections average around 38 percent. In fact, this senior midterm measure beats most voting blocs even in presidential election years. The 55–64 year old group turned out in large numbers in the 2016 presidential election, about 66 percent, but still somewhat lower than their elders whose turnout was about 71 percent.

Seniors have flocked to the Republican Party from the Democratic Party, a consistent trend that began in 2006 and held true on election night in 2016. From 1992 until 2006, they had been a primarily Democratic voting group. At that time, many survivors of the New Deal Coalition—that massive coalition of Americans who voted for Franklin Roosevelt and Democrats after him—still cast Democrat ballots. But since then, many from the Silent Generation have died and their Cold War culture warriors have replaced them.

The shift of this generation is due in part to the shift in policy positions by each of the major parties. The Democratic Party, though redefined as "liberal" economically in the New Deal era, still held somewhat conservative views and dominated in the South into the 1970s and 1980s. As the party took on more liberal social views, supporting the right to abortion, same-sex marriage, and affirmative action, followers of Roosevelt and their children have shifted to the Republican Party.

Lifecycle Effects

Just as each generation experiences dynamic social changes, people experience change as they move through the life cycle. **Lifecycle effects** include the variety of physical, social, and psychological changes that people go through as they age. These can affect political socialization in several ways. For one, they can shift focus to issues that are important at different age levels. For example, many college-age students are concerned about the accumulation of student debt and the challenges in finding a job that provides both a good income and health insurance benefits. In part because of these concerns, many Millennials were drawn to the candidacy of U.S. Senator Bernie Sanders (I-VT) in the Democratic presidential primaries in 2016 because he called for a free education at public colleges and an expansion of Medicare—the health insurance program for seniors managed by the government—to include everyone.

When people in this group move into the next stage of life, which often involves marriage and family, their priorities might shift to other issues related to a stable or growing economy and to schools their children might attend. At this point, a second lifecycle effect also becomes apparent. The demands of adult responsibility and raising children may limit the amount of active political participation people in this stage of the lifecycle can manage. They may be less able to volunteer in election efforts or to participate in demonstrations.

Just as young adults focus on the issues that matter at their life stage, seniors are worried about things that matter most as they age. The American Association of Retired Persons (AARP), the powerful interest group that directly represents more than 40 million seniors, lists among its major issues on its website: Social Security, health issues, Medicare, retirement, and consumer protection. Retirees who have paid into the Social Security system start collecting their benefits, and trips to the doctor become necessary and more expensive. According to a 2016 AARP study, 81 percent of seniors think prescription drug prices are too expensive and 87 percent say they support a tax credit to help families afford caregivers. Scammers and con artists prey on vulnerable targets living in their golden years and make the work of consumer protection agencies especially important.

By the time they become seniors, people have had a full life to forge their political attitudes and to practice political habits—consuming news, interacting with government on a local level, and developing the habit of voting. They have likely already registered to vote and are familiar with voting routines, and they don't have to schedule voting around work.

Measuring Public Opinion

Mining the views of Americans has become a keen interest of political scientists and a major industry in this age of data. Candidates running for office need to know their chances of winning and which groups support them. Once elected, members of Congress want to know how their constituents regard proposed bills and how they view different types of government spending. These elected officials can determine public opinion by reading letters or emails, holding a town hall meeting, or conducting a survey in their districts while news services rely on polls to see where the public stands on important issues.

Polling is the most reliable way to assess public opinion. It entails posing well developed, objective questions to a small, random group of people to find out what a much larger group thinks. Public opinion polling, developed in the early to mid-twentieth century, now follows a sophisticated methodology.

Since the polling industry began in the mid-1930s, the field of measuring Americans' views has become increasingly sophisticated. Many universities have established polling centers, and major television networks and large newspapers have created their own polling departments.

POLLING ORGANIZATIONS
Gallup
Harris Interactive
Pew Research Center
Rasmussen Reports
Quinnipiac University

Types of Polling

Pollsters use different kinds of polls to gather information. **Benchmark polls** are often the first type of poll used in an election, often before a potential candidate has declared his or her intentions. Benchmark polls are used to gather general information about people's views and concerns. **Tracking polls** ask people the same or similar questions over time to "track" the path of public opinion. These are used heavily during election season to show how public opinion changes or to assess a candidate's strength. Candidates also use tracking polls to shape their campaigns. **Entrance polls** and **exit polls** are conducted outside a polling place on Election Day to predict the outcome of the election later in the news day, to gain insight into the thoughts and behaviors of voters, or to identify and analyze how different voting demographics actually voted.

Focus groups are small groups of citizens—10 to 40 people—gathered to hold conversations about issues or candidates. Though less scientific than many types of polls, focus groups allow for deeper insight into a topic. Pollsters can ask follow-up questions and examine body language and intensity that would be missed in a simple automated questionnaire over the phone. For example, Republican presidential candidate Mitt Romney began wearing jeans more often when campaigning in the 2012 election after focus groups responded more positively to him in jeans than in formal clothes.

Polls regularly ask about presidential approval. **Approval ratings** are gauged by pollsters asking whether the respondent approves, yes or no, of the president's job performance. Presidents usually begin their term with a fairly high approval as the people and the press get to know them during the so-called "honeymoon period," typically the first 100 days after their inauguration.

According to Gallup, presidents since Harry Truman left office averaging 45 to 49 percent approval over their term of office. Some of the highest presidential approval ratings came when the nation prospered economically or when the country found itself in an international standoff and rallied around the president. The two highest recorded presidential approval ratings came after al-Qaeda attacked the United States in September 2001, when President

George W. Bush scored 90 percent approval, and when his father, President George H. W. Bush, received 89 percent approval after leading a military coalition to oust Iraqi dictator Saddam Hussein from Kuwait in 1991.

Of the 12 presidents before 2017, 6 averaged an approval rating of about 47 percent and 6 averaged about 60 percent. According to *RealClearPolitics,* President Donald Trump's job approval average at the end of his first full year was 39 percent.

Respondents are also often asked: "Is the nation on the right track or wrong track?" That question is commonly asked to determine Americans' satisfaction with government leaders. A positive right-track response usually means incumbents will fare well in their re-election campaigns, while a high wrong-track response will make incumbents uncomfortable at election time. The generic party ballot simply asks respondents if they will be voting for "Republicans" or "Democrats" during an upcoming election without mentioning candidates' names. Analyzing responses to these questions together serves as a relative measure of citizen support for each party.

Methodology

Pollsters take great pains to ensure their measurements are legitimate. They do so by constructing questionnaires with properly worded and appropriately ordered questions and selecting a representative sample after which they analyze the data and draw the appropriate conclusions.

Pollsters phrase survey questions so as not to skew the results. The wording should be objective and not emotionally charged. Poll results on highly emotional issues such as abortion, same-sex marriage, and affirmative action can be distorted depending on the wording. On foreign aid, imagine how the following two questions would bring noticeably different results: "Should the U.S. provide foreign aid to other nations?" and "Should the U.S. give foreign aid to other nations leading to a tax increase? "

Question order can also affect the results. In a 2002 poll on President George W. Bush's performance, for example, researchers asked the same questions but in a different sequence to two different groups. When people were asked first about the performance of the president and then the direction of the country, the president fared better. If respondents were asked about the state of the country first, which many said was bad, then the president's approval dropped by 6 percent.

How a question is framed also affects responses. *Framing* a question means posing it in a way that emphasizes a certain perspective. For example, researchers found that respondents had widely varying views on whether abortion should be legal depending on how the question was framed. Only 28 percent of Americans believe abortion should be legal under all circumstances, while many more supported abortion when the question was framed with a certain condition emphasized, as the chart on the next page shows.

BY THE NUMBERS WHEN SHOULD ABORTION BE LEGAL?	
When a woman's life is endangered	84%
When a woman's physical health is endangered	81%
When the pregnancy was caused by rape or incest	78%
When the woman's mental health is endangered	64%
When there is evidence the baby may be physically or mentally impaired	53%
When the woman or family cannot afford to raise the child	34%

Source: *R. Michael Alvarez and John Brehm, Hard Choices, Easy Answers, 2002.* © Princeton University Press

What do the numbers show? How does wording the question differently affect opinions? How do people differ on the legality of abortion? What factors in the question make the policy more or less favorable?

Sampling Techniques Which people are polled is just as important as the question's nature and wording. The pollster takes a **representative sample**, a group of people meant to represent the large group in question, known as the **universe**. A representative sample needs to have about 1,500 respondents, whether it is a sample of all U.S. adults or the population of a single state.

Pollsters must obtain a **random sample**. That is, every single member of the universe must have an equal chance of selection into the sample. A reporter or marketer standing on a street corner asking questions to passersby may determine some indication of public opinion, but this system is not random, because the person collecting the data may have biased who was included in the sample by approaching only those people who look "safe" or who otherwise look like they might be more willing to participate in the study. Since the 1980s, pollsters have used telephones as the primary contact for surveys, though there are concerns with this method. For example, roughly 30 percent of the populace has an unlisted number either by choice or because of mobility. To make telephone polling more reliable and efficient, pollsters use **random-digit dialing**. A computer randomly calls possible numbers in a given area until enough people respond to establish a representative sample.

Though technology has advanced, reaching voters has become more challenging. Landline use is dropping. In other measures, about 95 percent of American adults own a cell phone and a majority of homes have a wireless-only operation. More than 70 percent of all adults aged 25 to 34 years old use cell phones only and do not have landlines.

Pollsters are trying to combat this phenomenon in a few ways. One is mixing their broadly dialed, automated random phone surveys with more actual human interviewers. Federal law prohibits pre-recorded interactive surveys to cell phones. The Pew Research Center requires that 75 percent of their samples are cell phone participants.

Once the pollster has enough respondents, he or she checks to see if the demographics in the sample are reflective of those of the universe. If disproportionately more women than men answer the phone and take the poll, the pollster will remove some female respondents from the sample in order to make it proportional. If a congressional district contains roughly 25 percent African Americans, the sample needs to mirror that. Manipulating the sample to compensate for this is known as **weighting** or **stratification**—that is, making sure demographic groups are properly represented in a sample.

Sampling Error Even the most cautious survey with appropriate sampling techniques cannot guarantee absolute precision. The only way to know what everyone thinks is to ask everyone and assure they are entirely honest, both of which are impossible. Every poll has a **margin of error**. The sample size and the margin of error have an inverse relationship. That is, as the sample gets larger, the margin of error decreases. The way to determine this **sampling error**, the difference between poll results, is to measure the results in two or more polls. For example, the same basic poll with two similar samples revealed that 55 percent of the first sample opposed a particular congressional bill, while 58 percent of the second sample opposed the law. This poll has a sampling error of 3 percent. A margin of error of plus-or-minus 4 percent or less is usually considered satisfactory.

The simplest yet most perplexing problem in public opinion polling is the presence of non-attitudes. Many people do not have strong opinions on the issues of the day, or they are uninformed or simply concerned about their privacy. Just over half of eligible voters actually cast votes in presidential elections. Matters of extreme importance to journalists and policymakers may be unimportant to average citizens, so while poll results measure the views of average citizens on these matters, they don't show the relative importance of the matters to citizens. In a similar way, matters important to citizens may not be of interest to journalists, so polls may not reflect what is really on the minds of voters.

Another phenomenon affecting poll results is the high frequency of uninformed citizens responding. Political scientist Herb Asher explains a poll asking about the repeal of the Public Affairs Act. In reality, no such act or repeal effort existed, but fully 43 percent of those questioned had an opinion of the nonexistent law. Pollsters often ask screening questions to establish a respondent's knowledge or to ensure they are registered voters, such as "Do you plan to vote in the November election?" Such a question, however, does not eliminate the problem entirely. In fact, more than 90 percent of people answering phone surveys claim they will vote while far fewer do. Discerning polls may even ask if the respondent knows when the upcoming Election Day is to increase the chances that the respondent is a bona fide voter.

How the interviewer contacts and interacts with the respondent and how the respondent views the interviewer can also impact a poll. The difference between mailed questionnaires and telephone interviews are stark. People are more honest or frank with the anonymity of a paper questionnaire than a live telephone call. Some studies show women and men answering differently to male or female callers. Eighty-four percent of females agreed to a woman's right to choose an abortion when interviewed by females, while only 64 percent gave a pro-choice response to a male caller. Race, or perceived race, can matter as well. Asher claims that African Americans are more critical of the political and criminal justice system to black interviewers while more supportive or positive to white interviewers. White respondents are less likely to reveal attitudes of racial hostility when interviewed by blacks than by whites.

Still other problems exist because not everyone conducting a poll represents an objective journalist or an academic. Fundraising under the guise of polling has cheapened polling's reputation. Political parties and candidates use phone and mail surveys to assess where their followers stand and then ask for a donation. Also, **push polling** via telephone has become a common practice. This is basically a telephone poll with an ulterior motive. Rather than a series of neutral questions meant to determine public opinion on a candidate, the caller, or more commonly a tape-recorded voice, offers positive points about the candidate or negative points about the opponent, attempting to "push" the receiver one way or the other. Sometimes the voice takes an almost sinister tone. The call may end with a request for a vote on Election Day or a negative impression of the other candidate.

Internet polling can be problematic due to self-selection, administration, and the nature of people who go online. When directed toward an Internet poll, only those strongly motivated will participate. With some online polls, there's no limit to how many times one can take it. Internet users also tend to be younger, better educated, more affluent, white, and suburban and do not represent a genuine cross section of society.

Evaluating Claims Based on Public Opinion Data

As participants in democracy either at or approaching voting age, you will be surrounded by public opinion polls and the claims based on them. Knowing how to evaluate the quality and credibility of those claims will help you make informed decisions.

Public Opinion as a Source of Political Influence

Polls lend themselves to "horse race" news coverage in which elections are reported as if the most important aspect was which candidate is in the lead, not who is better qualified or more principled. That kind of media coverage can translate into significant political influence as well.

Influence on Elections For example, early in the Republican primary season in 2016, the first debate among the party's candidates was being planned. There were 17 candidates vying for the nomination. How could a reasonable debate be carried out with so many people on stage? The host of the debate, Fox News, made a decision to limit the number of participants to 10. Fox would choose from the 17 candidates those who registered in the top 10 percent in an average of five national polls as the debate grew near. If anyone in the top ten failed to earn at least a 5 percent ranking in the polls, that person would be eliminated from the debate. National polling, then, influenced whose voice would be heard at the televised debate and whose would be silenced. Candidates with the highest poll ratings also receive more media coverage than those with low ratings.

National polling also exerts influence on elections through the **bandwagon effect**—a shift of support to a candidate or position holding the lead in public opinion polls and therefore believed to be endorsed by many people. The more popular a candidate or position, the more likely increasing numbers of people will "hop on the bandwagon" and add their support. People like to back a winning candidate. For this reason, most media outlets do not report the findings from their statewide Election Day exit polls until polls have closed in that state. If people who have not yet voted learn that Candidate A is way ahead in votes, they may not bother going to the polls if they either supported Candidate A (that candidate will win anyway) or supported a rival who was behind (that candidate has no chance of winning).

The bandwagon effect is also partly responsible for the direct link between a candidate's rank in national polls and the ability to raise campaign funds. The higher the national ratings, the more campaign contributions a candidate can elicit. The larger a candidate's war chest—the funds used to pay for a campaign—the more ads a candidate can buy and the larger the staff a candidate can maintain. Both greatly influence the outcome of an election.

Influence on Policy Debate Scientific polling also exerts an influence on government policy and decision-making, although its effects are less clear than on elections. The three branches of the government tend to respond to public opinion polling in somewhat different ways, if at all.

The legislative branch is sometimes responsive to public opinion polls, especially the House of Representatives in which lawmakers face reelection every two years. Many try to represent their constituencies and to keep them satisfied with their performance to encourage fundraising and subsequent votes, so taking constituent views seriously pays off. Senators, with longer terms, do not seem as sensitive to pressure from public opinion.

The executive branch has sometimes been influenced by public opinion and at other times has tried to use the power of the "bully pulpit" to shift public opinion. A president usually enjoys high approval ratings in the first year of office and tries to use that popularity as a "mandate" to advance his or her agenda as quickly as possible.

The judicial branch may be influenced by public opinion, even though justices are appointed for life and are not at the mercy of the ballot box. Different studies have drawn varying conclusions about why. However, many have concluded that when the general mood of the nation is liberal, the Court will hand down more liberal rulings. When the general mood of the nation is conservative, the Court will issue more conservative rulings.

Reliability and Veracity of Public Opinion Data

One way to gauge the accuracy of a pre-election poll is to measure "candidate error"—the percentage point difference in the poll's estimate and the candidate's actual share of the vote after the election. Candidate error has gradually declined as polling techniques became more sophisticated. But in the last few years, what has been a consistently improving science and practice, with the occasional setback, has had some less-than-stellar predictions.

For example, Gallup predicted Mitt Romney as the winner of the 2012 presidential election with 50 percent of the vote and President Obama at 49 percent, the separation of one point. In reality, Obama won nationally by nearly four points. This failure led to Gallup's eventual decision to no longer predict presidential election outcomes, the so-called horse-race polls, but to stick to its vast polling of issues and views in other areas of public policy. Gallup wasn't the only firm that had an erroneous prediction outside the margin of error in 2012.

In the waning days of the 2016 presidential election, polls projected that Hillary Clinton would defeat Donald Trump. Election forecasters, those that aggregate polls and other data to make bold predictions, put Clinton's chances at 70 to 99 percent. The final round of polling by most major firms had Clinton winning by anywhere from 1 to 7 percentage points in the national vote. Once the vote was counted, Clinton won the popular vote by only 2 points but lost the Electoral College vote.

Several factors may explain why polls may be inaccurate and unreliable. One factor relates to the psychology of the respondents. Another factor relates to undecided voters and when they finally make up their minds.

Social-Desirability Bias The psychology behind these recent poll misreads and errors is at least in part explained by *social desirability bias*. That is, respondents and declared voters may tell the pollster what they think the pollster wants to hear.

Social desirability bias affects the predictions of voter turnout. Respondents may give the interviewer the impression that they will indeed vote, because they do not want to be seen as shirking a responsibility, but often on Election Day they do not vote. In a recent estimate, when asked their likelihood of voting on a scale of 1 to 9, U. S. citizens tend to say 8 or 9, yet only about 60 percent of eligible voters cast ballots.

Social desirability bias can fool pollsters beyond inflated turnout. Voters do not want to be perceived negatively, so they may give the interviewers a socially acceptable response, or what they perceive as the acceptable response, and yet act or vote in a different way. This phenomenon was noticeable in the 1982 California governor's race. The election included a popular candidate, Los Angeles Mayor Tom Bradley, who would have been the state's first African American governor. Bradley led strongly in the polls throughout the campaign but lost on Election Day. Most experts attributed the discrepancy to interviewees' falsely claiming they supported Bradley only later to vote for a white candidate. These poll participants did not want to appear bigoted or *against* the black candidate. In what has become known as the Bradley effect, later African American candidates have also underperformed against their consistently inflated poll predictions.

Pundits in 2017 encouraged speculation as public opinion polls shifted in the special U.S. Senate election in Alabama. Republican candidate Roy Moore, the favorite for weeks, was suddenly losing to Democrat Doug Jones, in some polls, after Moore was alleged to have committed sexual assault or aggressions toward several women when they were teenagers. Skeptics of the new polls pointed out that voters might not willingly admit on the phone that they were going to vote for this accused candidate. In fact, one famous political pundit, Nate Silver, pointed out that in polls using robocalls, or automated pre-recorded polls, Moore was ahead, and in polls using live interviews, Jones was ahead. Jones won in the close contest.

Undecideds Breaking Late According to exit polling and research after the election, a likely explanation for Trump's surprise win was that a larger than usual share of undecided voters "broke" (made their final decision) late and broke for Trump. Nate Cohn of the *New York Times* explains how likely voters who said they were voting for a third party candidate mostly did so. But 26 percent of those voters turned to Trump and only 11 switched to Clinton. Pollsters theorize that a disproportionate number of so-called "shy Trump voters" turned away the opportunity to be counted altogether. Perhaps the same anti-establishment, anti-media attitude that drew them to the outsider candidate also turned them away from pollsters, a phenomenon known as *non-response bias.*

Opinions in Social Media The willingness of people to take part in polls is declining. About 37 percent of randomly called citizens would participate in a telephone poll in 1997. Today, pollsters get about a 10 percent response rate for live callers, and about 1 percent participation with robocalls. But as Kristin Soltis Anderson, author of *The Selfie Vote*, points out, "The good news is, at the same time people are less likely to pick up the phone and tell you what they think, we are more able to capture the opinions and behaviors that people give off passively." We can take the public's pulse from available platforms widely used by a large swath of the general public. Examining what is said on social media and in the Google toolbar, what Anderson calls the "modern-day confessional," can tell us a lot about public opinion.

However, though blogs and the Twitter-verse constitute a massive sample, the people active on social media may have very different views from those who are not active on social media. A 2015 study found that people who discuss politics on Twitter tend to be overwhelmingly male, urban, and extreme in their ideological views. Another problem that makes this endeavor less-than-scientific is that researchers use computer programs to gauge the Internet's dialogue, but cannot easily discern sarcasm and unique language. And overly vocal people can go onto the Internet repetitively and be tabulated multiple times, dominating the conversation disproportionately.

Biased Pollsters and Data vs. Fact Reputable pollsters seek ways to avoid bias in sampling techniques and the wording of their questions. However, many polls are funded by special interest groups who want the poll results to tip a certain way. They then use those results to move their agendas forward, claiming that the data generated by their polls represented fact. "The numbers don't lie," they might say.

Unless you know about the organization doing the polling, the methods it used, the wording of the questions, and the context of the poll, you will not be able to evaluate a poll's veracity, or truthfulness. You have already read about how push polls slant their questions to produce certain outcomes. Political Action Committees (PACs), special interest groups, and partisan organizations all have a vested interest in getting a response from a poll that supports their cause. To help journalists evaluate the reliability and veracity of polls, the National Council on Public Polls (NCPP) provides 20 questions journalists should ask and answer before reporting on a poll. You can find that list on the NCPP website. The checklist below provides some of the key questions to ask about any poll.

QUESTIONS FOR EVALUATING CLAIMS BASED ON PUBLIC OPINION POLLS	
1. Who conducted the poll, and who paid for it?	If it was done by a reputable polling organization, it is probably mainly accurate; if it is done (or paid for) by a special interest, you need to consider possible bias.
2. What methodology did the pollsters use?	Reliable polls are often released with a report that explains how the results were obtained: the sampling methods, whether or not the results are weighted, and the margin of error.
3. What were the exact questions, and in what order were they presented?	As you read, the wording and ordering of questions can have a significant impact on the poll results.
4. How were the results obtained?	People tend to be more honest in mailed polls than when interacting with an interviewer because of social desirability bias.
5. In what context was the poll taken?	The date information is collected can be a factor in poll results. For example, if a statewide poll was taken in the days following a barrage of media ads for a certain candidate, the poll results may inflate the candidate's actual popularity.
6. Whose opinion might be missing from the poll?	Good polls need to make an accommodation for people who refused to participate in the poll in order to provide a fair sample.
7. How do the poll results compare with other poll results?	If the results of a poll match up with other polls taken under the same circumstances and at the same time, chances are good the poll is reliable.

REFLECT ON THE ESSENTIAL QUESTION

Essential Question: How do political culture, demographics, and dynamic social and personal change shape citizen beliefs about government, and how are those beliefs measured? On separate paper, complete a chart like the one below to gather details to answer that question.

Political Culture	Demographics	Social and Personal Change	Measuring Public Opinion

KEY TERMS AND NAMES

Citizen Beliefs
Baby Boomers/365
conservative/349
free enterprise/351
Generation X/365
globalization/362
ideology/353
individualism/349
liberal/349
libertarian/355
lifecycle effects/368
limited government/352
Millennials/365
moderate/353
party identification/358

political
  socialization/356
populist/356
progressive/356
rule of law/352
saliency/353
Silent Generation/365
valence issues/353
wedge issues/353

Polling
approval rating/370
bandwagon effect/375
benchmark polls/370
entrance polls/370
exit polls/370

focus group/370
margin of error/373
push polling/374
random-digit
  dialing/372
random sample/372
representative
  sample/372
sampling error/373
stratification/373
tracking polls/370
universe/372
weighting/373

Questions 1 and 2 refer to the passage below.

> Must the citizen, ever for a moment, or in the least degree, resign his conscience to the legislator? Why has every man a conscience, then? It is not desirable to cultivate a respect for the law, so much as for the right. The only obligation which I have a right to assume is to do at any time what I think right. . . . . Law never made men a whit more just; and, by means of their respect for it, even the well-disposed are daily made the agents of injustice. A common and natural result of an undue respect for law is, that you may see a file of soldiers, colonel, captain, corporal, privates . . . marching in admirable order over hill and dale to the wars, against their wills, ay, against their common sense and consciences, which makes it very steep marching indeed, and produces a palpitation of the heart. They have no doubt that it is a damnable business in which they are concerned; they are all peaceably inclined.
>
> —Henry David Thoreau, "Civil Disobedience," 1849

1. Which of the following perspectives reflects Thoreau's beliefs based on this passage?

   (A) War is immoral.

   (B) Law is less important than an individual's beliefs.

   (C) Soldiers fight against their wills.

   (D) Legislators are not to be trusted.

2. Which American cultural value does Thoreau highlight in this passage?

   (A) Rule of law

   (B) Individualism

   (C) Free enterprise

   (D) Equality of opportunity

3. Which of these federal officers are most influenced by public opinion polling?

   (A) Senators

   (B) Cabinet secretaries

   (C) Federal judges

   (D) Representatives in the House

4. Which of the following is necessary for a public opinion poll to be valid?

(A) The poll must use objective, open-ended questions.

(B) Equal numbers of people from different demographics need to be polled.

(C) The poll must be conducted by a responsible news organization.

(D) The poll must have a low margin of error.

5. Millennials' political socialization was colored by the 9/11/2001 attacks by al-Qaeda terrorists, showing most clearly which effect on the formation of political views?

(A) The generational effect

(B) The lifecycle effect

(C) The effect of social media

(D) The effect of globalization

6. Which of the following is an accurate comparison of Millennials and members of the Silent Generation?

	MILLENNIALS	SILENT GENERATION
(A)	Favor tough punishments for criminals	Favor lenient punishments for criminals
(B)	Generally oppose same-sex marriage	Generally support same-sex marriage
(C)	Tend to believe the United States should stay out of foreign countries	Tend to see the United States as a world guardian of freedom and democracy
(D)	Tend to be Republicans	Tend to be Democrats

Questions 7 and 8 refer to the passage below.

> So-called "Push polls" are not polls at all. They are a form of political telemarketing whose intent is not to measure public opinion but to manipulate—"push"—voters away from one candidate and toward the opposing candidate. Such polls defame selected candidates by spreading false or misleading information about them. The intent is to disseminate campaign propaganda under the guise of conducting a legitimate public opinion poll.
>
> —American Association for Public Opinion Research, "Condemned Survey Practices," 2017

7. Which of the following questions is most likely to appear on a push poll?

   (A) Do you approve of increasing the military budget?

   (B) Do you approve of raising property taxes slightly to help fund schools?

   (C) Do you approve of the waste of money on failing social service agencies under the current governor?

   (D) Do you approve of rolling back environmental regulations to encourage business investment?

8. Based on the text, with which of the following statements would the authors most likely agree?

   (A) As long as all sides use push polling equally, the effect should be minimal.

   (B) Despite its problems, push polling gives pollsters a fair sense of public opinion.

   (C) The government should provide campaign funding and regulate campaign practices.

   (D) Telemarketing disguised as research has decreased response rates and harmed public opinion polling.

Questions 9 and 10 refer to the graphic below.

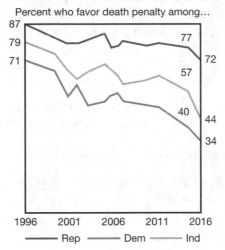

Death Penalty Support by Party

Percent who favor death penalty among...

1996 2001 2006 2011 2016
——— Rep ——— Dem ——— Ind

87
79
71
77
72
57
40
44
34

Source: *Pew Research Center*

9. Which of the following best describes a trend in the graph?

   (A) More Democrats than Republicans support the death penalty.

   (B) Support for the death penalty among Republicans, Democrats, and independents has dropped.

   (C) Democratic support for the death penalty has gradually risen.

   (D) More independents than Republicans support the death penalty.

10. Which of the following is an accurate conclusion based on the trends in the line graph above and your knowledge of political attitudes?

   (A) Young people are more likely to support the death penalty than older people.

   (B) Well educated people are more likely to support the death penalty than people with a high school diploma only.

   (C) Activism against the death penalty has failed to influence public opinion.

   (D) Conservatives tend to support the death penalty more than liberals.

1. "Consider the motives of the media reporting on the polls. Conservative and liberal media outlets are more likely to report on polls more favorable to their candidates or portray outlier polls as the true state of the race. And even nonpartisan media outlets know that 'New Poll Shows Race Hasn't Changed' isn't a great headline. Additionally, a media company that sponsors a poll is probably going to want to hype up their own findings."

> Harry Enton, 13 Tips for Reading General Election Polls
> Like a Pro, 9/2/2016, fivethirtyeight.com

After reading the tip above, respond to A, B, and C below:

(A) Describe the behavior the author recommends consumers demonstrate in response to polls.

(B) In the context of the scenario, explain how the behavior described in part A affects elections.

(C) In the context of the scenario, explain how the interactions between media and voters affect government.

2. Use the line graphs on the next page to answer the questions below.

(A) Identify the information conveyed in the graphs.

(B) Describe a similarity or difference in public opinion of job approval for President Obama and President George W. Bush.

(C) Explain why presidential approval ratings can fluctuate, and draw a conclusion about when President Bush would have had his best chance of moving his agenda forward.

3. In the mid-1970s, California resident Allan Bakke, a white, 35-year old man, applied to the University of California-Davis medical school. The school's affirmative action policy set aside 16 of the 100 spots exclusively for qualified minority applicants. The medical school denied Bakke's admission while it accepted minorities with lower grade point averages (GPAs) and test scores. Bakke alleged the state university violated both the 1964 Civil Rights Act and the Constitution in rejecting his application based on his race while accepting applicants of a minority status with lower GPAs and test scores.

In the decision of *Regents of the University of California v. Bakke* (1978), the U.S. Supreme Court held in a unique 5:4 ruling, that the university had violated the 1964 statute, but that using race as a criterion in higher education admissions was constitutionally permissible. The Court

President Obama Job Approval Rating

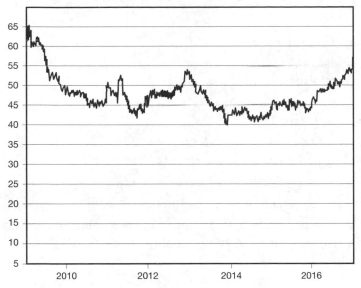

President George W. Bush Job Approval Rating

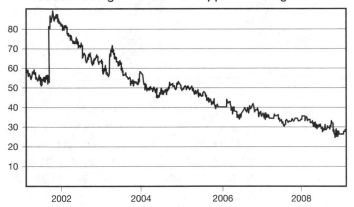

did not declare the practice of affirmative action unconstitutional but did declare that overly strict racial guidelines violate the Constitution.

(A) Identify the constitutional clause relevant to both *Regents of the University of California v. Bakke* (1978) and *Brown v. Board of Education* (1954). (See page 305.)

(B) Explain how the ruling differed in the *Bakke* and *Brown* cases.

(C) Describe an action students who oppose the *Bakke* ruling can take to limit its impact.

4. Develop an argument that explains whether public opinion polling during an election has a positive or negative effect on American political life.

In your essay you must:

- Articulate a defensible claim or thesis that responds to the prompt and establishes a line of reasoning
- Support your claim with at least TWO pieces of accurate and relevant information
  - At least ONE piece of evidence must come from one of the following foundational documents:
    - The First Amendment of the Constitution
    - Articles I and II of the Constitution
  - Use a second piece from another foundational document from the list above or your study of political beliefs and public opinion polling
- Use reasoning to explain why your evidence supports your claim/thesis
- Respond to an opposing or alternative perspective using refutation, concession, or rebuttal

WRITING: *USE REBUTTAL*

When you address an opposing or alternative perspective, you can refute it by showing logically why it is not as sound a perspective as yours, you can concede a point (usually a minor one), giving credit to an opposing view where credit is due, or you can use rebuttal. Not everyone agrees on the differences between refutation and rebuttal, but many see the difference this way: to refute means to use facts, evidence, and logic to successfully disprove an opposing or alternative view; to rebut means to offer a counterargument, even if you can't necessarily prove it with facts. Both, however, share the meaning of countering an opposing view. To rebut effectively, you need to carefully think through opposing or alternative views so you can clearly see why you disagree with them and then make your best assertion about what is wrong with them.

11

Political Ideology and Policy

"No matter where you stand politically—even if you're unsure of what your political ideology is— it is important to take part in the process of shaping our government."

—Brad Henry, Governor of Oklahoma (D, 2003–2011)

Essential Question: How do political ideologies shape policy debates and choices in American politics?

Political ideology is the grand set of political beliefs one holds. As you read in Chapter 2, public policy is the set of laws, regulations, funding priorities, executive actions, and court rulings that the government has implemented to address various problems. America's domestic policy includes all such programs that directly affect the people in the nation. Widely held political ideologies shape policy debates and choices, including those related to the government's role in regulating the economy and addressing social issues.

Policy is created and shaped by the federal government, even in small ways, such as when a member of Congress inserts language into a bill, when the president discusses relations with another head of state, when the U.S. Postal Service changes its delivery schedule, or when a court sets a precedent. The impetus for those policies, however, stems from Americans' values, attitudes, and beliefs. These drive the formation, goals, and implementation of public policy over time.

Party Ideology and Policymaking

The modern Republican Party holds a conservative party doctrine. Republicans for decades have preached against wasteful spending and for a strong national defense, limited regulation of businesses, and maintaining cultural traditions.

Democrats, on the other hand, uphold a liberal doctrine, believing strongly in civil rights, women's rights, and civil liberties. Democrats also desire more government services to solve public problems and greater regulations to protect the environment. These general positions of the two major parties tend to determine the terms of debate on public policy issues. Additional minor parties are players in this political game and have a degree of influence in policymaking. Minor parties are discussed in Chapter 13, which includes an in-depth look at the operations and influence of political parties.

Party Platforms

Divisions exist within both major parties. At no time do all party members agree on how to tackle all the issues. Yet the best way to determine a party's primary ideology is to read its platform, or list of principles and plans it hopes to enact. Platform committee members argue over the wording of this document during drafting. The arguments have revealed strong in-party differences or fractures.

In addition to basic principles, the party platforms drafted in 2016 include the legacies of each party's noted historical heroes, some specific proposals, and accusations against the opposite party. Below and on the next page are some selected quotes from the Democratic and Republican platforms on a wide range of issues.

Democratic Party Platform 2016

- **On health care for the poor:** "We will keep fighting until the [Affordable Care Act's] Medicaid expansion has been adopted in every state. Nineteen states have not yet expanded Medicaid. This means that millions of low-income Americans still lack health insurance and are not getting the care they need."

- **On equal rights for women:** "We are committed to ensuring full equality for women. Democrats will fight to end gender discrimination in the areas of education, employment, health care, or any other sphere."

- **On equality and sexual orientation:** 'Democrats will fight for the continued development of sex discrimination law to cover LGBT people."

- **On immigration:** "Democrats believe we need to urgently fix our broken immigration system—which tears families apart and keeps workers in the shadows—and create a path for citizenship for law-abiding families...."

- **On climate change:** "Democrats share a deep commitment to tackling the climate challenge. . . We believe America must be running entirely on clean energy by mid-century."

- **On abortion:** "Democrats are committed to protecting and advancing reproductive health, rights, and justice. We believe unequivocally, like the majority of Americans, that every woman should have access to quality reproductive health care services, including safe and legal abortion—regardless of where she lives, how much money she makes, or how she is insured."

Republican Party Platform 2016

- **On poverty and welfare:** "We propose . . . the dynamic compassion of work requirements in a growing economy, where opportunity takes the place of a hand-out, where true self-esteem can grow from the satisfaction of a job well done."

- **On the death penalty:** "With the murder rate soaring in our great cities, we condemn the Supreme Court's erosion of the right of the people to enact capital punishment in their states."

- **On marriage:** "[Family] is the foundation of civil society, and the cornerstone of the family is natural marriage, the union of one man and one woman."

- **On immigration:** "Our highest priority . . . must be to secure our borders and all ports of entry and to enforce our immigration laws."

- **On gun control:** "We salute the Republican Congress for defending the right to keep and bear arms by preventing the President from installing a new liberal majority on the Supreme Court.

- **On abortion:** "We oppose the use of public funds to promote or perform abortion .... We will not fund or subsidize healthcare that includes abortion coverage."

These statements reveal why each party has a unique following of voters. The Democrats have claimed that they are an inclusive party that works for minority rights. Republicans, on the other hand, rely on conservative voters who support limited gun regulation, anti-abortion legislation, and increased national security. The electoral map of recent years shows these same geographic trends. The Democratic Party generally carries the more liberal northeastern states and those on the West Coast, while Republicans carry most of the South and rural West and Midwest. In recent decades, Democrats have increased their votes among women, African Americans, and the fastest-growing minority in the United States, Hispanics.

Democrats and Republicans also tend to disagree on economic matters and issues related to law and order. Democrats, for example, tend to support increasing government services for the poor, including health care, and they tend to support regulations on business to promote environmental quality and equal rights. Republicans tend to oppose wasteful government spending and the expansion of entitlements—programs such as Social Security and Medicare—while supporting a strong national defense. They also tend to support limited regulation of business. On law and order, Democrats tend to prefer rehabilitation for prisoners over severe punishments and often oppose the death penalty. Republicans tend to favor full prison sentences with few opportunities for parole and, as their platform states, they support the right of courts to impose the death penalty in certain cases.

Libertarians are much, much fewer in number than Democrats and Republicans. However, dislike of the candidates in the two major parties—Democrat Hillary Clinton and Republican Donald Trump—led 3.2 percent of voters in the presidential election of 2016 to cast their votes for Libertarian candidate Gary Johnson, former Republican governor of New Mexico. Libertarians tend to believe as liberals do on most social issues and as conservatives do on many economic issues. Their central tenet is that the government's role should be limited to protecting private property, resolving disputes, and supporting free trade.

Libertarian influence on policy is considerably weaker than that of the major parties. However, a network of billionaire donors has succeeded in electing a number of Republicans with libertarian leanings to local offices. "We've made more progress in the last five years than I had in the previous 50," said Charles Koch, a key leader in the libertarian movement.

Influences on Public Policy

As you read in Chapter 10, Americans have a range of values, attitudes, and beliefs. These influence the development, goals, and implementation of public policy over time. Policies in place at any given time represent the success of the parties whose ideologies they represent and the political attitudes and beliefs of citizens who choose to participate in politics at a given time. Following are some of the key theories or pathways to policy. These differing pathways reflect some of the different types of democracy you read about in Chapter 1, since the United States has elements of each of them.

Majoritarian Policymaking Majoritarian policymaking emerges from the interaction of people with government in order to put into place and carry out the will of the majority. Democratic government, a foundational principle in America, is meant to represent the people's views through elected representatives. Popular ideas will work their way into the body politic via state and national legislatures. A president seeking a second term may go with public opinion when there is an outcry for a new law or a different way of enforcing an existing law. State referenda and initiatives, too, are a common way for large grassroots efforts to alter current policy when state assemblies refuse to make the public will the public law. (See page 487.) These are examples of participatory democracy at work.

This democratic system sounds fair and patriotic. But the framers also put into place a republic of states and a system to ensure that the tyranny of the majority did not run roughshod over the rights of the minority. Additionally, the framers warned, factions—often minority interests—will press government to address their needs, and at times government will comply.

Source: *DigitalVision*
State referenda give voters direct power over policy.

Interest Group Policymaking Interest groups have a strong influence and interact with all three branches in the policymaking process. They fund candidates who support their agendas, experts sympathetic to their concerns provide testimony at hearings, and they push for specific areas of policy to satisfy their members and their philosophy.

Interest groups represent a pluralist approach to policymaking. The interests of the diverse population of the United States, ethnically and ideologically, compete to create public policy that addresses as many group concerns as compromise allows.

Balancing Liberty and Order No matter the approach to public policymaking, two underlying principles guide debate. One is the core belief in individual liberties (pages 233–236). The other is the shared belief that one important role of government is to promote stability and social order. Policy debates are often an effort to find the right balance between these fundamental values. **BIG IDEA:** Governmental laws and policies balancing order and liberty are based on the Constitution and have been interpreted differently over time.

Decision-Making Process

In creating policy, public officials follow a general routine. Legislators and bureaucrats develop and reshape an **agenda**—a list of potential policy ideas, bills, or plans to improve society. These could be new methods of law enforcement, alterations of the tax system, or a long-term plan to improve relations with a foreign nation. With each new policy idea comes a cost-benefit analysis, a full look into the strains and efforts that come with a new policy compared to the benefits the new policy would bring. For example, building an overhead skywalk at every intersection would reduce pedestrian injuries and deaths, but the costs—the actual price, the disruption caused by their construction, the unsightliness, and pedestrian confusion from such a network of skywalks—might outweigh the benefits.

Sequence Ideally, governments at all levels recognize an issue, study it, and try to solve it. First an issue gains attention. The attention may come from a widespread citizen push to ban smoking in public places, for example, or it may come from a defense contractor's proposed design for new fighter jets. Once the issue becomes of public concern, Congress may exercise its investigatory power to better understand the issue. If interest in an issue reaches this stage, the relevant committee(s) will hear experts testify. Ideally all sides of the issue and particular concerns about solving the problem will be heard.

Then, government formulates the policy on paper, whether it is a new bill or a new way for police to enforce existing law. As the topic is discussed in theory and the language of a bill or an executive directive is developed and refined, the government will work toward adopting the policy. Sweeping changes in law usually come incrementally, with the most passable ideas coming before any major overhauls.

The government must also figure out a way to finance the enforcement of new laws. Each new policy requires the executive branch to enforce it, which means either creating an additional agency to oversee the law or putting more responsibilities on an existing one. Finally, the government will evaluate the new policy sometime after its implementation. This evaluation could be achieved through required agency reports or with congressional oversight. (See pages 172–174.)

Challenges to new policies quickly come from those who oppose the law. Opponents often file suit to overturn the law in the courts. Many times a state legislature will pass a controversial bill with a marginal vote only to see the citizenry rise up and repeal it through a referendum. In Ohio, for example, the state legislature had passed a bill (Senate Bill 5) limiting collective bargaining for 400,000 public workers employed by the state, preventing them from striking and limiting their ability to conduct collective bargaining for better pay and benefits. The bill was signed into law on March 31, 2011. Opponents of the law, however, collected more than one million signatures to put the law on the ballot as a referendum. The voters repealed the law in November 2011.

POLICY MATTERS: *POLITICAL CULTURE AND THE POLICYMAKING PROCESS OVER TIME*

BIG IDEA: Popular sovereignty, individualism, and republicanism are important considerations of U.S. laws and policymaking and assume citizens will engage and participate. The movement to legalize marijuana is a good example of how policy reflects the attitudes and beliefs of citizens who choose to participate at a given time and the balancing act between individual liberty and social order. A gradual but consistent change in public opinion on the issue over the past 20 years, especially by younger voters, has caused a fairly consistent state-by-state path of legalizing marijuana.

Order Over Liberty Marijuana, or cannabis, entered the United States in large amounts with Mexican immigrants who came across the border after the Mexican Revolution of 1910. Smoking the plant was part of their culture. Soon, awareness of the mind-altering drug and its potential danger spread. States, exercising their police powers, began outlawing marijuana. As the substance moved further into the country, more states followed suit in criminalizing it.

Critics not only denounced the drug but also demonized Mexican immigrants. Some historians argue that the criminalization of marijuana was likely an attempt to keep tabs on the Mexican immigrants. A short-lived nativism accompanied the criminalization effort while likely exaggerating the drug's effects. For example, critics declared that marijuana, or "pot," caused users to commit rape, murder, theft, and other acts of violence. Newspapers published by mogul William Randolph Hearst spread sensational stories about marijuana and violence and the supposed threat it represented to social order.

Congressional Policy The federal government first acted with a 1932 policy, the Uniform State Narcotics Act, which strongly urged states to make marijuana and other drugs illegal. Meanwhile a propaganda campaign that reached a peak with the release of the film *Reefer Madness* brought attention to the drug and alleged that cannabis caused users to become deranged. In 1937, the House of Representatives held hearings on the issue; only the American Medical Association spoke against criminalizing marijuana because there was no evidence it was anything more than a mild intoxicant. After only a half hour of floor debate, the House passed the 1937 Marijuana Tax Act in an effort to regulate the substance. By the end of the 1930s, most states and Congress had criminalized marijuana. Drug enforcement, other than interstate drug trafficking, was largely handled by state and local police.

Source: *Public Domain*

The film *Reefer Madness* places the blame for all the lurid crimes in the story on cannibas.

The 1960s counterculture brought further attention to drug use and abuse. By 1970, the Controlled Substances Act, a comprehensive federal drug policy that was part of President Richard Nixon's war on drugs, was the first federal law with any teeth to enforce and heavily punish marijuana dealers and users. The law categorized heroin, cocaine, and other illegal substances in terms of potential harm and placed marijuana in the same category with no medical benefits. At the time, the Gallup organization found that only about 12 percent of respondents thought it should be legal.

Citizen Influence Balancing Liberty and Order Through the 1970s and 1980s, attitudes toward pot slowly shifted. Advocates for legalizing marijuana formed the special interest group National Organization for the Reform of Marijuana Laws (NORML) in 1970. Other advocacy groups formed as well. Additional research and public education through advocacy brought growing acceptance of marijuana use. Some states began to decriminalize (keeping the drug illegal, but reducing punishments, in some cases down to a small fine for a small amount), as the trajectory toward acceptance and legalization grew. Some in the medical community recognized its palliative properties for patients with glaucoma, depression, and other conditions and helped strengthen a movement to legalize the plant for medical purposes.

California became the first state to legalize medicinal marijuana through a statewide vote, Proposition 215, in 1996—participatory democracy at work. Over the next two decades, additional states legalized marijuana by ballot measures. As citizens legalized, more state legislatures have taken up similar bills and approved them. In October 2013, one year after full legalization in Colorado and Washington state, Gallup reported for the first time that a majority of Americans supported legalizing pot.

Not every state that has sought to legalize pot has succeeded. Ohio placed an initiative on the ballot in 2015 that failed to pass by a vote of 65 to 35 percent. Analysts believe that the measure's attempt to legalize both medicinal and recreational pot at the same time may have brought its failure, since changes in government policy are usually incremental baby steps toward what might in time become sweeping policy change. Additionally, the ballot proposal would have placed the exclusive rights to grow the plant in the hands of 10 state-approved vendors. Conservatives who opposed legalization emphasized not the nature of marijuana itself but the near-monopoly that would come with legalization.

Presidential and Judicial Policymaking The 1970 Controlled Substances Act remains as federal law. What happens, then, when a state legalizes marijuana while the drug remains illegal at the national level? That depends on whom you ask, which level and branch of government are being asked, and the political mood of the nation and states.

As the legalization movement was underway but before it had crossed a tipping point, federal authorities in Republican president George W. Bush's administration began a crackdown on marijuana growing operations and medical marijuana dispensaries in California. Legalization advocates and patients sued the federal government, arguing that states had the authority under the 10th Amendment and the police powers doctrine to determine the status of the drug's legality. However, on appeal, in *Gonzales v. Raich* (2005), the Supreme Court ruled that the Constitution's commerce clause entitles Congress to determine what may be bought and sold. And thus federal marijuana crimes were upheld.

Though that precedent still stands, the Justice Department under Democratic president Barack Obama and the attorney general took a different approach. The attorney general announced early in Obama's presidency that federal resources would not go toward enforcing the national law in states where the people had voted to legalize the drug. Through his eight years as president, the states—those laboratories of democracy—legalized marijuana, and federal arrests for marijuana became nearly nonexistent.

Until recently, Democrats and Independents supported legalization more than Republicans. However, as Gallup reports, most Republicans now support legalizing marijuana. The policy debate on legalization and how federal law would be enforced surfaced in the 2016 primary and general elections for president with a variety of responses from candidates in both parties. After Donald Trump took office and Attorney General Jeff Sessions—an anti-drug conservative—was sworn in, pot users and medical marijuana proponents watched closely. Whatever policy this administration takes, most analysts predict more localities will legalize the drug.

Support for Marijuana Legalization

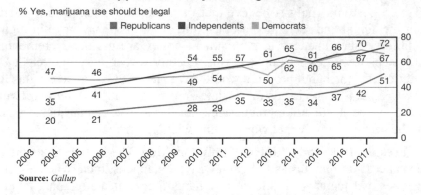

% Yes, marijuana use should be legal

■ Republicans ■ Independents ■ Democrats

Source: *Gallup*

How might the publication of polls on the subject affect people's attitudes toward marijuana?

Political Ideologies and the Marketplace

The philosophy of the president and the collective attitude of Congress can drastically impact the federal budget, taxes paid into the federal purse, the value of the dollar, and trade relationships with foreign nations. Except for partisan identification, there are no greater determiners on Election Day than a voter's view of the economy and the economic scorecard for politicians in power. Incumbent presidents who sought reelection during a bad economy invariably lost their chances for a second term. The classic example is Herbert Hoover, who in 1932 sought reelection during the worst economy in history and suffered a landslide loss to Franklin Roosevelt. Presidents Ford in 1976, Carter in 1980, and Bush Sr. in 1992 all lost their quests for a second term during poor economic times. In 1992, with the Cold War over and the economy in bad shape, Bill Clinton's campaign manager, James Carville, reminded his candidate, "It's the economy, stupid." People who are adversely affected by the economy will vote against members of the incumbent party.

Governing economic and budgeting issues is challenging, especially considering the general desires of the citizenry. Most people have three desires for government finances: lower taxes, no national debt, and enhanced government services. Having all three is impossible. So how do politicians satisfy these wants? "Don't tax me, don't tax thee, tax that fellow behind the tree," Democratic Senator Russell Long of Louisiana (1948–1987) allegedly used to say. Long came from a family of adept Louisiana politicians who knew that the answer was to raise taxes on "other people." For example, governments create excise taxes on particular products or services, such as cigarettes or gambling (often called "sin taxes"), hitting only a few people, many of whom won't stop making such purchases even when taxes lead to higher prices.

A key difference between political ideologies is a set of beliefs about the extent to which the government should be involved in the economy. Liberal ideologies favor considerable government involvement in the economy as a way to keep it healthy and protect the public good. For example, during the economic decline of the Great Recession (2007–2013), Democrats in power under the leadership of President Obama supported a high level of government spending to stimulate the economy. The law received practically no Republican support in Congress. Republicans criticized the bill for its emphasis on government spending rather than tax cuts, which is what the previous president, George Bush, had supported in the Economic Stimulus Act of 2008. The tax cuts put more money into the hands of citizens, giving them more control over how to spend it, they argued. Libertarian opposition was even stronger, since libertarians saw the law as an inappropriate expansion of government power.

Varying views on the role of government involvement and regulation of the economy are based on different economic theories. Liberals use the theory of English economist John Maynard Keynes (1883–1946) to support their views. Conservatives rely on so-called "supply-side" theories developed by economists during the presidency of Republican Ronald Reagan (1981–1989). Libertarians have been influenced by economists such as Alan Greenspan, who was Chairman of the Board of the Federal Reserve System from 1987–2006, and Milton Friedman, winner of the Nobel Prize in Economics in 1976.

Keynesian Economics

Keynesian economics addresses **fiscal policy**, that part of economic policy that is concerned with government spending and taxation. Keynes offered a theory regarding the aggregate demand (the grand total spent) in an economy. He theorized that if left to its own devices, the market will not necessarily operate at full capacity. Not all persons will be employed and the value of the dollar may drop. Much depends on how much people spend or save. Saving is wise for individuals, but when too many people save too much, companies will manufacture fewer products and unemployment will rise. When people spend too much, conversely, their spending will cause a sustained increase in prices and shortages of goods.

Keynes believed that the government should create the right level of demand. When demand is too low, the government should put more money into the economy by reducing taxes and/or increasing government spending, even if doing so requires borrowing money. This approach led to the 2009 American Recovery and Reinvestment Act. If demand is too high, the government should take money out of the economy by taxing more (taking wealth out of citizens' pockets) and/or spending less.

Keynesian economics also recognizes a *multiplier effect*, a mechanism by which an increase in spending results in an economic growth greater than the amount of spending. That is, output increases by a multiple of the original change in spending that caused it. For example, with a multiplier of 1.5, a

$10 billion increase in government spending could cause the total output of goods and services to rise by $15 billion. In concrete terms, consider what happens if the government begins public construction projects. Not only are unemployed construction contractors put to work, but bricklayers, electricians, and plumbers are too. With an income once again, these workers can afford to buy products and services from other retail businesses, whose income and demand for more employees increases.

Keynesian economics represents one end of the spectrum on the role of government regulation of the marketplace, calling for significant government involvement. Liberal ideologies tend to favor this level of government involvement. Democrat Franklin Roosevelt based his New Deal concept largely on the Keynesian model. The federal government built an array of public works during the Great Depression (1929–1939). Agencies such as the Works Progress Administration, the Public Works Administration, and the Civilian Conservation Corp built new schools, dams, roads, libraries, and other capital investments. The government had to borrow money while it pumped money into the economy and provided jobs. More recently, as you read, the American Recovery and Reinvestment Act (ARRA) of 2009 helped create new jobs by investing in education, infrastructure, health, and renewable energy resources.

Supply-Side Theory

At the other end of the economic ideological spectrum are supply-side theorists. They, too, address fiscal policy, but they approach it in a different way. Harvard economist Arthur Laffer, a key advisor to Republican President Ronald Reagan, came to define **supply-side economics**. Supply-siders—fiscal conservatives—believe that the government should leave as much of the money supply as possible with the people, letting the laws of the marketplace—supply and demand, for example—govern the market. This approach, known as *laissez-faire* (French for "let it be") or free-market theory, means taxing less and leaving that money in citizens' pockets. According to this theory, such a stance serves two purposes: 1) people will have more money to spend and will spend it, and 2) this spending will increase purchasing, jobs, and manufacturing. Under this concept, the government will still earn large revenues via the taxes collected from this spending. The more people spend, the more the state collects in sales taxes. The federal government will take in greater amounts of income tax because more people will be employed, will earn higher salaries, or both. Government will also take in greater revenues in corporate taxes from company profits. Supply-siders try to determine the right level of tax to strengthen firms and increase overall government revenues.

Keeping taxes low also provides incentives for people to work more and earn more, knowing they will be able to save more money. They will also invest more in other ways. If they are not spending money at the store, they may put more money into the economy with larger investments, such as purchasing stocks or bonds. These activities boost the economy and show consumer confidence.

Conservative ideologies favor this supply-side theory with its limits on government regulations and reduced taxation. The Republican Congress in late 2017 passed the Tax Cuts and Jobs Act, promoted by President Trump, which overhauled the tax code, temporarily lowering taxes for individuals and permanently lowering taxes for corporations. Proponents of the bill, which passed in the Senate with no votes from Democrats, argued that the lower taxes for corporations will induce them to pass some of the savings on to workers in the form of higher wages and to hire more workers, both of which would help the economy grow.

Libertarians favor even fewer government regulations. Libertarians believe the government should do no more than protect property rights and voluntary trade but in other ways let the free market work according to its own principles.

Differing Views on Revenue and Spending

In addition to conflicting views on the extent of government involvement in the economy, liberals and conservatives have differing views on the tax laws that produce revenue and policies that guide government spending.

Revenue Article I of the Constitution gives Congress the power to lay and collect taxes and to borrow money. It is through this power that the United States taxes, charges fees, and borrows money to collect revenue.

When the framers empowered Congress to lay and collect taxes, they only vaguely defined how Congress would assess and collect those taxes. For the first several decades, customs duties on imports supplied most of the government revenues. During this time, however, the federal government provided many fewer services than it does in modern times.

Congress passed the first income tax to support the Union cause during the Civil War. In the later 1800s, Congress instituted the first-ever peacetime income tax to support the growing federal government. In *Pollock v. Farmers' Loan and Trust* (1892) the Supreme Court ruled income taxes unconstitutional because Article I did not specifically grant Congress the power to directly tax individuals. This was a classic case that exemplified the Court's late-1800s judicial activism and adherence to *laissez-faire* or free-market thought.

To trump the Court's decision in *Pollock*, Congress proposed and the states ratified the **Sixteenth Amendment (1913)**, which allows Congress to tax people's incomes. Soon after, Congress began defining the income tax system and later created the **Internal Revenue Service (IRS)** to oversee the collection process. Today, the largest share of federal revenue comes from these income taxes on individuals.

Over the last century, Congress has regularly altered the tax code for a variety of reasons. Our national income tax is a **progressive tax**, meaning one's tax rate increases, or progresses, as one's income increases. During World War II, the highest tax bracket required a small number of Americans, only those making the equivalent of $2.5 million a year in today's dollars, to pay 94 percent of their income in tax. Since President Kennedy encouraged a major drop in the tax rate in 1962, the top tax bracket has gradually diminished. In the 1970s, the richest taxpayers paid around 70 percent. While conservative Ronald Reagan was in office in the 1980s, it fell to below 30 percent, and in the most recent decades, it has hovered between 35 and 40 percent. The Trump administration's Tax Cuts and Jobs Act of 2017 lowered the highest individual tax bracket to 37 percent.

Paying nearly 40 percent of what one earns to the national government seems high, but only the richest Americans do so. Today, only people earning hundreds of thousands of dollars per year are paying at this high rate. In fact, more than 18 million people in the United States need not even file a tax return, and well over 30 million others still end up paying no federal income tax at all. Middle-class Americans—families earning under $165,000 per year, pay roughly between 12 and 22 percent of their incomes to the federal government. Public opinion supports a mildly progressive tax code, and that has been the standard since the Progressive Era (1890–1920). Some conservatives on the far right, however, argue for a **flat tax**, one that taxes citizens at the same rate. Libertarians go even further, arguing that the government should not coerce people to do anything, including paying taxes.

Tax as Social Policy Congress has used taxing power not only as a revenue source but also as a way to draft social policy, by encouraging certain behaviors and discouraging others. When liberals have been in charge of drafting tax laws, Congress has created incentives to encourage people to purchase energy-efficient cars, appliances, solar panels, doors, and windows for their homes in order to protect the environment. The Trump tax reform eliminated some of those incentives while providing incentives for families who hold what many call traditional values. These incentives include increased child tax credits to encourage having children, with married couples receiving the greatest benefits. Special interest groups have also pushed for loopholes in the tax code to favor certain people.

Spending The budget process has become very partisan as Republicans and Democrats differ on spending priorities. Republicans tend toward fiscal conservatism; Democrats tend to spend federal dollars more liberally on social programs to help the disadvantaged or to support the arts.

The President initiates the annual budget, the plan for how revenue will be spent. (See pages 96–101 for more on the budget process.) Members of Congress from the party opposite the president commonly claim the president's budget plan is "dead on arrival." The reality is that typically both parties vote to spend more than the federal government takes in, increasing the national debt, while they argue about philosophical differences on parts of the budget that make up a fraction of the total. For example, some argue against spending money on NASA and other scientific endeavors. For the 2017 budget, all funds going to science, space exploration, and technology totaled $19.6 billion, a huge sum, but less than 1 percent of the overall budget. The National Endowment for the Arts, always a target for criticism from fiscal conservatives, was eliminated completely from President Trump's 2018 budget proposal, as was the National

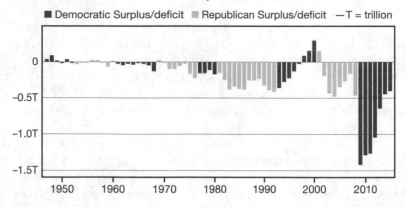

Federal Surplus and Deficit

■ Democratic Surplus/deficit   ■ Republican Surplus/deficit   —T = trillion

Source: *Office of Management and Budget as of December 2016.*
What policy explains the very large deficit starting in 2009?

Endowment for the Humanities, even though these endowments represented a mere 0.009 percent of the budget. In the final budget, however, their funding was extended. Welfare programs, an easy slice of the federal pie to rile taxpayers, typically amounts to between one and two percent.

Balancing the budget—spending no more than the revenue takes in—is a nearly impossible task. Democrat Bill Clinton (1993–2001) has been the only president in recent time to balance the budget, which he accomplished with no Republican support by raising taxes on the wealthy. Neither party has been able to sustain a balanced budget with all of the demands on government spending, though Democrats have done a slightly better job.

Political Ideologies on Monetary Policy

The basic forces of supply and demand that determine prices on every product or service from lemonade to cars also determine the actual value of the U.S. dollar. Of course, a dollar is worth 100 cents, but what will it buy? Diamonds and gold are worth a lot because they are in short supply. Paper clips are cheap for the opposite reason. These same principles affect the value of money. **Monetary policy** is how the government manages the supply and demand of its currency and thus the value of the dollar. How much a dollar is worth depends on how many printed dollars are available and how much people (both Americans and those around the world) want them.

Inflation (rising prices and devaluation of the dollar) occurs, monetarists will tell you, when there are too many dollars in circulation. If a government prints few dollars or closely monitors how much currency makes its way into circulation, the value of a dollar will remain relatively high. Conservatives tend to prefer monetary policy adjustments to regulate the economy over fiscal policies, which they tend to regard as wasteful government spending and unnecessary interference.

The Federal Reserve System

To manage the money supply, Congress created the Federal Reserve System in 1913. It consists of the **Federal Reserve Board** and 12 Federal Reserve Banks. The Federal Reserve Board, typically referred to as "The Fed," is a board of seven "governors" appointed by the president and approved by the Senate for staggered 14-year terms. One governor serves as the chairman for a four-year term. This agency sets monetary policy by buying and selling securities or bonds, regulating money reserves required at commercial banks, and setting interest rates.

The 12 Federal Reserve Banks serve as the intermediaries for money traveling from the government printing press to the commercial banks in your hometown. The letter code in the Federal Reserve seal on the face of a dollar bill represents one of these 12 banks. The U.S. government loans these printed dollars to the commercial banks.

The Fed also determines the rates for government **bonds,** or securities (government IOUs), and when to sell or purchase these. In addition to taxes, our federal government takes in revenue when individual Americans or even foreign governments purchase U.S. bonds or other Treasury notes on a promise that the United States will pay them back later with interest. The Fed both sells these to and purchases these from commercial banks. When it buys them back with interest, it is giving the banks more money with which to operate and to loan out to customers.

The Fed also sets the **discount rate**, the interest rate at which the government loans actual dollars to commercial banks. Since 1990, this rate has fluctuated from 4 to 6 percent; more recently it has dropped below 1 percent. Raising or lowering the discount rate has a direct impact on commercial banking activity and the economy in general. Commercial banks will borrow larger sums when the rate is lower and drop their interest rates accordingly in order to loan more money to its customer-borrowers. When banks can offer lower interest rates to consumers, people purchase more cars and houses. When more homes or cars are purchased, employment rises as more car sales associates, realtors, and housing contractors are needed, and demand is generated for lumber, bricks, rubber, and gasoline.

Reserve Requirement The Fed also regulates how much cash commercial banks must keep in their vaults. This amount is known as the **reserve requirement**. While these banks give you an incentive to keep your money with them by offering small interest rates on savings or checking accounts, they charge higher rates to those borrowing from them. The Fed sets reserve requirements, the amount of money that the bank must keep on hand as a proportion of how much money the bank rightfully possesses (though much of it is loaned out to borrowers). These reserves and this requirement have a direct effect on how much the bank can loan out. If the reserve requirement declines from $16 on hand for every $100 it loans out to $12 on hand per $100, the bank will be encouraged to loan out more. If the reserve requirement rises, the interest rates will also rise.

Independence and Stability As you can see, decisions at the Fed can have monumental impact on the value of the dollar and the state of the economy. That is why the Federal Reserve Board is an independent agency in the executive branch with a unique structural design. Presidents can shape the Fed with appointments, but once confirmed, these governors and the chairman act in the best interest of the nation, not at the whims of the president or of a political party. Their lengthy 14-year terms allow for continuity. The chairman's term is a four-year period that staggers the president's term to prevent making the appointment an election issue. The president can remove these governors for stated causes if they do not act in the best interest of the nation.

Differing Views on Monetary Policy

Supporters of monetary policy as the best stabilizing factor in an economy—mainly conservatives—look to the work of Milton Friedman and Alan Greenspan (Fed chairman from 1987–2007) as their theoretical base. Both disagree with the Keynesian analysis of the economy and have supported an "easy-money" policy of lowering interest rates to stimulate banks to loan more money, which in turn stimulates consumption and economic growth. This policy also guards against inflation. Critics of this approach, including many liberals, point to studies that show it has not had the desired effects and may have even been part of the cause of the Great Recession, when housing prices fell dramatically, stranding homeowners who borrowed with easy money and then found themselves with mortgage amounts exceeding the value of their homes. Many were forced to abandon their homes and the equity they had invested.

Individual libertarians differ in their views on monetary policy, but the Libertarian Party has taken a position on it: It opposes all national controls of the economy and believes the free market does the best job of adjusting to economic downturns. It favors doing away with the Federal Reserve Bank and all regulations on banking.

Political Ideologies on Trade

Globalization is the process of an ever-expanding and increasingly interactive world economy. Nations have increased their trading over the past two generations. Today, most products you find in your local department store were produced overseas. The U.S. government, mostly through Congress, can decide to increase or decrease this trade. A government wants to encourage its firms to export to larger world markets so that wealth from other nations enters the U.S. economy. A nation that exports more than it imports has a favorable

trade balance. One that purchases more goods from other nations than it sends out has a trade deficit. The size of this surplus or deficit is but one measure of U.S. economic success. On the other hand, Congress imposes import duties on products coming into the country to protect U.S. manufacturers.

According to the U.S. Constitution, Article I, Section 9, to encourage American production, Congress cannot tax exports. The framers did, however, expect Congress to tax imported goods, charging fees to foreign manufacturers in order to give American manufacturing an advantage. Import taxes require foreign firms to raise prices on their goods once they arrive in the United States. The idea was to create a favorable trade balance, hoping Americans would produce and export more than they imported.

NAFTA Since trade has an impact on the economy, trade agreements generate ideological differences of opinion. For example, the 1994 **North American Free Trade Agreement (NAFTA)** lifted trade barriers among the three largest North American countries: the United States, Canada, and Mexico. This agreement effectively removed import taxes among these powers. The debate about this agreement created a battle between generally conservative corporations and generally liberal labor unions. The business community, manufacturing firms, and economic conservatives generally favor free trade. To *laissez-faire* economists, lifting barriers and government interference will create a free flow of goods and services on a global scale. These same proponents of globalization argue that the process has decreased poverty and enhanced the general quality of life in foreign nations as well as opening new markets for U.S. goods and services.

A vessel stacked with containers filled with Chinese goods approaches Port Angeles in Washington state. China is the nation's number-one trading partner. The United States imported $479 billion in goods and services from China in 2016 and exported to China $170 billion.

Many laborers, however, feared that American firms would outsource their labor requirements, which they have done. The auto industry suffered a major blow over the past decade and the automakers in Detroit closed plants and laid off workers. The free traders responded that the Mexican economy has grown and Mexico has bought more goods and services from the United States.

Ideological Differences on Social Issues

Just as political ideologies vary on the issue of government involvement in the economy, so do they vary on the extent to which the government should address social issues. The Preamble to the Constitution declares that the government will "promote the general welfare" of its citizens. How that is interpreted, however, varies according to political theories.

For example, many people believe the goals of the Constitution are best served when the government plays a key role in providing **social welfare**—support for disadvantaged people to meet their basic needs. The nation's social welfare policy has enacted that goal, especially the New Deal programs of the 1930s and the Great Society programs of the 1960s. More recently, Congress passed and President Obama signed into law a national health care law, although it has been under attack by a Republican-dominated Congress and the Trump administration.

A Social Safety Net

In the liberal view of social policy, the government should provide a safety net for people in need and pay for it with higher taxes. This safety net takes the form of entitlements—government services Congress has promised by law to citizens—that are major contributors to both annual deficits and the overall debt. (See pages 99–101.) Congress frequently defines criteria that will award cash to individuals, groups, and state or local governments. Congress must cover this **mandatory spending**, paying those who are legally "entitled" to these funds. **Entitlements** include Social Security, Medicare, Medicaid, block grants, financial aid, food stamps, money owed on bonds, and the government's other contractual obligations.

The largest entitlement program is Social Security. This mandatory government-run retirement plan constitutes more than 20 percent of the budget. Compared to the 1930s, Americans are living much longer. Some predict the Social Security trust fund—an account set aside and protected to help maintain the system—will become exhausted in 2042. At that time, the annual revenue for the program is projected to drop by 25 percent.

Politicians began realizing the potential hazards with this program years ago. Political daredevils have discussed privatizing the program or raising the retirement age. However, people who have paid into the system for most of their lives become upset when they hear politicians planning to tamper with Social Security or to change the rules in the middle of their life-game. Older citizens vote reliably, and the American Association of Retired Persons (AARP) is the largest and one of the most influential interest groups in the nation. These factors have made Social Security the "third rail" of politics: Nobody wants to touch the third rail of a train track because it carries the electrical charge, and no politician wants to touch Social Security because of the shockwave in constituent disapproval.

Combined, Medicare and Medicaid make up nearly 20 percent of the federal budget. Once a patient is 65 years old, the government pays for most doctor visits, hospitalization, and prescription drugs. Medicare is largely administered by the states while the federal government pays the bill.

Congress must pay entitlements, but these could be altered. The rules and criteria can change to trim the payments to those entitled. And, for the future, some could surely be scrapped. The problem is that most entitlements are on autopilot, and the government need not review them annually. And, like the third rail of Social Security, politicians have little nerve to take away money from those who have paid into the system their entire working lives.

Other Western nations provide more social welfare services to their needy citizens than does the United States and begin providing services much earlier. Factors such as federalism and differing views on responsibility have slowed the United States in this regard. To some degree, American society has taken care of its elderly and its poor. Philanthropists and most states had some type of programs to support widows, orphans, and the less fortunate. However, not until Social Security was established to provide modest income to those who qualify did the poverty rate among the elderly decline from about 50 percent during the Great Depression to just under 10 percent now, though it is somewhat higher for senior women.

Social Security Act Amid the Great Depression, Franklin Delano Roosevelt (FDR) and his team of advisors created a federal safety net for the elderly and supported those who were put out of work, and in so doing greatly expanded the role of government, creating what some call the welfare state. The economic disaster had bankrupted local charities and state treasuries, forcing the national government to act. The **Social Security Act of 1935** created an insurance program that required the employed to pay a small contribution via a payroll tax into an insurance fund designed to assist the unemployed and to help financially strapped retirees. An additional assistance program helps blind, elderly, and less fortunate people. The act guaranteed that all who paid into the system would collect retirement benefits via Social Security checks beginning at age 65. But for the less fortunate under 65, only those who did not have the means to survive would be provided benefits. The government developed a **means test** to determine which citizens qualify for this aid.

Officially called Old Age, Survivors, and Disability Insurance (OASDI), Social Security requires most employed citizens to pay 12.4 percent (the employer pays 6.2 percent and the employee pays 6.2 percent) into a trust fund that is kept separate from the general treasury as an independent agency to protect it. The Social Security Administration handles the fund and distributes the checks. It is a large agency composed of almost 60,000 employees and more than 1,400 offices nationwide.

Medicare and Medicaid FDR's plan to pay for the elderly's medical care was tabled until Congress passed the **Medicare** law in 1965 during the Democratic administration of President Lyndon Johnson. Medicare helps ease the medical costs of seniors over the age of 65. It is administered by an agency in the Department of Health and Human Services and is funded by a payroll tax of 1.45 percent paid by both employer and employee. For those earning more than $200,000 per year, the rate has recently increased to 3.8 percent. The law, which has since been amended, is broken into four parts that cover hospitalization, physicians' services, a public-private partnership known as Medicare Advantage that allows companies to provide Medicare benefits, and a prescription drug benefit. For those over age 65 who qualify, Medicare can cover up to 80 percent of their health care costs. **Medicaid** provides health insurance coverage for the poorest Americans. To be eligible for Medicaid services, the applying citizen must meet minimum-income thresholds or be disabled or pregnant.

Liberals supported other measures in President Johnson's Great Society initiative, including programs in a War on Poverty that provided additional aid for the poor, subsidized housing, and job retraining programs, with the total increasing from nearly $10 billion in 1960 to about $30 billion in 1968. The percentage of people living in poverty fell dramatically, especially among African Americans.

Source: *LBJ Presidential Library*

President Lyndon Johnson toured poverty-stricken areas of the country in 1964 as part of his War on Poverty to offer hope for better times.

Conservative Opposition Conservatives and libertarians, however, had long opposed these expensive government programs. As early as 1964, Ronald Reagan clearly articulated the conservative view in a speech in supporting the candidacy of conservative Republican presidential candidate Barry Goldwater:

> The Founding Fathers knew a government can't control the economy without controlling people. And they knew when a government sets out to do that, it must use force and coercion to achieve its purpose. So we have come to a time for choosing . . . You and I are told we must choose between a left or right, but I suggest there is no such thing as a left or right. There is only an up or down. Up to man's age-old dream—the maximum of individual freedom consistent with order—or down to the ant heap of totalitarianism.

When Reagan became president in 1981 he built on efforts he made while governor of California to cut back on government social spending. "Reaganomics," as the economic programs of Reagan have come to be called, stressed lowering taxes and supporting free market activity. With lower taxes, welfare programs, such as the food stamp program and construction of public housing, were cut back.

Health Care American citizens purchase health insurance coverage either through their employer or on their own. Health insurance eases the cost of doctor visits, prescription medicines, operations, and other medical costs. Many politicians and several presidents have favored the idea of a government-based health care system for decades. Some health insurance regulations have existed for years, sometimes differing from state to state. Recently, with the continual increases in insurance prices and the diminishing level of coverage, more Americans have bought into the idea of expanding government regulation of health insurance and making the service more affordable.

This idea finally became law with the passage of the **Patient Protection and Affordable Care Act** in 2010. Sometimes referred to as "Obamacare" because of President Obama's support for the law, the comprehensive Affordable Care Act became a divisive issue in party politics, with opponents concerned about the overreach of government. Conservative legislators, many of them backed by wealthy campaign donors with libertarian leanings, objected to the government's involvement in health care and fought it fiercely. The Republicans lacked the power in Congress to prevent it from becoming law, but after they gained control of both houses and the White House with the election of President Trump in 2016, they have chipped away at the plan repeatedly and several times tried to repeal it completely.

Conservatives tend to believe that private companies can do a better job providing social services, including health care, than the government. They push for privatization of Medicare and Medicaid as a way to reduce mandatory spending and energize the private sector. In their view, privatizing health care would increase competition among providers, which in turn will lead to generally lower health care costs.

Labor

Labor is both an economic and a social issue. As an economic issue, conservatives tend to view labor as an element of the free market that should not be regulated by the government. Wages, according to this view, should be determined by supply and demand. Liberals, in contrast, view labor as a unique element in the marketplace because of the complexities of human behavior. For example, workers with higher wages tend to be more motivated to do a good job and remain with an employer longer than workers with lower wages, factors not considered in the supply-and-demand model.

As a social issue, conservatives tend to view organized labor as a negative influence. In some states at some places of business, whether they want to join a union or not, workers are required to pay union dues. Many people believe that such requirements are an infringement of their individual liberties, especially since labor unions actively campaign for candidates and not all workers support the candidates the unions endorse, as the election of Donald Trump in the Rustbelt states shows. Liberals have a much more positive view of organized labor as a force that has lifted workers into a position of some power through collective bargaining, which has resulted in the 40-hour work week, employer-provided health care, and many other benefits.

Corporations and workers struggled as the labor union movement developed from the late 1800s into the Great Depression. During periods of liberal or progressive domination of the federal government, Congress passed various laws that prevented collusion by corporations, price fixing, trusts, and yellow dog contracts (forcing newly hired employees into a promise not to join a labor union). Different presidents implemented these laws with varying degrees of enforcement. As part of the New Deal program, Congress passed the Wagner Act (also known as the National Labor Relations Act) in 1935 and the Fair Labor Standards Act in 1938. The Wagner Act created the National Labor Relations Board, a federal executive branch commission that regulates labor organizations and hears complaints of unfair labor practices. It also ensured workers' rights to collectively bargain with management. The second law established minimum wage, defined the 40-hour work week, and required companies to pay employees overtime pay.

After World War II, Republicans gained control of Congress in the 1946 mid-term elections and passed the Taft-Hartley Act (1947), generally favored by business and partly counteracting the labor movement. It enabled states to outlaw the closed shop—a company policy or labor contract that requires all employees to join the local union. States could now pass "right to work" laws. Taft-Hartley also allowed the federal government to block any labor strike in an industry that might put into jeopardy the "national health or safety." With Democratic support, Congress created the Occupational Safety and Health Act in 1970, which established the Occupational and Safety and Health Administration, or OSHA. OSHA inspects factories and other workplaces for occupational hazards. Like other regulatory agencies, OSHA can fine a company or can close it down until problems are fixed.

Source: *Getty Images*

President Ronald Reagan (C), with his Transportation Secretary Andrew L. Lewis (R) and Attorney General William French Smith

During the conservative presidency of Ronald Reagan, however, organized labor received a blow that has been hard to overcome. Reagan spoke out against the August 1981 strike by air traffic controllers. He declared the strike illegal because the controllers were public employees, and he fired them. Their union was later decertified. Reagan was in general a supporter of workers' rights to collective bargaining, but his firm stand against the air traffic controllers, according to labor expert Joseph A. McCartin, "shaped the world of the modern workplace," which has seen dramatically fewer participants in labor walkouts.

Ideological Differences on Government and Privacy

Other social issues besides government spending also divide liberals and conservatives. These concern matters related to personal choice and individual freedoms. Liberals tend to think that the government should not regulate private, personal matters, while many modern social conservatives believe the government needs to protect core values even if doing so intrudes on some individual freedoms.

Privacy and Intimacy

Many of the issues that divide liberals and conservatives on privacy relate to intimate decisions. With the 1965 ruling in *Griswold v. Connecticut* (page 287), the Court established a precedent for a right to privacy on intimate matters. That decision found that a Connecticut state law forbidding married persons from using contraception and forbidding people such as health care professionals from helping or advising someone else to use contraception was unconstitutional. Most liberals agree with this position. Similar cases with strong liberal support include *Roe v. Wade* (1973), which legalized abortion under certain conditions (see page 288); *Lawrence v. Texas* (2003), which ruled that laws banning consensual same-sex intimacy violated the Fourteenth Amendment's equal protection clause; and *Obergefell v. Hodges* (2015), which found that denying marriage to same-sex couples violated their rights.

Conservative Supreme Court Justice Antonin Scalia, however, said in a 2012 television interview, "There is no right to privacy," adding that the Griswold case "was wrong." Conservatives tend to believe that if the states pass laws in these areas of personal privacy, the federal government does not have authority to overrule them since the right to privacy is not explicit in the Constitution.

A number of recent cases highlight the difference between liberal and conservative views on privacy. For example, does the federal government through the Supreme Court have a right to overrule a state law that requires transgender people to use public bathrooms that match their birth sex rather than their gender identity? Conservatives argue that the state law should stand. Some students argue that being forced to use a school bathroom with people of the opposite physical sex violates *their* right to privacy.

Informational Privacy

Liberals and conservatives often disagree on issues of informational privacy as well. Though both perspectives value the privacy of an individual's personal data, they sometimes disagree on where the balance between individual liberty and national security lies. Conservatives tend to be more supportive of government surveillance efforts, especially when the nation may be under threat. Liberals tend to favor stricter limits on government surveillance.

However, over the years, as technology has made sweeping data collection simple, liberals and conservatives have joined in opposing the National Security Agency's collection of bulk data. Both support the requirement that requests for information need to be approved by the court authorized under the Foreign Intelligence Surveillance Act (FISA), but people with both liberal and conservative ideologies worry about the easy access the government may have to personal information. (For a full discussion of informational privacy and the Fourth Amendment, see pages 277–282.)

Education and Religion

On some matters related to education and religion, conservatives want less government intrusion than liberals. For example, many parents choose to send their children to private schools, which are often associated with a religious denomination. However, they still must pay local taxes that support the public schools. A number of states provide vouchers—diversions of public funds—to these families to defray the costs of these private schools.

Conservatives argue that the freedom to choose the educational environment and curriculum of their children is fundamental. They also argue that private schools create competition for public schools, which, to keep their students, will have an incentive to improve.

This free market approach to education is very different from the free public education value cherished by liberals, who worry that funds diverted from public schools will weaken an already challenged system. Liberals tend to want more government involvement in education than conservatives. For example, most liberals supported President Obama's "Race to the Top" initiative, which encouraged states to compete for grants to help them adopt rigorous standards, use data efficiently, establish data-driven evaluations of teachers, and address under-performing schools.

Conservatives are likewise more opposed to government interference in the practice of their religious beliefs, even when that practice may clash with federal nondiscrimination law. For example, some businesses that provide services for weddings, such as caterers and bakeries, have refused to work with same-sex couples on the grounds that doing so violates their religious beliefs. They do not deny service to same-sex couples on non-wedding related items—only those that support same-sex marriage. Cases of discrimination are working their way up to the Supreme Court, with the proprietors emphasizing their First Amendment freedom of religious exercise and the customers emphasizing the state and federal laws that assure equal access to merchants.

COMPARISON OF COLLEGE-EDUCATED DEMOCRATS AND REPUBLICANS ON SOME SOCIAL ISSUES BASED ON GALLUP POLLS IN 2016 AND 2017		
Issue	**Democrats**	**Republicans**
Prefer government-run health care	72%	8%
Government should make sure all have health care	84%	22%
Taxed too little or the right amount	71%	30%
Poor people pay too much in taxes	57%	27%
Abortion is morally acceptable	82%	41%
Homosexuality is morally acceptable	86%	49%

Public policy at any time is a reflection of the success of liberal or conservative perspectives in political parties. When Republicans are in power, conservative policies on marketplace regulation, social services, and privacy are often voted or adjudicated into law. When Democrats are in power, they tend to promote liberal social, economic, and privacy policies.

REFLECT ON THE ESSENTIAL QUESTION

Essential Question: *How do political ideologies shape policy debates and choices in American politics?* On separate paper, create a chart like the one below to help you answer that question.

Type of Policy	Conservatives	Liberals
Fiscal Policy		
Monetary Policy		
Social Policy		

KEY TERMS AND NAMES

agenda/391

bonds/402

discount rate/402

entitlements/405

Federal Reserve Board/402

fiscal policy/397

flat tax/400

globalization/403

inflation/401

Internal Revenue Service (IRS)/399

mandatory spending/405

means test/406

Medicaid/407

Medicare/407

monetary policy/401

North American Free Trade Agreement (NAFTA)/404

Patient Protection and Affordable Care Act (2010)/408

progressive tax/399

reserve requirement/402

Sixteenth Amendment/399

Social Security Act (1935)/406

social welfare/405

supply-side economics/398

trade balance/404

1. Which of the following best describes the sequence of the policy decision-making process?

   (A) Respond to challenges, plan for funding, cost-benefit analysis

   (B) Plan for funding, cost-benefit analysis, development of agenda

   (C) Public hearings, cost-benefit analysis, development of agenda

   (D) Development of agenda, cost-benefit analysis, plan for funding

2. Which of the following best describes how policy reflects the attitudes and beliefs of citizens who choose to participate at a given time?

   (A) Congress passes a new tax code.

   (B) Marijuana is legalized with pressure from interest groups.

   (C) The president issues an executive order on immigration.

   (D) The Supreme Court rules on school prayer.

3. Which argument do supporters of supply-side economics make?

   (A) The more revenue the government takes in and spends the better off the economy will be.

   (B) Leaving more money in the citizens' pockets will stimulate the economy and generate government revenues through other taxes.

   (C) The federal government should follow the ideas of John Maynard Keynes.

   (D) The government should increase the supply of currency into circulation to bring down inflation.

Questions 4 and 5 refer to the cartoon below.

Source: *Nick Anderson's Editorial Cartoons*

4. With which of the following statements would the cartoonist agree?

(A) The government is working hard to fix problems in Social Security.

(B) To provide tax cuts, politicians want to make Social Security less stable.

(C) Tax cuts are going to boost the economy and save Social Security.

(D) Nothing can be done to save Social Security.

5. Which of the following ideologies most likely aligns with the cartoonist's perspective?

(A) Libertarian

(B) Conservative

(C) Liberal

(D) Independent

6. Which of the following is an accurate comparison of contemporary conservative and liberal political views?

	CONSERVATIVE	LIBERAL
(A)	Believes government should do less	Believes in expanding government's role
(B)	Believes fiscal policy is the best stabilizing approach	Believes monetary policy is the best stabilizing approach
(C)	Believes in increasing the minimum wage	Accepts higher taxes in return for more government services
(D)	Believes government should not intrude on personal intimacy decisions	Believes government should set limits on personal intimacy decisions

Questions 7 and 8 refer to the graphic below.

FEDERAL RECEIPTS BY SOURCE

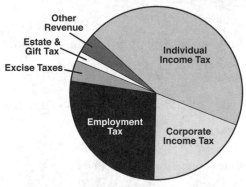

Source: *OMB Historical tables, FY 2011*

7. The pie graph above represents a key element of which of the following?

(A) Fiscal policy

(B) Monetary policy

(C) Keynesian economic theory

(D) Supply-side theory

8. To reduce the deficit, Democrats would most likely recommend increasing which source of revenue?

(A) Individual Income Tax

(B) Corporate Income Tax

(C) Employment Tax

(D) Excise Taxes

Questions 9 and 10 refer to the passage below.

There are two theories of prosperity and of well-being: The first theory is that if we make the rich richer, somehow they will let a part of their prosperity trickle down to the rest of us. The second theory [is] the theory that if we make the average of [hu]mankind comfortable and secure, their prosperity will rise upward, just as yeast rises up, through the ranks.

–President Franklin D. Roosevelt, Campaign address at Detroit, Michigan, 10/2/1932

9. To which economic theory does Roosevelt refer in his first example?

(A) Laissez-faire

(B) Supply-side

(C) Keynesian

(D) Monetarist

10. In Roosevelt's second theory, which agent is making "the average of [hu]mankind comfortable and secure"?

(A) The free market

(B) The Federal Reserve Board

(C) Social safety nets

(D) Corporate tax cuts that create jobs

1. "[The *College for All Act*] would provide $47 billion per year to states to eliminate undergraduate tuition and fees at public colleges and universities.

   Today, total tuition at public colleges and universities amounts to about $70 billion per year. Under the *College for All Act*, the federal government would cover 67% of this cost, while the states would be responsible for the remaining 33% of the cost. . . .

   States would be able to use funding to increase academic opportunities for students, hire new faculty, and provide professional development opportunities for professors. . . .

   [This program would be] fully paid for by imposing a Robin Hood tax on Wall Street. This legislation is offset by imposing a Wall Street speculation fee oninvestment houses, hedge funds, and other speculators of 0.5% on stock trades (50 cents for every $100 worth of stock), a 0.1% fee on bonds, and a 0.005% fee on derivatives. It has been estimated that this provision could raise hundreds of billions a year which could be used not only to make tuition free at public colleges and universities in this country, it could also be used to create millions of jobs and rebuild the middle class of this country."

   —Senator Bernie Sanders, Summary of *College for All Act*, April 2017

   After reading the above, respond to A, B, and C below.

   (A) Describe the political ideology behind Senator Sanders's proposed law.

   (B) Explain how the proposed law would affect federal fiscal policy.

   (C) Explain how the early stages of the policymaking process led to the proposed law.

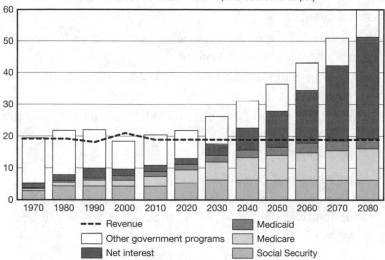

Projected Government Spending on Entitlements

Percent of Gross Domestic Product (total economic output)

Legend:
- Revenue
- Other government programs
- Net interest
- Medicaid
- Medicare
- Social Security

Source: *Government Accounting Office*

2. Use the information in the graphic above to answer the questions below.

(A) Describe the information conveyed in the graph.

(B) Describe a trend conveyed in the graph and draw a conclusion about the causes of that trend.

(C) Explain how liberals and conservatives would disagree on how to address the trend in the graph.

3. In *Everson v. Board of Education of the Township of Ewing* (1947), the Court considered whether state reimbursements for transportation costs to parents of children who used public busing to get to school, even if they attended a religious school, violated the Constitution. A divided Court ruled that busing, like fire or police protection, is a general program and available on an equal basis to families no matter what their religion.

(A) Identify the constitutional clause that is common to *Everson v. Board of Education* and *Engel v. Vitale* (1962). (See page 254.)

(B) Based on the constitutional clause identified in part A, explain why the facts of *Engel v. Vitale* led to a different holding than the holding in *Everson v. Board of Education*.

(C) Describe the likely political ideology of people who strongly agreed with the decision in *Everson v. Board of Education*.

4. Develop an argument that explains whether or not the federal government's involvement in education promotes democracy.

In your essay you must:

- Articulate a defensible claim or thesis that responds to the prompt and establishes a line of reasoning
- Support your claim with at least TWO pieces of accurate and relevant information:
  - ✦ At least ONE piece of evidence must be from one of the following foundational documents
    - − The First Amendment
    - − The Fourteenth Amendment
  - ✦ Use a second piece of evidence from the other foundational document from the list above or from your study of political ideologies
- Use reasoning to explain why your evidence supports your claim/thesis
- Respond to an opposing or alternative perspective using refutation, concession, or rebuttal

WRITING: *EXPLAIN WHY EVIDENCE SUPPORTS A CLAIM*

One requirement of the argumentative essay on the exam is that it shows how the evidence you choose supports your claim or thesis. The way you show that is by providing a *warrant*—a statement connecting the evidence to your thesis, often with a transitional word such as *because* or *therefore*. Suppose, for example, your claim is that the federal government should make cigarettes illegal. Your evidence is that cigarette smoking is harmful. Without a warrant, you do not show why, just because smoking is harmful, the government should make it illegal. A warrant would provide that glue:

Claim: The government should make cigarettes illegal.

Evidence: Cigarette smoking is harmful.

Warrant: Because one role of government is to protect health and safety, banning harmful cigarette smoking is a desirable action since it will save people's lives.

UNIT 4: Review

Those in government need to understand public opinion to create democratic laws. Opinion polls are useful to the news media, politicians, and academics.

Polling has its limits as well as its benefits. A poll is only valid if it has properly worded questions and a representative sample. In measuring public opinion, pollsters find that Americans fall into many political categories. People following liberal or conservative ideology tend to align with the Democrats or Republicans, respectively. The largest segment of the United States, however, is moderate and made up of independent voters and nonvoters. Countless other ideologies also exist. These are formed by many factors in the political socialization process, such as the influence of family, schooling, religion, and geographic region.

The values, attitudes, and beliefs of Americans influence the development, goals, and implementation of public policy over time. Policies in place at any given time represent the success of the parties whose ideologies they represent and the political attitudes and beliefs of citizens who choose to participate in politics at a given time.

THINK AS A POLITICAL SCIENTIST: *CONSTRUCT A GRAPH OF A PRESIDENT'S APPROVAL RATING*

Using one of the web sources below, select a recent president and examine that president's approval rating while in office. What major shifts in public opinion occurred? What were the highs and lows? When did these occur? Plot three distinct approval ratings on your own line chart, with dates on the *x-axis* and approval percentages on the *y-axis*. You can create your graph either on paper with a ruler or on a computer using a graphing program.

Then, using online newspapers, databases, timelines, or other sources, determine what brought the high or low approval ratings. Explain your findings in a brief paper or place quotes from reliable sources next to the high or low points on your chart. Or you could arrange the chart, with minimal text, atop an accompanying paragraph that explains the shifts of opinion in context.

- **The Roper Center**: http://www.ropercenter.uconn.edu/. Go to "Presidential Approval."

- **The American Presidency Project**: http://www.presidency.ucsb. edu/. Under "Data" you will find "Presidential Job Approval."

Review Learning Objectives

As you review Unit Four, be sure you can complete the following learning objectives. Page numbers are provided to help you locate the necessary information to fulfill the learning objective.

UNIT FOUR LEARNING OBJECTIVES	
MPA-1.A: Explain the relationship between core beliefs of U.S. citizens and attitudes about the role of government.	Pages 348–356
MPA-1.B: Explain how cultural factors influence political attitudes and socialization.	Pages 356–369
MPA-2.A: Describe the elements of a scientific poll.	Pages 371-374
MPA-2.B: Explain the quality and credibility of claims based on public opinion data.	Pages 374–378
PMI-4.A: Explain how the ideologies of the two major parties shape policy debates.	Pages 387–390
PMI-4.B: Explain how U.S. political culture (e.g., values, attitudes, and beliefs) influences the formation, goals, and implementation of public policy over time.	Pages 390–396
PMI-4.C: Describe different political ideologies regarding the role of government in regulating the marketplace.	Pages 396–399, 401–403
PMI-4.D: Explain how political ideologies vary on the government's role in regulating the marketplace.	Pages 399–401, 403-405
PMI-4.E: Explain how political ideologies vary on the role of the government in addressing social issues.	Pages 405–412

Review the following political science disciplinary practices and reasoning processes as well.

UNIT FOUR POLITICAL SCIENCE DISCIPLINARY PRACTICES AND REASONING PROCESSES	
Analyze and Interpret Visual Information	Page 360
Construct a Graph of a President's Approval Rating	Page 421

UNIT FOUR CONTEMPORARY ISSUES AND POLICY	
Policy Matters: Political Culture and the Policymaking Process Over Time	Pages 393–396

UNIT FOUR WRITING	
Use Rebuttal	Page 386
Explain Why Evidence Supports a Claim	Page 420

UNIT 5: Political Participation

On the edge of U.S. government, organized groups interact with government to shape policy. These so-called **linkage institutions**—political parties, interest groups, and the media—connect people with the government, keeping people informed and trying to shape public opinion and policy. Since the 1820s, two political parties, Democrats and Republicans, have dominated, battling back and forth for control of the government. On a national, state, and local level, parties recruit candidates, campaign, and play watchdog when the other party is in power.

Elections themselves also serve as a way to link citizens—who have constitutionally protected rights to vote—and the government. Elections are held for offices from president to sheriff. Presidential candidates spend massive amounts of money as they travel a hard road to the White House through a series of primary elections, a national convention, and televised debates. Congressional and state candidates also compete in distinct yet smaller campaigns en route to state-level office.

Interest groups adopt formal goals and raise money for their causes. Some are larger and more powerful than others and thus have more influence. They engage in several activities throughout the United States to influence policymaking.

The media are also a major force in U.S. politics. The press shapes public opinion, voter perceptions, campaign strategies, and the agenda. For this reason, candidates and members of government have a symbiotic and conflict-prone relationship with the media.

Enduring Understandings: Political Participation

MPA-3: Factors associated with political ideology, efficacy, structural barriers, and demographics influence the nature and degree of political participation.

PMI-5: Political parties, interest groups, and social movements provide opportunities for participation and influence how people relate to government and policymakers.

PRD-2: The impact of federal policies on campaigning and electoral rules continues to be contested by both sides of the political spectrum.

PRD-3: The various forms of media provide citizens with political information and influence the ways in which they participate politically.

Source: *AP® United States Government and Politics Course and Exam Description*

12

Voting and Voter Behavior

"Nobody will ever deprive the American people of the right to vote except the American people themselves—and the only way they could do that is by not voting at all."

—President Franklin D. Roosevelt, Radio Address, *October 5, 1944*

Essential Question: How are voting rights protected, and how have voting procedures been altered to respond to challenges?

The framers decided state governments were the best judges for determining **suffrage**, or which citizens were qualified to vote, and managing elections. (See Article I, Sections 2 and 4 and Article 2, Section 1.) In early U.S. history, only property-owning men could vote. Even when President Roosevelt addressed the nation about the right to vote (see the quote above), state legal barriers kept most African Americans from voting in the South. Today, legislation and constitutional amendments assure almost all adult citizens the **franchise**, or right to vote. In November 2016, about 138 million people, just over 60 percent of America's voting-eligible population, cast a vote, and Donald Trump was elected president. The **voting-eligible population** are citizens over the age of 18, and in nearly all states, they must also be non-felons.

Redefining "We the People"

The most common form of political participation is voting. Every four years, a large percentage of Americans, known as the **electorate**, "go to the polls" to cast a vote for the American president and some lower offices. Elections also occur between those four years at the local, state, and federal levels. BIG IDEA: These elections give political scientists much data to analyze to understand factors that shape voter behavior. Over the nation's history, voter eligibility expanded, redefining "We, the People" to include the working class, African Americans, women, residents of Washington, D.C., and young adults.

An Expanding Electorate

The franchise was extended to white working-class men in the United States much earlier than in other countries, but for decades, only property-owning white males were able to vote. The first presidential election (1788–1789) was decided by these political elites. The Constitution originally called for state legislatures to appoint electors who then later elected the president in an electoral college. On a designated day, every state's electors met in their capitals to cast votes for president. There was no popular vote for George Washington, but every one of the 69 electors cast their first ballots for Washington. By the 1800 presidential election, five of 16 states expanded participation by using popular elections to name the electors, and by 1823 popular selection of electors was practiced nationwide.

The framers had also endorsed the elite model of democracy (see pages 6 and 15) by calling for the election of senators by state legislatures. However, with the ratification of the **Seventeenth Amendment** in 1913, popular elections for senators became the law of the land.

State governments typically did not grant suffrage equally. The Constitution forbade religious tests for federal office but did not prevent such tests in determining who could vote. In addition to religious tests, states imposed property requirements and poll taxes. They also barred women, African Americans, and immigrants from the political process. Courageous activists worked for more than 100 years to persuade states to alter voting practices and state laws and to ratify amendments to extend suffrage. Until they were enfranchised, citizens participated in politics in the only channels available to them—through protest and expression of opinion in other ways.

Jacksonian Era Voter participation continued to grow in the 1830s. President **Andrew Jackson**, a popular leader and advocate for expanding suffrage to all white men, was influential in increasing citizen participation. Jackson embodied the common man, the non-son-of-privilege who bravely rose through military ranks and through Congress to become the seventh president of the United States. He called for the end of the property requirement to vote. In the Jacksonian Era (1828–1848), universal male suffrage became a reality, greatly increasing voter turnout. In 1824, four candidates had tallied a collective 350,671 votes. Four years later the popular vote total reached 1,155,350. By 1830, almost all states had removed the property requirement.

The citizenry played a role in pushing to expand the right to vote beyond property owners. In 1829, a Rhode Island gathering of some 300 demonstrators petitioned the state's general assembly for the extension of suffrage. It was finally granted in 1840. North Carolina was the last state to abandon the property requirement in 1856.

Suffrage by Constitutional Amendment and Legislation

By the 1860s, America had yet to give the franchise to blacks, women, and other minorities. That situation changed with the passage of three constitutional amendments: the Fifteenth, Nineteenth, and Twenty-Sixth. Two other amendments, the Twenty-Third and Twenty-Fourth, extended suffrage further. These allowed residents of the nation's capital to vote for the president and outlawed poll taxes, respectively.

- **Fifteenth Amendment (1870):** Citizens shall not be denied the right to vote by the states or the United States "on account of race, color, or previous condition of servitude."

- **Nineteenth Amendment (1920):** Citizens shall not be denied the right to vote by the states or the United States "on account of sex."

- **Twenty-Third Amendment (1961):** For presidential and vice presidential elections, "the District constituting the seat of government" shall appoint a number of electors "in no event more than the least populous State."

- **Twenty-Fourth Amendment (1964):** Citizens shall not be denied the right to vote by states or the United States "by reason of failure to pay any poll tax or other tax."

- **Twenty-Sixth Amendment (1971):** Citizens "eighteen years of age or older" shall not be denied the right to vote by the states or the United States "on account of age."

All suffrage amendments state in Section 2, "The Congress shall have the power to enforce this article by appropriate legislation." This enforcement clause has allowed Congress to assure that the spirit of the amendments is carried out. (See pages 640–644.)

African American Suffrage As suffrage expanded in its first phase, legislatures and groups of people discussed the potential for free blacks to vote. In the 1830s, six northern states permitted blacks to vote. After the North defeated the South in the Civil War, Congress passed the Reconstruction Amendments that freed the slaves, made them citizens, and gave them a vote. The **Fifteenth Amendment**, ratified in 1870, gave former slaves and free blacks the right to vote and was the first federal mandate affecting state voting requirements.

The Fifteenth Amendment, like the other amendments, passed through a northern-dominated Congress without southern support. The federal government enforced the amendment during Reconstruction when African Americans voted in large numbers. The Union Army's continued presence in the former Confederacy ensured that blacks could vote, and several were elected to public office. In 1876, Rutherford B. Hayes won a disputed presidential election and soon after withdrew Union troops from the South. A decade later, as the era of Jim Crow began, southern legislatures segregated their citizens and established loopholes to circumvent the Fifteenth Amendment. White citizens, including members of the Ku Klux Klan, intimidated and abused blacks to turn them away from the polls.

Structural Barriers Several southern states denied suffrage to African Americans as they began requiring property or literacy qualifications to vote. Several states elevated the **literacy test** into their state constitutions. The **poll tax**—a simple fee required to vote—became one of the most effective ways to discourage the potential black voter. And the **grandfather clause**, which allowed states to recognize a registering voter as it would have recognized his grandfather, prevented scores of blacks from voting, while it allowed illiterate and poor whites to circumvent the literacy test and poll tax requirements.

These state-level loopholes suppressed the black vote but never explicitly violated the letter of the Constitution because they never prevented blacks from voting, "on account of race, color, or previous condition of servitude." Rather, these barriers placed before African Americans prevented them from registering to vote. The impact on black voting was demonstrated by the number of registered black voters in Louisiana as the state sought to alter the law. Historian C. Vann Woodward reveals that in 1896, the state had 130,334 registered black voters, and African Americans outnumbered registered white voters in 26 parishes (counties). By 1900, white voters dominated every parish, and by 1904, only 1,342 blacks were on the poll books and registered to vote.

The **white primary**, too, became a popular method for southern states to keep African Americans from voting. State Democratic Party organizations set rules for their primaries, defining their membership as white men's clubs. By 1915, thirteen southern states had established the white primary. A generation of intimidation, lynching, and a host of public policies to prevent blacks from voting resulted in a steady decline in turnout that began as soon as the Union pulled out of the South. Black voting reached an all-time low in the 1920s.

Progress Through Law The growing quest for equality and the post-World War II Civil Rights Movement brought the greatest increases in African American turnout in a century. Some inroads to making the Fifteenth Amendment a reality had been made. In 1915, in *Guinn v. United States*, the Supreme Court ruled the grandfather clause unconstitutional. In 1944, the Court declared the white primary a violation of the Constitution's equal protection clause in *Smith v. Allwright*. One estimate of southern black registration before and after the white primary shows a statewide increase from 151,000 to 595,000 registered voters. Southern black voter turnout increased from 4.5 percent in 1940 to 12.5 percent in 1947. The Democratic Party included a pro-civil rights plank in its 1948 platform that called for equal treatment regardless of race, creed, or color. The Civil Rights Movement of the 1950s and 1960s caused greater increases in voter participation following key congressional acts, additional Supreme Court rulings, and one more constitutional amendment.

The **1957 Civil Rights Act**, the first such bill since Reconstruction, addressed discrimination in voter registration and established the U.S. Office of Civil Rights, an enforcement agency in the Justice Department. Before World War II, about 3 percent of the South's black voting-age populace was registered. In 1964, that percentage varied from 6 to 66 percent, averaging 36 percent.

The expansive **1964 Civil Rights Act** also addressed voting. That same year Congress proposed and the states ratified the **Twenty-Fourth Amendment**, which outlawed poll taxes in any federal elections. By the time the amendment was introduced in Congress in 1962, only four states still charged such a tax. The Supreme Court later ruled taxes on any election, such as state and local elections, unconstitutional because they violated the equal protection clause of the Fourteenth Amendment.

The 1965 **Voting Rights Act** was the most effective bill to bring the black populace into the political process. This law outlawed literacy tests and put states with low voter turnout under the watchful eye of the Justice Department. The law gave the department jurisdiction over states that had any type of voting test and less than 50 percent turnout in the 1964 election. These states became subject to federal election examiners and the **preclearance** provision of the act's Section Five. If these states attempted to invent new, legal loopholes to diminish black suffrage, such as moving polling places or gerrymandering, the federal government could stop them. By 1967, black voter registration in six southern states increased from about 30 to more than 50 percent. African Americans soon held office in greater numbers. The original law expired in 1971, but Congress has renewed the Voting Rights Act several times since.

Recently, the preclearance provision landed in the Supreme Court. Shelby County, Alabama, challenged the 1965 point of law, and the Court declared in a 5:4 decision that this section of the law imposes burdens that are no longer responsive to current conditions.

Women's Suffrage The push for women's suffrage began in the mid-1800s. Wyoming, Idaho, and Utah were among the first states to admit women to the polls. In the late 1800s, women entered the workplace and, later, in World War I served the nation on the home front. Women's suffrage became a national reality with ratification of the **Nineteenth Amendment** in 1920.

Activists had worked hard and courageously to secure the amendment's passage. Susan B. Anthony became a leading suffragist. She spoke at political conventions and helped organize different associations. In 1872, in direct violation of New York law, she walked into a polling place and cast a vote. She was tried and convicted by an all-male jury.

Suffragists continued the fight. By 1914, eleven states allowed women to vote. In the 1916 election, both major political parties endorsed the concept of women's suffrage in their platforms, and Montana elected the first woman to Congress, Jeanette Rankin. More western states granted suffrage to women; eastern and southern states did so later. Women's groups picketed the White House to persuade President Woodrow Wilson to get behind the cause. He finally supported the amendment, and it was ratified in 1920. Females became more and more accustomed to voting and became active participants in politics.

Source: *Library of Congress*

In July 1919, Missouri Governor Frederick Gardner signed the resolution ratifiying the Nineteenth Amendment.

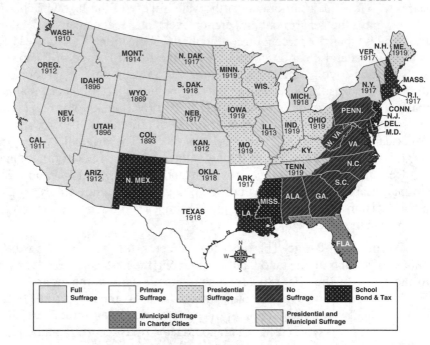

WOMEN'S SUFFRAGE BEFORE THE NINETEENTH AMENDMENT

The District of Columbia The Electoral College system awards each state the same number of electors that it has senators and representatives. Washington, D.C., is not a state and had no electors until passage of the **Twenty-Third Amendment**. The Founding Fathers were skeptical and concerned about the potential political influence of those living in and near the nation's capital. When they created the federal government, a debate ensued about the location of the national seat of government. Delegates at the constitutional convention feared the advantages a state might gain if it also housed the capital city. The Constitution therefore empowers Congress to "exercise exclusive Legislation in all Cases whatsoever, over such District…[to] become the Seat of the Government of the United States." After short terms of government in New York City and Philadelphia, the national capital moved to Washington, D.C., on a parcel of land (the Constitution mandated that it not exceed 10 square miles) ceded by Virginia and Maryland. The town's population remained small for decades, but as the role of government and the size of the town grew, the permanent population of citizens desired representation.

The Constitution, however, does not give this district "state" status, and therefore it has no voting representatives in the House or the Senate and no presidential electors, though it does have delegates who cannot introduce or vote on legislation but can vote at the committee level. The nation's least populous state, Wyoming, has 544,270 residents represented by three total members to Congress and three electoral votes. The District of Columbia has

599,657 residents with no voting representation in Congress. The Twenty-Third Amendment provides that the District shall appoint electors, but never more than those of the smallest state so that the District never has stronger influence than the smallest state. In 1964, the District voted for Democrat Lyndon Johnson and has voted for the Democratic candidate every year since.

Young Adults States used to generally require voters to be 21 years old. In the post-World War II years, however, a move to enfranchise 18-year-olds gained momentum. The president and Congress had sent scores of 18-, 19-, and 20-year-old draftees to Vietnam, most of whom had no right to vote for president or Congress. Some states, however allowed residents younger than 21 to vote, and four states allowed 18-year-olds to vote. In 1970, Congress passed amendments to the 1965 Voting Rights Act that lowered the national voting age to 18 for presidential and congressional elections. States challenged the new law in the Supreme Court based on reserved powers. The Court narrowly ruled that Congress did have the authority to set a voting age on *federal* elections but not for state and local offices. This ruling prompted Congress to propose and the states to ratify the **Twenty-Sixth Amendment** which prevents states from denying citizens 18 and over the right to vote, in July 1971.

The rapid ratification of the measure with strong majorities in each state put younger citizens on the road to voting. President Nixon proclaimed that some 11 million young men and women who "have participated in the life of our nation through their work, their studies, and their sacrifices for its defense now are to be fully included in the electoral process of our country."

Voting and Nonvoting

Voter turnout is the number of voters who actually cast votes as a percentage of the voting-age population. During the late 19th century, voter turnout was the highest in American history, though with restrictions on race, sex, and age, those eligible to vote were a minority of the population. Some estimates show that up to 90 percent of the legal electorate voted. However, manipulation of the ballot box and fraudulent practices such as voting more than once surely skewed those estimates.

From 1928 to 1968, the November voter turnout in presidential elections hovered generally over 60 percent. In 1972, an election year that embraced a new voting bloc of young voters, turnout actually dipped down to 57 percent. The anti-government feelings about the unpopular Vietnam War and later Nixon's Watergate scandal resulted in a number of people disengaging from politics during the next two decades. Party loyalty in elections became weaker and weaker. The connection between money and elections further disturbed Americans and required Congress to regulate the flow of dollars through campaigns. From 1972 to 2000, presidential election turnout hovered just above 50 percent of the voting-age population.

According to the U.S. Elections Project, in 2016, 59.3 percent of the **voting-eligible population**—citizens over the age of 18—voted for president, while 54.7 of the **voting-age population**—everyone over the age of 18— voted. However, as a percentage of *registered* voters, voter turnout is higher. Of those citizens registered to vote, about 70 percent voted in 2016.

Turnout varies based on the type of election. More voters show and cast ballots during the presidential contest than any other. Congressional midterm elections, those federal elections that occur midway through a president's term, have lower turnout. Turnout in the 2014 midterm congressional elections was 36 percent. Turnout for county-level and municipal races is even less, ranging from 15 to 30 percent.

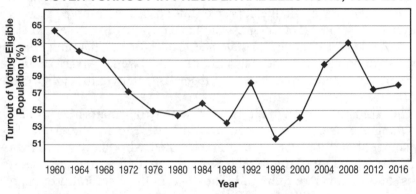

VOTER TURNOUT IN PRESIDENTIAL ELECTIONS, 1960–2016

Some people don't vote because logistical factors interfere—they are sick on Election Day or they can't arrange childcare. Also, certain people are excluded by law from voting in some states, including felons and people determined to be mentally incompetent. Others may not have the kind of ID their states require. (See page 318.)

However, many people who have the right to vote choose not to exercise it. This **voter apathy**, a lack of concern for the election outcome, has different causes. Some citizens feel no **political efficacy**, or sense that their vote makes a difference. Voters who have supported losing candidates or did not experience the change promised during a campaign feel a lack of efficacy, and they may see little reason to participate and vote in the next election.

Also, many people are generally satisfied with the government and don't feel the need to participate. Since the United States has a high number of elections, not all citizens vote in every election, reducing turnout. Nonvoters get involved in other ways by volunteering in their communities, for example.

If we had an election and everyone showed up, would it change the outcome of elections? Many believe that Democrats would benefit if restrictions were lifted on felons and people without the required ID. Those without IDs are typically among the working poor, minorities, and transient or homeless people, who tend to be liberal. Others believe nonvoters are as different from one another as voters are.

BY THE NUMBERS VOTER TURNOUT IN SELECTED DEMOCRACIES	
Country	**Turnout**
Denmark	83.2
Australia	82.7
Italy	79.1
France	76.8
Israel	71.2
Portugal	69.2
Japan	66.6
United Kingdom	58.3
United States	**58.2**
Switzerland	39.8

Source: *The International Institute for Democracy and Electoral Assistance*

What do the numbers show? Which countries lead in voter turnout? Which countries have the lowest turnout? What are the different reasons why turnout would be high or low?

Demographics

BIG IDEA Political scientists have long noticed the correlation between demographics and voting behavior. After elections, exit polls and other surveys are conducted to draw conclusions about which people vote and how and why they voted as they did. Age, education level, and personal income appear to correlate to rates of voting. Older, better-educated, wealthier voters show up to vote in higher numbers. Activists, people who attend church, military veterans, and members of civic organizations also turn out to vote in higher numbers. Some groups tend to vote in noticeable patterns. These are known as **voting blocs**.

Gender

One of the easiest ways to divide and analyze voters is along gender lines. The **gender gap** is the difference in political views between men and women and how these views are expressed at the voting booth. Women tend to oppose harsh punishments and the death penalty more than men; they favor government spending on welfare; and they are less war-prone. These leanings have resulted in more women voting with the Democratic than the Republican party. Men tend to believe in harsher punishments against accused criminals and are more fiscally conservative; they have a tendency to vote Republican. In 2016, 53 percent of men voted for Trump, and 41 percent voted for Clinton. For women, 54 percent voted for Clinton, and 42 percent voted for Trump.

Since the 1980 election, women turn out to vote in slightly higher numbers than men. There is a division in voting patterns among females who are married and unmarried. In 2000, unmarried females strongly voted with Democrats. Single women tend to care about health care, employment, education, job security, and retirement benefits. In contrast, in the 2002 midterms, 56 percent of married women voted for Republicans compared to 39 percent of unmarried women. Married women tend to be "moral traditionalists" with concerns for traditional marriage and family. In the 2016 presidential election, 56 percent of married women voters chose Trump, compared to 42 percent for Clinton. Unmarried female voters, in contrast, chose Clinton by a 62 to 35 percent margin.

Age

Since ratification of the Twenty-Sixth Amendment in 1971, the nation's youngest voters have had the lowest turnout. Reasons include their undeveloped views of candidates, lack of strong views on political issues, and mobility. Working a full-time job, owning a home, paying a substantial amount of one's income to taxes—activities of older people—are all things that make people notice the details of public policy.

Yet young voter turnout and interest in politics have risen. Authors Dan Balz and Haynes Johnson found in the 2008 election that citizens in the larger bloc of 18-to-30-year-olds turned out in the highest numbers in a generation, and the group is dominated by self-described liberals, 38 percent, while only 23 percent considered themselves conservative. A U.S. Census report on the 2016 election shows the 18-to-29-year-old bloc turned out at 46 percent.

In contrast, senior citizens vote in reliably high numbers. In 2012, voter turnout among those 65 and over was nearly 72 percent. This disparity in turnout results from older citizens having more experience and understanding of the political process, regular voting habits, and likely more at stake—property, investments, and Social Security and Medicare. Senior citizens turned out at nearly 71 percent, with 52 percent voting for Trump and 45 percent for Clinton.

Minorities

Minorities are increasing as a percentage of the U.S. population, and along with the increase in numbers comes an increase in political clout. However, with the exception of the 2012 presidential election in which African American voters outnumbered white voters, turnout among minorities has stalled or declined.

African Americans The disenfranchising and intimidation of black would-be voters in the South for generations created a consistently low voter turnout among African Americans. Because the Republican Party freed the slaves and enfranchised African Americans after the Civil War, blacks largely sided with the Republican Party during their first generation at the voting booth. By 1932, however, these voters began a relationship with the Democratic Party that only became stronger under Democratic presidents Truman, Johnson, and Obama. (See page 468.) Blacks tend to have a less favorable view of the criminal justice system than whites. A recent University of Cincinnati poll shows that African Americans favor abolishing the death penalty by 51 percent, compared with 23 percent of white respondents. They also want less attention and money focused on international affairs and foreign policy and more on Americans in need. Upon the 2012 presidential election, the PEW Research Center estimated that 95 percent of the voting-eligible African Americans voted for Democrat Barack Obama. For the first time ever, African American turnout in 2012 surpassed that of whites; 66.2 percent of eligible blacks voted, while 64.1 percent of eligible whites did so.

Hispanics Hispanics are the fastest growing minority in the United States, now numbering well over 43 million. Hispanics live in large numbers in the southwestern and western states, the Sunbelt states, New York, and Florida. Hispanic turnout rose from 2.5 million nationally in 1980 to more than 11 million in 2012. Hispanics turn out in lower percentages than whites and blacks. Hispanic participation peaked at 50 percent in 2008; in 2016 it was 47.6 percent.

The Latino voting population has sided with Democrats on urban, minority, and labor issues, although Cuban Americans have a history of favoring Republicans. Also, conflict over immigration laws has created a wedge between Hispanic voters and conservative lawmakers. Heightened rhetoric and a Republican desire for strict citizenship requirements have driven Hispanics closer to Democrats.

Asian Americans Asian Americans come mostly from China, the Philippines, India, Japan, Korea, and Vietnam. They make up only about 3 percent of the U.S. voting population, though that figure is higher in the West Coast states. They have concerns like other minorities for civil liberties and equal protection, but for years Asian Americans have voted conservatively, probably because the Republican Party has been stronger against the repressive regimes some have departed. Also, Republican leaders have pushed for fewer regulations on business, which satisfies the Asian business community, and because conservative values often align with ethical beliefs in Asian cultures. Yet in 2012, exit polls reveal that roughly 73 percent of Asians voted for Obama, and Indian Americans, many of them in the United States for less than 10 years, voted overwhelmingly for Hillary Clinton in 2016.

VOTER TURNOUT AMONG BLOCS	
Voting Bloc	**Turnout**
Males	59.3
Females	63.3
Whites	65.3
Black	59.6
Hispanic	47.6
Asian	49
18 to 29	46.1
65 and older	70.9
No High School Diploma	33

Source: *U.S. Census, United States Elections Project, 2016*

Religious Affiliation

Religions tend to share certain beliefs among their members and often tend to vote as blocs. By far the largest religious group is made up of Protestant and other Christian denominations. A majority of this group has consistently voted for Republican candidates.

Evangelicals White, born-again evangelical Christians have become the second largest religious group. They tend to hold conservative beliefs. They have become ardent supporters of the Republican Party and have joined Republicans to create the "religious right." Televangelists and leaders of conservative family-oriented groups have large followings and thus great political influence. Most members of this group do not believe in human evolution and don't want their sons or daughters to be taught this science in public schools. They are frustrated by the removal of prayer from school and the public square. They are a strong political force in the South and Midwest. Evangelicals supported Donald Trump in the 2016 presidential election by 80 percent and have become one of the president's most reliable groups within his base.

Catholics Catholics make up almost as large a group as evangelicals. Catholic voters have historically voted with the Democratic Party but today cast votes for both parties because they constitute such a large swath of the electorate. Catholic faith and custom is defined largely by papal decrees (the Pope's orders) from Rome, which have established some strict rules and beliefs.

The historical alliance between Catholics and Democrats began in 1856 when the party denounced the anti-immigrant, anti-Catholic American (or "Know Nothing") party and instead called for a "spirit of tolerance" in their platform. The relationship continued into the twentieth century, as Catholics played a large role in the politics of the urban North. According to Gallup, Catholic votes for Democrats in presidential elections peaked when John Kennedy, himself a Catholic, won in 1960 with roughly 78 percent of those voters.

Today, the Catholic vote seems to lean Democrat nationwide, but is no longer a monolith; it straddles the ideological spectrum. Roughly 25 percent of the country, Catholics overlap so many other demographics—rich and poor, young and old, white and Latino, northeast urban and Midwest suburbs—that they defy categorization. The Papacy denounces birth control and abortion, for example, thereby aligning with Republican ideals; yet the church opposes the death penalty and promotes charity, positions embraced by more Democrats than Republicans.

"Cafeteria Catholics," those who pick and choose elements of the religion, sometimes reject the church's teaching on abortion, birth control, homosexuality, and euthanasia. As author George Marlin explains, by 2004, approximately 70 percent of the congressional Catholic membership had cast pro-choice votes. A recent finding of the National Election Study shows that 36 percent of Catholics identify themselves as conservative, while 35 percent say they are moderate, and 29 percent claim to be liberal.

Jews Jews vote in large numbers and vote mainly with the Democrats. Jewish voters comprise a small fraction of the electorate, about 2 percent, but their participation in elections averages about 10 percent higher than the general population. Some estimates show that roughly 90 percent of Jews vote.

Jewish-American political history parallels American Catholic history—with ethnic, often immigrant, minorities occupying larger, northern urban centers. Subject to discrimination, Jews have developed strong concerns about the power of the state and infringements on civil liberties. Jewish voters place a high priority on privacy, on ensuring basic rights for the accused, and supporting charities. These factors have caused the Jewish vote to swing in a liberal direction.

The first measurable Jewish vote went to Woodrow Wilson with 55 percent in 1916. The 1920s Red Scare sent many Socialist Jews, fearing the "Communist" label, toward the Democratic party. When the United States entered World War II and later defeated the Jews' worst enemy—Adolf Hitler and Nazi Germany—FDR gained full backing from American Jewish voters. When his successor Harry Truman embraced the idea of creating a Jewish state in the Middle East in what became Israel, it sealed a generation of Jewish support for Democrats. From 1952 to 1968, Jewish support for Democratic presidential candidates ran 20 to 30 percent higher than that of the general population. According to exit polls, about 71 percent of Jews voted for Hillary Clinton over Republican Donald Trump in 2016.

Business, Labor, and Unions

Entrepreneurs, leaders in the business community, CEOs of companies, shareholders, and much of the upper class tend to embrace a conservative political philosophy and capitalist principles. Small business owners also want less regulation and interference by the state in the business world. They want lower taxes and an ability to make more profits. This voting profile usually results in their voting Republican.

In contrast, the wage earner, the craftsman, and the factory line worker tend to view politics through the lens of the workplace and often in line with their labor union. Since their rise in the late 1800s and early 1900s, labor unions such as the American Federation of Labor have supported government-mandated fair wage laws, child labor laws, safety regulations in the workplace, and fairness on the job. Aligned with Socialists in their earlier years, the labor unions struck a tight relationship with FDR's party during the implementation of New Deal policies. Unions have lost much of their influence today, and membership is down from the prior generation. The decline is explained in part by laws in 28 states that prohibit making union membership mandatory in places of business that have voted to unionize. In the 2016 election, estimates show that the Democratic presidential candidate still carried the union vote, by perhaps 16 percentage points, but by 2 points less than four years ago and a noticeable drop from the prior generation.

Voting Models

In addition to demographic influences, many other factors help explain voting behavior. One is the decision-making process voters use when choosing a candidate. All of these models play into voters' decision-making process with various levels of influence.

Rational-Choice Voting

Rational-choice voting takes place when a voter has examined an issue or candidate, evaluated campaign promises or platform points, and consciously decided to vote in the way that seems to most benefit the voter. What matters most to one rational-choice voter might mean much less to another voter. One voter might be approaching the voting booth with her own individual interest atop her priority list—who will help me obtain medical care, for example—while another could be acting out of concern for a larger group, posing such questions as, "What is best for America?" or "What is best for our schools?"

Either way, the rational-choice voter has consciously decided what would be the best choice and votes accordingly. A retiring citizen about to collect Social Security votes for the candidate promising to protect the Social Security system. A young voter might have a genuine interest in securing retirees' quality of life, and though this issue has little direct implication on this voter's life, he or she may rationally choose to vote with that issue as a priority.

Analysts point out that sometimes people vote against their self-interest to support larger issues. For example, Donald Trump gained much support from the non-college educated, wage-earning voters. Critics point out that the president's policies of lowering the marginal tax rate and deregulating businesses will possibly harm these voters. If those voters made their choice over concerns about immigration and protecting the Second Amendment rather than their economic interests, they still made their own rational choice.

Retrospective Voting

Citizens who apply the **retrospective voting** model look backward to consider candidates' track records. If the race for local office includes an incumbent, the voter will assess the official seeking reelection and her accomplishments while in office before deciding. If the race is for an open seat, the voter will likely consider the respective parties' recent track records, or maybe the candidates' accomplishments or shortcomings in other, prior offices. If Republicans are in control of Congress and the White House, and a bad economy ensues on their watch, a retrospective voter will likely cast his vote for the Democrats.

Prospective Voting

In contrast, using **prospective voting**, citizens anticipate the future. They consider how candidates or proposed ballot initiatives might affect their lives or the operation of government. For example, casinos and gambling companies have recently backed efforts to alter gambling laws and to legalize casinos in several states. Prospective voters, looking ahead, see the prospect of new jobs and increased tax revenues and decide on that basis to support legalizing gaming.

Barack Obama campaigned on the chief promise of a comprehensive government health care program. Senator Bernie Sanders (I-VT), seeking the Democratic nomination, campaigned on working toward free tuition at public colleges and a $15 minimum wage. Both gained millions of backers who were trying to choose the candidate with a vision for the future they supported.

Party-Line Voting

Citizens who affiliate with a political party or hold a strong party loyalty will more than likely vote with that party at most opportunities. In some states, voters register with a party; in others there is no legal state-level affiliation. All partisans have various levels of loyalty or strength of relationship with their party, but when one "self-identifies" with a party, acknowledging their membership or openly referring to themselves as a Democrat or Republican, then chances are good they will vote for that party. This **party identification**, rather than party registration, is the easiest way to predict a voter's habits. According to the 2016 CNN exit poll, 89 percent of Democrats voted for Clinton; 90 percent of Republicans voted for Trump.

Other Factors: Candidates and Issues

Party loyalists are occasionally drawn to a candidate from the other team. A voter may consider the track record of the incumbent while simultaneously considering the promises of the challenger, using both retrospective and prospective thinking.

Another impact on the voter's selection is the personality, integrity, or competence of a candidate. In fact, candidate-centered campaigns (as opposed to those focusing on party loyalty) will often forgo the party label or refrain from printing "Democrat" or "Republican" on their yard signs or including such information in their commercials and instead emphasize the candidate's military service or successes at managing a business before entering a campaign. (See pages 462–463.)

The candidate's character may also be a factor in how a voter decides to cast a ballot. In 2017, for example, Alabama held a special election to fill a Senate seat left vacant when Jeff Sessions was appointed attorney general by Donald Trump. The Republican candidate, Judge Roy Moore, received an endorsement from President Trump, and the state of Alabama had voted solidly for Trump in the 2016 election, and solidly Republican for 20 years. However, Moore's past defiance of court orders, remarks denigrating people of color and the LGBT community, allegations of sexual abuse, and an effort to paint his accusers as accomplices to his opposition and spreaders of "fake news" turned public opinion against him. Even the other Republican Senator from Alabama, Richard Shelby, said he would not vote for Moore. Democrat Doug Jones, with an exemplary character and a strong record—including convictions against Ku Klux Klan members responsible for the 1963 church bombing in Birmingham that killed four children—won a close victory. The Alabaman African American vote played a decisive role.

The most important political issues of the day also have an influence on how citizens choose to cast their votes, and the economy is often at the top of the list. If the nation is in an economic downturn, the incumbent is usually held responsible for it, so votes tend to go for the challenger. If a challenger from a party other than a voter's preference has a good idea for improving the economy, the candidate's position on that issue can sway the vote.

Government Policies and Voter Participation

Although states have the authority to administer elections, the federal government has passed election laws that the states must follow. For example, Congress passed the **National Voter Registration Act (NVRA)** in 1993 to increase citizen participation and to alleviate the burden of having to make a special effort to register to vote. Also known as the **motor-voter law,** it addresses national standards and enforcement of voter registration, mail-in registration, and government agency-based registration. The law requires states to offer citizens a chance to register at state-run agencies, such as the bureaus of motor vehicles (hence the "motor-voter law" nickname). The NVRA increases the number of eligible citizens who register to vote, expands the number of locations where voters can register, and protects the integrity of elections by ensuring that accurate voter rolls are maintained.

A recent U.S. Census Bureau report shows that 21 percent of voters registered at a county registration office; another 21 percent did so at a motor vehicle agency. More than 13 percent mailed in their registration, and 6 percent reported registering at the polls on Election Day (15 states allow that) at a school, hospital, campus, or registration booth.

Federal Response to the 2000 Election

The 2000 presidential election between Texas Governor George W. Bush and Vice-President Al Gore was one of the closest and most controversial elections in U.S. history. The outcome was finally decided by a Supreme Court ruling that the recount procedures violated the equal protection clause. As a result of the decision, George W. Bush became president. This unusual election focused great attention on voting processes and heightened concern for election reform.

Florida's vote in that election was extremely close. A confusing punch-card ballot, which allowed for fragments of paper called "chads" to remain partially attached to the ballot even after a voter punched the hole, made vote counting complicated. Some voters erroneously punched more than one hole, making accurate vote counting difficult. Similar voting problems had occurred in previous elections but none had received this level of attention.

Congress responded by passing the national **Help America Vote Act (HAVA)** in 2002. HAVA imposes a number of requirements on states, mostly to create national standards for voting and election management. All states had to upgrade their voting systems to an electronic format. The law required states to replace punch card and lever systems and provided funds for the changeover. HAVA also addresses voting for people with disabilities. States and counties must make polling places accessible for blind people and those with physical handicaps to "ensure full participation in the electoral process." Largely due to the confusion among Florida's voters in 2000, the law requires states to use a voting system that allows the voter to glance at his or her choices before confirming the vote. Through this provision, voters have an opportunity to change their vote if they make a mistake.

To prevent voter fraud, registering voters must provide a driver's license or the last four digits of a Social Security number that they must verify at the polling place on Election Day. The law also makes sure that military personnel serving overseas are provided with absentee ballots, registration forms, and election information.

Since the "hanging chad" debacle, 75 percent of the nation has changed the way it votes. Elections are now more accurate. There is less chance that voters will make mistakes and more safeguards in place if they do. Access has been expanded, and millions now vote by mail.

Voter Registration

Election schemes during the age of organized corruption in politics at the end of the nineteenth century brought the need for **voter registration**. Registration enables governments to prepare for an election, verify voter qualifications, and assign a voter to only one polling place to prevent repeat voting. In some places, the process for registering to vote became a barrier to would-be voters.

Though registration systems and requirements vary slightly, most states require a voter to be 18 years old, a U.S. citizen, and a resident of the state. A criminal record can effect one's voting right. All but two states prevent felons from voting while in prison. Most states, however, reinstate felons' voting rights after they are paroled. Twelve states deny felons who committed severe crimes the right to ever vote again.

Many states allow 17-year-olds to vote in primary elections if the voter will be 18 by the November general election. The Supreme Court has ruled that no state can require registration more than 30 days before an election.

Source: *Voice of America*
Washington University in St. Louis students register people to vote in the 2016 election.

Citizens can register to vote in a few ways. At a local board of elections, any adult resident can walk in during business hours with ID and Social Security number and register. The laws discussed earlier require states to offer opportunities by mail as well. In most cases, voters can find a printable form online, complete it, and mail it in. Because of the motor-voter law, registration forms are also available at public libraries and where motorists obtain a drivers' license.

Nearly 40 states allow citizens to register online. One of the first studies examining online registration showed a per-registrant cost to the state dropping from 83 cents to 3 cents. These savings do not take into account the expensive implementation costs, but considering those will diminish over time, it is no wonder so many states have made this possible. A handful of states offer Election Day registration at the same polling places where voting takes place.

Types of Ballots

Not only registration but also voting has been upgraded in an effort to increase accuracy and voter participation.

Election Day Ballots The ballot used today, known as the **Australian ballot** since a version of it was first used in Australia in 1872, helps make elections fair. Some form of the Australian ballot is used in all U.S. states. The ballot must 1) be printed and distributed at public expense, 2) show all qualifying candidates' names, 3) be available only at the polling places, and 4) be completed in private.

Other administrative procedures are followed to make the ballot and voting legitimate. Candidates can list their names how they wish on the ballot, with a familiar nickname instead of full legal name. Election officials in some states will rotate the order in which the candidates' names appear, precinct-by-precinct, so no one candidate is always atop the list.

Sometimes registration records can be incomplete or incorrect. Citizens' names may be purged from voting rolls after years of inactivity. Voters move residences from one precinct to another and forget to change their registration. When discrepancies like these occur at the polling place, states offer **provisional ballots**. These are set aside until election officials investigate to make certain that the voter voted at the correct polling place based on the voter's registration address. When these controversies of residency or registration come up, citizens may feel questioned or partially disfranchised. But these modern procedures afford a greater chance of a fair and accurate election.

On Election Day, officials update the media as they count the votes. Toward the end of the evening, when a large majority are counted, the media will likely "call" the winner, but elections are not officially over until the elections officials count every vote—provisional ballots included—and certify the election. Most states provide for a 7- to 21-day period to complete the process.

Absentee Ballots Voters can also vote by **absentee ballot**. If a voter cannot make it to the polls, he or she can mail a completed ballot instead. In the past, voters needed an excuse, such as illness or travel, to vote absentee.

But states have embraced no-excuse absentee and early voting. Thirty-seven states and D.C. allow any qualified voter to cast a ballot in person during a designated period before the election. Early voting is not only convenient to the voter—it also makes for easier management and vote counting on Election Day. Voting lines decrease, and fewer poll workers are needed. In the 2012 election, one-third of Americans had already voted when Election Day arrived. Today, only 15 states require in-person Election Day voting.

These convenience voting changes usually bring noticeable increases in participation, followed by a leveling out of turnout. As ProPublica reported in 2016, the research on how convenience voting has increased turnout is mixed. Some research shows that early voting has increased turnout by 2 to 4 percent. One report shows that early in-person voting actually *decreased* voter turnout. More consistent findings are that African American turnout has increased with early, in-person voting, and that same-day voting and registration has increased turnout. Oregon's automatic registration process may have been the key factor in a 4-point increase in participation and one of the top turnout states in the United States.

Online Voting? Scholars, technology specialists, and fiscal conservatives have put forth good points in favor of using the Internet to conduct elections online or at least as an alternative to traveling to a voting booth. Voting online would be easier for some, could lower the administration cost of elections, and could propel younger tech-savvy voters into an influential and formidable force. However, Internet users tend to be white, wealthy, well-educated, and male. The difference between that constituency and those without Internet access is known as a "digital divide," and that divide would disadvantage voters without Internet access. Online voting also opens the door to hacking and other manipulation, so paper receipts are important.

Voter ID Laws

State laws requiring voters to present some form of identification at the voting booth have passed in 34 states, generally put forth by Republican majorities. Like other election laws, they vary in detail from state to state. Some states accept multiple forms of ID, including a utility bill or a paycheck stub. Others require government-issued photo identification. Some allow citizens to cast provisional ballots if they don't have their ID with them. If they return with the necessary ID, their provisional ballots can be cast.

These requirements have brought criticism and constitutional challenges. Some conservatives say the IDs are necessary to decrease the chances of voter fraud and to further guarantee accuracy in elections. Liberals and progressives, in contrast, believe Republicans are trying to set up barriers to those voters less likely to have an ID, most of whom tend to vote Democratic.

Liberal critics say these laws create a structural impediment and unfairly disenfranchise the lower socioeconomic groups—minorities, workers, the poor, and immigrants. Those voters are less likely than others to have IDs. Liberals point out that very little coordinated voter fraud actually goes on in the United States. A 2007 Justice Department study issued as these laws began to sprout found virtually no proof of organized skewing of elections as a result of voter fraud. A 2014 Loyola Law School study of elections since 2000 found just 31 examples of voter impersonation.

In the courts, legal challenges to photo-ID policies emphasize the way these laws disproportionately impact people of different classes. In 2008, the Supreme Court upheld an Indiana voter-ID statute that requires a photo ID, but since then, federal appeals courts have struck down similar laws from other states.

What is the practical impact of these measures? Are these voter ID requirements suppressing the vote? The Brennan Center for Justice reports that about 25 percent of eligible black voters and 16 percent of Hispanics do not have IDs compared to 9 percent of whites. It's likely that at least some of the 33 to 35 percent of eligible African-American voters who did not participate before the voter ID requirements are among those without IDs. Participation among these groups has generally grown in recent years, and voter ID laws could interfere with that growth. At the same time, voter ID laws seemed to serve as a rallying cry against voter suppression and actually help increase turnout of the groups claimed to be suppressed.

Long Lines at the Polls Most voters wait an average of 14 minutes to cast their votes. However, 5 percent of voters—which amounts to several million people—have to wait much longer, up to two hours. Minority voters are six times as likely as whites to wait more than an hour to vote. Since their historic turnout rates have been lower than those of whites, they may have fewer voting machines and poll workers in their precincts, and those deficits slow down the voting process. For hourly workers, long wait times result in lower wages for the day. However, these long waits in line have a significant consequence beyond lost wages. One study estimates that for every hour spent in line, a voter is 1 percent less likely to vote in the next election. Long lines, then, are a voter suppression mechanism.

REFLECT ON THE ESSENTIAL QUESTION

Essential Question: *How are voting rights protected, and how have voting procedures been altered to respond to challenges?* On separate paper, complete a chart like the one below to gather details to answer that question.

Protections for Voting Rights	Responses to Challenges

When you **develop an argument**, you go through several processes of refinement. For example, you might have a general feeling that your city council should not vote to close the local branch of your library, as it is considering. From that general feeling, the first step in developing an argument is to articulate a **claim,** a statement you assert to be true: The library is too important a public facility to be closed. Then you look for **appropriate evidence** to support your claim, to prove that it is true. You might begin researching the benefits of libraries on the performance of children in school or the relationship between branch libraries and the level of teenage crime. You may also find that the city council is experiencing a budget shortfall and cannot both keep the local branch of the library open and support the public health clinic. Your research leads you to examine your original claim and refine it based on your new information. Maybe your refined claim is "City council should actively seek alternate funding for the clinic and continue to keep the branch library open." Now the evidence you provide to support your claim can be very focused and should show that other funding is available for the health clinic and that the benefits of the branch library are worth city funding.

Practice: Write an elected official expressing your reasoned position on an issue of concern. Formulate and refine an argument for or against a law or policy or governmental action or inaction and support it with appropriate evidence. Follow the process below.

- Find a public issue that concerns you. It could be the nation's most recent involvement in the Middle East or the potholes in your local streets.
- Become well acquainted with the issue through research in a variety of print and online sources. If appropriate, talk to local experts or perhaps contact local offices.
- Find a poll or some measure of public opinion on the issue. What do other citizens, constituents, and your neighbors think? How are they affected? How do their views and the impact of the issue on your neighbors affect your argument?
- What specific position do you take? Develop a well reasoned claim, refined through research, and support it with relevant and sufficient evidence appropriate to the topic.
- Select the appropriate public official and present your argument in a formal letter.

KEY TERMS AND NAMES

absentee ballot/442
apathy/432
Australian ballot/442
Civil Rights Act (1957, 1964)/428
Fifteenth Amendment/427
franchise/425
gender gap/433
grandfather clause/427
Help America Vote Act (2002)/440
Jackson, Andrew/426
linkage institutions/424
literacy test/427
National Voter Registration Act

(motor-voter law) (1993)/440
Nineteenth Amendment/429
party identification/439
political efficacy/432
poll tax/427
preclearance/429
prospective voting/438
provisional ballots/442
rational-choice voting/438
retrospective voting/438
Seventeenth Amendment/426
suffrage/425

Twenty-Fourth Amendment/428
Twenty-Sixth Amendment/431
Twenty-Third Amendment/430
voter apathy/432
voter registration/441
voter turnout/431
voting-age population/432
voting blocs/433
voting-eligible population/425
Voting Rights Act (1965)/429
white primary/428

MULTIPLE-CHOICE QUESTIONS

Questions 1 and 2 refer to the following table.

TOP REASONS FOR NOT VOTING	
Too Busy	17.5%
Illness/Disability	14.9%
Not Interested	13.4%
Didn't Like Candidates/Issues	12.9%
Out Of Town	8.8%
Registration Problems	6.0%

Source: *U.S. Census, 2010*

1. Which of the following is an accurate conclusion based on the data in the table?

    (A) Voter registration problems have become the chief deterrent to full participation in U.S. elections.

    (B) Not having enough time leads the reasons for not voting.

    (C) Lack of political efficacy is the chief reason people do not vote.

    (D) Voter identification laws have reduced voter turnout.

2. How have states responded to the reasons offered for non-voting?

   (A) States have required more accurate media coverage of candidates and issues.

   (B) States have switched to online voting.

   (C) States have moved Election Day to Saturdays and Sundays.

   (D) States have provided for early voting and no-excuse voting by mail.

Questions 3 and 4 refer to the Supreme Court opinion below.

> A photo identification requirement imposes some burdens on voters that other methods of identification do not share. For example, a voter may lose his photo identification, may have his wallet stolen on the way to the polls, or may not resemble the photo in the identification because he recently grew a beard. Burdens of that sort arising from life's vagaries, however, are neither so serious nor so frequent as to raise any question about the constitutionality of SEA 483 [the Indiana law requiring photo IDs]; the availability of the right to cast a provisional ballot provides an adequate remedy for problems of that character.
>
> —Justice John Paul Stevens, Majority Opinion, *Crawford v. Marion County Elections Board*, 2008

3. Which of the following statements best summarizes the Supreme Court's opinion?

   (A) Election Day burdens on citizens are acceptable if there are comparable burdens placed on the government to guarantee fair elections.

   (B) As long as a citizen can cast a temporary vote to be checked later, the citizen need not prove his or her identity on Election Day.

   (C) A state's goal to conduct an accurate and legitimate election does not outweigh the citizen's burden to show photo ID to cast a vote.

   (D) The burdens of providing photo-ID are so frequent that they make the provision unconstitutional.

4. Which of the following constitutional provisions did the Supreme Court follow in letting states implement the policy referred to in the opinion?

   (A) Article I, Section 4

   (B) Suffrage Amendments

   (C) Necessary and Proper Clause

   (D) Commerce Clause

5. Which of the following constitutional amendments did Congress seek to enforce when it passed the Voting Rights Act of 1965?

(A) Fifteenth Amendment

(B) Twenty-Third Amendment

(C) Twenty-Sixth Amendment

(D) Twenty-Seventh Amendment

6. Which of the following statements best summarizes the voter registration process in the United States?

(A) Voter registration is a national process that is uniform among the states.

(B) States can require citizens to register to vote as much as one year in advance of an election.

(C) Voter registration helps assure accuracy in the elections process.

(D) Efforts to ease registration have increased voter turnout.

7. A wage-earner who identifies as a political independent has heard a Senate candidate promise to push for an increase in the national minimum wage while her opponent does not support that. The citizen votes for this candidate primarily for this reason so his own pay might increase. Which of the following models best explains this citizen's voting behavior?

(A) Rational-choice voting

(B) Retrospective voting

(C) Prospective voting

(D) Party-line voting

8. Which of the following is an accurate comparison of the National Voter Registration Act and the Help America Vote Act?

	NATIONAL VOTER REGISTRATION ACT	HELP AMERICA VOTE ACT
(A)	Allows for absentee voting	Makes punch cards more reliable
(B)	Addresses voting for people with disabilities	Allows military personnel to return home to vote
(C)	Allows voter registration at state agencies	Requires systems for voters to confirm vote
(D)	Requires voter ID at the polls	Requires states to pay for upgrades

9. Which of the following demographic voting blocs has the most identifiable partisan voting behavior?

(A) African Americans

(B) Jewish voters

(C) Catholics

(D) Voters aged 18 to 24 years old

10. Both state and federal governments are involved in elections and make and enforce election law. Which is a responsibility of the federal government?

(A) Setting times and locations for voting

(B) Assuring groups are not prevented from voting

(C) Determining the format of the ballot

(D) Establishing voter registration procedures

FREE-RESPONSE QUESTIONS

1. "It is well established that minorities turn out less than whites in most elections in the United States. Our research shows that the racial turnout gap doubles or triples in states that enact strict ID laws. Latinos are the [most disadvantaged]. Their turnout is 7.1 percentage points lower in general elections and 5.3 percentage points lower in primaries in strict ID states than it is in other states. Strict ID laws lower African American, Asian American and multi-racial American turnout as well. In fact, where these laws are implemented, white turnout goes *up* marginally, compared with non-voter ID states."

—Zoltan L. Hajnal, *Los Angeles Times*, September 8, 2016

After reading the above scenario, respond to A, B, and C below.

(A) Describe an action Congress can take to address the comments in the scenario.

(B) In the context of this scenario, explain how the use of congressional power in part A can be affected by interactions between Congress and the state legislatures.

(C) In the context of this scenario, explain how voter ID laws affect democratic representation.

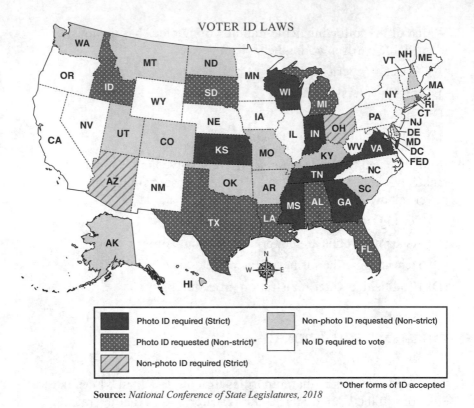

VOTER ID LAWS

■ Photo ID required (Strict)	▨ Non-photo ID requested (Non-strict)
▦ Photo ID requested (Non-strict)*	☐ No ID required to vote
▨ Non-photo ID required (Strict)	

*Other forms of ID accepted

Source: *National Conference of State Legislatures, 2018*

2. Use the information in the map to respond to the questions..

   (A) Identify the voter ID policy in Michigan.

   (B) Describe a similarity or difference in voter ID laws by state or region, as illustrated in the information graphic, and draw a conclusion about that similarity or difference.

   (C) Explain how voter ID laws as shown in the information graphic demonstrate a principle of federalism.

3. Virginia Minor, a leader in the Missouri women's suffrage movement, tried to register to vote in Missouri in 1872 as part of a nationwide civil disobedience effort but was denied because she was female. In a lawsuit asserting that as a citizen she had the right to vote, Minor argued for being registered as a legal voter based on constitutional protections as a citizen. The case, *Minor v. Happersett* (1875), reached the Supreme Court, which upheld the state supreme court's determination that the litigants failed to show that anything in the Constitution called for the federal government to take away from states the right to define voting qualifications. The Court ruled that citizenship conferred "membership of a nation and nothing more." States would still have the authority to define suffrage.

(A) Identify the constitutional clause that is common to both *Minor v. Happersett* and *Brown v. Board of Education* (1954). (See page 305.)

(B) Based on the constitutional clause identified in part A, explain how the facts of the case led to a different holding in *Brown v. Board of Education* than the holding in *Minor v. Happersett*.

(C) Describe an action supporters of women's suffrage in the 1870s could take to further their cause after the court defeat.

4. Develop an argument that explains whether voting in the United States should be mandatory, as it is in Australia, Belgium, Mexico, Singapore, and 18 other nations.

In your essay, you must:

- Articulate a defensible claim or thesis that responds to the prompt and establishes a line of reasoning
  - Support your claim with at least TWO pieces of accurate and relevant information:
    At least ONE piece of evidence must be from one of the following foundational documents:
    - Article I of the Constitution
    - First Amendment of the Constitution
  - Use a second piece of evidence from the list above or from your study of modern voting and voter behavior and elections
- Use reasoning to explain why your evidence supports your claim/ thesis
- Respond to an opposing or alternative perspective using refutation, concession, or rebuttal

WRITING: CONCLUDE WITH STRENGTH

Follow the line of reasoning you establish in your introduction all the way through your argument essay. After you have responded to an opposing or alternate perspective with refutation, concession, or rebuttal, take your argument to its logical conclusion. Your concluding paragraph should not simply restate your claim or thesis. Instead it should summarize how your evidence and your response to an opposing or alternative view demonstrate the soundness of your claim.

13

Political Parties

*"The common and continual mischiefs of the spirit of
party are sufficient to make it the interest and
duty of a wise people to discourage and restrain it."*

—George Washington, Farewell Address, 1797

Essential Question: What are the functions and impacts of political parties,
and how have they adapted to change?

Political parties are organized groups of people with similar political
ideologies and goals. They work to have candidates elected to public office
who will represent those ideologies and accomplish those goals. Political
parties developed in the aftermath of the American Revolution because of
social and economic divisions that already existed in our society. In his farewell
address, George Washington warned that parties were mischievous and said
that Americans should not split into factions. The founders viewed political
parties as being driven by self-interest rather than by a desire to enhance the
wellbeing of the new nation.

However, it seems that when like-minded people desire certain policy
changes in a democratic society, political parties are the inevitable result.
Organized parties provide important opportunities for people to participate
in politics. These parties are often influenced by special interest groups and
social movements, and their goal is always to capture the largest share of the
votes possible so that they can wield power. For this reason, political parties
must adapt and change as society and technology evolve. The United States
has traditionally had a **two-party system** that discourages third-party and
independent candidates, especially at the national level.

Functions and Impact of Political Parties

Political parties (1) mobilize and educate voters, (2) create platforms that define
their ideas and goals, (3) recruit candidates and manage their campaigns, and
(4) govern in hopes of implementing their desired public policy. Through these
functions they link the citizenry to the government. Two major parties, the
Democrats and the Republicans, have dominated U.S. politics for more than
150 years. Both major parties operate in every state.

Impact on Voters

Political parties exert a great influence on voters. They both shape and reflect voters' political ideologies. They play a large role in deciding which candidates will run for office, and they exercise significant control over the drawing of legislative districts, a process that can tilt the likelihood of election victory to the party in power.

Parties also engage voters in the routines of public life. Republican or Democratic party "members" could be lifelong party loyalists, just common voters who tend to vote for the party on Election Day, or somewhere in between. Parties have no restrictions on who can become members. Neither party charges dues nor requires any loyalty pledge. People who refer to themselves as Republicans or Democrats, or who regularly vote that way, are considered party members. More active and dedicated members volunteer for the party, make donations, or run for office.

For example, more active members of the local branch of a national party may hold monthly meetings, make calls to get voters to the polls, volunteer at the polling places on Election Day, and then gather at a neighborhood restaurant to watch the election results come in. Through these activities, the party is connecting with the electorate and members are connecting with other members, building social and political bonds. These activities link the voters to government and provide access to participation.

Mobilization of Voters Political parties are always looking to add rank-and-file members, because winning elections is essential to implementing party policy. Local parties target their outreach to mobilize and register voters in their effort to recruit more members—not just the party regulars but those who are on the fence about which side to take. They contact citizens via mail, phone, email, or at the door. Volunteers operate phone banks and make personal phone calls to citizens. Parties also use robocalls to remind people to vote for their candidates and to discourage voting for opposing candidates. **Robocalls** are prerecorded messages that can be delivered automatically to large numbers of people. (See page 374 for information on push polling, a technique for calling potential voters and asking questions framed to achieve a certain result.)

Political parties also hold voter registration drives. As elections draw near, small armies of volunteers canvass neighborhoods, walking door to door spreading the party philosophy, handing out printed literature and convincing citizens to vote for their causes and candidates. What is sometimes termed a "shoe-leather campaign" can gain more votes than a less personalized email blast. On Election Day, volunteers will even drive people to the polls.

Education of Voters Parties at national, state, and local levels make efforts to educate their membership on key issues and candidates. Parties also inform members of the activities of the government, both good and bad. They may tout accomplishments of local officeholders they support and criticize officeholders from the opposing party in an effort to stop unwanted policies.

Parties provide extensive training to candidates in how to run an effective campaign. They also train volunteers in the process of building party membership, getting out the vote, and interacting with elected officials.

This education effort goes both ways. To make sure their officeholders make decisions that reflect the voters' desires, parties conduct opinion surveys on the issues and share results with officeholders and candidates to educate them on party members' positions.

Creation of Party Platforms A party expresses its primary ideology in its **platform**—a written list of beliefs and political goals. In drafting a platform, national party leaders try to take into account the views of millions of voters, perhaps a third of the country.

As you read in Chapter 11, the modern **Republican Party** supports a conservative doctrine. Republicans for decades have advocated for a strong national defense, a reduction of wasteful government spending, and limited regulations on businesses. Democrats, on the other hand, support aggressive efforts for minority rights and stronger protections for the environment. Democrats also desire more government services to solve public problems and to provide public services. These views are reflected in each party's platform.

Members are drawn to political parties in part because of the position the parties take on these and other issues. However, the party leadership also takes into account the positions of the voters, leading to some flexibility and adaptability in party positions. For example, in the 1970s, the opposition of vocal members of the Republican Party to the proposed Equal Rights Amendment forced the party to change its position from support for the amendment to opposition to it (page 545).

The developing **Democratic Party** and its leaders drafted and approved their first formal party platform at the 1840 Democratic National Convention, the gathering of party representatives from all over the nation who come together for the purpose of nominating the party's presidential candidate. That first platform contained just over 500 words. The first Republican platform, written in 1854, took a stance on only two main issues. Today's platforms, in contrast, each contain a wide array of issues and concerns for government and are more than 25,000 words long. Party members don't necessarily agree on all the issues. Platform committee members argue over the wording, and these arguments have even caused some parties to split.

Democrats and Republicans arrive at their respective **conventions** with drafts of their platforms constructed weeks earlier. Each party has an official platform committee appointed by its leadership. As multiple candidates for president compete for the nomination, party leaders address the concerns of the different factions of the party. For this reason, even the runners-up in a nominating contest have strong input to the platform. In 2016, for example, second-place Democratic candidate Bernie Sanders of Vermont got to name five members of the platform-writing committee of 15; the winning presidential nominee, Hillary Clinton, got to name six members;

and the party chair appointed the others. Because of the influence from the Sanders members, the final platform included a desire for a $15 minimum wage—one of Sanders's most popular positions—and a commitment that the U.S. government would fight for LGBT rights in an international effort.

Giving a runner-up this much influence on the document is both principled and practical. A good portion of the party voted for the runner-up in the primary phase of the election, and the party needs those same dedicated voters to come out in the general election to support the candidate in the general election.

Political parties try to define their principles, which are shaped by the more ideological and active members, while remaining practical and looking ahead to the next election. They must strategize how to attract voters. After the Republicans lost their second straight presidential election in 2012, the party took a step back to evaluate its performance and assess how it could gain members and thus voters. Their so-called "autopsy report" suggested that the GOP needed to do more to reach out to Hispanics and younger citizens. Instead, however, during the 2016 election, the party platform and Republican winner Donald Trump took a strong position against illegal immigration—an issue affecting large numbers of Hispanics—and voiced the party's continued opposition to gay marriage—an issue that younger citizens tend to support. These policies appealed to a traditional, mostly white voter base. Trump also promoted protectionist trade policies, expanded oil and gas

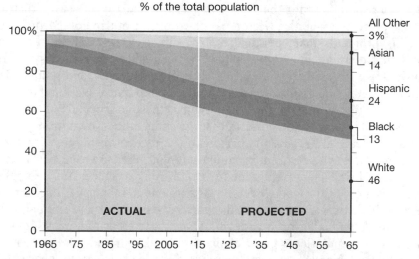

Demographic Trends, 1965–2065

% of the total population

Source: *Pew Research Center 2014 report, "Modern Immigration Wave Brings 59 Million to U.S., Driving Population Growth and Change Through 2065"*

Note: Whites, blacks, and Asians include only single-race non-Hispanics; Asians include Pacific Islanders. Hispanics can be of any race.

Political party leaders follow the population trends to determine the demographics of future voters so they can anticipate effective outreach.

drilling, and an America-first program, attracting a significant number of blue-collar voters who traditionally voted with the Democrats. Trump didn't win the popular vote, but, despite not following the recommendations of the autopsy report, he did win the majority of Electoral College votes, in part thanks to conservative voters who wanted a change in leadership.

As official statements of position, platforms matter to party leaders. However, most citizens do not follow the platform fight at the convention or read the final draft once it is available on the Internet. Nuances in platform language do not affect too many voters, but they could signal the beginning of an evolution in the party that may take a few election cycles to appear.

Candidate Recruitment Parties are always looking for talented candidates to run for office, especially those with their own financial resources or a strong, established following. For instance, at the national level, both parties sought to recruit General Dwight Eisenhower after World War II to run for president. Because he was a career soldier, mostly apolitical, and widely popular for his role in the victory over the Axis powers, a "Draft Eisenhower" movement started among some Democrats for the 1948 election. The Republicans succeeded in making him their candidate in 1952.

Party officials do sometimes court presidential candidates, but typically for the top offices, there's no shortage of experienced and well-funded contenders who have had their eye on higher office for years and are eager to compete for each party's nomination.

The party apparatus will look more aggressively for candidates to run for the state legislature or for the U.S. Congress, especially in "safe" districts where a party is assured a victory at the polls. Both major parties have recruiting programs that operate from Washington, D.C. These recruiters mark swing districts and swing states on maps and keep an eye on rising talent in those areas. Ideally, they find energetic, telegenic, and scandal-free candidates with good resumés and a talent for fundraising. National officials from Washington will sometimes call or visit these prospects and convince them to run. Those who can contribute large sums of their own money to the effort are appealing, because the party can use its own resources elsewhere. Also, candidates who fund their campaigns with their own money tend to have a high level of commitment to establishing a successful campaign. Candidates moving from one level of government up to the next may already have established a war chest of funds to carry over to the new campaign.

For the down-ballot, or local level, offices where partisan campaigns are likely, a local county-level party chair might talk a friend into running for city commissioner or school board member. Party leaders look for charismatic people who have a good grasp of the issues and who can articulate the party's positions. They also want candidates who can connect with voters. First-time candidates might include lifelong party volunteers, community leaders known around town, or people energized about a particular political issue.

Campaign Management As election season draws near, political parties get busy. Some of the regular, everyday activities continue, but an increase in engaging voters, holding campaign events, raising money, and trying to win elections for their candidates will consume the party for a months-long battle to take office and ultimately shape policy according to their ideology.

Most higher-office campaigns have a two-stage process. In the first stage, the party's rank-and-file voters nominate their candidates in a primary election. Since multiple candidates compete against one another for the party's nomination, the party will sometimes act more like a referee in the process of candidate selection than a coach. Multiple factions of members will coalesce around their favorite candidates. Sometimes these divisions are split along ideological beliefs—a primary might pit a liberal or conservative candidate against a moderate one—or they could be based on differences in personality or region.

One key part of the first stage is party-sponsored debates or forums featuring the party's declared candidates. Debates enable voters to get a sense of each candidate's principles and issue positions.

The second stage of the campaign process is the general election, in which the party candidates try to defeat their opposition. In this second phase, the party typically unites around its slate of nominees for different offices and works hard to get them elected. Parties seek success by hosting political rallies or fundraisers; canvassing for votes; distributing literature and campaign items, such as bumper stickers, signs, and buttons; and making "get-out-the-vote" phone calls.

The party assists candidates in preparing for debates, helps them create web pages, and does what it can to coordinate public events. Parties will run field offices, usually in a rented office space or a building donated by a wealthy party member, where party members coordinate local campaign efforts such as phone banks or door-to-door canvassing efforts.

Fundraising and Regulations Among the parties' most important campaign functions are raising and spending money in order to win elections. Campaign finance laws at the national and state levels limit how much donors can contribute to candidates, parties, and interest groups; define what types of items or activities the money can be used for, and regulate an enforcement mechanism that monitors this cash flow. You will learn more about campaign finance law—its evolution and how it works today—in Chapter 13. (See also page 470.)

The Federal Election Commission (FEC), an executive branch agency, monitors the flow of money and enforces financial limits. National and state party organizations must register with the FEC once they spend more than $1,000 toward any federal election effort in a calendar year. If a party organization conducts any activities with expenses within 120 days of a federal election, even generic voter registration, voter identification, or get-out-the-vote drives, those activities must be funded with money subject to federal limits.

Current party contribution limits dictate that state, local, and district-level party organizations can give a federal candidate's campaign committee up to a total of $5,000 per election. The national party can also give up to $5,000 per election (a combined $10,000 for the primary and general elections). For the 2016 federal elections, the Democratic National Committee (including its auxiliary committees) received a little more than $755 million and spent all but $20 million of it. The Republican National Committee received more than $652 million and had nearly $44 million remaining after the election.

Media Strategy One reason fundraising is such an important function of political parties is that the cost of buying TV, radio, and other media ads is very high, but an effective media strategy is fundamental to winning votes. Over the past 50 years, people received the bulk of their news from television. Even today, the average adult watches about 3.5 hours of TV per day. About three-quarters of all voters say television is where they obtain most of their information about elections. For this reason, political parties try to develop the most effective media strategy possible, taking full advantage of the power of television.

Candidates rely on two forms of TV placement: the news story and the commercial. A news story is typically a short news segment showing the candidate in action—touring a factory, speaking to a civic club, visiting a classroom, or appearing at a political rally. Candidates send out press releases announcing their events, usually scheduled early enough in the day to make the evening news. This is free media coverage because, unlike expensive television commercials, the campaign does not have to pay for it. A campaign commercial, on the other hand, has to be paid for. In fact, the most expensive part of nearly any campaign is television advertising. The typical modern campaign commercial includes great emphasis on imagery, action-oriented themes, emotional messages, negative characterizations of the opponent, and quick production turnaround.

A candidate's appearance on camera can influence voters more deeply than words. For instance, in the first televised debate in 1960, John F. Kennedy's youthful, handsome, and charming demeanor was a stark contrast to Richard M. Nixon's nervous sweating. Kennedy won the election. In 2016, Democrat Hillary Clinton actively modulated her voice, which had a reputation for grating on voters' ears. She also used careful wardrobe selection to find a balance between appealing to women voters and maintaining a powerful image. For certain events she wore her trademark white pantsuits, which served as a reminder of the white clothing women in the suffrage movement wore in the early 20th century.

Although television is still central to media strategy, the trend in how people get their news is shifting. As of 2017, about two-thirds of Americans got at least part of their news from social media. Examples of **social media** include Facebook, Instagram, Snapchat, and Twitter (all social networks), YouTube (video posting), WordPress and Tumblr (blog sites), or Quora and Digg (discussion groups). These social media outlets share certain traits that make them powerful tools for parties and candidates to spread a message and build a brand:

Source: *Granger, NYC*

Television shines a spotlight on image and appearance. More than 33 million TV viewers watched Hillary Clinton deliver a speech at the Democratic National Convention in July, 2016.

- they allow people to connect online to build relationships

- they support brand awareness and permit unlimited sharing (posts can "go viral" and be shared without cost among millions of followers)

- they permit visual images that reinforce the message

- they engage people by allowing them to share their own opinions (sometimes anonymously)

Just as Kennedy became the first "television president" because he used the medium so well, Barack Obama is often called the first "social media" president. His campaign, especially for reelection in 2012, spent years on research and development creating complex programs that could link data available through social media and the party's own paper records in such a way that organizing became highly efficient and voter outreach precisely targeted. Digital ad costs were also much lower than those of television ads. For about $14.5 million, Obama's campaign bought YouTube advertising that would have cost $47 million on television.

Many supporters gave permission to the Obama campaign to access their connections on social media, which were then cross-checked in the campaign's vast data repository. Rather than being asked to share an Obama ad with all their connections, supporters were told which of their connections, in which key states, would be most helpful to share an ad with. Since people are much more likely to trust the outreach of a friend than the outreach of a political volunteer, this strategy won many votes for Obama. Since then, parties try to develop the most efficient social media strategies to gather data for targeted outreach.

Despite the positive aspects of connectedness and free/low cost advertisement on social media, there is a negative side. Facebook and Twitter, in particular, ran thousands of "dark ads" during the 2016 election. **Dark ads** are anonymously placed status updates, photos, videos, or links that appear only in the target audience's social media news feeds but not in the general feeds. They are created to match the personality types of their audience to the message and to manipulate people's emotions—especially anger or fear—in order to sway their votes. Facebook and Twitter have both promised to provide more transparency to voters.

Impact of Political Parties on Government

In addition to their impact on voters, political parties have a significant influence on the way government works at all levels. On the national level, political committees work to write policy, elect candidates who will transform policies preferences into legislation, and maintain power. Holding onto power not only funnels funding for projects to members' home states, it also gives the dominant party the opportunity to appoint judges who will rule on the constitutionality of laws. The majority party also fills the leadership roles in the House and Senate, controlling the flow of legislation in both houses and the appointment of party members to key committee chairmanships. The most coveted prize for a president is to appoint judges to lifelong positions on the U.S. Supreme Court who are expected to represent, as much as an impartial judge can, the ideology of the president's party.

Party control over state legislatures and governorships is also important. Holding power at the state level can help parties enact legislation and create policy reflecting their party's ideology. In addition, it gives the majority party an advantage in drawing legislative district maps that can strengthen the likelihood of remaining in power (page 103) at the state level and maintaining or increasing the number of U.S. House of Representatives seats from the state's majority party . Following the 2016 election, a number of states had to redraw their voting district maps because federal courts determined that they were unfairly and unconstitutionally designed to keep incumbents in office.

Party Structures in Legislatures Both the **Democratic National Committee (DNC)** and the **Republican National Committee (RNC)** comprise a hierarchy of hundreds of employees and a complex network dedicated to furthering party goals. Each committee includes public leaders and other elite activists. The RNC and DNC meet formally every four years at their national conventions and on occasion between presidential elections to sharpen policy initiatives and to increase their influence.

Natlonal Chairs The **party chairperson** is the chief strategist and spokesperson. Though a leading official such as the president or an outspoken congressional leader tends to be the public face of the party, the party chair runs the party machinery. The chairperson's jobs include the following:

- appearing on political television shows and at major party events

- guiding the party's daily operations

- building up the membership

- seeking funding

- recruiting quality candidates for office

- conveying to voters the party philosophy

The position is nongovernmental, though some chairs have simultaneously served in Congress or as state governors. Some famous party chairpersons include Republican George H. W. Bush (before serving as vice president and then president) and former Vermont governor and Democrat Howard Dean (after his failed campaign for the presidential nomination). Republicans recently chose as their new chair Ronna Romney McDaniel of Michigan, a former state-level leader (and niccc of 2012 Republican presidential nominee Mitt Romney), and the Democrats elected Tom Perez, former U.S. secretary of labor.

Both the RNC and the DNC have subcommittees that manage recruitment, oversee communications and get-out-the-vote operations, and draft the party platform. Employees conduct surveys to ensure the party's philosophy aligns with that of its members and vice versa. Staffers meet with interest groups that have similar goals. They also regularly meet with their congressional leaders to further their policy agenda.

Hill Committees Both parties also have non-lawmaking committees in each house of Congress. Their purpose is to strategize how to win seats in the House and Senate. These four groups are sometimes referred to as the Hill Committees (page 86). Hill Committee members are also members of Congress. The chair of each party's Hill Committee holds a leadership position in his or her respective chamber. All four Hill Committees have permanent offices and support staff. They recruit candidates for open seats and seats held by the other party and try to reelect incumbents. They conduct polls, help candidates with fundraising activities, contribute to campaigns, create political ads, and purchase television time. Candidates running for election spend great amounts of time and energy seeking the parties' help and endorsement. During the 2016 federal election effort, the four groups each raised and spent between $130 million and $220 million in trying to keep or put their members into Congress.

PARTY COMMITTEES IN CONGRESS
National Republican Senatorial Committee (NRSC)
National Republican Congressional Committee (NRCC)
Democratic Senatorial Campaign Committee (DSCC)
Democratic Congressional Campaign Committee (DCCC)

State and Local Parties Every state has a statewide party organization. Usually headquartered in the state's capital city, this organization carries out many of the same activities as the national party. The state party chairperson makes public appearances on local television, recruits new members, and registers voters. Within states, many counties have a party chair as well. At the state and local levels, population size, the history of the local party, and its relative strength determine its size and influence. Some chairs are full-time employees who collect a generous annual salary. Some parties have permanent office space or their own building. Some county-level chairpersons from less populated counties are volunteers on a part-time basis and operate out of their homes with nothing more than a basic web page and a box of voter registration cards.

All these organizational elements at various levels create a mammoth party operation that is loosely structured across state lines. The national party chairperson and the national committees are at the top of this operation, but no official hierarchy really exists. There is no streamlined top-down flow of money, ideas, or directives. State and local organizations can operate independently of the national party committee. Popular, self-funded candidates often have more influence on campaigns than the local party. At times, state or local parties differ from the national party on a policy stance.

Party Changes and Adaptations

Since the beginning of the party system, two parties have dominated. However, for a variety of political, social, economic, and legal reasons, parties have undergone significant transformation over the years, adapting to new conditions. One reason parties have changed is the shift from party-centered to candidate-centered campaigns. Because charismatic candidates, especially those who are self-funded, can appeal directly to voters through mainstream and social media, the parties' role in nominating candidates has been weakened. Parties often have to revise their platforms to accommodate these candidates' desires. Parties also find themselves having to keep track of shifting demographics in order to clarify the message and policies that best attract voters.

Candidate-Centered Campaigns

Historically, voters identified with political parties more than with individual candidates. Even the mechanical voting booth— by which a person could pull one lever and vote for a single party's entire slate of candidates—encouraged this party identification. In the 1960s, this trend began to shift, for two main reasons. First, the more widespread use of television allowed candidates to build a following based on their own personalities rather than on party affiliation. Second, during the 1960s, society seriously questioned all public institutions, including political parties, as the Vietnam War dragged on, race riots burned cities across America, and the press revealed that President Nixon lied about both personal and public issues.

One result was the rise of the candidate-centered campaign. Increasingly—especially with social media and Internet technologies—candidates speak directly to the people, weakening the power of the parties. With so much access to information, people became more willing to learn about different candidates and cross party lines to vote for split tickets. Candidates who build their own campaigns are less beholden to party elites and can wield more personal power once they're in office. For this reason, parties are forced to work closely with charismatic candidates on both platform development and getting help with campaigning for down-ticket candidates.

Appeals to Demographic Coalitions

Each party has its core demographic groups, and each continually attempts to broaden its appeal to gain more voters. A demographic group—such as Hispanics, African Americans, Millennials, women, blue-collar workers, or LGBT persons—voting as a bloc can determine the outcome of an election. A party's image during televised events such as nominating conventions can convey how inclusive it is—or isn't—of various demographic groups.

For example, the 1968 Democratic National Convention in Chicago revealed deep divisions within the party and brought major changes in how the Democratic Party nominated its presidential candidate. Old-line conservative party regulars, who favored Vice President Hubert Humphrey as the presidential candidate, faced off against the anti-Vietnam War wing, who favored Senator Eugene McCarthy. Dominated by party elites and older members, the convention nominated Humphrey, who had not run in a single primary or caucus but entered the race after the assassination of Robert Kennedy, while young antiwar protesters battled in the streets with the Chicago police. The spectacle sent the ugly message that the old, white, and still somewhat conservative delegates inside the arena made party decisions, while the younger members—who were eligible for the draft in the unpopular Vietnam conflict but ineligible in many states to vote for a candidate responsible for sending them to war—were relegated to expressing themselves in the streets. The media focused on the party's imperfect and undemocratic nominating procedure.

The Democratic Party created the **McGovern-Fraser Commission** to examine, consider, and ultimately rewrite convention rules. Headed by Senator George McGovern, the commission brought significant changes that ensured minorities, women, and younger voters representation at future conventions. However, a decade later, after having won only one presidential contest, largely as a reaction to Nixon's Watergate scandal, the Democrats radically modified the system's emphasis on the party's rank-and-file voting to give more independence to the party's elites. The party created **superdelegates**, high-ranking delegates not beholden to any state primary vote. Superdelegates include members of Congress, governors, mayors of large cities, and other party regulars who comprise roughly 20 percent of the Democratic delegates.

Before the Democratic Convention in 2016, however, a DNC Unity Reform Commission met to reform the superdelegates' role in elections in the interest of making elections more democratic. Reforms included reducing the percentage of uncommitted delegates—those free to vote for whomever they chose—to one third, requiring the remaining two-thirds of the superdelegates to cast their votes according to the popular vote in their states.

The Republican Party faced its own challenges in appealing to a wider swath of voters. Even today, its convention delegates are overwhelmingly white, in contrast to the Democrats' now-inclusive and diverse participants. The president's State of the Union televised speeches also reflect these differences between the parties. The Republican side of the aisle tends to be older, white, and male. The Democratic side of the aisle includes more women and people of color.

Another vital way parties appeal to their demographic coalitions is through their policy views. Will party members, if elected to office, try to overturn abortion laws, thereby appealing to social conservatives, including many older white people? Will party members in office support same-sex marriage and thereby appeal to social liberals, including many young people? Will these persons provide immigration protection to Deferred Action on Childhood Arrivals (DACA) recipients and thereby appeal to Hispanics and other immigrant populations? What about making good on a promise to maintain broad rights to gun ownership, thereby appealing to mainly conservative white males? How will the party address climate change, the economy, taxes, and the national debt? Different demographic coalitions have different views on these issues, and party members will shape their policy positions in part to attract the demographic groups they believe they need to win elections while still working for their ideological principles.

Changes Influencing Party Structure

Parties have also adjusted to developments that affect their structure. At times throughout history, shifts in voter alignments transferred power to the opposition party and redefined the mission of each party. Campaign finance laws have brought about structural changes as well, altering the relationships among donors, parties, candidates, and interest groups. And in order to remain relevant, parties must continually adjust to changing communication technology and voter-data management systems to spread and control their message and appeal to voters.

Critical Elections and Realignments At certain points, new parties have emerged, and old ones have faded into the background. Additionally, large groups of voters have switched allegiance from one party to another over divisive issues or in times of crisis. These political **party realignments** are changes "in underlying electoral forces due to changes in party identification," according to the *Oxford Concise Dictionary of Politics*. They are marked by **critical elections**, those that reveal sharp, lasting changes in loyalties to political parties. Although there are various ways to classify realignments, many historians recognize political realignments occurring five times in U.S. history—associated with the elections of 1800, 1860, 1896, 1932, and 1968 — each realignment marking the emergence of a different party system. There are at least two causes of realignments: (1) a party is so badly defeated it fades into obscurity as a new party emerges, or (2) large blocs of voters shift allegiance from one party to another.

The First Alignment In 1800, power shifted from the Federalists, followers of Washington, Adams, and Hamilton, who were supporters of a strong national government that invested in national infrastructure and banking, to the **Jeffersonians**, later called the Democratic-Republicans, who favored states' rights, limited national government, and generally fewer laws. Federalists and Jeffersonians were deeply and passionately divided on the best course for the nation, yet this shift marked America's first peaceful transition of power. Federalist influence faded, and voters shifted to the **Democratic-Republicans**. In fact, for approximately two decades after the 1800 election, the only party in the United States was the Democratic-Republican Party.

In 1824, Andrew Jackson founded the Democratic Party, which emerged out of the Democratic-Republican Party and continued many of the principles of that party, while the National Republican Party formed that same year. In 1828, Jackson won the presidency with support from small Western farmers. By this time, suffrage had expanded because property qualifications had been dropped in most states, and many more citizens voted. This shift toward greater democracy for the common man (women were not permitted to vote) and away from the aristocracy that had previously held the power was called **Jacksonian Democracy**. Opponents formed the **Whig Party** and advocated for a strong central government that would promote westward expansion and investment in infrastructure and support these investments with a strong national bank. Both Northerners and Southerners joined the Whig party, with some Southern Whigs opposing slavery and some Northern Whigs supporting a lenient attitude toward Southern slaveholders. In time, the slavery issue would fracture the Whig party.

Several party innovations developed in this period that influenced the structure of parties. The Democrats started building state and local party organizations to help support the national party efforts. They established the **party principle**, the idea that the party exists independent of the government, and that, if victorious, it can reward with government jobs those who help the campaign. The Whigs and Democrats also developed more modern campaigns by holding nominating conventions. The Whigs elected only two presidents, while the Democratic Party dominated and became the party of the people.

New Alliances for the Republicans: The Second Realignment The 1850s marked a controversial time of intense division on the issue of slavery. Democrats broke into northern and southern wings.

By 1854, Northern Democrats became part of an alliance formed of abolitionists and old Whigs. They held their first national presidential nominating convention in Philadelphia in 1856, choosing John C. Fremont, who ran under the "Free Soil" banner, committed to not allowing the spread of slavery into new territories (hence "free soil"). Fremont lost to Democrat James Buchanan. At their next convention in Chicago in 1860, the alliance of abolitionists and Whigs formally took the label "Republican" and nominated Abraham Lincoln, who won the presidency.

The 1860 election marked the second national realignment. Though the new Republican Party was technically a third party at the time—the last third party to win the White House—it quickly began to dominate national politics. Today, the Republicans are often referred to as the **"Grand Old Party"** or **GOP**. From 1860 to 1932, Republicans dominated national politics with their pro-growth, pro-business agenda. Democrats became the party of the South.

Expanding Economy and the Realignment of 1896 America witnessed the third realignment period during the era of big business and expansion, with Republicans still dominant. The critical 1896 election realigned voters along economic lines. The economic depressions of the 1880s and 1890s (or *panics,* as they were often called in those years) hit the South and the Midwest hard. The Democratic Party joined with third parties such as the Greenbacks and Populists to seek a fair deal for the working class and represent voters in the South and West. Democrats also supported Protestant reformers who favored prohibition of alcohol.

For the 1896 presidential election, congressman and orator William Jennings Bryan captured the Democratic nomination. The Populist Party also endorsed him. However, anti-Bryan Democrats realigned themselves with the Republican Party, which nominated William McKinley. The Republicans were still aligned with big business, industry, capitalists, urban interests, and immigrant groups. These groups feared the anti-liquor stance of so many in the evolving Democratic Party, which increasingly focused on class conflict and workers' rights. As Democratic legislatures began to regulate industry to protect laborers, conservative Republican judges declared such regulations unconstitutional. These differences began the division that continues today between Republican free-market capitalists and Democrats who favor regulation.

Democrats, the Depression, and the Fourth Realignment In the 1930s during the Great Depression, America went from being mostly Republican to being solidly Democratic thanks to Franklin Delano Roosevelt's **New Deal coalition**, which was made up of Democratic state and local party organizations, labor unions and blue-collar workers, minorities, farmers, white Southerners, people living in poverty, immigrants, and intellectuals. At this time, blacks shifted from the Republican Party to the Democrats. The 1932 presidential election marks the first time that more blacks voted Democrat

Source: *Clifford Berryman, Library of Congress*

The 1928 presidential election pitted Democrat Al Smith against Republican Herbert Hoover. When interpreting a political cartoon, first notice the symbols and read the labels. What symbols does the cartoonist provide to indicate the party that nominated each candidate? What are the tools of persuasion in campaigning?

than Republican. This New Deal coalition sent Roosevelt to the White House four times. His leadership during the economic crisis and through most of World War II allowed the Democrats to dominate Congress for another generation. The New Deal implemented social safety nets and positioned the federal government as a force in solving social problems. It reined in business, promoted union protections and civil liberties, and increased participation by including women—granted suffrage through the Nineteenth Amendment in 1919—and minorities.

Source: *Franklin D. Roosevelt Presidential Library and Museum*

Franklin Roosevelt's public works programs employed the unemployed and boosted the nation's infrastructure. It's no wonder such a large coalition of voters supported President Roosevelt and his Democratic Party well after the New Deal. Roosevelt is pictured in the center of the photo with his wife Eleanor beside him.

Shifts Since the 1960s Although a mix of politicians from both parties favor equality among the races, the post-World War II fight for equality for African Americans was dominated by the Northern, liberal wing of the Democratic Party. President Lyndon Johnson quietly predicted the Democratic Party would lose the South for a generation when he signed the Civil Rights Act in the summer of 1964 (page 312). He was right.

This regional realignment became apparent in the 1964 presidential election between President Johnson and Arizona Republican Barry Goldwater. Johnson handily won the election, while Goldwater won the Deep South states, a region that had been the Solid South for Democrats for most presidential elections over the previous century. Southern white voters have all but left the New Deal coalition in opposition to civil rights reforms and joined the Republican Party. Additionally, decisions that resulted in busing public school children for racial balance and those that legalized abortion convinced conservative voters to move to the GOP.

Since 1968, the major parties have continued on similar ideological paths, especially on economic issues. However, a growing number of citizens became independents or turned away from politics altogether, resulting in a **party dealignment.** The unpopular Vietnam War and Richard Nixon's Watergate scandal brought mistrust of government and a mistrust of the parties. Voter turnout dropped over the following three decades. Party loyalty decreased, a fact made obvious by an increased number of independent voters. These voters split their tickets—or voted for candidates from both parties—which resulted in phases where the presidency was held by one party and one or both houses of Congress by the other. This **divided government** has been common at the federal level.

The Democratic Party has gone from being a states' rights advocate to believing in big government, while the Republican Party has gone from being the progressive anti-slavery party of Abraham Lincoln to being conservative. These drastic transitions did not happen overnight but through a series of changing voter habits and adjusted party alignments over more than a century.

Source: *Library of Congress*

African American and white children ride a bus from the suburbs to the inner city of Charlotte, North Carolina as part of a school integration plan in 1973.

	BY THE NUMBERS			
	PRESIDENT, RUNNER-UP, AND MAJORITY			
	PARTY IN CONGRESS			
Year	President	Runner-up	House	Senate
1968	Nixon (R)	Humphrey (D)	DEM	DEM
1970			DEM	DEM
1972	Nixon (R)	McGovern (D)	DEM	DEM
1974			DEM	DEM
1976	Carter (D)	Ford (R)	DEM	DEM
1978			DEM	DEM
1980	Reagan (R)	Carter (D)	DEM	REP
1982			DEM	REP
1984	Reagan (R)	Mondale (D)	DEM	REP
1986			DEM	DEM
1988	Bush, G. H. W. (R)	Dukakis (D)	DEM	DEM
1990			DEM	DEM
1992	Clinton, W. J. (D)	Bush (R)	DEM	DEM
1994			REP	REP
1996	Clinton, W. J. (D)	Dole (R)	REP	REP
1998			REP	REP
2000	Bush, G. W. (R)	Gore (D)	REP	REP
2002			REP	REP
2004	Bush, G. W. (R)	Kerry (D)	REP	REP
2006			DEM	DEM
2008	Obama (D)	McCain (R)	DEM	DEM
2010			REP	DEM
2012	Obama (D)	Romney (R)	REP	DEM
2014			REP	REP
2016	Trump (R)	Clinton, H. (D)	REP	REP

What do the numbers show? Since 1968, how many times did Democrats hold the majority? How many did Republicans dominate? In what years do you see a president governing with a Congress dominated by the opposing party? In which years was the Congress split? In what elections do you see a change in party power? What caused these changes?

PARTY SYSTEMS AND REALIGNMENT PERIODS		
1789–1800	**Federalists** won ratification of the Constitution and the presidency for the first three terms.	**Anti-Federalists** opposed strong national government and favored states' rights and civil liberties.
1800–1824	**Federalists** maintained beliefs in a loose interpretation of the Constitution to strengthen the nation.	**Democratic-Republicans** (Jeffersonians) put less emphasis on a strong Union and more on states' rights.
1824–1860	**Democrats** (Jacksonians) encouraged greater participation in politics and gained a Southern and Western following.	**Whigs** were a loose band of eastern capitalists, bankers, and merchants who wanted internal improvements and stronger national government.
1860–1896	**Democrats** became the second-place party, aligned with the South and the wage earner and sent only Grover Cleveland to the White House.	**Republicans** freed the slaves, reconstructed the Union, and aligned with industrial interests.
1896–1932	**Democrats** join with Populists to represent the Southern and Midwestern farmers, workers, and Protestant reformers.	**Republicans** continue to dominate after a realignment based on economic factors.
1932–Present (including dealignment starting in 1968)	The Great Depression created the **New Deal coalition** around FDR's programs. **Democrats** dominated politics until the mid-1990s.	**Republicans** have taken on a *laissez-faire* approach to economic regulation and a brand of conservatism that reflects limited government.

Campaign Finance Laws Since the early 1970s, national law and recent landmark Supreme Court cases have governed campaign finance rules. These laws, covered in Chapter 14, have affected the structure and strength of political parties.

Campaign finance laws differentiate between "hard money" and "soft money." **Hard money** is any contribution subject to the regulation of the Federal Election Commission (FEC), which was established in 1974 as the monitoring agency for campaign contributions. There are strict limits on how much can be donated, and donations can come from only individuals, political action committees, and political parties, not corporations or labor unions. A **political action committee (PAC)** is an organization that collects political donations from its members and uses the funds to influence an election, either by supporting or opposing a candidate. (See pages 503–505.)

However, donors found a way around these limits through a provision that allowed parties to receive **soft money**—donations not regulated by the FEC—as long as those contributions were for the purpose of "party-building activities," not for supporting specific candidates. Nonetheless, the parties found ways to use the money in campaigns by creating **issue ads**—advertisements highlighting an issue of concern. Such ads could point out the opposition's stand on those issues and leave a negative impression, but as long as they didn't say, "Vote for our candidate!" they were a permissible use of soft money. In this way soft money was making its way from the pockets of influential billionaires to the political parties, and the political parties' strength was increased.

The Bipartisan Campaign Reform Act (BCRA) of 2002 put an end to this practice. As a result, money that would have gone to the parties as soft money went instead to special interest groups in support of a candidate, so candidate-centered campaigns became the norm. This change weakened the influence of political parties, which are recognized as a moderating force, and gave more power to the special interest groups to back candidates who were often at extreme ends of the political spectrum. Candidates supported by big money interests often won their seats, and the political divide in Washington widened. Observers noted that as the party influence weakened, grassroots organizing efforts also declined.

The Supreme Court decisions in *Citizens United v. FEC* (2010) and *McCutcheon v. FEC* (2014) in essence reversed the soft money prohibitions. (See page 510.) The rulings allowed a new kind of organization, the **Super PAC**, to collect unlimited funds from a variety of sources, including corporations and labor unions, as long as the money did not go directly to a candidate's election campaign or to a political party. However, the money could be used for advertising to support or disparage any candidate as long as the Super PAC did not formally coordinate with the candidate. Ads of this kind are known as **independent expenditures**, and even parties can make them.

Also, while upholding the maximum contributions for individual candidates or committees, the ruling in *McCutcheon* removed the limit imposed by BCRA on how much an individual could donate to multiple candidates in a two-year cycle. This change greatly increased the popularity of the joint fundraising committee (JFC)—a coordinated fundraising effort of a number of candidates and committees. Rich donors can now write just one large check (more than $1 million depending on how many candidates and committees are in the JFC). The contributions are then shared among the members of the JFC according to their own agreement.

These changes affected political parties in several ways. First, state party committees are often members of JFCs, so they received a share of the contributions. Once the money was in their coffers, there was no law against returning a sizable amount of it to the national committees. Through this process, the political parties worked around their limits on hard money and once again had a strong hand in passing around campaign donations and thereby influencing candidate choice and results. Second, the unofficial structure of the party has changed from a top-down vertical organization to more of a horizontal network. Although the joint fundraising committees and Super PACs are not officially part of the party, they are key players in campaigns, so the political party has become part of a web of actors, dependent on elements outside of the party for funds.

BY THE NUMBERS DEMOCRATIC AND REPUBLICAN EXPENDITURES, PRESIDENTIAL CAMPAIGNS, 1952–1968 (IN MILLIONS)					
Year	Democrats	Spent	Republicans	Spent	Total
1952	Stevenson	$5.03	Eisenhower	$6.61	$11.64
1956	Stevenson	$5.11	Eisenhower	$7.78	$12.89
1960	Kennedy	$9.80	Nixon	$10.13	$19.93
1964	Johnson	$8.76	Goldwater	$16.03	$24.79
1968	Humphrey	$11.59	Nixon	$25.40	$36.99

What do the numbers show? What happened to the cost of presidential campaigns in the post-World War II era? Which party spent more during each cycle? How often did the higher-spending party win the election? What factors may have caused the trend(s) in this table?

Changes in Communication and Data-Management Technology Political parties rely heavily on polling and on mining databases to gain insights into voter preferences, so they must quickly adapt to changes in technology that affect these efforts. As you read, Obama's campaigns, especially for his reelection in 2012, devoted many resources to using available technology and media to their fullest to understand and target voters.

Parties use this information to craft, control, and clarify their messages. Voter data can reveal where people eat and shop, the people they're connected to, and which media sources they use to access news and information. Increasingly, political organizations are able to target with pinpoint accuracy who gets which message thanks to data-management technology. Data-management technology is a field that uses skills, software, and equipment to organize information and then store it and keep it secure.

These digital resources are so valuable in learning about voters that they have been abused. Before the 2016 election, a British political data firm called Cambridge Analytica managed to obtain 50 million Facebook user profiles from another company's personality quiz app. The data firm was an offshoot of the SCL Group, a company owned largely by the Mercer family, which includes conservative billionaire Republican Party supporters. Cambridge Analytica then created detailed "psychographic" profiles used to target voters during the campaign. Facebook suspended Cambridge Analytica and found itself in the crosshairs over its oversight and corporate policies and the role it played in presidential politics.

Managing Political Messages and Political Outreach

Psychographic segmentation uses data about personality, lifestyle, and social class to categorize groups of voters. Demographics explain "who" the voters are—race, gender, age, neighborhood, church or political affiliation, and similar traits. Psychographics, in contrast, explain "why" they vote the way they do. What are their values, hobbies, habits, and likes? This valuable data helps candidates and parties tailor their messages and conduct political outreach.

Part of a message's appeal is based on the candidate's appearance and choice of venues for delivery. A Western state candidate might appear wearing a cowboy hat and boots, riding on horseback along a river. An urban candidate could roll up her sleeves and visit a public works project that rehabilitates neighborhoods. Language is carefully crafted in messages to remind voters of key ideas and values espoused by the party.

Another key element of messaging and outreach is timing. In the early stages of a campaign, more abstract messages resonate. That's when the candidate will remind voters about core values and ideals. For instance, during the 2008 presidential primaries, Democrat Barack Obama spoke soaringly of hope and change, while his rivals focused on the concrete details of managing the Iraq War and closing a "doughnut hole" in Medicaid that made drug costs out of reach for some. Closer to Election Day, voters become receptive to messages that are more concrete. Candidates can specify the programs they plan to implement and how those changes will improve the lives of Americans.

Perhaps the greatest challenge for parties is to spark interest in unaligned or apathetic voters. In recent elections, Barack Obama succeeded in doing this and won two four-year terms in 2008 and 2012 with his brand and message of hope and change. In 2016, Donald Trump won the election by promising a very different brand of change—draining the Washington swamp of corrupt insiders.

Structural Barriers to Third-Party and Independent Candidates

Though a two-party system has generally dominated the American political scene, competitive **minor parties**, often called **third parties**, have surfaced and played a distinct role. Technically, the Jacksonian Democrats and Lincoln's Republicans began as minor parties. Since Lincoln's victory in 1860, no minor party has won the White House, but several third-party movements have met with some levels of success. These lesser-known groups have sent members to Congress, added amendments to the Constitution, and forced the larger parties to take note of them and their ideas. Despite these victories, structural barriers in our political system have limited the impact and influence—and therefore the success—of third-party and independent candidates.

Why Third Parties Form

Because the two major parties compete to win the majority of voters, and majorities always occupy the center, the more ideological citizens may not believe that their agenda is being heard and implemented in either party, so they create their own party. For instance, in the early 1900s as a response to conservative robber barons, uncontrolled industrial growth, and massive wealth inequality, the Socialist Party formed and was able to push a leftist agenda whose ideas were eventually incorporated into American politics. During the 1970s, following a long period of Democratic dominance, the

Libertarian party formed. Its supporters wanted a more traditional liberalism: *laissez-faire* (unregulated) capitalism, abolition of the welfare state, non-intervention in foreign affairs, and individual rights—such as the right to opt out of Social Security. Socialists and Libertarians are **ideological parties**.

Sometimes third parties form as **splinter parties**—broken off from a major party. For example, in 1968 segregationist George Wallace splintered off from the liberal Democratic Party and formed the American Independent Party. White southerners followed him, splitting the Democratic vote, and that —along with opposition to the Vietnam conflict and Humphrey's non-democratic nomination—led to the election of Republican Richard Nixon.

Some parties form as **economic protest parties**. In the late 19th century, the Greenback Party opposed monopolies. During that same period, farmers founded the Populist Party to fight against railroads, big banks, corporations, and the politicians those interests controlled. Other third parties rise and fall as **single-issue parties**. The Prohibition Party, for example, was founded in 1869 as part of the temperance movement to ban alcohol. The Green Party arose in the 1970s to advocate for environmental awareness, social justice, and nonviolence. Some of these parties still exist in America today. Protest parties are formed within a specific context—a social condition that demands reform.

MINOR PARTY TYPES AND EXAMPLES
Ideological parties: Socialist, Libertarian
Splinter parties: Bull Moose, American Independent
Economic protest parties: Greenback, Populist
Single-issue parties: American (Know-Nothings), Prohibition

Modern Third Parties

Since 1968, there have been additional minor party candidates seeking office, but no such candidate has won a plurality in any one state, and therefore none has ever earned even one electoral vote. Texas oil tycoon H. Ross Perot burst onto the political scene in 1992 to run for president as an independent. Funded largely from his own wealth, Perot created United We Stand America (later renamed the Reform Party) and campaigned in every state. He won nearly 20 percent of the national popular vote. But with no strong following in any one state, he failed to earn any electoral votes. However, more importantly, he pulled enough votes from Republican President George H. W. Bush that Democrat Bill Clinton won the presidency.

Ralph Nader was the Green Party candidate in the 2000 election. The votes he drew from Democrat Al Gore helped propel Republican George W. Bush into the presidency in an election that was so close, it was decided by a Supreme Court decision regarding "hanging chads" on ballots in Florida. Third-party candidates are feared by the two major parties, and for this reason, there are many barriers to prevent third-party and independent candidates from gaining enough traction to mount a campaign.

MINOR PARTY CANDIDATES AND INDEPENDENT POLITICAL LEADERS	
Recent Minor Party Presidential Candidates	**Becoming Independent**
• **H. Ross Perot**—Texas millionaire ran with United We Stand America, 1992 and 1996	• **Jim Jeffords**—Vermont Republican Senator, 2001
• **Ralph Nader**—Consumer advocate ran with the Green Party, 1996 and 2000	• **Joe Lieberman**—Connecticut Democratic Senator, 2006
• **Pat Buchanan**—Conservative aide to Nixon and Reagan ran with Reform Party, 2000	• **Michael Bloomberg**—New York Republican Mayor, 2007
• **Gary Johnson**—Former governor of New Mexico ran as Libertarian, 2012, 2016	
• **Jill Stein**—Physician and activist ran as Green Party candidate in 2012, 2016	

Barriers to Third-Party Success

No minor party has won the presidency since 1860, and no third party has risen to second place in the meantime. Minor parties have a difficult time competing with the highly organized and well-funded Republicans and Democrats. The minor parties that come and go cannot effectively participate in the political process in the United States because the institutional reasons for the dominance of the two major parties are many and complex. They include single-member districts, money and resources, winner-take-all voting, and the ability of the major parties to incorporate third-party agendas.

Single-Member Districts The United States generally has what are called single-member districts for elective office. In **single-member districts**, the candidate who wins the most votes, or a plurality in a field of candidates, wins that office. Many European nations use proportional representation. In that approach, multiple parties compete for office, and voters cast ballots for the party they favor. After the election those offices are filled proportionally. For example, a party that wins 30 percent of the votes cast in the election is then awarded 30 percent of the seats in that parliament or governing body. This method encourages and rewards third parties, even if minimally. In most elections in the United States, however, if three or more candidates seek an office, the candidate winning the most votes—even if it is with a minority of the total—wins the office outright. There is no rewarding second, much less third, place.

Money and Resources Minor party candidates also have a steeper hill to climb in terms of financing, ballot access, and exposure. Both the Republican and Democratic parties have organized operations to raise money to convince donors of their candidates' ability to win—and by so doing attract even more donors. Full-time employees at the DNC and RNC constantly seek funding between elections. Even more importantly, according to campaign finance law, the nominee's party needs to have won a certain percentage of the vote in the previous election in order to qualify for government funding in the current election. Political candidates from minor parties have a difficult time competing financially unless they're self-financed, as Ross Perot was.

Independents also have a difficult time with ballot access. Every state has a prescribed method for candidates to place their names on the ballot. It usually involves a fee and getting as many as 1.5 million signatures, which is what Ross Perot did in 1992. Favored candidates in the Democratic and Republican parties can simply dispatch party regulars and volunteers throughout a state's counties to collect signatures for the ballot petition. Green Party, Libertarian, or independent candidates must first secure assistance or collect those signatures themselves. Since the ballot petition requires thousands of registered voters, this task alone is daunting and discouraging to would-be third-party candidates.

The media tend not to cover minor party candidates. Reporters are less likely to show up at an event held for a minor candidate. Independents are often not invited to public debates or televised forums at the local and national levels, especially if they aren't on the ballot in all 50 states. Buying exposure and support through advertising costs millions of dollars.

Winner-Take-All Voting Perhaps the largest barrier to third-party and independent candidates is the winner-take-all system of the Electoral College. The founders created this process as a compromise between an election of the president by Congress and an election of the president by a popular vote. The Electoral College determines the presidential candidate, but the popular vote determines how the electors cast their ballots.

Each state has a certain number of electoral votes based on population. All states, with the exception of Maine and Nebraska, award all their electoral votes to the candidate who wins the majority of the popular vote—called the **winner-take-all voting** system. The biggest problem with the Electoral College for mainstream candidates is that they may assume the presidency without having earned a mandate by winning the majority of the popular vote. The biggest problem for third-party and independent candidates is that they very rarely win a state's popular vote and thus can't accumulate the required minimum 270 (out of 538) electoral votes needed to win the presidency.

The winner-take-all system can make politics highly contentious when people feel disenfranchised. Because only two states have proportionate voting, certain voters rarely if ever see their candidates win. For instance, a Democrat in Arizona or a Republican in California might believe that there's little point in voting. However, there have been only five times when the winner of the electoral vote lost the popular vote:

ELECTORAL VOTE WINNERS WHO LOST POPULAR VOTE	
1824	John Quincy Adams
1876	Rutherford B. Hayes
1888	Benjamin Harris
2000	George W. Bush
2016	Donald Trump

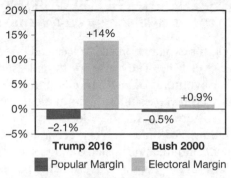

Popular Margin vs. Electoral Margin

Trump 2016: Popular Margin –2.1%, Electoral Margin +14%

Bush 2000: Popular Margin –0.5%, Electoral Margin +0.9%

■ Popular Margin   ■ Electoral Margin

Source: *Dave Leip's Atlas of US Presidents*

The final problem with winner-takes-all voting is that **swing states**—those that could go either way in an election—tend to get most of the attention. Swing states shift party resources to certain regions, and it is always difficult for third-party and independent candidates to match that level of investment.

Incorporation of Third-Party Agendas

Throughout U.S. history, there have been 52 independent political parties, yet none of them has gained traction. No one other than a Democrat or a Republican has been elected since 1860. Does that mean third parties play no role other than as gadfly and spoiler? Definitely not.

In order to attract the third-party candidate's voters, the most closely aligned party will often incorporate items from that person's agenda into its agenda. Although this practice serves to discourage third-party candidates from running, it can also result in positive social change. For instance, Socialists promoted women's suffrage and child labor laws in the early 1900s, now taken for granted by both parties. Populists eventually got Americans a 40-hour work week. Ross Perot planted the idea of a balanced federal budget in the national consciousness. Ralph Nader fought for consumer protections and a clean environment. Minor parties play an important role as the conscience of the nation.

* * * * *

Political parties are responsible for creating many national customs, involving great numbers of people in the electoral process, and elevating political leaders into national office. Since the first political contests before the Republic was created, most citizens have fallen into two camps with very different points of view about how government should be run. Parties provide an identity that simplifies the task of parsing major issues for members. Yet, this simplification can also be divisive. More and more Americans are looking for ways to stop being "red" or "blue." They want practical compromises to solve big problems. This is the challenge for the two-party system: for each to hold on to its base voters while appealing to the middle.

THINK AS A POLITICAL SCIENTIST: *EXPLAIN CAUSATION AND CHANGE OVER TIME IN AMERICA'S TWO-PARTY SYSTEM*

Political scientists look for explanations of causes and effects when trying to understand change over time. They also try to understand what issues endure over time. The evolution of the nation's political parties affords an opportunity to study both causes and effects and constants. The causes include fundamental differences in the most important principles of government, an expanding electorate, slavery, economic booms and busts, wars, social movements, and the emergence of huge social programs. The enduring issues include big vs. small government, personal liberty vs. regulation for the public good, democratic participation vs. the power and influence of wealthy interests, and equal rights vs. racial discrimination. Today's parties take positions on these issues as well as others that are more concrete.

Practice: Using information from this chapter, create a visual or write a paper explaining the causes and effects of the shifting alignments of political parties. Also address continuity—what is the lineage of the positions of today's political parties? From which historic parties have today's parties built their policy positions, and where is there overlap in the enduring issues?

REFLECT ON THE ESSENTIAL QUESTION

Essential Question: *What are the functions and impacts of political parties, and how have they adapted to change?* On separate paper, complete a chart like the one below to gather details to answer that question.

Functions and Impacts	Adaptations to Change

KEY TERMS AND NAMES

conventions/454
critical election/465
dark ads/460
Democratic National
  Committee (DNC)/460
Democratic-
  Republicans/465
Democratic Party/454
divided
  government/468
economic protest
  parties/474
Grand Old Party
  (GOP)/466
hard money/470
Hill Committees/461
ideological parties/474

independent
  expenditures/471
issue ads/470
Jacksonian
  Democracy/465
Jeffersonians/465
McGovern-Fraser
  Commission/463
minor parties/473
New Deal coalition/466
party chairperson/461
party dealignment/468
party realignments/465
platform/454
political action
  committee (PAC)/470
psychographic
  segmentation/472

Republican National
  Committee (RNC)/460
Republican Party/454
robocalls/453
single-issue parties/474
single-member
  districts/475
social media/458
soft money/470
splinter parties/474
superdelegates/464
swing states/477
Super PAC/471
third parties/473
two-party system/452
Whig Party/465
winner-take-all
  voting/476

MULTIPLE-CHOICE QUESTIONS

Questions 1 and 2 refer to the passage below:

> "In this campaign, I've met so many people who motivate me to keep fighting for change. And, with your help, I will carry all of your voices and stories with me to the White House. I will be a president for Democrats, Republicans, and Independents. For the struggling and the successful. For those who vote for me and those who don't. For all Americans."
>
> —Hillary Clinton, Acceptance Speech,
> Democratic National Convention, 2016

1. Why was this passage most likely included in the candidate's message?
   (A) To cast a positive light on her opponent
   (B) To gain voters outside the Democratic Party
   (C) To show how much effort it takes to win to the White House
   (D) To promise her voters that she would implement Democratic policies

2. What guidelines of messaging best align with this passage?

(A) Since the nominating process is over, she can start to be specific about which groups to mention.

(B) Since the general election is months away, she needs to keep her message general and ideological.

(C) Since the nominating process is over, she doesn't have to worry about trying to gain the support of other party members.

(D) Since the general election is months away, she needs to start addressing specific solutions to specific problems.

Questions 3 and 4 refer to the following table.

EXIT POLL, 2016 PRESIDENTIAL ELECTION			
Voters	**Clinton**	**Trump**	**Other**
Men	41%	52%	7%
Women	54%	41%	5%
Ages 18–29	55%	36%	9%
Ages 30–44	51%	41%	8%
Ages 45–64	44%	52%	4%
Ages 65 and older	45%	52%	3%

Source: *CNN.com*

3. Which of the following statements is reflected in the data in the chart?

(A) The youngest voting bloc favored Trump over Clinton.

(B) Trump likely won because of the Southern and rural vote.

(C) The support for each candidate reveals a gender gap.

(D) The largest bloc voting for third-party candidates was the 45-64-year olds.

4. Based on the information in the table, what conclusion can you draw?

   (A) There are very few Democrats over 65 years old.

   (B) A minor party candidate will likely win the presidency this century.

   (C) Young voters tend to be more liberal than old voters.

   (D) Younger men voted for Trump more than older women did.

1968 DEMOCRATIC NATIONAL CONVENTION DELEGATES' VOTES ON FIRST BALLOT	
Candidate	Votes
Hubert Humphrey	1759 ¼
Eugene McCarthy	601
Others	146

5. Based on the data in the table above, what was the likely outcome of this convention?

   (A) The Democrats would lose the general election.

   (B) The Republicans would lose the general election.

   (C) Eugene McCarthy would become the vice presidential nominee.

   (D) Hubert Humphrey would receive the party's nomination.

6. You believe in expanding gun-control legislation, and you support more affirmative action efforts. You oppose the death penalty. Which party best aligns with your beliefs?

   (A) Libertarian

   (B) Democratic

   (C) Republican

   (D) Green

Questions 7 and 8 refer to the following cartoon.

Source: *davegranlund.com*

7. The cartoonist likely believes that the pointing fingers represent a conflict between which two entities?

(A) The two houses of Congress

(B) The Democratic majority and minority leaders of the House

(C) The state and federal governments

(D) The two political parties within Congress

8. When was the cartoon likely published?

(A) During partisan gridlock in Congress

(B) After the passage of a bipartisan bill

(C) When Democrats controlled both Congress and the White House

(D) After the president's inaction

9. Which of the following is an accurate comparison of Democrats and Republicans?

	DEMOCRATS	REPUBLICANS
(A)	Lost the Solid South in a regional realignment	Have shifted the party ideology from a more liberal stance to a more conservative stance over time
(B)	Constitute the majority party in the Mountain West	Became a strong party after the creation of the New Deal coalition
(C)	Have stronger support among Asian Americans	Have stronger support among younger voters
(D)	Believe the law should forbid abortions	Believe in a woman's right to choose to have an abortion

10. Which of the following is an accurate comparison of winner-take-all voting districts and proportional voting districts?

	WINNER-TAKE-ALL	PROPORTIONAL
(A)	Guarantees occasional third or minor party success in elections	Used for U.S. House elections but not Senate elections
(B)	Common in European nations	Typical in American elections
(C)	Limits the promotion of the views of citizens who voted for second and third-place candidates	Allots seats or government positions relative to party's success in an election
(D)	Not used in the Electoral College System	Used in the Electoral College System of electing a president

FREE-RESPONSE QUESTIONS

1. "According to the Center for Responsive Politics, of the $3.7 billion spent in the 2014 congressional midterms, Super PACs, nonprofits and other outside spenders made up around $560 million, or roughly 15%. In contrast, $1.5 billion, or 42%, was spent by candidates themselves, with the rest left to party committees. . . . The hard money chase marinates our elected representatives in the mindsets of the wealthy and special interests — and takes them away from doing the job we voters pay them to do."
   —Nick Penniman and Wendell Potter, *Los Angeles Times*, March 8, 2016

   Based on the scenario above, respond to A, B, and C below.

   (A) Describe the authors' claim.

   (B) In the context of this scenario, explain how the evidence provided supports the claim described in part A.

   (C) In the context of this scenario, explain how the funding situation affects the effectiveness of the political party as a linkage institution.

INDEPENDENT EXPENDITURES IN CONGRESSIONAL ELECTIONS, 2006–2014 ($ MILLIONS)						
	Primaries		General Elections		Combined	
Year	Party	Non-Party	Party	Non-Party	Party	Non-Party
2006	5.9	8.7	211.5	30.3	217.4	38.9
2008	3.9	8.5	215.7	32.9	219.6	41.3
2010	0.2	16.6	175.3	170.3	175.5	186.4
2012	0.2	54.8	205.5	402.5	205.7	457.3
2014	0.3	102.0	222.0	418.6	222.2	520.6

SOURCE: *Campaign Finance Institute, derived from FEC data.*

2. Use the information in the graphic above to respond to the items below.

(A) Identify the first year in which the combined spending of non-party actors exceeded that of party actors.

(B) Describe a spending trend of non-party actors, and draw a conclusion about what caused the trend.

(C) Explain how interactions between Congress and the judiciary led to the current state of campaign finance law.

3. After 1890, in some Southern states, the Democratic Party denied African Americans participation in primary elections, creating the so-called white primary. During the Democrats' hold on the Solid South, most officeholders were determined by the primary election rather than the general election. Blacks were therefore prevented from participating in the part of the electoral process that actually picked the candidate. Proponents of the white primary argued that all voters were free to vote in the general election. Since political parties are private institutions without government funding, they are not subject to the Constitution in defining their members. Lonnie Smith, a black Texan, tried to vote in the 1940 primary but was denied by S. S. Allwright, a county elections official. In 1944, attorney Thurgood Marshall argued in the Supreme Court that the party was so intertwined with elections and government in this process that the Constitution did, in fact, apply.

In *Smith v. Allwright*, the Court agreed, admitting the party was a voluntary association but arguing that state statutes governed the selection of party leaders and that the party operated primary elections under state authority. A state cannot permit a private organization to practice racial discrimination in elections.

(A) Identify a difference in a constitutional provision at issue between *Smith v. Allwright* (1944) and *Shaw v. Reno* (1993). (See page 107.)

(B) Based on the difference in part A, explain why the holding in *Smith v. Allwright* is different from the holding in *Shaw v. Reno*.

(C) Explain how the ruling in *Smith v. Allwright* demonstrates the linkage between political parties and government.

4. Develop an argument that explains whether political parties strengthen or weaken American democracy.

In your essay, you must:

- Articulate a defensible claim or thesis that responds to the prompt and establishes a line of reasoning
- Support your claim with at least TWO pieces of accurate and relevant information:
    - At least ONE piece of evidence must be from one of the following foundational documents:
        - *Federalist No. 10*
        - *Brutus No.1*
    - Use a second piece of evidence from the other document in the list above or your study of modern political parties
- Use reasoning to explain why your evidence supports your claim/thesis
- Respond to an opposing or alternative perspective using refutation, concession, or rebuttal

WRITING: USE TRANSITIONS FOR COHERENCE

A strong argumentative essay has clearly connected ideas and sentences that flow smoothly. Transitional words and phrases can help you achieve this coherence. Good transitions for argumentative essays include the following:

on the other hand	in contrast	though
nonetheless	however	although
first	second	the most important
because	despite	finally

14

Campaigns and Elections

"The overflow of big money in politics drowns out the voices of everyday people . . . The more money you have the more speech you have. That leaves everyday people out of the equation."

—Nina Turner, Democratic State Senator from Ohio
2008–2014, interview March 4, 2017

Essential Question: How do electoral processes and campaign finance laws affect political participation?

Every four years, millions of Americans go to the polls to cast a vote for the American president and lower offices. Sometimes a candidate will win in a "landslide" with a strong margin and claim victory before sunset. Sometimes close elections require careful vote counting, and no victor is declared for days. In November 2016, some 138 million people, slightly over 60 percent of America's voting-eligible population, cast a vote, and Donald Trump was elected president. **BIG IDEA:** Popular sovereignty is a fundamental principle in representative government, which assumes the engagement and participation of citizens.

There are broad statements regarding voting and elections in the Constitution. Article I states in part that "The Times, Places and Manner of holding Elections for Senators and Representatives, shall be prescribed in each State by the Legislature thereof," but Congress may "make or alter such Regulations." It also states, "Each House shall be the Judge of the Elections, Returns and Qualifications of its own Members."

Congress has set federal elections to occur every two years, in even-numbered years, on the Tuesday after the first Monday in November. Congressional and presidential terms begin the next January. With constitutional amendments and federal law, Congress has some oversight on elections, but administering elections is a state responsibility.

State and Local Administration of Elections

Most states require a voter to register in advance of an election and to be at least 18 years old, a citizen of the United States, a resident of the state where voting will take place, and a non-felon. States can require **voter registration** 30 days in advance of the election so county boards of elections can create and maintain the voter rolls, or poll books.

States' election laws authorize some state department, bureaucratic agency, and/or a secretary of state to oversee elections statewide. Certain customs and procedures are consistent statewide, such as voter registration guidelines, the times voting locations are open, procedures for candidates to file candidacy, and the criteria for candidates to get their names on the ballot. County or local governments conduct and oversee local elections even when the election is for federal offices.

Typically, a county-level elections board governs the election and vote-counting process and serves as a referee when controversies arise. For purposes of voting, counties, cities, and towns are subdivided into **wards**, which are broken into **precincts**. A precinct is a small geographic area of about 500–1,000 voters, who all vote at an assigned **polling place**, often a school or community center. Its size is determined by the supervisor of elections. States can allow 17-year-olds to vote, and many do so in the primary elections if the voter will be 18 by the date of the general election in November. A state elections official oversees the process statewide, while the county-level boards of elections tabulate and report the election returns. Typically, winning candidates are known late on election night or by the following day, but election authorities do not certify the election for days or weeks while they verify the count and wait for absentee ballots to come in.

| WHO GOVERNS ELECTIONS? ||
State	Federal
Sets times and locations for elections (based on federal, state, and local criteria), most dates	Sets date for federal, general elections
Chooses format of acceptable ballots and how to file for candidacy	Has judicial jurisdiction on election policy
Creates rules and procedures for voter registration	Addresses suffrage in constitutional amendments
Draws congressional district lines	Enforces relevant civil rights legislation
Certifies election results days or weeks after Election Day	Administers and enforces campaign finance rules

Ballot Measures

In several states, citizens can change the law with elections or end an elected official's term early. Through ballot measures developed mostly during the Progressive Era—the initiative petition, referendum, and recall—citizen-voters can exercise great influence in shaping policy. They are examples of the participatory model of democracy at work.

Initiatives With **initiatives**, citizens or an organized group formulate a law in writing, then gather the necessary number of registered voters' signatures on a petition to place the proposal on the ballot for approval by the electorate at-large. The procedure as a statewide tool has existed since South Dakota established it in 1898. There are direct and indirect initiatives. Direct initiatives go directly from the citizen-effort to the ballot for citizen approval. The indirect initiative must first go to the state legislature. If the lawmaking institution does not pass the proposal, then it goes to the ballot for citizen approval into law. In some states, the procedure allows the legislature to offer competing proposals in an election. The initiative can create state law, such as a statewide smoking ban or legalization of marijuana. Today, 24 states have a statewide initiative procedure.

Referendum A similar procedure known as a **referendum** can repeal an unpopular law. Legislative referenda are required for certain policies in many states. The most common are certain statewide taxes, bond issues, and constitutional amendments. The legislature will draft the policy and propose it to the people for approval. The legislative referendum is available in all 50 states. The popular referenda allow voters to approve or repeal an already-passed law. When enough signatures are collected, the new law does not go into effect until after the contesting vote, and only if that vote loses.

Recall Nineteen states allow citizens to **recall** elected officials in the middle of their elected term. If the effort makes the ballot, and if over half of the voters vote to recall the official, he or she will be out of a job. On the same ballot for a recall election is a list of candidates to replace the official, if recalled. Probably the most famous recall election removed California Democrat Gray Davis and replaced him with body-builder-turned-actor Arnold Schwarzenegger. As of 2016, about three-fourths of recalls and recall attempts are directed at city or school board officials.

With most of the above citizen-oriented elections, a simple majority is the threshold for change. None of these measures exists at the national level, and states cannot pass laws allowing citizens to recall U.S. Senate or House members. For an up-to-date examination of these state-level methods, consult the National Council of State Legislatures.

Road to the White House

The U.S. presidential race is more complex and more involved than any other election. The road to the White House is long and arduous, with layers of rules and varying state election laws. A presidential campaign requires two or more years of advance work to make it through two fierce competitions—securing the party's nomination and winning a majority of electoral votes. Before presidential hopefuls formally announce their candidacy, they test the waters. Most start early, touring the country and making television appearances. Some author a book, typically a memoir that relies heavily on their political philosophy. As the election year nears, announced and unannounced candidates compete in the **invisible primary** (sometimes called the media primary or money primary), as public opinion polls and comparisons of fundraising abilities begin to tell the score, long before the first states have voted.

An **incumbent** president—one already holding the office—seeking a second term has a much easier time securing the nomination than a challenger, because of the **incumbent advantage phenomenon**—the ability to use all the tools of the presidency to support candidacy for a second term. At the end of a president's second term, the field opens up again for candidates, since the president has served as long as he can.

Although being an incumbent does not guarantee reelection, the rate of reelection is high, about 80 percent. The chart below shows some of the factors in the incumbent advantage phenomenon.

ADVANTAGES OF AN INCUMBENT PRESIDENT IN AN ELECTION
• The incumbent is already very well known, having commanded the national spotlight as the head of the country for four years.
• The incumbent now has four years of experience doing the job and a record people can use to evaluate the president's performance.
• The incumbent still commands the "bully pulpit," the president's ability to use his position to get messages out to the American people.
• The president has already proven he can win elections.
• The president already has a network of campaign contributors who can raise a large amount of money.
• The president already has a network of campaign staff and volunteers who know how to do voter outreach.
• The president is already seen as "presidential," a quality other candidates have to earn.

Primaries and Caucuses

To win the presidential nomination, candidates must first win state **primary elections** or caucuses. Technically, citizen-voters in these contests cast votes for delegates to attend the party's national convention. With their vote, the citizen-voters advise those delegates whom to nominate at that national convention. The Republican and Democratic rules for nomination differ, but both require a majority of votes by the appointed delegates at the convention. To win the nomination, candidates must win the requisite number of these state contests from January into the summer.

Types of Primaries Today, most states hold a primary election. For years, the closed primary was standard. In a **closed primary**, voters must declare their party affiliation in advance of the election, typically when they register to vote. The **open primary**, used by about half of the states today, allows voters to declare party affiliation on Election Day. Poll workers hand these voters one party's ballot from which they select candidates.

The rarest primary is the **blanket primary.** California and other western states pioneered the blanket primary, which allows voters to cast votes for candidates in multiple parties. In other words, voters can cast a **split ticket**, picking Republicans in some races and Democrats in others. California voters instituted a nonpartisan primary in 2010. This new runoff system includes all candidates—both party members and independents. The top two vote-getters, regardless of party affiliation, compete for office in the general election. The quest for inclusiveness created a unique dynamic that caused the press to dub it the "jungle primary" because the winners emerge through the law of the jungle—survival of the fittest without regard to party.

Iowa Caucuses Since 1976, the Iowa caucuses have taken place before any other contest. **Caucuses** differ from primary elections. Across Iowa, rank-and-file party members meet at community centers, schools, and private homes where they listen to endorsing speeches, discuss candidates, and then finally cast their vote before leaving the caucus. In comparison to standard elections, caucuses are less convenient and more public. This two-hour commitment makes attendance hard for some, especially those who might have to skip work. Others dislike the public discussion and the somewhat public vote (voters usually cast a vote at a table set aside for their candidate). So, those who do show up at caucuses tend to be more dedicated voters who hold strong opinions and often fall on the far left or far right of the ideological spectrum, thus causing more liberal or conservative figures to win nominations.

New Hampshire Primary New Hampshire follows Iowa on the primary schedule. Candidates travel the state and hold town hall forums. Candidates spend time and money to seek the endorsement of the *Manchester Union-Journal*. They campaign in grocery stores and on the streets of relatively small New Hampshire towns. During this time, the voters actively engage these presidential candidates. When asked their opinion on a particular candidate, a typical New Hampshire voter might respond, "I don't know if I'm comfortable with him; I've only met him twice."

This contest has such great influence that candidates cautiously frame their primary election night speeches to paint themselves as front-runners. In 1992, the news came to light that Bill Clinton had been part of a sex scandal when he was governor of Arkansas, but he survived his diminished poll numbers to earn a second-place spot in New Hampshire. During his speech late that night, Clinton confidently referred to himself as "The Comeback Kid." This sound bite made its way into headlines that gave the impression that Clinton had actually won the New Hampshire primary.

Front-Loading Iowa and New Hampshire receive immense national attention during these events. Campaign teams and the national media converge on these states well in advance of Election Day. Hotels and restaurants fill with out-of-state customers bringing massive revenues. Politically, these states hold more influence than those that conduct their elections much later. This reality has brought on **front-loading**—states scheduling their primaries and caucuses earlier and earlier to boost their political clout and to enhance their tourism.

Following Iowa and New Hampshire, candidates then travel an uncertain path through several more states, hoping to secure enough delegates to win the nomination. In recent years, South Carolina has followed New Hampshire and has served as a barometer for the southern voting bloc. A few weeks later, several states coincidentally hold primaries on **Super Tuesday** (so known because of the large number of primaries that take place on that day), when the nomination contest narrows and voters start to converge around fewer, or perhaps one nominee.

According to a Pew study, since 1980, voter turnout in presidential primaries has ranged from 15 to 30 percent of the voting-eligible population. In 2016, about 57.6 million primary voters or about 28.5 percent of the estimated eligible voters, voted in Republican and Democratic primaries. The year 2008 still ranks as having the highest primary turnout in American history, but turnout in 2016 was considerably higher than in 2012, when the incumbent Barack Obama was running for reelection. Voter turnout increases when there are open seats to fill.

Party Conventions

The party conventions have become less suspenseful in modern times because the nominees are determined long before the convention date. Both parties have altered rules and formulas for state delegation strength.

State Delegates States determine their convention delegates in different ways and hold them to differing rules. Some states give their delegates complete independence at the convention. Some presidential primaries are binding on "pledged delegates." But even in those cases, states differ on how these delegates are awarded. Some operate by congressional district. Some use a statewide winner-take-all system, and some use proportional distribution for assigning delegates. For instance, if Candidate A receives 60 percent and Candidate B receives 40 percent of the popular primary vote, the state sends the corresponding percentage of delegates to the national gathering. The parties at the state and national level change their rules at least slightly every election cycle. The Democrats' use of superdelegates (see page 464) also leaves room for uncertainty in the process.

Geographic Strength At the Democratic convention, strength has shifted away from delegations from the South and toward the North and West, while Republican voting strength rests in the southern and western states. Democrats take into account the strength of each state's electoral vote and compare it to the record of how the state has cast votes for Democratic candidates in past general elections. Republicans place more value on the number of GOP representatives in Congress from those states and whether states have cast their electoral votes for Republican presidential candidates. In other words, Democrats give more delegates to large states, while Republicans give extra delegates to loyal states. Democrats have also instituted the idea of "fair reflection" to balance delegates by age, gender, and race in relation to the superdelegates or party elders.

The convention usually ends after three or four days of televised coverage, an acceptance speech by the nominee, and a balloon drop, followed by a bounce up in the polls for the winning candidate.

By The Numbers Presidential Nominations (Selected Conventions)			
Year & Convention	Candidates on First Ballot (in order of votes received)	Eventual Nominee	Required Ballots
1924 Dem	William Gibbs McAdoo, Al Smith, James Cox, John W. Davis	Davis	103
1932 Dem	Franklin Roosevelt, Al Smith, John Nance Garner	Roosevelt	4
1952 GOP	Dwight Eisenhower, Robert Taft, Earl Warren	Eisenhower	1
1960 Dem	John Kennedy, Lyndon Johnson	Kennedy	1
1968 Dem	Hubert Humphrey, Eugene McCarthy, George McGovern	Humphrey	1
1976 GOP	Gerald Ford, Ronald Reagan	Ford	1
1980 GOP	Ronald Reagan, John Anderson	Reagan	1
1992 Dem	Bill Clinton, Jerry Brown	Clinton	1

What do the numbers show? Who were the party nominees in selected years? How frequently is the leader on the first ballot the final nominee? How many ballots are usually required to choose the party's candidate? How frequently did a losing candidate receive the party's nomination in a later convention?

The General Election

The **general election** season starts after party nominations and kicks into high gear after Labor Day. Candidates fly around the country, stopping at key locations to deliver speeches. As the public and press begin to compare the two major party candidates, the issues become more sharply defined. Different groups and surrogates (spokespersons) support each candidate and appear on cable shows. The major party candidates debate, usually in three televised events over the course of several weeks. The vice presidential candidates usually debate once. Major newspapers endorse a candidate in their editorial pages. The media's daily coverage provides constant updates about which candidate is ahead and behind as measured by public opinion polls and campaign funding. By November, candidates have traveled to most states and have spent millions of dollars.

Swing States Where candidates spend those millions depends on where they have the best chance to influence outcomes. Republicans and Democrats live in all 50 states, but in some states Republicans have a long history of being victorious, while in others Democrats win most often. The patterns have changed over the course of the nation's growth and development, but in recent times the so-called "red states," those in which Republicans usually win, and "blue states," those in which Democrats usually win, have remained fairly constant.

However, some states have a less regular pattern. They are known as **swing states**, because the victories swing from one party to another in different elections. Candidates concentrate their campaign resources in those states. They travel to most of the states, meeting with wealthy donors to raise money. But they hold campaign events and spend advertising money in the swing states.

RED, BLUE, AND SWING STATES

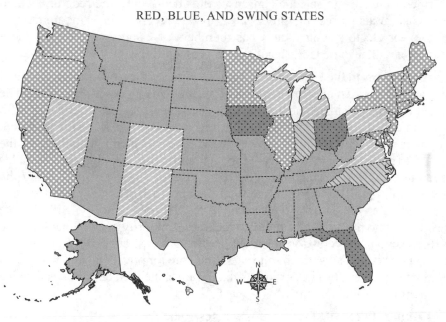

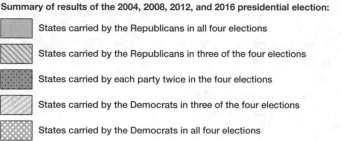

Summary of results of the 2004, 2008, 2012, and 2016 presidential election:

States carried by the Republicans in all four elections

States carried by the Republicans in three of the four elections

States carried by each party twice in the four elections

States carried by the Democrats in three of the four elections

States carried by the Democrats in all four elections

If you were managing the campaign for a Republican presidential candidate in the 2020 election, in what states would you spend most of your television advertising budget? Why? If you were managing the campaign for a Democratic presidential candidate for the same election, which states would you be targeting with your advertising money? Why?

Electoral College The **Electoral College** system is both a revered and a frustrating part of the presidential election—one that shapes a presidential candidate's strategy. The system to elect the president has several features. The "college" is actually a simultaneous gathering of **electors** in their respective capital cities to vote on the same day. The framers included this system in Article II of the Constitution to temper public opinion and to allow the more informed statesmen to select a consensus president. State and federal law and party custom also affect the process. Each state receives the same number of electors (or electoral votes) as it has members of Congress; however, these electors cannot also be U.S. senators or representatives.

Alterations to the Electoral System Originally, the Constitution provided that each elector cast one vote for each of his top two choices for president. The winner became president and the runner-up became vice president. The Twelfth Amendment altered the system so that electors cast one vote for president and another for vice president. To win, candidates must earn a majority of the electoral votes. Since the **Twenty-Third Amendment**, Washington, D.C, adds three electoral votes. This brings the vote total to 538—435 replicating the House total, plus 100 to match the total Senate seats, plus the three for D.C. The candidate who earns 270 electoral votes, a simple majority, will become president. If no presidential candidate receives a majority, then the U.S. House of Representatives votes for president, by delegations, choosing from among the top three candidates. Each state casts one vote for president, and whichever candidate receives 26 states or more wins. The Senate then determines the vice president in the same manner.

Winner-Take-All Today, most states require their pledged electors (people already committed to a party's ticket) to follow the state's popular vote. Besides, electors are typically long-time partisans or career politicians who are ultimately appointed by the state party. The candidate who wins the **plurality** of the popular vote (the most, even if not the majority) in a given state will ultimately receive all of that state's electoral votes. This is known as the **winner-take-all** system. Only Nebraska and Maine allow for a split in their electoral votes and award electors by congressional district rather than on a statewide basis.

In early December, electors meet in state capitals and cast their votes. The ballots are transported to Washington in locked boxes. When Congress opens in January, the sitting vice president and speaker of the House count these votes before a joint session of Congress. Since most states now require their electors to follow the popular vote, the electoral vote total essentially becomes known on election night in November. Television newscasters typically show a U.S. map with Republican victories depicted in red and Democratic victories in blue. Soon after popular votes are tabulated, losing candidates publicly concede, and the winner gives a victory speech. The constitutionally required procedures that follow—states' electors voting in December and the Congress counting those votes in January—thus become more formal ceremony than suspenseful events.

Five times in American history, the winner of the popular vote did not win the electoral vote. Hillary Clinton's loss to Donald Trump in 2016 is the most recent example. This possibility has led some to criticize the Electoral College system. Others see the process as a way to ensure balance and to guarantee that a consensus candidate becomes president. Gallup has found that more than 60 percent of those polled want a constitutional amendment to change the electoral system, while only about 33 percent want to keep it in its current form. A proposed constitutional amendment to scrap the system and replace it with a popular vote has been offered repeatedly in Congress for years.

BENEFITS OF THE ELECTORAL COLLEGE	DRAWBACKS OF THE ELECTORAL COLLEGE
• States retain their importance in electing the president.	• One candidate can win the popular vote and not win the electoral vote.
• Candidates must campaign and seek votes in most states rather than only heavily populated states.	• Electoral vote strength is higher, per capita, in smaller states.
• The practice guarantees a consensus president with broad support.	• The winner-take-all system discourages those who voted for the runner-up.
• States retain primacy if the election goes into the House and Senate.	• If the election goes to the House and Senate, these delegations can vote independently of their states.

The 2016 Presidential Campaign

The unusual 2016 presidential campaign is perhaps the worst example to study for understanding norms and trends in voting, campaigns, and elections, since it was dominated by an unconventional candidate. It drew the attention of more than 20 viable candidates, brought an intense intra-party contest in both major parties, set a new record for money spent, sparked attempts to manipulate election rules to stop that unconventional candidate, and took the candidates down in the mud like no other public campaign in memory.

The Frontrunners Former Secretary of State Hillary Clinton was the heir-apparent for the Democratic nomination. She stepped down after one term at the State Department. She had survived criticism and an FBI investigation into her use of a personal email server for official State Department and classified communications and had been exonerated.

Also entering the race was Senator Bernie Sanders of Vermont. Sanders, a self-described democratic socialist and champion of the common person, promised to work for a $15 minimum wage, free college tuition at public universities, and a universal health care policy. Four other viable candidates took part in early Democratic primary elections but dropped out after failing to gain much support. The nomination quest came down to a race between Clinton and Sanders, one the darling of the elite wing of the party able to raise huge amounts of campaign money, the other bragging about his $27 average campaign donations.

On the other side was a field of 16 Republicans, some with executive experience or time in Congress. Young senators Ted Cruz (TX) and Marco Rubio (FL) entered the race. Governors Chris Christie (NJ), John Kasich (OH), and Jeb Bush (FL) all had a level of support. Dr. Ben Carson, a retired neurosurgeon from Michigan, also joined the race. New York real estate mogul and media hound Donald J. Trump, who had flirted with running for president more than once, announced in the summer of 2015 in an orchestrated descent down the escalator in golden Trump Tower that he was a candidate for the Republican nomination. The race was on.

Trump, Carson, and Cruz exchanged places for coming in first in the Iowa state polls leading up to the state's caucus vote, dwarfing the establishment candidates. It was clearly a year for the outsiders.

The pre-primary election campaigns were characterized by the enthusiastic chants for economic equality from Sanders crowds and Donald Trump's personal attacks against fellow Republican candidates. Trump's key promises involved tightening up the border with Mexico with a wall and repealing the North American Free Trade Agreement (NAFTA) (see page 404). He also found support among a Republican base by adopting a pro-gun, pro-life, pro-America position.

Caucuses and Primaries When Iowa held its caucuses in early February, Clinton beat Sanders by only two-tenths of one percent. In New Hampshire a week later, Sanders defeated her with 60 percent of the vote to Clinton's 38 percent. In the Republican contest, Cruz won the Iowa Republican caucuses with 28 percent, Trump came in second with 24 percent, and Rubio sneaked into third with 23 percent. In New Hampshire for the next round of rank-and-file party voters, Trump won with 35 percent, John Kasich came in second and kept his bid alive with 17 percent, and Ted Cruz came in third with 12 percent. The nation was in for a competitive nomination contest in both major parties.

Over the next few state primaries, Trump continually attacked whichever candidate seemed to pose a threat to him, creating insulting nicknames for them—"Low-energy Jeb," "Little Marco," and "Lyin' Ted." He continued to accumulate primary and caucus wins and was perhaps underestimated as a formidable presidential candidate.

The GOP contest got uglier. Trump pointed to a tabloid magazine story of Cruz's marital infidelity and alleged that Cruz's father, a Cuban immigrant, was somehow involved in JFK's assassination. With these tactics and others like them, Trump plowed over his opponents and clinched enough convention delegates after Indiana's primary vote on May 3 to become the Republican candidate. Cruz bowed out of the race that evening, and Kasich bowed out the next morning. Kasich never endorsed Trump; Cruz did so only after Trump won the nomination.

Nominees Over the remaining nine states, Trump, the only candidate still in the contest, received an average of 73 percent of the primary vote (some other candidates' names appeared on ballots, though they had withdrawn their candidacy). With some strong anti-Trump feelings within the Republican

Party, a few conservative leaders tried to stop Trump's nomination at the Cleveland convention with creative use of the technical delegate rules to nominate someone else. It didn't work.

For the Democrats, Clinton remained ahead of Sanders in the delegate count, but he won 23 of the 57 state and territorial contests through the spring. Though Clinton handily had the support of superdelegates and the delegates resulting from the primaries, in many ways Sanders won the heart and soul of the party. Despite his low average donation, he received more than $200 million in total campaign contributions. But she was the presumptive nominee.

"We are all standing under a glass ceiling right now," she said from a New York stage, and declared that this would be the "the first time in our nation's history that a woman will be a major party's nominee for president." Clinton carefully enjoyed the moment but did not yet claim the nomination. Sanders had yet to concede, and the official vote would take place at the convention.

Before conceding, Sanders wanted some of his policy positions to be added to the Democratic platform. After a White House meeting with President Obama and five days to think things over, he personally gave Hillary a full endorsement in a high school gym in New Hampshire. "She will be the Democratic nominee for president," he declared, "and I intend to do everything I can to make certain she will be the next president." A number of his ideas on the minimum wage, environmental regulations, and drug policy did influence the Democratic platform.

Campaign for the General Election As the post-convention campaign began, a late August poll showed perhaps the widest gap between the candidates, Clinton with 45 percent to Trump's 33. That gap narrowed. The candidates' respective poll averages from September through Election Day had Clinton outpolling Trump by only 45.5 percent to 42.2 percent.

Third-Party Candidates Some minor party candidates entered the race. Former Republican New Mexico governor Gary Johnson was the Libertarian nominee, and Dr. Jill Stein of Massachusetts received the Green Party nomination, as she had in 2012. Former CIA official Evan McMullen gave Republicans against Trump someone to vote for, but his name appeared only on the Utah ballot.

The general election campaign put a Democrat candidate from the heart of D.C. politics against a bombastic and sometimes crude TV persona whose most recent public gig was firing people on NBC's *The Apprentice*. By the time Trump earned the nomination, he had insulted prior Republican nominee John McCain for getting captured by the enemy in Vietnam. Trump had also questioned the judicial ethics of a federal judge because he was Hispanic, and he had refused to denounce the support of a head Ku Klux Klansman. Meanwhile, his heavily-attended rallies were characterized by altercations between Trump supporters and Democratic interlopers and harsh threats to members of the media. The party's most recent nominee, Mitt Romney, had suggested Republicans nominate "anybody but Trump."

An Ugly Campaign What followed was what many termed "a race to the bottom." Trump continued his unconventional and, to many, unstatesmanlike approach to campaigning, winning support among many middle-class workers who responded well to his America First ideology and the concern he expressed for average working persons who may have lost their jobs as industry steadily declined.

As of early October, Clinton's campaign had spent $145 million on TV commercials to Trump's $32 million. Trump, however, received an estimated $200 million in free media. Top cable news reporters stood by at his rallies awaiting his grand entrance and anticipating some shocking behavior or pronouncement that would boost ratings. Meanwhile, his "Make America Great Again" message resonated with those who felt shut out by traditional politicians. He had strong support among independents, who believed the Democratic party had gone soft on illegal immigration and no longer protected the American worker. He had capitalized on a cultural patriotism that put him in reach of defeating Clinton if he focused on the right states.

Meanwhile Clinton took a jab at some of Trump's supporters, referring to them as "a basket of deplorables." This pejorative phrase delivered at an expensive Democraticm Party fundraiser was likely directed at the pro-Trump Klansman and those ruffians hissing at reporters, but it was perceived by many as a broad-brush painting of any voter who did not support her. Trump strategists were able to turn the comment into another liberal elite's uptown view of Middle America.

The October surprise came with the release of a decade-old *Access Hollywood* video of Trump on a hot mic bragging about how he could have his way with women, kissing and grabbing them. When this news broke, he apologized before quickly pointing to Bill Clinton's dalliances, affairs, and aggressions toward women, suggesting that Hillary enabled this behavior. He invited Bill Clinton's past victims to the next televised debate to showcase the former president's behavior.

The campaign had sunk to a new low. Then, on October 28, then-FBI Director James Comey announced the FBI had come across a new batch of Clinton emails and felt compelled to let it be known that the FBI was obligated to examine these and warned that more investigation was possible. As it turned out, there was nothing new in those emails and the investigation was closed once again.

The Vote When citizen voters cast their popular votes on Tuesday, November 8, and such states as North Carolina, Florida, and Ohio went for Trump, the Clinton team became very nervous. Into the late evening and early morning, Trump won Pennsylvania, Wisconsin, and by the closest of margins, Michigan. The networks and the pundits started calling the election. In the final tally, Trump won 306 electoral votes to Clinton's 232. However, Clinton's large-margin successes in states like New York and California took her over the top in the national popular vote. Once provisional and absentee ballots were counted, Clinton had 3 million more votes than Trump did. She received 48 percent of the national total, he received 46, and the minor party candidates split the remainder. But with the winner-take-all system and the razor-thin victories in the Rust Belt (parts of the Northeast and Midwest where industry is in decline), Trump took the Electoral College. In his 2:45 a.m. victory speech, the president-elect said in a partially scripted and partly ad-lib address, "Now it's time for America to bind the wounds of division; have to get together. To all Republicans and Democrats and independents across this nation, I say it is time for us to come together as one united people."

Congressional Elections

All House seats and one-third of Senate seats are up for election every two years. Federal elections that take place halfway through a president's term are called **midterm elections**. The midterm elections receive a fraction of the media attention and fewer voters cast ballots. The Council of State Governments reports that since 1972, voter turnout in midterm elections is on average 17 points lower than in presidential elections. The down-ballot federal races that take place on the same day as presidential elections are overshadowed by the big contest. Yet, in terms of policymaking, these campaigns are important and deserve attention.

To compete in a modern campaign for the U.S. House or Senate, a candidate must create a networked organization that resembles a small company, spend much of his or her own money, solicit hundreds of contributions, and sacrifice many hours and days. Senator Sherrod Brown of Ohio explains how a candidate "must hire a staff and make wise use of volunteers . . . craft a cogent, clear message . . . budget carefully in spending money on mail, radio, television and printed material . . . and be able to successfully sell the product—himself—to the public and to the media." Large campaigns divide these tasks into several categories, such as management, public relations, research, fundraising, advertising, and voter mobilization.

Incumbency As with presidential candidates, the incumbent in congressional elections has an advantage over a challenger. With rare exception, a congressional incumbent has a stronger chance of winning than the challenger.

The incumbent's financial and electoral advantage is so daunting to challengers that it often dissuades viable candidates from ever entering the race. House incumbents tend to win reelection more than 95 percent of the time. Senators have an incumbency advantage too, but theirs is not quite as strong. Incumbents capitalize on their popularity and war chest, showering their districts with mail and email throughout the congressional term. During campaign season, they purchase commercials and load up the district with yard signs while ignoring their opponent and sometimes refusing to take part in public debates.

Incumbents have several built-in advantages. Name recognition is a powerful factor. For two or more years, all federal incumbents have appeared in the news, advocated legislation, and sent newsletters back to constituent voters. Nine out of ten voters recognize their House member's name, while fewer than six out of ten recognize that of the challenger.

Incumbents nearly always have more money than challengers because they are highly visible and often popular, and they can exploit the advantages of the office. They also already have a donor network established. **Political action committees (PACs)**, formal groups formed from interest groups, donate heavily to incumbents. PACs give $12 to an incumbent for every $1 they donate to a challenger.

Party leaders and the Hill Committees (see page 461) realize the advantage incumbents have and invariably support the incumbent when he or she is challenged in a primary. In the general elections, House representatives receive roughly three times more money than their challengers. Challengers receive a mere 9 percent of their donations from PACs, while House incumbents collect about 39 percent of their receipts from these groups.

A substantial number of incumbents keep a small campaign staff or maintain a campaign office between elections. Officeholders can provide services to constituents, including answering questions about issues of concern to voters, such as Medicare payments and bringing more federal dollars back home.

Certainly not all incumbents win. The single greatest predictor of an incumbent's loss is a poor economy while his or her party is in power. In hard economic times, the voting public holds incumbents and their party responsible.

In midterm elections, regardless of the condition of the economy, the president's party usually loses some seats in Congress. Based on results from five recent midterm elections, the president's party lost an average of 26.4 House seats and 3.6 Senate seats.

However, during presidential election years, congressional candidates can often ride the popularity of their party's presidential candidate. When a Democrat presidential candidate wins by wide margins, fellow Democratic congressional candidates down the ballot typically do well also. This is called the **coattail effect**.

Districts and Primaries Legislative elections in several states have resulted in one-party rule in the statehouse. When drawing congressional districts for the reapportionment of the U.S. House, these legislatures have gerrymandered congressional districts into one-party dominant units. (See page 106.) This situation dampens competitiveness in the general election. In 2016, only 33 House races, less than 10 percent, were decided by 10 points or less. Nearly three-quarters of all House seats were decided by 20 points or more.

These "safe" districts make House incumbents unresponsive to citizens outside their party, and they have shifted the competition to the primary election. Several candidates from the majority party will emerge for an open seat, all trying to look more partisan than their competitors, while one or two sacrificial candidates from the minority party will run a grassroots campaign. When House incumbents do not act with sufficient partisan unity, candidates will run against them, running to their ideological extreme.

Campaign Strategies

Winning elections requires the expertise of professional consultants. These may include a campaign manager, a communications or public relations expert, a treasurer, an advertising agent, a field organizer, and a social media consultant. The campaign profession has blossomed as a consulting class has emerged. Staffers on Capitol Hill, political science majors, and those who have worked for partisan and nonprofit endeavors also overlap with political campaigns. Entire firms and partisan-based training organizations prepare energetic civic-minded citizens to enter this field that elects officials to implement desired policy.

Consultants will help candidates understand what voters think. A typical campaign spends about 3 percent of its resources on polling and surveys to gather this information. Candidates also want to build a base of support and mobilize members of their coalition to get to the voting booths.

Polling results can help candidates frame their message. Polling helps determine which words or phrases to use in speeches and advertising. Campaigns occasionally use tracking polls to gain feedback after changing campaign strategy. They may also hold focus groups, and incumbents rely on constituent communication over their term. Candidates also keep an eye on Internet blogs, listen to radio call-in shows, and talk with party leaders and political activists to find out what the public wants. Campaigns also set up registration tables at county fairs and on college campuses. They gather addresses from voter registration lists and mail out promotional pieces that highlight the candidate's accomplishments and often include photos of the candidate alongside spouse and family. Campaigns also conduct robocalls, automated mass phone calls to promote themselves or to denounce an opponent.

Showcasing the Candidate Most voters, like most shoppers, make their decision based on limited information with only a small amount of consideration. For this reason, electronic and social media, television, and focus groups are essential to winning an election. A candidate's message is often centered on common themes of decency, loyalty, and hard work.

A typical campaign is divided into three segments: the biography, the issues, and the attack. Successful candidates have a unique story to tell. Campaign literature and television ads show candidates in previous public service, on playgrounds with children, on a front porch with family, or in church. These images attract a wide variety of voters. After the biography is told, a debate over the issues begins as voters shop for their candidate. Consultants and professionals believe issues-oriented campaigns motivate large numbers of people to come out and vote.

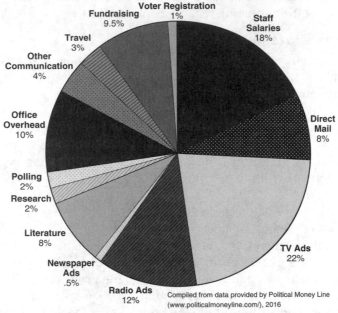

BY THE NUMBERS
Typical House Candidate Campaign Budget

- Voter Registration 1%
- Fundraising 9.5%
- Staff Salaries 18%
- Travel 3%
- Other Communication 4%
- Direct Mail 8%
- Office Overhead 10%
- Polling 2%
- Research 2%
- Literature 8%
- TV Ads 22%
- Newspaper Ads .5%
- Radio Ads 12%

Compiled from data provided by Political Money Line (www.politicalmoneyline.com/), 2016

Source: *Paul S. Herrnson, Congressional Elections, 2008*

What do the numbers show? What are the chief expenses in a House campaign? What portion of a candidate's expenditures are for marketing/showcasing the candidate? What percent goes to support staff or some type of research?

Defining the Opponent Candidates competing for independent voters find it necessary to draw sharp contrasts between themselves and their opponents. An attack phase begins later in the race, often motivated by desperation. Underdogs sometimes resort to cheap shots and work hard to expose inconsistencies in their opponent's voting records. Campaigns do opposition research to reveal their opponent's missteps or any unpopular positions taken in the past. Aides and staffers comb over the *Congressional Record*, old interview transcripts, and newspaper articles to search for damaging quotes. They also analyze an opponent's donor list in order to spotlight special-interest donations or out-of-state money.

Debates As the election nears, candidates participate in formal public debates, highly structured events with strict rules governing response time and conduct. These events are risky because candidates can suffer from gaffes (verbal slips) or from poor performances. Incumbents and front-runners typically avoid debates because they have everything to lose and little to gain. Appearing on a stage with a lesser-known competitor usually helps the underdog. For races with large fields, those organizations sponsoring the debates typically determine which candidates get to participate. Their decisions are sometimes based on where candidates stand in the polls.

Television Appearances The candidate's campaign team also strategizes about appearances on television, either in news coverage or in a commercial. Veteran Democratic speechwriter and campaign consultant Bob Shrum laments, "Things are measured by when a campaign will go on television, or if they can and to what degree they can saturate the air waves." (See page 458 for more on a candidate's television strategy.)

Social Media Connecting to voters via social media has become essential in campaigning. Campaigns use Facebook as a way to connect with other Facebook users. Also, for a fee, Facebook offers consultants from their company to political groups to help reach voters, much as they offer consulting connections to a corporation. As Trump's key digital campaign manager, Brad Parscale, explained on *60 Minutes*, the Trump team took Facebook's offer of help; the Clinton team did not.

The Facebook platform and technology allow campaigns to microtarget—identify by particular traits and criteria—independent voters who could be persuaded and learn what might persuade them. Perhaps an intense, issues-oriented ad would sway their opinions, or maybe the color of a button might enhance the chances for a donation. Marketers use psychographics—profiles of a person's hobbies, interests, and values—to create image-based ads that would appeal to certain personalities. Different personality types will see different ads.

Some of the ad systems or strategies employed dark ads, those that go to a particularly selected small audience and then disappear. It is suspected that campaigns have used these for shaky or even false messages, as there is less of a trail to connect them to their source. (See page 460.)

Campaign Finance

"There are two things that are important in politics," asserted political boss Mark Hanna more than 100 years ago. "The first is money, and I can't remember what the second is."

Hanna was neither the first nor the last politician to realize that money is at the heart of politics. The entanglement of money and politics reached new levels when people with unscrupulous business practices became fixtures in the political process in the late 19th century in an effort to influence and reduce the federal government's regulation of commerce. The bulk of today's relevant campaign finance regulations, however, came about much later—in the early 1970s—and other laws and Supreme Court decisions followed.

In 1971, Congress passed the **Federal Election Campaign Act (FECA)**, which tightened reporting requirements and limited candidates' expenditures. Despite this law, spending in the 1972 presidential race between Richard Nixon and George McGovern reached $91 million. As the Watergate scandal unfolded, Americans became disenchanted with their president and with the flow of money in national politics. The White House-sponsored Watergate break-in and subsequent investigation was not initially about money, but as investigators and reporters looked closer at the scandal, Americans soon realized how much money was going through the campaign process and how donors had subverted the groundbreaking yet incomplete 1971 act. Congress followed up with the 1974 amendment to the FECA.

The 1974 law prevented donors from giving more than $1,000 to any federal candidate and more than $5,000 to a political committee in each election (primaries and general elections are each considered "elections"). It capped the total a candidate could donate to his or her campaign and set a maximum on how much the campaign could spend. The law created the **Federal Election Commission (FEC)** to monitor and enforce the regulations. It also created a legal definition for political action committees (PAC) making donations to campaigns, declaring that they must have at least 50 members, donate to at least five candidates, and register with the FEC at least six months in advance of the election.

KEY PROVISIONS OF THE FEDERAL ELECTION CAMPAIGN ACT
• Limited an individual's contributions to $1,000 per election
• Limited a candidate's own contribution to $50,000 per election
• Defined and regulated donations of political action committees (PACs)
• Created a voluntary public fund to assist viable presidential candidates

Types of PACs Campaign finance laws define several different types of political action committees, distinguished by how they are formed, how they are funded, and how they can disperse their funds. Some also have different limits on the donation amount from individuals per year or election.

Connected PACs Corporations, labor unions, and trade organizations are not allowed to use money from their treasuries to influence elections. However, they are allowed to form **connected PACs**—political action committees funded separately from the organization's treasury through donations from members—and make limited campaign contributions in that way. Connected PACs are also known as Separate Segregated Funds (SSF) because of the way the money is separated from the sponsoring organizations' treasuries. They cannot solicit donations from anyone who is not a member of the organization.

Nonconnected PACs These political action committees have no sponsoring organization and often form around a single issue. They can solicit funds from anyone in the general public and they can make direct donations to candidates up to limits set by law. Like the connected PACs, nonconnected PACs must register with the FEC and disclose their donors.

Leadership PACs are a type of nonconnected PAC. They can be started by any current or former elected official and can raise money from the general public. Though they cannot be used to fund the officials own campaigns, funds in a leadership PAC can be used to cover travel and other expenses for other candidates.

Super PACs These are the newest kind of political action committee, whose creation resulted from the Supreme Court ruling in *Citizens United v. FEC* and the U.S. District Court ruling in *Speechnow v. FEC*, both cases decided in 2010. The *Citizens United* ruling opened the door for corporations to make political contributions to a committee as long as that committee did not formally coordinate with a candidate. (See page 471.) The *Speechnow* ruling determined that those contributions should have no limit placed on them.

TYPE	FORMED BY	REQUIREMENTS	DONATION LIMITS	EXAMPLE
Connected PAC (SSF—Separate Segregated Funds)	Corporations, labor unions, trade groups	Can collect contributions only from their members; can donate directly to candidates	Strict	Coca-Cola Company Nonpartisan Committee for Good Government KochPAC
Nonconnected PAC	No sponsoring (connected) organization	Can collect from general public; can donate directly to candidates	Strict	National Rifle Association Emily's List
Leadership PAC (type of nonconnected)	Current or former elected official	Can collect from general public; can donate directly to candidates	Strict	Leadership Fund (Mitch McConnell)
Super PAC (independent expenditure-only committee)	Anyone	Can collect from anyone; cannot coordinate with candidates	No limits	Vote Latino Super PAC Cryptocurrency Alliance Super PAC

Buckley v. Valeo (1976) One of the first challenges to FEC law came with the case of *Buckley v. Valeo*. In January 1975, a group of conservatives and liberals joined to overturn the Federal Election Campaign Act in the courts. Conservative New York Senator James Buckley teamed up with Democratic senator and past presidential candidate Eugene McCarthy, the American Civil Liberties Union, and the American Conservative Union to file suit against Secretary of the U.S. Senate Francis Valeo. They argued that the early 1970s law unconstitutionally limited free speech. The Court upheld the law's $1,000 limit on individual donations and the $5,000 limit on political action committee (PAC) donations, claiming such limits did not violate free speech guarantees. However, the Court also ruled that Congress cannot limit a candidate's donation to her own campaign or spending her own money, nor can it place a maximum on the overall receipts or expenditures for a federal campaign.

Fundraising

Since the passage of the early 1970s campaign finance laws, money and politics have gone hand in hand, yet most Americans have become concerned by one's influence on the other. Since the Federal Election Campaign Act created the Federal Election Commission to monitor donations and spending, the amount of cash that has flowed through federal elections has skyrocketed. Meanwhile, Congress has further regulated the campaign finance system while free-speech advocates have won concessions for less regulation.

Some candidates finance their own campaigns, but most rely on the party organization and thousands of individual donors for contributions. The size of a candidate's **war chest**, or bank account for campaigning, can play a role in determining victory or loss. The campaign for financial resources begins long before the campaign for votes. Fundraising allows candidates to test their chances. Those who can gather funds begin to prove a level of support that makes them viable. Most successful House candidates spend more than $1 million during a two-year campaign. In more competitive districts with strong media markets, that number will rise. To raise that cash over a two-year period, candidates spend about one-fourth of their campaign schedule making personal phone calls and holding formal fundraisers. Senate candidates, because they are running statewide and may attract wealthier opponents, begin raising money much earlier than House candidates and devote more time to soliciting cash. Senate candidates spend an average of $12 million and seek funds on a more national scale than House candidates.

The Internet became a campaign and fundraising tool in 1998. By 2002, 57 percent of all House candidates and virtually every Senate candidate used the Web or email to gather funds. This type of solicitation is free, compared with an average of $3 to $4 for every direct mail request. Candidates also hold parties, picnics, and formal dinners with higher-level officials or celebrities as guest speakers. The president or other high-level party leaders can attract many donors to such events. During the 2006 midterm campaigns, 23 Republican incumbents who hosted a visit by then-President George W. Bush raised 159 percent more money than GOP incumbents who did not host such a visit.

The Federal Election Commission

The FEC has unique structural traits so it can carry out several responsibilities. The president appoints the FEC's board of commissioners to oversee election law and the Senate approves them. This commission always has an equal number of Democrats and Republicans. The FEC requires candidates to register, or file for candidacy, and to report campaign donations and expenses on a quarterly basis. A candidate's entire balance sheet is available to the government and the public. The FEC has a staff of professionals that maintains these records and places the information online. The site www.fec.gov is a database that allows anyone to see which individuals or PACs contributed to the candidates and in what amounts.

The FEC also has a legal department that prosecutes candidates who do not follow the prescribed laws. From 1980 to 2005, the FEC was involved in more than 530 court cases and prevailed in 90 percent of the cases that went to court. From 2000 to 2013, the commission closed 2,623 cases and issued fines to candidates for late filing and non-filing that amounted to nearly $5 million.

Matching Money After the 1976 Supreme Court ruling in *Buckley v. Valeo*, Congress and the Court ultimately reached consensus that unlimited donations make for unfair elections. Despite the Court ruling in *Buckley*, however, television advertising and money became more important in campaigns as interest groups, politicians, and lawyers found loopholes in the law.

Also in 1976, the federal government established a system to offer some public financial support for presidential candidates who met the qualifications. In this system today, everyone who files a tax return is offered a chance to contribute $3 of taxes they already owe to be redirected to the presidential campaign fund. The federal government then uses that voluntarily directed money to match specified donations given to candidates in both the primary and general elections. In short, the federal government will match, dollar for dollar, individual donations of $250 or less. To qualify, candidates must contribute no more than $50,000 of their own money. They must also raise at least $5,000 in each of 20 states in increments of $250 or less. The guidelines for the federal matching money ensure that candidates have a broad base of support from smaller donors. Minor party candidates can qualify for matching money too, but only if the party's candidate won more than 5 percent of the vote in the prior election. This is the only public finance system for candidates across the United States.

The FECA only covered money going directly to and from a candidate's treasury. If a non-candidate wanted to spend money to impact an election—for example, to buy a radio ad for or against a candidate—there were no limits. **Hard money**, donations given directly to a candidate, could be traced and regulated. But **soft money**, donations to a party or interest group, was not tracked. Therefore the party could flood a congressional district with television ads that paint the opponent in a bad light, causing large, ultimately untraceable spending on electioneering at the end of a campaign. Unsurprisingly, soft money spending escalated.

Bipartisan Campaign Reform Act This situation brought greater attention to soft money's influence on elections and highlighted how much that influence was able to subvert the spirit of the 1970s reforms. Senators John McCain (R–AZ) and Russ Feingold (D–WI) had pushed for greater campaign finance regulations since the mid-1990s. After some modification, the **Bipartisan Campaign Reform Act (BCRA)** of 2002, also known as the McCain-Feingold law, finally passed the House with a 240–189 vote and the Senate with 60–40 vote, and President Bush signed it. The act banned soft money contributions to the national parties, increased the limits on hard money donations to $2,000 from individuals with an adjustment for inflation, $5,000 from PACs, and $25,000 from the national parties per election cycle. The law also placed an aggregate limit on how much an individual could donate to multiple candidates in a two-year cycle.

The BCRA prohibited corporations, trade associations, and labor organizations from paying for electioneering communications on radio or TV using campaign treasury money within 60 days of the general election and 30 days of a primary. To clear up who or what organization is behind a broadcasted advertisement, the McCain-Feingold law also requires candidates to explicitly state, "I'm [candidate's name] and I approve this message." That statement must last at least four seconds.

Though the law was dubbed bipartisan, the vote in Congress and the reaction to the law has been somewhat partisan, with more Democratic support than Republican. It was challenged immediately by a leading Republican in the courts, and largely upheld. The 2010 case of *Citizens United v. Federal Election Commission (FEC)*, however, overturned key parts of the law.

MUST-KNOW SUPREME COURT DECISIONS: *CITIZENS UNITED V. FEC* (2010)

The Constitutional Questions Before the Court: Does the Bipartisan Campaign Reform Act's (McCain-Feingold law) donation disclosure requirement violate the First Amendment's free speech clause, and is a negative political documentary that never communicates an expressed plea to vote for or against a candidate subject to the BCRA?

Decision: No and Yes for Citizens United, 5:4

Before *Citizens United*: *Buckley v. Valeo* (1976) upheld the limits on campaign contributions from individuals ($1,000) and PACs ($5,000) but ruled that candidates could contribute unlimited funds from their own money to their campaigns. It also ruled that there was no limit on total revenue or expenditures for campaigns.

Facts: The BCRA prevented corporations or nonprofit agencies from engaging in "electioneering communications," primarily TV and radio campaign ads, 60 days before the general election. In 2008, the conservative group Citizens United produced *Hillary: The Movie*, a critique meant to derail Hillary Clinton's chance for the presidency. The law prevented the film's airing, regarding it as "electioneering communications," but the group appealed to the Supreme Court. The opportunity to broadcast the movie had passed by the time the Court issued its ruling, which has had a dramatic impact on campaign financing.

Reasoning: The Court ruled that part of the BCRA violated the First Amendment's free speech clause and that corporations, labor unions, and other organizations could use funds from their treasuries to endorse or denounce a candidate at any time, provided ads are not coordinated with any candidate. The majority opinion reasoned that the limitations amounted to censorship.

The Court reasoned further that just because a PAC or any entity entitled to free speech supports a candidate via advertising, that candidate does not necessarily owe anything to that PAC. There's no assumption that the donation is buying a favor from the candidate, which in any event is already criminal and punishable by statute.

The Court's Majority Opinion by Mr. Justice Anthony Kennedy, joined by Chief Justice John G. Roberts and Justices Antonin G. Scalia, Samuel A. Alito, and Clarence Thomas: The law before us . . . makes it a felony for all corporations—including nonprofit advocacy corporations—either to expressly advocate the election or defeat of candidates or to broadcast electioneering communications within 30 days of a primary election and 60 days of a general election . . . These prohibitions are classic examples of censorship. . . . Were the Court to uphold these restrictions, the Government could repress speech by silencing certain voices at any of the various points in the speech process. . . . If [this part of the law] applied to individuals, no one would believe that it is merely a time, place, or manner restriction on speech. Its purpose and effect are to silence entities whose voices the Government deems to be suspect.

Speech is an essential mechanism of democracy, for it is the means to hold officials accountable to the people. The right of citizens to inquire, to hear, to speak, and to use information to reach consensus is a precondition to enlightened self-government and a necessary means to protect it. . . .

For these reasons, political speech must prevail against laws that would suppress it, whether by design or inadvertence. . . . .

We find no basis for the proposition that, in the context of political speech, the Government may impose restrictions on certain disfavored speakers. Both history and logic lead us to this conclusion.

The Court, like the country, split along ideological lines. Those dissenting argued that corporations are not people and do not have the same rights, and that limiting corporate money in local and national elections would be favorable to fair, democratic elections.

Dissenting Opinion by Mr. Justice John Paul Stevens, joined by Justices Ruth Bader Ginsburg, Stephen G. Breyer, and Sonia Sotomayor:
The Court's ruling threatens to undermine the integrity of elected institutions across the Nation. . . .

It is simply incorrect to suggest that we have prohibited all legislative distinctions based on identity or content. Not even close. . . We have, for example, allowed state-run broadcasters to exclude independent candidates from televised debates. We have upheld statutes that prohibit the distribution or display of campaign materials near a polling place. . . . And we have consistently approved laws that bar Government employees, but not others, from contributing to or participating in political activities . . . .

The same logic applies to this case with additional force because it is the identity of corporations, rather than individuals, that the Legislature has taken into account. . . .

The Court's blinkered and aphoristic approach to the First Amendment may well promote corporate power at the cost of the individual and collective self-expression the Amendment was meant to serve. It will undoubtedly cripple the ability of ordinary citizens, Congress, and the States to adopt even limited measures to protect against corporate domination of the electoral process.

Since *Citizens United*: In 2014, in *McCutcheon v. FEC*, the Supreme Court ruled that the limit on how much a donor can contribute over a two-year election cycle was unconstitutional. To stay within that limit, the plurality of the Court argued, donors who could afford to give the maximum amount to a number of candidates would have to rule out some candidates and causes they might also wish to support. In that way, the Court ruled, their freedom of expression was unconstitutionally limited.

Political Science Disciplinary Practices: Analyze and Interpret Supreme Court Decisions

As you analyze the ruling in *Citizens United v. FEC* (or any other court case or law), compare it to other related cases or laws. Identify specific categories for comparison. If you are comparing Supreme Court cases, for example, the categories for comparison might include the constitutional principle at stake, the facts of the case, the decision, the makeup of the court, the historic time of the decision, and dissenting opinions, among others. Creating these specific and relevant categories will help you sharpen the comparisons you make.

Apply: Complete the activities below.

1. Explain the Court's ruling in *Buckley v. Valeo*.
2. Describe the facts of the *Citizens United v. FEC* case and the congressional regulation at issue.
3. Describe the claim the group Citizens United made about BCRA.
4. Explain how the Court's reasoning in *Citizens United* led to its ruling.
5. Relate the ideas expressed in *Federalist No. 10* to the decision in *Citizens United*.
6. Identify specific categories you can use as a basis of comparison between the case of *Citizens United* and the case of *Buckley,* and then describe similarities and differences.

Impact of Citizens United

Debates over free speech and competitive and fair elections have increased since *Citizens United*. Free speech advocates, libertarians, and many Republicans view most campaign finance regulations as infringements on their freedoms, so they hailed the ruling. Others agreed with President Obama when he criticized the ruling at his 2010 State of the Union address as a decision that would "open the floodgates to special interests."

Dark Money In addition to allowing ads by outside or soft money groups immediately before an election, the Court's ruling also allowed for unlimited contributions to these groups from individual citizens and other organizations. This dark money has penetrated political campaigning, causing a lack of transparency about where the money originates. Even though political ads must express who is behind them, determining exactly where the money ultimately comes from is hard to do.

"*Citizens United* changed the culture at the same time that it changed the law," according to Zephyr Teachout, Fordham University law professor and author of *Corruption in America*. "Before *Citizens United*, corporate or individual money could be spent with a good enough lawyer. But after *Citizens United v. FEC*, unlimited corporate money spent with intent to influence was named, by the U.S. Supreme Court, indispensable to the American political conversation."

The ruling also concentrates who dominates the political discussion. Five years after the ruling, the Brennan Center at New York University found that of the $1 billion spent, about 60 percent of the donations to PACs came from 195 people or couples. More recently, an analysis by OpenSecrets.org found that during the 2016 election cycle, the top 20 individual donors gave more than $500 million to PACs. The 20 largest organizational donors also gave a total of more than $500 million to PACs. And more than $1 billion came from the top 40 donors. About one-fifth of political donations spent in all federal elections in 2016 came from dark money sources.

In the 2016 election cycle, special interests spent at least $183.5 million in dark money, up from $5.2 million in 2006. Of that, liberal special interests spent at least $41.3 million, or 22.5 percent; conservatives spent most of the rest.

Though Democrats are more prone to use *Citizens United* as a rallying cry against corporate special interests, Democrats have also benefitted from the ruling. As Sarah Kleiner of the Center for Public Integrity points out, "Many Democrats have taken full advantage of the fundraising freedoms *Citizens United* has granted them." Candidate Hillary Clinton, especially, "benefited from a small army of super PACs and millions of dollars in secret political money." More specifically, in 2016 the Clinton presidential campaign received 18 percent of its contributions, about $220 million, from such sources, whereas Trump received 12 percent of his overall contributions, or roughly $80 million, from PACs.

REFLECT ON THE ESSENTIAL QUESTION

Essential Question: How do electoral processes and campaign finance laws affect political participation? On a separate paper, complete a chart like the one below to gather details to answer that question.

Issue	Effect on Political Participation
Electoral Process	
Campaign Finance Laws and Rulings	

KEY TERMS AND NAMES

Bipartisan Campaign Reform Act (BCRA) (2002)/507

blanket primary/489

Buckley v. Valeo (1976)/505

caucuses/490

Citizens United v. FEC (2010)/508

closed primary/489

coattail effect/500

Electoral College/494

electors/494

Federal Election Campaign Act (FECA)/503

Federal Election Commission (FEC)/504

front-loading/490

general election/492

hard money/507

incumbent/489

incumbent advantage phenomenon/489

initiative/487

invisible primary/488

Iowa caucuses/490

matching money/507

midterm elections/499

New Hampshire primary/490

open primary/489

plurality/494

political action committees (PACs)/500

polling place/487

precincts/487

primary election/489

recall/488

referendum/488

soft money/507

split ticket/489

Super Tuesday/491

Twenty-Third Amendment/494

voter registration/486

war chest/506

wards/487

winner-take-all/494

MULTIPLE-CHOICE QUESTIONS

1. Which of the following is an accurate comparison of congressional and presidential campaigns?

	Congressional	Presidential
(A)	Are conducted at three-year intervals	Are conducted every four years
(B)	Have lower turnouts than presidential elections	Are decided by the Electoral College
(C)	Nominate candidates at national conventions	Second-highest vote-getter in primaries becomes vice presidential candidate
(D)	Have candidates that compete for federal matching money	Can accept higher donations from individuals than congressional candidates

Questions 2 and 3 refer to the table below.

CALIFORNIA PRESIDENTIAL PRIMARY ELECTION RESULTS, 2016 (TOP FIVE VOTE-GETTERS)					
Democrat	Total Votes	Percent	Republican	Total Votes	Percent
Hillary Clinton	2,745,302	53.1	Donald Trump	1,665,135	74.8
Bernie Sanders	2,381,722	46	John Kasich	252,544	11.3
Willie Wilson	12,014	0.2	Ted Cruz	211,576	9.5
Michael Steinberg	10,880	0.2	Ben Carson	82,259	3.7
Roque De La Fuente	8,453	0.2	Jim Gilmore	15,691	0.7
Total Democratic votes	5,158,371	100	Total Republican votes	2,227,205	100

Source: *California Secretary of State*

2. Which of the following statements is reflected in the data in the table above?
   (A) Hillary Clinton received more California primary votes than Bernie Sanders or Donald Trump.
   (B) More voters participated in California's Republican primary than in the state's Democratic primary.
   (C) John Kasich was the runner-up candidate in the Democratic field.
   (D) Based on this election outcome, Donald Trump will receive all the state's electoral votes.

3. Based on the data in this table, which statement is accurate?

(A) In California, Donald Trump likely earned a greater proportion of Republican convention delegates than Hillary Clinton earned Democratic convention delegates.

(B) The outcome of this state election will have no impact on which candidates receive their party nominations.

(C) Regardless of the second-place candidate's political ideology or personalities, the winning nominee will choose that person as his or her vice presidential running mate.

(D) Because California holds the first primary election, this outcome will have great impact on subsequent primary elections.

4. To find how much money a political candidate spent on a campaign for U.S. House, Senate, or the presidency, which agency should one consult or contact?

(A) Federal Election Commission

(B) Internal Revenue Service

(C) Federal Bureau of Investigation

(D) Office of Management and Budget

5. The words "I'm Ready for Hillary" appeared on bumper stickers and T-shirts during the 2016 presidential campaign. Which of the following campaign messages do those words convey?

(A) The candidate's name recognition and an argument for progress

(B) The candidate's foreign policy stance

(C) The candidate's pick for vice president

(D) The candidate's compassion and approach to governing

Question 6 refers to the table below.

MICHIGAN 2016 ELECTION NIGHT RESULTS			
Candidate	Party	Votes	Pct
Donald Trump	Republican	2,279,543	47.3%
Hillary Clinton	Democrat	2,268,839	47.0%
Gary Johnson	Libertarian	172,136	3.6%
Jill Stein	Green	51,463	1.1%
Others	Independent, U.S.Taxpayers	50,070	1.0%

Source: *New York Times*

6. Which of the following most accurately describes the information in the table?

   (A) The table shows the percentage of voting age population in Michigan voting for each candidate.

   (B) The table shows the percentage of the voter-eligible population in Michigan voting for each candidate.

   (C) The table shows the percentage of votes cast for each candidate.

   (D) The table shows the increasing influence of Libertarian candidates.

7. Which type of primary election provides the greatest choice for voters?

   (A) Blanket primary

   (B) Open primary

   (C) Closed primary

   (D) Caucus

8. The Bipartisan Campaign Reform Act

   (A) lowered limits on soft money

   (B) lowered limits on hard money

   (C) raised limits on soft money

   (D) raised limits on hard money

9. Which of the following is an accurate comparison of challengers and incumbents?

	Challengers	Incumbents
(A)	Tend to win in a bad economy	Spend less money
(B)	Have an easier time raising money because of their fresh appeal	Are viewed skeptically because they have an open voting record
(C)	Have generally fewer resources than incumbents	Use the tools of their office to help support their candidacy
(D)	Mainly use federal matching money	Coordinate with Super PACs

Source: *CartoonStock.com*

10. Which message does the cartoonist convey?

(A) The free speech considerations in Super PAC ads help strengthen democracy.

(B) Super PAC ads try to be truthful even if they put forward a strong point of view.

(C) A good Super PAC ad promotes a candidate and disparages opponents.

(D) Super PAC advertising is likely highly untrue.

FREE-RESPONSE QUESTIONS

1. "I confess to having supported the ACLU position in *Buckley*. As the corrosive effects on democracy of uncontrolled campaign spending became increasingly clear, however, I joined several former ACLU leaders . . . in opposing the organization's campaign finance position [on *Citizens United* that the Bipartisan Campaign Reform Act limited free speech]. We have argued . . . that spending massive amounts of money during an election campaign is not "pure" speech when the spending level is so high that it drowns out competing voices . . . ; that a compelling interest in equality justifies preventing wealthy speakers from buying up an unfair proportion of the speech . . . that massive campaign spending by 'independent' entities poses a serious risk of postelection corruption; and that corporations lack the attributes of conscience and human dignity that justify free-speech protection."

— Burt Neuborne, *The Nation,* March 21, 2012

After reading the scenario, respond to A, B, and C below:

(A) Describe the political behavior that has resulted from the *Citizens United* ruling, according to the author.

(B) In the context of the scenario, explain how the behavior described in part A affects elected officials.

(C) In the context of the scenario, explain how the effect on elected officials can be influenced by linkage institutions.

TV Ad Spending by State
(2012 Presidential Election Cycle)

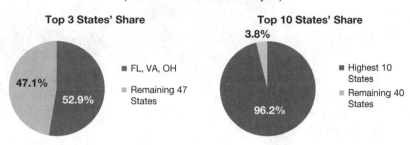

Top 3 States' Share

47.1% 52.9%

■ FL, VA, OH
■ Remaining 47 States

Top 10 States' Share

3.8% 96.2%

■ Highest 10 States
■ Remaining 40 States

2. Use the information graphic to answer the questions.

(A) Describe the information presented in the graphs.

(B) Describe differences in the television ad spending in different states, and draw a conclusion about the reasons for those differences.

(C) Explain how the patterns of ad expenditures demonstrate a strength or weakness of the election process.

3. After passage of the Bipartisan Campaign Reform Act (BCRA) in 2002, groups including the Democratic Party of California, the National Rifle Association, and individuals, including Mitch McConnell who was at the time the Senate Majority Whip, brought a case against the Federal Election Commission arguing that the provisions of BCRA violated constitutional protections of free speech. In 2003, the Supreme Court upheld most of the law in its ruling in *McConnell v. FEC*. It reasoned that since the law's ban was on soft money, which could not be used to help elect a candidate directly but rather was spent on party activities such as get-out-the-vote efforts, then its limits on free speech were minimal. It argued further that even if ads paid for by unions and corporations were not shown to lead to corruption, to protect the legitimacy of its institutions, the state had an interest in protecting against "both the actual corruption threatened by large financial contributions and . . . the appearance of corruption."

(A) Identify the constitutional clause that is common to both *McConnell v. FEC* (2003) and *Citizens United v. FEC* (2010).

(B) Based on the constitutional clause identified in part A, explain why the facts of *Citizens United v. FEC* led to a different holding than the holding in *McConnell v. FEC*.

(C) Describe an action that interest groups who disagree with the holding in *Citizens United v. FEC* could take to limit its impact.

4. Develop an argument that explains whether or not *Citizens United v. FEC* (2010) should be overturned.

In your essay, you must:

- Articulate a defensible claim or thesis that responds to the prompt and establishes a line of reasoning
    - Support your claim with at least TWO pieces of accurate and relevant information:
      At least ONE piece of evidence must be from one of the following foundational documents:
        - First Amendment of the Constitution
        - *Federalist No. 10*
    - Use a second piece of evidence from another document from the list above or from your study of modern campaigns and elections
- Use reasoning to explain why your evidence supports your claim/ thesis
- Respond to an opposing or alternative perspective using refutation, concession, or rebuttal

WRITING: *USE CONCISE LANGUAGE*

Keep your writing as crisp and clear as possible. To improve the clarity of your writing, eliminate wordy phrases and avoid inflated language. For example, instead of the wordy phrases "due to the fact that" and "in light of the fact that," use the simpler, clear word "because." And instead of such inflated language as "is cognizant of" and "is desirous of" use the simpler and clearer "knows" and "wants."

15

Interest Groups

"By a faction, I understand a number of citizens . . . united and actuated by some common impulse of passion, or of interest, adversed to the rights of other citizens, or to the . . . aggregate interests of the community."

—James Madison, *Federalist No.10*, 1787

Essential Question: How do citizens, businesses, and other interests influence lawmaking and policy, and how has government regulated their actions?

At any level of government, people differ on the question of how to shape the law. Some citizens naturally become part of formal groups based on their common beliefs. James Madison and other founders expressed concern about factions, groups of "interested" people motivated by the pursuit of wealth, religious beliefs, or alliances with other countries. Today, these special interests, sometimes referred to as pressure groups or lobbies, are concerned with corporate profits, workers' rights, the environment, product safety, or other issues. They are *linkage institutions* because they connect citizens to government and provide organizations through which citizen voices can be expressed. Historic and recent accounts of bribery, scandal, and other unethical tactics have shaped the public's impression of these groups. Yet, the First Amendment guarantees the right of special interests to operate and express opinions.

Benefits of Interest Groups

Since Madison wrote *Federalist No. 10* (pages 23 and 644), the United States has developed into a complex web of viewpoints, each seeking to influence government at the national, state, and local levels. The nation's constitutional arrangement of government encourages voices in all three branches of government and at all three levels. This **pluralism**, a multitude of views that ultimately results in a consensus on some issues, has intensified the ongoing competition among interests.

The three separate and equal branches of government, Madison argued in *Federalist No.10*, would prevent the domination and influence of factions or interests. The American system of government, however, with policymaking bodies in multiple branches at multiple levels, encourages the rise of interest groups. Modern interest groups have become adept at influencing policies in all three branches. Within each branch there are people and entities—individual members of Congress, a president's appointed staff, agency directors, and scores of federal courts—that have helped to increase special interest group efforts.

The division of powers among national and state governments has also encouraged **lobbying,** applying pressure to influence government, not only in Washington but also in every state capital across the land. State governments are based on the federal model: within each state branch is a multi-member legislature, state agencies, and various courts, all of which provide targets for interest groups. County and city governments also make major decisions on school funding, road construction, fire departments, water works, and garbage collection. Many of the national interest groups, such as the Fraternal Order of Police (FOP) or national teachers' unions, have local chapters to influence local decisions. Thus interests have an incentive to meet not only with national and state legislators but also with mayors, county administrators, and city council members.

BIG IDEA: This opportunity for multiple access points for people to have their voices heard and influence government policy is a key benefit of interest groups. Interest groups must compete in the "marketplace of ideas" just as products must compete in a free enterprise system. This competition tends to increase democratic participation, since people cannot take for granted that their interests will be considered. Interest groups also devote time and resources to creating practical solutions to real problems and have the power to

Source: *Dreamstime*
In September 2012, the 26,000 members of the Chicago Teachers Union (CTU) went on strike for the first time in 25 years in part to protest Mayor Rahm Emanuel's policy of using standardized test scores as part of teacher performance evaluations. The strike won higher wages for the teachers, but they lost the fight on the use of standardized tests for evaluation. The CTU is affiliated with the American Federation of Teachers and the National Education Association and is also a member of the Illinois Federation of Teachers, a part of the AFL-CIO.

get their solutions accepted. In exercising those benefits, interest groups also educate the public and use their resources to mobilize support for their point of view. They even draft legislation and work with lawmakers and government agencies to see it put into law and enforced.

Some interest groups represent broad issues, such as civil rights or economic reform. Others, such as those focusing on drunk driving or gun rights, represent very specific or narrow interests. Both types form in response to changing times and circumstances and both demonstrate the benefits of interest groups—their ability to have their voices heard, gain support for their position, and influence government policies and elections. Interest groups, along with the protest movements that sometimes brought them into being, form with the goal of making an impact on society and influencing policy.

Broad Interests

Interest groups arose in response to the dynamic changes in the United States as the nation developed from a mainly agrarian economy to a manufacturing nation. Immigrants arrived on both coasts, bringing a wide variety of viewpoints into the country. Factory workers banded together for protection against their bosses. War veterans returning from armed conflicts looked to the government for benefits. Women and minorities sought equality, justice, and the right to vote. Congress began taking on new issues, such as regulating railroads, addressing child labor, supporting farmers, and generally passing legislation that would advance the nation. As democracy increased, the masses pushed to have their voices heard.

Labor One interest group that represented a broad issue is the American Federation of Labor (AFL), organized in 1886 under the leadership of Samuel Gompers. Initially the organization had about 140,000 members. The AFL's most useful tool was the labor strike—skilled workers simply banding together and refusing to work until the company met their demands. Labor unions also entered the political arena and pushed for legislation that protected workers against unhealthy and hazardous conditions. New state (and sometimes national) laws addressed child labor, maximum workday hours, and eventually minimum wages.

The power of labor organizations reached new levels in the 1950s. In 1955 the American Federation of Labor merged with the Congress of Industrial Organizations (CIO), a large union composed of steelworkers, miners, and unskilled workers. The AFL-CIO became the leading voice for the working class. American union membership peaked in 1954 with roughly 28 percent of all households belonging to unions. In 1964, the nation's largest truckers' union, the Teamsters, signed a freight agreement that protected truckers across the country and increased the union's power. Union membership hovered near the levels of the 1950s until the early 1980s. Today, about 13 percent of households, or about 7 percent of American workers, belong to organized labor. (For more on the competing interests of labor and business, see page 409.)

The AFL-CIO comprises 57 smaller unions, including the United Mine Workers and United Automobile, Aerospace and Agricultural Implement Workers of America, with about 12 million total members. After the decline in manufacturing starting in the 1960s, and the related decline in union membership, union organizers turned to the public sector. Between 1958 and 1978, public sector union membership more than doubled, from about 7.8 million to 15.7 million. Today, most states have laws allowing collective bargaining for such public employees as teachers, firefighters, and police.

Labor unions have been instrumental in achieving the 40-hour workweek, employer-sponsored health care, family and medical leave, and an end to child labor, and although their strength is diminished in comparison to the mid-1900s, labor unions as a type of interest group continue to have an influence on policy.

Business Associations Businesses soon organized in response to the growing labor movement so they could gain influence for their positions. Manufacturing and railroad firms sent men to influence decisions in Washington. As more and more influential "lobby men" roamed the Capitol, these interests became known as the "third house of Congress."

The National Association of Manufacturers (NAM) was founded in 1895. Its members include such regional organizations as the Georgia Employers' Association, New Haven Manufacturers Association, and the San Antonio Manufacturers Association. The U.S. Chamber of Commerce formed in 1912 from the many local chambers of commerce in cities across the country, as well as private firms and individuals. Heavily financed, the NAM and the Chamber became deeply involved in politics. They both backed conservative presidential candidate William Howard Taft. The number of **trade associations** grew from about 800 in 1914 to 1,500 in 1923. By 2010, that number had grown to more than 90,000.

The U.S. Chamber of Commerce seeks to protect business interests and has used its influence to oppose the Dodd-Frank Wall Street Reform and Consumer Protection Act, which regulates banking and other investment and became federal law in 2010 following the financial crisis of 2007–2008. It opposed the Affordable Health Care for America Act and spent more than $16 million to elect senators to write a competing plan more favorable to the health insurance companies among their membership. It has also opposed government action on climate change. It supported the American Recovery and Reinvestment Act of 2009, sometimes called the stimulus bill, which provided government money to businesses to preserve jobs and improve the nation's infrastructure. The U.S. Chamber of Commerce has been the top spender on lobbying for many years. In 2017, the organization spent more than $1.4 billion to help promote the interests of its members. In contrast, organized labor spent only $46 million, most of it in support of the interests of public sector and transportation employees.

Social Movements The Progressive Era (1890–1920) was a fertile period of American reform. The growing country and the rise in immigration resulted in a push for greater levels of democracy and policies to assist the average American. The push for a women's suffrage amendment had been growing. African-American leaders and compassionate northern intellectuals sought to ease racial strife in both the South and the North. The Woman's Christian Temperance Union wanted to eliminate consumption of alcohol. Many believed that the nation's cities had become overcrowded, filthy denizens of vice, and various groups formed to clean them up.

The ratification of three amendments—the Sixteenth, Seventeenth, and Nineteenth—contributed to interest group growth and activity. First, the **Sixteenth Amendment** (1913) empowered Congress to tax individual incomes, which enhanced the national treasury and encouraged groups to push for more services. The **Seventeenth Amendment** (1913) empowered citizens to elect their U.S. senators directly, replacing the old system in which state legislators and party caucuses picked the senators. Senators now had to consider the views of all voters, not just the elites. When the **Nineteenth Amendment** (1920) guaranteed women the right to vote, it doubled the potential voting population. Caring and civic-minded women drew attention to urban decay, child labor, alcoholism, and other humanitarian concerns.

PROGRESSIVE ERA INTEREST GROUPS		
Group	**Purpose**	**Founded**
Veterans of Foreign Wars	To secure rights for military veterans	1899
National Association for the Advancement of Colored People	To advocate for racial justice and civil rights	1909
Urban League (originally called Committee on Urban Conditions Among Negroes)	To prevent discrimination, especially in northern cities	1910
U.S. Chamber of Commerce	To unify businesses and protect commercial affairs	1912
Anti-Defamation League	To stop bigotry and defamation of Jewish people	1913
American Farm Bureau	To make farming more profitable; to secure farmers' benefits	1919
American Legion	To assist war veterans, service members, and communities	1919
League of Women Voters	To assure good government	1920
American Civil Liberties Union	To guarantee free speech, separation of church and state, and fair trials	1920

After World War II, civil rights and women's equality, environmental pollution, and a rising consumer consciousness were the focus of leading social movements. Backing for these causes expanded during the turbulent 1960s as citizens began to rely less on political parties with general platforms and more on interest groups addressing broad issues but working toward very specific goals. Interest groups tied to social movements cannot match the financial resources of the Chamber of Commerce or even unions to lobby policymakers, but they have another tool to help sway opinion—grassroots movements.

Civil Rights The National Association for the Advancement of Colored People (NAACP) and the Urban League were founded in 1909 and 1910, respectively, to seek racial equality and social fairness for African Americans. In the 1950s and 1960s, these groups experienced a dramatic rise in membership, which increased their influence in Washington. NAACP attorneys worked tirelessly to organize black communities to seek legal redress in the courts. The Urban League worked to increase membership to enhance its influence. Additional civil rights groups surfaced and grew. The Congress of Racial Equality (CORE) was founded at the University of Chicago and became instrumental in the nonviolent civil disobedience effort to desegregate lunch counters. Reverend Martin Luther King's Southern Christian Leadership Conference (SCLC), an organization of leading black southern clergymen, began a national publishing effort to create public awareness of racist conditions in the South. And the Student Nonviolent Coordinating Committee (SNCC) was a leading force in the dangerous Freedom Rides to integrate interstate bus lines and terminals. Whether in the courts, in the streets, or on Capitol Hill, most changes to civil rights policy and legislation, especially the Civil Rights Act of 1964 and the Voting Rights Act of 1965, resulted from these organizations' efforts.

Women's Movement A growing number of women entered public office. Federal laws began to address fair hiring, equal pay, and workplace discrimination. Both the 1963 Equal Pay Act and the 1964 Civil Rights Act addressed occupational equality but left unsettled equal pay for equal work and a clear definition of sex discrimination.

Leading feminist Betty Friedan wrote *The Feminine Mystique* in 1963 and formed the National Organization for Women (NOW) in 1966. NOW had 200 chapters by the early 1970s and was joined by the National Women's Political Caucus and the National Association for the Repeal of Abortion Laws (NARAL) to create a coalition for feminist causes. The influence of these groups brought congressional passage of the Equal Rights Amendment (which failed in the state ratification battle; see page 544) and Title IX (1972), which brought more focus and funding equality to men's and women's school athletics. They also fought for the *Roe v. Wade* Supreme Court decision that prevented states from outlawing abortion.

Environmental Movement As activists drew attention to mistreatment of blacks and women, they also generated a consciousness about the misuse of our environment. Marine biologist Rachel Carson's best-selling book *Silent*

Spring (1962) made a dramatic impact. Carson criticized the use of insecticides and other pesticides that harmed birds and other wildlife. Her chosen title referenced the decreased bird population that silenced an otherwise cheerful springtime. Organizations such as the Sierra Club, the Wilderness Society, and the Audubon Society expanded their goals and quadrupled their membership. In 1963 and 1964, Congress passed the first Clean Water Act and Clean Air Act, respectively, in part through the efforts of the environmental groups. The years of disregard of pollution and chemical dumping into the nation's waterways reached a crisis point in 1969 when Cleveland's Cuyahoga River was so inundated with chemicals that it actually caught on fire. This crisis led to even stronger legislation and the creation of the Environmental Protection Agency in 1970. Earth Day became an annual event to focus on how Americans could help to preserve the environment. In 1980, environmental interest groups celebrated the creation of the Superfund under the Comprehensive Environmental Response, Compensation, and Liability Act (CERCLA). The Superfund taxes chemical and petroleum companies and puts the revenue into a trust fund to be used for cleaning up environmental disasters. The first disaster to use Superfund resources was at Love Canal in New York, an abandoned canal project into which a chemical company had dumped 21,000 tons of hazardous chemicals between 1942 and 1953, putting the health of residents in the area at risk.

Consumer Movement Consumers and their advocates began to demand that manufacturers take responsibility for making products safe. No longer was *caveat emptor* ("let the buyer beware") the guiding principle in the exchange of goods and services. In 1962 President Kennedy put forth a Consumers' Bill

Source: *Massachusetts Department of Environmental Protection*

The Shpack Landfill in Attleboro and Norton, Massachusetts was the site of a Superfund cleanup effort to remove hazardous waste materials, including low-level radioactive waste.

of Rights meant to challenge manufacturers and guarantee citizens the rights to product safety, information, and selection. By the end of the decade, the Consumers Union established a Washington office, and activists formed the Consumer Federation of America. With new access to sometimes troubling consumer information, the nation's confidence in major companies dropped from 55 percent in 1966 to 27 percent in 1971.

Ralph Nader emerged as America's chief consumer advocate. As early as 1959 he published articles in *The Nation* condemning the auto industry. "It is clear Detroit is designing automobiles for style, cost, performance, and calculated obsolescence," Nader wrote, "but not for safety." In 1965 he published *Unsafe at Any Speed*, an exposé of the industry, especially General Motors' (GM) sporty Corvair. To counter Nader's accusations, GM hired private detectives to tail and discredit and even blackmail him. When this effort came to light, a congressional committee summoned GM's president to testify and to apologize to Nader. The publicity helped catapult Nader's book sales and his career. In 1966, Congress also passed the National Traffic and Motor Vehicle Safety Act, which, among other things, required seat belts in all new cars.

After the financial crisis of 2008–2009, consumer interest groups united under an umbrella organization called Americans for Financial Reform which helped pressure lawmakers to create the Consumer Financial Protection Bureau. Its responsibilities include regulating debt and collection practices, monitoring mortgage lending, investigating complaints about financial institutions, and obtaining refunds for consumers who were owed them.

Narrow Interests

Some interest groups form to address a narrow area of concern. For example, the Woman's Christian Temperance Union (WCTU), founded in 1874, wanted to eliminate consumption of alcohol. It was one of the first interest groups to have a professional lobbyist in Congress, and through its organizing efforts it succeeded in getting the Eighteenth Amendment ratified, ushering in the era of Prohibition—a time when it was illegal to make, sell, or transport alcohol. The Eighteenth Amendment was repealed in 1933 by the Twenty-first Amendment. Long before then, WCTU had branched out to cover other issues as well. However, they continue to focus on the importance of abstinence, not just from tobacco but from drugs as well.

National Rifle Association This "single-issue" group (see page 531) is the interest group most associated with narrow interest lobbying. The National Rifle Association (NRA) has gone from post–Civil War marksmen's club to pro-gun Washington powerhouse, especially in the last 30 years under the leadership of lobbyist Wayne LaPierre. Its original charter was to improve the marksmanship of military soldiers. After a 1968 gun control and crime law, the NRA appealed to sportsmen and Second Amendment advocates. Its revised 1977 charter states the NRA is "generally to encourage the lawful ownership and use of small arms by citizens of good repute." In 2001 *Fortune* magazine named the NRA the most powerful lobby in America. Hundreds of employees work at its Fairfax, Virginia, headquarters, a short 20-minute ride to Washington, D.C. The NRA appeals to law enforcement officers and outdoorsmen with insurance policies, discounts, and its magazine *American Rifleman*. The group holds periodic local dinners for "Friends of the NRA" to raise money. The annual convention provides a chance for gun enthusiasts to mingle and view the newest firearms, and attendance reaches beyond 50,000 gun enthusiasts.

The Brady Handgun Violence Prevention Act of 1993 (see page 263), which mandates automatic waiting periods and background checks for handgun purchasers, along with the 1992 election of President Bill Clinton, caused NRA membership to soar from 2.5 million to 3.4 million. The NRA endorses candidates from both major political parties but heavily favors Republicans. From 1978 to 2000 the organization spent more than $26 million in elections; $22.5 million went to GOP candidates and $4.3 went to Democrats.

Drawbacks of Interest Groups

Interest groups, as you have read, have many benefits as a way for people to have their voices heard and influence policy. They also, however, have potential problems and have been the subject of much criticism. President Woodrow Wilson (1913–1921) often expressed his frustration over the tactics lobbyists employed. "Washington has seldom seen so numerous, so industrious, or so insidious a lobby," he once lamented when corporations opposed his tariff bill. "The newspapers are being filled with paid advertisements calculated to mislead the judgments of public men … [and] the public opinion of the country itself."

Alabama Senator Hugo Black (D, 1927–1937) investigated one utility company's 1930s lobbying effort, as recounted by Kenneth Crawford in *The Pressure Boys*. Black became suspicious when very similarly worded letters opposing a bill to regulate electric utilities began to flood Capitol Hill. Black exposed the scheme when a 19-year-old Western Union messenger testified before the investigating Senate committee. A gas and electric company had paid a group of telegraph messenger boys to persuade Pennsylvania citizens to send telegrams opposing the bill to their congressmen. The company provided the talking points for the messages. One congressman received 816 of these telegrams in two days, mostly from citizens with last names that began with *A*, *B*, or *C*. As it turned out, the young messenger had pulled the names from a phone book starting from the beginning.

"The lobby has reached such a position of power that it threatens government itself," an outraged Senator Black said in a radio address. He went on to condemn the lobby's "capacity for evil, its greed, trickery, deception, and fraud." To Black's dismay, it turned out that the utility company had done nothing illegal, and this tactic continues today with email and social media. Interest groups send members and supporters legislative alerts when an issue of concern is about to come up for a vote. Along with the alerts they send sample messages for supporters to use a base for writing their own messages, although many just send the sample message. Some cell phone apps will even fax the message to a person's representatives.

Another potential problem is that interest groups by definition promote the interests of their members over more general interests. When groups pull in many different or completely opposite directions, compromise becomes impossible and gridlock can result. This phenomenon is called *hyperpluralism*.

In such a situation, a form of elitism can also develop. Groups with more power and resources are more likely to achieve their goals than groups with smaller memberships or more limited funding, putting interest groups on an uneven footing in the "marketplace of ideas" (see page 520).

Interest groups also have the potential to lead to corruption and fraud. In 2009, for example, the tobacco industry was found guilty of defrauding the American public about the dangers of smoking, intentionally suppressing research that showed a cause-and-effect relationship between smoking and lung cancer. As their PACs contribute to political campaigns, interest groups also apply financial pressure to lawmakers that some believe exert undue influence on lawmakers.

Interest groups also do not participate on a level playing field. Some are well funded and have much more power than smaller or relatively underfunded groups. That power gives them access to government decision makers that other interest groups may not have. Relationships between interest groups and government representatives develop, deepen, and expand over time (see page 534 on iron triangles and issue networks for more information), so the inequality of resources and access widens even more.

Groups, Members, and Resources

Interest groups fall into a handful of categories. These consist of institutional (corporate and intergovernmental groups), professional, ideological, member-based, and public interest groups. There is some overlap among these. For example, business groups want to make profits, but they also have a distinct ideology when it comes to taxation and business regulation. Likewise, citizens groups have members who may pay modest dues, but these groups mostly push for laws that benefit society at large.

The types and resources of interest groups affect their ability to influence elections and policy. For example, nonprofit interest organizations fall into two categories based on their tax classification. The **501(c)(3)** organizations, such as churches and certain hospitals, receive tax deductions for charitable donations and can influence government, but they cannot lobby government officials or donate to campaigns. By comparison, **501(c)(4)** groups, such as certain social welfare organizations, can lobby and campaign, but they can't spend more than half their expenditures on political issues. Available resources also affect the ability of groups to influence policy. Well-funded groups are usually able to wield more power and to have greater access to government decision makers than groups with fewer resources.

Institutional Groups

Institutional groups break down into several different categories, including intergovernmental groups, professional associations, and corporations.

Intergovernmental Groups The U.S. system of redistributing federal revenues through the state governments encourages government-associated interest groups. Governors, mayors, and members of state legislatures are all interested in receiving funding from Washington. The federal grants system and marble cake federalism (see page 54) increase state, county, and city interest in national policy. Governments and their employees— police, firefighters, EMTs, and sanitation workers—have a keen interest in government rules that affect their jobs and funding that impacts their salaries. This interest has created the **intergovernmental lobby**, which includes the National Governors Association, the National League of Cities, and the U.S. Conference of Mayors, all of which have offices in the nation's capital.

Professional Associations Unlike labor unions that might represent pipefitters or carpenters, **professional associations** typically represent white-collar professions. Examples include the American Medical Association (AMA) and the American Bar Association (ABA). They are concerned with business success and the laws that guide their trade. Police and teachers unions, such as the Fraternal Order of Police or the National Education Association, are often associated with the labor force, but in many ways they fall into this category. The AMA endorsed the 2010 Affordable Care Act. The ABA rates judicial nominees and testifies before Congress about proposed crime bills.

Corporations In the 1970s, the consumer and environmental movements brought an increase in business and free enterprise lobbyists. The National Association of Manufacturers and the U.S. Chamber of Commerce merged resources to form a joint effort. By the late 1970s, both groups had convinced Congress to deregulate. The Chamber's membership grew at a rate of 30 percent per year, expanding its $20 million budget and 50,000 members to $65 million and 215,000 members by 1983.

The Business Roundtable, formed in 1973, represents firms that account for nearly half of the nation's gross domestic product. New conservative **think tanks**—research institutions, often with specific ideological goals— emerged and old ones revived, such as the American Enterprise Institute and the Heritage Foundation, largely to counter the ideas coming from liberal think tanks and philanthropic foundations.

Some think tanks are associated with universities, even though their funding comes entirely from corporations, philanthropic foundations, and private individuals. For example, the Mercatus Center at George Mason University in Virginia was founded to promote free market ideas and solutions in higher education with the backing of billionaire Charles Koch and other free market proponents.

As writer John Judis explains, in 1971, only 175 businesses registered lobbyists in Washington. By 1982, there were 2,445 companies that had paid lobbyists. The number of corporate offices in the capital jumped from 50 in 1961 to 500 in 1978 and to 1,300 by 1986. By 1978, 1,800 trade associations were headquartered in the nation's capital. Today, Washington has an army of lawyers and public relations experts whose job it is to represent corporate interests and lobby the government for their corporate clients.

Member Groups

Most groups have a defined membership and member fees, typically ranging from $15 to $40 annually. (Corporate and professional associations typically charge much higher fees.) When groups seek to change or protect a law, they represent their members and even nonmembers who have not joined. For example, there are many more African Americans who approve of the NAACP's goals and support their actions than there are actual NAACP members. There are more gun advocates than members of the National Rifle Association (NRA). These nonmembers choose not to bear the participation costs of time and fees but do benefit from the associated group's efforts. This results in what is known as the **free rider** problem. Groups that push for a collective benefit for a large group inevitably have free riders.

To encourage membership, interest groups offer incentives. **Purposive incentives** are those that give the joiner some philosophical satisfaction. They realize their money will contribute to some worthy cause. If they donate to an organization addressing climate change, for example, they might feel gratified that their contribution will help future generations. **Solidary incentives** are those that allow people of like mind to gather on occasion. Such gatherings include monthly organizational meetings and citizen actions. Many groups offer **material incentives**, such as travel discounts, subscriptions to magazines or newsletters, or complimentary items such as bags or jackets.

One study found that the average interest group member's annual income is $17,000 higher than the national average and that 43 percent of interest group members have advanced degrees, suggesting that interest group membership has an **upper-class bias**. Though annual membership fees in most interest groups are modest, critics argue that the trend results in policies that favor the higher socioeconomic classes.

As opposed to special interest groups, **public interest groups** are geared to improve life or government for the masses. Fully 30 percent of such groups have formed since 1975, and they constitute about one-fifth of all groups represented in Washington.

Common Cause In 1970, Republican John Gardner, Lyndon Johnson's Secretary of Health, Education, and Welfare, took what he called the biggest gamble of his career to create Common Cause. "Everybody's organized but the people," Gardner declared when he put out the call to recruit members to build "a true citizens' lobby." Within six months Common Cause had more than 100,000 members. The antiwar movement and the post-Watergate reform mindset contributed to the group's early popularity. Common Cause's accomplishments include the Twenty-sixth Amendment to grant voting rights to those 18 and over, campaign finance laws, transparent government, and other voting reforms. More recently, the group pushed for the 2002 Bipartisan Campaign Reform (McCain-Feingold) Act and the 2007 lobbying regulations in the Honest Leadership and Open Government Act, which called for better public disclosure of lobbying activities and limits gifts for Congress members. Today Common Cause has nearly 400,000 members and 38 state offices.

Public Citizen With money from a legal settlement with General Motors, Ralph Nader joined with other consumer advocates to create Public Citizen in 1971. He hired bright, aggressive lawyers who came to be known as Nader's Raiders. In 1974, *U.S. News and World Report* ranked Nader as the fourth most influential man in America. Carrying out ideals similar to those that Nader had emphasized in the 1960s—consumer rights and open government—Public Citizen tries to ensure that all citizens are represented in the halls of power. It fights against undemocratic trade agreements and provides a "countervailing force to corporate power." Nader went on to create other watchdog organizations, such as the Center for Responsive Law and Congress Watch, to address the concerns of ordinary citizens who don't have the resources to organize and lobby government.

Single-Issue and Ideological Groups

You have already read about the National Rifle Association, the best-known **single-issue group.** (See page 526.) Single-issue groups focus narrowly on one topic. Two other well-known single-issue groups are the American Civil Liberties Union (ACLU) and the American Association of Retired Persons (AARP).

American Civil Liberties Union Activists created the American Civil Liberties Union after World War I to counteract government's authoritarian interpretation of the First Amendment. At that time, the federal government deported radicals and threw dissenters of the war and the military draft in jail. Guaranteeing free expression became the ACLU's central mission. In 1925, the organization went up against Tennessee state law to defend John Scopes's right to teach evolution in a public school.

Over the following decades, the ACLU opened state affiliates and took on other civil liberties violations. It remains very active, serving as a watchdog for free speech, fair trials, and racial justice and against overly aggressive law enforcement. The ACLU has about half a million members, about 200 attorneys, a presence on Capitol Hill, and chapters in all 50 states.

American Association of Retired Persons AARP has the largest membership of any interest group in the nation. AARP has twice the membership of the AFL-CIO, its own zip code in Washington, and its own registered in-house lobbyists. Its magazine has the largest circulation of any monthly publication in the country. People age 50 and over can join by paying

$16 per year. The organization's main concerns are members' health, financial stability and livelihood, and the Social Security system. "AARP seeks to attract a membership as diverse as America itself," its Web site claims. With such a large, high voter-turnout membership, elected officials tend to pay very close attention to AARP.

You have also already read about a number of **ideological groups**— interest groups formed around a political ideology. On the liberal side of the ideology spectrum are groups such as the NAACP and NOW. On the other end of the spectrum, conservative ideological interest groups include the Christian Coalition and the National Taxpayers Union.

Political Action Committees

Many interest groups create **political action committees (PACs)**. Typically defined as the political arm of a labor union, interest group, or corporation, PACs involve themselves in a wide array of election season activities, such as sending direct mail, creating advertising, staging rallies, and campaigning door-to-door. Politicians and party-driven organizations can also form what are known as **leadership PACs**. Leading up to her 2008 presidential run, Hillary Clinton created Hill-PAC, a committee to raise money that she distributed to other candidates in return for support in her presidential campaign. She created a similar PAC in conjunction with the Democratic National Committee, the Hillary Victory Fund.

Interest groups, corporations, and unions are forbidden from donating directly to candidates, but their PACs can contribute up to $5,000 per election cycle ($10,000 combined for primary and general elections). Since costly television advertising dramatically impacts elections, PAC support is a valuable asset. To get a return on their investment, PACs tend to support incumbents that side with them. The 1970s campaign finance laws caused a drastic increase in the number of PACs. In 1974, 608 committees registered with the Federal Elections Commission. Ten years later, 4,009 did so. Direct contributions rose from $23 million in 1975–76 to nearly $260 million in the 1999–2000 cycle. In 2008, contributions to House and Senate candidates reached nearly $400 million. By the 2015-2016 election cycle, contributions to House and Senate candidates totaled more than $443 million.

Interest groups and their PACs can also spend money to affect the election without directly writing a check to the candidate. These soft-money contributions or independent expenditures pay for fund-raisers, meet-and-greets, ads, and other campaign activities.

The landmark decision in *Citizens United v. FEC* in 2010 declared that corporations and other organizations have a similar right to free speech as individuals (see page 508). Corporations, labor unions, and other organizations can now use funds from their treasuries to endorse or denounce a candidate at any time provided ads are not coordinated with any candidate.

BY THE NUMBERS GROWTH IN POLITICAL ACTION COMMITTEES, 1974–2016					
Year	Corporate	Labor	Trade/ Member	Other	Total
1974	89	201	318	NA	608
1978	433	224	489	873	1,146
1982	1,469	380	649	873	3,371
1984	1,682	394	698	1,235	4,009
1988	1,816	354	786	1,312	4,268
1992	1,735	347	770	1,343	4,195
1996	1,642	332	838	1,267	4,079
2000	1,523	316	812	1,055	3,706
2004	1,555	303	877	1,305	4,040
2008	1,551	264	962	1,474	4,251
2012	1,851	300	1,033	2,319	5,503
2016	1,803	289	973	1,981	5,046

Source: *Federal Elections Commission. "Other" includes nonconnected, privately owned companies and leadership PACs.*

What do the numbers show? To what extent have PACs grown since 1974? When did the total PAC count peak or level off? What types have grown at the fastest rates?

Super PACs Not long after, the **super PAC**, known in legal terms as an independent expenditure-only committee, became a player in national politics. Powerful PACs receive unlimited donations, and they can raise and spend as much as they want on electioneering communication provided they disclose their donors and don't coordinate with any candidate. The 501(c)(4) groups, so named for the relevant part of the tax code, need not disclose donors but cannot spend as freely. Critics refer to them as **dark money** groups. They accounted for more than one-fourth of outside group spending in 2012. Dark money contributions in the 2016 election increased tenfold over the 2012 amount.

Some 501(c)(4)s are getting around the 50% expenditure limit on politics by donating to super PACs, which can take unlimited donations but have to disclose their donors—that is, the names of the contributing nonprofit organizations, not the names of the actual donors themselves.

The spending by nonparty outside groups tripled during the period 2008–2012 and topped the historic outside group record at $1 billion. Super PACs accounted for more than $600 million of that, according to information from the Center for Responsive Politics. Michael Beckel and Russ Choma from that organization report that conservative groups were responsible for 69 percent of outside spending and liberal groups for 28 percent. Only 7 percent of the money spent by American Crossroads, one of the largest and best-funded groups, went to candidates who actually won.

According to Molly Ball of *The Atlantic*, during the 2012 campaign, "groups on the left were some of the most skilled exploiters of the 2010 *Citizens' United* decision." The AFL-CIO had actually filed an *amicus curiae* brief with the court to allow unions to campaign to the general public. This action returned labor to a powerhouse position during campaigns.

Iron Triangles and Issue Networks

As you read in Chapter 5, **iron triangles** are the bonds among an agency, a congressional committee, and an interest group. The three entities establish relationships that benefit them all. Bureaucrats benefit by cooperating with congressional members who fund and direct them. Committee members benefit by listening to interest groups that reward them with PAC donations.

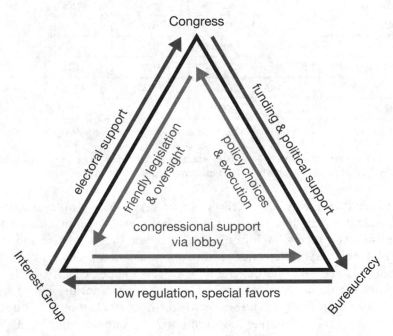

Follow the arrows in the above graphic so you can explain how the stages of the give and take process in an iron triangle relate to one other. How does the interest group benefit? How does the congressional committee benefit? How does the bureaucracy benefit?

Issue networks are also collectives with similar goals, but they have come together to support a specific issue and usually do not have the long-term relationships that characterize iron triangles. If and when their issue of common concern is resolved, the networks break up. Issue networks often include a number of different interest groups who share an opinion on the issue at hand but may have strongly differing opinions on other matters. For example, religious interest groups and some civic organizations might have differing views on abortion or same-sex marriage, but they may agree on the importance of health care for children living in poverty and work together to advance that cause.

Influencing Policy

"Agitate, educate, legislate!" were the watchwords of the WCTU, neatly summarizing the ways in which many interest groups spread their influence and use it to bring about change. They agitate through public demonstrations, such as the 1963 march in Selma, Alabama after which Dr. Martin Luther King Jr. was arrested. Dr. King described agitation when he wrote, "Nonviolent direct action seeks to create such a crisis and foster such a tension that a community which has constantly refused to negotiate is forced to confront the issue. It seeks so to dramatize the issue that it can no longer be ignored."

Once the issue has been brought to the surface, the education of both voters and legislators can begin. Interest groups use many different channels to educate the public and legislators on their concerns, as you will read below.

With enough public support, interest groups can help draft legislation to support their cause. This process requires ongoing relationships with legislators and others in government. To keep up the pressure on legislators to produce the desired result, interest groups mobilize their members and the public to take to the streets in demonstrations or make phone calls or in-person visits to representatives.

Interest groups take on a variety of activities using a variety of techniques to "agitate, educate, and legislate." **Insider strategies** quietly persuade government decision makers through exclusive access. The most common form of insider activity is **direct lobbying** of legislators. **Outsider strategies** involve lawsuits or get-out-the vote drives. Groups also try to sway public opinion by issuing press releases, writing op-ed articles for newspapers, appearing as experts on television, and purchasing print and TV advertising. They also mobilize their membership to call or write legislators on pending laws or to swing an election. Interest groups have become skilled in influencing all three branches of government.

Lobbying Legislators

The term *lobbying* came into vogue in the mid-1600s when the anteroom of the British House of Commons became known as "the lobby." **Lobbyists** were present at the first session of the U.S. Congress in 1789. As Kaiser reports, wealthy New York merchants engaged House and Senate members to delay action on a tariff bill they thought would hurt their profits. They soon employed what would become a classic tactic—a good dinner with plenty of alcohol to help create the type of warm, friendly atmosphere the favor seeker needed to make his case.

Lobbyists attend Washington social gatherings to develop relationships through their contacts who have **access** to government officials, or a way of approaching them. They monitor legislators' proposed bills and votes. They assess which lawmakers support their cause and which do not. They also help

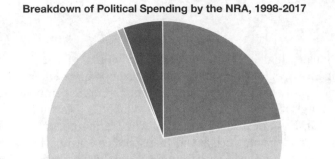

Breakdown of Political Spending by the NRA, 1998-2017

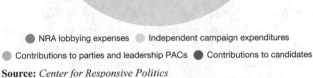

● NRA lobbying expenses   ● Independent campaign expenditures

● Contributions to parties and leadership PACs   ● Contributions to candidates

Source: *Center for Responsive Politics*

In what category of spending does the NRA expect to see the greatest return on investment?

draft bills that their congressional allies introduce. They find which lawmakers are undecided and try to bring them over to their side. "Influence peddler" is a derogatory term for a lobbyist, but influencing lawmakers is exactly what lobbyists try to do.

Give and Take Lobbyists want access to legislators, and Congress members appreciate the information lobbyists can provide. Senators and House members represent the individual constituents living in their districts. Sometimes so-called special interests actually represent large swaths of a given constituency. A lobbyist for a defense contractor that sells fighter jets to the Pentagon represents her company but might also speak for hundreds of plant workers. Democracy purists argue that a lawmaker should disregard a heavily financed influence peddler, but most members of Congress recognize the useful byproduct—the resources lobbyists offer.

For example, imagine a North Carolina representative has a meeting with a tobacco lobbyist, who is concerned about a pending bill that further taxes and regulates the sale of cigarettes. The tobacco company sees the bill as dangerous to its bottom-line profits.

The lobbyist presents the legislator with the results of an opinion poll— an expensive endeavor—that shows 57 percent of registered voters in his district oppose the bill. The lobbyist also points out that the tax increase will lead to a rise in black market sales. The lobbyist then hands the lawmaker a complete report at the end of the meeting. Could the poll or report be bogus?

Probably not. Lobbyists have an agenda, but they are generally looking to foster a long-term relationship. "[T]hey know that if they lie, they lose," Congressman Barney Frank once declared. "They will never be allowed to come back to this office." Imagine further that the following day the lawmaker meets with a representative from the American Heart Association. He provides a medical research study about cigarette prices as a deterrent to new smokers. He also provides poll results from a nationwide survey on smoking in public places.

The elected official has now spent only a couple hours to obtain valuable information with no money spent by his office. With that information, he can represent more of his constituents while considering attitudes and factors across the country. "I help my boss the most," declared one congressional staffer, "when I can play the good lobbyists off each other."

Key Targets and Strategizing No one is more effective in lobbying a legislator than another lawmaker. In the early stages of a legislative fight, influential members of Congress, especially those serving on key committees, become interest group targets. Some legislators give cues to other members, so lobbyists target them first.

To what degree do lobbyists move legislators on an issue? Do they persuade members to change their votes? Little evidence exists, Cigler and Loomis offer, to show that lobbyists actually change legislators' votes. Most findings do not prove lobbyists are successful in "bribing" legislators. Also, lobbyists tend to interact mostly with those members already in favor of the group's goals. So the money didn't bring the legislators over to the interest group; the legislator's position on the issue brought the interest group to him or her.

ACTIVITIES OF LOBBYISTS
Client interaction: informing clients, discussing strategy
Legislative activity: providing information/researching bills/ drafting bills
Social media: monitoring congressional activity, targeting outreach
Implementation: testifying on bills/filing amicus briefs
Electoral activity: advertising, making PAC donations
Other activity: meetings, business development/media commentary, etc.

What different skills must congressional lobbyists have?

Researcher Rogan Kersh conducted a unique two-year study of corporate lobbyists. "I'm not up here to twist arms and change somebody's vote," one lobbyist told him in a Senate anteroom crowded with lobbyists from other firms, "and neither are most of them." These lobbyists seem more concerned with waiting, gossiping, and rumor trading. A separate study conveyed that lobbyists want information or legislative intelligence as much as the lawmakers do. "If I'm out playing golf with some congressman or I buy a senator lunch, I know I'm not buying a vote," one lobbyist declared before recent reforms. The lobbyist is simply looking for the most recent views of lawmakers in order to act upon them. Kersh tabulated congressional lobbyists' legislative activities. A lobbyist attempting to alter a legislator's position occurred only about 1 percent of the time.

Research and Expertise Large interest groups have created entire research departments to study their concerns. "How many lives would be saved if government raised the drinking age from 18 to 21?" Mothers Against Drunk Driving wanted to know. "What kind of a Supreme Court justice would nominee Clarence Thomas make?" the American Bar Association pondered. These are the kinds of questions that members of Congress also ask as they contemplate legislative proposals. During the investigatory phase of lawmaking, experts from these groups testify before congressional committees to offer their findings. Since they represent their own interest, researchers and experts from interest groups and think tanks will often focus on the positive aspects of supporting their desired outcomes.

Campaigns and Electioneering As multiple-term congressional careers have become common, interest groups have developed large arsenals to help or hinder a legislator's chances at election time. Once new methods—TV ads, polling, direct mail, and marketing—determined reelection success, politicians found it increasingly difficult to resist interest groups that had perfected these techniques and that offered greater resources to loyal officials.

A powerful interest group can influence the voting public with an **endorsement**—a public expression of support. The Fraternal Order of Police can usually speak to a lawmaker's record on law enforcement legislation and financial support for police departments. The NRA endorses its loyal congressional allies on the cover of the November issue of its magazine, printed uniquely for each district. Groups also rate members of Congress based on their roll call votes, some with a letter grade (A through F), others with a percentage. Americans for Democratic Action and the American Conservative Union, two ideological organizations, rate members after each congressional term.

Grassroots lobbying, generally an outsider technique, takes place when an interest group tries to inform, persuade, and mobilize large numbers of people. Originally practiced by the more modest citizens and issue advocacy groups, such as students marching against the war in Vietnam, Washington-based interests are increasingly relying on grassroots techniques to influence officials.

Grassroots lobbying focuses on the next election, regardless of how far away it might be. In 1982, soon after Republican Senator Bob Dole and Democratic Representative Dan Rostenkowski introduced a measure to withhold income taxes from interest earned on bank accounts and dividends, the American Banking Association went to work encouraging banks to persuade their customers to oppose the measure. *The Washington Post* called it the "hydrogen bomb of modern day lobbying." Banks used advertisements and posters in branch offices; they also inserted flyers in monthly bank statements mailed out to every customer, telling them to contact their legislators in opposition to the proposed law. Banks generated nearly 22 million constituent communications. Weeks later the House voted 382–41, and the Senate 94–5, to oppose the previously popular bipartisan proposal.

Framing the Issue When the debate over the Clean Air Bill of 1990 began, *Newsweek* asked how automakers could squash legislation that improved fuel efficiency and reduced both air pollution and America's reliance on foreign oil. A prominent grassroots consultant reasoned that smaller cars—which would be vital if the act were to be successful—would negatively impact child safety, senior citizens' comfort, and disabled Americans' mobility. Opponents of the bill contacted and mobilized senior organizations and disability rights groups to create opposition to these higher standards. What was once viewed as an anti-environment vote soon became a vote that was pro-disabled people and pro-child.

Use of Media Television and telephones have encouraged grassroots lobbyists and issue advocacy groups. Depending on their tax classification, some groups cannot suggest a TV viewer vote for or against a particular congressperson. So instead they provide some detail on a proposed policy and then tell the voters to call the senator and express their feelings on the issue. Such ads have become backdoor campaigning. They all but say, "Here's the congressperson's position. You know what to do on Election Day."

The restaurant industry responded rapidly to a 1993 legislative idea to remove the tax deduction for business meals. Everyday professionals conducting lunchtime business in restaurants are able to write off the expense at tax time. As Congress debated changing that deduction, special interests acted. The National Restaurant Association (sometimes called "the other NRA") sponsored an ad that showed an overworked server-mother: "I'm a waitress and a good one….But I might not have a job much longer. President Clinton's economic plan cuts business-meal deductibility. That would throw 165,000 people out of work. I need this job." Opposition to eliminating the tax benefit no longer came from highbrow, lunchtime dealmakers but instead from those wanting to protect hardworking servers, cooks, and dishwashers. At the end of the ad, the server directed concerned viewers to call a toll-free number. Callers were put through to the corresponding lawmaker's office with the push of a button. The "other NRA" successfully stopped the bill.

Interest groups increase their chances of success when they reach the masses, but they also target opinion leaders, those who can influence others. Lobbying firms try to connect with business owners or lesser officials in a community—the **grasstops**—to shape opinion on the local level. Some lobbyists charge $350 to $500 for getting a community leader to communicate his or her feelings to a legislator in writing or on the phone. They also set up personal meetings between high-profile constituents and members of Congress. Grasstops lobbying sometimes shifts public opinion in the desired direction; for example, it might cherry-pick selected opinions that create an artificial view, sometimes called "Astroturf."

Congressional lobbyists sometimes also use grassroots techniques in tandem with their Washington, D.C., operations. Once they determine a legislator's anticipated position, especially if it is undecided, lobbyists can pressure that congressperson by mobilizing constituents in his or her district. Interest group leaders send out letters that provide an outline or talking points so their member can easily create a factual letter to send to their representative. With email, this technique became easier, cheaper, and more commonly used than ever before. With the click of a mouse, interest group members can forward a message to a lawmaker to signal where they stand and how they will vote. Such organizing has also become commonplace on social media. Lobbyists are also developing ways to mine social media for data so they can create highly targeted outreach.

Connecting with the Executive

Interest groups and industry representatives also lobby the executive branch. Leaders of major organizations, from the civil rights groups of the 1960s to business leaders today, visit the White House and gain access to the president. Martin Luther King Jr., Roy Wilkins of the NAACP, and others met with Lyndon Johnson to shape civil rights legislation and enforcement. And President Obama heard from members of the Chamber of Commerce as he fashioned his health care bill. More often, liaisons from powerful interest groups connect with White House staffers to discuss policy. This practice is particularly useful in view of the fact that so much policy—legislation and enforcement—comes from the president.

Bureaucratic agencies write and enforce specific policies that regulate industries. High-level experts at television networks might connect with the Federal Communications Commission as it revises its rules. Representatives of the National Association of Manufacturers may attempt to influence the implementation of environmental legislation by meeting with officials at the Environmental Protection Agency.

In the Courts

Interest groups also shape policy in the courts. Federal judges are not elected and cannot accept donations from PACs, and lobbyists don't try to woo judges over lunch or in their closed chambers. Yet an open and honest presentation by an interest group in a trial or in an appeals court hearing is quite common. This can be done in three major ways: representing clients in court, filing an *amicus curiae* brief, and challenging executive regulatory action.

Representing Clients Established interest groups have legal departments with expert attorneys who both seek out clients to represent—sometimes even paying their legal fees if the case seems promising for a victory in court that would promote the special interest—and accept those who request them. Compassionate groups defend those who cannot provide their own counsel or those who are wrongly accused, to assure justice. The NAACP Legal Defense Fund has represented scores of wrongly accused African-American defendants. The ACLU has defended free speech rights and regularly defends those facing the death penalty. At other times, test cases are taken to establish a higher principle or to declare an unjust law unconstitutional. If an interest group wins a case in the Supreme Court, the victory can create a new national policy.

Amicus Curiae Legal departments often file an *amicus curiae*, or "friend of the court," brief in cases in which they have an interest but no client. The amicus brief argues why the court should side with one party in the case. In this instance, the interest group acts as a third party merely expressing an outside opinion. Groups include their research findings in these briefs as experts on matters that are important to them to persuade judges.

ACLU ACTION IN SUPREME COURT		
Year	Case	Outcome
1962	*Engel v. Vitale*	Outlawed New York's state-sponsored school prayer
1967	*Loving v. Virginia*	Ended state laws against interracial marriage
1969	*Tinker v. Des Moines*	Overturned student suspensions for protesting Vietnam War
1971	*New York Times Co. v. US*	Prevented government prior restraint of news publication
1997	*Reno v. ACLU*	Internet speech gained full First Amendment protection
2003	*Lawrence v. Texas*	Overturned state laws against same-sex intimacy

*The ACLU has **represented** clients or filed amicus briefs in the above cases.*

Challenging Regulatory Decisions Federal regulatory agencies such as the Food and Drug Administration or the Environmental Protection Agency can issue fines and other punishments to companies that violate regulations. Corporations can challenge these decisions in the U.S. District of Columbia Circuit Court of Appeals.

In recent times, new media forms and changing government customs have allowed people outside of Washington to keep abreast of the events and actions within the capital. Congress opened its committee hearings decades ago, and today these are televised via C-SPAN and other media outlets. Roll call votes are more accessible as well. This visibility enables groups and their members to monitor and understand government, which in turn allows them to find effective ways to influence it. In this process interest groups compete at key stages of policymaking and to varying degrees with professional organizations, social movements and the advocacy organizations they spawned, the military, and bureaucratic agencies. Perhaps no other issue demonstrates these interactions better than the federal budget process. That process begins with a proposal from the president, moves to each house of Congress for legislative review and debate, and ideally ends with budgetary legislation that is approved by both houses and signed by the president. Along the way, various points of entry allow for the input of citizen interests expressed by special interest groups and social movements.

Influence on the President's Proposal Preparing a spending plan for an entire department or just one federal agency is a complex process in itself. The FBI, the Navy, and all other agencies create annual operating budgets to cover federal employees' salaries, equipment, services, new initiatives, and many more expenses. As a yardstick, these agencies consider their spending in the prior year. If their goals are similar, and inflation has not taken off, they will require about the same amount. They submit their spending requests up to their department secretaries. The 15 departments consider these requests, perhaps tweak them, and then send these up to the president's Office of Management and Budget (OMB) for review. The budget director, in consultation with the president, his Council of Economic Advisors, and the Treasury Secretary, draft what becomes the president's budget proposal to Congress.

During the period of review by the OMB, which includes a public comment period, interest groups can play an influential role. Since an executive order by President Reagan in 1981, the public can comment directly to the OMB, expressing views on budgetary and other regulations before the final draft moves on to Congress. Much more of this public input comes from interest groups than from individual members of the public. For a time, powerful lobbyists could meet in private with OMB officials, arguing for the interests of the group they represented. In 1993, President Clinton signed an executive order requiring that all lobbying to the OMB be publicly recorded so that the influence from special interest groups could be transparent. Most of the interest group influence at this stage of the budgeting comes from businesses.

The OMB, as a representative of the president, uses public input to gauge the popularity of the administration's priorities, and studies have shown that interest group influence has resulted in changes at the this stage of the process, especially if the interest groups tend to agree on broad objectives.

Influence on Congress The president's final draft of the budget proposal moves to Congress for its consideration. Congressional budget committees in both houses, created by the **Budget and Impoundment Control Act of 1974**, examine the president's budget. The Act was a response to the practice of some presidents of impounding funds, refusing to spend monies Congress had appropriated if they disagreed with the policy. President Nixon, particularly, impounded funds in an attempt to curb spending. Yet, saving federal dollars by refusing to spend what Congress deemed necessary was seen as undemocratic and a violation of separation of powers. The Congressional Budget and Impoundment Control Act outlawed such impoundments.

The various legislative committees (those with jurisdiction over particular areas, such as education, transportation, or the military) hold public hearings to listen to the concerns of constituents. Both business interest groups and nonprofit interest groups use these hearings to press the budgetary needs of their group. They might send experts to testify before congressional committees to educate the legislators. Nonprofits might highlight the plight of a person in the community they serve—a homeless veteran, for example—by bringing that person in to tell a personal story to a committee to show legislators why the interests of their organization need funding. Organizations representing the needs of people with mental illness might call on their members to contact their representatives and senators during this period to urge them to increase spending for mental health treatment. Organizations such as the Natural Resources Defense Council, an outgrowth of the environmental movement, might send experts to argue for renewed funding for the National Environmental Policy Act, a key piece of legislation that ensures public safety and the participation of citizens. After listening to public input, these committees take up appropriations bills for the coming fiscal year, ideally staying within the guidelines set by the budget resolution.

A relevant player in the congressional budgeting process is the **Government Accountability Office (GAO)**, an independent, nonpartisan arm of Congress. The GAO serves as a watchdog of congressional funds and keeps track of where and how money is spent. Sometimes viewed as Congress's accounting firm, it is headed by the U.S. Comptroller General. The comptroller is a presidential appointee chosen from a slate of nominees recommended by a nonpartisan, bicameral congressional commission and confirmed by the Senate. The GAO's work is based on requests from committees and committee chairs. The agency audits federal spending, examines efficiency, and in many ways acts as policy developer in the spending process.

After each of these committees considers and passes these appropriations bills, and after Congress passes the overall budget bill—by this time the result of the competing interests of input from interest groups, professional organizations, social movements, the military, and bureaucratic agencies—it then goes back to the president for signing.

Interest Group Pressure on Political Parties

Political parties and interest groups are both linkage institutions, creating connections between people and government. Political parties and interest groups also have connections between them. Some interest groups align with political parties that share their ideology and goals and endorse candidates in that party, encouraging their membership to vote for those candidates. However, interest groups can also exert pressure on political parties in areas of disagreement, and sometimes the result is that the official party ideology shifts in the direction of the interest group pressure.

Republican Party's Pull to the Right Several examples in recent history show the power of interest groups to influence policy positions of political parties. For example, as early as 1940, the Republican Party declared in its platform, "We favor submission by Congress to the States of an amendment to the Constitution providing for equal rights for men and women," and with that statement set the stage for becoming the first party to endorse the Equal Rights Amendment (ERA) after Congress proposed submitting it to the states for their ratification in 1972. By 1980, however, the Republican platform expressed a different stance to the ERA: "We acknowledge the legitimate efforts of those who support or oppose ratification of the Equal Rights Amendment." What happened during the eight years between those statements to shift the Republican position?

Phyllis Schlafly (1924–2016) was a lifelong Republican, playing an active role in the party and even running for office. She founded a conservative interest group, now called the Eagle Forum, in 1972, but refocused her energy on stopping the Equal Rights Amendment by founding the interest group STOP ERA (STOP stands for "Stop Taking Our Privileges"). By this time the ERA had won overwhelming support in Congress and ratification of 30 of the required 38 states. Schlafly's organization took the position that the ERA would disadvantage women—that it would deprive them of certain spousal rights, require them to serve in the armed forces and in combat, force them to use unisex bathrooms—and lead to same-sex marriage. Against the backdrop of the Supreme Court's 1962 ban on school prayer in *Engel v. Vitale* (page 254) and the legalization of abortion in *Roe v. Wade* in 1973 (page 288), women from a variety of backgrounds, especially conservative and Christian, feared that their traditional values were under attack, and they feared the consequences of the ERA that Schlafly predicted.

Source: *Florida Memory Project, State Archive of Florida*

A solemn group of anti-ERA women line the wall of the Florida Senate Rules Committee room in Tallahassee, where standing room only was available. The Senate Rules Committee defeated, then tabled consideration of, the Equal Rights Amendment, virtually killing the bill for the 1979 session.

The anti-ERA movement gained so much strength that the Republican Party could not ignore its influence, and it withdrew its support for the ERA from its platform. STOP ERA and other anti-ERA interest groups, including Concerned Women for America, Women for Constitutional Government, the John Birch Society, and Daughters of the American Revolution, carried out well-organized efforts and were successful in halting the ratification of the amendment and at the same time in pulling the Republican Party toward more conservative policy positions.

When President Nixon resigned in 1974 under the shadow of impeachment, only 18 percent of Americans identified as Republicans. STOP ERA and similar groups revitalized the Republican Party, and by 1980, Republican Ronald Reagan won the presidency by a landslide.

In a similar way, after President Obama's Patient Protection and Affordable Care Act passed in 2010, the Tea Party ("Tea" stands for "Taxed Enough Already") movement appeared on the scene to combat it and other government spending considered to be handouts to undeserving people. A number of interest groups arose as a result of this movement, and they helped elect very conservative replacements for more moderate Republicans at every level of government. Once again, the Republican Party was pulled to the right as a result of pressure from interest groups.

Democratic Party's Push to the Left The Democratic Party had experienced a similar shift in policy positions. Until the 20th century, it was more conservative than the Republican Party (the party of Abraham Lincoln) and was opposed to civil rights. However, during the administration of Franklin D. Roosevelt in the 1930s and 1940s, African Americans aligned with the Democrats. During the administration of Lyndon Johnson in the 1960s, powerful interest groups such as NAACP exerted pressure for progress in civil rights legislation, and the Democratic Party welcomed more African American and other minority voters, as well those favoring the ERA and opposing war, as its policy positions became more liberal in the party's shift to the left.

Other interest groups have also greatly influenced the Democratic Party. In 1984, the National Organization for Women (NOW) made its first-ever presidential endorsement when it endorsed Democratic candidate Walter Mondale, and the Democratic Party made history by nominating Geraldine Ferraro as his running mate, the first woman to be nominated for vice president by a major party. In 1985, EMILY's List was founded to help Democratic women to office. (EMILY stands for "Early Money Is Like Yeast," referring to the importance of securing donations early in a candidate's campaign in order to ensure donations later as well, to help a campaign rise as yeast makes dough rise.) Its first victory was the election of Senator Barbara Mikulski of Maryland, who became the longest-serving woman in the history of Congress. EMILY's List has gone on to help many Democratic women, including women of color and openly gay women, get elected. These strong associations between women's interest groups and the Democratic Party influenced the party's stand on women's issues.

The Sierra Club, a large environmental interest group, also carries influence with the Democratic Party. Many of its resources go to lobbying for environmental protection, and nearly all of its super PAC money goes to Democratic candidates.

Ethics and Reform

Lobbyists work for many different interests. The Veterans of Foreign Wars seeks to assist military veterans. The Red Cross, United Way, and countless public universities across the land employ lobbyists to seek funding and support. Yet the increased number of firms that have employed high-paid consultants to influence Congress and the increased role of PAC money in election campaigns have given lobbyists and special interests a mainly negative public reputation. The salaries for successful lobbyists typically outstrip those of the public officials they seek to influence. Members of Congress and their staffs can triple their salaries if they leave Capitol Hill to become lobbyists. This situation has created an era in which careers on K Street—the noted Washington street that hosts a number of interest group headquarters or lobbying offices—are more attractive to many than careers in public service. Still, old and recent bribery cases, lapses of ethics, and conflicts of interest have led to strong efforts at reform.

Scandals Bribery in Congress, of course, predates formal interest groups. In the 1860s Credit Mobilier scandal, a holding company sold nominally priced shares of railroad stock to congressmen in return for favorable votes on pro-Union Pacific Railroad legislation. A century ago, *Cosmopolitan* magazine ran a series entitled "Treason in the Senate" that exposed nine senators for bribery. In the late 1940s, the "5 percenters," federal officials who offered government favors or contracts in exchange for a 5 percent cut, went to prison. Over the years, Congress has had to pass several laws to curb influence and create greater transparency.

CONGRESSIONAL ACTS ON LOBBYING
• Federal Regulation of Lobbying Act (1946)
• Lobbying Disclosure Act (1995)
• Honest Leadership and Open Government Act (2007)

The high-profile cases of congressmen Randall "Duke" Cunningham and William Jefferson and lobbyist Jack Abramoff created headlines in 2006 that exposed lawlessness taking place inside the lawmaking process. Cunningham, a San Diego Republican representative, took roughly $2.4 million in bribes to direct Pentagon military defense purchases to a particular defense contractor. A California contractor supplied Cunningham with lavish gifts and favors such as cash, a Rolls-Royce, antique furniture, and access to prostitutes. He was convicted in 2006. In Louisiana Congressman William Jefferson's case, an FBI probe uncovered $90,000 in cash hidden in his home freezer, which led to his bribery conviction.

A more publicized scandal engulfed lobbyist Jack Abramoff, whose client base included several Native American casinos. He was known to trade favors—fancy dinners, golf trips to Scotland, lavish campaign contributions—for legislation. He pled guilty in January 2006 to defrauding four wealthy tribes and other clients of nearly $25 million as well as evading $1.7 million in taxes, and he went to jail.

Recent Reform Congress responded with the Honest Leadership and Open Government Act (HLOGA) in 2007. New rules banned all gifts to members of Congress or their staff from registered lobbyists or their clients. It also banned members from flying on corporate jets in most circumstances and restricted travel paid for by outside groups. The 2007 law also outlawed lobbyists from buying meals, gifts, and most trips for congressional staffers. Lobbyists must now file reports quarterly instead of twice a year. The new law also requires members to report the details of any **bundling**—raising large sums from multiple donors for a candidate. Lobbyists who bundle now have to report it if the combined funds equal more than $15,000 in any six-month period. Also, for the first time ever, lobbyists who break ethics rules will face civil and criminal penalties of up to $200,000 in fines and five years in prison. The Abramoff scandal brought an end to former House and Senate members' Capitol Hill gym privileges. Many of those former members had become lobbyists, and the gym had become a place where both heavy lifting and heavy lobbying took place.

Revolving Door However, the HLOGA had loopholes that have been repeatedly exploited. One relates to the problem of the **revolving door**—the movement from the job of legislator or regulator to a job within an industry affected by the laws or regulations. Many officials leave their jobs on Capitol Hill or in the executive branch to lobby the government they departed. Some members of Congress take these positions after losing an election. Others realize they can make more money by representing industry instead of citizens.

While serving in the House or Senate, legislators gain hands-on understanding of the legislative process. When they leave office, they have the phone numbers of key committee chairs already in their cell phones. Later as lobbyists, they can serve their clients with both expertise and immediate access. Congressional staffers, too, are known for seeking jobs as lobbyists—especially if they have worked on key committees. The average term for a congressional staffer is about two years. Many who work under the president also find it lucrative to leave the Pentagon to lobby for defense contractors or to leave the Department of Agriculture to lobby for large agricultural firms.

A Public Citizen study found that half the senators and 42 percent of House members who left office between 1998 and 2004 became lobbyists. Another study found that 3,600 former congressional aides had passed through the revolving door. The Center for Responsive Politics identified 310 former Bush and 283 Clinton appointees as lobbyists working in the capital. As of late 2014, 143 former members of Congress serve as registered lobbyists.

As author Robert Kaiser explains, when former Senate Majority Leader Trent Lott abruptly announced his retirement, it soon became clear why. He wanted to leave within a year of his new six-year term to avoid the impact of a 2007 law and join friend and former Louisiana senator John Breaux to start a lobbying firm. Recent reform requires outgoing senators, their senior aides, and officials in the executive branch to wait two years before becoming lobbyists. House members must wait only one year. This period is meant to at least slow down the revolving door. Lott got around the requirement by leaving office just before the new reform law took effect. Others follow the letter of the law but work in the shadows—cultivating relationships that will pay off when their waiting period expires.

The problems with powerful interest groups have led some critics to wish to silence their voices. However, these critics need look no further than the First Amendment to understand why they can't. Interest groups are legal and constitutional because the amendment protects free speech, free association, and the right to petition the government. In response to escalating lobbying efforts over the years, however, Congress began in 1946 to require lobbyists to register with the House or Senate. The Supreme Court upheld lobbyists' registration requirements but also declared in *United States v. Harriss* (1954) that the First Amendment ensures anyone or any group the right to lobby.

REFLECT ON THE ESSENTIAL QUESTION

Essential Question: *How do citizens, businesses, and other interests influence lawmaking and policy, and how has government regulated their actions?* On a separate paper, complete a chart like the one below to gather details to answer that question.

How Groups Influence Lawmaking	Government Regulations

THINK AS A POLITICAL SCIENTIST: *DETERMINE RELATIONSHIPS, PATTERNS, OR TRENDS*

To contextualize historical and present-day events and ideas, researchers need to be able to determine relationships, patterns, and trends among them over time. To do so, they use both qualitative and quantitative research methods.

Qualitative research is a type of exploratory research that helps researchers understand human motivations and other underlying factors and reasons for how and why events, problems, or ideas take shape. It is subject to interpretation. Qualitative research presents a broad, mostly verbal view of a research topic. Examples of qualitative research include focus groups and one-on-one interviews. It typically uses only semistructured research techniques and small sample sizes.

Quantitative research, on the other hand, generates data that can be charted numerically to arrive at relevant statistical information. It is used to narrow a qualitative research topic. Quantitative research most often relies on surveys and polls and data collected by the Census Bureau and American National Election Studies. The surveys and polls can be given in person, online, or by telephone.

Practice: Choose two well-known super PACs—one liberal and one conservative—such as Americans for Prosperity (Koch brothers) or Workers' Voice (AFL-CIO). Use quantitative information from online sources and/or print media to track and compare the issues and causes these super PACs support and the levels of funding they apply to influence American politics. Illustrate your findings in a graph or chart.

KEY TERMS AND NAMES

access/535

amicus curiae/541

Budget and
    Impoundment Control
    Act (1974)/543

bundling/547

Citizens United v. FEC
    (2010)/532

dark money/533

direct lobbying/535

endorsement/538

501(c)(4)/528

501(c)(3)/528

free rider/530

Government
    Accountabiity
    Office/544

grassroots
    lobbying/538

grasstops/540

ideological group/532

insider strategies/535

intergovernmental
    lobby/529

issue networks/534

iron triangles/534

leadership PACs/532

lobbying/520

lobbyists/535

material incentives/530

Nineteenth Amendment
    (1920)/523

outsider strategies/535

pluralism/519

political action
    committees
    (PACs)/532

professional
    associations/529

public interest
    group/530

purposive
    incentives/530

revolving door/548

Seventeenth
    Amendment
    (1913)/523

single-issue group/531

Sixteenth Amendment
    (1913) /523

solidary incentives/530

Super PAC/533

think tanks/529

trade associations/522

upper-class bias/530

MULTIPLE-CHOICE QUESTIONS

Questions 1 and 2 refer to the table below.

INTEREST GROUP INFLUENCE ON SELECT POLICY ISSUES, 1945–2012		
Issue Area	**Percent of policy enactments with interest group influence**	**Type of interest group credited**
Agriculture	63.2	Advocacy groups*
Civil Rights and Liberties	67.2	Advocacy groups
Criminal Justice	30.8	Advocacy groups
Energy	36.4	Business interests
Environment	69.1	Advocacy groups
Science and Technology	36.8	Business interests
Transportation	57.8	Business interests

Advocacy groups include public interest groups, single-issue groups, and representatives of identity groups, such as African Americans, Hispanics, LGBT persons, and women

Source: Matt Grossman, "Interest Group Influence on US Policy Change." *Interest Groups & Advocacy,* Oct. 2012, Vol 1, 2, p. 181.

1. Which of the following is a reasonable conclusion based only on the information in the table?

   (A) Advocacy groups appear more effective at influencing policy than business interests.

   (B) Business interests are the main interest groups for agriculture.

   (C) Environmental issues draw the most support from interest groups.

   (D) There are more advocacy groups than business interest groups.

2. Which of the following issue areas would have more grassroots reach with conservatives?

   (A) Transportation

   (B) Civil Rights and Liberties

   (C) Criminal Justice

   (D) Environment

Questions 3 and 4 refer to the passage below.

[T]he largest empirical study of actual decisions by our government in the history of political science, published last year, related what our government did to the attitudes of the economic elites, organized interest groups, and the average voter. What they found was, what our government actually did was strongly correlated with the views of the economic elites. If zero percent of the elites support something, very low chance it's going to pass, if 100% support something, very high chance it's going to pass. Same thing for organized interest groups. But for the average voter, it's a flat line. Which says it doesn't matter whether zero percent of the public believes something or 100% of the average voters believe something—it doesn't affect the probability that that thing will be enacted. . . .

There's a whole raft of studies that look at the voting behavior of Senators. And they relate their voting behavior to the average views of voters in their district, to the party view, and to the funders' or donors' view. What they find is: almost no relation to what the average voter wants, some relation to what the party wants, but a very tight relation to what the donor wants.

—Lawrence Lessig, Democratic candidate for president, October 2015

3. Which of the following best reflects Lessig's argument in this passage?

   (A) Organized interest groups have little actual effect on policy.

   (B) The economic elites and organized interest groups share policy priorities.

   (C) If people want to influence policy, they should support interest groups whose ideas they share.

   (D) Unlike interest groups, the economic elites buy their power through lobbying efforts and campaign contributions.

4. Which of the following legislative initiatives would Lessig be most likely to support?

(A) Congressional term limits

(B) Reform of nonprofit tax status

(C) Campaign finance reform

(D) Automatic voter registration

5. Which interest group action would most greatly influence rulings in the courts?

(A) Rating senators and representatives based on roll call votes

(B) Directly lobbying House and Senate members

(C) Filing an *amicus curiae* brief

(D) Purchasing an ad in a newspaper

6. Which statement about recent trends in grassroots lobbying is true?

(A) Only citizen groups employ grassroots lobbying.

(B) Grassroots lobbying uses mail and telephone, but not television.

(C) This technique is often used to target particular congressional districts.

(D) The average citizen and the grasstops are of equal value to a lobbyist.

7. Which of the following statements about interest groups and lobbying is true?

(A) Lobbying is protected by the Fourth Amendment.

(B) Lobbyists spend most of their time persuading lawmakers to change their political views.

(C) A Capitol Hill lobbyist's most precious asset is access.

(D) Free riders rarely benefit from interest group activity.

Questions 8 and 9 refer to the table below.

PAC CAMPAIGN DONATIONS (IN MILLIONS)			
	2000	2004	2008
Incumbents	$195.4	$246.8	$304.7
Challengers	$27.5	$22.3	$48.8
Open Seats	$36.9	$41.3	$32.4

Source: *FEC*

8. Which trend does the table on the previous page support?

(A) PAC donations tend to change legislators' votes.

(B) PAC donations to challengers have diminished in recent years.

(C) Republican candidates receive more donations from labor PACs than do Democrats.

(D) Interest group PACs tend to donate to incumbents more than challengers.

9. What implication can be drawn from the information in the table?

(A) To be effective, PACs need to spend more on challengers than on open seats.

(B) Issue networks have incumbents at their center.

(C) Iron triangles depend on longstanding relationships that challengers can't provide.

(D) Open seats provide the opportunity for a new access point for interest groups.

10. Which statement reflects the perspective of the cartoonist?

Source: *Nick Anderson, Cartoonist/Group*

(A) Interest groups working together improve legislation.

(B) Health care reform has been threatened by special interests.

(C) Special interests make surgically precise changes to proposed policy.

(D) Government involvement in health care is unwise.

1. "Most Nevadans don't have a choice. We don't get to decide how much our health care costs go up. No one's asking us if older Americans should be charged five times more for coverage than everyone else. And it's not our decision if Congress cuts Medicaid, leaving millions of seniors without the care they need . . . Just one vote could be enough to stop this bill. And Senator Heller, that vote is yours. Call Senator Heller today. Tell him to vote NO on the healthcare bill."

—AARP Radio Ad, June 20, 2017

After reading the above scenario, respond to A, B, and C below.

(A) Describe the goal of this interest group's radio ad.

(B) In the context of such radio ads aired by interest groups, explain the strategy AARP used to achieve the goal described in part A.

(C) Considering government interactions, explain one factor that could inhibit the success of this radio ad.

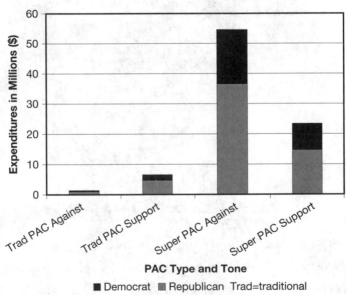

PAC Expenditure Totals According to Political Party in the 2014 Congressional General Election

Source: *Federal Election Commission*

2. Use the information in the graphic on the previous page to respond to the tasks below.

(A) Identify the most common type and tone of super PAC spending.

(B) Describe a difference between traditional PAC and super PAC spending, and draw a conclusion about the cause of that difference.

(C) Explain how the information in the graphic may demonstrate a factor in the public's view of Congress as a whole.

3. In June 1985, the Michigan State Chamber of Commerce wanted to run a newspaper ad in support of a candidate in the special election to fill a vacant seat in the Michigan House of Representatives. Although the organization had a separate political fund, it wanted to use money from its general treasury to pay for the ad. However, the Michigan State Campaign Finance Act prohibited the use of general treasury funds for political purposes. The Michigan State Chamber of Commerce argued that it was "nonprofit ideological corporation" and as such should not be bound by the Michigan law, which it argued suppressed the Chamber's First Amendment rights to free speech. A Michigan court upheld the application of the law; an appeals court reversed that decision, and the case came before the Supreme Court.

In 1990, in *Austin v. Michigan Chamber of Commerce,* the Supreme Court once again reversed, upholding the Michigan law that prohibited corporations from spending general treasury funds for political purposes. The Court disagreed with the designation of the organization, noting that most of its members were corporations. It reasoned further that since corporations are allowed to make political expenditures through their separate political funds their right to free speech is not unduly burdened.

(A) Identify a similarity between *Austin v. Michigan* (1990) and *Citizens United v. FEC* (2010). (See page 508.)

(B) Given the similarity identified in part A, explain why the reasoning in *Citizens United v. FEC* led to a different holding than the holding in *Austin v. Michigan.*

(C) Describe the effect of the ruling in *Citizens United* on corporate influence in policymaking.

4. Develop an argument that explains whether or not interest groups help achieve the type of representative democracy the founders envisioned.

In your essay, you must:

- Articulate a defensible claim or thesis that responds to the prompt and establishes a line of reasoning
- Support your claim with at least TWO pieces of accurate and relevant information:
  - At least ONE piece of evidence must be from one of the following foundational documents:
    - *Federalist No. 10*
    - First Amendment
  - Use a second piece of evidence from another foundational document from the list above or from your study of interest groups
- Use reasoning to explain why your evidence supports your claim/thesis
- Respond to an opposing or alternative perspective using refutation, concession, or rebuttal.

WRITING: *ESTABLISH A LINE OF REASONING*

An effective claim carries within it the direction your argument will take. For example, if you are arguing that the school day for teenagers should start later, you might develop this thesis:

School days should begin later to allow students to get the sleep they need to function at their physical, intellectual, and social best.

This claim establishes that the evidence you will provide will follow the line of reasoning that physical, intellectual, and social performance improve if students get the recommended amount of sleep.

16

The Media

*"Were it left to me to decide whether we should have a government
without newspapers, or newspapers without government,
I should not hesitate a moment to prefer the latter."*

—Thomas Jefferson, letter to a friend, 1787

Essential Question: How do changes in the media as a linkage institution
influence political institutions and behavior?

Soon after Johannes Gutenberg created the printing press, reporting and
commenting on government became commonplace. In late colonial America,
pamphleteers and newspaper editors printed ideas that helped bring about
the American Revolution. The media have since evolved from those hard-
copy publications intended for elite audiences to instant reporting and citizen
interaction via the Internet. Governments have a love-hate relationship with
the press, because journalists and commentators can affect public opinion,
government operation, and policy. In fact, the media wield power that rivals
that of the three branches of government. For that reason, the media are often
referred to as the "Fourth Estate," or the fourth branch of government. They have
the power to influence society and politics almost as effectively as government
itself.

Media as a Linkage Institution

In 1734, New York writer and publisher John Peter Zenger faced an American
colonial court on a charge of seditious libel. Zenger had criticized the royal
governor in his weekly *New York Journal*, which constituted an illegal action
at the time. Zenger's attorney argued that the truth, which was not a legitimate
defense under the law at the time, should be an absolute defense. The jury agreed
and found Zenger not guilty. This radical verdict, at odds with legal standards
in England, marked the beginning of an American **free press**—an uninhibited
institution that places an additional check on government to maintain honesty,
ethics, and transparency—later enshrined in the First Amendment.

No matter what form it takes, the free press serves to link citizens to
their government. Newspapers and television report on citizen concerns and
what their government does. Web-based news organizations provide constant
updates as news develops. Social media has become a chief way for citizens

and government to exchange information. All media ultimately help shape how people engage with government, including voting, and how the government acts.

Traditional News Media

Colonial newspapers served a major function during the American Revolution. Later, they fostered a spirit of unity for the new nation's course. Only large cities could maintain a regular newspaper, however, and most of them were only four pages and printed weekly. The first daily paper did not appear until 1784.

President Washington and Secretary of the Treasury Alexander Hamilton wanted a newspaper to convey Federalist Party ideas. They hired a printer to create the *Gazette of the United States*, which became a tool of the Washington administration and the developing Federalist Party. Thomas Jefferson's followers responded by publishing the *National Gazette*. The warring political factions debated and sometimes attacked each other through these printed journals.

The partisan press ceased to dominate national media as newspapers expanded their circulation with mass-production and the creation of national news organizations. The 1860 opening of the **Government Printing Office (GPO)**—a permanent federal agency to print government publications—broke the patronage relationship between government and publishers. The GPO prints only government documents, not news stories or editorials.

In 1833, the *New York Sun* became the first successful daily newspaper to be priced moderately. The paper cost one penny per copy and was sold at outdoor city markets. It consisted primarily of human-interest stories and recipes, which were what the average reader desired. Government activity no longer dominated the front pages. Other similar papers also began to thrive as America's readership grew and newspaper owners sought a mass audience.

Associated Press Wire Service The telegraph altered communication even further. In 1841, Congress funded inventor Samuel Morse's telegraph line from Washington to Baltimore. This was the first direct government involvement in private-sector telecommunications. In 1848, New York's leading editors gathered in the *New York Sun* offices to finalize plans for a formal news organization, the **Associated Press (AP)**. By pooling resources, the editors could gather, share, and sell the news beyond their respective cities. By expanding the telegraph lines, reporters could send information quickly from anywhere in the world to AP headquarters in New York. Editors could then shape the story and send it out to client newspapers in cities across the country.

During its first year, the AP covered a presidential campaign, a women's rights convention, and other national stories. It established **news bureaus**, or offices beyond a newspaper's headquarters, in Albany, New York, and Washington, D.C. Because it wrote for a national audience in so many different newspapers, the AP standardized unbiased reporting in order to appeal to a range of customers. The wire service set the standard for other news outlets to follow. Today, other wire services such as United Press International and Reuters compete with the AP, but they all follow the same standards of reporting.

Investigative Reporting In the early 20th century, Washington became a common dateline—the locale listed atop an article in a newspaper. Dispatches from the capital described such major news stories as the progress of the pure food and drug legislation, the efforts at trust busting, and the controversy over railroad rates. Progressive Era (1890–1920) journalism fostered integrity in reporting and a publication's ability to create real change. Magazines such as *McClure's*, *The Nation*, and *The New Republic* employed aggressive reporters to offer in-depth stories on national issues. **Investigative reporting** became a new genre, as reporters dug deep into stories to expose corruption in government and other institutions. Reporter Ida Tarbell wrote a damaging exposé of John D. Rockefeller's Standard Oil monopoly. Others such as Lincoln Steffens and Jacob Riis wrote stories and published photos that revealed the tragic conditions in cities. These journalists changed the national mindset to bring about reforms. For example, breaking up monopolies became easier once the public was aware of the harsh and sometimes illegal business practices of some industries. Newspapers were serving as a link between citizens and their government by reporting situations that called for new legislation.

Theodore Roosevelt shared the progressive spirit of these investigative journalists, though he did not always appreciate how they threatened his image or that of the United States. He dubbed the journalists muckrakers, a derogatory term that compared them to "the man with the muck rake" in the novel *Pilgrim's Progress*. They were too busy looking down and stirring up filth to gaze upon the stars. Lincoln Steffens proudly reflected on the label years later, "The makers of muck . . . bade me to report them."

Modern Print Media New media have emerged recently, profoundly influencing how citizens receive news. Yet, national newspapers such as the *Washington Post, Wall Street Journal, New York Times,* and *USA Today* remain influential, even if they've had to adapt to new modes of delivery. These newspapers continue to set the tone for national reporting, even if a majority of citizens no longer receive a hard copy on their front step every morning.

For decades, magazines such as *Time*, *Newsweek*, and *U.S. News and World Report* dominated in-depth news coverage with middle-of-the-road perspectives. These publications still operate today, though now they compete with news magazines that originated online. Other magazines cover national and international politics with a particular editorial slant. Some of the more liberal publications—*The New Republic*, *The Nation*, and *The Progressive*—have been around since the Progressive Era. Others, like *National Review* and *The Weekly Standard*, attract a conservative readership.

LEADING IDEOLOGICAL POLITICAL MAGAZINES	
Liberal	**Conservative**
The Nation	National Review
The New Republic	Human Events
The Progressive	The Weekly Standard
Mother Jones	American Spectator

New Communication Technologies

In the 20th century, radio and television both emerged as powerful new communication technologies. Citizens became fascinated with headlines and brief reports coming to them through the air. Broadcast stations developed news departments to shape an industry that competed with—and later surpassed—print media. Citizens began to rely on and become influenced by information relayed through sound and moving images.

Radio The first new form of technology was radio, which appeared shortly after World War I. The concept of a **broadcast network**—the broadcasting from one central location to several smaller stations called **affiliates**—was in full force by 1926, just seven years after the end of the First World War. Early newscasts included readings from *Time* magazine and news dramatizations featuring narrators and voice-over artists playing the parts of world leaders.

Radio journalism transitioned into more fact-based reporting as journalists moved from print to broadcast media. Edward R. Murrow was a key pioneer of this style. In 1940, Murrow broadcast from a rooftop in London in the midst of the Second World War, reporting on Germany's massive bombing efforts. The bombing had stopped temporarily, but radio listeners could still hear anti-aircraft weapons and air raid warnings. Films of the war appeared in movie theaters at the time, but, as Murrow biographer Bob Edwards put it, "Newsreel footage of the Blitz is in black and white; Ed's radio reports were in color." By the end of World War II, Murrow's voice was the most familiar in radio.

In the postwar period, broadcast companies shifted efforts toward television. By 1951, six years after the end of the Second World War, 10 million American homes had a television. Networks worked to develop news departments, and they covered the 1948 Democratic and Republican conventions. Television reporters wore headsets, carried 30-pound transmitters on their backs, and roamed the convention floor to interview delegates. Presidential contenders highlighted their credentials in front of the television cameras. Citizens were introduced to candidates for a live look at the individuals vying for each party's nomination. How a politician looked on television suddenly mattered.

Big Three Networks Over the next few years, the **Big Three networks** of ABC, CBS, and NBC set the tone for television journalism that is still largely followed today. Developing technology encouraged the networks to create in-depth programming that examined national affairs, international relations, and the lives of celebrities.

Edward R. Murrow moved from radio to television in 1951 to host *See It Now*, a precursor to *60 Minutes*. Murrow exposed Senator Joseph McCarthy by presenting examples of McCarthy's abusive tactics toward alleged American communists, which ultimately helped bring about McCarthy's downfall. Citizens trusted the voice—and now the image—of a trusted World War II reporter over an aggressive and corrupt politician. Television journalism had asserted itself as a watchdog, which made it an even more influential medium and strengthened its linkage function.

Television President In 1960, Senator John F. Kennedy became one of the first politicians to use the power of television to his advantage. The televised presidential debates between Kennedy and his opponent, Richard Nixon, began a new era of campaigning. Those who viewed the debates on television felt Kennedy won, while those who listened to the debates on the radio felt Nixon won.

Once elected president, Kennedy proved a master of the television medium, working with reporters and holding the first televised live press conferences. In 1963, CBS extended its 15-minute newscast to 30 minutes when Walter Cronkite interviewed President Kennedy. On November 22, 1963, Cronkite announced the president's death to the nation on live television. Coverage of Kennedy's assassination and funeral became the largest television event to date, and it remains embedded in the nation's collective memory.

Cable News In 1980, Atlanta TV station owner Ted Turner created the **Cable News Network (CNN)**. Americans had access to national news 24 hours a day for the first time. Cable companies added MSNBC and the Fox News Channel in the mid-1990s. These three cable news networks changed television news from a daily cycle with one evening peak to an all-day cycle with updates and analysis on the hour.

This change explains why President Bill Clinton's White House affair with Monica Lewinsky was so widely reported and why previous presidential affairs had not. Veteran White House reporter Helen Thomas noted how news reporting changed in the wake of the Lewinsky scandal: "Although gossip was also rampant about previous presidents, it remained just that—gossip—and reporters did not attempt to verify it."

Today, Fox, MSNBC, and CNN lead in viewership of cable TV news channels, though others like Bloomberg and BBC America have also become sources of 24-hour news delivery. Viewership of the top three channels peaked in 2008 at 4.3 million viewers per evening, and has declined somewhat as more channels are offered and as people turn to the Internet for news and entertainment. The Pew Research Center reported in 2016 that about 3.1 million combined viewers tune into those channels nightly. Though viewership has dropped, ad revenues for the cable's big three have steadily increased.

The original Big Three's (CBS, NBC, and ABC) 30-minute evening news broadcasts even today lead as America's key venue for political news consumption, hovering between 23 to 25 million combined viewers each night. These news sources have been around the longest, strive more for objectivity, provide short but inclusive top stories, and are still free for those citizens who get their broadcasts through the air. It should also be noted that though local TV news has lost some of its audience over the past decade, it still has more viewers than the chief national networks or cable TV channels. More Americans turn on the local news for traffic and weather than the national news for politics.

The Internet The Internet was created and developed by the U.S. military as a tool to connect its vast network of computers. The technology became generally available to the public in the early 1990s. It is now an ever-present source of news, information, and entertainment.

In the early days of the Internet, journalists and news-savvy citizens scoffed at news traveling across the web. Because the Internet is mostly free and accessible, skeptics originally feared merging the news business with the new medium because they could not see how to make money. But major news magazines, dailies, and other traditional media outlets have now followed their audience to the Internet. While some people still receive a daily subscription of their favorite printed newspaper, the newsprint rolling off the presses for home delivery has shrunk drastically. Today, nearly all Americans (93 percent) rely on the Internet somewhat to get their news. People under 30 have made the web their preferred news source. Pew reports about 38 percent of people primarily get their news from a digital platform, versus about 20 percent from print.

Internet news sources can be divided into those outlets that were "born on the web," and "legacy" news sources. In the first category, websites such as *Huffington Post* and *Politico* are setting the standards for online political reporting. These and other digital media organizations, such as Yahoo News and BuzzFeed, have spent millions to bring well-known print and TV journalists into their ranks.

Meanwhile, traditional news outlets, the legacy sources, have developed strong and popular Internet platforms for reporting, such as nytimes.com and the *Wall Street Journal's* platform, wsj.com. These organizations have turned to digital platforms to compete and remain afloat financially. Promoting their mobile apps, hiring full-time online editors and graphic designers, and selling digital versions of their newspapers has helped ease the transition from print to digital somewhat, though the number of full-time journalists has dropped from almost 55,000 in 2007 to just under 24,000 in 2015.

The shift from print to electronic journalism and the intense competition to "scoop" competitors in a fast-paced news environment has sped up publishing, shortened stories, enabled sloppy reporting, and caused journalists to seek out anything unique on an almost hourly basis to grab attention. This shift has not only encouraged sensationalism, but it also has increased the number of errors and after-story corrections.

Social Media Advances

In 2004, Harvard student Mark Zuckerberg launched Facebook, originally a campus social networking site that has since grown into a multibillion dollar corporation that engages as many as 400 million users daily worldwide. Competitors and other social media sites soon followed until social media became a primary vehicle for a vast number of Americans to consume their news. In 2018, about 86 percent of 18- to 29-year-olds used social media, and about 34 percent of senior citizens did. Of people who say they use Facebook, 76 percent use it every day.

Social Media and News This social media interaction between consumers and news outlets has encouraged the outlets to use social media to their advantage. Even the Big Three networks now have a strong social media presence. News outlets engage readers online, allowing direct conversations between journalists and consumers. Consumers also produce citizen-journalism by posting on-the-scene videos or other consumer-created content. Consumers also use social media to help organize newsworthy events, such as the nationwide Women's March in January 2017 and the student-organized March for Our Lives in March 2018. Social media therefore plays an increasingly large role in shaping news presentation and consumption.

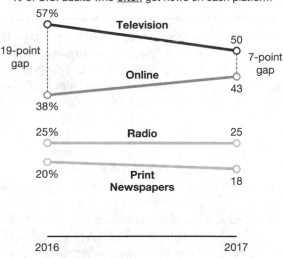

Television and Online News Consumption, 2016–2017
% of U.S. adults who <u>often</u> get news on each platform

	2016	2017	
Television	57%	50	7-point gap
Online	38%	43	
	19-point gap		
Radio	25%	25	
Print Newspapers	20%	18	

Source: *Pew Research Center*

What do the numbers show? From what media platform do Americans often obtain news the most? What portion of citizens often obtain news via the Internet? What percentage often read a printed newspaper?

Media and Political Participation

Various types of media coverage—reports of our three branches, breaking news, election coverage, and commentary—influence political participation and policy as they inform the public to make educated decisions and sometimes sway parts of the public to their way of thinking or problem solving.

Political Reporting

Government and its leaders have always been topics of interest to the press and the public, and much of the coverage of a topic in the press takes the form of **political reporting**, standard "just-the-facts" kinds of stories.

Using media is an efficient and free way for government officials to make announcements, to test the popularity of ideas (sometimes called "trial balloons"), or to assist in operating the government. Politicians try to interact with the press in a way that paints themselves and the government institutions they run in a positive light. The press's ability to influence public opinion has always kept government officials on their toes, and the sometimes adversarial relationship between journalists and government officials creates a rift between the two. Though candidates and officeholders cannot do without the press, an unfavorable headline can sometimes make or break an official's reputation. Today, an unfortunate snapshot or video clip suddenly available on YouTube can ruin a politician's career.

This dynamic has created a love-hate relationship between the government and the press. Candidates and officeholders will frequently contact reporters to offer up a news story about themselves, their platforms, or their new programs, which in reality may be nothing but a public-relations campaign. Depending on the day's events and how much news is happening, a reporter may be grateful for the easy story that will result in a "puff piece" highlighting the positive side of a politician on the front page. The same reporter, weeks later, might have to explain allegations of corruption made toward the same politician.

Reporters sometimes have their own agenda or bias, and how they present information in **sound bites**—short excerpts edited from a longer remark that are especially vivid in presenting an issue—can have drastically different effects on the public depending on how they are worded. A politician or his communications chief may deem a reporter as hostile and not return calls if the reporter seems to be painting the politician in a bad light. This tenuous and sometimes confusing relationship between government and media influences how the Fourth Estate covers the three branches of government.

The **Freedom of Information Act (FOIA),** signed into law in 1966, allows the public to gain access to nonclassified federal documents. This law has helped journalists uncover information that was otherwise not released. However, there are many exemptions to this act. The president, for example, can request that certain documents remain sealed for a number of years and can redact content.

Congress and Press Coverage The House of Representatives voted during the first Congress to open its doors to the public and the press. In the late 1800s, many reporters preferred to cover Congress instead of the White House. In the 1950s, Americans became familiar with Congress during Senator McCarthy's televised committee hearings and in the 1970s during the Watergate hearings.

Congressional stories include members' roles on committees and in the legislative process—these are typically technical story lines, not easily conveyed in short headlines or brief TV news segments. Yet those interested in lawmaking continue to monitor the legislature closely. Two traditional print outlets that cover Congress, *Roll Call* and *The Hill*, have gained national popularity with their websites. Large newspapers and most TV news services have at least one Capitol Hill correspondent. On the Sunday talk shows—such as *Meet the Press* and *Face the Nation*—hosts will commonly have a lawmaker from each party at the table to debate the issues.

In the late 1970s, the cable industry created **C-SPAN**—the Cable Satellite Public Affairs Network—a privately funded, nonprofit public service. Cable and satellite affiliates pay fees that in turn fund the network. C-SPAN began covering the House in 1979. The Senate decided to allow cameras into its chamber in 1986, which gave rise to C-SPAN 2. Congress owns and controls the cameras in the two chambers, but C-SPAN receives the feed and can broadcast House and Senate floor debates. When Congress is not holding debate in its respective chambers, the network covers committee hearings, seminars at university campuses and think tanks, public meetings, and political rallies.

Presidents and Press Coverage Significant media resources are assigned to cover the president. The press delves into the president's mind, relations with fellow policymakers, the first family, and interactions with other world leaders. Beyond the regular 100 or so top reporters who might cover the president in person daily, another 2,000 have White House press credentials. Some travel on *Air Force One* (the president's plane) or on the chartered press plane that follows it.

John F. Kennedy did the first live televised press conferences in the early 1960s. By President Richard Nixon's term (1969–1974), the dynamic between president and press had changed drastically. Nixon's paranoia, complicated by the release of the Pentagon Papers and the Watergate scandal, pitted him directly against the press. He had offending reporters' phones tapped, his vice president spoke publicly about "disloyal" reporters, his Department of Justice tried to subpoena reporters' notes, and a White House aide threatened antitrust lawsuits against TV networks if they did not let more conservatives on the air.

In recent times, a full-time White House press secretary has served the president. The press secretary holds regular **press conferences** in the James Brady Press Briefing Room (named for President Reagan's press secretary, who was shot in an assassination attempt against President Reagan in 1981). The White House controls these media events. TV networks and wire services get preferential seating, as do the other major outlets, such as the *New York Times* and the *Washington Post*. The more senior reporters are called on first, and the press secretary typically signals the close of the session by calling on the senior wire service reporter.

Presidents appear at a podium to field questions much less frequently than their press secretaries do, usually only a few times each year. In their first year, Presidents George W. Bush, Barack Obama, and Donald Trump held 19, 27, and 21 overall press conferences respectively.

Donald Trump's candidacy and his first year in office led to tense relationships with the press. While on the campaign trail, Trump encouraged crowds at his rallies to rough up reporters. From his inauguration onward he and his team have misled and battled with the press. The pattern started with a combative first press conference when Press Secretary Sean Spicer offered exaggerations of the actual crowd size at Trump's swearing-in ceremony but otherwise did not take questions from the reporters present at the press conference.

Media coverage of President Trump's initial year reflected some of the adversarial relationships between the president and the press by tending to include more stories on personality, character, and leadership than on policy. The Pew Research Center found that two-thirds of the coverage during his first year concentrated on the president's political skills, immigration, his appointees, U.S.-Russia relations, and health care. Another finding was the more sources a reporter quoted, the more negative the story. And about one in six stories on the president included a direct tweet from Trump's Twitter account.

Courts and Press Coverage The press covers crime, lawsuits, courtroom activity, and appeals court decisions. The Sixth Amendment requires that trials be public and thus makes regular press coverage possible. At the national level, major newspapers and television news typically assign a legal affairs correspondent to cover the Supreme Court and high-profile trials throughout the country. Viewers often see footage of a trial from the state level, especially one involving celebrities or a horrific crime. In the federal courts, however, cameras are generally not allowed. Instead, pastel drawings depicting courtroom people and events usually appear on screen during TV news coverage.

Attempts to bring cameras into the Supreme Court for increased understanding and transparency will likely fail. For every person who sees court coverage on C-SPAN gavel-to-gavel, the late Justice Antonin Scalia once warned, "10,000 will see 15-second take outs on the network news, which, I guarantee you, will be uncharacteristic of what the court does."

Political Commentary

Journalism in the late 20th century made distinctions between fact and opinion. In print newspapers, the front pages offered more of an Edward R. Murrow-style of objectivity, while subjective views were kept on the editorial or Op-Ed pages, where the organization's editorial board would publish **editorials**— the organization's opinion pieces—including endorsements of political candidates. Television newscasters and newsroom editors would occasionally go on the air and read their written **commentary** as the word "Commentary" appeared on the screen, meaning opinion and interpretation rather than "just-the-facts" reporting.

As more media outlets have appeared and as the political conversation has widened to include more extreme positions, at times the lines between objective and slanted presentations have blurred. Though the solid wall between newsrooms and editorial departments remains in the offices at some news outlets, in other places the wall between what is news and what is commentary is not strong or apparent.

Ideologically slanted websites and TV channels compete with and are often as powerful and present as those following traditional standards of journalism. Born-on-the-web ideological outlets and cable TV networks hire partisans, political strategists, and former Congress members and give them prominence on their web pages and in their studios. Many columns and blogs are not clearly labeled as "opinion," and thus the nondiscerning reader may not immediately realize the voice of an ideological extremist and may accept those views as if they were coming from the old-guard reporter dedicated to objectivity. CNN's *Anderson Cooper 360,* for example, often provides a panel of four commentators on each side of the political spectrum, competing not only to express their political goals but perhaps also for a more-permanent position with the network or a higher-paying offer from another channel. In other words, their statements are unlikely to be purely objective.

In a news environment of frequent commentary, observers have noticed two major trends. "One is a fixation on small concerns that have little or nothing to do with official actions of governments, such as whose statues should be displayed in public and what NFL players do during the national anthem," Josh Barro of *Business Insider* has pointed out, referring to controversies about the statues of confederate leaders in the South and the practice during the 2017 football season of some NFL players to kneel during the national anthem as a sign of protest. The other trend is how fixated these commentators are on concerns "so large and amorphous they cannot obviously be addressed by public policy."

Cable networks have employed more and more commentators, in part because of so many expanded outlets but mainly to draw audiences. The basic news can be presented in only so many unique ways, but commentators often have their own colorful personalities or backgrounds that serve to draw viewers looking for something different.

"Make politics boring again," says Noah Rothma, oddly enough in *Commentary* magazine. His bland solution might help Americans have a realistic understanding of governmental functions and would allow the press to neutralize politicians who incite controversies that exacerbate tensions. He admits, however, that his approach "would murder a lucrative industry that has turned societal divisiveness into a sport."

Political Analysis

A form of journalistic expression that explores and provides opinions on a topic in depth is called **political analysis**. This form offers explanations on topics, usually by experts, which help readers understand complex subjects. Political analysis is valuable as a way to educate news consumers on likely causes, effects, and implications of proposed legislation, court rulings, or budget proposals. Experts examine the topic from a variety of angles but do not include their own opinions on the subject.

For example, in 2014, there was discussion in the Senate about a constitutional amendment to limit campaign contributions that would have undone both *Citizens United v. FEC* (2010) (page 508) and *Buckley v. Valeo* (page 505). No one expected the amendment to come into being, but it provided an opportunity to reexamine the extremely complex issues intertwined in those cases. Mark Schmitt, Director of Political Reform at New America, a nonprofit, nonpartisan think tank, wrote an analysis for the *Washington Post* that explored what would happen if such an amendment were to be ratified ("A constitutional amendment wouldn't really limit the power of money in politics," May 29, 2014). He used his decades of policy experience to write his analysis. Pieces such as these provide important information and explanations for engaged citizens who want to take seriously the consequences of government actions.

New America is a think tank that "does not engage in research or educational activities directed or influenced in any way by financial supporters," according to its website, so its political analysis is likely objective. Other think tanks, however, have strong ideological bases, liberal and conservative, and analysis from such a think tank would be likely to have a biased perspective.

Election Coverage: Media as Scorekeeper

As you read in Chapter 10, public opinion polling becomes a major news item during elections, a situation that casts media in the role of **scorekeeper**. As scorekeepers, the media track political successes and failures. During campaign seasons, reporters update readers and viewers nonstop on the ups and downs of competing candidates. The result is **horse-race journalism**, in which reporters find new ways to discuss who is leading and who is falling behind. As a result, they tend to over-emphasize public opinion polls, mainly because these are the only data that tend to change day to day. Candidates' ideas, policies, or biographies remain fairly static, so once those are reported, they are no longer considered newsworthy. The scorekeeping continues after an election by examining an elected official's approval rating or by crediting or blaming the successes and failures of government proposals and programs.

Scorekeeping, especially before an election, can be criticized for many reasons. When the media devotes time and emphasis to polling, it is not sharing candidates' proposals or examining the intricacies of a bill. When it delves into approval ratings, it is not properly evaluating government delivery of services.

When numbers and statistics dominate the conversation and the analysis, the media sacrifice time that could be used to publicize ideas that could affect real change. This constant—often circular—style of reporting also causes media outlets to turn political events into popularity contests, rather than contests in which voters make decisions based on candidate qualifications and platforms.

Bandwagon Effect Constant reporting on poll numbers may also cause a **bandwagon effect**, or a phenomenon in which people do something only because other people are doing it. (See page 375.) If Candidate A is ahead in the polls, undecided voters may begin to favor Candidate A because others do. Citizens may also jump on the bandwagon because they trust the wisdom of the masses or because they simply accept an inevitability and want to vote for a winner. Citizens may even start to genuinely admire the person who they believe will likely win.

What Gets Covered: Media as Gatekeeper

Much more is happening in the world than can fit into a 30-minute broadcast of the evening news or even fit onto a single online news magazine. Most news outlets have an **editorial board**, a group of veteran journalists who guide the editorial philosophy of the organization.

The editorial boards of news media therefore act as a **gatekeeper** by determining what is newsworthy and therefore deciding what information the public will receive. Print and radio editorial boards fulfill the same function by setting their own news agenda. What the media decide to publish directly influences the issues people regard as important. From what they learn through the media, citizens will contact their member of Congress, write letters to the editor, and assemble in support of a cause.

For example, a 2017 news story that implicated powerful filmmaker Harvey Weinstein as a serial womanizer and sexual assault offender sparked a movement for women to speak out against sexual aggression and rape. Before, such accusations may have resulted in powerful people in the film industry scoffing at them or ending the accuser's movie career. The coverage of Weinstein and many more sexual victims of powerful men followed. As the media accurately portrayed these women as victims, the news spread quickly and encouraged additional victims (recent and old) to make similar accusations. With what became the #MeToo Movement, the press had directly or indirectly facilitated an organized effort to stop sexual aggression in the workplace. This effort was highlighted at the end of 2017 when a special U.S. Senate election pitted Alabama Republican Roy Moore against Democrat Doug Jones. As the election approached, several women alleged that Moore had propositioned them or had a relationship with them back when he was a prosecutor in his 30s and they were teenagers. In a usually reliable Republican state, Jones defeated Moore for the Senate seat. Had the accusations against Moore been in isolation or barely covered, it is hard to imagine those accusations having the same political impact, and it might have been difficult for Jones to win.

Digging for the Truth: Media as Watchdog

Journalists' obligations to keep an eye on government or industry is part of the press's function as a **watchdog**. Investigative reporters look for corruption, scandal, or inefficiency. In fact, Congress may not even decide to address an issue until after the press has brought it into the light of day. In the age of Teddy Roosevelt's muckrakers, *McClure's* magazine published a series entitled "Railroads on Trial" that ultimately led Congress to strengthen train regulations. More recently, the Pulitzer Prize for Investigative Journalism, the industry's top honor, was awarded to journalists who investigated the flood of opioids into West Virginia counties with the highest overdose rates in the nation; the responsibility of the state of Florida for violence and neglect toward mental patients in state hospitals; the influence of lobbyists on congressional leaders and state attorneys general to favor the rich; and a rigged system orchestrated by doctors and lawyers to deny benefits to coal miners with black lung disease. The investigative work on the coal miners led to changes in the law.

Investigative Reporting in Vietnam Several investigative journalism efforts have become iconic examples of the power of the press to bring about change. One involves reporting from Vietnam during the war (1955–1975). Unlike the patriotic press corps of both world wars and the Korean War, journalists stationed in Vietnam began to question information presented by the United States military and diplomats. Television images brought the war into citizens' living rooms, and journalists did not hold back on showing the tough realities of the war. Roughly 10 American journalists were assigned to Vietnam in 1960. By 1968, about 500 full-time correspondents representing print, television, and radio were in South Vietnam. "Government's interpretations of events did not coincide with what we learned on our own," said NBC Vietnam Bureau Chief Ron Steinman. "We listened, hoping to discover a kernel of truth in a fog of lies." The reporting from Vietnam helped inspire the mass protests against the war that eventually led to U.S. withdrawal. In early 1968, after a trip to Vietnam, CBS anchor Walter Cronkite—known as the "most trusted man in America"—closed the evening news with an opinionated report that had big consequences. "We have been too often disappointed by the optimism of American leaders, both in Vietnam and Washington, to have faith any longer in the silver linings they find in the darkest clouds." President Lyndon Johnson, commander in chief at the time, reportedly remarked that if he had lost Cronkite, he had also lost America.

The Watergate Scandal A few years after the conflict in Vietnam waned, President Nixon sought reelection. *Washington Post* reporters Bob Woodward and Carl Bernstein served as watchdogs by uncovering the Watergate burglary scandal. In 1972, while reporting on a burglary of the

Democratic National Committee office in the Watergate Hotel, Woodward and Bernstein eventually discovered that the burglars stole information in order to help Nixon's reelection campaign. These investigative reporters kept the story alive throughout a congressional investigation and the eventual resignation of the president.

Torture at Abu Ghraib When the U.S. Army discovered its soldiers were mistreating Iraqi prisoners at Abu Ghraib, a prison in Iraq, journalist Seymour Hersh reported the horrific abuses in *The New Yorker* magazine in 2004. The TV show *60 Minutes* aired the story with photographic evidence. The terrible abuses, which occurred halfway around the world, would never have reached the American public if not for the Fourth Estate's check on government. A number of military personnel were charged and sentenced, and, in 2008, the military instituted reforms in its Iraqi prisons.

Media Ownership and Bias

The increasingly diverse options presented by so many media outlets have altered how citizens rely on the media. The around-the-clock demand for information has created a fast-paced, competitive market of outlets. They constantly vie for readers, viewers, and consumers, becoming increasingly partisan in their efforts to do so. As a result, demand for more media content also encourages the growth of media outlets with a specific political agenda and a targeted audience—a concept known as **narrowcasting.**

The rapid surge of new media outlets has therefore altered the political landscape. The lifting of the **Fairness Doctrine**—a former federal policy that required radio and television broadcasters to present alternative viewpoints—has allowed broadcasters more leeway and freedoms in what they air. A generations-long reputation of the news media having a liberal bias has allowed for conservative alternatives to succeed. For example, Sinclair Broadcast Group, reaching 40 percent of American households, is known for its conservative slant. Cable television has given birth to a variety of unique outlets that have altered news delivery to specialized audiences. The Internet has also created seemingly endless choices. All of these changes have redefined the roles and relationships between media and citizens.

For example, conservative radio talk show host Rush Limbaugh emerged as a national conservative voice and gained a strong following in the early 1990s. One reason he succeeded was because he created a sense of community among people already inclined to agree with one another. By 2008, this pioneer of the new medium had as many as 20 million listeners. Over the same period, **talk radio**—those syndicated political shows that air at stations coast-to-coast—grew apace and became a common way for Republicans to get political news. Without the Fairness Doctrine, there was no need to provide other viewpoints to challenge the community's beliefs, which became self-reinforcing on both the right and left.

Media Ownership

In 1934, Congress passed the Federal Communications Act, which created the **Federal Communications Commission (FCC)**. The FCC regulates electronic media, and it has authority over the content of radio, television, wire, and satellite broadcasts. It also regulates ownership by attempting to prevent monopolies. In 1941, for example, the FCC forbade NBC from operating two networks. NBC sold one of its two networks, which led to the establishment of ABC. In the last years of the 20th century, the popularity of cable news exploded, the Internet became a viable news source, and the entire landscape of media ownership changed.

The Influence of Fox Though Ted Turner and CNN invented cable news in general, the **Fox News Channel (FNC)** drastically altered it when it started in 1996. As media critic David Folkenflick claims in his book *Murdoch's World*, "No other news organization has done more in recent years to reshape that terrain than Fox." The time was ripe for an alternative news channel. The Republicans had gained control of Congress. A longstanding conservative disdain for the media had reached its zenith. And an era of polarization had begun. Media mogul Rupert Murdoch hired Nixon ad man and longtime Republican media strategist Roger Ailes to launch the endeavor.

Ailes assembled a team of capable journalists, many who leaned to the right or desired the breathing space an alternative news channel might offer. And Ailes knew there were enough viewers in middle America who thirsted for that alternative. On its maiden broadcast, Fox host Bill O'Reilly asked, "How did television news become so predictable and in some cases so boring?" After emphasizing too many news channels had become "politically correct," he offered, "Well, we're going to try to be different, stimulating and a bit daring, but at the same time, responsible and fair." It was code for "we're not going to be the typical liberal TV news." Sharper graphics, more dramatic show introductions, noticeable red-white-and-blue patriotism, and a nightly lineup dominated by conservative hosts, conservative guests, and attractive reporters became the hallmarks of the Fox model.

The news at Fox is presented in ways, Folkenflick shows, "that reflect and further stoke a sense of grievance among cultural conservatives against coastal elites." Since its early days, the motto "Fair and Balanced" has suggested that the other networks are not and Fox is here to correct that. Another catchphrase, "We Report, You Decide," suggested that the others—the liberal media elite—are indoctrinating viewers.

The risk paid off. After September 11, 2001, and the initial years of the George W. Bush presidency, Fox took the number one slot as the most-watched of the cable TV news channels and it has never lost it. In fact, after the 2016 election year, Fox became the most-watched cable TV channel of any kind.

A 2014 study showed that Fox had edged the Big Three networks as the "most trusted" news overall, though not likely due to Fox's journalistic standards. When lining up several TV news outlets, right-leaning citizens from the sample consistently back Fox News, while moderates and liberals list as their top choice those from a variety of other not-conservative networks as the most trustworthy. Among self-described conservatives, Fox was trusted by 48 percent. Among self-described liberals, the Big Three led as most trusted, with CNN and PBS essentially tied for second.

Since America has such an ideologically diverse audience, producers, viewers, and TV journalists responded. As Fox News was born and developed, so too were other cable news networks. MSNBC was also established in 1996. Over time, it became the liberal alternative to Fox. However, the world of cable television is more fragmented than having a simple split between two networks. Channels as varied as ESPN and The History Channel have found ways to draw shares of viewers to them, seeking niche audiences to sell their product. CNBC is a 24-hour news channel that focuses on financial news. Large numbers of social conservatives tune into the Christian Broadcasting Network. Some networks, like Univision, have Hispanic audiences. Bloomberg News is yet another up-and-coming news channel that broadcasts much political news.

Impact of Ownership This market fragmentation has only encouraged network owners to find more potential viewers to turn to their channel. For those presenting political news while in search of profits—competing for viewers in order to attract advertisers—Fox, CNN, and MSNBC have each gone further away from objectivity and have revealed their bias. Studies show that 24-hour news channels actually show little substantive news, repeat sensational stories over and over all day often with nothing new to add, have reporters do more general talking about their story than traditional reporting on it, and the journalistic drive to answer the hard questions is spotty. The regular newscasters and anchors tend to ignite tempers, employ sarcasm, stoke fear, and conduct their presentations with a sense of moral righteousness. Sometimes their partisan guests deliver ad hominem attacks.

Politically savvy citizens in search of more than what the main networks offer turn to their choice of cable media, especially during election season. More Americans watch the evening Big Three in general, but during campaign season, more Americans say they turn to one or more cable channels for election coverage. In 2016, all news channels advanced in the ratings. Fox led all basic cable networks with an average of 2.5 million viewers during its prime-time lineup, up 36 percent from the previous year. CNN went up 77 percent to 1.3 million viewers and MSNBC increased at the same rate to 1.1 million.

As Pew Research Center confirms, "Those on the right and left have significantly different media diets." In a study done in late 2016, Pew found about 40 percent of Trump voters relied on Fox News as their "main source" for news. Clinton voters, on the other hand, listed CNN as their main source, but only 18 percent did so. MSNBC was second, and Fox didn't make it into their top ten.

Fox viewers include a high number of self-described conservatives, 60 percent. Meanwhile both CNN and MSNBC viewers claimed to be split with roughly one-third conservative, liberal, and moderate.

Media Bias

With the explosion of niche cable networks and online news sources, there is no longer any doubt as to whether bias in the media exists. Now, it is merely a question of where it exists and which way it leans. In fact, bias has become essential to the business model of several news outlets. Meanwhile, what is sometimes termed the **mainstream media**, or the collection of traditional news organizations, still operates an objective news model. Conservative critics have called the media liberal for nearly two generations, and researchers have found liberal tendencies in the media both in its membership and less obviously in its delivery. But to understand bias in the media, one has to ask, "Which media are you talking about?"

Traditional Bias Label The media have been accused of a liberal bias since the early 1970s, when the press hounded President Nixon. But that is a simplistic characterization that circumvents the real challenges of measuring bias. Today, with thousands of national reporters for every entity from Fox News to the *Huffington Post*, a sound method to determine the question of bias is challenging. One measurement is to examine the professionals who report the news. Overwhelmingly, national reporters who shape political coverage vote with the Democratic Party, and they have for some time. A 1972 poll showed that 70 percent of reporters voted for Nixon's opponent, George McGovern. A 1992 election study discovered that 89 percent of reporters voted for Bill Clinton, who received only 43 percent of the popular vote.

Studies that examine ideological slants also find that leading news outlets describe Republican and Democrat officials differently. David Brady and Jonathan Ma found that the *New York Times* and the *Washington Post* tend to treat liberal senators as cooperative bipartisans and malign conservative senators. Their study saw a distinct difference in favorable or unfavorable adjectives that preceded "liberal" or "conservative" in their reporting. These outlets too often painted liberal senators as bipartisan lawmakers and iconic leaders of a noble cause but portrayed conservatives as hostile, combative, and out of the mainstream.

In a study of 20 major print and TV news outlets, researchers found that only two leaned conservative, Fox News and *The Washington Times*, but the other 18 ranged from slightly to substantially left of center.

Contemporary Bias While professional journalists may still strive for objectivity, the increasing choices of media driven by writers and broadcasters of different ideological persuasions have in some cases made objectivity a minor concern at best. Slanted media predated the Internet, but now legacy outlets—*The New Republic*, *Slate*, and *Salon* on the left; *National Review* and *The Weekly Standard* on the right—mesh with other news sites, and readers may or may not discern source bias as they read their stories. Newer, born-on-the-web outlets, such as *Red State* or *Huffington Post*, are noticeably ideological. They and the nightly cable broadcasts provide diametrically opposite presentations and narratives of the same basic stories.

One Pew study at the end of the 2012 presidential election found President Obama received far more negative than positive coverage on Fox. About 46 percent of Fox stories on Obama were negative, while only 6 percent were positive (the remainder being neutral). The same study found MSNBC was harsher on Republican nominee Mitt Romney, where 71 percent of election stories were negative and only 3 percent were positive. Based on the viewership differences and where citizens are going to get their information online, people on the left and right have distinctly different information streams from those of people with mixed political beliefs.

Meanwhile, as "news sources" are playing fast and loose with journalistic norms, citizens are communicating more frequently via the Internet, and people are choosing more selectively what they read. People of like mind are supplying one another with a tailored diet of news and commentary that only confirms what they already believe. While the exercise of First Amendment rights allows people to read or not read what they want, the self-reinforcing and isolated loop of "news" is not helpful in developing consensus policy or in finding the best solutions for America's problems, nor is it helpful in understanding the alternative viewpoints.

Media and Democratic Debate

Scholar and political expert Cass Sunstein calls the phenomenon of people remaining in echo chambers of their own creation "cyberpolarization." He believes public life would be better served if people relied on what he calls "the general interest intermediary," streams of information from those traditional, objective outlets. Without these, the level of political knowledge of citizens is reduced, and the result is a decline in the quality of public debate. At least four factors affect the quality of public debate and level of political knowledge: increased media choices, ideologically oriented programming, consumer-driven media and technology, and the credibility of news sources.

Increased Media Choices

In 1960, the average American home received three television stations. By 2014, Nielsen Research estimated that the number had risen to nearly 200. Evening news telecasts on the Big Three networks changed very little from Presidents Kennedy to Clinton. Viewers could expect the time slots around the dinner hour and before bedtime to be reserved for news broadcasts. But

Media consumers have more choices than ever before as a result of producers appealing to niche markets. These often one-sided media outlets have also popped up in new media through podcasts, streaming content on YouTube, and social media outlets such as Twitter. The line between traditional journalistic content and uninformed citizen editorialization is often blurred.

the explosion of cable news channels and their wide variety of programming have given consumers many more choices for their time in front of the TV. While at one time viewers were regularly exposed to the news no matter what channel they tuned to, now they can choose to watch entertainment of a seemingly endless variety instead. Studies have shown that while some people use the increased amount of news broadcasting to try to deepen their understanding of politics, others simply tune out news and politics by choosing to watch entertainment. This situation creates a gap not only in political knowledge but also in political participation because people with greater political knowledge turn out to vote more than people with less political knowledge. Public debate is diminished by the uneven distribution of political knowledge as well.

Ideologically Oriented Programming

Fox News is by far the most-watched cable news channel, outpacing its more centrist or liberal competitors CNN and MSNBC by a significant margin. The ideologically oriented programming on cable news channels has made the outlets a subject of great interest to political scientists, who ask a number of questions about their influence on voters and public debate. How much influence do the ideologically oriented news programs actually have on viewers, especially if viewers are attracted to a channel because they already share that channel's ideology?

A 2017 study by Emory University political scientist Gregory Martin and Stanford economist Ali Yurukoglu found that Fox News has a sizable influence on viewers' political attitudes, which in turn influence how they vote. They estimate that if Fox News hadn't been on the scene, John Kerry would likely have won the 2004 presidential election instead of George W. Bush.

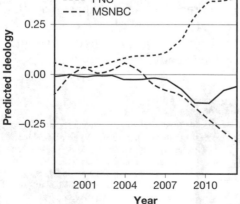

Researchers Martin and Yurukoglu studied the changes over time of the liberal or conservative slant of CNN, FNC, and MSNBC. Their study focused on the choice of phrases used in broadcasts that convey different connotations. For example, does the broadcaster refer to the "war in Iraq" or the "global war on terrorism"? The researchers studied transcripts of broadcasts from 1998 to 2012 and then analyzed the results using a system for interpreting similar statistics on speech by members of Congress, whose voting records show their political slant. The higher the score, the more conservative the slant.

Source: Adapted from Martin and Yurukoglu 2017

They also found that CNN tried to develop its political ideology to match it to the maximize number of viewers it could attract, while Fox took a different approach. The political views of Fox are more conservative than those of their viewers, but Fox has had the effect of shifting their viewers' attitudes to the right. Fox is more successful at persuasion than the other cable news outlets and in this way is a major political agent.

As people are drawn to ideologically oriented programming, they demonstrate **confirmation bias,** the tendency to seek out and interpret information in a way that confirms what they already believe. They have no incentive, then, to consider opposing views, and yet the clash of ideas is vital for democratic debate and the democratic process. Sunstein writes, "Unplanned, unanticipated encounters [of ideas] are central to democracy itself. Such encounters often involve topics and points of view that people have not sought out and perhaps find quite irritating—but that might nevertheless change their lives in fundamental ways."

Consumer-Driven Media and Technology

Confirmation bias is evident on social media as well, where more than 60 percent of Americans get news. On Facebook, for example, people exchange political links and memes in a circle of like-minded friends, in the process reinforcing their own and other group members' beliefs and even accepting as true statements that have been proven false as long as they fit in with their beliefs.

While people are creating their own "bubbles" for information sharing, usually without critical evaluation, professionally trained journalists are being laid off and printing presses are shutting down. Reliable, ethical news outlets are disappearing. Cities that once had multiple newspapers that kept one another in check as they competed to provide the best news possible may now have only one paper.

Information outlets—newspapers, television stations, and radio stations—have always had to make decisions about what issues to cover, exercising their gatekeeper function. They considered what issues they believed would be most important to their consumers and assigned their resources to cover those issues accordingly. They always had to attract readers or go out of business. In today's highly competitive media environment, however, consumer-driven media has entered a new dimension. **Consumer-driven media** refers to media whose content is influenced by the actions and needs of consumers.

While at one time experienced professionals with a commitment to ethical journalism decided what to cover based on their best understanding of their consumers' interests and concerns, today such decisions are strongly influenced by the data that technology provides—what stories do people click on and read the most?

Now news companies and tech companies figure out what the average consumer will click on and generate stories from there. In other words, the role of gatekeeper has been passed on from experienced journalists to average online surfers. Responsible news outlets still try to balance the forces of genuine newsworthiness and popular interests. But in the competitive media world, too often the citizen-gatekeepers, perhaps more interested in the Kardashians than foreign policy, have become the gatekeepers. When more trivial topics are covered at the expense of serious issues, the level of political knowledge and public debate declines.

Continuously monitored ratings provide similar data for television news stations, which now have to compete with not only other news stations but also a wide array of other programming—including on-demand services such as Netflix and Amazon Prime Video. Some analysts believe the hunger for ratings contributed to Donald Trump's rise to the Republican presidential nomination among a field of experienced politicians. As journalist and Fox contributor Michael Goodwin explains, at first the media treated Donald Trump's candidacy as a publicity stunt, until "television executives quickly made a surprising discovery; the more they put Trump on the air, the higher their ratings climbed." Cable news shows started devoting hours to simply pointing the cameras at Trump as he gave off-the-cuff speeches at his rallies. By one estimate, Goodwin notes, Trump received so much free airtime that if it had been purchased, it would have cost $2 billion.

Managers of legacy news organizations are changing their business model and operating differently to survive. "Dependence generates desperation," laments Franklin Foer, former editor at the *New Republic*. "A mad, shameless chase to gain clicks through Facebook, a relentless effort to game Google's algorithms," has altered the role of one of progressive journalism's century-old magazines. When Google changes an algorithm—such as the rules by which autocomplete fills in possibilities after a user enters a few words to start, or the rules determining the order in which search results appear—web traffic can change significantly, benefiting some media companies and hurting others. In this way, tech companies can influence the ethics and ethos of an entire profession.

Credibility of News Sources

While Americans have more media choices and more control over what information to seek, consumers are simultaneously sent information from people with an agenda: friends and family who are of like mind, media sources with the goal of gaining more clicks, American political groups trying to impact public opinion, or American adversaries trying to stoke the flames of discord or to influence an election. The result is an era of dubious credibility and impulsive clicks.

Pew discovered when citizens access political news digitally, most often (46 percent of the time) they go to a news organization's website. Social media is the second most frequently used source, 31 percent of the time; 20 percent go through a search engine such as Google; and 24 percent seek out news links after receiving email alerts from a news organization or friend. Those who willingly go to a reliable news organization are more likely to get credible information.

Consumers are not always as responsible in their consumption of news as an informed and engaged citizenry would require. For example, this same Pew study found that citizens who received an article via social media could recall and name the original news outlet only 56 percent of the time. Another finding was that fully 10 percent cited "Facebook" as the news outlet, when of course Facebook is not a news outlet at all.

If indeed this is an era of consumer-driven media, then consumers demanding credibility and objectivity would have influence in the content news outlets provide. Author Clay Johnson in *The Information Diet* compares consumers' intake of news to their consumption of food and argues that the problem is not that people consume too much information but rather that they take in too much "junk" information. Just as people have to consciously make choices about healthy eating, they need to make responsible choices about news consumption. He advocates for education in media literacy so people can develop the critical evaluation skills needed to make informed choices about information.

 THINK AS A POLITICAL SCIENTIST: *EVALUATE SOURCES*

Political scientists carefully consider the source of all the information they acquire. The following checklists will guide you as you evaluate your information sources and distinguish genuine from "fake" news.

Checklist for Evaluating Books

- ✓ What is the publication date? Is the book likely to include up-to-date information?
- ✓ What are the author's credentials? Read the book jacket, online catalog entries, or a biographical reference work to get information about the author.
- ✓ Is the author a recognized expert? See if other people frequently cite this author.
- ✓ Is there anything in the author's background or associations that might suggest a biased viewpoint?
- ✓ Who is the publisher? Major publishers, including university presses and government agencies, review what they publish and are likely to be reputable sources.

Checklist for Evaluating Print Articles

- ✓ When was the article published? Is the article likely to include up-to-date information?
- ✓ Who is the author? What are his or her credentials? You can find these in a note at the beginning or end of the article.

✓ Does the magazine or newspaper appeal to a special interest group that may have a biased viewpoint on the subject? For example, a magazine called *Free Enterprise* would probably have a conservative leaning and appeal to free market advocates who want only minimal government in people's economic lives. A periodical called *Equal Justice*, on the other hand, might appeal to liberals who expect the government to intervene when needed to guarantee equality.

Checklist for Evaluating Websites

✓ If you receive a link through social media, consider the views of the person or organization that sent it. What bias might that sender have?

✓ When you follow the link, start by identifying the top-level domain name. Is the site maintained by a for-profit company (.com) that might be trying to sell something? Is it an educational institution (.edu), which tends to be more reliable, or an independent organization (.org)? If it is an organization, is it one whose name you recognize or is it one that you have never heard of before? Be aware that ".org" sites are often owned by nonprofit organizations that may support a particular cause.

✓ If the website contains an article, is it signed? If it is not signed, you should be skeptical of its credibility. If you do not recognize the author's name, you can do a web search using the author's name as the keyword to get more information.

✓ Does it use reasonable and sufficient facts and examples from reliable sources to make its points?

✓ Is it free from obvious errors?

✓ Do the language and graphics avoid sensationalism?

✓ Has the site been recently updated? Is the information still current? Look for a date on the main web page indicating the last time it was updated.

Whether you are evaluating print or online sources, you will need to verify information by finding corroboration in a number of sources. Some errors may be obvious, but unless you check the facts and find an agreement about them among sources, you might miss some bias, misinformation, and outright untruths.

Practice: Choose several links you have received through one or more of your social media accounts and evaluate the information in the link by using the checklist for evaluating websites. Write your comments to each point on the checklist and share your comments with the class as your teacher directs.

REFLECT ON THE ESSENTIAL QUESTION

Essential Question: *How do changes in the media as a linkage institution influence political institutions and behavior?* On separate paper, complete a chart like the one below to gather details to answer that question.

Changes in the Media	Influence of the Media

KEY TERMS AND NAMES

affiliates/560

Associated Press (AP)/558

bandwagon effect/569

Big Three networks/560

broadcast network/560

Cable News Network (CNN)/561

commentary/567

confirmation bias/577

consumer-driven media/577

C-SPAN/565

editorial boards/569

editorials/566

Fairness Doctrine/571

Federal Communications Commission (FCC)/572

Fox News Channel (FNC)/572

Freedom of Information Act (FOIA)/564

free press/557

gatekeeper/569

Government Printing Office (GPO)/558

horse-race journalism/568

investigative reporting/559

mainstream media/574

narrowcasting/571

news bureaus/558

political analysis/568

political reporting/564

press conferences/565

scorekeeper/568

sound bites/564

talk radio/571

watchdog/570

Questions 1 and 2 refer to the passage below.

> Shortly after Richard Nixon resigned the presidency, Bob and I were asked a long question [which] we answered with a short phrase that we've used many times since to describe our reporting on Watergate and its purpose and methodology. We called it the "best obtainable version of the truth." It's a simple concept for something very difficult to get right because of the enormous amount of effort, thinking, persistence, pushback, removal of ideological baggage and the sheer luck that is required, not to mention some unnatural humility. Underlying everything reporters do in pursuit of the best obtainable version of the truth, whatever our beat or assignment, is the question "what is news?" What is it that we believe is important, relevant, hidden, perhaps, or even in plain sight and ignored by conventional journalistic wisdom or governmental wisdom?
>
> I'd say this question of "what is news" becomes even more relevant and essential if we are covering the president of the United States. Richard Nixon tried to make the conduct of the press the issue in Watergate, instead of the conduct of the president and his men. We tried to avoid the noise and let the reporting speak.
>
> —Reporter Carl Bernstein, White House Correspondents Dinner, 2017

1. Which of the following statements best summarizes Bernstein's views?

   (A) Journalists' egos often get in the way of determining what stories to cover.

   (B) For a variety of reasons, most journalism is unfortunately shallow.

   (C) Reporters use professional judgment about what to cover as they filter out a variety of distractions and follow the facts.

   (D) Partisan spokespeople color the facts and are not reliable sources of information.

2. Which of the following reasons likely explains why Bernstein thinks the question of "what is news" is especially important when covering the president?

(A) The question of "what is news" is easier to determine when covering Congress than the president.

(B) The president can get a strong message out to the public asserting his interpretation of events.

(C) The Freedom of Information Act provides access to virtually unlimited presidential documents.

(D) News reports about the president help increase a newspaper's circulation.

3. During political campaigns before an election, the news media is said to cover the campaigns like a horse race. Which of the following statements best explains the reason for this analogy?

(A) The press relies heavily on measurements like poll numbers as a constant comparison of candidates' relative success in a campaign.

(B) The results of an election, like the results of a horse race, can't be predicted until the very end.

(C) The candidates are groomed and trained for the campaign just as racehorses are groomed and trained for a race.

(D) As gatekeepers, members of the press officially begin the horse race.

4. Which of the following is an accurate comparison of objective news and commentary?

	Objective News	Commentary
(A)	Factual accounts of events and people	Opinions of experts or people with political goals
(B)	Includes endorsements as long as they are on the editorial pages	Less common today than in the past and found in fewer places
(C)	Delivered by the guests on a talk show	Avoids criticizing government or government officials
(D)	A hallmark of talk radio after the removal of the Fairness Doctrine	Usually found on the front pages of traditional newspapers

Pathways to Online News

Twice a day for one week, online news consumers were asked **if they got news in the past two hours.**

When they did, average % of the times they got it through...

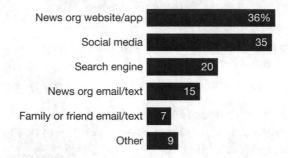

News org website/app — 36%
Social media — 35
Search engine — 20
News org email/text — 15
Family or friend email/text — 7
Other — 9

Note: Respondents were asked about the news they got on their main topic in each instance. Numbers add to more than 100% because respondents could report using more than one pathway in each survey.

"How Americans Encounter, Recall and Act Upon Digital News," Survey conducted Feb. 24-March 1, 2016

Source: *Pew Research Center*

5. Which accurately describes the information presented in the above chart?

(A) People obtain news online mostly through social media or a news organization's website.

(B) More Americans are getting news through social media than via television.

(C) Most Americans use Google, Bing, or other search engines to find relevant news stories.

(D) Texts from family and friends are what most often lead people to online news.

6. Which of the following is a reasonable conclusion based on the data in the graph?

(A) Americans prefer watching video to reading text for their news.

(B) News outlets face stiff competition for consumers.

(C) Email will soon be the main way news outlets deliver news.

(D) Search engines provide an unbiased index to the news.

7. Which of the following is a legitimate limitation to the information presented in the graph?

   (A) The graph does not consider Twitter or Snapchat.

   (B) The graph does not distinguish between email, text, and alerts.

   (C) The graph fails to consider how often people get their news from word of mouth.

   (D) The graph does not distinguish consumption of online news versus print media.

Main Sources of News for Voters in 2016 Presidential Election

% of voters who named__as their "main source" for news about the 2016 campaign

ALL VOTERS		TRUMP VOTERS		CLINTON VOTERS	
Fox News*	19%	Fox News*	40%	CNN*	19%
CNN*	13	CNN	8	MSNBC	9
Facebook	8	Facebook	7	Facebook	8
Local TV	7	NBC	6	Local TV	8
NBC	5	Local TV	5	NPR	7
MSNBC	5	ABC	3	ABC	6
ABC	5	CBS	3	New York Times	5
NPR	4	Local radio	3	CBS	5
CBS	4			NBC	4
New York Times	3			Local newspapers	4
Local newspapers	3			Fox News	3

*Among this group of voters, this source was named at significantly higher rates than the source below it. Significance of any other relationships provided upon request.
Note: Sources shown are only those that were named by at least 3% of each group. Results are based on responses to open-ended questions; respondents could write in any source they chose.
Source: Pew Research Center survey conducted Nov. 29-Dec. 12, 2016.
"Trump, Clinton Voters Divided in Their Main Source for Election News"

8. Which statement accurately reflects the information presented in the above illustration?

   (A) More Clinton voters watched CNN than any other outlet for their election news.

   (B) Trump voters tended to watch a wider variety of news outlets than Clinton voters.

   (C) One of the Big Three led in viewership/audience when voters were asked what they watched for election news.

   (D) For election news viewing, CNN ranked highest in all three categories.

9. What conclusion can you draw from the data in the information graphic?

   (A) Fox News built its viewership on its reputation for credibility.

   (B) Fox News targets conservatives as their niche audience.

   (C) Trump voters tend to rely more on print journalism than television.

   (D) Social media plays a very small role in getting election news.

10. What is one effect of consumer-driven media?

(A) It replaces content from professionals with content from nonexperts.

(B) It increases the quality of public debate by engaging so many people.

(C) It helps establish the importance of fact and research before sharing stories.

(D) It overcomes ideological divides and brings people together.

FREE-RESPONSE QUESTIONS

1. "For it seems now more certain than ever that the bloody experience of Vietnam is to end in a stalemate . . . To say that we are mired in stalemate seems the only realistic, yet unsatisfactory, conclusion. On the off chance that military and political analysts are right, in the next few months we must test the enemy's intentions, in case this is indeed his last big gasp before negotiations. But it is increasingly clear to this reporter that the only rational way out then will be to negotiate, not as victors, but as an honorable people who lived up to their pledge to defend democracy, and did the best they could."

—Anchorman Walter Cronkite, CBS News Broadcast, 1968

After reading the scenario, respond to A, B, and C below:

(A) Describe the nature of the reporting in the passage above.

(B) In the context of the passage, explain how the nature of reporting in part A affects elected officials.

(C) In the context of the passage, explain how the media serves as a linkage institution.

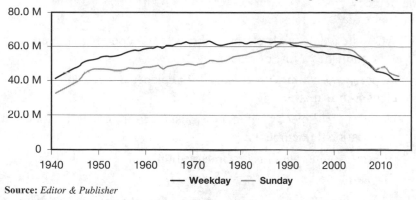

Total Estimated Circulation for U.S. Daily Newspapers

80.0 M

60.0 M

40.0 M

20.0 M

0

1940   1950   1960   1970   1980   1990   2000   2010

— Weekday — Sunday

Source: *Editor & Publisher*

2. Use the information graphic to answer the questions.

   (A) Identify a decade during which both weekday and Sunday circulation declined.

   (B) Describe a difference in the trend between weekday and Sunday circulation, and draw a conclusion about that difference.

   (C) Explain how newspaper circulation as shown in the graphic demonstrates the changing media landscape.

3. Jay Near was the publisher of a newspaper in Minneapolis in the late 1920s called *The Saturday Press*. In it he accused public officials of corruption in sensational exposes and took an anti-Catholic, anti-Semitic, and anti-labor posture. A 1925 Minnesota state law known as the Public Nuisance Law or Minnesota Gag Law banned future publication of *The Saturday Press* on the grounds that its bigoted attitudes constituted a public nuisance. Near sued, arguing that the rights to a free press were violated. A state court upheld the ban, but the newly formed American Civil Liberties Union became interested in the case and it came before the Supreme Court in 1931 as *Near v. Minnesota*. In a 5:4 vote, the Court ruled that the state law preventing publication in advance was unconstitutional even if what was going to be published was untrue.

   (A) Identify the principle that is common to both *Near v. Minnesota* (1931) and *New York Times Co. v. United States* (1971). (See page 250.)

   (B) Based on the principle identified in part A, explain a difference between the facts of *Near v. Minnesota* and those in *New York Times Co. v. United States* (1971).

   (C) Describe an action that a person or organization could take after publication of a controversial, libelous, or offensive article.

4. Develop an argument that explains whether a free press is essential to democracy.

In your essay, you must:

- Articulate a defensible claim or thesis that responds to the prompt and establishes a line of reasoning.
- Support your claim with at least TWO pieces of accurate and relevant information:
  - At least ONE piece of evidence must be from one of the following foundational documents:
    - First Amendment of the Constitution
    - *Brutus No. 1*
  - Use a second piece of evidence from the other document from the list above or your study of the media
- Use reasoning to explain why your evidence supports your claim/thesis.
- Respond to an opposing or alternative perspective using refutation, concession, or rebuttal.

WRITING: *PLAN AND REVISE*

Take time before digging into your writing to gather your thoughts. What position are you taking? What evidence will you use to support that position? What are alternate positions? How will you respond to them? A graphic like the one below might help you prepare to write.

My position	
Evidence (include at least two pieces)	
Alternate positions	
Rebuttals	

Leave time to revise your essay after you complete a first draft. Check it over to make sure you have addressed each required task. Also check your organization and transitions. Does your essay flow smoothly? Read it over from the beginning with fresh eyes and try to make your ideas as clear as possible.

UNIT 5: Review

The chapters in Unit 5 have explored how political parties, interest groups, campaigns and elections, and the media are conduits to voters and democracy. If it weren't for parties, elections, interest groups, and the press, many American voices would never be heard, and fewer citizens would understand government. Political parties, very broad coalitions, choose candidates and try to place them into office. Countless people also have more narrowly tailored interests, and they coalesce to create interest groups. These groups represent everyone from police officers to Wall Street financiers. Many form Political Action Committees (PACs) and develop relationships with lawmakers. The pluralist theory holds that many interests are better than few and that they create opposing political forces and operate as a check and balance outside the Constitution. Because there is so much interest in who will govern and that winning elections takes so much money and public effort, the government has passed laws to properly and fairly administer elections. Most notably, the Congress created the Federal Election Commission to monitor campaign finance limits.

The media report on government, help set a national agenda, and often give their opinions. They have gone from party-financed printed publications to a fast-paced, interactive platform. Select language or images can heavily enhance or ruin candidates or stop a policy idea. Since the Supreme Court has ruled that government has no right to prior restraint, the freedom of the media to express a wide range of ideas is guaranteed.

THINK AS A POLITICAL SCIENTIST: *RESEARCH THE ROLE OF THE PRESS*

Political scientists, like journalists, ask and try to answer questions when doing research. In this chapter, for example, you read about the role of the press in the U.S. political system. What are some questions you might ask to create meaty question worthy of further research?

Practice: Look up the following articles: "GOP Security Aide Among Five Arrested in Bugging Affair," Bob Woodward and Carl Bernstein (*Washington Post*, June 19, 1972) and "Donald Trump for President" (*Las Vegas Review-Journal*, November 7, 2017). Look at the headlines and dates, and consider the overall editorial slant of each of the publications. Determine the purpose of each article. Look for patterns that link and separate the two articles. Then write down a succinct theory about what they indicate about the role of the press in U.S. politics. Also identify two more questions for additional research.

Review Learning Objectives

As you review Unit Five, be sure you can complete the following learning objectives. Page numbers are provided to help you locate the necessary information to fulfill the learning objective.

UNIT FIVE LEARNING OBJECTIVES	
MPA-3.A: Describe the voting rights protections in the Constitution and in legislation.	Pages 426–431
MPA-3.B: Describe different models of voting behavior.	Pages 438–440
MPA-3.C: Explain the roles that individual choice and state laws play in voter turnout in elections.	Pages 431–432, 443–444
PMI-5.A: Describe linkage institutions.	Page 424
PMI-5.B: Explain the function and impact of political parties on the electorate and government.	Pages 452–462
PMI-5.C: Explain why and how political parties change and adapt.	Pages 462–473
PMI-5.D: Explain how structural barriers impact third-party and independent candidate success.	Pages 473–477
PMI-5.E: Explain the benefits and potential problems of interest-group influence on elections and policy making.	Pages 519–528
PMI-5.F: Explain how variation in types and resources of interest groups affects their ability to influence elections and policy making.	Page 528
PMI-5.G: Explain how various political actors influence public policy outcomes.	Pages 535–545
PRD-2.A: Explain how the different processes work in a U.S. presidential election.	Pages 488–495
PRD-2.B: Explain how the Electoral College impacts democratic participation.	Pages 494–495
PRD-2.C: Explain how the different processes work in U.S. congressional elections.	Pages 499–501
PRD-2.D: Explain how campaign organizations and strategies affect the election process.	Pages 501–503
PRD-2.E: Explain how the organization, finance, and strategies of national political campaigns affect the election process.	Pages 503–511
PRD-3.A: Explain the media's role as a linkage institution.	Pages 557–563
PRD-3.B: Explain how increasingly diverse choices of media and communication outlets influence political institutions and behavior.	Pages 571–581

Review the following Supreme Court case and political science disciplinary practices and reasoning processes.

UNIT FIVE SUPREME COURT CASE	
Citizens United v. Federal Election Commission (2010)—determined that political spending by corporations, associations, and labor unions is a form of protected speech under the First Amendment	Pages 508–510

UNIT FIVE POLITICAL SCIENCE DISCIPLINARY PRACTICES AND REASONING PROCESSES	
Develop and Support an Argument to an Elected Official	Page 445
Explain Causation and Change Over Time in America's Two-Party System	Page 478
Analyze, Interpret, and Apply Supreme Court decisions *Citizens United v. Federal Election Commission* (2010)	Page 510
Determine Relationships, Patterns, or Trends	Page 549
Evaluate Sources	Page 579

UNIT FIVE CONTEMPORARY ISSUES AND POLICY	
Policy Matters: The Influence of Competing Actors on the Budget Process	Pages 542–544

UNIT FIVE WRITING	
Conclude with Strength	Page 451
Use Transitions for Coherence	Page 485
Use Concise Language	Page 518
Establish a Line of Reasoning	Page 556
Plan and Revise	Page 588

Think Tank:
Making a Civic Connection

Think tanks are organizations devoted to researching social, political, economic, and technological policies and their application. (See page 529.) Here, in association with your civics project, the term takes on a different meaning: it's a way in which you use critical thinking, disciplinary practices and reasoning processes, deliberative skills, and civic virtues to engage in a real-world application of the principles of government and politics you have learned or are learning in the course. You have been developing **critical thinking, disciplinary practices,** and **reasoning processes** throughout this course as you have analyzed and interpreted foundational documents and Supreme Court cases, completed the Think as a Political Scientist activities, and answered the questions at the end of each chapter. **Deliberative skills** are strategies for resolving issues amidst differences of opinion or ideology, as the framers did when they hashed out their differences to compromise on the details of the Constitution. Public officials use deliberative skills to engage with those who disagree with them to find solutions that work for everyone. **Civic virtues** are those practices of relating to others, even those you disagree with, with respect, honesty, cooperation, and openness to diversity. Together, these elements of an engaged, informed citizen make you and those you work with a Think Tank for social understanding and progress.

The Advanced Placement Government and Politics course calls for students to engage in a political science research or applied civics project. The project must connect with the course framework and must culminate with your presentation of findings. Think broadly as you consider topics and project ideas, and think openly as you begin to consider your presentation format. Projects can range from an explanation of how local city government works presented in multimedia format to a competent and persuasive letter-to-the-editor seeking to alter public policy on an issue of importance to you or your community.

Local educators and school officials will govern which project types and subjects are acceptable. Your AP Government teacher will guide the research and presentation process. He or she will also determine the scope and timing based on your interests, available resources and transportation, and the community's political climate. Your teacher will assist you in choosing topics and will give you feedback so you can refine them. Projects can be group-based or individual, also determined by your teacher, but in either case, they should involve or end with a formal presentation to an actual audience.

Any projects that satisfy this course will encourage your engagement in a sustained, real-world activity that deepens understanding of course content and helps you apply the disciplinary practices tested on the national exam. A good project will apply course concepts to actual political issues, institutions, people, procedures, interactions, and/or policymaking. The key is choosing an appropriate issue or inquiry. What question or questions are you ultimately asking? Whether researching and writing a traditional research paper or scripting and cutting a digital documentary, what question are you trying to answer? Like a political scientist, you might answer a conceptual question, or like a citizen activist, you might shine light on a specific issue, work on persuading others, or even institute or change a policy.

The project must:

- Connect course concepts to real-world issues

- Demonstrate disciplinary practices

- Present or communicate findings in an authentic way

Think Local

The College Board has included a Project Guide in the Course and Exam Description available on the College Board website (see pages 67–72 of that document for project ideas). The guide encourages students to submerge themselves into real-world observance of and interaction with government. This activity could be as simple as becoming involved in a local municipal government meeting or interviewing local public officials. Find the local governments in your community. Visit your local county or city government websites, and determine what responsibilities each entity covers, what services it provides. What actions, plans, or concerns do they have? How do they spend taxpayer money? Attend one or more meetings and interview officials involved.

In addition to local, county, and state governments, organized nonprofit agencies interact with government regularly. Linkage institutions such as public sector labor unions (police, firefighters, teachers, and other public employees unions, for example) are somewhat accessible and would assist your understanding of their role. National and local interest groups concerned about the environment, civil rights, and taxpayer burdens have local chapters that regularly interact with government. Television reporters and community newspaper journalists engage with government and policy daily. Interacting with these professionals would enhance your understanding of the media.

Connect and engage with local real-world experts. For example, if looking into the 2016 presidential election or any other election, think about interviewing a local elections official, party chair, field staffer, or precinct captain living around the corner to get an authoritative, real-world perspective. If your government-based or political topic involves events or people from the past, connect with a local historian or visit the local history section of your library for ideas and information.

Activities and Sources for Thinking Local

- Attend meeting(s)

- Conduct interview(s)

- Contact your city council members, county commissioner, or state representative

- Collect and study local news articles, video clips, and radio segments/podcasts

- Examine local government publications online and at your public library

- Read the minute books from a local governing body

Think National

Though you may live far from Washington, D.C., the institutions of national government have never been more accessible. You can monitor your elected members of Congress and examine their voting records. You can listen to audio of the Supreme Court's oral arguments days after they occur. The National Archives, the Library of Congress, the executive departments and agencies all have an abundance of information, documents, and ways to connect via their websites. National research organizations and think tanks offer documents, data, and secondary sources online at no charge. Events from hours ago are archived online, whether in a summary of a White House press briefing at the *Washington Post*'s site or full-length videos of committee hearings at C-SPAN's video library. Additionally, though the federal government is headquartered in the nation's capital, government buildings and operations exist throughout the country and beyond. Within miles, you can likely find a federal agency building, U.S. courthouse, or military base.

National politics is worthy of deeper analysis to understand and connect with the course content and concepts. American presidential elections are well documented with differing dynamics, accompanied with available primary sources. Think of political personalities—Speakers of the House, Supreme Court justices, and White House chiefs of staff who have been involved in the policymaking arena. A thorough look into their experiences and interactions with other branches and the public to craft policy would facilitate your practice with the skills and reasoning of this course. On a national scale, a thorough look into the passage of landmark legislation, a pivotal presidential decision, or a Supreme Court ruling could be interesting and engaging.

Activities and Sources for Thinking National
- Interview an officer of the federal courts or a federal employee
- Research a database of national newspapers
- Contact your member(s) of Congress, an executive agency, or federal court
- Examine the *Congressional Record*, presidential speeches/briefings, and Court rulings
- Attend a portion of a trial or public agency hearing
- Study reports from reliable think tanks
- Read books and other secondary sources from public libraries
- Explore the National Archives website
- Visit presidential libraries' websites

Think Numbers

Collecting and analyzing data is essential in the study of political science. Think about election data, budget expenditures, census data, polling and survey results, roll call votes in Congress or at the local city council, and other quantifiable measures that could help you answer your question(s). If numbers are your chief source, be sure to round out your statistical findings with other narrative information to understand your findings and to give your presentation context.

Statistics and reports with measurements rely on a technical language that goes with explaining stats. Assertions and qualifications, precise language, and apples-to-apples comparisons are necessary when dealing with stats whether you are writing a paper, creating a slide presentation, or narrating a digital broadcast. So when you present an analysis of figures, use proper language to explain your findings.

- Conduct an original survey/measure public opinion on a topic or issue
- Examine polling data from Gallup, Pew Research Center, or other organizations
- Obtain and review local reports, surveys, and budgets
- Collect and compare statistics from government agencies (Census Bureau, FEC, OMB, for example)
- Explore election data and methods of statisticians at such organizations as fivethirtyeight.com

Think Presentation

As you develop your project, consider potential project presentation formats. You will share your findings with others, either classmates, a governing body, or other citizens, so plan for a real-world or at least authentic audience and consider their needs. Some findings and presentation pieces will be of a statistical nature, so creating your own charts and graphs to express something may be necessary. If you are trying to generate a discussion in the process, perhaps an interactive blog would be useful. Sometimes a comprehensive and well-developed white paper or letter to the editor, though maybe not as colorful or tech-centered, might make more sense for your topic and purposes.

Ideas for Thinking Presentation
- In-person presentation with oral, visual, and Q & A component
- An informative or persuasive documented website
- A published op-ed, letter to the editor, or article for publication
- A display for a political science fair
- A regular, interactive blog for a defined period
- A detailed, supported letter to a government official
- An analysis of media coverage with embedded video or audio clips
- Interview(s) of public official(s)
- A documentary film
- A report on a public action as part of a community organizing effort
- Research paper or portfolio on an issue
- An ad campaign/series of advertisements

Practice Exam

SECTION 1: MULTIPLE-CHOICE

1. Which element of the Electoral College system causes some people's votes to be discounted?

   (A) Variation in electoral votes per state

   (B) Winner-take-all system

   (C) The closed primary

   (D) The Australian ballot

2. Which of the following is an accurate comparison of the Articles of Confederation and the U.S. Constitution?

	ARTICLES OF CONFEDERATION	CONSTITUTION
(A)	Supported by arguments made in *The Federalist*	Takes reserved powers from the state governments
(B)	Declared and listed reasons for a political break from Great Britain	Included a bill of rights in its original form
(C)	Created a loose union of states, each receiving one vote in Congress	Proposed in 1787, sets up a framework for national government
(D)	Allowed the United States to raise national troops and fund a war	Was ratified by the 13 states within the first year it was issued

3. Two citizens are arguing over the role and influence of the many organized interest groups that try to impact public policy. The first citizen suggests that interest groups should be banned from engaging Congress members and other policymakers. The second suggests that since there are so many groups looking to impact policy from so many different perspectives, these competing groups will bring about only policies acceptable to a consensus of the citizenry. The second citizen believes in which type of political theory?

   (A) Elitist theory

   (B) Direct democracy theory

   (C) Politico theory

   (D) Pluralist theory

Questions 4 and 5 refer to the map below.

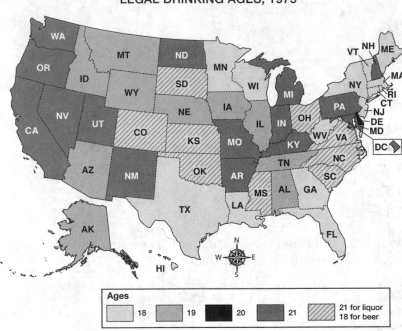

LEGAL DRINKING AGES, 1975

Ages: 18 | 19 | 20 | 21 | 21 for liquor 18 for beer

Source: *U.S. Department of Transportation*

4. Which of the following accurately describes the information in the map?

   (A) States with a legal drinking age of 18 were clustered together in one region.

   (B) Most states in the Northeast were among those with the lowest drinking age.

   (C) Federal laws on drinking and driving caused the differences displayed in the map.

   (D) The West Coast states maintained different ages for different beverages.

5. Which of the following constitutional principles or policies best explains the information in the map?

   (A) The amendment process

   (B) National supremacy

   (C) Congress's commerce power

   (D) Federalism

6. Due to Supreme Court rulings, state schools can no longer conduct morning prayer, local police must warn suspects of their right to remain silent, and public schools must respect students' right to non-disruptive symbolic speech. The Court has established these policies through which process?

(A) Prior restraint

(B) Judicial restraint

(C) Selective incorporation

(D) Plea bargaining

Questions 7 and 8 refer to the graph below.

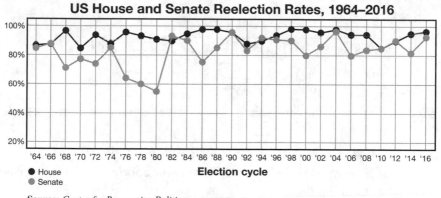

US House and Senate Reelection Rates, 1964–2016

● House
● Senate

Election cycle

Source: *Center for Responsive Politics*

7. Which of the following statements is reflected in the data in the line graph?

(A) Congressional incumbents win reelection a majority of the time.

(B) Incumbent success was at the lowest point in both houses in 1980.

(C) Voter turnout for both houses was at a high point in 2004.

(D) House incumbents rarely win at rates above 80 percent.

8. Which of the following is a chief cause for the trend shown in the line chart?

(A) Unbiased, nonpartisan drawing of congressional districts maintains this trend.

(B) Different campaign finance rules apply to incumbents and challengers.

(C) Incumbents do not need to raise as much money as challengers.

(D) Citizens are familiar with incumbents, who use their office for outreach.

Questions 9 and 10 refer to the chart below.

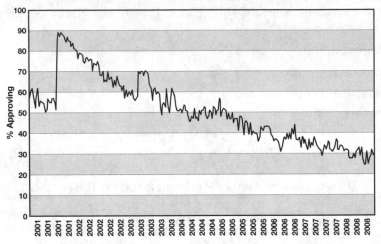

Presidential Approval Rating, George W. Bush (2001–2009)

Source: *The Presidency Project, UCSB*

9. Which of the following accurately describes the information presented in the chart above?

   (A) George W. Bush had a better approval rating than most presidents.

   (B) George W. Bush left office with a lower approval rating than when he entered office.

   (C) George W. Bush had his best approval rating during the lame duck period.

   (D) George W. Bush's approval rating reached a peak in his second term.

10. Which of the following was a likely consequence of the trend illustrated in the graph?

   (A) President Bush's political party lost the 2008 presidential election.

   (B) President Bush's honeymoon period came at the end of his term.

   (C) President Bush used his second term to forward his policy agenda.

   (D) President Bush's low approval rating actually made it easier for him to govern.

11. A member of the president's cabinet disagrees strongly with the president on how executive branch policy should be carried out and has publicly expressed those views. Which of the following outcomes will likely happen?

(A) The president will reassign the official to another cabinet position.

(B) The president will remove the official with the Senate's approval.

(C) The president will remove the official from his or her administration.

(D) The remainder of the cabinet will vote to remove or keep the official.

12. Which of the following statements is an accurate interpretation of the law on obscene speech in America?

(A) Governments cannot outlaw obscene materials as long as the material has a warning label.

(B) Governments cannot limit speech, and therefore cannot ban obscene speech.

(C) Obscene speech is not protected unless it can meet established standards of value.

(D) The law on obscene speech is uniform across the United States.

13. Which of the following best supports an argument that the national news media is a liberal-leaning institution?

(A) The Democratic Party tends to win more elections due to media coverage.

(B) A high percentage of national journalists are self-described Democrats.

(C) Corporations run the media, and most corporate executives are Democrats.

(D) More journalists donate to the Republican Party than to the Democratic Party.

14. Which of the following actions may Congress take to limit the president's power?

(A) Refuse to spend money that the president has allotted

(B) Override a presidential veto with a two-thirds vote

(C) Name new cabinet secretaries opposed by the president

(D) Raise taxes on the president's supporters

Questions 15 and 16 refer to the political cartoon below.

"*I'm not so sure about this 'life, liberty and pursuit of happiness' bit. Whaddya say we look at some polling numbers first?*"

Source: *cartoonstock.com, cartoon by Tim O'Brien*

15. The central message of this political cartoon is best summarized by which of the following statements?

(A) The founders drew their ideas by sampling public opinion.

(B) "Life, liberty, and the pursuit of happiness" were negotiable principles.

(C) The founders used debate and compromise to write the founding documents.

(D) The founding principles are more enduring than public opinion.

16. What implication does the cartoon convey about today's government officials?

(A) They are too willing to stray from principles in the interest of pleasing the public.

(B) They take seriously the concerns of the public and shape policy accordingly.

(C) Small groups of powerful officials make important decisions in secret.

(D) They would rather be true to the founding principles than popular with voters.

17. Which of the following is an accurate statement about the necessary and proper clause?

    (A) After *United States v. Lopez*, the clause allowed Congress to bar guns near schools.

    (B) The clause empowers Congress to overrule Supreme Court decisions.

    (C) The clause empowers Congress to act as required to carry out its expressed powers.

    (D) The clause has mainly been used to return authority to the states in contested laws.

18. Which of the following sequences accurately follows the impeachment and removal process as outlined in the Constitution?

    (A) The Senate votes to accuse the official; the House determines if the charges warrant removal.

    (B) The House accuses an official; the Senate judges and decides whether to remove the official.

    (C) The cabinet, by a majority vote, impeaches the president out of office; the Senate convicts or acquits.

    (D) The Justice Department impeaches the official; the Supreme Court convicts or acquits.

19. Which of the following best describes Congress's use of the commerce clause over time?

    (A) Congress has used it to protect workers and the environment.

    (B) The Supreme Court has denied Congress much of its commercial regulation authority.

    (C) Congress can legislate only on products that involve interstate commerce.

    (D) Congress has used its commerce power sparingly and there are few federal commercial laws.

20. Which of the following statements about the Declaration of Independence is accurate?

    (A) It provides a legal and moral justification for rebellion.

    (B) It sets forth the new system of national government.

    (C) American colonists unanimously agreed to it.

    (D) It was drafted in 1787 and eventually ratified by the states.

Questions 21 and 22 refer to the graph below.

**Equal Employment Opportunity Commission (EEOC)
Complaints Filed, 2016**

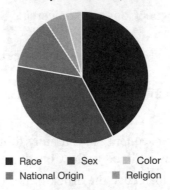

■ Race   ■ Sex   ■ Color
■ National Origin   ■ Religion

Source: *EEOC, 2016. 91,503 total complaints*

21. Which of the following is an accurate statement based on the data in the pie chart?

   (A) Racial prejudice has declined as a problem in the United States.

   (B) Terrorism has spiked discrimination complaints based on national origin.

   (C) Discrimination based on race and sex are the most common complaints.

   (D) Discrimination based on natural origin and religion have about the same percent of complaints.

22. Which of the following is a reasonable conclusion based on the information in the chart?

   (A) African Americans and women suffered discrimination before national laws protected them.

   (B) Enforcing racial equality and equality of the sexes is a reserved power.

   (C) Government employers cannot discriminate in hiring and firing, but private employers can.

   (D) A majority of these complaints were justified and punished.

Questions 23 and 24 refer to the table below.

Opinions about Legalizing Marijuana Use

% who say marijuana should be...	Legal	Illegal	DK
	%	%	%
Total	61	37	3
Men	64	33	3
Women	57	41	3
White	62	36	2
Black	71	25	4
Hispanic	52	44	4
College grad+	65	32	3
Some college	65	32	3
HS or less	54	43	2
Republican	43	55	2
Democrat	69	28	3
Independent	65	32	3
White evangelical Protestant	38	60	2
White mainline Protestant	64	33	2
Catholic	52	45	4
Unaffiliated	78	20	2

Oct. 25-30, 2017. DK=Don't Know
Note: Figures may not add to 100 because of rounding.

Source: *Pew Research Center*

23. Which of the following statements reflects the data in the chart?

(A) Most religious groups tend to have the same opinion about legalizing marijuana.

(B) A higher percentage of women than men want to legalize marijuana.

(C) Less educated citizens favor legalization more than well-educated citizens.

(D) More people today want marijuana to be legal than illegal.

24. Based on the information in the table, which of the following is implied?

(A) Democrats would be more likely to support marijuana use than Republicans.

(B) White, evangelical Protestants have the strongest pro-legalization views.

(C) African Americans and Hispanics believe in legalizing at the same levels.

(D) Women favor legalizing marijuana for medical, not recreational, purposes.

Questions 25 and 26 refer to the passage below.

> It looked like I was going to win the popular vote, maybe by a significant margin. There was some comfort in that fact. It meant that a majority of Americans hadn't embraced Trump's "us versus them" campaign, and that despite all our troubles more people chose our platform and vision for the future. I had been rejected—but also affirmed. It was surreal. . . . I'd been saying since 2000 that the Electoral College gave disproportionate power to less populated states and therefore was profoundly undemocratic. It made a mockery of the principle of "one person, one vote."

> —Hillary Clinton, *What Happened*, 2017

25. Which of the following statements best summarizes candidate Hillary Clinton's argument?
    (A) The Electoral College system impedes citizen participation.
    (B) The Electoral College system is the constitutional way to elect a president.
    (C) Clinton should be president because she received more votes than her opponent.
    (D) States with fewer people are disadvantaged by the Electoral College system.

26. Based on this passage, with which of the following statements would Clinton most likely agree?
    (A) The Electoral College is at odds with the Voting Rights Act of 1965.
    (B) The Electoral College is at odds with a principle established in *Shaw v. Reno*.
    (C) Congress should pass a law eliminating the Electoral College.
    (D) The winner-take-all system should be adopted by all 50 states.

27. In a primary election for the U.S. House of Representatives, a citizen votes for a candidate whose record she has studied carefully. What model of voting is she using?
    (A) Rational-choice
    (B) Prospective
    (C) Retrospective
    (D) Party-line

28. Which of the following is true about Super PACs?

(A) They can collect limited donations from members of their organization and donate directly to candidates.

(B) They can collect donations from the general public up to a limit and donate directly to candidates.

(C) They can collect donations from the general public and can donate directly to candidates with no limits.

(D) They can collect donations from the general public with no limits but cannot coordinate with candidates.

29. Which of the following statements most accurately reflects voter trends in U.S. midterm elections?

(A) Voter turnout in midterm elections is higher than in presidential elections.

(B) The president's party typically loses seats in Congress during a midterm election.

(C) Incumbents in the House of Representatives have about a 50 percent chance of reelection.

(D) Voters' biggest influence on election outcomes is in safe districts.

Questions 30 and 31 refer to the passage below.

> In republican government, the legislative authority necessarily predominates. The remedy for this inconveniency is to divide the legislature into different branches; and to render them, by different modes of election and different principles of action, as little connected with each other as the nature of their common functions and their common dependence on the society will admit. It may even be necessary to guard against dangerous encroachments by still further precautions. As the weight of the legislative authority requires that it should be thus divided, the weakness of the executive may require, on the other hand, that it should be fortified.
>
> —James Madison, *Federalist No. 51*, 1788

30. What constitutional principle does Madison address in the above passage?

(A) Bicameralism

(B) Federalism

(C) Freedom of speech

(D) The power to tax and spend

31. Which of the following statements is most consistent with Madison's views in the passage?

(A) A three-branch design makes the legislature a safe branch.

(B) The president should be on the same level as the legislature.

(C) Checks in the lawmaking process limit the legislature's power.

(D) The commander in chief should create most of the laws.

Questions 32 and 33 refer to the infographic below.

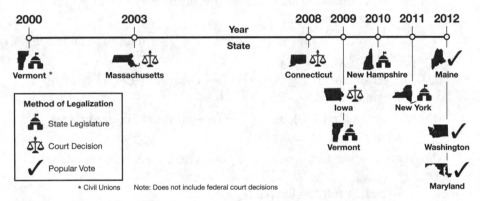

32. Based on the infographic, which of the following statements is most accurate?

(A) Same-sex marriage was legalized nationally within a decade after Massachusetts legalized it.

(B) Southern and Midwest states legalized same-sex marriage the earliest.

(C) Strong majorities approved same-sex marriage in states that legalized through ballot measures.

(D) The first states to legalize same-sex marriage did so through courts; later states used more democratic methods.

33. Which of the following constitutional clauses has motivated these changes?

(A) Commerce clause

(B) Necessary and proper clause

(C) Free exercise of religion clause

(D) Equal protection clause

34. Which of the following best defines the term *judicial activism*?

(A) The demands on judges to increase their caseload and issue more rulings

(B) Rulings based on the assumption that judges can make policy as well as interpret it

(C) The efforts of judges to actively lobby Congress for increased funding for their staffs

(D) Judges refusing to recuse themselves from cases in which they have a conflict of interest

35. A local police officer searched a person's car on a slight suspicion, and happened to find the person possessed an illegal gun. The person never consented to a search, nor did the officer obtain a warrant. Which of the following might prevent the gun from being introduced as evidence in a trial?

(A) The ban on double jeopardy

(B) The exclusionary rule

(C) Stare decisis

(D) Failure to read the Miranda warning

36. Which of the following is an accurate comparison of the Fourteenth and Fifteenth Amendments?

	FOURTEENTH AMENDMENT	FIFTEENTH AMENDMENT
(A)	Established that states had to assure citizens equal protection	Assured states could not deny citizens the right to vote based on color or race
(B)	Abolished slavery	Assured states could not deny women the right to vote
(C)	Gave Congress the power to enforce voting rights	Assured citizenship to all persons born in the United States
(D)	Required businesses to serve all citizens regardless of race or heritage	Prevented states from determining voting rights without federal preclearance

Questions 37–39 refer to the graph below.

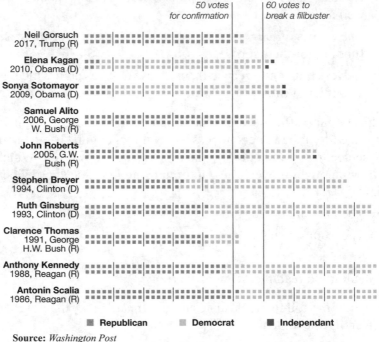

Total Senate Votes for Confirmation (by Party)
Supreme Court Justices

Source: *Washington Post*

37. Based on the infographic, which of the following is an identifiable trend?

(A) Several justices received confirmation votes from only one party.

(B) Senators from the president's party vote to confirm nominated justices more than senators from the opposing party.

(C) Intense partisan voting on Supreme Court nominees was more common two decades ago than it is more recently.

(D) Decisions of justices confirmed by party-line votes have generally not aligned with views of the party that confirmed them.

38. What conclusion can you draw from the information in the graphic?

(A) Each senator has to vote yes or no on a confirmation.

(B) Republicans controlled the Senate when Justice Kagan was confirmed.

(C) Justice Kennedy appealed about equally to Republicans and Democrats.

(D) Controversy surrounding Justice Ginsburg led to a close vote.

39. Which of the following strategies might a president follow to receive greater support for Supreme Court nominees?

   (A) Using public opinion polls for judges' approval ratings before naming them

   (B) Naming ideologically moderate justices to the Supreme Court

   (C) Broadcasting party-supported television ads to influence senators

   (D) Nominating more women and minorities to the Court

40. Which of the following is a result of the *Gideon v. Wainwright* decision?

   (A) Evidence acquired without a warrant will be excluded from the defendant's trial.

   (B) No state can prevent a woman from having an abortion.

   (C) Police must tell arrested suspects that they have a right against self-incrimination.

   (D) States must provide indigent or poor defendants with public defense attorneys.

41. How can public opinion polling affect political participation?

   (A) Random samples leave too many people out of the poll.

   (B) It contributes to "horse-race" journalism so voters don't engage with the real issues.

   (C) Confirmation bias makes people vote for candidates whose policies align with their own.

   (D) It predicts results so accurately that there's little need for an actual election.

42. Which of the following groupings constitute an "iron triangle"?

   (A) Executive agency, congressional committee, interest group

   (B) President, House majority leader, Senate majority leader

   (C) Interest group, Senate majority leader, House majority leader

   (D) Executive department, House majority leader, president

43. Which of the following statements about the federal government and economic policy is true?

   (A) Supply-side economics requires more taxes in order to increase government services.

   (B) The secretary of the treasury holds the power of the purse.

   (C) The House Budget Committee chair initiates the budget process each year.

   (D) The Federal Reserve Board uses monetary policy to aid the health of the economy.

44. A Congress member and several other sponsors are ready to introduce a bill into the legislative process. The bill is designed to reduce tax rates on people with lower incomes. In which committee will these House members introduce their bill?

(A) Finance Committee

(B) Budget Committee

(C) Ways and Means Committee

(D) Welfare Committee

45. Which of the following is an accurate comparison of how the legislative branch and the executive branch can influence the federal courts?

	LEGISLATIVE BRANCH	EXECUTIVE BRANCH
(A)	Withholding or decreasing judges' salaries	Issuing executive orders to override Court decisions
(B)	Pressuring justices to resolve matters a certain way	Giving advice and consent on judicial decisions
(C)	Impeachment and removal of poor or improper judges	Implementation of decisions through administrative bureaucracy
(D)	Refusing to carry out judicial decisions	Setting jurisdiction between federal and state courts

46. Which of the following principles protects a citizen from imprisonment without the government taking certain prescribed steps?

(A) Substantive due process

(B) Stare decisis

(C) Procedural due process

(D) Selective incorporation

47. Which of the following is a fair criticism of the federal bureaucracy?

(A) Overlapping bureaucratic authority can cause wasteful spending and duplication.

(B) Senior-level bureaucrats keep their jobs because they cannot earn comparable salaries working elsewhere.

(C) After Congress creates a bureaucratic agency, it has little impact over how that agency operates.

(D) The bureaucracy does not rely on experts in their fields to formulate regulations.

48. Which of the following would most likely be in violation of the Twenty-Fifth Amendment?

(A) The president-elect asks to delay his inauguration until January 22.

(B) The president writes and uses his own oath of office rather than saying the words in the Constitution.

(C) The president refuses to sign or veto a bill without giving reasons for his refusal.

(D) The president puts his secretary of defense in charge of the executive branch while he undergoes a medical procedure.

49. Which of the following is an accurate statement regarding congressional leaders?

(A) The House speaker and the Senate majority leader have about the same amount of power and influence within their respective chambers.

(B) In case of a tie vote in the Senate, the vice president breaks the tie.

(C) The vice president regularly presides over and casts votes in the Senate.

(D) The minority and majority whips focus primarily on fundraising for the party.

50. Which of the following is an accurate comparison of state and local governments and federal government with respect to jurisdiction over national elections?

	STATE & LOCAL GOVERNMENTS	FEDERAL GOVERNMENT
(A)	Endorse candidates once they have filed for office	Certifies statewide vote totals once votes are fully counted
(B)	Monitor campaign donations and expenditures	Determines the type(s) of ballots to be used in federal elections
(C)	Define campaign donation limits from political action committees	Sets a national standard for voter-identification laws
(D)	Administer elections and designate voting districts	Can pass voting legislation to enforce constitutional suffrage amendments

51. A Republican president has nominated a federal judge for an opening on a U.S. court. A number of senators have declared they are not supportive of the nominee, including many senators within the president's own party, which holds only a simple majority of the Senate seats. No Democrats support the candidate. Which of the following scenarios will likely occur?

(A) The House of Representatives will withdraw the nomination.

(B) The Senate will likely vote to confirm the nominee.

(C) The president will withdraw the nomination or the nominee will withdraw.

(D) A split in the vote will occur and the vice president will break the tie.

52. An interest group's political action committee has donated to Representative Jones's campaign, yet Jones has signaled she opposes a proposed bill that the same interest group favors. Which of the following actions is the interest group most likely to take?

(A) Create and air negative ads about Representative Jones

(B) File an *amicus curiae* brief in court against Ms. Jones

(C) Ask for the donation to be returned to the political action committee

(D) Ask to meet with the representative to explain and persuade her to vote otherwise

53. Which of the following is true regarding the public's perception of Congress?

(A) A House member's individual approval rating is usually higher than Congress's approval rating.

(B) Most Americans see Congress as hardworking, ethical, and responsive to people's needs.

(C) Congress's approval rating tends to be higher than that of the president.

(D) The public appreciates the bipartisan spirit in Congress that brings people together.

54. Which of the following is an accurate comparison of traditional media and new media?

	TRADITIONAL MEDIA	NEW MEDIA
(A)	Radio and television stations are licensed and regulated by the federal government.	Cable stations and Internet news platforms appeal to niche markets.
(B)	Print media usually provides shorter and simpler stories than broadcast media.	Cable news tends to be objective and uphold high journalistic standards.
(C)	Local newspapers as a practice do not endorse candidates for office.	Social media is a reliable news source.
(D)	The national broadcast networks typically endorse the Democratic presidential nominee.	Cable television networks blossomed with the development of wire services.

55. Which of the following best describes a frequent source of contention between the executive branch and the legislative branch?

(A) Power of the purse

(B) War powers and foreign affairs

(C) Homeland security

(D) Voter ID laws

FREE-RESPONSE QUESTIONS

1. "If trends continue . . . Mr. Trump will win or come very close to winning by the convention in July. If party forces succeed in finagling him out of the nomination, his supporters will bolt, which will break the party. And it's hard to see what kind of special sauce . . . would make them come back in the future. If [he] is given the crown in Cleveland [at the national convention], party political figures, operatives, loyalists, journalists and intellectuals . . . sophisticated suburbanites and . . . donors will themselves bolt. . . . And again it's hard to imagine the special sauce— the shared interests, the basic worldview—that would allow them to reconcile with Trump supporters down the road."

—Peggy Noonan, *Wall Street Journal,* March 5, 2016

After reading the scenario, respond to A, B, and C below:

(A) Describe the nomination process referred to in the scenario.

(B) In the context of the above scenario, explain how the process described in part A can be affected by interactions with the media.

(C) In the context of the scenario, explain what citizens can do to affect the impact of the interactions between elections and the media.

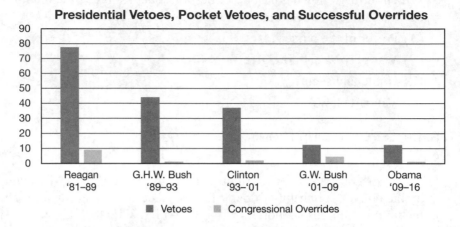

Presidential Vetoes, Pocket Vetoes, and Successful Overrides

Legend: ■ Vetoes ■ Congressional Overrides

(X-axis categories: Reagan '81–89, G.H.W. Bush '89–93, Clinton '93–'01, G.W. Bush '01–09, Obama '09–16; Y-axis: 0 to 90)

2. Use the bar graph above to answer the questions.

   (A) Identify the president who rejected the most laws through vetoes.

   (B) Describe a similarity or difference in the use of the veto as illustrated in the chart, and draw a conclusion about that similarity or difference.

   (C) Explain how the information represented in the graph demonstrates checks and balances in the lawmaking process.

3. The Alabama legislature passed laws (1978–1982) that authorized the state's public school teachers to set aside time to conduct a moment of silence for individual students to pray or meditate. Ishmael Jaffree, on behalf of his children who were students in the Mobile, Alabama, schools, filed suit against school and state officials, namely Governor George C. Wallace, seeking to stop such religious observances and "maintaining or allowing the practice of regular religious prayer services or other forms of religious observances" during the school day.

   In Jaffree's case, *Wallace v. Jaffree* (1985), the Supreme Court held in a 6:3 decision in favor of Jaffree that Alabama law and this practice were not only a deviation from the state's duty to maintain neutrality toward religion but represented an affirmative endorsement of religion and clearly lacked any secular purpose.

   (A) Identify the constitutional clause that is common to both *Wallace v. Jaffree* (1985) and *Engel v. Vitale* (1962).

   (B) Based on the constitutional clause identified in part A, explain why the facts of *Engel v. Vitale* led to a similar holding as the holding in *Wallace v. Jaffree*.

   (C) Describe an action that citizens who disagree with the holding in *Wallace v. Jaffree* could take to limit its impact.

4. Develop an argument to explain whether or not federal judges should continue to have life terms.
In your essay you must:

- Articulate a defensible claim or thesis that responds to the prompt and establishes a line of reasoning

- Support your claim with at least TWO pieces of accurate and relevant information:
  - At least ONE piece must come from one of the following foundational documents:
    - Article III
    - Federalist No. 78
  - Use a second piece of evidence from the other foundational document from the above list or from your study of public policy and the judiciary

- Use reasoning to explain why your evidence supports your claim/thesis

- Respond to an opposing or alternative perspective using refutation, concession or rebuttal

Foundational Documents Sourcebook

Note: Throughout the foundational documents, paragraphs have been numbered for easy reference. If numbers appear in brackets [ ], they were not part of the original document.

The Declaration of Independence

IN CONGRESS, JULY 4, 1776
The unanimous Declaration of the thirteen united States of America

[1] When in the Course of human events it becomes necessary for one people to dissolve the political bands which have connected them with another and to assume among the powers of the earth, the separate and equal station to which the Laws of Nature and of Nature's God entitle them, a decent respect to the opinions of mankind requires that they should declare the causes which impel them to the separation.

[2] We hold these truths to be self-evident, that all men are created equal, that they are endowed by their Creator with certain unalienable Rights, that among these are Life, Liberty and the pursuit of Happiness. — That to secure these rights, Governments are instituted among Men, deriving their just powers from the consent of the governed, — That whenever any Form of Government becomes destructive of these ends, it is the Right of the People to alter or to abolish it, and to institute new Government, laying its foundation on such principles and organizing its powers in such form, as to them shall seem most likely to effect their Safety and Happiness. Prudence, indeed, will dictate that Governments long established should not be changed for light and transient causes; and accordingly all experience hath shewn that mankind are more disposed to suffer, while evils are sufferable than to right themselves by abolishing the forms to which they are accustomed. But when a long train of abuses and usurpations, pursuing invariably the same Object evinces a design to reduce them under absolute Despotism, it is their right, it is their duty, to throw off such Government, and to provide new Guards for their future security. — Such has been the patient sufferance of these Colonies; and such is now the necessity which constrains them to alter their former Systems of Government. The history of the present King of Great Britain is a history of repeated injuries and usurpations, all having in direct object the establishment of an absolute Tyranny over these States. To prove this, let Facts be submitted to a candid world.

[3] He has refused his Assent to Laws, the most wholesome and necessary for the public good.

[4] He has forbidden his Governors to pass Laws of immediate and pressing importance, unless suspended in their operation till his Assent should be obtained; and when so suspended, he has utterly neglected to attend to them.

[5] He has refused to pass other Laws for the accommodation of large districts of people, unless those people would relinquish the right of Representation in the Legislature, a right inestimable to them and formidable to tyrants only.

[6] He has called together legislative bodies at places unusual, uncomfortable, and distant from the depository of their Public Records, for the sole purpose of fatiguing them into compliance with his measures.

[7] He has dissolved Representative Houses repeatedly, for opposing with manly firmness his invasions on the rights of the people.

[8] He has refused for a long time, after such dissolutions, to cause others to be elected, whereby the Legislative Powers, incapable of Annihilation, have returned to the People at large for their exercise; the State remaining in the mean time exposed

to all the dangers of invasion from without, and convulsions within.

[9] He has endeavoured to prevent the population of these States; for that purpose obstructing the Laws for Naturalization of Foreigners; refusing to pass others to encourage their migrations hither, and raising the conditions of new Appropriations of Lands.

[10] He has obstructed the Administration of Justice by refusing his Assent to Laws for establishing Judiciary Powers.

[11] He has made Judges dependent on his Will alone for the tenure of their offices, and the amount and payment of their salaries.

[12] He has erected a multitude of New Offices, and sent hither swarms of Officers to harass our people and eat out their substance.

[13] He has kept among us, in times of peace, Standing Armies without the Consent of our legislatures.

[14] He has affected to render the Military independent of and superior to the Civil Power.

[15] He has combined with others to subject us to a jurisdiction foreign to our constitution, and unacknowledged by our laws; giving his Assent to their Acts of pretended Legislation:

[16] For quartering large bodies of armed troops among us:

[17] For protecting them, by a mock Trial from punishment for any Murders which they should commit on the Inhabitants of these States:

[18] For cutting off our Trade with all parts of the world:

[19] For imposing Taxes on us without our Consent:

[20] For depriving us in many cases, of the benefit of Trial by Jury:

[21] For transporting us beyond Seas to be tried for pretended offences:

[22] For abolishing the free System of English Laws in a neighbouring Province, establishing therein an Arbitrary government, and enlarging its Boundaries so as to render it at once an example and fit instrument for introducing the same absolute rule into these Colonies

[23] For taking away our Charters, abolishing our most valuable Laws and altering fundamentally the Forms of our Governments:

[24] For suspending our own Legislatures, and declaring themselves invested with power to legislate for us in all cases whatsoever.

[25] He has abdicated Government here, by declaring us out of his Protection and waging War against us.

[26] He has plundered our seas, ravaged our coasts, burnt our towns, and destroyed the lives of our people.

[27] He is at this time transporting large Armies of foreign Mercenaries to compleat the works of death, desolation, and tyranny, already begun with circumstances of Cruelty & Perfidy scarcely paralleled in the most barbarous ages, and totally unworthy the Head of a civilized nation.

[28] He has constrained our fellow Citizens taken Captive on the high Seas to bear

Arms against their Country, to become the executioners of their friends and Brethren, or to fall themselves by their Hands.

[29] He has excited domestic insurrections amongst us, and has endeavoured to bring on the inhabitants of our frontiers, the merciless Indian Savages whose known rule of warfare, is an undistinguished destruction of all ages, sexes and conditions.

[30] In every stage of these oppressions we have petitioned for redress in the most humble terms; our repeated petitions have been answered only by repeated injury. A Prince, whose character is thus marked by every act which may define a Tyrant, is unfit to be the ruler of a free people.

[31] Nor have We been wanting in attentions to our British brethren. We have warned them from time to time of attempts by their legislature to extend an unwarrantable jurisdiction over us. We have reminded them of the circumstances of our emigration and settlement here. We have appealed to their native justice and magnanimity, and we have conjured them by the ties of our common kindred to disavow these usurpations, which would inevitably interrupt our connections and correspondence. They too have been deaf to the voice of justice and of consanguinity. We must, therefore, acquiesce in the necessity, which denounces our Separation, and hold them, as we hold the rest of mankind, Enemies in War, in Peace Friends.

[32] We, therefore, the Representatives of the United States of America, in General Congress, Assembled, appealing to the Supreme Judge of the world for the rectitude of our intentions, do, in the Name, and by Authority of the good People of these Colonies, solemnly publish and declare, That these united Colonies are, and of Right ought to be Free and Independent States, that they are Absolved from all Allegiance to the British Crown, and that all political connection between them and the State of Great Britain, is and ought to be totally dissolved; and that as Free and Independent States, they have full Power to levy War, conclude Peace, contract Alliances, establish Commerce, and to do all other Acts and Things which Independent States may of right do. — And for the support of this Declaration, with a firm reliance on the protection of Divine Providence, we mutually pledge to each other our Lives, our Fortunes, and our sacred Honor.

(You may find it useful to use the worksheet at EDSITEment! to analyze the Declaration of Independence. You can find it at http://edsitement.neh.gov/sites/ edsitement.neh.gov/files/worksheets/worksheet02-declaration-six-parts.pdf.)

1. Describe the perspective, or point of view, of the authors of the Declaration of Independence and the philosophical assumptions underlying their argument.

2. The key claim in the Declaration of Independence—the claim on which the revolution was based—is in the second paragraph. Identify that claim and describe it in your own words.

3. What role do the facts "submitted to the candid world" play in the argument?

4. What is the purpose in the argument of paragraph 31, beginning with "Nor have we been wanting . . ."?

5. Describe the final claim made in the Declaration of Independence.

6. An implication is a conclusion that can be drawn even if it is not stated directly. Identify the implications of the argument in the Declaration of Independence about the nature of the new government. Even though the new government was not yet formed, what implications about its political principles, processes, institutions, and behaviors does the Declaration of Independence suggest?

Articles of Confederation (1777)

[1] To all to whom these Presents shall come, we, the undersigned Delegates of the States affixed to our Names send greeting. Whereas the Delegates of the United States of America in Congress assembled did on the fifteenth day of November in the year of our Lord One Thousand Seven Hundred and Seventy seven, and in the Second Year of the Independence of America agree to certain articles of Confederation and perpetual Union between the States of New Hampshire, Massachusetts-bay, Rhode Island and Providence Plantations, Connecticut, New York, New Jersey, Pennsylvania, Delaware, Maryland, Virginia, North Carolina, South Carolina, and Georgia in the Words following, viz. "Articles of Confederation and perpetual Union between the States of New Hampshire, Massachusetts-bay, Rhode Island and Providence Plantations, Connecticut, New York, New Jersey, Pennsylvania, Delaware, Maryland, Virginia, North Carolina, South Carolina, and Georgia.

Article I. The Stile of this confederacy shall be, "The United States of America."

Article II. Each state retains its sovereignty, freedom and independence, and every Power, Jurisdiction and right, which is not by this confederation expressly delegated to the United States, in Congress assembled.

Article III. The said states hereby severally enter into a firm league of friendship with each other, for their common defense, the security of their Liberties, and their mutual and general welfare, binding themselves to assist each other, against all force offered to, or attacks made upon them, or any of them, on account of religion, sovereignty, trade, or any other pretense whatever.

Article IV.

[1] The better to secure and perpetuate mutual friendship and intercourse among the people of the different states in this union, the free inhabitants of each of these states, paupers, vagabonds and fugitives from Justice excepted, shall be entitled to all privileges and immunities of free citizens in the several states; and the people of each state shall have free ingress and regress to and from any other state, and shall enjoy therein all the privileges of trade and commerce, subject to the same duties, impositions and restrictions as the inhabitants thereof respectively, provided that such restrictions shall not extend so far as to prevent the removal of property imported into any state, to any other State of which the Owner is an inhabitant; provided also that no imposition, duties or restriction shall be laid by any state, on the property of the united states, or either of them.

[2] If any Person guilty of, or charged with, treason, felony, or other high misdemeanor in any state, shall flee from Justice, and be found in any of the united states, he shall upon demand of the Governor or executive power of the state from which he fled, be delivered up, and removed to the state having jurisdiction of his offence.

[3] Full faith and credit shall be given in each of these states to the records, acts and judicial proceedings of the courts and magistrates of every other state.

Article V.

[1] For the more convenient management of the general interests of the united states, delegates shall be annually appointed in such manner as the legislature of each state shall direct, to meet in Congress on the first Monday in November, in every year, with a power reserved to each state to recall its delegates, or any of them, at any time within the year, and to send others in their stead, for the remainder of the Year.

[2] No State shall be represented in Congress by less than two, nor by more than seven Members; and no person shall be capable of being delegate for more than three years, in any term of six years; nor shall any person, being a delegate, be capable of holding any office under the united states, for which he, or another for his benefit receives any salary, fees or emolument of any kind.

[3] Each State shall maintain its own delegates in a meeting of the states, and while they act as members of the committee of the states.

[4] In determining questions in the united states, in Congress assembled, each state shall have one vote.

[5] Freedom of speech and debate in Congress shall not be impeached or questioned in any Court, or place out of Congress, and the members of congress shall be protected in their persons from arrests and imprisonments, during the time of their going to and from, and attendance on congress, except for treason, felony, or breach of the peace.

---

1. How do the authors describe the relationship between the States, and what responsibilities do the States have in relationship to the federal government and to each other?

2. The final paragraph of Article V protects the speech of members of Congress and prevents their arrests while serving, except for grievous crimes. Explain why this clause might have been necessary.

Article VI.

[1] No State, without the Consent of the united States, in congress assembled, shall send any embassy to, or receive any embassy from, or enter into any conference, agreement, alliance, or treaty, with any King prince or state; nor shall any person holding any office of profit or trust under the united states, or any of them, accept of any present, emolument, office, or title of any kind whatever, from any king, prince, or foreign state; nor shall the united states, in congress assembled, or any of them, grant any title of nobility.

[2] No two or more states shall enter into any treaty, confederation, or alliance whatever between them, without the consent of the united states, in congress assembled, specifying accurately the purposes for which the same is to be entered into, and how long it shall continue.

[3] No State shall lay any imposts or duties, which may interfere with any stipulations in treaties, entered into by the united States in congress assembled, with any king, prince, or State, in pursuance of any treaties already proposed by congress, to the courts of France and Spain.

[4] No vessels of war shall be kept up in time of peace, by any state, except such number only, as shall be deemed necessary by the united states, in congress assembled, for the defense of such state, or its trade; nor shall any body of forces be kept up, by any state, in time of peace, except such number only as, in the judgment of the united states, in congress assembled, shall be deemed requisite to garrison the forts necessary for the defense of such state; but every state shall always keep up a well regulated and disciplined militia, sufficiently armed and accounted, and shall provide and constantly have ready for use, in public stores, a due number of field pieces and tents, and a proper quantity of arms, ammunition, and camp equipage.

[5] No State shall engage in any war without the consent of the united States in congress assembled, unless such State be actually invaded by enemies, or shall have received certain advice of a resolution being formed by some nation of Indians to invade such State, and the danger is so imminent as not to admit of a delay till the united states in congress assembled, can be consulted: nor shall any state grant commissions to any ships or vessels of war, nor letters of marque or reprisal, except it be after a declaration of war by the united states in congress assembled, and then only against the kingdom or State, and the subjects thereof, against which war has been so declared, and under such regulations as shall be established by the united states in congress assembled, unless such state be infested by pirates, in which case vessels of war may be fitted out for that occasion, and kept so long as the danger shall continue, or until the united states in congress assembled shall determine otherwise.

Article VII. When land forces are raised by any state, for the common defense, all officers of or under the rank of colonel, shall be appointed by the legislature of each state respectively by whom such forces shall be raised, or in such manner as such state shall direct, and all vacancies shall be filled up by the state which first made appointment.

Article VIII. All charges of war, and all other expenses that shall be incurred for the common defense or general welfare, and allowed by the united states in congress assembled, shall be defrayed out of a common treasury, which shall be supplied by the several states, in proportion to the value of all land within each state, granted to or surveyed for any Person, as such land and the buildings and improvements thereon shall be estimated, according to such mode as the united states, in congress assembled, shall, from time to time, direct and appoint. The taxes for paying that proportion shall be laid and levied by the authority and direction of the legislatures of the several states within the time agreed upon by the united states in congress assembled.

Article IX.

[1] The united states, in congress assembled, shall have the sole and exclusive right and power of determining on peace and war, except in the cases mentioned in the sixth article - of sending and receiving ambassadors - entering into treaties and alliances, provided that no treaty of commerce shall be made, whereby the legislative power of the respective states shall be restrained from imposing such imposts and duties on foreigners, as their own people are subjected to, or from prohibiting the exportation or importation of any species of goods or commodities whatsoever - of establishing rules for deciding, in all cases, what captures on land or water shall be legal, and in what manner prizes taken by land or naval forces in the service of the united Sates, shall be divided or appropriated - of granting letters of marque and reprisal in times of peace - appointing courts for the trial of piracies and felonies committed on the high seas; and establishing courts; for receiving and determining finally appeals in all cases of captures; provided that no member of congress shall be appointed a judge of any of the said courts.

[2] The united states, in congress assembled, shall also be the last resort on appeal, in all disputes and differences now subsisting, or that hereafter may arise between two or more states concerning boundary, jurisdiction, or any other cause whatever; which authority shall always be exercised in the manner following. Whenever the legislative or executive authority, or lawful agent of any state in controversy with another, shall present a petition to congress, stating the matter in question, and praying for a hearing, notice thereof shall be given, by order of congress, to the legislative or executive authority of the other state in controversy, and a day assigned for the appearance of the parties by their lawful agents, who shall then be directed to appoint, by joint consent, commissioners or judges to constitute a court for hearing and determining the matter in question: but if they cannot agree, congress shall name three persons out of each of the united states, and from the list of such persons each party shall alternately strike out one, the petitioners beginning, until the number shall be reduced to thirteen; and from that number not less than seven, nor more than nine names, as congress shall direct, shall, in the presence of congress, be drawn out by lot, and the persons whose names shall be so drawn, or any five of them, shall be commissioners or judges, to hear and finally determine the controversy, so always as a major part of the judges, who shall hear the cause, shall agree in the determination: and if either party shall neglect to attend at the day appointed, without showing reasons which congress shall judge sufficient, or being present, shall refuse to strike, the congress shall proceed to nominate three persons out of each State, and the secretary of congress shall strike in behalf of such party absent or refusing; and the judgment and sentence of the court, to be appointed in the manner before prescribed, shall be final and conclusive; and if any of the parties shall refuse to submit to the authority of such court, or to appear or defend their claim or cause, the court shall nevertheless proceed to pronounce sentence, or judgment, which shall in like manner be final and decisive; the judgment or sentence and other proceedings being in either case transmitted to congress, and lodged among the acts of congress, for the security of the parties concerned: provided that every commissioner, before he sits in judgment, shall take an oath to be administered by one of the judges of the supreme or superior court of the State where the cause shall be tried, "well and truly to hear and determine the matter in question, according to the best of his judgment, without favor, affection, or hope of reward: "provided, also, that no State shall be deprived of territory for the benefit of the united states.

---

1. Describe the authorities granted to "the united states, in congress assembled," regarding foreign relations and war.
2. Explain the steps in the process of resolving disputes between states.

---

[3] All controversies concerning the private right of soil claimed under different grants of two or more states, whose jurisdictions as they may respect such lands, and the states which passed such grants are adjusted, the said grants or either of them being at the same time claimed to have originated antecedent to such settlement of jurisdiction, shall, on the petition of either party to the congress of the united states, be finally determined, as near as may be, in the same manner as is before prescribed for deciding disputes respecting territorial jurisdiction between different states.

[4] The united states, in congress assembled, shall also have the sole and exclusive right and power of regulating the alloy and value of coin struck by their own authority, or by that of the respective states— fixing the standard of weights and measures throughout the united states —regulating the trade and managing all affairs with the Indians, not members of any of the states; provided that the legislative right of any state, within its own limits, be not infringed or violated —establishing and regulating post-offices from one state to another, throughout all the united states, and exacting such postage on the papers passing through the same, as may be requisite to defray the expenses of the said office—appointing all officers of the land forces in the service of the united States, excepting regimental officers—appointing all the officers of the naval forces, and commissioning all officers whatever in the service of the united states; making rules for the government and regulation of the said land and naval forces, and directing their operations.

[5] The united States, in congress assembled, shall have authority to appoint a committee, to sit in the recess of congress, to be denominated, "A Committee of the States," and to consist of one delegate from each State; and to appoint such other committees and civil officers as may be necessary for managing the general affairs of the united states under their direction - to appoint one of their number to preside; provided that no person be allowed to serve in the office of president more than one year in any term of three years; to ascertain the necessary sums of money to be raised for the service of the united states, and to appropriate and apply the same for defraying the public expenses; to borrow money or emit bills on the credit of the united states, transmitting every half year to the respective states an account of the sums of money so borrowed or emitted, - to build and equip a navy - to agree upon the number of land forces, and to make requisitions from each state for its quota, in proportion to the number of white inhabitants in such state, which requisition shall be binding; and thereupon the legislature of each state shall appoint the regimental officers, raise the men, and clothe, arm, and equip them, in a soldier-like manner, at the expense of the united states; and the officers and men so clothed, armed, and equipped, shall march to the place appointed, and within the time agreed on by the united states, in congress assembled; but if the united states, in congress assembled, shall, on consideration of circumstances, judge proper that any state should not raise men, or should raise a smaller number than its quota, and that any other state should raise a greater number of men than the quota thereof, such extra number shall be raised, officered, clothed, armed, and equipped in the same manner as the quota of such state, unless the legislature of such state shall judge that such extra number cannot be safely spared out of the same, in which case they shall raise, officer, clothe, arm, and equip, as many of such extra number as they judge can be safely spared. And the officers and men so clothed, armed, and equipped, shall march to the place appointed, and within the time agreed on by the united states in congress assembled.

[6] The united states, in congress assembled, shall never engage in a war, nor grant letters of marque and reprisal in time of peace, nor enter into any treaties or alliances, nor coin money, nor regulate the value thereof nor ascertain the sums and expenses necessary for the defense and welfare of the united states, or any of them, nor emit bills, nor borrow money on the credit of the united states, nor appropriate money, nor agree upon the number of vessels of war to be built or purchased, or the number of land or sea forces to be raised, nor appoint a commander in chief of the army or navy, unless nine states assent to the same, nor shall a question on any other point, except for adjourning from day to day, be determined, unless by the votes of a majority of the united states in congress assembled.

[7] The congress of the united states shall have power to adjourn to any time within the year, and to any place within the united states, so that no period of adjournment be for a longer duration than the space of six Months, and shall publish the Journal of their proceedings monthly, except such parts thereof relating to treaties, alliances, or military operations, as in their judgment require secrecy; and the yeas and nays of the delegates of each State, on any question, shall be entered on the Journal, when it is desired by any delegate; and the delegates of a State, or any of them, at his or their request, shall be furnished with a transcript of the said Journal, except such parts as are above excepted, to lay before the legislatures of the several states.

Article X. The committee of the states, or any nine of them, shall be authorized to execute, in the recess of congress, such of the powers of congress as the united states, in congress assembled, by the consent of nine states, shall, from time to time, think expedient to vest them with; provided that no power be delegated to the said committee, for the exercise of which, by the articles of confederation, the voice of nine states, in the congress of the united states assembled, is requisite.

Article XI. Canada acceding to this confederation, and joining in the measures of the united states, shall be admitted into, and entitled to all the advantages of this union: but no other colony shall be admitted into the same, unless such admission be agreed to by nine states.

Article XII. All bills of credit emitted, monies borrowed, and debts contracted by or under the authority of congress, before the assembling of the united states, in pursuance of the present confederation, shall be deemed and considered as a charge against the united States, for payment and satisfaction whereof the said united states and the public faith are hereby solemnly pledged.

Article XIII. Every State shall abide by the determinations of the united states, in congress assembled, on all questions which by this confederation are submitted to them. And the Articles of this confederation shall be inviolably observed by every state, and the union shall be perpetual; nor shall any alteration at any time hereafter be made in any of them, unless such alteration be agreed to in a congress of the united states, and be afterwards confirmed by the legislatures of every state.

And Whereas it hath pleased the Great Governor of the World to incline the hearts of the legislatures we respectively represent in congress, to approve of, and to authorize us to ratify the said articles of confederation and perpetual union, Know Ye, that we, the undersigned delegates, by virtue of the power and authority to us given for that purpose, do, by these presents, in the name and in behalf of our respective constituents, fully and entirely ratify and confirm each and every of the said articles of confederation and perpetual union, and all and singular the matters and things therein contained. And we do further solemnly plight and engage the faith of our respective constituents, that they shall abide by the determinations of the united states in congress assembled, on all questions, which by the said confederation are submitted to them. And that the articles thereof shall be inviolably observed by the states we respectively represent, and that the union shall be perpetual. In Witness whereof, we have hereunto set our hands, in Congress. Done at Philadelphia, in the State of Pennsylvania, the ninth Day of July, in the Year of our Lord one Thousand seven Hundred and Seventy eight, and in the third year of the Independence of America.

---

1. Explain what may have caused the authors to set term limits for members of the Committee of the States.
2. Explain the political process by which the Articles of Confederation could be modified.
3. Describe the type of democracy implied by the election and purpose of the representatives.

The Constitution of the United States of America

Note: The passages that have been amended or superseded have been struck out. In sections with more than one paragraph, paragraph numbers have been added in brackets to help you locate passages easily.

Preamble

We the people of the United States, in order to form a more perfect Union, establish justice, insure domestic tranquility, provide for the common defense, promote the general welfare, and secure the blessings of liberty to ourselves and our posterity [descendants], do ordain [issue] and establish this Constitution for the United States of America.

ARTICLE I. CONGRESS

Section 1. Legislative Power All legislative powers herein granted shall be vested in a Congress of the United States, which shall consist of a Senate and House of Representatives.

Section 2. House of Representatives

[1] The House of Representatives shall be composed of members chosen every second year by the people of the several states, and the electors [voters] in each state shall have the qualifications requisite [required] for electors of the most numerous branch of the state legislature.

[2] No person shall be a representative who shall not have attained to the age of twenty-five years, and been seven years a citizen of the United States, and who shall not, when elected, be an inhabitant of that state in which he shall be chosen.

[3] ~~Representatives and direct taxes shall be apportioned among the several states which may be included within this Union according to their respective numbers [population], which shall be determined by adding to the whole number of free persons, including those bound to service for a term of years [indentured servants], and excluding Indians not taxed, three-fifths of all other persons~~. The actual enumeration [census] shall be made within three years after the first meeting of the Congress of the United States, and within every subsequent term of ten years, in such manner as they shall by law

direct. The number of representatives shall not exceed one for every thirty thousand, but each state shall have at least one representative; ~~and until such enumeration shall be made, the State of New Hampshire shall be entitled to choose three, Massachusetts eight, Rhode Island and Providence Plantations one, Connecticut five, New York six, New Jersey four, Pennsylvania eight, Delaware one, Maryland six, Virginia ten, North Carolina five, South Carolina five, and Georgia three.~~

[4] When vacancies happen in the representation from any state, the executive authority [governor] thereof shall issue writs of election to fill such vacancies.

[5] The House of Representatives shall choose their Speaker and other officers; and shall have the sole power of impeachment.

Section 3. Senate

[1] The Senate of the United States shall be composed of two senators from each state, ~~chosen by the legislature thereof,~~ for six years; and each senator shall have one vote.

[2] Immediately after they shall be assembled in consequence of the first election, they shall be divided as equally as may be into three classes. The seats of the senators of the first class shall be vacated at the expiration of the second year, of the second class at the expiration of the fourth year, and of the third class at the expiration of the sixth year, so that one-third may be chosen every second year; and if vacancies happen by resignation, or otherwise, during the recess of the legislature of any state, the executive [governor] thereof may make temporary appointments until the next meeting of the legislature, which shall then fill such vacancies.

[3] No person shall be a senator who shall not have attained to the age of thirty years and been nine years a citizen of the United States, and who shall not, when elected, be an inhabitant of that state for which he shall be chosen.

[4] The vice president of the United States shall be president of the Senate, but shall have no vote, unless they be equally divided [tied].

[5] The Senate shall choose their other officers, and also a president pro tempore [temporary presiding officer], in the absence of the vice president, or when he shall exercise the office of president of the United States.

[6] The Senate shall have sole power to try all impeachments. When sitting for that purpose, they shall be on oath or affirmation. When the president of the United States is tried, the chief justice [of the United States] shall preside; and no person shall be convicted without the concurrence of two-thirds of the members present.

[7] Judgment in cases of impeachment shall not extend further than to removal from office, and disqualification to hold and enjoy any office of honor, trust, or profit under the United States; but the party convicted shall nevertheless be liable and subject to indictment, trial, judgment, and punishment, according to law.

Section 4. Elections and Meetings of Congress

[1] The times, places, and manner of holding elections for senators and representatives shall be prescribed [designated] in each state by the legislature thereof; but the Congress may at any time by law make or alter such regulations, except as to the places of choosing senators.

[2] The Congress shall assemble at least once in every year, ~~and such meeting shall be on the first Monday in December,~~ unless they shall by law appoint a different day.

Section 5. Rules and Procedures of the Two Houses

[1] Each house shall be the judge of the elections, returns, and qualifications of its own members, and a majority of each shall constitute a quorum to do business; but a smaller number may adjourn from day to day, and may be authorized to compel the attendance of absent members, in such manner, and under such penalties, as each house may provide.

[2] Each house may determine the rules of its proceedings, punish its members for disorderly behavior, and with the concurrence of two-thirds, expel a member.

[3] Each house shall keep a journal of its proceedings, and from time to time publish the same, excepting such parts as may in their judgment require secrecy; and the yeas [affirmative votes] and nays [negative votes] of the members of either house on any question shall, at the desire of one-fifth of those present, be entered on the journal.

[4] Neither house, during the session of Congress, shall, without the consent of the other, adjourn for more than three days, nor to any other place than that in which the two houses shall be sitting.

Section 6. Members' Privileges and Restrictions

[1] The senators and representatives shall receive a compensation for their services, to be ascertained [fixed] by law and paid out of the treasury of the United States. They shall in all cases except treason, felony [serious crime], and breach of the peace [disorderly conduct], be privileged [immune] from arrest during their attendance at the session of their respective houses, and in going to and returning from the same; and for any speech or debate in either house, they shall not be questioned in any other place.

[2] No senator or representative shall, during the time for which he was elected, be appointed to any civil office under the authority of the United States, which shall have been created, or the emoluments [salary] whereof shall have been increased, during such time; and no person holding any office under the United States shall be a member of either house during his continuance in office.

Section 7. Lawmaking Procedures

[1] All bills for raising revenue shall originate in the House of Representatives; but the Senate may propose or concur with amendments as on other bills.

[2] Every bill which shall have passed the House of Representatives and the Senate shall, before it becomes a law, be presented to the president of the United States; if he approve, he shall sign it, but if not, he shall return it, with his objections, to that house in which it shall have originated, who shall enter the objections at large on their journal, and proceed to reconsider it. If after such reconsideration two-thirds of that house shall agree to pass the bill, it shall be sent, together with the objections, to the other house, by which it shall likewise be reconsidered, and, if approved by two-thirds of that house, it shall become a law. But in all such cases the votes of both houses shall be determined by yeas and nays, and the names of the persons voting for and against the bill shall be entered on the journal of each house respectively. If any bill shall not be returned by the president within ten days (Sundays excepted) after it shall have been presented to him, the same shall be a law, in like manner as if he had signed it, unless the Congress by their adjournment prevent its return, in which case it shall not be a law.

[3] Every order, resolution, or vote to which the concurrence of the Senate and House of Representatives may

be necessary (except on a question of adjournment) shall be presented to the president of the United States; and before the same shall take effect, shall be approved by him, or, being disapproved by him, shall be repassed by two-thirds of the Senate and House of Representatives, according to the rules and limitations prescribed in the case of a bill.

Section 8. Powers of Congress The Congress shall have power:

[1] To lay and collect taxes, duties, imposts, and excises, to pay the debts and provide for the common defense and general welfare of the United States; but all duties, imposts, and excises shall be uniform [the same] throughout the United States;

[2] To borrow money on the credit of the United States;

[3] To regulate commerce with foreign nations, and among the several states, and with the Indian tribes;

[4] To establish a uniform rule of naturalization [admitting to citizenship], and uniform laws on the subject of bankruptcies throughout the United States;

[5] To coin money, regulate the value thereof, and of foreign coin, and fix [set] the standard of weights and measures;

[6] To provide for the punishment of counterfeiting the securities and current coin of the United States;

[7] To establish post offices and post roads;

[8] To promote the progress of science and useful arts by securing for limited times to authors and inventors the exclusive right to their respective writings and discoveries;

[9] To constitute tribunals [establish courts] inferior to [lower than] the Supreme Court;

[10] To define and punish piracies and felonies committed on the high seas and offenses against the law of nations [international law];

[11] To declare war, grant letters of marque and reprisal, and make rules concerning captures on land and water;

[12] To raise and support armies, but no appropriation of money to that use shall be for a longer term than two years;

[13] To provide and maintain a navy;

[14] To make rules for the government and regulation of the land and naval forces;

[15] To provide for calling forth the militia to execute [carry out] the laws of the Union, suppress insurrections [rebellions], and repel invasions;

[16] To provide for organizing, arming, and disciplining [training] the militia, and for governing such part of them as may be employed in the service of the United States, reserving to the states respectively the appointment of the officers, and the authority of training the militia according to the discipline [regulations] prescribed by Congress;

[17] To exercise exclusive legislation in all cases whatsoever, over such district (not exceeding ten miles square) as may, by cession of particular states, and the acceptance of Congress, become the seat of government of the United States, and to exercise like authority over all places purchased by the consent of the legislature of the state in which the same shall be, for the erection of forts, magazines [warehouses for explosives], arsenals, dockyards, and other needful buildings; and

[18] To make all laws which shall be necessary and proper for carrying into execution the foregoing powers, and all other powers vested by this Constitution in the government of the United States, or in any department or officer thereof.

Section 9. Powers Denied to the Federal Government

[1] ~~The migration or importation of such persons as any of the states now existing shall think proper to admit shall not be prohibited by the Congress prior to the year 1808; but a tax or duty may be imposed on such importation, not exceeding ten dollars for each person.~~

[2] The privilege of the writ of habeas corpus shall not be suspended, unless when in cases of rebellion or invasion the public safety may require it.

[3] No bill of attainder or ex post facto law shall be passed.

[4] No capitation [head] or other direct tax shall be laid, ~~unless in proportion to the census or enumeration herein before directed to be taken.~~

[5] No tax or duty shall be laid on articles exported from any state.

[6] No preference shall be given by any regulation of commerce or revenue to the ports of one state over those of another; nor shall vessels bound to, or from, one state be obliged to enter, clear, or pay duties in another.

[7] No money shall be drawn from the treasury, but in consequence of appropriations made by law; and a regular statement and account of the receipts and expenditures of all public money shall be published from time to time.

[8] No title of nobility shall be granted by the United States; and no person holding any office of profit or trust under them shall, without the consent of the Congress, accept of any present, emolument, office, or title, of any kind whatever, from any king, prince, or foreign state.

Section 10. Powers Denied to the States

[1] No state shall enter into any treaty, alliance, or confederation; grant letters of marque and reprisal; coin money; emit bills of credit; make anything but gold and silver coin a tender [legal money] in payment of debts; pass any bill of attainder, ex post facto law, or law impairing the obligation of contracts, or grant any title of nobility.

[2] No state shall, without the consent of the Congress, lay any imposts or duties on imports or exports, except what may be absolutely necessary for executing its inspection laws; and the net produce [income] of all duties and imposts, laid by any state on imports or exports, shall be for the use of the treasury of the United States; and all such laws shall be subject to the revision and control of the Congress.

[3] No state shall, without the consent of Congress, lay any duty of tonnage, keep troops or ships of war in time of peace, enter into any agreement or compact with another state or with a foreign power, or engage in war unless actually invaded or in such imminent [threatening] danger as will not admit of delay.

---

1. Identify four relevant categories for comparing the House and the Senate, and explain the similarities and differences within those categories.

2. Explain the reasons for the differences between the House and Senate. What did the framers accomplish with these structures?

3. Explain the significance of the difference between the powers of Congress described in Article I, Section 8, paragraphs 1–17 and the power described in Article I, Section 8, paragraph 18.

ARTICLE II. THE PRESIDENCY

Section 1. Executive Power

[1] The executive power shall be vested in a president of the United States of

America. He shall hold his office during the term of four years, and, together with the vice president, chosen for the same term, be elected as follows:

[2] Each state shall appoint, in such manner as the legislature thereof may direct, a number of electors, equal to the whole number of senators and representatives to which the state may be entitled in the Congress; but no senator or representative, or person holding an office of trust or profit under the United States, shall be appointed an elector.

[3] ~~The electors shall meet in their respective states, and vote by ballot for two persons, of whom one at least shall not be an inhabitant of the same state with themselves. And they shall make a list of all the persons voted for, and of the number of votes for each; which list they shall sign and certify, and transmit sealed to the seat of the government of the United States, directed to the president of the Senate. The president of the Senate shall, in the presence of the Senate and House of Representatives, open all the certificates, and the votes shall then be counted. The person having the greatest number of votes shall be the president, if such number be a majority of the whole number of electors appointed; and if there be more than one who have such majority, and have an equal number of votes, then the House of Representatives shall immediately choose by ballot one of them for president; and if no person have a majority, then from the five highest on the list the said House shall in like manner choose the president. But in choosing the president, the votes shall be taken by states, the representation from each state having one vote; a quorum for this purpose shall consist of a member or members from two-thirds of the states, and a majority of all the states shall be necessary to a choice. In every case, after the choice of the president, the person having the greatest number~~ ~~of votes of the electors shall be the vice president. But if there should remain two or more who have equal votes, the Senate shall choose from them by ballot the vice president.~~

[4] The Congress may determine the time of choosing the electors, and the day on which they shall give their votes; which day shall be the same throughout the United States.

[5] No person except a natural-born citizen, ~~or a citizen of the United States at the time of the adoption of this Constitution,~~ shall be eligible to the office of the president; neither shall any person be eligible to that office who shall not have attained to the age of thirty-five years and been fourteen years a resident within the United States.

[6] ~~In case of the removal of the president from office, or of his death, resignation, or inability to discharge the powers and duties of the said office, the same shall devolve on the vice president, and the Congress may by law provide for the case of removal, death, resignation, or inability, both of the president and vice president, declaring what officer shall then act as president, and such officer shall act accordingly, until the disability be removed, or a president shall be elected.~~

[7] The president shall, at stated times, receive for his services, a compensation, which shall neither be increased nor diminished during the period for which he shall have been elected, and he shall not receive within that period any other emolument from the United States, or any of them.

[8] Before he enter on the execution of his office, he shall take the following oath or affirmation:

"I do solemnly swear (or affirm) that I will faithfully execute the office of President of the United States, and will, to the best of my ability, preserve, protect, and defend the Constitution of the United States."

Section 2. Powers of the President

[1] The president shall be commander in chief of the army and navy [all the armed forces] of the United States, and of the militia of the several states, when called into the actual service of the United States; he may require the opinion in writing of the principal officer in each of the executive departments upon any subject relating to the duties of their respective offices; and he shall have power to grant reprieves and pardons for offenses against the United States except in cases of impeachment.

[2] He shall have power, by and with the advice and consent of the Senate, to make treaties, provided two-thirds of the senators present concur; and he shall nominate, and, by and with the advice and consent of the Senate, shall appoint ambassadors, other public ministers and consuls, judges of the Supreme Court, and all other officers of the United States whose appointments are not herein otherwise provided for and which shall be established by law; but the Congress may by law vest the appointment of such inferior officers as they think proper in the president alone, in the courts of law, or in the heads of departments.

[3] The president shall have power to fill up all vacancies that may happen during the recess of the Senate, by granting commissions which shall expire at the end of their next session.

Section 3. Duties and Responsibilities of the President

He shall, from time to time, give to the Congress information of the state of the Union, and recommend to their consideration such measures as he shall judge necessary and expedient [advisable]; he may, on extraordinary [special] occasions, convene both houses, or either of them, and in case of disagreement between them with respect to the time of adjournment, he may adjourn them to such time

as he shall think proper; he shall receive ambassadors and other public ministers; he shall take care that the laws be faithfully executed, and shall commission [appoint] all the officers of the United States.

Section 4. Impeachment

The president, vice president, and all civil officers of the United States, shall be removed from office on impeachment for, and conviction of, treason, bribery, or other high crimes and misdemeanors [offenses].

---

1. On September 8, 1974, President Gerald Ford issued former President Richard Nixon "a full, free, and absolute pardon" for any wrongdoings while he was president, especially in relation to the Watergate scandal. Describe the executive power Ford used to accomplish this act and the relationship of that power to the duty outlined in Section 3 to "take care that the laws be faithfully executed."

2. Compare the powers of the president with those of the legislature, and explain how those differences affect the government.

ARTICLE III. THE SUPREME COURT AND OTHER COURTS

Section 1. Federal Courts

The judicial power of the United States shall be vested in one Supreme Court, and in such inferior [lower] courts as the Congress may from time to time ordain and establish. The judges, both of the Supreme and inferior courts, shall hold their offices during good behavior, and shall, at stated times, receive for their services a compensation, which shall not be diminished during their continuance in office.

Section 2. Jurisdiction of Federal Court

[1] The judicial power shall extend to all cases in law and equity arising under this Constitution, the laws of the United States, and treaties made, or which shall be made, under their authority; to all cases affecting ambassadors, other public ministers, and consuls; to all cases of admiralty and maritime jurisdiction; to controversies to which the United States shall be a party; to controversies between two or more states, ~~between a state and citizens of another state,~~ between citizens of different states, between citizens of the same state claiming lands under grants of different states, and between a state, or the citizens thereof, and foreign states, citizens, or subjects.

[2] In all cases affecting ambassadors, other public ministers, and consuls, and those in which a state shall be a party, the Supreme Court shall have original jurisdiction. In all the other cases before mentioned, the Supreme Court shall have appellate jurisdiction, both as to law and fact, with such exceptions and under such regulations as the Congress shall make.

[3] The trial of all crimes, except in cases of impeachment, shall be by jury; and such trial shall be held in the state where the said crimes shall have been committed; but when not committed within any state, the trial shall be at such place or places as the Congress may by law have directed.

Section 3. Treason

[1] Treason against the United States shall consist only in levying [carrying on] war against them, or in adhering to [assisting] their enemies, giving them aid and comfort. No person shall be convicted of treason unless on the testimony of two witnesses to the same overt [open; public] act, or on confession in open court.

[2] The Congress shall have power to declare the punishment of treason, but no attainder of treason shall work corruption of blood or forfeiture except during the life of the person attainted.

---

1. Based on Article III, under what jurisdiction did the Supreme Court hear the cases that are required for this course? Explain how the cases reached the Court.

2. Compare the process for settling disputes between states outlined in the Articles of Confederation with the process outlined in the Constitution. Draw a conclusion about the purpose of the plan for the courts outlined in the Constitution that was lacking in the plan in the Articles of Confederation.

ARTICLE IV. INTERSTATE RELATIONS

Section 1. Official Acts and Records

Full faith and credit shall be given in each state to the public acts, records, and judicial proceedings of every other state. And the Congress may, by general laws, prescribe the manner in which such acts, records, and proceedings shall be proved, and the effect thereof.

Section 2. Mutual Obligations of States

[1] The citizens of each state shall be entitled to all privileges and immunities of citizens in the several states.

[2] A person charged in any state with treason, felony, or other crime, who shall flee from justice and be found in another state, shall, on demand of the executive authority of the state from which he fled, be delivered up, to be removed to the state having jurisdiction of the crime.

[3] ~~No person held to service or labor in one state, under the laws thereof, escaping into another, shall, in consequence of any law or regulation~~

~~therein, be discharged from such service or labor, but shall be delivered up on claim of the party to whom such service or labor may be due.~~

Section 3. New States and Territories

[1] New states may be admitted by the Congress into this Union; but no new state shall be formed or erected within the jurisdiction of any other state; nor any state be formed by the junction [joining] of two or more states, or parts of states, without the consent of the legislatures of the states concerned as well as of the Congress.

[2] The Congress shall have power to dispose of and make all needful rules and regulations respecting the territory or other property belonging to the United States; and nothing in this Constitution shall be so construed [interpreted] as to prejudice [damage] any claims of the United States, or of any particular state.

Section 4. Federal Guarantees to the States
The United States shall guarantee to every state in this Union a republican form of government, and shall protect each of them against invasion; and on application of the legislature, or of the executive (when the legislature cannot be convened), against domestic violence [riots].

---

1. Describe ways in which the United States government can "guarantee to every state in this Union a republican form of government."

2. Much of the remaining conflict related to Article IV centers on family law issues. For example, the legal adoption of a child by unmarried partners in one state is not recognized in another state that does not allow unmarried partners to adopt. Based on the example of *Obergefell v. Hodges* (2015), what might be necessary to make such adoptions uniformly recognized?

ARTICLE V. AMENDING THE CONSTITUTION

The Congress, whenever two-thirds of both houses shall deem [think] it necessary, shall propose amendments to this Constitution, or, on the application of the legislatures of two-thirds of the several states, shall call a convention for proposing amendments, which, in either case, shall be valid, to all intents and purposes, as part of this Constitution when ratified by the legislatures of three-fourths of the several states, or by conventions in three-fourths thereof, as the one or the other mode [method] of ratification may be proposed by the Congress; provided ~~that no amendment which may be made prior to the year 1808 shall in any manner affect the first and fourth clauses in the ninth section of the first article; and~~ that no state, without its consent, shall be deprived of its equal suffrage in the Senate.

---

1. Describe the steps in one of the legal processes for amending the Constitution.

2. Describe the steps in another legal process for amending the Constitution.

ARTICLE VI. MISCELLANEOUS PROVISIONS

Section 1. Public Debts
All debts contracted and engagements [agreements] entered into before the adoption of this Constitution shall be as valid [binding] against the United States under this Constitution as under the Confederation.

Section 2. Federal Supremacy This Constitution, and the laws of the United States which shall be made in pursuance thereof, and all treaties made, or which shall be made, under the authority of the United States, shall be the supreme law of the land; and the judges in every state shall be bound thereby, anything in the Constitution or laws of any state to the contrary notwithstanding.

Section 3. Oaths of Office The senators and representatives before mentioned, and the members of the several state legislatures, and all executive and judicial officers, both of the United States and of the several states, shall be bound by oath or affirmation to support this Constitution; but no religious test shall ever be required as a qualification to any office or public trust under the United States.

ARTICLE VII. RATIFICATION

~~The ratification of the conventions of nine states shall be sufficient for the establishment of this Constitution between the states so ratifying the same.~~

Done in convention, by the unanimous consent of the states present, the 17th day of September, in the year of our Lord 1787, and of the independence of the United States of America the twelfth. In witness whereof we have hereunto subscribed our names.

Signed by

George Washington

[President and Deputy from Virginia]

and 38 other delegates

---

1. Explain the reasons the Constitution, in contrast to the Articles of Confederation, made the federal government the "supreme law of the land."

2. The absence of a religious test was a matter of debate in many state ratification conventions. At the 1788 convention in Massachusetts, Theophilus Parsons expressed his views: "But what security is it to government, that every publick officer shall swear that he is a christian? . . . . Sir, the only evidence we can have of the sincerity and excellency of a man's religion, is a good life—and I trust that such evidence will be required of every candidate by every elector. That man who acts an honest part to his neighbour, will most probably conduct honourably towards the publick." Has the electorate lived up to Parsons's expectations? Provide an example to explain your position.

Amendments to the Constitution

Note: The first ten amendments to the Constitution, adopted in 1791, make up the Bill of Rights. The year of adoption of later amendments (11 to 27) is given in parentheses.

AMENDMENT I. FREEDOM OF RELIGION, SPEECH, PRESS, ASSEMBLY, AND PETITION

Congress shall make no law respecting an establishment of religion, or prohibiting the free exercise thereof; or abridging [reducing] the freedom of speech or of the press; or the right of the people peaceably to assemble, and to petition the government for a redress [correction] of grievances.

AMENDMENT II. RIGHT TO BEAR ARMS

A well-regulated militia being necessary to the security of a free state, the right of the people to keep and bear arms shall not be infringed [weakened].

AMENDMENT III. QUARTERING OF TROOPS

No soldier shall, in time of peace, be quartered [assigned to live] in any house without the consent of the owner, nor in time of war, but in a manner to be prescribed by law.

AMENDMENT IV. SEARCHES AND SEIZURES

The right of the people to be secure [safe] in their persons, houses, papers, and effects [be-longings] against unreasonable searches and seizures shall not be violated; and no [search] warrants shall issue but upon probable cause, supported by oath or affirmation, and particularly describing the place to be searched, and the persons or things to be seized.

AMENDMENT V. RIGHTS OF THE ACCUSED; PROPERTY RIGHTS

No person shall be held to answer for a capital or otherwise infamous crime unless on a presentment or indictment of a grand jury, except in cases arising in the land or naval forces, or in the militia, when in actual service in time of war or public danger; nor shall any person be subject for the same offense to be twice put in jeopardy of life or limb; nor shall be compelled in any criminal case to be a witness against himself; nor be deprived of life, liberty, or property without due process of law; nor shall private property be taken for public use without just compensation.

AMENDMENT VI. ADDITIONAL RIGHTS OF THE ACCUSED

In all criminal prosecutions [trials], the accused shall enjoy the right to a speedy and public trial by an impartial [fair] jury of the state and district wherein the crime shall have been committed, which district shall have been previously ascertained by law; and to be informed of the nature and cause of the accusation; to be confronted with the witnesses against him; to have compulsory process for obtaining witnesses in his favor; and to have the assistance of counsel for his defense.

AMENDMENT VII. CIVIL SUITS

In suits at common law where the value in controversy shall exceed twenty dollars, the right of trial by jury shall be preserved, and no fact tried by a jury shall be otherwise reexamined in any court of the United States, than according to the rules of the common law.

AMENDMENT VIII. BAILS, FINES, AND PUNISHMENTS

Excessive bail shall not be required, nor excessive fines imposed, nor cruel and unusual punishments inflicted.

AMENDMENT IX. RIGHTS NOT LISTED

The enumeration [listing] in the Constitution of certain rights shall not be construed to deny or disparage [weaken] others retained by the people.

AMENDMENT X. POWERS RESERVED TO THE STATES AND PEOPLE

The powers not delegated to the United States by the Constitution, nor prohibited by it to the states, are reserved to the states respectively, or to the people.

---

1. Describe the philosophical and political assumptions underlying the provisions in the Bill of Rights.

2. On the basis of the Ninth and Tenth Amendments, describe the powers the states and the people have in the federalist system.

AMENDMENT XI. SUITS AGAINST STATES (1798)

The judicial power of the United States shall not be construed to extend to any suit in law or equity, commenced or prosecuted against one of the United States by citizens of another state, or by citizens or subjects of any foreign state.

AMENDMENT XII. ELECTION OF PRESIDENT AND VICE PRESIDENT (1804)

[1] The electors shall meet in their respective states, and vote by ballot for president and vice president, one of whom at least shall not be an inhabitant of the same state with themselves; they shall name in their ballots the person voted for as president, and in distinct [separate] ballots the person voted for as vice president; and they shall make distinct lists of all persons voted for as president, and of all persons voted for as vice president, and of the number of votes for each, which lists they shall sign and certify, and transmit sealed to the seat of the government of the United States, directed to the president of the Senate.

[2] The president of the Senate shall, in the presence of the Senate and House of Representatives, open all the certificates, and the votes shall then be counted; the person having the greatest number of votes for president shall be the president, if such number be a majority of the whole number of electors appointed; and if no person have such majority, then from the persons having the highest numbers not exceeding three on the list of those voted for as president, the House of Representatives shall choose immediately, by ballot, the president. But in choosing the president, the votes shall be taken by states, the representation from each state having one vote; a quorum for this purpose shall consist of a member or members from two-thirds of the states, and a majority of all the states shall be necessary to a choice. And if the House of Representatives shall not choose a president whenever the right of choice shall devolve upon them, ~~before the fourth day of March next following~~, then the vice president shall act as president, as in the case of the death or other constitutional disability of the president.

[3] The person having the greatest number of votes as vice president shall be the vice president, if such number be a majority of the whole number of electors appointed; and if no person have a majority, then from the two highest numbers on the list, the Senate shall choose the vice president; a quorum for the purpose shall consist of two-thirds of the whole number of senators, and a majority of the whole number shall be necessary to a choice. But no person constitutionally ineligible to the office of president shall be eligible to that of vice president of the United States.

AMENDMENT XIII. ABOLITION OF SLAVERY (1865)

Section 1. Slavery Forbidden   Neither slavery nor involuntary servitude [compulsory service], except as a punishment for crime whereof the party shall have been duly convicted, shall exist within the United States, or any place subject to their jurisdiction.

Section 2. Enforcement Power   Congress shall have power to enforce this article [amendment] by appropriate [suitable] legislation.

AMENDMENT XIV. CITIZENSHIP AND CIVIL RIGHTS (1868)

Section 1. Rights of Citizens   All persons born or naturalized in the United States, and subject to the jurisdiction thereof, are citizens of the United States and of the state wherein they reside. No state shall make or enforce any law which shall abridge the privileges or immunities of citizens of the United

States; nor shall any state deprive any person of life, liberty, or property, without due process of law; nor deny to any person within its jurisdiction the equal protection of the laws.

Section 2. Apportionment of Representatives in Congress
Representatives shall be apportioned among the several states according to their respective numbers, counting the whole number of persons in each state, excluding Indians not taxed. But when the right to vote at any election for the choice of electors for president and vice president of the United States, representatives in Congress, the executive and judicial officers of a state, or the members of the legislature thereof, is denied to any of the *male* inhabitants of such state, being *twenty-one* years of age and citizens of the United States, or in any way abridged, except for participation in rebellion or other crime, the basis of representation therein shall be reduced in the proportion which the number of such *male* citizens shall bear to the whole number of *male* citizens *twenty-one* years of age in such state.

Section 3. Persons Disqualified from Public Office
No person shall be a senator or representative in Congress, or elector of president and vice president, or hold any office, civil or military, under the United States, or under any state, who, having previously taken an oath, as a member of Congress, or as an officer of the United States, or as a member of any state legislature, or as an executive or judicial officer of any state, to support the Constitution of the United States, shall have engaged in insurrection or rebellion against the same, or given aid or comfort to the enemies thereof. But Congress may, by a vote of two-thirds of each house, remove such disability.

Section 4. Valid Public Debt Defined
The validity [legality] of the public debt of the United States, authorized by law, including debts incurred for payment of pensions and bounties [extra allowances] for services in suppressing insurrection or rebellion, shall not be questioned. But neither the United States nor any state shall assume or pay any debt or obligation incurred in aid of insurrection or rebellion against the United States, or any claim for the loss or emancipation [liberation] of any slave; but all such debts, obligations, and claims shall be held illegal and void.

Section 5. Enforcement Power
The Congress shall have power to enforce, by appropriate legislation, the provisions of this article.

AMENDMENT XV. RIGHT OF SUFFRAGE (1870)

Section 1. African Americans Guaranteed the Vote
The right of citizens of the United States to vote shall not be denied or abridged by the United States or by any state on account of race, color, or previous condition of servitude [slavery].

Section 2. Enforcement Power
The Congress shall have power to enforce this article by appropriate legislation.

---

1. All three "Reconstruction Amendments"—the Thirteenth, Fourteenth, and Fifteenth—conclude with an "Enforcement of Power" section. Explain how this differs from the necessary and proper clause in Article I, Section 8.

2. The Fourteenth Amendment, especially its due process clause, has been called the "Second Bill of Rights." Explain the effect of the Fourteenth Amendment on incorporation of the Bill of Rights.

AMENDMENT XVI. INCOME TAXES (1913)

The Congress shall have power to lay and collect taxes on incomes, from whatever source derived, without apportionment among the several states, and without regard to any census or enumeration.

AMENDMENT XVII. POPULAR ELECTION OF SENATORS (1913)

[1] The Senate of the United States shall be composed of two senators from each state, elected by the people thereof, for six years; and each senator shall have one vote. The electors [voters] in each state shall have the qualifications requisite for electors of the most numerous branch of the state legislatures.

[2] When vacancies happen in the representation of any state in the Senate, the executive authority of such state shall issue writs of election to fill such vacancies: Provided, that the legislature of any state may empower [authorize] the executive thereof to make temporary appointments until the people fill the vacancies by election as the legislature may direct.

[3] This amendment shall not be so construed as to affect the election or term of any senator chosen before it becomes valid as part of the Constitution.

AMENDMENT XVIII. PROHIBITION (1919)

Section 1. Intoxicating Liquors Prohibited After one year from the ratification of this article, the manufacture, sale, or transportation of intoxicating liquors within, the importation thereof into, or the exportation thereof from the United States and all territory subject to the jurisdiction thereof, for beverage purposes is hereby prohibited.

Section 2. Enforcement Power The Congress and the several states shall have concurrent power to enforce this article by appropriate legislation.

Section 3. Conditions of Ratification This article shall be inoperative unless it shall have been ratified as an amendment to the Constitution by the legislatures of the several states, as provided in the Constitution, within seven years from the date of the submission hereof to the states by the Congress.

AMENDMENT XIX. WOMEN'S SUFFRAGE (1920)

[1] The right of citizens of the United States to vote shall not be denied or abridged by the United States or by any state on account of sex.

[2] Congress shall have power to enforce this article by appropriate legislation.

AMENDMENT XX. PRESIDENTIAL AND CONGRESSIONAL TERMS (1933)

Section 1. Terms of Office The terms of the president and vice president shall end at noon on the 20th day of January, and the terms of senators and representatives at noon on the 3d day of January, of the years in which such terms would have ended if this article had not been ratified; and the terms of their successors shall then begin.

Section 2. Convening Congress The Congress shall assemble at least once in every year, and such meeting shall begin at noon on the 3rd day of January, unless they shall by law appoint a different day.

Section 3. Presidential Succession If, at the time fixed for the beginning of the term of the president, the president-elect shall have died, the vice president-elect shall become president. If a president shall not have been chosen before the time fixed for the beginning of his term, or if the president-elect shall have failed to qualify, then the vice president-elect shall act as president until a president shall have qualified; and the Congress may by law provide for the case wherein neither a president-elect nor a vice president-elect shall have qualified, declaring who shall then act as president, or the manner in which one who is to act shall be selected, and such person shall act accordingly until a president or vice president shall have qualified.

Section 4. Selection of President and Vice President   The Congress may by law provide for the case of the death of any of the persons from whom the House of Representatives may choose a president whenever the right of choice shall have devolved upon them, and for the case of the death of any of the persons from whom the Senate may choose a vice president whenever the right of choice shall have devolved upon them.

Section 5. Effective Date   ~~Sections 1 and 2 shall take effect on the 15th day of October following the ratification of this article.~~

Section 6. Conditions of Ratification   ~~This article shall be inoperative unless it shall have been ratified as an amendment to the Constitution by the legislatures of three-fourths of the several states within seven years from the date of its submission.~~

AMENDMENT XXI. REPEAL OF PROHIBITION (1933)

Section 1. Amendment XVIII Repealed   The eighteenth article of amendment to the Constitution of the United States is hereby repealed.

Section 2. Shipment of Liquor into "Dry" Areas   The transportation or importation into any state, territory, or possession of the United States for delivery or use therein of intoxicating liquors in violation of the laws thereof is hereby prohibited.

Section 3. Conditions of Ratification   ~~This article shall be inoperative unless it shall have been ratified as an amendment to the Constitution by conventions in the several states, as provided in the Constitution, within seven years from the date of the submission hereof to the states by the Congress.~~

AMENDMENT XXII. LIMITING PRESIDENTIAL TERMS (1951)

Section 1. Limit Placed on Tenure   No person shall be elected to the office of the president more than twice, and no person who has held the office of president, or acted as president, for more than two years of a term to which some other person was elected president shall be elected to the office of the president more than once. ~~But this article shall not apply to any person holding the office of president when this article was proposed by the Congress, and shall not prevent any person who may be holding the office of president, or acting as president, during the term within which this article becomes operative from holding the office of president or acting as president during the remainder of such term.~~

Section 2. Conditions of Ratification   ~~This article shall be inoperative unless it shall have been ratified as an amendment to the Constitution by the legislatures of three-fourths of the several states within seven years from the date of its submission to the states by the Congress.~~

AMENDMENT XXIII. SUFFRAGE FOR WASHINGTON, D.C. (1961)

Section 1. D.C. Presidential Electors   The district constituting [making up] the seat of government of the United States shall appoint in such manner as the Congress may direct:

A number of electors of president and vice president equal to the whole number of senators and representatives in Congress to which the district would be entitled if it were a state, but in no event more than the least populous state; they shall be in addition to those appointed by the states, but they shall be considered, for the purposes of the election of president and vice president, to be electors appointed by a state; and they shall meet in the district and perform such duties as provided by the Twelfth Article of amendment.

Section 2. Enforcement Power   The Congress shall have power to enforce this article by appropriate legislation.

AMENDMENT XXIV. POLL TAXES (1964)

Section 1. Poll Tax Barred   The right of citizens of the United States to vote in any primary or other election for president or vice president, for electors for president or vice president, or for senator or representative in Congress, shall not be denied or abridged by the United States or any state by reason of failure to pay any poll tax or other tax.

Section 2. Enforcement Power   The Congress shall have the power to enforce this article by appropriate legislation.

AMENDMENT XXV. PRESIDENTIAL SUCCESSION AND DISABILITY (1967)

Section 1. Elevation of Vice President   In case of the removal of the president from office or his death or resignation, the vice president shall become president.

Section 2. Vice Presidential Vacancy   Whenever there is a vacancy in the office of the vice president, the president shall nominate a vice president who shall take the office upon confirmation by a majority vote of both houses of Congress.

Section 3. Temporary Disability   Whenever the president transmits to the president pro tempore of the Senate and the Speaker of the House of Representatives his written declaration that he is unable to discharge the powers and duties of his office, and until he transmits to them a written declaration to the contrary, such powers and duties shall be discharged by the vice president as acting president.

Section 4. Other Provisions for Presidential Disability

[1] Whenever the vice president and a majority of either the principal officers of the executive departments or of such other body as Congress may by law provide, transmit to the president pro tempore of the Senate and the Speaker of the House of Representatives their written declaration that the president is unable to discharge the powers and duties of his office, the vice president shall immediately assume the powers and duties of the office as acting president.

[2] Thereafter, when the president transmits to the president pro tempore of the Senate and the Speaker of the House of Representatives his written declaration that no inability exists, he shall resume the powers and duties of his office unless the vice president and a majority of either the principal officers of the executive department or of such other body as Congress may by law provide, transmit within four days to the president pro tempore of the Senate and the Speaker of the House of Representatives their written declaration that the president is unable to discharge the powers and duties of his office. Thereupon Congress shall decide the issue, assembling within 48 hours for that purpose if not in session. If the Congress, within 21 days after receipt of the latter written declaration, or, if Congress is not in session, within 21 days after Congress is required to assemble, determines by two-thirds vote of both houses that the president is unable to discharge the powers and duties of his office, the vice president shall continue to discharge the same as acting president; otherwise, the president shall resume the powers and duties of his office.

AMENDMENT XXVI. VOTE FOR 18-YEAR-OLDS (1971)

Section 1. Lowering the Voting

Age The right of citizens of the United States, who are 18 years of age or older, to vote shall not be denied or abridged by the United States or by any state on account of age.

Section 2. Enforcement Power The Congress shall have power to enforce this article by appropriate legislation.

AMENDMENT XXVII. CONGRESSIONAL PAY (1992)

No law, varying the compensation for the services of the Senators and Representatives, shall take effect, until an election of Representatives shall have intervened.

Federalist No. 10

The Same Subject Continued—The Utility of the Union as a Safeguard Against Domestic Faction and Insurrection

November 23, 1787—To the People of the State of New York:

[1] Among the numerous advantages promised by a well-constructed Union, none deserves to be more accurately developed than its tendency to break and control the violence of faction. The friend of popular Governments never finds himself so much alarmed for their character and fate, as when he contemplates their propensity to this dangerous vice. He will not fail, therefore, to set a due value on any plan which, without violating the principles to which he is attached, provides a proper cure for it. The instability, injustice, and confusion introduced into the public councils, have, in truth, been the mortal diseases under which popular Governments have everywhere perished; as they continue to be the favorite and fruitful topics from which the adversaries to liberty derive their most specious [misleading but appealing] declamations. The valuable improvements made by the American Constitutions on the popular models, both ancient and modern, cannot certainly be too much admired; but it would be an unwarrantable partiality, to contend that they have as effectually obviated [bypassed] the danger on this side, as was wished and expected. Complaints are everywhere heard from our most considerate and virtuous citizens, equally the friends of public and private faith, and of public and personal liberty, that our Governments are too unstable; that the public good is disregarded in the conflicts of rival parties; and that measures are too often decided, not according to the rules of justice, and the rights of the minor party, but by the superior force of an interested and overbearing majority. However anxiously we may wish that these complaints had no foundation, the evidence of known facts will not permit us to deny that they are in some degree true. It will be found, indeed, on a candid review of our situation, that some of the distresses under which we labor have been erroneously charged on the operation of our Governments; but it will be found, at the same time, that other causes will not alone account for many of our heaviest misfortunes; and, particularly, for that prevailing and increasing distrust of public engagements, and alarm for private rights, which are echoed from one end of the continent to the other. These must be chiefly, if not wholly, effects of the unsteadiness and injustice, with which a factious spirit has tainted our public administrations.

[2] By a faction, I understand a number of citizens, whether amounting to a majority or a minority of the whole, who are united and actuated [motivated] by some

common impulse of passion, or of interest, adverse to the rights of other citizens, or to the permanent and aggregate interests of the community.

[3] There are two methods of curing the mischiefs of faction: the one, by removing its causes; the other, by controlling its effects.

[4] There are again two methods of removing the causes of faction: the one, by destroying the liberty which is essential to its existence; the other, by giving to every citizen the same opinions, the same passions, and the same interests.

[5] It could never be more truly said than of the first remedy, that it was worse than the disease. Liberty is to faction what air is to fire, an aliment [nourishment] without which it instantly expires. But it could not be less folly to abolish liberty, which is essential to political life, because it nourishes faction, than it would be to wish the annihilation of air, which is essential to animal life, because it imparts to fire its destructive agency.

[6] The second expedient is as impracticable, as the first would be unwise. As long as the reason of man continues fallible, and he is at liberty to exercise it, different opinions will be formed. As long as the connection subsists between his reason and his self-love, his opinions and his passions will have a reciprocal influence on each other; and the former will be objects to which the latter will attach themselves. The diversity in the faculties of men, from which the rights of property originate, is not less an insuperable obstacle to a uniformity of interests. The protection of these faculties is the first object of Government. From the protection of different and unequal faculties of acquiring property, the possession of different degrees and kinds of property immediately results; and from the influence of these on the sentiments and views of the respective proprietors, ensues a division of the society into different interests and parties.

[7] The latent causes of faction are thus sown in the nature of man; and we see them everywhere brought into different degrees of activity, according to the different circumstances of civil society. A zeal for different opinions concerning religion, concerning Government, and many other points, as well of speculation as of practice; an attachment to different leaders ambitiously contending for preëminence and power; or to persons of other descriptions whose fortunes have been interesting to the human passions, have, in turn, divided mankind into parties, inflamed them with mutual animosity, and rendered them much more disposed to vex and oppress each other, than to coöperate for their common good. So strong is this propensity of mankind to fall into mutual animosities, that where no substantial occasion presents itself, the most frivolous and fanciful distinctions have been sufficient to kindle their unfriendly passions, and excite their most violent conflicts. But the most common and durable source of factions has been the various and unequal distribution of property. Those who hold, and those who are without property, have ever formed distinct interests in society. Those who are creditors, and those who are debtors, fall under a like discrimination. A landed interest, a manufacturing interest, a mercantile interest, a moneyed interest, with many lesser interests, grow up of necessity in civilized nations, and divide them into different classes, actuated by different sentiments and views. The regulation of these various and interfering interests forms the principal task of modern Legislation, and involves the spirit of party and faction in the necessary and ordinary operations of the Government.

[8] No man is allowed to be a judge in his own cause; because his interest would certainly bias his judgment, and, not improbably, corrupt his integrity. With equal,

nay with greater reason, a body of men are unfit to be both judges and parties at the same time; yet what are many of the most important acts of legislation, but so many judicial determinations, not indeed concerning the rights of single persons, but concerning the rights of large bodies of citizens? and what are the different classes of Legislators, but advocates and parties to the causes which they determine? Is a law proposed concerning private debts? It is a question to which the creditors are parties on one side and the debtors on the other. Justice ought to hold the balance between them. Yet the parties are, and must be, themselves the judges; and the most numerous party, or, in other words, the most powerful faction, must be expected to prevail. Shall domestic manufactures be encouraged, and in what degree, by restrictions on foreign manufactures? are questions which would be differently decided by the landed and the manufacturing classes; and probably by neither, with a sole regard to justice and the public good. The apportionment of taxes on the various descriptions of property is an act which seems to require the most exact impartiality; yet there is, perhaps, no legislative act in which greater opportunity and temptation are given to a predominant party, to trample on the rules of justice. Every shilling, with which they overburden the inferior number, is a shilling saved to their own pockets.

[9] It is in vain to say, that enlightened statesmen will be able to adjust these clashing interests, and render them all subservient to the public good. Enlightened statesmen will not always be at the helm: Nor, in many cases, can such an adjustment be made at all, without taking into view indirect and remote considerations, which will rarely prevail over the immediate interest which one party may find in disregarding the rights of another, or the good of the whole.

[10] The inference to which we are brought is, that the causes of faction cannot be removed; and that relief is only to be sought in the means of controlling its effects.

[11] If a faction consists of less than a majority, relief is supplied by the republican principle, which enables the majority to defeat its sinister views by regular vote. It may clog the administration, it may convulse the society; but it will be unable to execute and mask its violence under the forms of the Constitution. When a majority is included in a faction, the form of popular Government, on the other hand, enables it to sacrifice to its ruling passion or interest both the public good and the rights of other citizens. To secure the public good, and private rights, against the danger of such a faction, and at the same time to preserve the spirit and the form of popular Government, is then the great object to which our inquiries are directed: Let me add, that it is the great desideratum [object desired], by which this form of Government can be rescued from the opprobrium [criticism] under which it has so long labored, and be recommended to the esteem and adoption of mankind.

[12] By what means is this object attainable? Evidently by one of two only. Either the existence of the same passion or interest in a majority, at the same time, must be prevented; or the majority, having such coexistent passion or interest, must be rendered, by their number and local situation, unable to concert and carry into effect schemes of oppression. If the impulse and the opportunity be suffered to coincide, we well know that neither moral nor religious motives can be relied on as an adequate control. They are not found to be such on the injustice and violence of individuals, and lose their efficacy in proportion to the number combined together; that is, in proportion as their efficacy becomes needful.

[13] From this view of the subject, it may be concluded, that a pure Democracy, by which I mean a Society consisting of a small number of citizens, who assemble

and administer the Government in person, can admit of no cure for the mischiefs of faction. A common passion or interest will, in almost every case, be felt by a majority of the whole; a communication and concert result from the form of Government itself; and there is nothing to check the inducements to sacrifice the weaker party, or an obnoxious individual. Hence it is, that such Democracies have ever been spectacles of turbulence and contention; have ever been found incompatible with personal security, or the rights of property; and have in general been as short in their lives, as they have been violent in their deaths. Theoretic politicians, who have patronized this species of Government, have erroneously supposed, that by reducing mankind to a perfect equality in their political rights, they would, at the same time, be perfectly equalized and assimilated in their possessions, their opinions, and their passions.

[14] A Republic, by which I mean a Government in which the scheme of representation takes place, opens a different prospect, and promises the cure for which we are seeking. Let us examine the points in which it varies from pure Democracy, and we shall comprehend both the nature of the cure, and the efficacy which it must derive from the Union.

[15] The two great points of difference, between a Democracy and a Republic, are, first, the delegation of the Government, in the latter, to a small number of citizens elected by the rest: Secondly, the greater number of citizens, and greater sphere of country, over which the latter may be extended.

[16] The effect of the first difference is, on the one hand, to refine and enlarge the public views, by passing them through the medium of a chosen body of citizens, whose wisdom may best discern the true interest of their country, and whose patriotism and love of justice will be least likely to sacrifice it to temporary or partial considerations. Under such a regulation, it may well happen, that the public voice, pronounced by the representatives of the People, will be more consonant to the public good, than if pronounced by the People themselves, convened for the purpose. On the other hand, the effect may be inverted. Men of factious tempers, of local prejudices, or of sinister designs, may by intrigue, by corruption, or by other means, first obtain the suffrages, and then betray the interests of the people. The question resulting is, whether small or extensive Republics are more favorable to the election of proper guardians of the public weal [wellbeing]; and it is clearly decided in favor of the latter by two obvious considerations.

[17] In the first place, it is to be remarked that however small the Republic may be, the Representatives must be raised to a certain number, in order to guard against the cabals of a few; and that however large it may be, they must be limited to a certain number, in order to guard against the confusion of a multitude. Hence, the number of Representatives in the two cases not being in proportion to that of the Constituents, and being proportionally greater in the small Republic, it follows, that if the proportion of fit characters be not less in the large than in the small Republic, the former will present a greater option, and consequently a greater probability of a fit choice.

[18] In the next place, as each Representative will be chosen by a greater number of citizens in the large than in the small Republic, it will be more difficult for unworthy candidates to practice with success the vicious arts, by which elections are too often carried; and the suffrages of the People, being more free, will be more likely to center in men who possess the most attractive merit, and the most diffusive and established characters.

[19] It must be confessed, that in this, as in most other cases, there is a mean, on both sides of which inconveniences will be found to lie. By enlarging too much the number of electors, you render the representatives too little acquainted with all their local circumstances and lesser interests; as by reducing it too much, you render him unduly attached to these, and too little fit to comprehend and pursue great and National objects. The Federal Constitution forms a happy combination in this respect; the great and aggregate interests being referred to the National, the local and particular to the State Legislatures.

[20] The other point of difference is, the greater number of citizens and extent of territory which may be brought within the compass of Republican, than of Democratic Government; and it is this circumstance principally which renders factious combinations less to be dreaded in the former, than in the latter. The smaller the society, the fewer probably will be the distinct parties and interests composing it; the fewer the distinct parties and interests, the more frequently will a majority be found of the same party; and the smaller the number of individuals composing a majority, and the smaller the compass within which they are placed, the more easily will they concert and execute their plans of oppression. Extend the sphere, and you take in a greater variety of parties and interests; you make it less probable that a majority of the whole will have a common motive to invade the rights of other citizens; or if such a common motive exists, it will be more difficult for all who feel it to discover their own strength, and to act in unison with each other. Besides other impediments, it may be remarked, that where there is a consciousness of unjust or dishonorable purposes, communication is always checked by distrust, in proportion to the number whose concurrence is necessary.

[21] Hence, it clearly appears, that the same advantage which a Republic has over a Democracy, in controlling the effects of faction, is enjoyed by a large over a small Republic, is enjoyed by the Union over the States composing it. Does the advantage consist in the substitution of Representatives, whose enlightened views and virtuous sentiments render them superior to local prejudices, and to schemes of injustice? It will not be denied, that the Representation of the Union will be most likely to possess these requisite endowments. Does it consist in the greater security afforded by a greater variety of parties, against the event of any one party being able to outnumber and oppress the rest? In an equal degree does the increased variety of parties, comprised within the Union, increase this security. Does it, in fine, consist in the greater obstacles opposed to the concert and accomplishment of the secret wishes of an unjust and interested majority? Here, again, the extent of the Union gives it the most palpable advantage.

[22] The influence of factious leaders may kindle a flame within their particular States, but will be unable to spread a general conflagration through the other States: A religious sect may degenerate into a political faction in a part of the Confederacy; but the variety of sects dispersed over the entire face of it, must secure the National Councils against any danger from that source; A rage for paper money, for an abolition of debts, for an equal division of property, or for any other improper or wicked project, will be less apt to pervade the whole body of the Union, than a particular member of it; in the same proportion as such a malady is more likely to taint a particular county or district, than an entire State.

[23] In the extent and proper structure of the Union, therefore, we behold a Republican remedy for the diseases most incident to Republican Government.

And according to the degree of pleasure and pride we feel in being Republicans, ought to be our zeal in cherishing the spirit, and supporting the character, of Federalists.—PUBLIUS.

---

1. Explain the distinctions Publius makes between a democracy and a republic in paragraphs 12–14.
2. Explain the effects of those distinctions on the ability to tame factions (paragraphs 15–19).
3. Explain how the federal constitution "forms a happy combination" regarding local versus national issues.

Brutus No. 1

18 October, 1787—To the Citizens of the State of New York

[1] When the public is called to investigate and decide upon a question in which not only the present members of the community are deeply interested, but upon which the happiness and misery of generations yet unborn is in great measure suspended, the benevolent mind cannot help feeling itself peculiarly interested in the result.

[2] In this situation, I trust the feeble efforts of an individual, to lead the minds of the people to a wise and prudent determination, cannot fail of being acceptable to the candid and dispassionate part of the community. Encouraged by this consideration, I have been induced to offer my thoughts upon the present important crisis of our public affairs.

[3] Perhaps this country never saw so critical a period in their political concerns. We have felt the feebleness of the ties by which these United States are held together, and the want of sufficient energy in our present Confederation, to manage, in some instances, our general concerns. Various expedients have been proposed to remedy these evils, but none have succeeded. At length a Convention of the States has been assembled, they have formed a Constitution which will now, probably, be submitted to the people to ratify or reject, who are the fountain of all power, to whom alone it of right belongs to make or unmake constitutions or forms of government, at their pleasure. The most important question that was ever proposed to the decision of any people under heaven, is before you, and you are to decide upon it by men of your own election, chosen specially for this purpose. If the Constitution, offered to your acceptance, be a wise one, calculated to preserve the invaluable blessings of liberty, to secure the inestimable rights of mankind, and promote human happiness, then, if you accept it, you will lay a lasting foundation of happiness for millions yet unborn; generations to come will rise up and call you blessed. You may rejoice in the prospects of this vast extended continent becoming filled with freemen, who will assert the dignity of human nature. You may solace yourselves with the idea, that society, in this favored land, will fast advance to the highest point of perfection; the human mind will expand in knowledge and virtue, and the golden age be, in some measure, realized. But if, on the other hand, this form of government contains principles that will lead to the subversion of liberty—if it tends to establish a despotism, or, what is worse, a tyrannic aristocracy; then, if you adopt it, this only remaining asylum for liberty will be shut up, and posterity will execrate [curse] your memory.

[4] Momentous then is the question you have to determine, and you are called upon by every motive which should influence a noble and virtuous mind, to examine it well, and to make up a wise judgment. It is insisted, indeed, that this Constitution must be received, be it ever so imperfect. If it has its defects, it is said, they can be best amended when they are experienced. But remember, when the people once part with power, they can seldom or never resume it again but by force. Many instances can be produced in which the people have voluntarily increased the powers of their rulers; but few, if any, in which rulers have willingly abridged their authority. This is a sufficient reason to induce you to be careful, in the first instance, how you deposit the powers of government.

[5] With these few introductory remarks, I shall proceed to a consideration of this Constitution.

[6] The first question that presents itself on the subject is, whether a confederated government be the best for the United States or not? Or in other words, whether the thirteen United States should be reduced to one great republic, governed by one legislature, and under the direction of one executive and judiciary; or whether they should continue thirteen confederated republics, under the direction and control of a supreme Federal head for certain defined, national purposes only?

[7] This inquiry is important, because, although the government reported by the Convention does not go to a perfect and entire consolidation, yet it approaches so near to it, that it must, if executed, certainly and infallibly terminate in it.

[8] This government is to possess absolute and uncontrollable powers, legislative, executive and judicial, with respect to every object to which it extends, for by the last clause of section eighth, article first, it is declared, that the Congress shall have power " to make all laws which shall be necessary and proper for carrying into execution the foregoing powers, and all other powers vested by this Constitution in the government of the United States, or in any department or office thereof." And by the sixth article, it is declared, " that this Constitution, and the laws of the United States, which shall be made in pursuance thereof, and the treaties made, or which shall be made, under the authority of the United States, shall be the supreme law of the land; and the judges in every State shall be bound thereby, any thing in the Constitution or law of any State to the contrary notwithstanding." It appears from these articles, that there is no need of any intervention of the State governments, between the Congress and the people, to execute any one power vested in the general government, and that the Constitution and laws of every State are nullified and declared void, so far as they are or shall be inconsistent with this Constitution, or the laws made in pursuance of it, or with treaties made under the authority of the United States. The government, then, so far as it extends, is a complete one, and not a confederation. It is as much one complete government as that of New York or Massachusetts; has as absolute and perfect powers to make and execute all laws, to appoint officers, institute courts, declare offences, and annex penalties, with respect to every object to which it extends, as any other in the world. So far, therefore, as its powers reach, all ideas of confederation are given up and lost. It is true this government is limited to certain objects, or to speak more properly, some small degree of power is still left to the States; but a little attention to the powers vested in the general government, will convince every candid man, that if it is capable of being executed, all that is reserved for the individual States must very soon be annihilated, except so far as they are barely necessary to the organization of the general government. The powers

of the general legislature extend to every case that is of the least importance—there is nothing valuable to human nature, nothing dear to freemen, but what is within its power. It has authority to make laws which will affect the lives, the liberty, and property of every man in the United States; nor can the Constitution or laws of any State, in any way prevent or impede the full and complete execution of every power given. The legislative power is competent to lay taxes, duties, imposts, and excises ;—there is no limitation to this power, unless it be said that the clause which directs the use to which those taxes and duties shall be applied, may be said to be a limitation; but this is no restriction of the power at all, for by this clause they are to be applied to pay the debts and provide for the common defence and general welfare of the United States; but the legislature have authority to contract debts at their discretion; they are the sole judges of what is necessary to provide for the common defense, and they only are to determine what is for the general welfare: this power, therefore, is neither more nor less than a power to lay and collect taxes, imposts, and excises, at their pleasure; not only the power to lay taxes unlimited, as to the amount they may require, but it is perfect and absolute to raise them in any mode they please. No State legislature, or any power in the State governments, have any more to do in carrying this into effect than the authority of one State has to do with that of another. In the business, therefore, of laying and collecting taxes, the idea of confederation is totally lost, and that of one entire republic is embraced. It is proper here to remark, that the authority to lay and collect taxes is the most important of any power that can be granted; it connects with it almost all other powers, or at least will in process of time draw all others after it; it is the great mean of protection, security, and defense, in a good government, and the great engine of oppression and tyranny in a bad one. This cannot fail of being the case, if we consider the contracted limits which are set by this Constitution, to the State governments, on this article of raising money. No State can emit paper money, lay any duties or imposts, on imports, or exports, but by consent of the Congress; and then the net produce shall be for the benefit of the United States: the only means, therefore, left for any State to support its government and discharge its debts, is by direct taxation; and the United States have also power to lay and collect taxes, in any way they please. Every one who has thought on the subject, must be convinced that but small sums of money can be collected in any country, by direct tax; when the Federal government begins to exercise the right of taxation in all its parts, the legislatures of the several States will find it impossible to raise moneys to support their governments. Without money they cannot be supported, and they must dwindle away, and, as before observed, their powers be absorbed in that of the general government.

[9] It might be here shown, that the power in the Federal legislature, to raise and support armies at pleasure, as well in peace as in war, and their control over the militia, tend not only to a consolidation of the government, but the destruction of liberty. I shall not, however, dwell upon these, as a few observations upon the judicial power of this government, in addition to the preceding, will fully evince the truth of the position.

[10] The judicial power of the United States is to be vested in a supreme court, and in such inferior courts as Congress may, from time to time, ordain and establish. The powers of these courts are very extensive; their jurisdiction comprehends all civil causes, except such as arise between citizens of the same State; and it extends to all cases in law and equity arising under the Constitution. One inferior court must be established, I presume, in each State, at least, with the necessary executive officers

appendant thereto. It is easy to see, that in the common course of things, these courts will eclipse the dignity, and take away from the respectability, of the State courts. These courts will be, in themselves, totally independent of the States, deriving their authority from the United States, and receiving from them fixed salaries; and in the course of human events it is to be expected, that they will swallow up all the powers of the courts in the respective States.

[11] How far the clause in the eighth section of the first article may operate to do away all idea of Confederated States, and to effect an entire consolidation of the whole into one general government, it is impossible to say. The powers given by this article are very general and comprehensive, and it may receive a construction to justify the passing almost any law. A power to make all laws, which shall be necessary and proper, for carrying into execution all powers vested by the Constitution in the government of the United States, or any department or officer thereof, is a power very comprehensive and definite, and may, for aught I know, be exercised in such manner as entirely to abolish the State legislatures. Suppose the legislature of a State should pass a law to raise money to support their government and pay the State debt; may the Congress repeal this law, because it may prevent the collection of a tax which they may think proper and necessary to lay, to provide for the general welfare of the United States? For all laws made, in pursuance of this Constitution, are the supreme law of the land, and the judges in every State shall be bound thereby, any thing in the Constitution or laws of the different States to the contrary notwithstanding. By such a law, the government of a particular State might be overturned at one stroke, and thereby be deprived of every means of its support.

[12] It is not meant, by stating this case, to insinuate that the Constitution would warrant a law of this kind or unnecessarily to alarm the fears of the people, by suggesting that the Federal legislature would be more likely to pass the limits assigned them by the Constitution, than that of an individual State, further than they are less responsible to the people. But what is meant is, that the legislature of the United States are vested with the great and uncontrollable powers of laying and collecting taxes, duties, imposts, and excises; of regulating trade, raising and supporting armies, organizing, arming, and disciplining the militia, instituting courts, and other general powers; and are by this clause invested with the power of making all laws, proper and necessary, for carrying all these into execution; and they may so exercise this power as entirely to annihilate all the State governments, and reduce this country to one single government. And if they may do it, it is pretty certain they will; for it will be found that the power retained by individual States, small as it is, will be a clog upon the wheels of the government of the United States; the latter, therefore, will be naturally inclined to remove it out of the way. Besides, it is a truth confirmed by the unerring experience of ages, that every man, and every body of men, invested with power, are ever disposed to increase it, and to acquire a superiority over every thing that stands in their way. This disposition, which is implanted in human nature, will operate in the Federal legislature to lessen and ultimately to subvert the State authority, and having such advantages, will most certainly succeed, if the Federal government succeeds at all. It must be very evident, then, that what this Constitution wants of being a complete consolidation of the several parts of the Union into one complete government, possessed of perfect legislative, judicial, and executive powers, to all intents and purposes, it will necessarily acquire in its exercise in operation.

[13] Let us now proceed to inquire, as I at first purposed, whether it be best the thirteen United States should be reduced to one great republic, or not? It is here taken for granted, that all agree in this, that whatever government we adopt, it ought to be a free one; that it should be so framed as to secure the liberty of the citizens of America, and such an one as to admit of a full, fair, and equal representation of the people. The question, then, will be, whether a government thus constituted, and founded on such principles, is practicable, and can be exercised over the whole United States, reduced into one State?

[14] If respect is to be paid to the opinion of the greatest and wisest men who have ever thought or wrote on the science of government, we shall be constrained to conclude, that a free republic cannot succeed over a country of such immense extent, containing such a number of inhabitants, and these increasing in such rapid progression, as that of the whole United States. Among the many illustrious authorities which might be produced to this point, I shall content myself with quoting only two. The one is the Baron De Montesquieu, Spirit of Laws, Chap. xvi. Vol. 1. "It is natural to a republic to have only a small territory, otherwise it cannot long subsist. In a large republic there are men of large fortunes, and consequently of less moderation; there are trusts too great to be placed in any single subject; he has interest of his own; he soon begins to think that he may be happy, great and glorious, by oppressing his fellow-citizens; and that he may raise himself to grandeur on the ruins of his country. In a large republic, the public good is sacrificed to a thousand views; it is subordinate to exceptions, and depends on accidents. In a small one, the interest of the public is easier perceived, better understood, and more within the reach of every citizen ; abuses are of less extent, and of course are less protected." Of the same opinion is the Marquis Beccarari.

[15] History furnishes no example of a free republic, any thing like the extent of the United States. The Grecian republics were of small extent; so also was that of the Romans. Both of these, it is true, in process of time, extended their conquests over large territories of country; and the consequence was, that their governments were changed from that of free governments to those of the most tyrannical that ever existed in the world.

[16] Not only the opinion of the greatest men, and the experience of mankind, are against the idea of an extensive republic, but a variety of reasons may be drawn from the reason and nature of things, against it. In every government the will of the sovereign is the law. In despotic governments, the supreme authority being lodged in one, his will is law, and can be as easily expressed to a large, extensive territory as to a small one. In a pure democracy, the people are the sovereign, and their will is declared by themselves; for this purpose they must all come together to deliberate and decide. This kind of government cannot be exercised, therefore, over a country of any considerable extent; it must be confined to a single city, or at least limited to such bounds as that the people can conveniently assemble, be able to debate, understand the subject submitted to them, and declare their opinion concerning it.

[17] In a free republic, although all laws are derived from the consent of the people, yet the people do not declare their consent by themselves in person, but by representatives, chosen by them, who are supposed to know the minds of their constituents, and to be possessed of integrity to declare this mind.

[18] In every free government, the people must give their assent to the laws by which they are governed. This is the true criterion between a free government and an arbitrary one. The former are ruled by the will of the whole, expressed in any manner they may agree upon; the latter by the will of one, or a few. If the people are to give their assent to the laws, by persons chosen and appointed by them, the manner of the choice and the number chosen must be such as to possess, be disposed, and consequently qualified to declare the sentiments of the people; for if they do not know, or are not disposed to speak the sentiments of the people, the people do not govern, but the sovereignty is in a few. Now, in a large, extended country, it is impossible to have a representation possessing the sentiments, and of integrity to declare the minds of the people, without having it so numerous and unwieldy as to be subject, in great measure, to the inconveniency of a democratic government.

[19] The territory of the United States is of vast extent; it now contains near three millions of souls, and is capable of containing much more than ten times that number. Is it practicable for a country, so large and numerous as they will soon become, to elect a representation that will speak their sentiments, without their becoming so numerous as to be incapable of transacting public business? It certainly is not.

[20] In a republic, the manners, sentiments and interests of the people should be similar. If this be not the case, there will be a constant clashing of opinions; and the representatives of one part will be continually striving against those of the other. This will retard the operations of government, and prevent such conclusions as will promote the public good. If we apply this remark to the condition of the United States, we shall be convinced that it forbids that we should be one government. The United States includes a variety of climates. The productions of the different parts of the Union are very variant, and their interests, of consequence, diverse. Their manners and habits differ as much as their climates and productions; and their sentiments are by no means coincident. The laws and customs of the several States are, in many respects, very diverse, and in some opposite; each would be in favor of its own interests and customs; and, of consequence, a legislature, formed of representatives from the respective parts, would not only be too numerous to act with any care or decision, but would be composed of such heterogeneous and discordant principles, as would constantly be contending with each other.

[21] The laws cannot be executed in a republic of an extent equal to that of the United States, with promptitude.

[22] The magistrates in every government must be supported in the execution of the laws, either by an armed force, maintained at the public expense for that purpose, or by the people turning out to aid the magistrate upon his command, in case of resistance.

[23] In despotic governments, as well as in all the monarchies of Europe, standing armies are kept up to execute the commands of the prince or the magistrate, and are employed for this purpose when occasion requires; but they have always proved the destruction of liberty, and are abhorrent to the spirit of a free republic. In England, where they depend upon the parliament for their annual support, they have always been complained of as oppressive and unconstitutional, and are seldom employed in executing the laws; never except on extraordinary occasions, and then under the direction of a civil magistrate.

[24] A free republic will never keep a standing army to execute its laws. It must depend upon the support of its citizens. But when a government is to receive its support from the aid of the citizens, it must be so constructed as to have the

confidence, respect, and affection of the people. Men who, upon the call of the magistrate, offer themselves to execute the laws, are influenced to do it either by affection to the government, or from fear; where a standing army is at hand to punish offenders, every man is actuated by the latter principle, and therefore, when the magistrate calls, will obey; but, where this is not the case, the government must rest for its support upon the confidence and respect which the people have for their government and laws. The body of the people being attached, the government will always be sufficient to support and execute its laws, and to operate upon the fears of any faction which may be opposed to it, not only to prevent any opposition to the execution of the laws themselves, but also to compel the most of them to aid the magistrate; but the people will not be likely to have such confidence in their rulers, in a republic so extensive as the United States, as is necessary for these purposes. The confidence which the people have in their rulers, in a free republic, arises from their knowing them, from their being responsible to them for their conduct, and from the power they have of displacing them when they misbehave; but in a republic of the extent of this continent, the people in general would be acquainted with very few of their rulers; the people at large would know little of their proceedings, and it would be extremely difficult to change them. The people in Georgia and New Hampshire would not know one another's mind, and therefore could not act in concert to enable them to effect a general change of representatives. The different parts of so extensive a country could not possibly be made acquainted with the conduct of their representatives, nor be informed of the reasons upon which measures were founded. The consequence will be, they will have no confidence in their legislature, suspect them of ambitious views, be jealous of every measure they adopt, and will not support the laws they pass. Hence the government will be nerveless and inefficient, and no way will be left to render it otherwise, but by establishing an armed force to execute the laws at the point of the bayonet—a government of all others the most to be dreaded.

[25] In a republic of such vast extent as the United States, the legislature cannot attend to the various concerns and wants of its different parts. It cannot be sufficiently numerous to be acquainted with the local condition and wants of the different districts, and if it could, it is impossible it should have sufficient time to attend to and provide for all the variety of cases of this nature that would be continually arising.

[26] In so extensive a republic, the great officers of government would soon become above the control of the people, and abuse their powers to the purpose of aggrandizing themselves, and oppressing them. The trust committed to the executive offices, in a country of the extent of the United States, must be various and of magnitude. The command of all the troops and navy of the republic, the appointment of officers, the power of pardoning offences, the collecting of all the public revenues, and the power of expending them, with a number of other powers, must be lodged and exercised in every State, in the hands of a few. When these are attended with great honor and emolument, as they always will be in large States, so as greatly to interest men to pursue them, and to be proper objects for ambitious and designing men, such men will be ever restless in their pursuit after them. They will use the power, when they have acquired it, to the purposes of gratifying their own interest and ambition, and it is scarcely possible, in a very large republic, to call them to account for their misconduct, or to prevent their abuse of power.

[27] These are some of the reasons by which it appears, that a free republic cannot long subsist over a country of the great extent of these States. If then this new Constitution is calculated to consolidate the thirteen States into one, as it evidently is, it ought not to be adopted.

[28] Though I am of opinion, that it is a sufficient objection to this government, to reject it, that it creates the whole Union into one government under the form of a republic, yet if this objection was obviated, there are exceptions to it which are so material and fundamental, that they ought to determine every man, who is a friend to the liberty and happiness of mankind, not to adopt it. I beg the candid and dispassionate attention of my countrymen, while I state these objections—they are such as have obtruded themselves upon my mind upon a careful attention to the matter, and such as I sincerely believe are well founded. There are many objections, of small moment, of which I shall take no notice. Perfection is not to be expected in any thing that is the production of man, and if I did not in my conscience believe that this scheme was defective in the fundamental principles—in the foundation upon which a free and equal government must rest—I would hold my peace.

—Brutus

1. Identify the assumptions Brutus implies about the nature of humans.
2. Identify the claims resulting from those assumptions.
3. Explain the reasoning Brutus uses to support his claims.
4. Identify the constitutional clause that worries Brutus the most (see paragraphs 8 and 11), and explain why it is such a cause of concern to him.
5. Explain the political implications of Brutus's argument on the outcome of the ratification process.

FEDERALIST No. 51

The Structure of the Government Must Furnish the Proper Checks and Balances Between the Different Departments

February 8, 1788—To the People of the State of New York:

[1] TO WHAT expedient, then, shall we finally resort, for maintaining in practice the necessary partition of power among the several departments, as laid down in the Constitution? The only answer that can be given is, that as all these exterior provisions are found to be inadequate, the defect must be supplied, by so contriving the interior structure of the government as that its several constituent parts may, by their mutual relations, be the means of keeping each other in their proper places. Without presuming to undertake a full development of this important idea, I will hazard a few general observations, which may perhaps place it in a clearer light, and enable us to form a more correct judgment of the principles and structure of the government planned by the convention.

[2] In order to lay a due foundation for that separate and distinct exercise of the different powers of government, which to a certain extent is admitted on all hands to

be essential to the preservation of liberty, it is evident that each department should have a will of its own; and consequently should be so constituted that the members of each should have as little agency as possible in the appointment of the members of the others. Were this principle rigorously adhered to, it would require that all the appointments for the supreme executive, legislative, and judiciary magistracies should be drawn from the same fountain of authority, the people, through channels having no communication whatever with one another. Perhaps such a plan of constructing the several departments would be less difficult in practice than it may in contemplation appear. Some difficulties, however, and some additional expense would attend the execution of it. Some deviations, therefore, from the principle must be admitted. In the constitution of the judiciary department in particular, it might be inexpedient to insist rigorously on the principle: first, because peculiar qualifications being essential in the members, the primary consideration ought to be to select that mode of choice which best secures these qualifications; secondly, because the permanent tenure by which the appointments are held in that department, must soon destroy all sense of dependence on the authority conferring them.

[3] It is equally evident, that the members of each department should be as little dependent as possible on those of the others, for the emoluments annexed to their offices. Were the executive magistrate, or the judges, not independent of the legislature in this particular, their independence in every other would be merely nominal. But the great security against a gradual concentration of the several powers in the same department, consists in giving to those who administer each department the necessary constitutional means and personal motives to resist encroachments of the others. The provision for defense must in this, as in all other cases, be made commensurate to the danger of attack. Ambition must be made to counteract ambition. The interest of the man must be connected with the constitutional rights of the place. It may be a reflection on human nature, that such devices should be necessary to control the abuses of government. But what is government itself, but the greatest of all reflections on human nature? If men were angels, no government would be necessary. If angels were to govern men, neither external nor internal controls on government would be necessary. In framing a government which is to be administered by men over men, the great difficulty lies in this: you must first enable the government to control the governed; and in the next place oblige it to control itself.

[4] A dependence on the people is, no doubt, the primary control on the government; but experience has taught mankind the necessity of auxiliary precautions. This policy of supplying, by opposite and rival interests, the defect of better motives, might be traced through the whole system of human affairs, private as well as public. We see it particularly displayed in all the subordinate distributions of power, where the constant aim is to divide and arrange the several offices in such a manner as that each may be a check on the other that the private interest of every individual may be a sentinel over the public rights. These inventions of prudence cannot be less requisite in the distribution of the supreme powers of the State. But it is not possible to give to each department an equal power of self-defense. In republican government, the legislative authority necessarily predominates. The remedy for this inconveniency is to divide the legislature into different branches; and to render them, by different modes of election and different principles of action, as little connected with each other as the nature of their common functions and their common dependence

on the society will admit. It may even be necessary to guard against dangerous encroachments by still further precautions. As the weight of the legislative authority requires that it should be thus divided, the weakness of the executive may require, on the other hand, that it should be fortified.

[5] An absolute negative on the legislature appears, at first view, to be the natural defense with which the executive magistrate should be armed. But perhaps it would be neither altogether safe nor alone sufficient. On ordinary occasions it might not be exerted with the requisite firmness, and on extraordinary occasions it might be perfidiously abused. May not this defect of an absolute negative be supplied by some qualified connection between this weaker department and the weaker branch of the stronger department, by which the latter may be led to support the constitutional rights of the former, without being too much detached from the rights of its own department? If the principles on which these observations are founded be just, as I persuade myself they are, and they be applied as a criterion to the several State constitutions, and to the federal Constitution it will be found that if the latter does not perfectly correspond with them, the former are infinitely less able to bear such a test.

[6] There are, moreover, two considerations particularly applicable to the federal system of America, which place that system in a very interesting point of view. First. In a single republic, all the power surrendered by the people is submitted to the administration of a single government; and the usurpations are guarded against by a division of the government into distinct and separate departments. In the compound republic of America, the power surrendered by the people is first divided between two distinct governments, and then the portion allotted to each subdivided among distinct and separate departments. Hence a double security arises to the rights of the people. The different governments will control each other, at the same time that each will be controlled by itself. Second. It is of great importance in a republic not only to guard the society against the oppression of its rulers, but to guard one part of the society against the injustice of the other part. Different interests necessarily exist in different classes of citizens. If a majority be united by a common interest, the rights of the minority will be insecure.

[7] There are but two methods of providing against this evil: the one by creating a will in the community independent of the majority that is, of the society itself; the other, by comprehending in the society so many separate descriptions of citizens as will render an unjust combination of a majority of the whole very improbable, if not impracticable. The first method prevails in all governments possessing an hereditary or self-appointed authority. This, at best, is but a precarious security; because a power independent of the society may as well espouse the unjust views of the major, as the rightful interests of the minor party, and may possibly be turned against both parties. The second method will be exemplified in the federal republic of the United States. Whilst all authority in it will be derived from and dependent on the society, the society itself will be broken into so many parts, interests, and classes of citizens, that the rights of individuals, or of the minority, will be in little danger from interested combinations of the majority.

[8] In a free government the security for civil rights must be the same as that for religious rights. It consists in the one case in the multiplicity of interests, and in the other in the multiplicity of sects. The degree of security in both cases will depend on the number of interests and sects; and this may be presumed to depend on the extent of country and number of people comprehended under the same government.

This view of the subject must particularly recommend a proper federal system to all the sincere and considerate friends of republican government, since it shows that in exact proportion as the territory of the Union may be formed into more circumscribed Confederacies, or States oppressive combinations of a majority will be facilitated: the best security, under the republican forms, for the rights of every class of citizens, will be diminished: and consequently the stability and independence of some member of the government, the only other security, must be proportionately increased. Justice is the end of government. It is the end of civil society. It ever has been and ever will be pursued until it be obtained, or until liberty be lost in the pursuit. In a society under the forms of which the stronger faction can readily unite and oppress the weaker, anarchy may as truly be said to reign as in a state of nature, where the weaker individual is not secured against the violence of the stronger; and as, in the latter state, even the stronger individuals are prompted, by the uncertainty of their condition, to submit to a government which may protect the weak as well as themselves; so, in the former state, will the more powerful factions or parties be gradually induced, by a like motive, to wish for a government which will protect all parties, the weaker as well as the more powerful.

[9] It can be little doubted that if the State of Rhode Island was separated from the Confederacy and left to itself, the insecurity of rights under the popular form of government within such narrow limits would be displayed by such reiterated oppressions of factious majorities that some power altogether independent of the people would soon be called for by the voice of the very factions whose misrule had proved the necessity of it. In the extended republic of the United States, and among the great variety of interests, parties, and sects which it embraces, a coalition of a majority of the whole society could seldom take place on any other principles than those of justice and the general good; whilst there being thus less danger to a minor from the will of a major party, there must be less pretext, also, to provide for the security of the former, by introducing into the government a will not dependent on the latter, or, in other words, a will independent of the society itself. It is no less certain than it is important, notwithstanding the contrary opinions which have been entertained, that the larger the society, provided it lie within a practical sphere, the more duly capable it will be of self-government. And happily for the REPUBLICAN CAUSE, the practicable sphere may be carried to a very great extent, by a judicious modification and mixture of the FEDERAL PRINCIPLE. —PUBLIUS

---

1. Explain how the process of a bill becoming law (see pages 93–97) demonstrates the checks and balances the two chambers of Congress exert on each other and the checks and balances between Congress and the executive branch.

2. Using Publius's example of Rhode Island (paragraph 9) as a starting point, develop an argument on how a welcoming national immigration policy benefits the republic.

3. How does Publius classify the ways to ensure the majority do not trample the minority (see paragraphs 6 and 7)?

4. Describe the characteristics of federalism identified in this document.

FEDERALIST No. 70

The Executive Department Further Considered

March 15, 1788—To the People of the State of New York:

[1] THERE is an idea, which is not without its advocates, that a vigorous Executive is inconsistent with the genius of republican government. The enlightened well-wishers to this species of government must at least hope that the supposition is destitute of foundation; since they can never admit its truth, without at the same time admitting the condemnation of their own principles. Energy in the Executive is a leading character in the definition of good government. It is essential to the protection of the community against foreign attacks; it is not less essential to the steady administration of the laws; to the protection of property against those irregular and high-handed combinations which sometimes interrupt the ordinary course of justice; to the security of liberty against the enterprises and assaults of ambition, of faction, and of anarchy. Every man the least conversant in Roman story, knows how often that republic was obliged to take refuge in the absolute power of a single man, under the formidable title of Dictator, as well against the intrigues of ambitious individuals who aspired to the tyranny, and the seditions of whole classes of the community whose conduct threatened the existence of all government, as against the invasions of external enemies who menaced the conquest and destruction of Rome.

[2] There can be no need, however, to multiply arguments or examples on this head. A feeble Executive implies a feeble execution of the government. A feeble execution is but another phrase for a bad execution; and a government ill executed, whatever it may be in theory, must be, in practice, a bad government.

[3] Taking it for granted, therefore, that all men of sense will agree in the necessity of an energetic Executive, it will only remain to inquire, what are the ingredients which constitute this energy? How far can they be combined with those other ingredients which constitute safety in the republican sense? And how far does this combination characterize the plan which has been reported by the convention?

[4] The ingredients which constitute energy in the Executive are, first, unity; secondly, duration; thirdly, an adequate provision for its support; fourthly, competent powers.

[5] The ingredients which constitute safety in the republican sense are, first, a due dependence on the people, secondly, a due responsibility.

[6] Those politicians and statesmen who have been the most celebrated for the soundness of their principles and for the justice of their views, have declared in favor of a single Executive and a numerous legislature. They have with great propriety, considered energy as the most necessary qualification of the former, and have regarded this as most applicable to power in a single hand, while they have, with equal propriety, considered the latter as best adapted to deliberation and wisdom, and best calculated to conciliate the confidence of the people and to secure their privileges and interests.

[7] That unity is conducive to energy will not be disputed. Decision, activity, secrecy, and despatch will generally characterize the proceedings of one man in a much more eminent degree than the proceedings of any greater number; and in proportion as the number is increased, these qualities will be diminished.

[8] This unity may be destroyed in two ways: either by vesting the power in two or more magistrates of equal dignity and authority; or by vesting it ostensibly in one man, subject, in whole or in part, to the control and co-operation of others, in the capacity of counsellors to him. Of the first, the two Consuls of Rome may serve as an example; of the last, we shall find examples in the constitutions of several of the States. New York and New Jersey, if I recollect right, are the only States which have intrusted the executive authority wholly to single men.(1) Both these methods of destroying the unity of the Executive have their partisans; but the votaries of an executive council are the most numerous. They are both liable, if not to equal, to similar objections, and may in most lights be examined in conjunction.

[9] The experience of other nations will afford little instruction on this head. As far, however, as it teaches any thing, it teaches us not to be enamoured of plurality in the Executive. We have seen that the Achaeans, on an experiment of two Praetors, were induced to abolish one. The Roman history records many instances of mischiefs to the republic from the dissensions between the Consuls, and between the military Tribunes, who were at times substituted for the Consuls. But it gives us no specimens of any peculiar advantages derived to the state from the circumstance of the plurality of those magistrates. That the dissensions between them were not more frequent or more fatal, is a matter of astonishment, until we advert to the singular position in which the republic was almost continually placed, and to the prudent policy pointed out by the circumstances of the state, and pursued by the Consuls, of making a division of the government between them. The patricians engaged in a perpetual struggle with the plebeians for the preservation of their ancient authorities and dignities; the Consuls, who were generally chosen out of the former body, were commonly united by the personal interest they had in the defense of the privileges of their order. In addition to this motive of union, after the arms of the republic had considerably expanded the bounds of its empire, it became an established custom with the Consuls to divide the administration between themselves by lot—one of them remaining at Rome to govern the city and its environs, the other taking the command in the more distant provinces. This expedient must, no doubt, have had great influence in preventing those collisions and rivalships which might otherwise have embroiled the peace of the republic.

[10] But quitting the dim light of historical research, attaching ourselves purely to the dictates of reason and good sense, we shall discover much greater cause to reject than to approve the idea of plurality in the Executive, under any modification whatever.

[11] Wherever two or more persons are engaged in any common enterprise or pursuit, there is always danger of difference of opinion. If it be a public trust or office, in which they are clothed with equal dignity and authority, there is peculiar danger of personal emulation and even animosity. From either, and especially from all these causes, the most bitter dissensions are apt to spring. Whenever these happen, they lessen the respectability, weaken the authority, and distract the plans and operation of those whom they divide. If they should unfortunately assail the supreme executive magistracy of a country, consisting of a plurality of persons, they might impede or frustrate the most important measures of the government, in the most critical emergencies of the state. And what is still worse, they might split the community into the most violent and irreconcilable factions, adhering differently to the different individuals who composed the magistracy.

[12] Men often oppose a thing, merely because they have had no agency in planning it, or because it may have been planned by those whom they dislike. But if they have been consulted, and have happened to disapprove, opposition then becomes, in their estimation, an indispensable duty of self-love. They seem to think themselves bound in honor, and by all the motives of personal infallibility, to defeat the success of what has been resolved upon contrary to their sentiments. Men of upright, benevolent tempers have too many opportunities of remarking, with horror, to what desperate lengths this disposition is sometimes carried, and how often the great interests of society are sacrificed to the vanity, to the conceit, and to the obstinacy of individuals, who have credit enough to make their passions and their caprices interesting to mankind. Perhaps the question now before the public may, in its consequences, afford melancholy proofs of the effects of this despicable frailty, or rather detestable vice, in the human character.

[13] Upon the principles of a free government, inconveniences from the source just mentioned must necessarily be submitted to in the formation of the legislature; but it is unnecessary, and therefore unwise, to introduce them into the constitution of the Executive. It is here too that they may be most pernicious. In the legislature, promptitude of decision is oftener an evil than a benefit. The differences of opinion, and the jarrings of parties in that department of the government, though they may sometimes obstruct salutary plans, yet often promote deliberation and circumspection, and serve to check excesses in the majority. When a resolution too is once taken, the opposition must be at an end. That resolution is a law, and resistance to it punishable. But no favorable circumstances palliate or atone for the disadvantages of dissension in the executive department. Here, they are pure and unmixed. There is no point at which they cease to operate. They serve to embarrass and weaken the execution of the plan or measure to which they relate, from the first step to the final conclusion of it. They constantly counteract those qualities in the Executive which are the most necessary ingredients in its composition—vigor and expedition, and this without any counterbalancing good. In the conduct of war, in which the energy of the Executive is the bulwark of the national security, every thing would be to be apprehended from its plurality.

[14] It must be confessed that these observations apply with principal weight to the first case supposed—that is, to a plurality of magistrates of equal dignity and authority a scheme, the advocates for which are not likely to form a numerous sect; but they apply, though not with equal, yet with considerable weight to the project of a council, whose concurrence is made constitutionally necessary to the operations of the ostensible Executive. An artful cabal in that council would be able to distract and to enervate the whole system of administration. If no such cabal should exist, the mere diversity of views and opinions would alone be sufficient to tincture the exercise of the executive authority with a spirit of habitual feebleness and dilatoriness.

[15] But one of the weightiest objections to a plurality in the Executive, and which lies as much against the last as the first plan, is, that it tends to conceal faults and destroy responsibility. Responsibility is of two kinds—to censure and to punishment. The first is the more important of the two, especially in an elective office. Man, in public trust, will much oftener act in such a manner as to render him unworthy of being any longer trusted, than in such a manner as to make him obnoxious to legal punishment. But the multiplication of the Executive adds to the difficulty of detection in either case. It often becomes impossible, amidst mutual accusations, to determine

on whom the blame or the punishment of a pernicious measure, or series of pernicious measures, ought really to fall. It is shifted from one to another with so much dexterity, and under such plausible appearances, that the public opinion is left in suspense about the real author. The circumstances which may have led to any national miscarriage or misfortune are sometimes so complicated that, where there are a number of actors who may have had different degrees and kinds of agency, though we may clearly see upon the whole that there has been mismanagement, yet it may be impracticable to pronounce to whose account the evil which may have been incurred is truly chargeable.[1]

[16] "I was overruled by my council. The council were so divided in their opinions that it was impossible to obtain any better resolution on the point." These and similar pretexts are constantly at hand, whether true or false. And who is there that will either take the trouble or incur the odium, of a strict scrutiny into the secret springs of the transaction? Should there be found a citizen zealous enough to undertake the unpromising task, if there happen to be collusion between the parties concerned, how easy it is to clothe the circumstances with so much ambiguity, as to render it uncertain what was the precise conduct of any of those parties?

[17] In the single instance in which the governor of this State is coupled with a council—that is, in the appointment to offices, we have seen the mischiefs of it in the view now under consideration. Scandalous appointments to important offices have been made. Some cases, indeed, have been so flagrant that ALL PARTIES have agreed in the impropriety of the thing. When inquiry has been made, the blame has been laid by the governor on the members of the council, who, on their part, have charged it upon his nomination; while the people remain altogether at a loss to determine, by whose influence their interests have been committed to hands so unqualified and so manifestly improper. In tenderness to individuals, I forbear to descend to particulars.

[18] It is evident from these considerations, that the plurality of the Executive tends to deprive the people of the two greatest securities they can have for the faithful exercise of any delegated power, first, the restraints of public opinion, which lose their efficacy, as well on account of the division of the censure attendant on bad measures among a number, as on account of the uncertainty on whom it ought to fall; and, second, the opportunity of discovering with facility and clearness the misconduct of the persons they trust, in order either to their removal from office or to their actual punishment in cases which admit of it.

[19] In England, the king is a perpetual magistrate; and it is a maxim which has obtained for the sake of the public peace, that he is unaccountable for his administration, and his person sacred. Nothing, therefore, can be wiser in that kingdom, than to annex to the king a constitutional council, who may be responsible to the nation for the advice they give. Without this, there would be no responsibility whatever in the executive department an idea inadmissible in a free government. But even there the king is not bound by the resolutions of his council, though they are answerable for the advice they give. He is the absolute master of his own conduct in the exercise of his office, and may observe or disregard the counsel given to him at his sole discretion.

[20] But in a republic, where every magistrate ought to be personally responsible for his behavior in office the reason which in the British Constitution dictates the propriety of a council, not only ceases to apply, but turns against the institution. In the monarchy

---

1This paragraph appeared in a slightly different form in a version published a few days later.

of Great Britain, it furnishes a substitute for the prohibited responsibility of the chief magistrate, which serves in some degree as a hostage to the national justice for his good behavior. In the American republic, it would serve to destroy, or would greatly diminish, the intended and necessary responsibility of the Chief Magistrate himself.

[21] The idea of a council to the Executive, which has so generally obtained in the State constitutions, has been derived from that maxim of republican jealousy which considers power as safer in the hands of a number of men than of a single man. If the maxim should be admitted to be applicable to the case, I should contend that the advantage on that side would not counterbalance the numerous disadvantages on the opposite side. But I do not think the rule at all applicable to the executive power. I clearly concur in opinion, in this particular, with a writer whom the celebrated Junius pronounces to be "deep, solid, and ingenious," that "the executive power is more easily confined when it is ONE"; that it is far more safe there should be a single object for the jealousy and watchfulness of the people; and, in a word, that all multiplication of the Executive is rather dangerous than friendly to liberty.

[22] A little consideration will satisfy us, that the species of security sought for in the multiplication of the Executive, is unattainable. Numbers must be so great as to render combination difficult, or they are rather a source of danger than of security. The united credit and influence of several individuals must be more formidable to liberty, than the credit and influence of either of them separately. When power, therefore, is placed in the hands of so small a number of men, as to admit of their interests and views being easily combined in a common enterprise, by an artful leader, it becomes more liable to abuse, and more dangerous when abused, than if it be lodged in the hands of one man; who, from the very circumstance of his being alone, will be more narrowly watched and more readily suspected, and who cannot unite so great a mass of influence as when he is associated with others. The Decemvirs of Rome, whose name denotes their number, were more to be dreaded in their usurpation than any ONE of them would have been. No person would think of proposing an Executive much more numerous than that body; from six to a dozen have been suggested for the number of the council. The extreme of these numbers, is not too great for an easy combination; and from such a combination America would have more to fear, than from the ambition of any single individual. A council to a magistrate, who is himself responsible for what he does, are generally nothing better than a clog upon his good intentions, are often the instruments and accomplices of his bad and are almost always a cloak to his faults.

[23] I forbear to dwell upon the subject of expense; though it be evident that if the council should be numerous enough to answer the principal end aimed at by the institution, the salaries of the members, who must be drawn from their homes to reside at the seat of government, would form an item in the catalogue of public expenditures too serious to be incurred for an object of equivocal utility. I will only add that, prior to the appearance of the Constitution, I rarely met with an intelligent man from any of the States, who did not admit, as the result of experience, that the UNITY of the executive of this State was one of the best of the distinguishing features of our constitution.

---

1. Based on this document, describe the traits needed in a good president.
2. Explain how a president might use ideas in this document—especially unity and energy—to support a presidency with expanded powers.

FEDERALIST No. 78

The Judiciary Department

May 28, 1788—To the People of the State of New York:

[1] WE proceed now to an examination of the Judiciary department of the proposed Government.

[2] In unfolding the defects of the existing Confederation the utility and necessity of a Federal Judicature have been clearly pointed out. It is the less necessary to recapitulate the considerations there urged, as the propriety of the institution in the abstract is not disputed; the only questions which have been raised being relative to the manner of constituting it, and to its extent. To these points, therefore, our observations shall be confined.

[3] The manner of constituting it seems to embrace these several objects:—1st. The mode of appointing the Judges;—2d. The tenure by which they are to hold their places;—3d. The partition of the Judiciary authority between different courts, and their relations to each other.

[4] First. As to the mode of appointing the Judges; this is the same with that of appointing the officers of the Union in general, and has been so fully discussed in the two last numbers, that nothing can be said here which would not be useless repetition.

[5] Second. As to the tenure by which the Judges are to hold their places: this chiefly concerns their duration in office; the provisions for their support; the precautions for their responsibility.

[6] According to the plan of the Convention, all Judges who may be appointed by the United States are to hold their offices during good behavior; which is conformable to the most approved of the State Constitutions, and among the rest, to that of this State. Its propriety having been drawn into question by the adversaries of that plan, is no light symptom of the rage for objection, which disorders their imaginations and judgments. The standard of good behavior for the continuance in office of the Judicial magistracy, is certainly one of the most valuable of the modern improvements in the practice of Government. In a monarchy, it is an excellent barrier to the despotism of the Prince; in a republic it is a no less excellent barrier to the encroachments and oppressions of the representative body. And it is the best expedient which can be devised in any Government, to secure a steady, upright, and impartial administration of the laws.

[7] Whoever attentively considers the different departments of power must perceive, that, in a Government in which they are separated from each other, the Judiciary, from the nature of its functions, will always be the least dangerous to the political rights of the Constitution; because it will be least in a capacity to annoy or injure them. The Executive not only dispenses the honors, but holds the sword of the community. The Legislature not only commands the purse, but prescribes the rules by which the duties and rights of every citizen are to be regulated. The Judiciary, on the contrary, has no influence over either the sword or the purse; no direction either of the strength or of the wealth of the society; and can take no active resolution whatever. It may truly be said to have neither force nor will, but merely judgment; and must ultimately depend upon the aid of the Executive arm even for the efficacy of its judgments.

[8] This simple view of the matter suggests several important consequences. It proves incontestably, that the Judiciary is beyond comparison the weakest of the three

departments of power; (1) that it can never attack with success either of the other two; and that all possible care is requisite to enable it to defend itself against their attacks. It equally proves, that though individual oppression may now and then proceed from the courts of justice, the general liberty of the People can never be endangered from that quarter: I mean so long as the Judiciary remains truly distinct from both the Legislature and the Executive. For I agree, that "there is no liberty, if the power of judging be not separated from the Legislative and Executive powers."(2) And it proves, in the last place, that as liberty can have nothing to fear from the Judiciary alone, but would have everything to fear from its union with either of the other departments; that as all the effects of such an union must ensue from a dependence of the former on the latter, notwithstanding a nominal and apparent separation; that as, from the natural feebleness of the Judiciary, it is in continual jeopardy of being overpowered, awed, or influenced by its coördinate branches; and that as nothing can contribute so much to its firmness and independence as permanency in office, this quality may therefore be justly regarded as an indispensable ingredient in its constitution; and in a great measure, as the citadel of the public justice and the public security.

[9] The complete independence of the Courts of justice is peculiarly essential in a limited Constitution. By a limited Constitution, I understand one which contains certain specified exceptions to the Legislative authority; such, for instance, as that it shall pass no bills of attainder, no ex post facto laws, and the like. Limitations of this kind can be preserved in practice no other way than through the medium of the Courts of justice; whose duty it must be to declare all Acts contrary to the manifest tenor of the Constitution void. Without this, all the reservations of particular rights or privileges would amount to nothing.

[10] Some perplexity respecting the rights of the Courts to pronounce Legislative acts void, because contrary to the Constitution, has arisen from an imagination that the doctrine would imply a superiority of the Judiciary to the Legislative power. It is urged that the authority which can declare the acts of another void, must necessarily be superior to the one whose acts may be declared void. As this doctrine is of great importance in all the American Constitutions, a brief discussion of the ground on which it rests cannot be unacceptable.

[11]There is no position which depends on clearer principles, than that every act of a delegated authority, contrary to the tenor of the commission under which it is exercised, is void. No Legislative act, therefore, contrary to the Constitution, can be valid. To deny this, would be to affirm, that the deputy is greater than his principal; that the servant is above his master; that the Representatives of the People are superior to the People themselves; that men acting by virtue of powers, may do not only what their powers do not authorize, but what they forbid.

[12] If it be said that the Legislative body are themselves the constitutional judges of their own powers, and that the construction they put upon them is conclusive upon the other departments, it may be answered, that this cannot be the natural presumption, where it is not to be collected from any particular provisions in the Constitution. It is not otherwise to be supposed, that the Constitution could intend to enable the Representatives of the People to substitute their will to that of their constituents. It is far more rational to suppose, that the Courts were designed to be an intermediate body between the People and the Legislature, in order, among other things, to keep the latter within the limits assigned to their authority. The interpretation of the laws is the proper and peculiar province of the Courts. A Constitution is, in fact, and must

be regarded by the Judges, as a fundamental law. It therefore belongs to them to ascertain its meaning, as well as the meaning of any particular Act proceeding from the Legislative body. If there should happen to be an irreconcilable variance between the two, that which has the superior obligation and validity ought, of course, to be preferred; or in other words, the Constitution ought to be preferred to the statute; the intention of the People to the intention of their agents.

[13] Nor does this conclusion by any means suppose a superiority of the Judicial to the Legislative power. It only supposes that the power of the People is superior to both; and that where the will of the Legislature, declared in its statutes, stands in opposition to that of the People, declared in the Constitution, the Judges ought to be governed by the latter rather than the former. They ought to regulate their decisions by the fundamental laws, rather than by those which are not fundamental.

[14] This exercise of judicial discretion, in determining between two contradictory laws, is exemplified in a familiar instance. It not uncommonly happens, that there are two statutes existing at one time, clashing in whole or in part with each other, and neither of them containing any repealing clause or expression. In such a case, it is the province of the Courts to liquidate and fix their meaning and operation; so far as they can, by any fair construction, be reconciled to each other, reason and law conspire to dictate that this should be done; where this is impracticable, it becomes a matter of necessity to give effect to one, in exclusion of the other. The rule which has obtained in the Courts for determining their relative validity is, that the last in order of time shall be preferred to the first. But this is a mere rule of construction, not derived from any positive law, but from the nature and reason of the thing. It is a rule not enjoined upon the Courts by Legislative provision, but adopted by themselves, as consonant to truth and propriety, for the direction of their conduct as interpreters of the law. They thought it reasonable, that between the interfering acts of an equal authority, that which was the last indication of its will should have the preference.

[15] But in regard to the interfering acts of a superior and subordinate authority, of an original and derivative power, the nature and reason of the thing indicate the converse of that rule as proper to be followed. They teach us that the prior act of a superior ought to be preferred to the subsequent act of an inferior and subordinate authority; and that accordingly, whenever a particular statute contravenes the Constitution, it will be the duty of the Judicial tribunals to adhere to the latter and disregard the former.

[16] It can be of no weight to say that the Courts, on the pretence of a repugnancy, may substitute their own pleasure to the constitutional intentions of the Legislature. This might as well happen in the case of two contradictory statutes; or it might as well happen in every adjudication upon any single statute. The Courts must declare the sense of the law; and if they should be disposed to exercise will instead of judgment, the consequence would equally be the substitution of their pleasure to that of the Legislative body. The observation, if it proved anything, would prove that there ought to be no Judges distinct from that body.

[17] If then the Courts of justice are to be considered as the bulwarks of a limited Constitution, against Legislative encroachments, this consideration will afford a strong argument for the permanent tenure of Judicial offices, since nothing will contribute so much as this to that independent spirit in the Judges, which must be essential to the faithful performance of so arduous a duty.

[18] This independence of the Judges is equally requisite to guard the Constitution and the rights of individuals, from the effects of those ill humors, which the arts of designing men, or the influence of particular conjunctures, sometimes disseminate among the People themselves, and which, though they speedily give place to better information, and more deliberate reflection, have a tendency, in the mean time, to occasion dangerous innovations in the Government, and serious oppressions of the minor party in the community. Though I trust the friends of the proposed Constitution will never concur with its enemies in questioning that fundamental principle of republican Government, which admits the right of the People to alter or abolish the established Constitution, whenever they find it inconsistent with their happiness, yet it is not to be inferred from this principle, that the Representatives of the People, whenever a momentary inclination happens to lay hold of a majority of their constituents, incompatible with the provisions in the existing Constitution, would, on that account, be justifiable in a violation of those provisions; or that the Courts would be under a greater obligation to connive at infractions in this shape, than when they had proceeded wholly from the cabals of the Representative body. Until the People have, by some solemn and authoritative act, annulled or changed the established form, it is binding upon themselves collectively, as well as individually; and no presumption, or even knowledge of their sentiments, can warrant their Representatives in a departure from it, prior to such an act. But it is easy to see, that it would require an uncommon portion of fortitude in the Judges to do their duty as faithful guardians of the Constitution, where Legislative invasions of it had been instigated by the major voice of the community.

[19] But it is not with a view to infractions of the Constitution only, that the independence of the Judges may be an essential safeguard against the effects of occasional ill humors in the society. These sometimes extend no farther than to the injury of the private rights of particular classes of citizens, by unjust and partial laws. Here also the firmness of the Judicial magistracy is of vast importance in mitigating the severity, and confining the operation of such laws. It not only serves to moderate the immediate mischiefs of those which may have been passed, but it operates as a check upon the Legislative body in passing them; who, perceiving that obstacles to the success of iniquitous intention are to be expected from the scruples of the Courts, are in a manner compelled, by the very motives of the injustice they meditate, to qualify their attempts. This is a circumstance calculated to have more influence upon the character of our Governments, than but few may be aware of. The benefits of the integrity and moderation of the Judiciary have already been felt in more States than one; and though they may have displeased those whose sinister expectations they may have disappointed, they must have commanded the esteem and applause of all the virtuous and disinterested. Considerate men, of every description, ought to prize whatever will tend to beget or fortify that temper in the Courts; as no man can be sure that he may not be to-morrow the victim of a spirit of injustice, by which he may be a gainer to-day. And every man must now feel, that the inevitable tendency of such a spirit is to sap the foundations of public and private confidence, and to introduce in its stead universal distrust and distress.

[20] That inflexible and uniform adherence to the rights of the Constitution, and of individuals, which we perceive to be indispensable in the Courts of justice, can certainly not be expected from Judges who hold their offices by a temporary commission. Periodical appointments, however regulated, or by whomsoever made,

would, in some way or other, be fatal to their necessary independence. If the power of making them was committed either to the Executive or Legislature, there would be danger of an improper complaisance to the branch which possessed it; if to both, there would be an unwillingness to hazard the displeasure of either; if to the People, or to persons chosen by them for the special purpose, there would be too great a disposition to consult popularity, to justify a reliance that nothing would be consulted but the Constitution and the laws.

[21] There is yet a further and a weightier reason for the permanency of the Judicial offices, which is deducible from the nature of the qualifications they require. It has been frequently remarked, with great propriety, that a voluminous code of laws is one of the inconveniences necessarily connected with the advantages of a free Government. To avoid an arbitrary discretion in the Courts, it is indispensable that they should be bound down by strict rules and precedents, which serve to define and point out their duty in every particular case that comes before them; and it will readily be conceived from the variety of controversies which grow out of the folly and wickedness of mankind, that the records of those precedents must unavoidably swell to a very considerable bulk, and must demand long and laborious study to acquire a competent knowledge of them. Hence it is, that there can be but few men in the society, who will have sufficient skill in the laws to qualify them for the stations of Judges. And making the proper deductions for the ordinary depravity of human nature, the number must be still smaller of those who unite the requisite integrity with the requisite knowledge. These considerations apprize us, that the Government can have no great option between fit characters; and that a temporary duration in office, which would naturally discourage such characters from quitting a lucrative line of practice to accept a seat on the Bench, would have a tendency to throw the administration of justice into hands less able, and less well qualified, to conduct it with utility and dignity. In the present circumstances of this country, and in those in which it is likely to be for a long time to come, the disadvantages on this score would be greater than they may at first sight appear; but it must be confessed, that they are far inferior to those which present themselves under the other aspects of the subject.

[22] Upon the whole, there can be no room to doubt that the Convention acted wisely, in copying from the models of those Constitutions which have established good behavior as the tenure of their Judicial offices, in point of duration; and that so far from being blamable on this account, their plan would have been inexcusably defective, if it had wanted this important feature of good Government. The experience of Great Britain affords an illustrious comment on the excellence of the institution.—PUBLIUS

---

1. Describe the function of the Supreme Court as Publius sees it.

2. Identify the opposing views on life terms and powers that Publius anticipates in this document, and explain how he addresses the opposition.

3. Identify the two powers the judiciary lacks that, according to Publius, make it the weakest branch.

4. Explain the role the judiciary plays in the system of checks and balances, not only among branches, but also between citizens and their government.

LETTER FROM BIRMINGHAM JAIL

Dr. Martin Luther King

16 April 1963

My dear Fellow Clergymen:

[1] While confined here in the Birmingham City Jail, I came across your recent statement calling our present activities "unwise and untimely." . . . since I feel that you are men of genuine goodwill and your criticisms are sincerely set forth, I would like to answer your statement in what I hope will be patient and reasonable terms.

[2] I think I should give the reason for my being in Birmingham, since you have been influenced by the argument of "outsiders coming in." . . . I am here, along with several members of my staff, because we were invited here. I am here because I have basic organizational ties here.

[3] Beyond this, I am in Birmingham because injustice is here. Just as the eighth century prophets left their little villages and carried their "thus saith the Lord" far beyond the boundaries of their home towns; and just as the Apostle Paul left his little village of Tarsus and carried the gospel of Jesus Christ to practically every hamlet and city of the Graeco-Roman world, I, too, am compelled to carry the gospel of freedom beyond my particular home town. Like Paul, I must constantly respond to the Macedonian call for aid. . . .

[4] You deplore the demonstrations that are presently taking place in Birmingham. But I am sorry that your statement did not express a similar concern for the conditions that brought the demonstrations into being. . . . I would not hesitate to say that it is unfortunate that so-called demonstrations are taking place in Birmingham at this time, but I would say in more emphatic terms that it is even more unfortunate that the white power structure of this city left the Negro community with no other alternative.

[5] In any nonviolent campaign there are four basic steps: 1) Collection of the facts to determine whether injustices are alive. 2) Negotiation. 3) Self-purification and 4) Direct Action. We have gone through all of these steps in Birmingham. There can be no gainsaying of the fact that racial injustice engulfs this community. Birmingham is probably the most thoroughly segregated city in the United States. Its ugly record of police brutality is known in every section of this country. Its unjust treatment of Negroes in the courts is a notorious reality. There have been more unsolved bombings of Negro homes and churches in Birmingham than any city in the nation. These are the hard, brutal and unbelievable facts. On the basis of these conditions Negro leaders sought to negotiate with the city fathers. But the political leaders consistently refused to engage in good faith negotiation.

[6] Then came the opportunity last September to talk with some of the leaders of the economic community. In these negotiating sessions certain promises were made by the merchants—such as the promise to remove the humiliating racial

signs from the stores. On the basis of these promises Rev. Shuttlesworth and the leaders of the Alabama Christian Movement for Human Rights agreed to call a moratorium on any type of demonstrations. As the weeks and months unfolded we realized that we were the victims of a broken promise. The signs remained. Like so many experiences of the past we were confronted with blasted hopes, and the dark shadow of a deep disappointment settled upon us. So we had no alternative except that of preparing for direct action, whereby we would present our very bodies as a means of laying our case before the conscience of the local and the national community. We were not unmindful of the difficulties involved. So we decided to go through a process of self-purificaton. We started having workshops on nonviolence and repeatedly asked ourselves the questions, "Are you able to accept blows without retaliating?" "Are you able to endure the ordeals of jail?" We decided to set our direct action program around the Easter season, realizing that with the exception of Christmas, this was the largest shopping period of the year. Knowing that a strong economic withdrawal program would be the by-product of direct action, we felt that this was the best time to bring pressure on the merchants for the needed changes. Then it occurred to us that the March election was ahead and so we speedily decided to postpone action until after election day. When we discovered that Mr. Connor [Police Commissioner Bull Connor] was in the run-off, we decided again to postpone action so that the demonstrations could not be used to cloud the issues. At this time we agreed to begin our nonviolent witness the day after the run-off.

[7] This reveals that we did not move irresponsibly into direct action. We too wanted to see Mr. Connor defeated; so we went through postponement after postponement to aid in this community need. After this we felt that direct action could be delayed no longer.

[8] You may well ask, "Why direct action? Why sit-ins, marches, etc.? Isn't negotiation a better path?" You are exactly right in your call for negotiation. Indeed, this is the purpose of direct action. Nonviolent direct action seeks to create such a crisis and establish such creative tension that a community that has constantly refused to negotiate is forced to confront the issue. It seeks so to dramatize the issue that it can no longer be ignored. I just referred to the creation of tension as a part of the work of the nonviolent resister. This may sound rather shocking. But I must confess that I am not afraid of the word tension. I have earnestly worked and preached against violent tension, but there is a type of constructive nonviolent tension that is necessary for growth. Just as Socrates felt that it was necessary to create a tension in the mind so that individuals could rise from the bondage of myths and half-truths to the unfettered realm of creative analysis and objective appraisal, we must see the need of having nonviolent gadflies to create the kind of tension in society that will help men to rise from the dark depths of prejudice and racism to the majestic heights of understanding and brotherhood. So the purpose of the direct action is to create a situation so crisis-packed that it will inevitably open the door to negotiation. We, therefore, concur with you in your call for negotiation. Too long has our beloved Southland been bogged down in the tragic attempt to live in monologue rather

than dialogue.

[9] One of the basic points in your statement is that our acts are untimely. . . . We know through painful experience that freedom is never voluntarily given by the oppressor; it must be demanded by the oppressed. Frankly, I have never yet engaged in a direct action movement that was "well timed," according to the timetable of those who have not suffered unduly from the disease of segregation. For years now I have heard the word "Wait!" It rings in the ear of every Negro with a piercing familiarity. This "Wait" has almost always meant "Never." It has been a tranquilizing thalidomide [a widely-used tranquilizer that was later found to result in birth defects when taken by pregnant women], relieving the emotional stress for a moment, only to give birth to an ill-formed infant of frustration. We must come to see with the distinguished jurist of yesterday that "justice too long delayed is justice denied." We have waited for more than three hundred and forty years for our constitutional and God-given rights. The nations of Asia and Africa are moving with jet-like speed toward the goal of political independence, and we still creep at horse and buggy pace toward the gaining of a cup of coffee at a lunch counter.

[10] I guess it is easy for those who have never felt the stinging darts of segregation to say, "Wait." But when you have seen vicious mobs lynch your mothers and fathers at will and drown your sisters and brothers at whim; when you have seen hate filled policemen curse, kick, brutalize and even kill your black brothers and sisters with impunity; when you see the vast majority of your twenty million Negro brothers smothering in an air tight cage of poverty in the midst of an affluent society; when you suddenly find your tongue twisted and your speech stammering as you seek to explain to your six-year-old daughter why she can't go to the public amusement park that has just been advertised on television, and see tears welling up in her little eyes when she is told that Funtown is closed to colored children, and see the depressing clouds of inferiority begin to form in her little mental sky, and see her begin to distort her little personality by unconsciously developing a bitterness toward white people; when you have to concoct an answer for a five-year-old son asking in agonizing pathos: "Daddy, why do white people treat colored people so mean?"; when you take a cross-county drive and find it necessary to sleep night after night in the uncomfortable corners of your automobile because no motel will accept you; when you are humiliated day in and day out by nagging signs reading "white" and "colored"; when your first name becomes "nigger" and your middle name becomes "boy" (however old you are) and your last name becomes "John," and when your wife and mother are never given the respected title "Mrs."; when you are harried by day and haunted by night by the fact that you are a Negro, living constantly at tip-toe stance never quite knowing what to expect next, and plagued with inner fears and outer resentments; when you are forever fighting a degenerating sense of "nobodiness;" then you will understand why we find it difficult to wait. There comes a time when the cup of endurance runs over, and men are no longer willing to be plunged into an abyss of injustice where they experience the bleakness of corroding despair. I hope, Sirs, you can understand our legitimate and unavoidable impatience.

[11] You express a great deal of anxiety over our willingness to break laws. This is certainly a legitimate concern. Since we so diligently urge people to obey the Supreme Court's decision of 1954 outlawing segregation in the public schools, it is rather strange and paradoxical to find us consciously breaking laws. One may well ask, "how can you advocate breaking some laws and obeying others?" The answer is found in the fact that there are two types of laws: There are *just* and there are *unjust* laws. Conversely, one has a moral responsibility to disobey unjust laws. I would agree with St. Augustine that "An unjust law is no law at all."

[12] Now, what is the difference between the two? How does one determine when a law is just or unjust? A just law is a man-made code that squares with the moral law or the law of God. An unjust law is a code that is out of harmony with the moral law. To put it in the terms of St. Thomas Aquinas, an unjust law is a human law that is not rooted in eternal and natural law. Any law that uplifts human personality is just. Any law that degrades human personality is unjust. All segregation statutes are unjust because segregation distorts the soul and damages the personality. It gives the segregator a false sense of superiority, and the segregated a false sense of inferiority. To use the words of Martin Buber, the great Jewish philosopher, segregation substitutes an "I-it" relationship for the "I-thou" relationship, and ends up relegating persons to the status of things. So segregation is not only politically, economically and sociologically unsound, but it is morally wrong and sinful. Paul Tillich has said that sin is separation. Isn't segregation an existential expression of man's tragic separation, an expression of his awful estrangement, his terrible sinfulness? So I can urge men to disobey segregation ordinances because they are morally wrong. . . .

[13] Let us turn to a more concrete example of just and unjust laws. An unjust law is a code that a majority inflicts on a minority that is not binding on itself. This is difference made legal. On the other hand a just law is a code that a majority compels a minority to follow that it is willing to follow itself. This is sameness made legal.

[14] Let me give another explanation. An unjust law is a code inflicted upon a minority which that minority had no part in enacting or creating because they did not have the unhampered right to vote. Who can say that the legislature of Alabama which set up the segregation laws was democratically elected? Throughout the state of Alabama all types of conniving methods are used to prevent Negroes from becoming registered voters and there are some counties without a single Negro registered to vote despite the fact that the Negro constitutes a majority of the population. Can any law set up in such a state be considered democratically structured?

[15] These are just a few of examples of unjust and just laws. There are some instances when a law is just on its face and unjust in its application. For instance, I was arrested Friday on a charge of parading without a permit. Now there is nothing wrong with an ordinance which requires a permit for a parade, but when the ordinance is used to preserve segregation and to deny citizens the First Amendment privilege of peaceful assembly and peaceful

protest, then it becomes unjust.

[16] I hope you can see the distinction I am trying to point out. In no sense do I advocate evading or defying the law as the rabid segregationist would do. This would lead to anarchy. One who breaks an unjust law must do it *openly, lovingly,* (not hatefully as the white mothers did in New Orleans when they were seen on television screaming "nigger, nigger, nigger") and with a willingness to accept the penalty. I submit that an individual who breaks a law that conscience tells him is unjust, and willingly accepts the penalty by staying in jail to arouse the conscience of the community over its injustice, is in reality expressing the highest respect for law. . . .

[17] I must make two honest confessions to you, my Christian and Jewish brothers. First, I must confess that over the past few years I have been gravely disappointed with the white moderate. I have almost reached the regrettable conclusion that the Negro's great stumbling block in his stride toward freedom is not the White Citizen's Council-er or the Ku Klux Klanner, but the white moderate who is more devoted to "order" than to justice; who prefers a negative peace which is the absence of tension to a positive peace which is the presence of justice; who constantly says "I agree with you in the goal you seek, but I can't agree with your methods of direct action;" who paternalistically feels that he can set the time-table for another man's freedom; who lives by the myth of time and who constantly advises the Negro to wait until a "more convenient season." Shallow understanding from people of goodwill is more frustrating than absolute misunderstanding from people of ill will. Lukewarm acceptance is much more bewildering than outright rejection. . . .

[18] I had hoped that the white moderate would understand that law and order exist for the purpose of establishing justice, and that when they fail to do this they become the dangerously structured dams that block the flow of social progress. I had hoped that the white moderate would understand that the present tension in the South is merely a necessary phase of the transition from an obnoxious negative peace, where the Negro passively accepted his unjust plight, to a substance-filled positive peace, where all men will respect the dignity and worth of human personality. Actually, we who engage in nonviolent direct action are not the creators of tension. We merely bring to the surface the hidden tension that is already alive. We bring it out in the open where it can be seen and dealt with . . . Like a boil that can never be cured as long as it is covered up but must be opened with all its pus-flowing ugliness to the natural medicines of air and light, injustice must likewise be exposed, with all of the tension its exposing creates, to the light of human conscience and the air of national opinion before it can be cured.

[19] In your statement you asserted that our actions, even though peaceful, must be condemned because they precipitate violence. But can this assertion be logically made? Isn't this like condemning the robbed man because his possession of money precipitated the evil act of robbery? Isn't this like condemning Socrates because his unswerving commitment to truth and his philosophical delvings precipitated the misguided popular mind to make him drink the hemlock? Isn't this like condemning Jesus because His unique God-Consciousness and never-ceasing devotion to His will precipitated the evil act of crucifixion? We must come to see, as federal courts have consistently affirmed, that it is immoral to urge an individual to withdraw his efforts to gain his basic constitutional rights because the quest precipitates violence. Society must protect the robbed and punish the robber. . . .

[20] I had also hoped that the white moderate would reject the myth of time. I received a letter this morning from a white brother in Texas which said: "All Christians know that the colored people will receive equal rights eventually, but it is possible that you are in too great of a religious hurry. It has taken Christianity almost 2000 years to accomplish what it has. The teachings of Christ take time to come to earth." All that is said here grows out of a tragic misconception of time. It is the strangely irrational notion that there is something in the very flow of time that will inevitably cure all ills. Actually time is neutral. It can be used either destructively or constructively. I am coming to feel that the people of ill-will have used time much more effectively than the people of good will. We will have to repent in this generation not merely for the vitriolic words and actions of the bad people, but for the appalling silence of the good people. We must come to see that human progress never rolls in on wheels of inevitability. It comes through the tireless efforts and persistent work of men willing to be co-workers with God, and without this hard work time itself becomes an ally of the forces of social stagnation. We must use time creatively, and forever realize that the time is always ripe to do right. Now is the time to make real the promise of democracy, and transform our pending national elegy into a creative psalm of brotherhood. Now is the time to lift our national policy from the quicksand of racial injustice to the solid rock of human dignity.

[21] You spoke of our activity in Birmingham as extreme. At first I was rather disappointed that fellow clergymen would see my nonviolent efforts as those of an extremist. I started thinking about the fact that I stand in the middle of two opposing forces in the Negro community. One is a force of complacency, made up of Negroes who, as a result of long years of oppression, have been so completely drained of self-respect and a sense of "somebodiness" that they have adjusted to segregation, and, of a few Negroes in the middle class who, because of a degree of academic and economic security, and because at points they profit by segregation, have unconsciously become insensitive to the problems of the masses.

[22] The other force is one of bitterness, and hatred and comes perilously close to advocating violence. It is expressed in the various black nationalist groups that are springing up over the nation, the largest and best known being Elijah Muhammad's Muslim movement. This movement is nourished by the contemporary frustration over the continued existence of racial discrimination. It is made up of people who have lost faith in America, who have absolutely repudiated Christianity, and who have concluded that the

white man is an incurable "devil." I have tried to stand between these two forces saying that we need not follow the "do-nothingism" of the complacent or the hatred and despair of the black nationalist. There is a more excellent way of love and nonviolent protest. I'm grateful to God that, through the Negro church, the dimension of nonviolence entered our struggle. If this philosophy had not emerged, I am convinced that by now many streets of the South would be flowing with floods of blood. And I am further convinced that if our white brothers dismiss as "rabble rousers" and "outside agitators" those of us who are working through the channels of nonviolent direct action and refuse to support our nonviolent efforts, millions of Negroes, out of frustration and despair, will seek solace and security in black nationalist ideologies, a development that will lead inevitably to a frightening racial nightmare.

[23] Oppressed people cannot remain oppressed forever. The urge for freedom will eventually come. This is what has happened to the American Negro. Something within has reminded him of his birthright of freedom; something without has reminded him that he can gain it. Consciously and unconsciously, he has been swept in by what the Germans call the *Zeitgeist*, and with his black brother of Africa, and his brown and yellow brothers of Asia, South America and the Caribbean, he is moving with a sense of cosmic urgency toward the promised land of racial justice. Recognizing this vital urge that has engulfed the Negro community, one should readily understand public demonstrations. The Negro has many pent up resentments and latent frustrations. He has to get them out. . . .

[24] But as I continued to think about the matter I gradually gained a bit of satisfaction from being considered an extremist. Was not Jesus an extremist in love— "Love your enemies, bless them that curse you, pray for them that despitefully use you." Was not Amos an extremist for justice— "Let justice roll down like waters and righteousness like a mighty stream." Was not Paul an extremist for the gospel of Jesus Christ—"I bear in my body the marks of the Lord Jesus." Was not Martin Luther an extremist—"here I stand; I can do none other so help me God." Was not John Bunyan an extremist—"I will stay in jail to the end of my days before I make a butchery of my conscience." Was not Abraham Lincoln an extremist—"This nation cannot survive half slave and half free." Was not Thomas Jefferson an extremist— "We hold these truths to be self evident that all men are created equal." So the question is not whether we will be extremist but what kind of extremist will we be. Will we be extremists for hate or will we be extremists for love? Will we be extremists for the preservation of injustice—or will we be extremists for the cause of justice? In that dramatic scene on Calvary's hill, three men were crucified. We must not forget that all three were crucified for the same crime—the crime of extremism. Two were extremists for immorality, and thusly fell below their environment. The other, Jesus Christ, was an extremist for love, truth, and goodness, and thereby rose above his environment. So, after all, maybe the South, the nation and the world are in dire need of creative extremists. . . .

[25] Let me rush on to mention my other disappointment. I have been so greatly disappointed with the white church and its leadership. Of course, there are some notable exceptions. I am not unmindful of the fact that each of you has taken some significant stands on this issue. I commend you, Rev. Stallings, for your Christian stand on this past Sunday, in welcoming Negroes to your worship service on a non-segregated basis. I commend the Catholic leaders of this state for integrating Spring Hill College several years ago.

[26] But despite these notable exceptions I must honestly reiterate that I have been disappointed with the church. I do not say that as one of those negative critics who can always find something wrong with the Church. I say it as a minister of the gospel, who loves the church; who was nurtured in its bosom; who has been sustained by its spiritual blessings and who will remain true to it as long as the cord of life shall lengthen. . . .

[27] I have heard numerous religious leaders of the South call upon their worshippers to comply with a desegregation decision because it is the *law*, but I have longed to hear white ministers say, "Follow this decree because integration is morally *right* and because the Negro is your brother." In the midst of blatant injustices inflicted upon the Negro, I have watched white churches stand on the sideline and merely mouth pious irrelevancies and sanctimonious trivialities. In the midst of a mighty struggle to rid our nation of racial and economic injustice, I have heard so many ministers say, "those are social issues with which the gospel has no real concern," and I have watched so many churches commit themselves to a completely other-worldly religion which made a strange distinction between body and soul, between the sacred and the secular. . . .

[28] I have traveled the length and breadth of Alabama, Mississippi and all the other southern states. On sweltering summer days and crisp autumn mornings I have looked at her beautiful churches with their lofty spires pointing heavenward. I have beheld the impressive outlay of her massive religious education buildings. Over and over again I have found myself asking: "What kind of people worship here? Who is their God? Where were their voices when the lips of Governor Barnett dripped with words of interposition and nullification? Where were they when Governor Wallace gave the clarion call for defiance and hatred? Where were their voices of support when tired, bruised and weary Negro men and women decided to rise from the dark dungeons of complacency to the bright hills of creative protest?"

[29] Yes, these questions are still in my mind. In deep disappointment, I have wept over the laxity of the church. But be assured that my tears have been tears of love. There can be no deep disappointment where there is not deep love. Yes, I love the church; I love her sacred walls. How could I do otherwise? I am in the rather unique position of being the son, the grandson and the great-grandson of preachers. Yes, I see the church as the body of Christ. But, oh! How we have blemished and scarred that body through social neglect and fear of being nonconformists. . . .

[30]   There was a time when the Church was very powerful. It was during that period when the early Christians rejoiced when they were deemed worthy to suffer for what they believed. In those days the Church was not merely a thermometer that recorded the ideas and principles of popular opinion; it was a thermostat that transformed the mores of society. Wherever the early Christians entered a town the power structure got disturbed and immediately sought to convict them for being "disturbers of the peace" and "outside agitators."" But they went with the conviction that they were "a colony of heaven," and had to obey God rather than man. They were small in number but big in commitment. They were too God-intoxicated to be "astronomically intimidated." They brought an end to such ancient evils as infanticide and gladiatorial contest. . . .

[31]   Maybe again, I have been too optimistic. Is organized religion too inextricably bound to the status-quo to save our nation and the world? Maybe I must turn my faith to the inner spiritual church, the church within the church, as the true *ecclesia* and the hope of the world. But again I am thankful to God that some noble souls from the ranks of organized religion have broken loose from the paralyzing chains of conformity and joined us as active partners in the struggle for freedom. They have left their secure congregations and walked the streets of Albany, Georgia, with us. They have gone through the highways of the South on tortuous rides for freedom. Yes, they have gone to jail with us. Some have been kicked out of their churches, and lost support of their bishops and fellow ministers. But they gone with the faith that right defeated is stronger than evil triumphant. These men have been the leaven in the lump of the race. Their witness has been the spiritual salt that has preserved the true meaning of the Gospel in these troubled times. They have carved a tunnel of hope through the dark mountain of disappointment.

[32]   I hope the church as a whole will meet the challenge of this decisive hour. But even if the church does not come to the aid of justice, I have no despair about the future. I have no fear about the outcome of our struggle in Birmingham, even if our motives are presently misunderstood. We will reach the goal of freedom in Birmingham and all over the nation, because the goal of America is freedom. Abused and scorned though we may be, our destiny is tied up with the destiny of America. Before the pilgrims landed at Plymouth, we were here. Before the pen of Jefferson etched across the pages of history the majestic words of the Declaration of Independence, we were here. For more than two centuries our fore-parents labored in this country without wages; they made cotton king; and they built the homes of their masters in the midst of brutal injustice and shameful humiliation—and yet out of a bottomless vitality they continued to thrive and develop. If the inexpressible cruelties of slavery could not stop us, the opposition we now face will surely fail. We will win our freedom because the sacred heritage of our nation and the eternal will of God are embodied in our echoing demands.

[33]   I must close now. But before closing I feel impelled to mention one other point in your statement that troubled me profoundly. You warmly commended the Birmingham police force for keeping "order" and "preventing violence." I don't believe you would have so warmly commended the police force if you had seen its angry violent dogs literally biting six unarmed, nonviolent Negroes. I don't believe you would so quickly commend the policemen if you would observe their ugly and inhuman treatment of Negroes here in the city jail; if you would watch them push and curse old Negro women and young Negro girls; if you would see them slap and kick old Negro men and young boys; if you will observe them, as they did on two occasions, refuse to give us food because we wanted to sing our grace together. I'm sorry that I can't join you in your praise of the police department.

[34]   It is true that they have been rather disciplined in their public handling of the demonstrators. . . . But for what purpose? To preserve the evil system of segregation
. . . they have used the moral means of nonviolence to maintain the immoral end of flagrant racial injustice. T. S. Eliot has said that there is no greater treason than to do the right deed for the wrong reason.

[35]   I wish you had commended the Negro sit-inners and demonstrators of Birmingham for their sublime courage, their willingness to suffer and their amazing discipline in the midst of the most inhuman provocation. One day the South will recognize its real heroes. They will be the James Merediths, courageously and with a majestic sense of purpose, facing jeering and hostile mobs and the agonizing loneliness that characterizes the life of the pioneer. They will be old oppressed, battered Negro women, symbolized in a seventy-two year old woman in Montgomery, Alabama, who rose up with a sense of dignity and with her people decided not to ride segregated buses, and responded to one who inquired about her tiredness with ungrammatical profundity: "my feet is tired, but my soul is rested." They will be the young high school and college students, young ministers of the gospel and a host of their elders courageously and nonviolently sitting-in at lunch counters and willingly going to jail for conscience sake. One day the South will know that when these disinherited children of God sat down at lunch counters, they were in reality standing up for the best in the American dream and the most sacred values in our Judeo-Christian heritage, and thusly, carrying our whole nation back to those great wells of democracy which were dug deep by the founding fathers in their formulation of the Constitution and the Declaration of Independence.

[36]   Never before have I written a letter this long (or should I say a book?). I'm afraid that it is much too long to take your precious time. I can assure you that it would have been much shorter if I had been writing from a comfortable desk, but what else is there to do when you are alone for days in the dull monotony of a narrow jail cell other than write long letters, think strange thoughts, and pray long prayers?

[37] If I have said anything in this letter that is an overstatement of the truth and is indicative of an unreasonable impatience, I beg you to forgive me. If I have said anything in this letter that is an understatement of the truth and is indicative of my having a patience that makes me patient with anything less than brotherhood, I beg God to forgive me. . . .

Yours for the cause of Peace and Brotherhood,

Martin Luther King, Jr.

---

1. Explain how Dr. King defines a just and an unjust law.
2. Describe the reasoning Dr. King uses to apply those definitions to actions.
3. Describe the spectrum of forces working on racial issues and where Dr. King positions his movement in relation to them.
4. What consequence might follow if the "white brothers" dismiss nonviolent action?
5. Explain how "Letter from a Birmingham Jail," written almost 200 years after the nation was created, can serve as a foundational document.
6. Of the other foundational documents, identify one that is most like "Letter from a Birmingham Jail." Give reasons for your choice.

Bibliography

Books

Aberback, Joel D. and Bert A. Rockman. In the Web of Politics: *Three Decades of the U.S. Federal Executive*. Washington: Brookings Institution Press, 2000.

Acheson, Dean. *Present at the Creation: My Years in the State Department*. New York: Norton, 1969.

Allen, Jonathan and Amie Parnes. *Shattered: Inside Hillary Clinton's Doomed Campaign*. New York: Crown, 2017.

Alter, Jonathan. *The Promise: President Obama, Year One*. New York: Simon and Schuster, 2010.

Alterman, Eric. *What Liberal Media? The Truth About Bias in the News*. New York: Basic Books, 2003.

Alvarez, R. Michael and John Brehm. *Hard Choices, Easy Answers*. Princeton: Princeton University Press, 2002.

Asher, Herbert. *Polling and the Public: What Every Citizen Should Know*. Washington: Congressional Quarterly Press, 2004.

Balz, Dan. *Collision 2012: Obama vs. Romney and the Future of Elections in America*. New York: Viking, 2013.

Balz, Dan and Haynes Johnson. *The Battle for America 2008: The Story of an Extraordinary Election*. New York: Viking, 2009.

Becker, Carl L. *The Declaration of Independence: A Study in the History of Political Ideas*. New York: Vintage Books, 1970.

Bowen, Catherine Drinker. *Miracle at Philadelphia*. Boston: Little, Brown and Co., 1966.

Brown, Sherrod. *Congress from the Inside*. Kent, Ohio: Kent State University Press, 2004.

Caesar, James W., Andrew E. Busch, and John J. Pitney, Jr. *Defying the Odds: The 2016 Elections and American Politics*. Lanham, MD: Rowan and Littlefield, 2017.

Cigler, Allan J. and Burdettt A. Loomis eds. *Interest Group Politics*. Washington: CQ Press, 2002.

Clinton, Hillary Rodham. *What Happened*. New York: Simon and Schuster, 2017.

Clyburn, James E. *Blessed Experiences: Genuinely Southern Proudly Black*. Columbia: University of South Carolina Press, 2014..

Crawford, Kenneth G. *The Pressure Boys: The Inside Story of Lobbying in America*. New York: J. Messner, 1939.

D'Antonio, Michael. *A Consequential Presidency: The Legacy of Barack Obama*. New York: Thomas Dunne Books, 2016.

David, Paul T., Ralph Goldman, and Richard Bain. *The Politics of National Party Conventions*. New York: Vintage Books (Brookings Institute), 1964.

Edwards, Bob. *Edward R. Murrow and the Birth of Broadcast Journalism*. Hoboken, NJ: John Wiley and Sons, 2004.

Elkins, Stanley and Eric McKitrick. *The Age of Federalism: The Early American Republic, 1788 to 1800*. New York: Oxford University Press, 1995.

Fauntroy, Michael K. *Republicans and the Black Vote*. Boulder: Lynne Rienner Publishers, 2007.

Frank, Nathaniel. Awakening: *How Gays and Lesbians Brought Marriage Equality to America*. Cambridge: The Belknap Press of Harvard University Press, 2017.

Gillespie, Nick and Matt Welch. *The Declaration of Independents: How Libertarian Politics Can Fix What's Wrong with America*. New York: Public Affairs, 2011.

Goldberg, Bernard. *Bias: A CBS Insider Exposes How the Media Distort the News*. Washington: Regnery Publishing, 2002.

Goldman, Ralph M. *The Democratic Party in American Politics*. New York: Macmillan Company, 1966.

Goldstein, Kenneth M. *Interest Group Lobbying, and Participation in America*. Cambridge, UK: Cambridge University Press, 1999.

Gould, Lewis. *The Most Exclusive Club: A History of the Modern United States Senate*. New York: Basic Books, 2005.

Gray, David. *The Fourth Amendment in an Age of Surveillance*. New York: Cambridge University Press, 2017.

Fleischer, Ari. *Taking Heat: The President, the Press, and My Years in the White House*. New York: William Morrow, 2005.

Halperin, Mark and John Heilemann. *Double Down: Game Change 2012*. New York: Penguin Press, 2013.

___. *Game Change: Obama and the Clintons, McCain and Palin, and the Race of a Lifetime*. New York: Harper, 2010.

Hamilton, Lee. *How Congress Works and Why You Should Care*. Bloomington: Indiana University Press, 2004.

Herrnson, Paul S. *Congressional Elections: Campaigning at Home and in Washington*. Washington: CQ Press, 2000..

Jensen, Merrill. *The Articles of Confederation: An Interpretation of the Social-Constitutional History of the American Revolution, 1774-1781*. Madison: University of Wisconsin Press, 1959.

Judis, John B. *The Paradox of Democracy: Elites, Special Interests and the Betrayal of Public Trust*. New York: Pantheon, 2000.

Kaiser, Robert G. So Damn Much Money: *The Triumph of Lobbying and the Corrosion of Government*. New York: Knopf, 2009..

Kelly, Kate. *Election Day: An American Holiday, An American History*. New York: Facts on File, 1991.

Krent, Harold J. *Presidential Powers*. New York: New York University Press, 2005.

Labunski, Richard E. *James Madison and the Struggle for the Bill of Rights*. Oxford: Oxford University Press, 2006.

Lazarus, Edward. *Closed Chambers: The Rise, Fall, and Future of the Modern Supreme Court*. New York: Penguin Books, 1998.

Mann, Thomas and Norman Ornstein. *The Broken Branch: How Congress Is Failing America and How to Get It Back on Track*. New York: Oxford, 2006.

Marlin, George J. *The American Catholic Voter: 200 Years of Political Impact*. South Bend, IN: St. Augustine Press, 2004.

Medoff, Rafael. *Jewish Americans and Political Participation*. Santa Barbara, CA: ABC-CLIO, 2002.

Newport, Frank. *Polling Matters: Why Leaders Must Listen to the Wisdom of the People*. New York: Warner Books, 2004.

Nichols, David. *A Matter of Justice: Eisenhower and the Beginning of the Civil Rights Revolution*. New York: Simon and Schuster, 2007.

Nichols, Tom. *The Death of Expertise: The Campaign Against Established Knowledge and Why it Matters*. New York: Oxford University Press, 2017.

Nixon, Richard. *The Memoirs of Richard Nixon. New York: Grosset and Dunlap, 1978.*

Patterson, Bradley H. The White House Staff: Inside the West Wing and Beyond. Washington: Brookings Institution Press, 2000.

Piven, Frances Fox, Lorraine C. Minnite, and Margaret Groarke. *Keeping Down the Black Vote: Race and the Demobilization of American Voters*. New York: The New Press, 2009.

Rehnquist, William. *The Supreme Court*. New York: Vintage Books, 2001.

Remeni, Robert V. *The House*. New York: Harper Collins, 2007..

Safire, William. *Safire's New Political Dictionary*. New York: Random House, 1993.

Schlesinger, Arthur M., Jr. *The Imperial Presidency*. Boston: Houghton Mifflin, 1989.

Sorenson, Theodore *C. Kennedy*. Old Saybrook, CT: Konecky & Konecky, 1965.

Steinman, Ron. *Inside Television's First War: A Saigon Journal*. Columbia: University of Missouri Press, 2002.

Sunstein, Cass R. #republic: *Divided Democracy in the Age of Social Media*. Princeton: Princeton University Press, 2017.

Teachout, Zephyr. *Corruption in America: From Benjamin Franklin's Snuff Box to Citizens United*. Cambridge: Harvard University Press, 2014.

Thomas, Helen. *Watchdogs of Democracy? The Waning Washington Press Corps and How It Has Failed the Public*. New York: Scribner, 2006.

Tocqueville, Alexis de. *Democracy In America*. Chicago: University of Chicago Press, 2002.

Toobin, Jeffrey. *The Nine: Inside the Secret World of the Supreme Court*. New York: Anchor, 2008.

Tribe, Laurence and Joshua Matz. *Uncertain Justice: The Roberts Court and the Constitution*. New York: Henry Holt, 2014.

Whitcover, Jules. *Party of the People: A History of the Democrats*. New York: Random House, 2003.

White, Theodore. *The Making of a President 1960*. New York: Atheneum, 1961.

Wood, Gordon S. *The Creation of the American Republic, 1776-1787*. Chapel Hill: UNC Press, 1998.

Woodward, C. Vann. *The Strange Career of Jim Crow*. New York: Oxford University Press, 2002.

Articles

Abello, Cristina. "Changes in Store at the FCC." *The News Media and the Law*. Winter 2009.

Alterman, Eric. "Bush's War on the Press." *The Nation*. May 9, 2005.

Baker, Peter. "The Education of a President." *New York Times*. October 12, 2010.

Basinger, Scott, and Maxwell Mak. "The Changing Politics of Federal Judicial Nominations." *Congress and the President*, vol. 37. 2010.

Beckel, Michael and Russ Choma. "Decision Helped Romney Neutralize Obama's Fundraising Advantage." Open Secrets <www.opensecrets.org>. October 30, 2012.

Biskupic, Joan. "Ellis Island: This Land is Whose Land?" *Washington Post*. January 11, 1998, and May 27, 1998.

Bogost, Ian. "Obama Was Too Good at Social Media." *The Atlantic*. January 6, 2017.

Bottum, Joseph. "There is No Catholic Vote." *The Weekly Standard*. November 1, 2010.

Brand, Rachel. "Judicial Appointments: Checks and Balances in Practice." *Harvard Journal of Law and Public Policy*. Volume 33, Number 1.

Brill, Steven. "On Sale: Your Government." *Time*. July 12, 2010.

Carney, Eliza Newlin. "K Street's Sea Change." *National Journal*. September 22, 2007.

Casey, Winter. "Why They Lobby." *National Journal*. May 31, 2008.

____. "Everything You Need to Know about the Voter ID Controversy." *The Week*. October 25, 2014.

Chamberlain, Craig. "Will White House Continue to Use Photos as a Social Media Tool?" *Illinois News Bureau*. December 20, 2016.

Cole, David. "Privacy 2.0: Surveillance in the Digital State." *The Nation*. April 16, 2015.

Conway, Kelly. "Primary Polling Problems: Can Horse Race Coverage Alter Results?" *Brown Political Review*. March 9, 2016.

Eilperin, Juliet. "Here's How the First President of the Social Media Age has Chosen to Connect with Americans." *Washington Post*. May 26, 2015.

Filisko, G.M. "Gun War: Congress Has Been Silent on Guns, But States Haven't, So Change is on the Horizon." *ABA Journal*. May 2017.

Fisher, Daniel, "Bureaucrats May be the Losers if Gorsuch Wins a Seat on Supreme Court." *Forbes*. Jan. 26, 2017.

Foer, Franklin. "When Silicon Valley Took Over Journalism." *The Atlantic*. September 2017.

Garrow, David. "The Once and Future Supreme Court." *American History*. February 2005.

Goldmacher, Shane. "Four Years Later." *National Journal*. June 8, 2014.

Goodwin, Michael. "The Collapse of Fair-Minded Journalism." *USA Today Magazine*. September 2017.

Greenberg, David. "Spinning With Obama." *Dissent*. Fall 2015.

Groseclose, Tim and Jeffery Milyo. "A Measure of Media Bias." Stuart Kallen ed., *Media Bias*. San Diego: Greenhaven Press, 2004.

Guiliano, Paola and Antonio Spilimebergo, "Growing Up in a Recession." *Review of Economic Studies*. November 2013.

Guldon, Bob. "Mr. X Speaks: An Interview with George Kennan." *Foreign Service Journal*. February 2004.

Huffman, Jim, "What the Supreme Court's Decision in Arlington v. FCC Means for America." *Daily Caller*. May 22, 2013.

Jackson, Jannie, Peter Hart and Rachel Coen. "The Media are Biased Against Conservative Economic Policies." Stuart Kallen ed., *Media Bias*. San Diego: Greenhaven Press, 2004.

Johnson, Fawn. "The End of No Child Left Behind." *National Journal*. October 29, 2011.

Jost, Kenneth. "Revising No Child Left Behind." CQ Researcher. April 16, 2010.

___. "Voting Controversies: Are U.S. Elections Being Conducted Fairly?" *Congressional Quarterly Researcher*. February 21, 2014.

Klein, Daniel B. and Charlotta Stern. "By the Numbers: The Ideological Profile of Professors." *The Politically Correct University*. Washington: AEI Press, 2009.

Kleiner, Sarah. "Democrats Say Citizens United Should Die. Here's Why That Won't Happen." *Time*. August 31, 2017.

Kohler, Peter. "The Unfairness of the 'Fairness Doctrine.'" *The Masthead*. Spring 2009.

Lewis, Charles. "Why I Left 60 Minutes." Politico Magazine. June 29, 2014..

McLeod, Ethan. "Will the GOP-Led Congress Further Loosen Gun Restrictions?" *CQ Researcher*. July 17, 2017.

Meyerson, Harold. "California's Jungle Primary: Tried it. Dump it." *Los Angeles Times*. June 21, 2014.

"New American Center," *Esquire*. November 2013.

Rendell, Steve. "The Fairness Doctrine: How We Lost It, and Why We Need it Back." *Extra!* January/February 2005.

Rothschild, David. "Understanding How Polls Affect Voters." *Huffington Post*. October 26, 2012.

Smock, Raymond W. "The Institutional Development of the House of Representatives, 1789–1801." Kenneth R. Bowling and Donald R. Kennon eds. The House and Senate in the 1790s: Petitioning, Lobbying, and Institutional Development. Athens: Ohio University Press, 2002.

Sohoni, Mila. "A Bureaucracy If You Can Keep It." Harvard Law Review. November 2017.

Thrall, A. Trevor and Erik Goepner. "Millennials and U.S. Foreign Policy: The Next Generation's Attitudes Toward Foreign Policy and War (and Why They Matter)." Cato Institute, 2015.

Turley, Jonathan. "The Rise of the Fourth Branch of Government." *Washington Post*. May 24, 2013.

Underwood, Julie. "The Privacy of a Student's Backpack." *Kappan*. October 2017.

Unger, Ross. "Boss Rove." *Vanity Fair*. September 2012.

"Voting Trends by Age Group." *Congressional Digest*. January 2017.

Walker, Jesse. "Beyond the Fairness Doctrine." *Reason*. November 2008.

Wolfensberger, Donald R. "The Return of the Imperial Presidency?" *The Wilson Quarterly*. Spring 2002.

Reports

American National Election Study (ANES). Stanford University, University of Michigan, and the National Science Foundation, 2014.

Congressional Research Service.

___. An Introduction to Judicial Review of Federal Agency Action. December 7, 2016.

Congressional Research Service. *An Introduction to Judicial Review of Federal Agency Action*. December 7, 2016.

___. *Declarations of War and Authorizations for the Use of Military Force: Historical Background and Legal Implications*. March 17, 2011.

___. *Lobbying Reform, Background and Legislative Proposals*, 109th Congress. March 23, 2006.

___. *Membership of the 115th Congress: A Profile*. March 14, 2014.

___. *Women in Congress: Historical Overview, Tables, and Discussion*. April 29, 2015.

Democratic National Committee. *Moving America Forward: Democratic National Platform*. 2012.

Gans, Curtis. *African-Americans, Anger, Fear and Youth Propel Turnout to Highest Level Since 1960*. American University. December 17, 2008.

___. Testimony Before Senate Rules Committee. March 11, 2009.

Klein, Daniel B. *By the Numbers: The Ideological Profile of Professors*. American Enterprise Institute Conference. November 14, 2007.

Pew Research Center. Digital News Fact Sheet. August 7, 2017.

___. *How Americans Encounter, Recall and Act Upon Digital News*. February 9, 2017.

___. *Local TV News Fact Sheet*. July 13, 2017.

___. *The Future of Free Speech, Trolls, Anonymity and Fake News Online*. March 29, 2017.

___. *Trump, Clinton Voters Divided in Their Main Source for Election News*. January 18, 2017.

U.S. Elections Project. *America Goes to the Polls 2016: A Report on Voter Turnout in the 2016 Election*.

U.S. Office of Personnel Management. *Biography of an Ideal: A History of the Federal Civil Service*. 2003.

___. *A New Day for the Civil Service*. Fiscal Year 2010 Annual Performance Report. 2011.

___. *Sizing Up the Executive Branch Fiscal Year 2016*. June 2017.

Films

Casino Jack and the United States of Money. Magnolia Home Entertainment, 2010.

The Most Dangerous Man in America: Daniel Ellsberg and the Pentagon Papers. First Run Features, 2009.

The War Room. Criterion Collection, 1994.

Index

A

Abolitionists, 201
Abortion, 372
Absentee ballots, 442
Access to government officials, 535
Act of clemency, 136
Adams, John, 46–47
Advice and consent, 31, 84, 213
Affiliates, 560
Affirmative action, 334
  seeking diversity, 334–335
Affordable Care Act (2010), 529
Affordable Health Care for America Act, 522
African Americans, 434
African American suffrage, 427
Agencies within departments, 164
Agenda, 391
Ambassador, 144
Amendments ratification, 523
American Association of Retired Persons, 531
American Bar Association (ABA), 214–215, 529
American Civil Liberties Union (ACLU), 235, 531
American Federation of Labor (AFL), 521
American independence and early national government
  Enlightenment political theory, 4–5
  representative democracies, 5–7
  road to revolution, 4
American Medical Association (AMA), 529
American revolutionaries, 3
Americans for Financial Reform, 526
Americans with Disabilities Act, 58, 315
Amicus curiae, 541
  brief, 218

Amnesty, 136
Amtrak, 165
Anti-ERA movement, 545
Anti-Federalists, 24, 44
Anti-slavery advocates, 201
Appellate courts, 195
Appellate jurisdiction, 190
Appropriations, 173
Approval ratings, 370
Article II, enhanced presidency, 121
Article III, 190
Articles of Confederation, 9, 16, 43, 189, 622
Asian Americans, 435
Associated Press (AP), 558
Associated Press wire service, 558–559
Austin v. Michigan Chamber of Commerce (1990), 555
Australian ballot, 442
Authorization of spending, 173
Autopsy report, 455

B

Baby Boomers, 365
Baker v. Carr (1962), 105
Balancing liberty and order, 391
Ballot
  initiatives, 330
  measures, 487–488
Bandwagon effect, 375, 569
Benchmark polls, 370
Biased pollsters, 378
Bicameral, 13, 79
Biden, Joe, 138–139
Big Three networks, 560
Bill of Rights, 26, 234–235
Binding precedent, 197
Bipartisan Campaign Reform Act (BCRA), 209, 471, 507
Blanket primary, 489

New communication technologies, 560–562

New Deal and Roosevelt's plan, 202–203

New Deal coalition, 467

New Federalism, 57, 63

New Hampshire primary, 490

New Jersey Plan, 13

New Jersey v. TLO (1985), 279

News bureaus, 558

News sources, credibility, 578–579

New York Times v. Sullivan (1964), 249

New York Times v. United States (1971), 250–252

New York v. Quarles, 283

Nineteenth Amendment (1920), 323, 429, 523

Nixon, Richard, 122

No Child Left Behind (NCLB) Act (2002), 61

Nominees, 496–497

Nonconnected PACs, 504, 505

Non-germane amendments, 93

Nonresponse bias, 376–377

North American Free Trade Agreement (NAFTA), 404–405

Nuclear option, 216

Nuclear Regulatory Commission (NRC), 173

Nullification, 47

O

Obama, Barack, 130, 148, 205

Obamacare, 81

Obergefell, issues since, 331–333

Obergefell v. Hodges (2015), 45, 330

Obscene speech, 247

Obscenity, 247–248

Office of Information and Regulatory Affairs (OIRA), 174

Office of Management and Budget (OMB), 97, 542

Office of Personnel Management (OPM), 161, 169–170

Olive Branch Petition, 4

Omnibus bill, 93–94

Online political reporting, 562

Online voting, 443

Open primary, 489

Opinions and caseload, 211–212

Opponent, 502

Order over liberty, 393

Organizations, bureaucracy, 161–165

Original jurisdiction, 190

Outsider strategies, 535

Overlap and uncertainty, 45

P

Panama Canal Zone, acquiring, 133–135

Panics, 466

Parchment barriers, 26

Participatory democracy, 5–6

Partisanship and polarization, 102–110

Party chairperson, 461

Party changes and adaptations, 462
  candidate-centered campaigns, 462–463
  demographic coalitions, appeals to, 463–464
  party structure, changes influencing, 464–472
  political messages and political outreach, 472

Party conventions, 491–492

Party dealignment, 468

Party identification, 358, 439

Party ideology and marketplace, 396–397
  Keynesian economics, 397–398
  revenue and spending, 399–401
  supply-side theory, 398–399

Party ideology and policymaking, 387
  decision-making process, 391–392
    citizen influence balancing liberty and order, 394–395
    congressional policy, 393–394
    order over liberty, 393
    presidential and judicial policymaking, 395
    sequence, 391–393
  influences on public policy, 390
    balancing liberty and order, 391
    interest group policymaking, 391
    majoritarian policymaking, 390

Respondent, 195
Retrospective voting, 438
Revenue, 399
    sharing, 52, 63
    and spending, 399–401
Revolving door, 548
Reynolds, George, 253
Riders, 93
Riding circuit, 192
Right ideology, 353
Right to Counsel, 283
Right to jury trial, 190
Right to privacy, 287
Roberts, John, 206
Robocalls, 453
Roe and later abortion rulings, 290
Roe v. Wade (1973), 204, 287–290, 293
Roosevelt, Theodore, 124, 125
Roth, Samuel, 247
Roth v. United States (1957), 247
Royal courts, 4
Rule of four, 210
Rule of law, 352
Rules and procedures unique to senate, 91–92
Rules Committee, 90

S

Safe seats, 106
Salesman in chief, 137
Saliency, 353
Same-sex marriage, 329–331
Sampling error, 373
Sampling techniques, 372
Scandals, 546–547
Schenck v. United States (1919), 239–241, 240
School and college, 358
Scorekeeper, 568. See also media
Search and seizure, 278
Second Amendment, 263–268
Second Realignment, 466
Secretaries, 139–140
Secretary of defense, 195
Select committees, 88
Selective exclusiveness, 50

Selective incorporation, civil liberties
    due process, 236
    early incorporation, 237–238
    Fifth Amendment, 236
    Fourteenth Amendment, 236–237
Self-incrimination, 282
Senate, 14
    leaders, 85–86
    majority leader, 86
    and presidential appointees, 142–144
    standoffs, 143–144
Senatorial courtesy, 214
Senior Executive Service, 169
"Separate but equal," 303
Separation of powers, 13, 29–31
September 11, civil liberties and national
    security, 291–292
Sequence, 391–393
Sequential referral, 94
Seventeenth Amendment (1913), 79, 426, 523
Shaping and supporting policy, 138–139
Shaw v. Reno (1993), 107
Shays's Rebellion and response, 11
Signing statements, 136
Silent Generation, 365, 366–367
Silent Spring (1962), 524–525
Single-issue and ideological groups, 531–532
Single-issue group, 531
Single-issue parties, 474
Single-member districts, 475
Sixteenth Amendment (1913), 168, 399, 523
Size and term length, bicameral, 79
Skeptics, 44
Slaughterhouse Cases, 287
Slavery, 14–15
Smith v. Allwright, 208, 484
Social contract, 3
Social-desirability bias, 376–377
Social environments, 359
Social insurance taxes, 98
Social issues, 366–367, 405
    social safety net, 405–406
        conservative opposition, 408

W

Wall of separation, 252
War chest, 506
Wards, 487
War Powers Act, 83, 131
Warren, Earl, 203–204, 278
Warren Court, 203–204, 277
Washington, George, 122
Washington's example, enhanced
    presidency, 122–123
Washington's Golden Age, 45–46
Watchdog, 570. See also media
Watergate scandal, 570–571
Ways and Means Committee, 90
"We, the People," 425
Weaver, Robert Clifton, 139
Wedge issues, 353
Weeks v. United States, 278
Weighting, 373
West Coast Hotel v. Parrish (1937),
    202–203
Whig party, 465
Whip, 85
Whiskey Rebellion, 46
Whistleblower Protection Act, 175, 177
White flight, 306
White House, 488
    general election, 492–495
    party conventions, 491–492
    2016 presidential campaign,
        495–499
    primaries and caucuses, 489–491

White House Staff, 141
White primary, 303, 304, 428
Wilson, Woodrow, 124–125
Winner-take-all system, 494
Winner-take-all voting, 476
Wisconsin v. Yoder (1972), 257
The Woman's Christian Temperance
    Union (WCTU), 523, 526
Women and equality, 323–326
Women's movement, 524
Women's rights, 322
    women and equality, 323–326
    women's suffrage, 322–323
Women's suffrage, 322–323, 429
    amendment, 523
Writing and enforcing regulations, 165
Writ of certiorari, 210, 211

Y

Young Adults, 431

Z

*Zivotofsky v. John Kerry, Secretary of
    State* (2015), 156